Mastering QuickBooks 2026

Seventh Edition

The complete guide to small business accounting with US QuickBooks Online

Crystalynn Shelton, CPA

<packt>

Mastering QuickBooks 2026

Seventh Edition

Portfolio Director: Pavan Ramchandani

Relationship Lead : Larissa Pinto

Content Engineer: Esha Banerjee

Technical Editor: Vidhisha Patidar

Copy Editor: Safis Editing

Proofreader: Esha Banerjee

Indexer: Pratik Shirodkar

Production Designer: Jyoti Kadam

Growth Lead: Nivedita Singh

First published: December 2019

Seventh edition: December 2026

Production reference: 1231225

Published by Packt Publishing Ltd.

Grosvenor House

11 St Paul's Square

Birmingham

B3 1RB, UK

ISBN 978-1-80638-689-5

`www.packtpub.com`

Contributors

About the author

Crystalynn Shelton is a CPA and an Advanced QuickBooks ProAdvisor. She has managed accounting teams at Fortune 500 companies such as Texaco and Paramount Pictures, operated her own bookkeeping and payroll practice for 10 years, and spent another three years at Intuit (QuickBooks) as a senior learning specialist. She is the author of the Amazon bestseller series Mastering QuickBooks, now in its Seventh edition. She serves as an adjunct instructor at UCLA Extension, teaching accounting, bookkeeping, and QuickBooks to numerous small business owners and accounting students for 14 years. She holds an accounting degree from the University of Texas, Arlington. In 2022, she was recognized as one of the Top 100 ProAdvisors in the United States.

For more information on her services and to subscribe to her weekly newsletter featuring QuickBooks tips and tricks, visit her website at `https://crystalynnshelton.com/`. Be sure to visit her YouTube Channel (`https://packt.link/du2BR`), where you will find videos on many of the concepts taught in this book.

I would like to thank my husband of 30 years, Charles, for supporting me – ALWAYS and in all ways. To the small business owners all over the world, you are my inspiration for writing this book. I do what I do so you can do what you love most. I hope this book helps you understand the crucial role that managing your business finances plays in the future success of your business.

About the reviewer

Dominique Waits is a CPA, a CGMA, and a Top 100 QuickBooks ProAdvisor with 30 years of experience in public and private accounting and was nominated as one of Ignition's Top 50 Women in Accounting. She received her degree in accounting from Transylvania University in Lexington, KY, where she completed multiple internships in non-profit accounting, the Volunteer Income Tax Assistance program, and public accounting. She has been a small business owner, running a successful restaurant for many years. Currently, Dominique serves as a senior manager in the CAS department at Blue & Co., a regional accounting firm with offices in Indiana, Ohio, Kentucky, Michigan, and Tennessee. She works with individuals and small businesses, providing full outsourced accounting and CFO, financial management and advisory, as well as tax preparation and planning services.

I would like to thank my husband, Chris, and daughter, Mackenzie, for always supporting me with my work endeavors, one of which is reviewing this book.

Table of Contents

Chapter 3: Company File Setup 41

Chapter 4: Customizing QuickBooks for Your Business 63

Part 4: Closing the Books and Generating Reports in QBO 371

Preface

Intuit QuickBooks is an accounting software package that helps small business owners manage all their bookkeeping tasks. Its complete range of accounting capabilities, such as tracking income and expenses, managing payroll, simplifying taxes, and accepting online payments, makes QuickBooks software a must-have for business owners and aspiring bookkeepers.

The goal of this book is to teach small business owners, bookkeepers, and aspiring accountants how to properly use QuickBooks Online. Using a fictitious company, we will demonstrate how to create a QuickBooks Online account; customize key settings for a business; manage customers, vendors, and products and services; enter transactions; generate reports; and close the books at the end of the period.

QuickBooks records debits and credits for you so that you don't have to know about accounting. However, we will show you what happens behind the scenes in QuickBooks so that you understand how your actions in QuickBooks impact financial statements. We will also provide tips, shortcuts, and best practices to help you save time and become a QuickBooks pro.

In this new edition, we introduce you to the new and improved user interface that Intuit released just a few months ago. It is a step up from previous editions and is very user-friendly. We also introduce you to AI technology that has been implemented, including AI agents that automate a number of tasks that you would have normally done manually, to save you time.

Who this book is for

If you're a small business owner, bookkeeper, or accounting student who wants to learn how to make the most of QuickBooks Online, this book is for you. Business analysts, data analysts, managers, professionals working in bookkeeping, and QuickBooks accountants will also find this guide useful. If you are planning to take the **QuickBooks Certified User** (**QBCU**) exam, this book is an excellent study guide. We have also provided a list of the topics covered in the QBCU exam and cross-referenced it with the chapters in the book so you can go directly to that content.

The QBCU syllabus can be found in *Appendix 2*. No experience with QuickBooks Online is required to get started; however, some bookkeeping knowledge would be helpful.

The US edition of QuickBooks Online was used to create this book. If you are using a version that is outside of the US, results may differ.

What this book covers

Chapter 1, Small-Business Bookkeeping 101, provides you with some basic bookkeeping knowledge that you will need to successfully use QuickBooks Online. We cover money coming in and money going out of your business, inventory and fixed asset purchases, tracking the money you owe (liabilities), how to set up and use the chart of accounts, cash versus accrual accounting, and double-entry bookkeeping.

Chapter 2, Getting Started with QuickBooks Online, starts off with a brief description of QuickBooks Online, then it outlines the key features in all four editions of the software. We also explain how to choose the right edition for your business. There are step-by-step instructions on how to create a QuickBooks Online account and how to navigate the software. In this chapter, we also introduce you to the AI technology that is now in QBO and the AI agents that help you save time.

Chapter 3, Company File Setup, shows you how to customize the QuickBooks Online account created in *Chapter 1* to meet your business needs. First, we explain the documents and key information you will need to have handy for the setup. Next, we walk you through all of the available settings in QuickBooks Online and explain the purpose and benefit of utilizing the various options available.

Chapter 4, Customizing QuickBooks for Your Business, introduces customization for the chart of accounts and then dives into the different ways of connecting bank accounts and credit cards to your QuickBooks Online account, followed by granting users access to your QuickBooks data. Finally, you will learn how to discover and install apps in QuickBooks Online. Apps are a great way to help you streamline day-to-day business tasks that can otherwise be time-consuming.

Chapter 5, Managing Customer and Vendor Lists, gives you detailed insight into how to manage your customers, vendors, products, and services. This includes importing customer, vendor, and product and service data from an Excel spreadsheet and manually entering it into the software.

Chapter 6, Managing Sales Tax, covers how to set up sales tax for the various tax jurisdictions you are required to collect sales tax for, how to create an invoice with sales tax, and what reports will help you to report and pay the appropriate sales tax amount when it becomes due.

Chapter 7, Recording Sales Transactions in QuickBooks Online, starts by giving detailed information on different forms of sales, followed by information on how the customer can record payments using different methods, and finally teaches you how to initiate refunds for your customers. You will also learn how to customize sales templates with your company branding, such as adding a name and logo.

Chapter 8, Customer Sales Reports in QuickBooks Online, focuses on reports that will give you insight into your customers and sales. We will discuss what information you will find on each report, how to customize the reports, and how to generate each report. Once they are generated, we will observe when to check these reports and what decisions they might encourage us to make.

Chapter 9, Recording Expenses in QuickBooks Online, teaches you how to enter and pay bills for your QuickBooks Online account. Then, we'll start exploring how to manage recurring expenses, followed by writing and printing checks.

Chapter 10, Vendor and Expenses Reports in QuickBooks Online, dives into reports that help you manage your outgoings and have a clearer view of your profitability. The main reports that are covered are the accounts payable aging report, unpaid bills report, expense by vendor summary report, and bill payments report. You will learn how to generate and customize these reports to help you manage your expenses and cash flow.

Chapter 11, Managing Bank Feeds and Reconciling Bank and Credit Card Accounts, gives you an overview of the Banking Center in QuickBooks Online and an understanding of how the bank rules work, followed by how to edit QuickBooks Online transactions and how to reconcile bank accounts. We wrap this chapter up with a few troubleshooting tips for reconciling bank/credit card accounts.

Chapter 12, Managing 1099 Contractors and Introducing QuickBooks Time in QBO, shows you what information and key documents are needed to add 1099 contractors by inviting them to provide their W9 information electronically. We will show you how to pay contractors and how to process 1099 forms at the end of the year. If you need to keep track of the hours a contractor or employee works, you can do so using QuickBooks Time. We provide you with an overview of how QuickBooks Time works.

Chapter 13, Managing Employees in QuickBooks Online, shows you what information and key documents are needed to set up payroll, how to sign up for an Intuit Payroll subscription plan, and how to generate payroll reports. You will also learn how to file payroll tax forms and payments.

Chapter 14, Report Center Overview, highlights the key reports that you need in order to keep track of your business finances. It takes you through the Report Center, its purpose, and how to navigate it. You will then go through instructions for generating and customizing the main reports that are available, as well as how to export reports and send them via email. You will learn how regularly you need to check these reports, what to look out for, and what actions or decisions these findings might prompt.

Chapter 15, Business Overview and Cash Management Tools and Reports, discusses the three primary reports that provide a good overview of your business: the profit and loss statement, balance sheet report, and statement of cash flows. You will learn when to check these reports and how to use them to evaluate your business's performance. It also introduces you to the Cash Flow Center, where you can find important tools such as the Cash Flow Planner and audit log.

Chapter 16, Closing the Books in QuickBooks Online, covers the steps needed to close your books each month or for the year, including, but not limited to, reconciling all bank and credit card accounts, making year-end accrual adjustments (if applicable), recording fixed asset purchases made throughout the year, recording depreciation, taking a physical inventory, adjusting retained earnings, and preparing financial statements.

Chapter 17, Integrating E-Commerce Platforms with QuickBooks Online, covers the basics of integrating your online store (e.g., Shopify or Etsy) with QuickBooks Online. We cover how to find your sales channel in the QuickBooks Apps Center, the pros and cons of connecting apps to QuickBooks Online, and how to connect your sales channel to QuickBooks Online.

Chapter 18, Managing Products and Services, takes a deeper dive into how to set up and manage the products that you sell to your customers. We begin by showing you how to turn on the inventory tracking feature, and then we show you how to add your products to QuickBooks, how to record product sales, how to create purchase orders to send to vendor suppliers to place orders, how to receive products in the inventory, and finally, how to generate inventory reports.

Appendix 1, Shortcuts and QBO Test Drive, you will find handy keyboard shortcuts in this chapter, along with instructions on how to access a QuickBooks sample company that you can use to test drive the product before you purchase a subscription.

Appendix 2, Intuit QuickBooks Online Certified User Exam Objectives, is a list of objectives that are covered on an exam administered by Certiport. We have provided you with a guide that shows you where each objective is covered in this book. This book covers the majority of the objectives that are in the certification exam.

To get the most out of this book

This book is ideal for anyone who has accounting/bookkeeping knowledge, as well as those who don't. Each chapter builds on the knowledge and information presented in the previous chapters. If you don't have any experience in bookkeeping, we recommend you start with *Chapter 1, Bookkeeping 101,* and complete the chapters in the order they are presented. If you have experience in using QuickBooks Online, feel free to advance to the chapters that cover the topics you need to brush up on.

Download templates

We've added some QuickBooks Online templates that you might find useful at the following link: `https://github.com/PacktPublishing/Mastering-QuickBooks-2026-Seventh-Edition`.

Download the color images

We also provide a PDF file that has color images of the screenshots/diagrams used in this book. You can download it here: `https://packt.link/gbp/9781806386895`

Conventions used

Bold: Indicates a new term, an important word, or words that you see on screen. For example, words in menus or dialog boxes appear in the text like this. Here is an example: Click on the **New account** button located in the upper-right corner of the screen.

`CodeInText`: Indicates text that the user should type into a field or search bar. For example: "The email address in our example is `AliciaK@gmail.com`."

> Warnings or important notes appear like this.

> Tips and tricks appear like this.

Get in touch

Errata: Although we have taken every care to ensure the accuracy of our content, mistakes do happen. If you have found a mistake in this book, we would be grateful if you would report this to us. Please visit `www.packtpub.com/support/errata`, selecting your book, clicking on the **Errata Submission Form** link, and entering the details.

Piracy: If you come across any illegal copies of our works in any form on the internet, we would be grateful if you would provide us with the location address or website name. Please contact us at `copyright@packtpub.com` with a link to the material.

If you are interested in becoming an author: If there is a topic that you have expertise in and you are interested in either writing or contributing to a book, please visit `http://authors.packtpub.com`.

Share your thoughts

Once you've read *Mastering QuickBooks 2026*, we'd love to hear your thoughts! Scan the QR code below to go straight to the Amazon review page for this book and share your feedback.

`https://packt.link/r/1806386895`

Your review is important to us and the tech community and will help us make sure we're delivering excellent quality content.

Free Benefits with Your Book

This book comes with free benefits to support your learning. Activate them now for instant access (see the "*How to Unlock*" section for instructions).

Here's a quick overview of what you can instantly unlock with your purchase:

PDF and ePub Copies

- Access a DRM-free PDF copy of this book to read anywhere, on any device.
- Use a DRM-free ePub version with your favorite e-reader.

Next-Gen Web-Based Reader

- **Multi-device progress sync**: Pick up where you left off, on any device.
- **Highlighting and notetaking**: Capture ideas and turn reading into lasting knowledge.
- **Bookmarking**: Save and revisit key sections whenever you need them.
- **Dark mode**: Reduce eye strain by switching to dark or sepia themes.

How to Unlock

UNLOCK NOW

Scan the QR code (or go to `packtpub.com/unlock`). Search for this book by name, confirm the edition, and then follow the steps on the page.

Note: *Keep your invoice handy. Purchases made directly from Packt don't require one.*

Part 1

Setting Up Your Company File

Before diving into QuickBooks Online, it's crucial to get the setup right. In this section, we'll walk you through creating and customizing your company file step by step. From choosing the right QuickBooks edition and understanding the software's features to setting up your chart of accounts and connecting bank accounts, you'll learn everything you need to tailor QuickBooks to your business. You'll also explore how to manage customer, vendor, and product and services lists and discover powerful apps to make your day-to-day tasks more efficient. This part comprises the following chapters:

- *Chapter 1, Small-Business Bookkeeping 101*
- *Chapter 2, Getting Started with QuickBooks Online*
- *Chapter 3, Company File Setup*
- *Chapter 4, Customizing QuickBooks for Your Business*
- *Chapter 5, Managing Customer and Vendor Lists*

1

Small-Business Bookkeeping 101

While you don't need to be a **Certified Public Accountant** (**CPA**) to use QuickBooks, there are some basic concepts that you need to know to set up and manage your books like a pro. If you are an **Enrolled Agent** (**EA**), CPA, or aspiring bookkeeper or accountant, the concepts that we cover in this section will be familiar to you. However, if you are brand new to bookkeeping, make sure you grab a notepad to take notes and a cup of coffee to stay alert.

One of the benefits of using QuickBooks to manage your books is that you don't need an accounting degree to learn how to use the software. However, you should have a basic understanding of how bookkeeping works and what's happening behind the scenes in QuickBooks when you record transactions.

The key aspects of small-business bookkeeping are the following:

- Money coming into your business (sales)
- Money going out of your business (expenses)
- Keeping track of inventory and fixed-asset purchases
- Tracking the money you owe (liabilities)
- Using the chart of accounts to properly track transactions
- Exploring accounting methods – cash versus accrual
- Learning double-entry bookkeeping
- Interpreting financial statements

Before we dive into each of these areas in more detail, I would like to introduce you to a fictitious business that we will use throughout this book. **Bedrock Professional Cleaning Services LLC** is the fictitious business that we will refer to throughout each chapter to demonstrate how to manage bookkeeping tasks in **QuickBooks Online** (**QBO**). Bedrock Professional Cleaning Services is a residential and commercial cleaning company. It is an LLC with two co-founders and six employees. They are a service-based business that offers one-time deep cleaning, recurring weekly/monthly cleanings, and move-in/move-out cleanup services. This is their first year in business, and they use accrual-based accounting.

The US edition of QBO was used to create this book. If you are using a version that is outside of the United States, results may differ.

Recording sales

Every business generates sales by selling either products, services, or a combination of the two. For example, Bedrock Professional Cleaning Services generates sales by providing various types of cleaning services to their clients. Meanwhile, a retailer that sells custom T-shirts in various sizes and colors provides a product to generate sales.

In general, there are two types of sales: **cash sales** and **credit sales**. The primary difference between the two is when you receive payment from your customer. Cash sales are sales that require payment at the time a product is sold or services have been provided. For example, let's say a customer walks into a T-shirt shop and buys a T-shirt. This sale would be considered a cash sale because the sale of the T-shirt and payment by the customer take place at the same time.

Credit sales are the opposite of cash sales because the sale and the payment by the customer take place at separate times. For example, let's say Bedrock Professional Cleaning Services spends four hours cleaning a home for one of their residential clients and sends the client a sales invoice at the end of the week. This is considered a credit sale because payment will take place sometime in the future, depending on the payment terms. For bookkeeping purposes, credit sales are recorded as accounts receivable. **Accounts receivable**, also referred to as **A/R**, is the money that is owed to a business by its customers. We will talk more about how to keep track of your A/R balances later in *Chapter 8, Customer Sales Reports in QuickBooks Online.*

Recording expenses

Most of the money that flows out of a business is used to pay for business expenses. Business expenses can be categorized as **recurring** or **non-recurring**. A recurring expense is one that repeats, such as rent, utilities, or insurance, which are typically paid on a monthly basis.

A non-recurring expense is one that is unexpected or takes place less frequently. For example, let's say the air conditioner is on the blink at your office and you need a repairman to come out and fix it. This would be considered a non-recurring expense because it isn't likely to happen routinely.

QuickBooks is designed to help you easily track both recurring and non-recurring expenses. In *Chapter 9, Recording Expenses in QuickBooks Online*, we cover how to create recurring transactions in QuickBooks so that you don't have to manually enter them each time they occur. Plus, you will learn how to pay non-recurring transactions by making online payments, paying with a credit or debit card, or writing a check.

Recording inventory and fixed-asset purchases

To keep track of all the costs and quantities for each item that you purchase, you create a purchase order and send it to your vendor or supplier to place an order. When you receive the goods, you record them in your inventory. As you sell products to customers, you record the sales in QuickBooks so that your inventory, cost, and quantities can be adjusted in real time. In *Chapter 18, Managing Products and Services*, we cover in detail how to set up and manage the products that you sell.

If you purchase computers, printers, or other equipment for your business, these items are called **fixed assets**. When you record these items in QuickBooks, they will be categorized as fixed assets. Fixed assets should be **depreciated** over their useful life. Depreciation is the reduction of the value of an asset due to wear and tear. In *Chapter 16, Closing the Books in QuickBooks Online*, we will cover how to add fixed assets to QuickBooks.

Be sure to refer to current IRS guidelines or your tax preparer regarding thresholds for capitalizing assets versus expensing them at the time of purchase. Also, keep track of all receipts for fixed-asset purchases so your tax preparer can calculate the amount of depreciation you are able to deduct on your tax return. Receipt capture can make it easy to upload receipts from your mobile device to QuickBooks. In *Chapter 9, Recording Expenses in QuickBooks Online*, we cover this in detail.

Recording liabilities

Many people think that liabilities are expenses, but they are not. A liability can be described as money that is owed to creditors, such as a loan you have with a financial institution or money that you owe to vendors or suppliers, which is also called **accounts payable**, or **A/P**. The primary difference between expenses and liabilities is that if you were to go out of business tomorrow, you would no longer have to pay expenses. Instead, you would stop making payments for utilities, and you would lay off employees to eliminate payroll expenses.

On the other hand, if you go out of business, you still have to pay your outstanding liabilities. They don't just disappear as expenses do. For example, if you have an outstanding loan with a bank, you still owe that money and will have to contact the financial institution to make payment arrangements. The same would apply to unpaid bills for products and/or services you received. This means you would have to contact the vendor/supplier and notify them you were going out of business in order to make payment arrangements.

Money you borrow is not income; it is a liability that you will repay. Loan repayments are not expenses; they are a reduction of the liability that you owe.

The chart of accounts

The chart of accounts is a systematic way of categorizing financial business transactions. Every transaction for your business can be categorized into one of five primary categories: assets, liabilities, owner's equity, income, and expenses. Here is a brief description of each category, with an example:

- **Assets**: Assets are items that your business owns. For example, the money in your business checking account is an asset, and the inventory that you have on hand is an asset until it is sold.

- **Liabilities**: As discussed, liabilities consist of money that you owe to creditors. This includes loans, lines of credit, and the money owed to vendors or suppliers (for example, A/P.
- **Equity**: Equity is everything the owner(s) have invested in the business. For example, any money that you invest in your business is equity. Depending on your entity type, equity can be an individual owner, partners, or shareholders. Consult with your tax advisor regarding your entity type and ownership classification.
- **Income**: Income refers to proceeds from the sale of products, such as T-shirts, or services such as photography or consulting.
- **Expenses**: Expenses are payments made to maintain daily business operations. This includes, but is not limited to, rent, utilities, payroll, and office supplies.

When setting up your QuickBooks company account, you don't have to worry about creating a chart of accounts from scratch. Instead, QuickBooks will create a default chart of accounts based on the industry your business falls into. However, you can add and edit accounts to fit the needs of your business. If you already have an existing chart of accounts that you would like to use, you can also create a customized chart of accounts list.

> Create a custom chart of accounts using a template.
>
> You can download the chart of accounts template from the Chapter 1 folder in the following link: `https://github.com/PacktPublishing/Mastering-QuickBooks-2026-Seventh-Edition`.

Choosing an accounting method

One of the key decisions a business will make when setting up their books is which accounting method to use. There are two accounting methods to choose from: **cash-basis accounting** and **accrual accounting**. The primary difference between the two accounting methods is the point at which you record sales and purchase transactions as having occurred in your books.

Cash-basis accounting involves recording sales and purchases when cash changes hands. Going back to our previous example, where Bedrock Professional Cleaning Services invoices a client for cleaning services provided, based on cash-basis accounting, Bedrock Professional Cleaning Services cannot count the cleaning services as income until they receive payment in cash, by check, or by credit card.

Accrual accounting involves recording sales as soon as you have shipped the products to your customer or have provided services. Going back to our example, Bedrock Professional Cleaning Services would count the cleaning services they provided as income once they completed the consultations, regardless of when the customer pays for the services.

In general, most small business owners will start out using the cash-basis accounting method. However, according to the **Internal Revenue Service** (**IRS**), there are certain types of businesses that are not allowed to use this method of accounting. If you are unsure of which method is best for your business, consult with an accounting or tax professional for guidance.

The following businesses should not use cash-basis accounting:

- Businesses that carry an inventory
- C-corporations (regular corporations) whose average annual gross receipts exceed $29 million over the prior three years
- Partnerships with a C corp partner and gross receipts that exceed $29 million over the prior three years

One of the benefits of using QuickBooks, regardless of which accounting method you choose, is that it does not change how you record transactions. As a matter of fact, you can start recording transactions in QuickBooks and decide later on which method you will use. This is because, at any time, you can run reports for either method (cash or accrual). QuickBooks will determine which transactions belong in the report based on the accounting method chosen. In *Chapter 14, Report Center Overview*, we will cover in detail how to generate reports.

Double-entry bookkeeping

One of the key reasons why you don't need to have prior bookkeeping knowledge to use QBO is that the software records all debits and credits for you in the background. However, I thought it would be helpful to explain what's actually taking place when you record an invoice, a bill, or other transactions in QBO. You may have heard the term **double-entry accounting/bookkeeping**. This means that for every financial transaction you record, there are at least two entries—a debit and a credit. This ensures that both sides of the **accounting equation** always remain in balance.

The accounting equation is as follows:

```
Assets = Liabilities + Owner's Equity
```

Let's look at the following example. A T-shirt business owner goes out and purchases $100 worth of T-shirts from a supplier. They don't pay for the T-shirts right away, but the supplier will send a bill later on. For this transaction, inventory increases by $100 and A/P increases by $100. Since inventory is an **asset** and A/P is a **liability**, both **assets** and **liabilities** increased, which keeps their books in balance.

The impact of this transaction on the accounting equation is as follows:

```
Assets = Liabilities + Owner's Equity
$100 = $100 + $0
```

The left side of the equation (*Assets*) goes up by $100 and the right side of the equation (*Liabilities*) goes up by the same amount, $100. Therefore, the equation has been kept in balance.

Behind the scenes in QuickBooks, the following journal entry would be recorded for this transaction:

Financial impact	Account	Amount
Debit (Dr.)	Inventory (T-shirts)	$100
Credit (Cr.)	Accounts Payable	$100

Table 1.1: Example journal entry

We will discuss journal entries in more detail in *Chapter 16, Closing the Books in QuickBooks Online.*

Financial statements

Having access to accurate and reliable financial statements is one of the benefits of tracking your business finances in QuickBooks as opposed to Excel spreadsheets or the dreaded "shoe box." There are five key reports that you should be familiar with: Profit and Loss report, Balance Sheet report, cash flow statement, Accounts Receivable Aging report, and Accounts Payable Aging report.

Next, you will find a brief description of each of these reports:

- **Profit and Loss report**: This report is sometimes referred to as the income statement. It provides you with a summary of all income generated from the sale of your products and/or services. In addition, a summary of all expenses incurred by your business is also provided in this report. The difference between the income and the expenses is calculated and shown on this report as either a net profit (if total income is greater than expenses) or a net loss (if your total expenses exceed your total income). We cover each section of this report in detail in *Chapter 15, Business Overview and Cash Management Tools and Reports.*

- **Balance Sheet report**: This report is sometimes referred to as the statement of financial position. It provides you with a summary of all assets, liabilities, and owner's equity for your business. At the top of the report, assets are listed first, which would include all bank accounts, A/R, and fixed assets. Next are all liabilities, such as A/P, loans, and payroll liabilities, for example. After liabilities, we have the equity section, which includes owner/shareholder contributions and withdrawals. Total assets equal the sum of all liabilities and equity accounts. We show you how to create a balance sheet report in *Chapter 15, Business Overview and Cash Management Tools and Reports.*
- **Cash flow statement**: This report reflects the cash inflows and outflows for a period of time. Cash flow activities are grouped into three categories: operating activities, investing activities, and financing activities. Operating activities include monies due from customers (A/R) as well as what is owed to vendors or suppliers (A/P). Investing activities include cash spent on the purchase of assets such as a business vehicle or machinery and equipment purchases. Financing activities include money coming into the business from a business loan or line of credit. You will learn how to generate a statement of cash flows in *Chapter 15, Business Overview and Cash Management Tools and Reports.*
- **Account Receivable Aging report**: One of the areas where small businesses struggle the most is maintaining a positive cash flow. The Accounts Receivable Aging report is a great tool to help you maintain positive cash flow. This report shows all unpaid customer invoices grouped by the number of days the payment remains outstanding. Reviewing this report and following up with customers on a weekly basis will help to minimize delinquent customer payments, which will ensure that you get paid on time. In *Chapter 8, Customer Sales Reports in QuickBooks Online,* we show you how to generate Accounts Receivable Aging reports.
- **Accounts Payable Aging report**: The Accounts Payable Aging report is the complete opposite of the Accounts Receivable Aging report. This report shows all unpaid bills grouped by the number of days the payments remain outstanding. In order to build and maintain a positive credit history, you should review this report on a weekly basis to ensure that your bills are paid on time. In *Chapter 10, Vendor and Expense Reports in QuickBooks Online,* we show you how to create Accounts Payable Aging reports.

Regularly reviewing key QBO reports—such as Profit and Loss, Balance Sheet, cash flow statement, Accounts Receivable Aging, and Accounts Payable Aging—provides essential insight into your business's financial health and supports informed decision-making for success.

> To demonstrate some of the concepts taught in this chapter and to give you some additional insights not covered, check out my YouTube channel:
>
> https://packt.link/du2BR

Summary

In this chapter, we have covered the eight main areas of focus when managing the books for your business: money coming into a business in the form of sales to customers; money going out of a business for expenses such as office supplies and rent; inventory and fixed-asset purchases, and how to record them in your books; money you owe to suppliers and creditors (liabilities); how to manage the chart of accounts; the two accounting methods (cash-basis versus accrual); how double-entry bookkeeping works, and a brief overview of five key financial statements. Now that you have a basic understanding of how QuickBooks works, you will be able to easily grasp the concepts taught throughout each chapter. In addition, you now understand the key areas of your business that you will need to keep track of to ensure complete and accurate financial statements.

In the next chapter, we will explain in detail what QuickBooks is, the subscription plans available, how to choose the right plan, and how to create your QBO account. We will also share some navigation tips and tricks.

Next steps

Things to start thinking about for your business

1. What does your business sell?
    a. Products
    b. Services
    c. Products and services

2. What type of sales do you envision your business having?

    a. Cash sales

    b. Credit sales

    c. Both

3. Do you currently have or plan to purchase any fixed assets for your business?
4. Do you have (or plan to have) a business loan or line of credit?
5. Do you have (or plan to have) a business credit card?
6. Do you already have an existing chart of accounts list that you (or your accountant) would like you to use in QBO?
7. What accounting method do you currently use or will use for your business?

    a. Cash basis

    b. Accrual basis

2

Getting Started with QuickBooks Online

QuickBooks is the most popular accounting software for small businesses. The desktop version has been around for more than 30 years, and the online version for more than 20 years. It is affordable, easily accessible, and ideal for non-accountants. Before diving into the nuts and bolts of setting up QuickBooks for your business, you should understand what QuickBooks is and what your options are when it comes to using it. Once you know what your options are, you will be in a better position to choose the version of QuickBooks that will best suit your business needs. We will then show you how to create a **QuickBooks Online** (**QBO**) account and how to navigate QBO.

> If you don't have previous experience as a bookkeeper, you will need to know a few bookkeeping basics before you get started. In *Chapter 1, Small-Business Bookkeeping 101,* we covered five key areas in terms of recording transactions in your business: money coming in, money going out, inventory purchases, fixed asset purchases, and liabilities. In this chapter, we also cover the importance of the chart of accounts and accounting methods, as well as what double-entry bookkeeping is.

We will cover the following key concepts in this chapter:

- What is QuickBooks?
- Understanding the role of AI agents in QBO
- Exploring QBO editions

- Choosing the right QBO edition
- Creating a QBO account
- Navigating in QBO

Once you've got these key concepts under your belt, you will be ready to dive into setting up your business in QBO.

> The US edition of QBO was used to create this book. If you are using a version that is outside of the US, results may differ.

What is QuickBooks?

QuickBooks is an accounting software program that allows you to track your financial transactions, such as income and expenses, for your business. One of the benefits of using QuickBooks is having access to key financial reports (such as profit and loss reports) so that you can see the overall health of your business at any time. Having access to these reports makes filing your taxes a lot easier. QuickBooks has been around for more than three decades and is the accounting software used by millions of small businesses around the globe.

QBO is a cloud-based program that is accessible from any mobile device or desktop computer with an internet connection. It is available in four editions, and we'll focus on discussing each edition in detail next.

The most recent addition to the Intuit product line is **Intuit Enterprise Suite** (**IES**). IES is for medium to large businesses that are growing rapidly and expect to outgrow QBO soon. It can help simplify complex operations with multiple entities and departments to keep track of. It has automated revenue recognition and multi-dimensional reporting, which give you key insights into what is going on with your business in real time. Use this link to schedule a free demo to find out whether IES is right for you: `https://www.intuit.com/enterprise/`.

Understanding the role of AI agents in QBO

Within the last several months, QuickBooks has completely transformed the user experience. In addition to the changes made to the user interface, you also have access to Intuit AI agents that will help you categorize transactions, detect and resolve anomalies, reconcile accounts, and more.

Here is a brief description of the Intuit AI agents that are currently available to help you manage your day-to-day work all in one place:

- **The accounting agent**: The accounting agent can categorize transactions, detect and resolve issues, and reconcile bank and credit card accounts. It can also flag something that needs your approval so that you can stay focused on other aspects of your business. The work performed by the accounting agent will appear in the business feed, which we will discuss later in this chapter.
- **The payments agent**: The payments agent automatically categorizes expenses and creates estimates and invoices from your existing data. It will also identify overdue invoices and draft reminders that you can review and approve with just a few clicks.
- **The customer agent**: The customer agent allows you to source leads from your inbox; it will draft personalized email responses and track every customer opportunity in the sales cycle so that you can grow your business efficiently.
- **The finance agent**: The finance agent analyzes financial data and automatically creates forecasts, highlights variances, and pinpoints the source of any issues that may arise.
- **The project management agent**: Currently in beta, the project management agent helps to streamline the bid-to-profit cycle. By collaborating with the sales and finance agents, the project management agent helps you manage projects efficiently while monitoring profitability for each project. It will highlight any deviations as well as recommend steps to take corrective action for you to review and approve.
- **The payroll agent**: The payroll agent manages payroll tasks proactively by collecting data and running payroll accurately and automatically. It will request confirmation or approval from payroll managers when necessary to ensure that payroll is done right.
- **The sales tax agent**: Currently in beta, the sales tax agent identifies potential issues and suggests fixes to ensure that your sales tax filing and payments are accurate.

You can always see the work performed by AI agents within the business feed. All updates will appear there for your review and approval. Soon, you will be able to see the AI agent status, as well as a past activity log, so you can have access to a history of the actions your AI agents have taken.

The following figure is an example of a task that an AI agent has completed. This notification will appear in the business feed as well as in the **Reports** center. In our example, we can click on the **Review Summary** link shown in *Figure 2.1* to review the key insights that the AI finance agent has prepared regarding our finances for November.

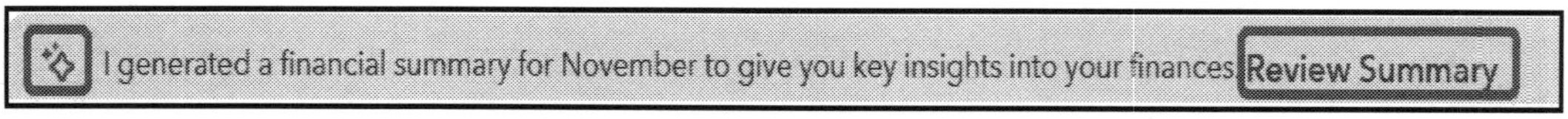

Figure 2.1: AI agent at work icon

This is just a brief introduction to how AI agents are working on your behalf to save you time and allow you to work on those areas of the business that you enjoy most. Unfortunately, not all AI agents are available in each QBO edition. Next, we will cover what AI agents and other features are available in each edition so that you can determine which plan is best for your business. While AI agents are great tools for day-to-day operations, they do not replace the knowledge and expertise of your **Certified Public Accountant** (**CPA**) or tax preparer for more complex issues.

Exploring QBO editions

As mentioned earlier, QBO comes in four editions:

- Simple Start
- Essentials
- Plus
- Advanced

Each edition varies in terms of price, number of users to whom you can give access, and features included.

The following table gives a summary of the pricing and features for each edition of QBO at the time of writing:

	Simple Start	**Essentials**	**Plus**	**Advanced**
Cost	$38	$75	$115	$275
Maximum number of users	1	3	5	25
Accountant users included	2	2	2	3
AI agents included	None	Accounting agent Payments agent	Customer agent Sales tax agent	Finance agent Project management agent

	Simple Start	**Essentials**	**Plus**	**Advanced**
Income and expenses tracking	✓	✓	✓	✓
Invoice and payments (**accounts receivable (A/R)**)	✓	✓	✓	✓
Maximize tax deductions	✓	✓	✓	✓
Reports included	40+	70+	90+	90+
Capture and organize receipts	✓	✓	✓	✓
Track mileage with a smartphone	✓	✓	✓	✓
Cash flow planning	✓	✓	✓	✓
Sales and sales tax tracking	✓	✓	✓	✓
Estimates	✓	✓	✓	✓
Pay 1099 contractors	✓	✓	✓	✓
Connect online sales channels	1	3	All available	All available
User management and permissions		Basic	Basic	Custom
Bill management (**accounts payable (A/P)**)		✓	✓	✓
Track billable hours by customer		✓	✓	✓
Class and location tracking			40	Unlimited
Inventory tracking			✓	✓

	Simple Start	Essentials	Plus	Advanced
Track project profitability			✓	✓
Data sync with Excel				✓
Track employee expenses				✓
Batch invoices and expenses				✓
Automate workflows				✓
Back up and restore data				✓
24/7 support and training				✓
Revenue recognition				✓

Table 2.1: QBO edition comparison

As you can see from the preceding table, all four editions of QBO include the following features:

- **Maximum number of users**: Each plan includes a set number of users. Simple Start includes 1 user, Essentials includes 3 users, Plus comes with 5 users, and Advanced includes up to 25 users. In *Chapter 4, Customizing QuickBooks for Your Business*, we will show you how to give other users permission to access your QBO file.
- **Accountant users included**: Each plan includes two or more accountant users. Simple Start, Essentials, and Plus include two accountant users, and Advanced includes three accountant users. Typically, you would give this level of access to a CPA or tax preparer who has the authority to make changes to your books. In *Chapter 16, Closing the Books in QuickBooks Online*, we will show you how to give your accountant access to your books.
- **Track income and expenses**: Keep track of all sales to customers and expenses paid to vendors.

- **Invoice and payments (A/R)**: Invoice customers, enter payments, and stay on top of unpaid invoices. In *Chapter 7, Recording Sales Transactions in QuickBooks Online*, we will cover how to manage accounts receivable.
- **Tax deductions**: Keeping track of all expenses will ensure that you don't miss out on any tax deductions you may qualify for.
- **Reports**: All plans include preset reports so you don't have to create them from scratch. The number of reports available is based on your subscription plan. Simple Start includes the minimum number of reports (40), and Advanced includes unlimited reports. In *Chapter 14, Reports Center Overview*, we will show you how to generate reports.
- **Receipt capture**: All plans allow you to use your phone or mobile device to snap a photo of a receipt and upload it to QuickBooks. You can also link expense receipts to transactions. In *Chapter 9, Recording Expenses in QuickBooks Online*, we will show you how this feature works.
- **Mileage tracking**: Automatically track miles with your phone's GPS and categorize them as business or personal trips.
- **Cash flow**: Stay on top of your cash flow by using the cash flow tools available in all QBO plans.
- **Track sales and sales tax**: Keep track of sales tax collected from customers, submit electronic payments to state and local authorities, and complete required sales tax forms and filings. In *Chapter 6, Managing Sales Tax*, we demonstrate how to turn on the **sales tax** feature and set up sales tax properly in QBO.
- **Estimates**: Create a quote or proposal and email it to prospective clients for approval.
- **Pay 1099 contractors**: You can keep track of payments made to independent contractors and generate 1099 forms at the end of the year. In *Chapter 12, Managing 1099 Contractors and Introducing QuickBooks Time in QBO*, we will show you how to manage and report payments made to contractors.
- **Sales channels**: E-commerce businesses can connect QBO to their Amazon, Shopify, or eBay accounts to sync sales with QBO. In *Chapter 17, Integrating E-Commerce Platforms with QuickBooks Online*, we will show you how to connect your online store to QBO.

We will discuss the features of each plan in more detail, as well as how to choose the right QBO edition for your business, in the next section.

Choosing the right QBO edition

Depending on the edition, QBO can be ideal for anyone from solopreneurs and freelancers all the way to mid-to-large-sized businesses.

The needs of your business will determine which edition of QBO is ideal for you. The following provides some additional insight into the ideal edition of QBO for different types of businesses.

> When you purchase a QBO subscription, you can track business finances for one business entity. If you need to track more than one business, you will need to purchase a QBO subscription for each business entity that you have. In general, any business with a unique tax ID number will need its own set of books.

Keep in mind that pricing is subject to change and that the pricing reflected in this book is based on what is reflected on the Intuit website at the time of writing.

QBO Simple Start

The Simple Start plan is the most economical, at $38 per month, on sale currently with the first 3 months at 50% off, costing $19.00 per month. It includes one user and two accountant users. QBO Simple Start is ideal for a freelancer or sole proprietor who sells services only, and no products. You may have employees that you need to pay, or 1099 contractors. Most of your expenses are paid via online banking or wire transfer, so you don't need to write or print checks to pay bills. While this edition does not include AI agents, it does include a tool called **Smart Expense Organization** that helps to review and organize your transactions for efficiency and accuracy.

QBO Essentials

The Essentials plan is the next tier and starts at $75 per month, on sale currently with the first 3 months at 50% off, costing $37.50 per month. It includes three users and two accountant users. Unlike Simple Start, you can manage bills (also known as A/P) with the Essentials plan.

QBO Essentials includes all the features found in QBO Simple Start. It is ideal for freelancers and sole proprietors who only sell services and no products (or those who sell "non-inventory" products, such as e-books, other digital items, or subscription offerings). You may have employees and/or contractors whose time you need to keep track of to bill back to clients. Unlike QBO Simple Start, you pay most of your bills by writing checks, and you need the ability to keep track of your unpaid bills. This plan includes the accounting agent and the payments agent, covered in the previous section. QBO Essentials is the next step for small businesses that may need more reporting options.

QBO Plus

The Plus plan is $115 per month, on sale currently with the first 3 months having 50% off, at $57.50 per month. It includes five users and two accountant users. Unlike the Simple Start and Essentials plans, you *can* track your inventory and project profitability with the Plus plan.

QBO Plus includes all of the features found in Simple Start and Essentials. Unlike QBO Simple Start and QBO Essentials, QBO Plus is ideal for small businesses that sell products, since it includes inventory tracking. Similar to QBO Simple Start and QBO Essentials, you can pay employees. If you tend to work on a project basis, QBO Plus is ideal because you can track the profitability of all of your projects, as well as create income and expense budgets. This plan includes the accounting agent, payments agent, customer agent, and sales tax agent, discussed in the previous section.

QBO Advanced

The Advanced plan is the top-tier QBO plan. It starts at $275 per month, currently on sale with 50% off for the first 3 months, costing $137.50 per month. It includes up to 25 users and 3 accountant users.

QBO Advanced includes all of the features found in Simple Start, Essentials, and Plus. It is ideal for businesses that have more than five users needing access to their data. With this plan, you get the accounting agent, payments agent, customer agent, sales tax agent, finance agent, and project management agent, discussed in the previous section. QBO Advanced is QBO Plus on steroids; it includes all of the features found in QBO Plus, along with some great bonus features, such as on-demand online training for your entire team, and spreadsheet sync with Excel.

The bonus features you will find in QBO Advanced are as follows:

- **Spreadsheet sync with Excel**: Connect QBO to Excel to gain access to pre-made templates and the ability to build consolidated reports for multiple companies and easily refresh your data.
- **Employee expenses tracking**: Employees can submit expenses directly to QuickBooks for easy tracking, review, and reimbursement.
- **Batch invoices and expenses**: Enter, edit, and email hundreds of invoices, checks, expenses, and bills instead of entering them one by one.
- **Custom access control**: It provides a deeper level of user permissions that allows you to manage access to sensitive data, such as bank accounts.

- **Exclusive premium apps**: Intuit has more than 700 best-in-class apps to customize QuickBooks for your business needs. For example, the Amazon Marketplace connector is available to automatically sync e-commerce sales to QuickBooks.
- **24/7 support and training**: With QBO Advanced, you get support 24 hours a day, 7 days a week, at no additional cost. In addition, on-demand online training videos are available to help you and your staff get up to speed on how to use QBO. This training has an annual value of $3,000 but is included with your subscription to QBO Advanced at no additional cost.
- **Workflow automation**: This feature helps you save time and minimize risk by implementing automation for repetitive tasks.
- **Data restoration**: This allows you to continuously back up changes to your company file or restore a specific version.
- **Revenue recognition**: This new feature allows you to automatically track and enter deferred revenue into your books so that you can stay compliant with standards that state how and when businesses should recognize their revenue.

Depending on your business and individual circumstances, you should now be able to determine whether you will need QBO Simple Start, Essentials, Plus, or Advanced. It is important to pick the right version for you so that you have access to the appropriate features you will need. However, you can upgrade or downgrade your QBO plan at any time. Now that you know about the QBO subscription plans, we will show you how to create a QBO account.

Creating a QBO account

The first step to setting up your business in QBO is to create a QBO account. In this section, we will create a QBO account for **Bedrock Professional Cleaning Services, LLC**, a fictitious business we will use to demonstrate features and explain concepts taught throughout this book. **Bedrock Professional Cleaning Services** is owned by a partnership that provides cleaning services to both professional and residential customers. Bedrock Professional Cleaning Services is in its first year of business and has no employees. Instead, the partners have hired contractors to help meet the demands of the business.

To create a QBO account, go to the Intuit website and select a QBO subscription plan.

Follow these steps to create a QBO account:

1. Open your web browser and go to the Intuit website: `www.intuit.com`.
2. Click on **Products** and select **QuickBooks**, as shown in *Figure 2.2*:

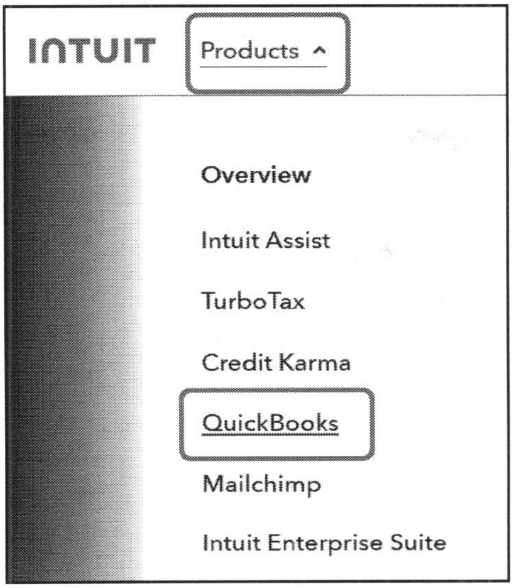

Figure 2.2: Navigating to QuickBooks

3. Click on **Plans & Pricing**, as indicated in *Figure 2.3*:

Figure 2.3: Choosing Plans & Pricing

4. Choose from four pricing plans (**Simple Start**, **Essentials**, **Plus**, or **Advanced**) as indicated in *Figure 2.4*:

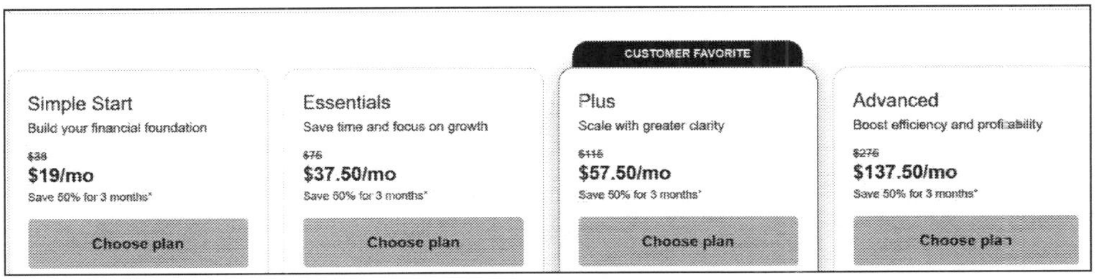

Figure 2.4: Choosing a pricing plan

The pricing shown here is correct as of the time of writing this book and is subject to change. To get a special discount on your QBO subscription, contact me at `www.crystalynnshelton.com`, and I will get you taken care of.

5. After selecting a plan, you will be asked whether you want to continue without payroll. Select this option; in *Chapter 13, Managing Employees in QuickBooks Online*, we will cover payroll in more detail.
6. Intuit has a service called **QuickBooks Live Bookkeeping** that connects you with a bookkeeper, who can assist you in getting things set up properly and managing ongoing tasks.

   Select **Off** for the **QuickBooks Live Bookkeeping** option. You can elect to add this service later or reach out to a QuickBooks ProAdvisor here: `https://quickbooks.intuit.com/find-an-accountant/`.

7. Create an Intuit account by providing your business email address, a secure password, and mobile number, as indicated in *Figure 2.5*:

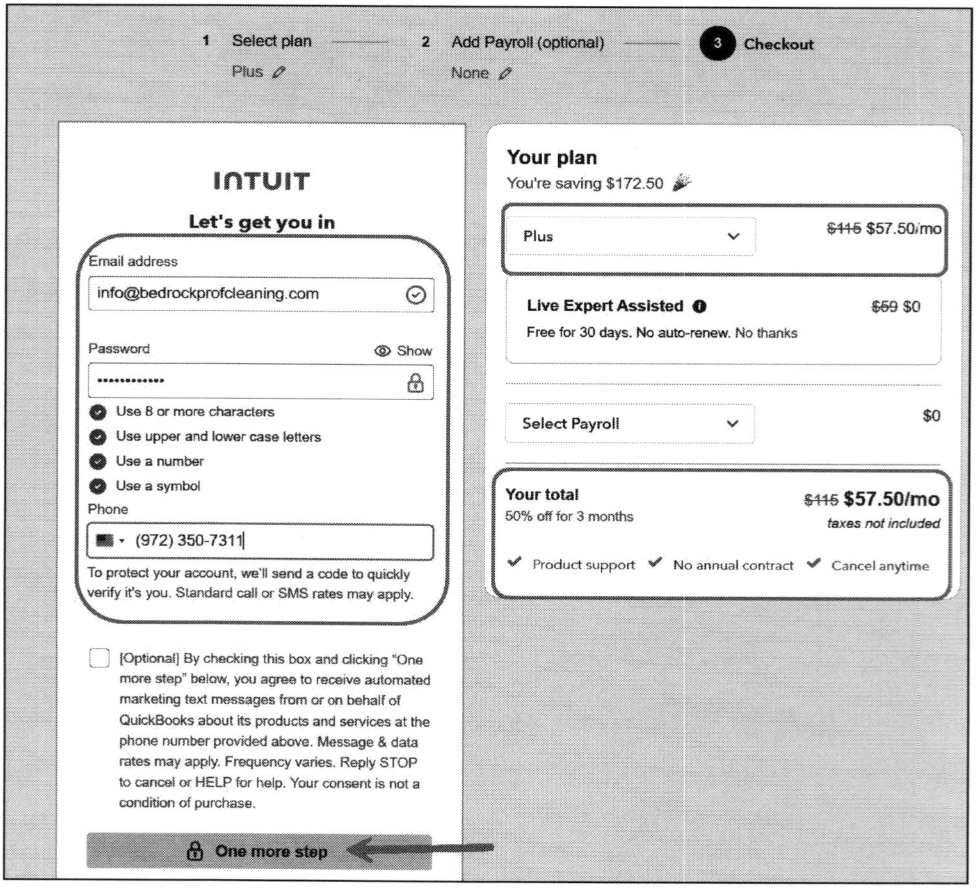

Figure 2.5: Creating an Intuit account

If you need to set up multiple companies, you will be able to use the same email address to set up additional companies. Instead of creating a new account, you will click on the **Sign In** option, as shown in *Figure 2.6*, to sign into your existing Intuit account. This will ensure that you can access *all* of your company files using one sign-on.

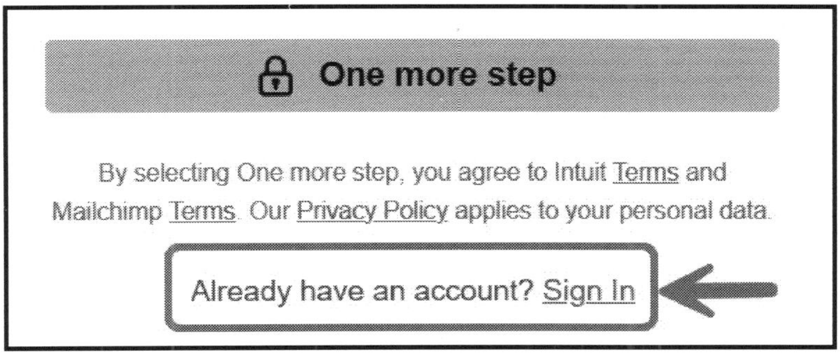

Figure 2.6: Signing into an existing QBO account

8. On the right, you will see the plan you have selected along with the monthly cost. After entering and saving your credit card info, the following welcome screen will appear:

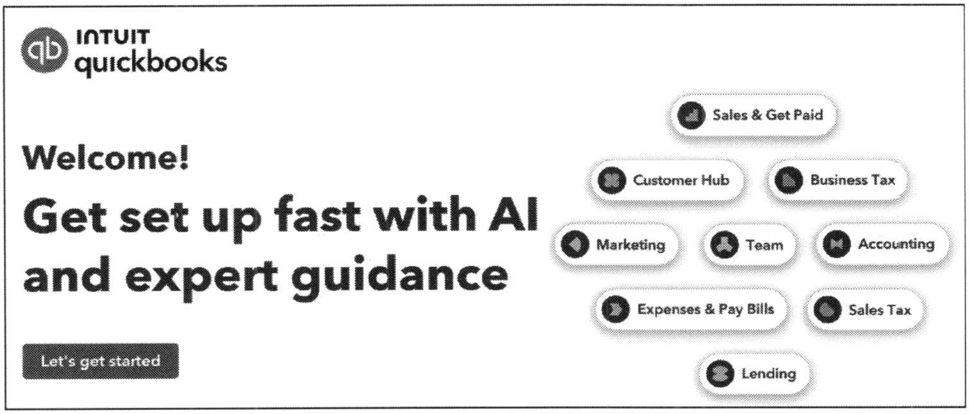

Figure 2.7: Welcome screen after account creation

9. Click **Let's get started**, as shown in *Figure 2.7*. The following screen will appear:

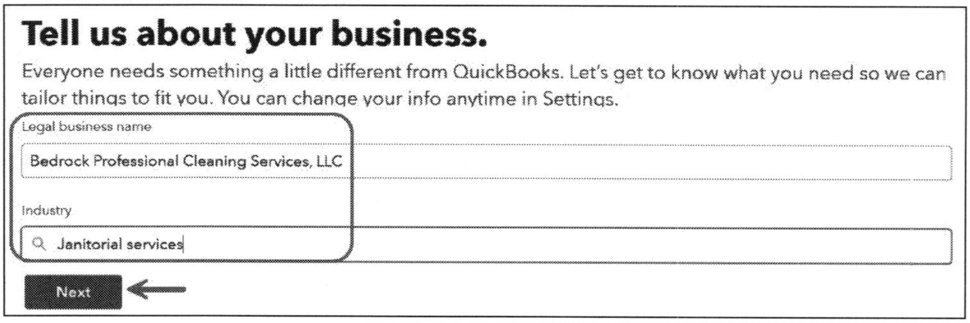

Figure 2.8: Entering your legal business name

10. Type your legal business name, as shown in the screenshot, and click the **Next** button. The following screen will appear:

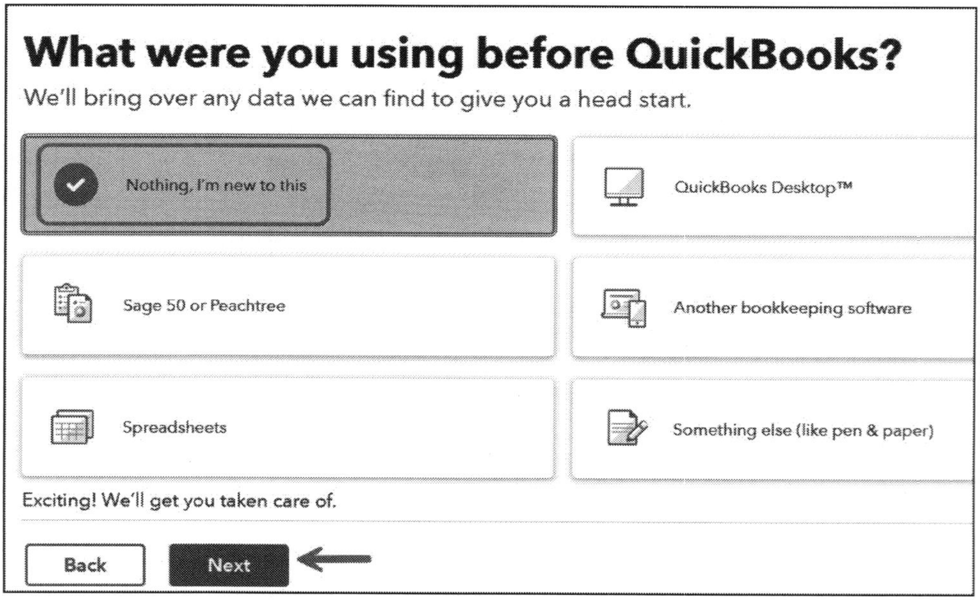

Figure 2.9: Confirm how you have been managing your finances

> QuickBooks uses industry selection to create a chart of accounts. Instead of having to create a chart of accounts list from scratch, QBO will provide you with a preset list of accounts that will include a few customized accounts commonly used by businesses in the industry that you select.

11. Select how you are currently keeping track of your finances. If you select **QuickBooks Desktop** or **Sage 50 or Peachtree**, instructions for how you can convert that data into QBO will come up. For Bedrock Professional Cleaning Services, select **Nothing, I'm new to this**.

    If you are migrating from another accounting software to QBO, check out the YouTube video tutorial by Intuit QuickBooks at *Migrating to QuickBooks Online* at `https://www.youtube.com/watch?v=Ddph_qKThYw` for step-by-step instructions.

12. On the next screen, indicate the structure of your business. Bedrock Professional Cleaning Services is an LLC with multiple partners that own the business, so select **Partnership**, as indicated in *Figure 2.10*:

Figure 2.10: Selecting business type

13. Click the **Next** button.

Most small businesses start out as sole proprietors. If you're not sure what your business structure is, talk to your accountant. You can always select **I'm not sure** and answer this question in the *Company settings* section, which we will explore in *Chapter 3, Company File Setup*. However, it's important that you select a business structure to customize QuickBooks for your business.

14. On the next screen, you can select how your business makes money so that QuickBooks can customize your user experience to meet your specific needs. For Bedrock Professional Cleaning Services, choose **Provides Services**, as shown in *Figure 2.11*:

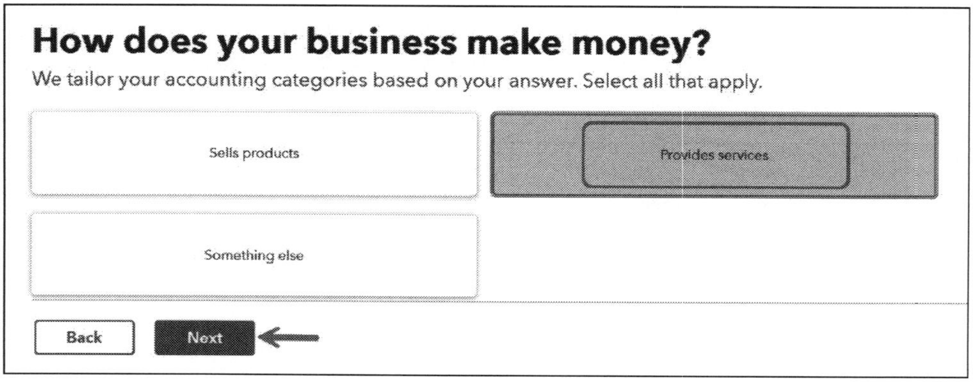

Figure 2.11: How does your business make money?

15. Click **Next**. On the next screen, you will select what you would like to do in QBO. Choose **Send & track invoices**, **Organize your expenses**, and **Track your bills**, as shown in *Figure 2.12*:

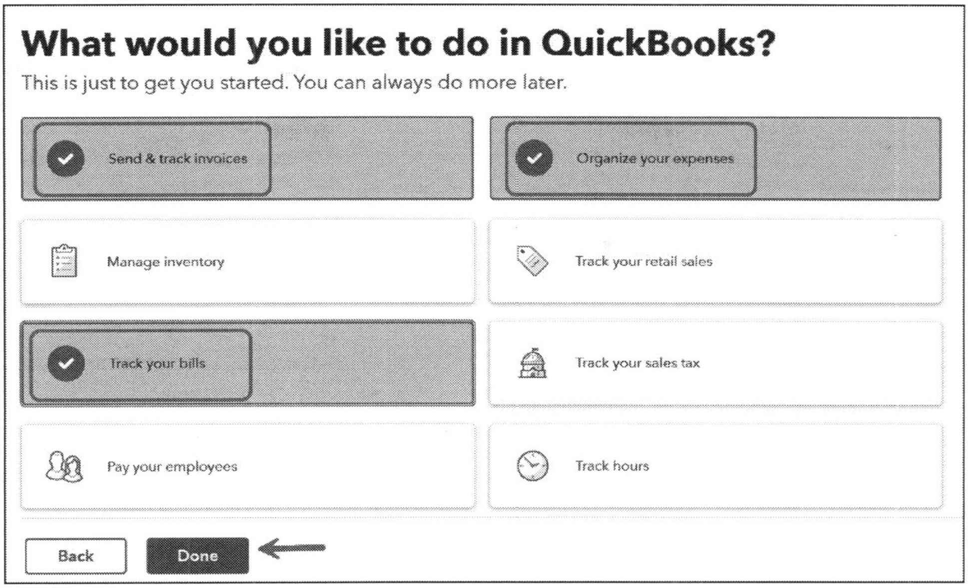

Figure 2.12: Selecting your role in the business

16. Click **Done**.

Congratulations! You have completed the initial QuickBooks setup, taking you one step closer to managing your books. Next, we will show you how to navigate through the program, which will help you locate what you need to complete your business setup.

Navigating in QBO

The QBO user interface is currently undergoing several changes as of the writing of this book. This means that screenshots in this section might vary slightly from what you see when you log in to your QBO account. There are a variety of ways you can navigate within the program, including via the following:

- Left navigation menu
- All apps/app carousel
- Home dashboard
- Gear menu

Let's look at the left navigation menu first.

QBO left navigation menu

To explore what the QBO left navigation menu looks like, we will use our sample company, Bedrock Professional Cleaning Services, LLC:

Figure 2.13: QBO left navigation menu

On the left menu bar, you will find several ways to navigate QBO. A brief description of what you will find, starting at the very top of the menu, is as follows:

- **Create** (formerly **New**): This allows you to access tasks related to customers, vendors, your team, and other tasks. We will provide you with a deeper dive into what you can find in this menu later on.
- **Bookmarks**: This is where you will find the apps that you have chosen to create a bookmark for so that you can quickly access them. You can bookmark any area that has the *bookmark* icon next to it.
- **Home** (formerly **Dashboard**): This is the page that will display when you log in to QBO. It will include a personalized greeting, and below that will be the apps carousel, **Business Feed**, **Create actions**, and your business at a glance. We will provide you with additional details about what you can find on the home page later in this chapter.
- **Feed**: Within the business feed, you will find work performed by the AI agents. For example, notifications about transactions that have been automatically posted, details about transactions that are ready for your approval, as well as transactions that need your attention, will be summarized here. This is a good place to start when you first log in to QBO for the day.
- **Reports**: This will take you directly to the **Reports** center. As mentioned previously, each QBO plan includes more than 40 report templates that you can generate in just a few clicks. In *Chapter 14*, *Reports Center Overview*, we will teach you how to navigate the **Reports** center.
- **All apps/app carousel**: Depending on the tasks you need to perform in QBO, you can access all areas of QBO via **All apps**. Another way to describe apps is the various "departments" of your company. **All apps** includes the following:
    - **Accounting**
    - **Expenses & Bills**
    - **Sales & Get Paid**
    - **Customer Hub**
    - **Team**
    - **Time**
    - **Projects**
    - **Inventory**
    - **Sales Tax**

- **Business Tax**
- **Lending**
- **Payroll**

Below **All apps**, you will find the various apps' departments that have been pinned for quick access. You can "pin" an app by clicking on the **Customize** button located at the very bottom of the left menu bar, shown in *Figure 2.13*.

QBO Home dashboard

The initial screen you will see when you log in is the **Home** dashboard. At the top of the screen, you will see the business feed. This is where you can go to see what work AI agents have performed, including items pending your review and approval. **Create actions** is toward the middle of the page, and this is where you can take quick actions to perform tasks such as create an invoice or pay a bill. Finally, apps that allow you to navigate to different areas, such as **Accounting**, **Sales & Get Paid**, are easily accessible from the **Home** dashboard. A brief description of what you will find on the **Home** page is as follows:

- **Business Feed**: The business feed is similar to the news "headlines." The items listed here are what you should pay attention to when you first log in. If you have not completed your QBO setup, you will see a **View setup** link, as shown in *Figure 2.14*, which will display a checklist of tasks that need to be done to complete your setup. As you finish a task, QBO will mark it completed. Once you have connected bank accounts and started to record transactions, the accounting agent will offer suggestions on actions that you can take. For example, if a customer's invoice is past due, the payments agent will prepare an email to remind the customer that their payment is due. You will have the opportunity to review the reminder and make any changes before sending it out.

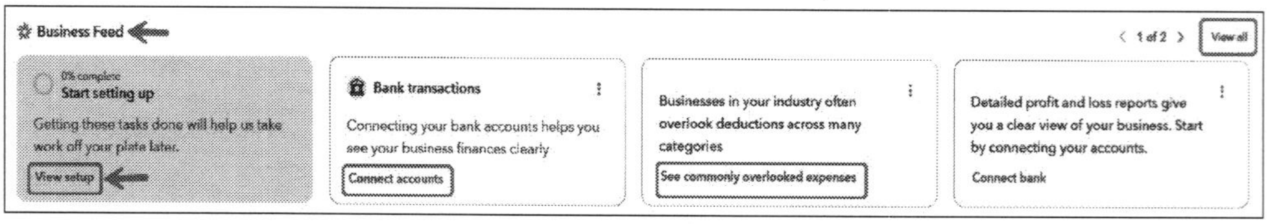

Figure 2.14: Business Feed overview

- **Create actions:** This section of the **Home** page includes buttons that allow you to quickly complete tasks. As shown in *Figure 2.15*, you can add an employee, add a time entry, get paid online, create an invoice, and record an expense. Click **Show all** to customize this list to include the most common tasks for your business.

Figure 2.15: Create actions in QBO

- **Business at a glance** appears below **Create actions** on the **Home** page. You can find your sales, mileage, bank accounts, profit and loss, accounts receivable, accounts payable, expenses, and outstanding invoices (paid and unpaid) here. Similar to **Create action**, you can customize the information that appears in this section.
- **All apps**: All apps is where you will find the various areas of QBO that you will be working in on a daily basis. When you hover your mouse over the **All apps** menu, it will show you the list of each area that you can navigate to.

  Within the **Accounting** app, you will find **Bank transactions**, **Integration transactions**, **Receipts**, **Reconcile**, **Rules**, **Chart of accounts**, **Recurring transactions**, **My accountant**, and **Live Experts**. A brief explanation of each of these follows:

- **Bank transactions**: You can manage all the transactions downloaded into QBO from the bank and credit card accounts you have linked to QuickBooks. In *Chapter 11, Managing Bank Feeds and Reconciling Bank and Credit Card Accounts*, we will show you what to do with bank transactions.
- **Integration transactions**: This is where you can manage transactions downloaded from the apps you have linked to QBO, such as PayPal, Shopify, Square, and so on. In *Chapter 17, Integrating E-Commerce Platforms with QuickBooks Online*, we will cover how to connect and manage transactions from your online store.
- **Receipts**: You can find any receipts you have uploaded using the QBO app.
- **Reconcile**: This allows you to match your bank and credit card statements with what has been recorded in QBO. In *Chapter 11, Managing Bank Feeds and Reconciling Bank and Credit Card Accounts*, we will show you how to reconcile bank and credit card transactions.

- **Rules**: This allows you to create bank rules so that QBO can automatically categorize recurring bank/credit card transactions. In *Chapter 11, Managing Bank Feeds and Reconciling Bank and Credit Card Accounts*, we will show you how to create bank rules.
- **Chart of accounts**: This is a list of categories you can use to organize income and expense transactions. In *Chapter 4, Customizing QuickBooks for Your Business*, we will show you how to add, edit, and delete accounts in QBO.
- **Recurring transactions**: This allows you to create a template for repeat expenses, such as rent and telephone expenses. In *Chapter 9, Recording Expenses in QuickBooks Online*, we will cover how to create and manage recurring transactions.

Now that you have a better understanding of how to navigate QBO from the left navigation menu and the **Home** dashboard, along with how to customize it to fit your needs, let's look at the next navigation tool: icons.

QBO icons

The following screenshot shows the common icons that can be found at the top right of any screen in QBO:

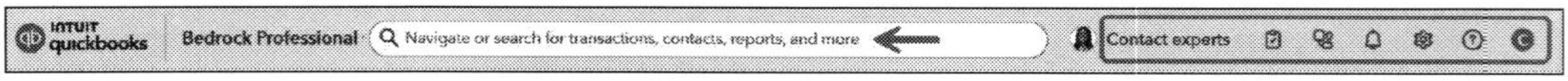

Figure 2.16: Icons on the home page

The following are explanations of the options in the preceding screenshot:

- **Search**: If you need to locate an invoice, bill, or any transaction, you can do a global search of the program by typing an account name, the name of a vendor, an amount, or any information in this field to search for it.
- **Contact experts**: This allows access to a live bookkeeper who can help you get your books set up and is available through this link; additional charges may apply.
- **Tasks**: The icon to the right of **Contact experts** is the checklist of tasks to complete setup, and a tab for ongoing tasks that you can use to create a to-do list with a due date to help you prioritize your work.

- **My integrations**: All sales channels and other apps you have connected with QBO will appear here so that you can easily manage them. You can also head over to the **Integrations** center to research software products that integrate with QBO.
- **Notifications**: Notifications about changes that have been made to your account or upgrades to your QBO subscription can be found here.
- **Gear**: This icon will display a menu of tasks that you can perform in QBO. Tasks related to global company settings, lists, and tools, such as reconciling and budgeting, can be found here. We will explore the *gear* menu next.
- **Help**: If you have a question or need to learn how to do something in QBO, you can click on this icon to launch the **Help** menu. You will find detailed support articles, video tutorials, and access to a sample company file in this section.
- **Account info**: This allows you to log out of QuickBooks or manage your Intuit account. If you need to update your email address, billing information, or even your user ID, you can do so within the **Manage Intuit account** section.

As we mentioned previously, the QBO icons allow you to navigate the program so that you can quickly get to the information you need. In addition to icons, the QBO menus allow you to access your overall company settings, lists, tools, and your company profile. We will cover the *gear* menu next.

Gear menu

In addition to the left navigation menu, there are a couple more menus you can use to navigate QBO.

The first menu is accessible through the gear icon, located in the upper right-hand corner, next to the *Notifications* icon. The following screenshot shows the menu that will display when you click on the *gear* icon:

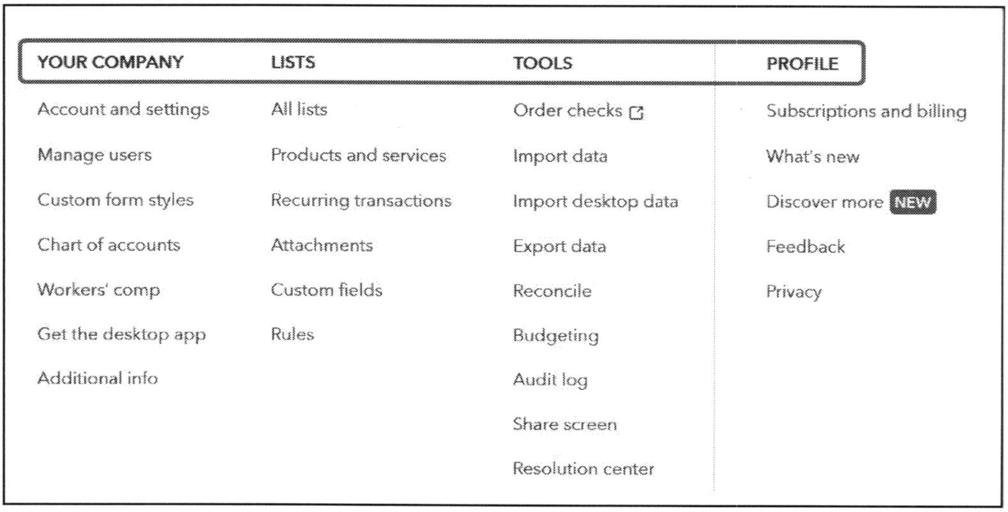

Figure 2.17: Gear menu options

A brief description of the areas of QBO that you can access through the *gear* icon is as follows:

- **YOUR COMPANY**: This menu includes global company accounts and settings, which we will explore in detail in the next chapter. It also allows you to access **Manage users**, which is where you can give other users access to your QuickBooks data. You can customize forms such as invoices and estimates, launch the chart of accounts, and access additional information, which shows you the keyboard shortcuts you can use to navigate QBO more efficiently.
- **LISTS**: This menu includes several QuickBooks lists, such as products and services, recurring transactions, attachments, custom fields, and rules. You can manage recurring transactions such as monthly rent or utility expenses from this menu. In addition, files or images that you have attached to QuickBooks transactions, such as receipts or signed contracts, are accessible in the form of attachments.
- **TOOLS**: If you need to order checks that you can print from QuickBooks, you can do so by selecting the **Order checks** option in this column. If you have customer, vendor, product, or service information that you need to import, you can select **Import data** and follow the on-screen instructions. If you are currently using QuickBooks Desktop, you can use the **Import desktop data** option to migrate your data from desktop to QBO. Also available are the bank and credit card reconciliation tool, the budgeting tool, and the audit log.

- **PROFILE**: You can manage your QBO subscription under the **Subscriptions and billing** section. **What's new** will provide you with info on the latest features, and **Discover more** will allow you to add apps, new features that you don't currently have, and AI agents. There is also a **Feedback** section where you can submit recommendations or issues to the Intuit team. The **Privacy** option provides you with information about the built-in privacy features included in QBO.

Another menu that is available in QuickBooks is the **Quick Create** menu. You can access this menu by clicking on the **Create** button located at the very top of the left navigation menu. The following screenshot shows the menu that you will see when you click on the **Create** button:

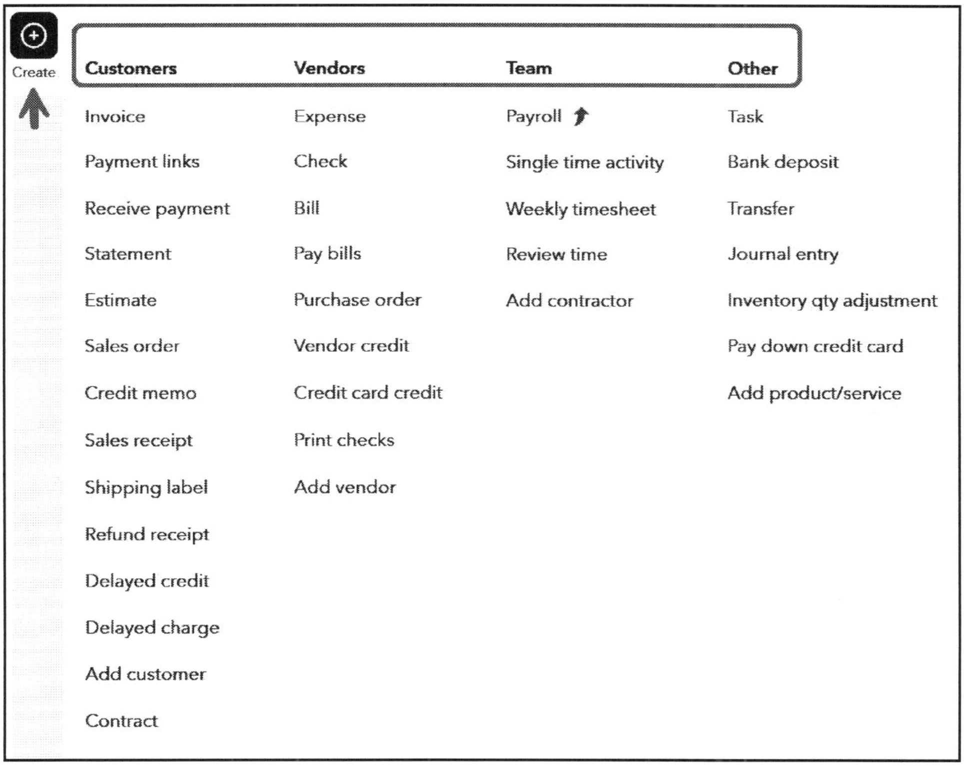

Figure 2.18: The Quick Create menu

The areas of QBO that you can access through the **Quick Create** menu are as follows:

- **Customers**: Most of the transactions that pertain to customers can be found here, from creating invoices and sales receipts to accepting customer payments and adding new customers, to name a few.

- **Vendors**: Tasks related to vendors can be found in this section. This includes recording expenses, writing checks, tracking unpaid bills, creating purchase orders, and adding new vendors.
- **Team**: If you sign up for a QuickBooks **Payroll** subscription, you can access all payroll-related tasks in this section. This includes adding new employees, setting up employee deductions, running payroll, and making payroll tax payments.
- **Projects**: If you have QBO Advanced, you will see a **Projects** menu. Within this menu, you can create projects and project estimates, as well as manage all projects.
- **Other**: This section includes creating tasks, making bank deposits and bank transfers, recording journal entries, making inventory adjustments, paying down credit cards, and adding products and services.

In this section, we learned how to access the menus of QBO, all of which give you access to your company information, lists, tools, and profile. In addition, the **Quick Create** menu allows you to access customers, vendors, employees, and other areas of QuickBooks. From *Chapter 3, Company File Setup*, onward, we will show you how to navigate through these menus to customize QuickBooks for your business.

Summary

In this chapter, we explained what QuickBooks is and introduced you to the QBO product line. We covered setting up your QBO account and basic navigation using dashboards, icons, and online menus in QBO. We also provided tips on how to choose the right software for your business. Having a good understanding of the QuickBooks product line will help you choose the best product for your business. In addition, having a basic knowledge of bookkeeping helps you understand the accounting that takes place behind the scenes in QuickBooks when you enter an invoice or pay a bill.

In the next chapter, we will show you how to customize QuickBooks for your business. This will include setting up company preferences and other key information you will need in order to tailor QuickBooks to your business needs.

Next steps

1. If you would like to take QBO for a test drive before you buy, just google *QuickBooks Online Test Drive*. You will have the option to test drive QBO Plus or QBO Advanced, as shown in the following screenshot. Click on one of the links and follow the on-screen instructions to confirm that you are not a robot:

> **Available QuickBooks test drives**
>
> Go to these links to test out QuickBooks in our "Craig's Design and Landscaping Services" demo company.
>
> - QuickBooks Online : https://qbo.intuit.com/redir/testdrive
> - QuickBooks Online Advanced: https://qbo.intuit.com/redir/testdrive_us_advanced

2. If you plan to hire a bookkeeper or accountant to manage your books, be sure to schedule time to meet with that person each month. However, make sure that you have already reviewed your financial reports and made a list of your questions prior to this meeting.

   Be sure to head over to my YouTube channel for step-by-step product demos in QBO. Use this link to access the channel:

   `https://packt.link/du2BR`

3

Company File Setup

Picking up where we left off in *Chapter 2, Getting Started with QuickBooks Online*, we will show you how to customize your **QuickBooks Online** (**QBO**) account using company preferences. Company preferences allow you to establish how sales and expenses are recorded, how payments are handled, and other advanced settings, such as selecting the start of your fiscal year and which accounting method to use.

Before we dive into company preferences, we will spend some time discussing key information and documents that you need to have handy. This will help you to include as much information as possible; otherwise, you will be missing key details that should appear on customer invoices, documents, and forms that can be produced in QuickBooks. In addition, we will show you how easy it is to edit information in this section whenever you need to.

In this chapter, we'll cover the following topics:

- Key information and documents required to complete the company file setup in QBO
- Setting up company preferences in QBO

> The US edition of QBO was used to create this book. If you are using a version that is outside of the United States, results may differ.

Key information and documents

Before we get into the mechanics of creating your company file, you will need to gather some key documents and answer a few questions first. This information is necessary so that you can customize QuickBooks for your business. Plus, having this information at your fingertips will help you complete the company setup a lot faster.

The information you will need to know includes the following:

- **Company name**: This needs to be the legal name or the business name that should appear on all legal documents and payroll forms.
- **Company contact information**: This will include the mailing address, business telephone number, business email address, and website address of the company.
- **Industry**: In QuickBooks, you will select the industry that your business falls into. Using this information, a default chart of accounts list will be created for you. Selecting the correct industry can open up additional reporting for KPIs and other industry-specific information, depending on which version of QBO you are using.
- **Federal tax ID number**: This is a nine-digit number that identifies your business to the IRS. If you don't have a federal tax ID number, you can use your social security number. If you plan to process payroll within QBO, be sure to have your state and local payroll tax account numbers available.
- **Company organization type**: In QuickBooks, you will need to select from one of the following organization types—sole proprietor, partnership or LLC, nonprofit organization, C-Corp, or S-Corp.

  If you are a new business, information on your company's organization type can be found in the letter from the IRS that includes your **Federal Employer Identification Number (FEIN)**. If you are an existing business, this information can be found on your most recently filed tax return for your business.
- **Fiscal year**: In QuickBooks, you will need to enter your company's fiscal year. For example, if you are on a calendar year, it will be January 1 to December 31.
- **List of products you sell**: If you have a lot of products, you should create an Excel or CSV spreadsheet that includes product name, product description, cost, price, and quantity on hand. If you track inventory, we will show you how to import this information in *Chapter 5, Managing Customer and Vendor Lists.*
- **List of services you sell**: Similar to products, you should create an Excel or CSV spreadsheet that includes the name of the service you offer, a brief description, and the price. We will show you how to import this information in *Chapter 5, Managing Customer and Vendor Lists.*
- **List of sales tax rates**: A list of each city, state, or jurisdiction and tax rate for which you are required to collect sales tax, along with the name of the tax authority that you pay, is required to properly set up sales tax in QuickBooks. In *Chapter 6, Managing Sales Tax*, we cover how to properly set up and manage your sales tax.

- **List of customers**: Customer contact details, such as address, email address, telephone number, Facebook handle, or other information you have on file, can be entered into an Excel or CSV file if you wish to import the information into QuickBooks. Like products and services, we will show you how to import this information in *Chapter 5, Managing Customer and Vendor Lists*.
- **List of vendor suppliers**: Vendor contact details, such as a remit-to address, email address, telephone number, primary contacts, and other information you have on file, can be entered into an Excel or CSV file and imported into QuickBooks. Like products, services, and customers, we will show you how to import this information in *Chapter 5, Managing Customer and Vendor Lists*.
- **Chart of accounts list**: While QBO will provide you with a sample chart of accounts, you can use an existing chart of accounts that you may have. Your current list of accounts can be entered into an Excel spreadsheet if you wish to easily import it into QuickBooks. We show you how to import this information in *Chapter 5, Managing Customer and Vendor Lists*.

> Be sure to have copies of your most recent bank and credit card statements, along with the last bank reconciliations completed.

By taking the time to gather these documents, you will ensure that you are not missing key information when you create forms such as customer invoices. In addition, your financial statements will be more accurate and reliable.

QuickBooks includes default settings called **Preferences**. You can edit **Preferences** to customize them to your specific business needs.

Setting up company preferences in QBO

Before you start entering data into QuickBooks, you should spend some time going through the company preferences, which allow you to activate features that you would like to use and deactivate features that you don't plan on using. If you are not sure of what to select in this section, you can always update the settings later. Click on the gear icon and select **Account and settings**, located below the **Your Company** column.

The company preferences are made up of eight key areas:

- Company settings
- Usage settings
- Payments settings
- QuickBooks Checking
- Sales settings
- Expenses settings
- Time settings
- Advanced settings

Let's look at each one of these in more detail.

Company settings

In your **Company** preferences, you will provide basic information about your business, such as the contact email and telephone number, where customers can reach you, your company logo, and your mailing address. The contact information that's included in this section will appear on customer invoices and emails that are sent to them, ensuring that they know how to get in contact with you. You will also provide your company name and entity type (sole proprietor, partnership, LLC, C-Corp, or S-Corp). It is also a good idea to enter your **employer identification number** (**EIN**) or social security number in this section. This information will be used to file payroll tax returns and 1099 forms, and it can also be used by your tax preparer when filing your taxes.

A brief explanation of the entity types is as follows:

- **Sole proprietor**: Individuals who own and operate a business alone, known as sole proprietors, generally file a Schedule C to report their business income and expenses, along with IRS Form 1040 or Schedule E for rental entities.
- **Partnership**: Businesses with two or more owners, known as partnerships, generally file IRS Form 1065 to report their business income and expenses to the IRS.
- **Limited Liability Company** (**LLC**): This refers to a company with one or more owners who are not personally liable for the LLC's debts or lawsuits. Your LLC can also be a partnership or S-Corp. Check your EIN letter or ask your accounting professional which entity type your LLC was set up as.
- **C-Corp**: This refers to a corporation that is taxed separately from its owners. C-Corps typically file IRS Form 1020 to report business income and expenses.

- **S-Corp**: These are closely held corporations that elect to be taxed under IRS Subchapter S. S-Corps typically file IRS Form 1020S to report business income and expenses.
- **Nonprofit**: A legal entity that operates for public or social benefit, rather than to generate profit for owners or shareholders. A nonprofit earns revenue through donations, grants, services, or product sales, and any surplus is reinvested into the organization's mission. Nonprofits are required to file an annual report, Form 990, to maintain transparency.

Once you have completed the **Company** settings, this page should resemble the one for our fictitious company, *Craig's Design & Landscaping*:

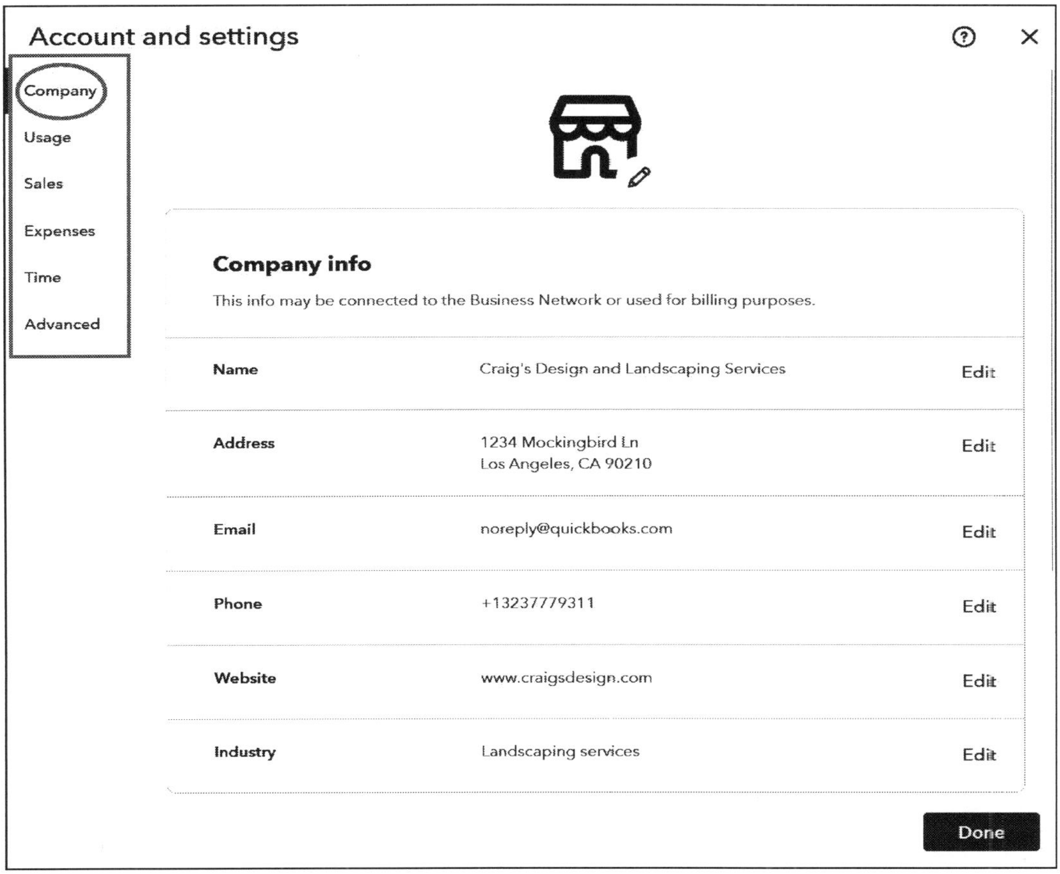

Figure 3.1: Company settings

The information provided in the **Company** preferences can impact several areas of QuickBooks, such as customer invoices, tax forms, and documents. Therefore, it's important to complete this information in its entirety before you begin using QuickBooks to track your business activity. Next, we will explain what information you will find in the **Usage** settings.

Usage settings

A few years ago, Intuit implemented usage limits on all QBO plans. What this means is that each plan will have a maximum number of billable users, non-billable users, classes, locations, accounts that you can add to the chart of accounts, custom fields, and QuickBooks Commerce accounting.

The following is a brief description of these:

- **Billable users**: This refers to the total number of users you can give access to your QBO account. This includes owners, bookkeepers, accountants, employees, contractors, or anyone you provide access to your accounting data.
- **Non-billable users**: Accounting firms, time tracking-only, and reports-only users fall into the non-billable users group. All plans include at least one accountant firm user, Essentials includes unlimited time-tracking only users but no reports-only users, and Plus and Advanced include unlimited time-tracking only and reports-only users. In *Chapter 4, Customizing QuickBooks for Your Business*, we discuss the different types of users you can grant access to your books.
- **Classes**: Depending on your business, a class can represent departments, office locations, or product lines. For example, our landscaping business could create a class for each type of service that they offer (for example, flowerbed upkeep, lawn maintenance, fertilizer services). One of the benefits of using classes is the ability to generate reports that you can filter by class.
- **Locations**: If you have multiple locations, you can turn on location tracking in QuickBooks. One of the benefits of using locations is that you can generate reports and filter by location.
- **Chart of accounts**: We discussed the chart of accounts in *Chapter 1, Small Business Bookkeeping 101*. The chart of accounts is used to classify your day-to-day business transactions. For example, office supplies and telephone expenses are two accounts that appear on the chart of accounts.
- **Custom fields**: A field that will allow you to capture information that is not already included in a transaction, form, or report in QBO. Custom fields are included in all QBO plans.

- **QuickBooks Commerce Accounting**: An integrated solution that is designed to help e-commerce businesses manage their sales, inventory, and overall business finances through multiple channels. Some examples include Shopify, Amazon Business, Square, and Wix.

The following is a summary table that includes the usage limits for each QBO plan:

Description	QBO Simple Start	QBO Essentials	QBO Plus	QBO Advanced
Billable users	1	3	5	25
Non-billable users	2	2	2	3
Classes & locations (combine)	0	0	40	Unlimited
Chart of accounts	250	250	250	Unlimited
Custom Fields per transaction	1	4	4	12
QuickBooks Commerce Accounting	1	3	Unlimited	Unlimited

Table 3.1: QBO usage limits for each plan

Here is a brief explanation of the usage limits for each QBO plan:

- **QBO Simple Start**: QBO Simple Start has one billable user and two non-billable users for accountants included. It does not have the ability to track classes or locations, but you can have up to 250 accounts on the chart of accounts list. It allows for one custom field per transaction and one sales channel.
- **QBO Essentials**: Three billable users (such as tax preparers or employees) and two non-billable users for accountants are included in this plan. In addition, it includes an unlimited number of time tracking users but no reports-only users. Similar to Simple Start, QBO Essentials does not have the ability to track classes or locations, but you can have up to 250 accounts on the chart of accounts list. It includes up to four custom fields per transaction and three sales channels.
- **QBO Plus**: Five billable users and two non-billable users for accountants are included in this plan. In addition to having an unlimited number of time-tracking users, it also includes an unlimited number of reports-only users. Unlike Simple Start and Essentials, QBO Plus allows you to track classes and locations. You can add up to a total of 40 classes and/or locations combined. You can add up to four custom fields per transaction and an unlimited number of sales channels.

- **QBO Advanced**: 25 billable users and 3 non-billable users for accountants are included in this plan. Like QBO Plus, you can have unlimited time-tracking and reports-only users. QBO Advanced allows you to track unlimited classes and locations. In addition, an unlimited number of custom fields per transaction is included, as well as unlimited sales channels. Your **Usage** settings should resemble the ones for our fictitious company, Craig's Design & Landscaping, as shown in *Figure 3.2*:

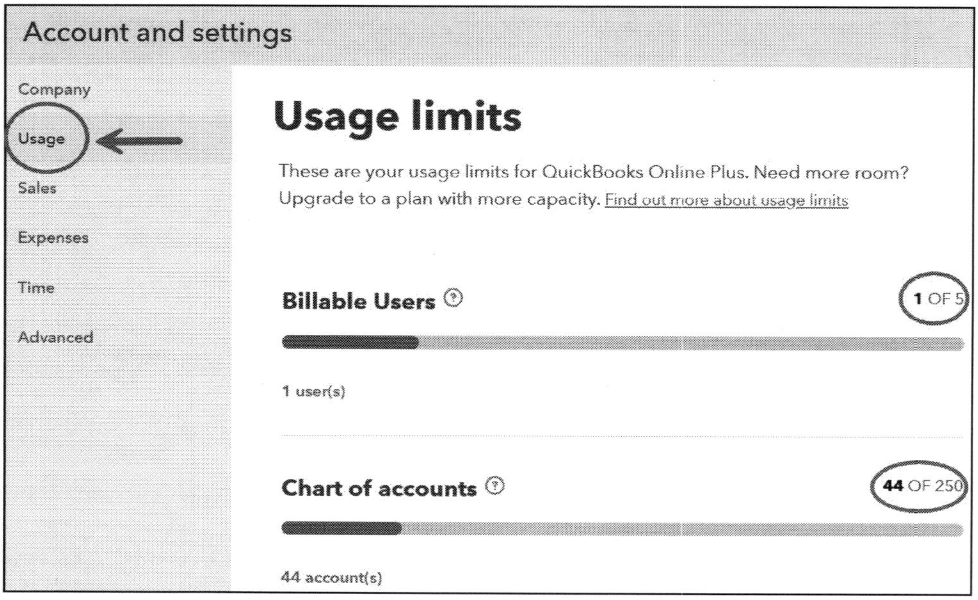

Figure 3.2: Usage settings

Usage limits can impact the number of users you can add to QBO and the classes, locations, and accounts you add to the chart of accounts. This can have a significant effect on how much you pay for your QBO subscription if you hit the maximum usage settings and need to upgrade.

> You can upgrade or downgrade your QBO plan at any time, and it only takes a few minutes.

Payments settings

QuickBooks **Payments** allows you to accept online payments from customers in the form of debit cards, credit cards, Apple Pay, ACH, and PayPal/Venmo. Once approved, all the invoices that you email to customers (directly from QuickBooks) will include a payment link. Your customers can click on the link, enter their payment details, and submit a payment in just a few minutes.

To apply for a QuickBooks **Payments** account, click on the **Activate payments** link and follow the onscreen instructions. Once your account is approved, it will resemble the information shown in *Figure 3.3*:

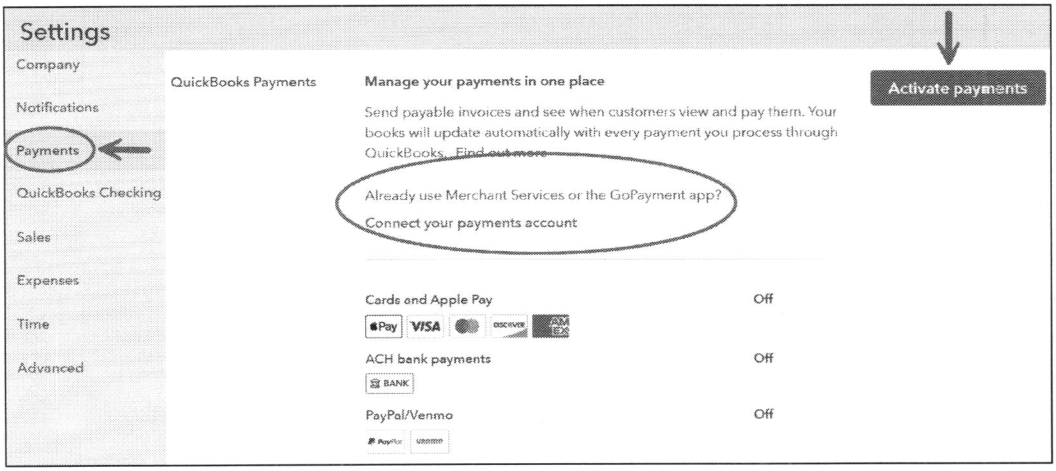

Figure 3.3: Payments settings

If you have an existing **Payments** account, you can connect it by clicking the **Connect your payments account** link and following the onscreen instructions.

As we mentioned previously, QuickBooks **Payments** makes it easier to get paid by customers in a timely manner. This will allow you to maintain a positive cash flow, which is important for your business.

QuickBooks Checking settings

QuickBooks Checking is a monthly fee-free checking account where all your customer payments get deposited. Use your **QuickBooks Checking** account like you do any bank account. You can save money or use features such as envelopes to save proactively and earn 3% APY (at the time of writing this book).

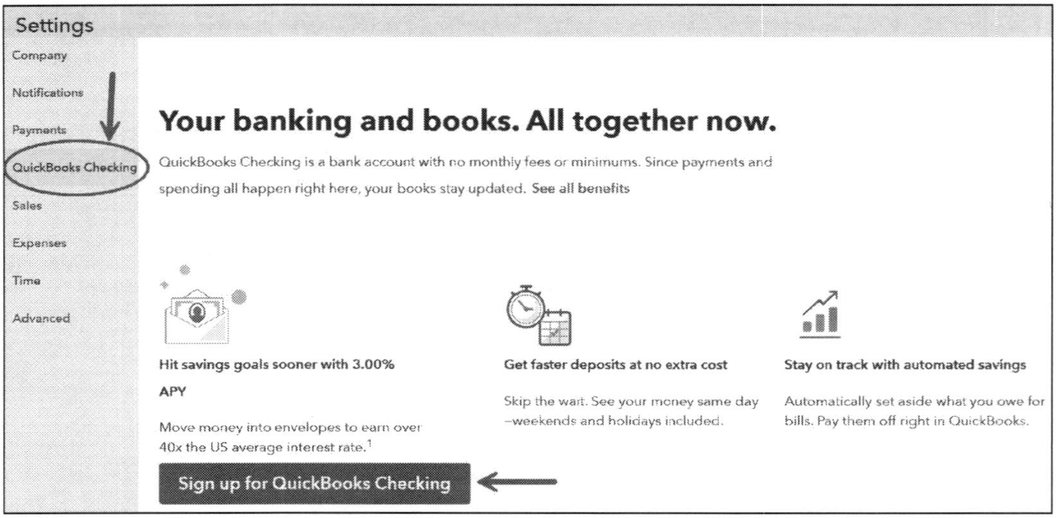

Figure 3.4: Sign up for QuickBooks Checking

Sales settings

The **Sales** settings allow you to select and customize invoices, estimates, and sales receipt templates. In this section, payment terms are set for customers. If you have a few customers whose payment terms differ, you can customize payment terms when you add a new customer. If you offer discounts to customers or require upfront deposits, you can turn these features on here.

The following is a screenshot of the settings for **Sales**:

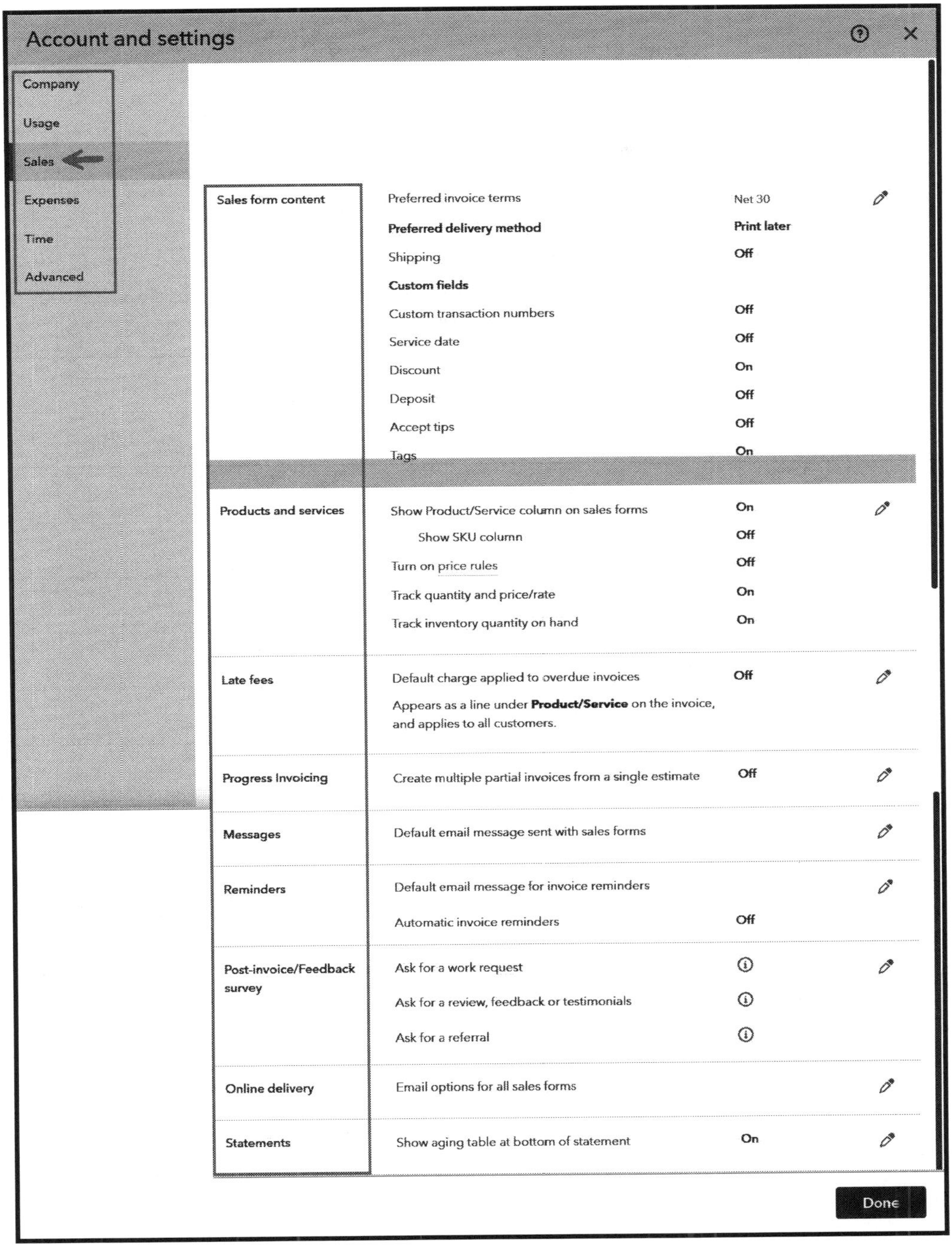

Figure 3.5: Sales settings

Here is a brief explanation of the information you can update/change in the **Sales** settings. You can click within each section or on the pencil icon to make the necessary changes:

- **Sales form content**: In this section, you can select the default payment terms for most customers. For example, if the invoice due date for most customers is *Net 30* days, you will make that selection in the **Preferred invoice terms** field (shown in *Figure 3.5*). If you have customers who have different payment terms, you can select those terms when you add the customer to QuickBooks.

  If you offer customer discounts, accept deposits, or want to add custom fields, you will also turn these features on in this section. The main reason why you may want to offer customer discounts is to incentivize customers to order more or use them to reward customers who make frequent purchases. If you typically need to include a shipping address on your sales form, you can turn this feature on here. QuickBooks will automatically assign transaction numbers (invoice numbers), but if you prefer to generate custom transaction numbers, you can turn this feature on. Keep in mind that you can always return to the **Sales form content** section to activate any of these settings later on.

- **Products and services**: The **Products and services** settings allow you to determine what information you would like to appear on the sales form. You can turn on **price rules**, which is a feature that allows you to set up automatic discounts for certain customers or on specific products and services. If you want to track inventory, you will need to turn on both the **Track quantity and price/rate** and **Track inventory quantity on hand** features. Keep in mind that inventory tracking is only available in QBO Plus and Advanced.
- **Late fees**: Create a default charge that is automatically applied to delinquent invoices. Please note that when you turn this feature on, it applies to all customers. You won't be able to pick and choose which customers you want to apply the feature to. Therefore, I recommend that you leave this feature off and set up reminders. We will cover how to set up reminders in the *Advanced settings* section at the end of this chapter.
- **Progress Invoicing**: **Progress Invoicing** allows you to bill a customer in installments. For example, imagine you have a job that is going to result in $100,000 in revenue, but you are required to complete certain milestones before you can submit an invoice. Progress invoicing allows you to create multiple invoices for one estimate. QuickBooks allows you to run reports that will show you how much you have billed against the estimate and the remaining amount to be billed.

- **Messages**: When you email invoices, sales receipts, or estimates directly from QuickBooks, you can customize the message that is included in the body of the email. You can also select whether you want the invoice to be attached to the email as a PDF document or whether you prefer the invoice details to be included in the body of the email.

Figure 3.6 shows a screenshot of the custom email message options you can choose from:

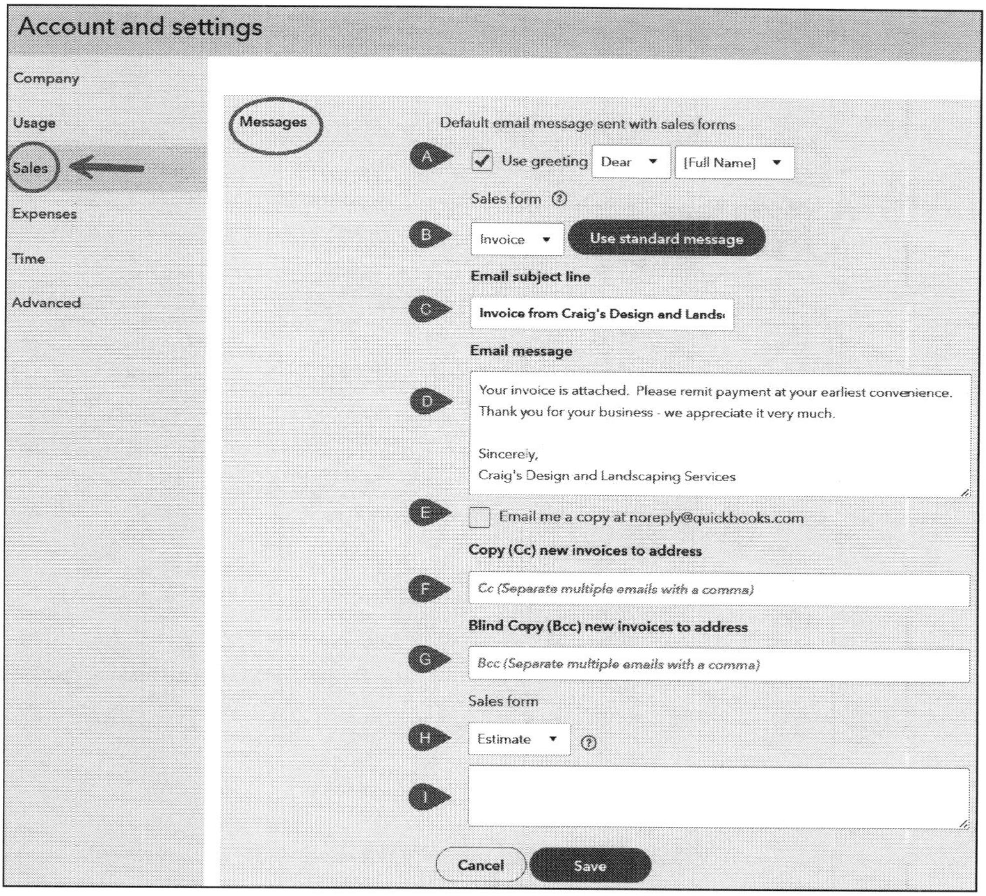

Figure 3.6: Customizing the email message for invoices, estimates, and sales receipts

To customize emails, you can choose to use a greeting (**A**), select the type of form (**B**), customize the email subject line (**C**), customize the email message (**D**), or choose to use the standard message shown. You can have a copy of the email sent to you (**E**), send a carbon copy to someone else (**F**), and **blind-copy** (**Bcc**) new invoices to multiple people (**G**). You can also customize emails for estimates and sales receipts by choosing the preferred option from the drop-down (**H**). You can type a custom email message or copy and paste the message used for invoices (**I**). After making your selections, be sure to click the **Save** button.

When sending invoices to customers via email, you now have the option to enter their mobile number so that they also receive a text message. This helps make it even easier for your customers to make a payment.

- **Reminders**: QuickBooks allows you to send payment reminder emails to customers. You can customize the message that goes out to your customers in this section.
- **Post-invoice/Feedback survey**: A brand-new feature that prompts a customer to complete a survey after they have paid their invoice online. The survey asks for a star rating, feedback on their experience, and whether they'd like to work with you again.

Now that you know how to customize sales forms, set payment terms for customers, and turn on discounts and deposits, it's time to learn how to manage expenses using the **Expenses** settings next.

Expenses settings

The settings in the **Expenses** section include preferences for managing bills, expenses, and purchase orders. In this section, you will determine what information you want to appear on expense and purchase forms, whether you want to track expenses and items by customer, and default payment terms.

The following is a screenshot of the **Expenses** settings:

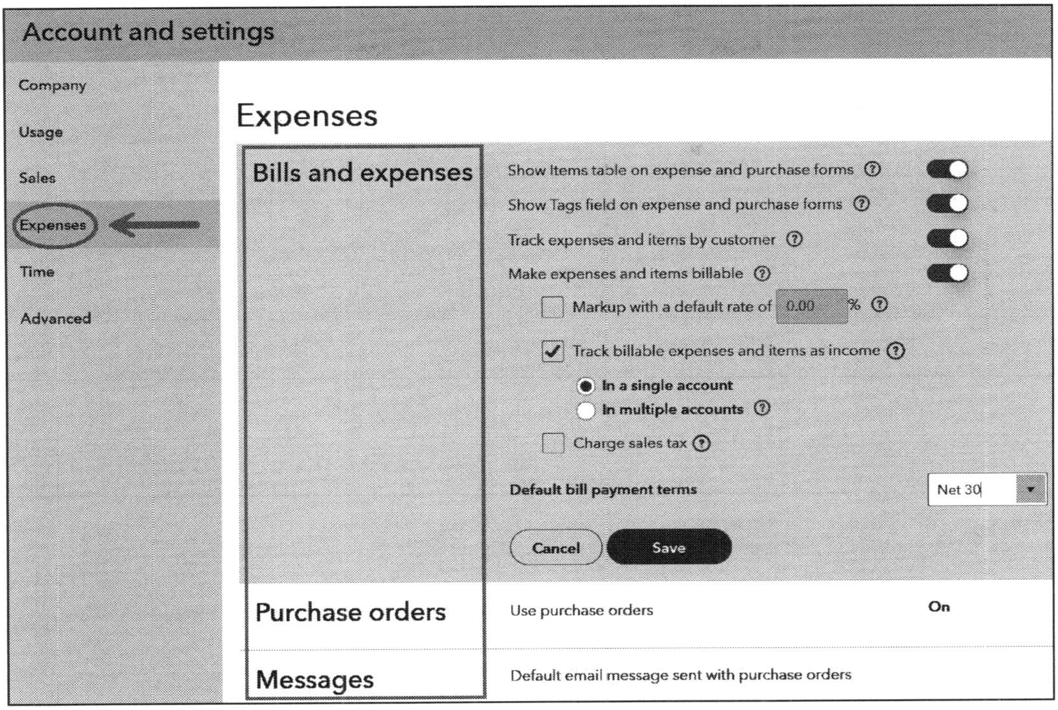

Figure 3.7: Expenses settings

The following is a brief explanation of what you can find in the **Expenses** preferences:

- **Bills and expenses**: This section includes the following five options for tracking expenses:
    - **Show Items table on expense and purchase forms**: This feature is automatically turned on, and it will add a *products and services* table to your expense and purchase forms so that you can itemize your products and services. You will learn more about products and services lists in *Chapter 5, Managing Customer and Vendor Lists.*
    - **Show Tags field on expense and purchase forms**: While tags are no longer available for new customers, existing customers who were using tags before they were discontinued will still have this feature.

  - **Track expenses and items by customer**: This feature allows you to track expenses with a specific customer. This is ideal for reporting purposes if you want to keep track of specific items that have been purchased but may or may not be billable to customers. For example, let's say we want to keep track of the hours worked by contractors for each client. If Craig's Design & Landscaping bills its customers a flat rate, then there is no need to bill the client back for those hours worked, but they need to keep track of them to ensure the flat rate is accurate.
  - **Make expenses and items billable**: This feature adds a billable column on all expense and purchase forms so that you can bill customers for items you've purchased on their behalf. Using our previous example, if Craig's Design & Landscaping did bill its customers by the hour, it could easily select the client and mark the billable column to bill its clients for the hours worked by contractors, as opposed to billing them a flat fee.
  - To see a list of unbilled expenses, you can run the *Unbilled Charges* report, which is located in the **Who Owes You** report group.
  - **Default bill payment terms**: If most of the bills you receive have similar payment terms (for instance, **Net 30**), you can set payment terms for all vendors here and then change the vendor profile for those vendors whose payment terms may differ. In *Chapter 5, Managing Customer and Vendor Lists,* we cover this in detail.
- **Purchase orders**: If you plan to create purchase orders, be sure to turn this feature on. If you don't need to create purchase orders, you can leave it turned off.
- **Messages**: You can email purchase orders directly from QuickBooks to vendor suppliers. This section allows you to customize the email message that your vendor supplier will receive along with the purchase orders.

Now that you are familiar with the **Expenses** settings that affect bills, purchase orders, and expenses, you can set up QuickBooks the way you need to track expenses that are incurred by your business. Next, we will discuss a way for you to keep track of the hours worked by employees and contractors.

Time settings

Basic time tracking is included in all QBO subscription plans. Time tracking allows your team to keep track of the hours they work, using a mobile app with GPS. With GPS, you can see the location that a worker clocked in from. In addition, workers can keep track of their mileage. As a business owner, you can schedule workers, manage time off, and review reports in real time. To learn more about the time tracking plans available, click on the **See plans** button, as shown in *Figure 3.8*:

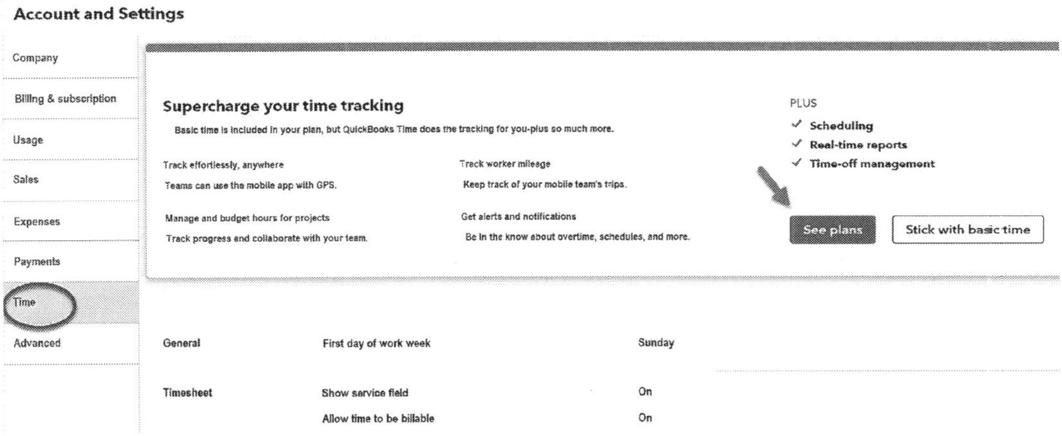

Figure 3.8: See plans button on the Time settings page

Advanced settings

The **Advanced** settings page includes eleven key settings: **Accounting method**, **Customer label**, **Accounting**, **Company type**, **Chart of accounts**, **Categories**, **Automation**, **Projects**, **Currency**, **Communications with Intuit**, and **Other preferences**.

The following is a screenshot of the **Advanced** settings section:

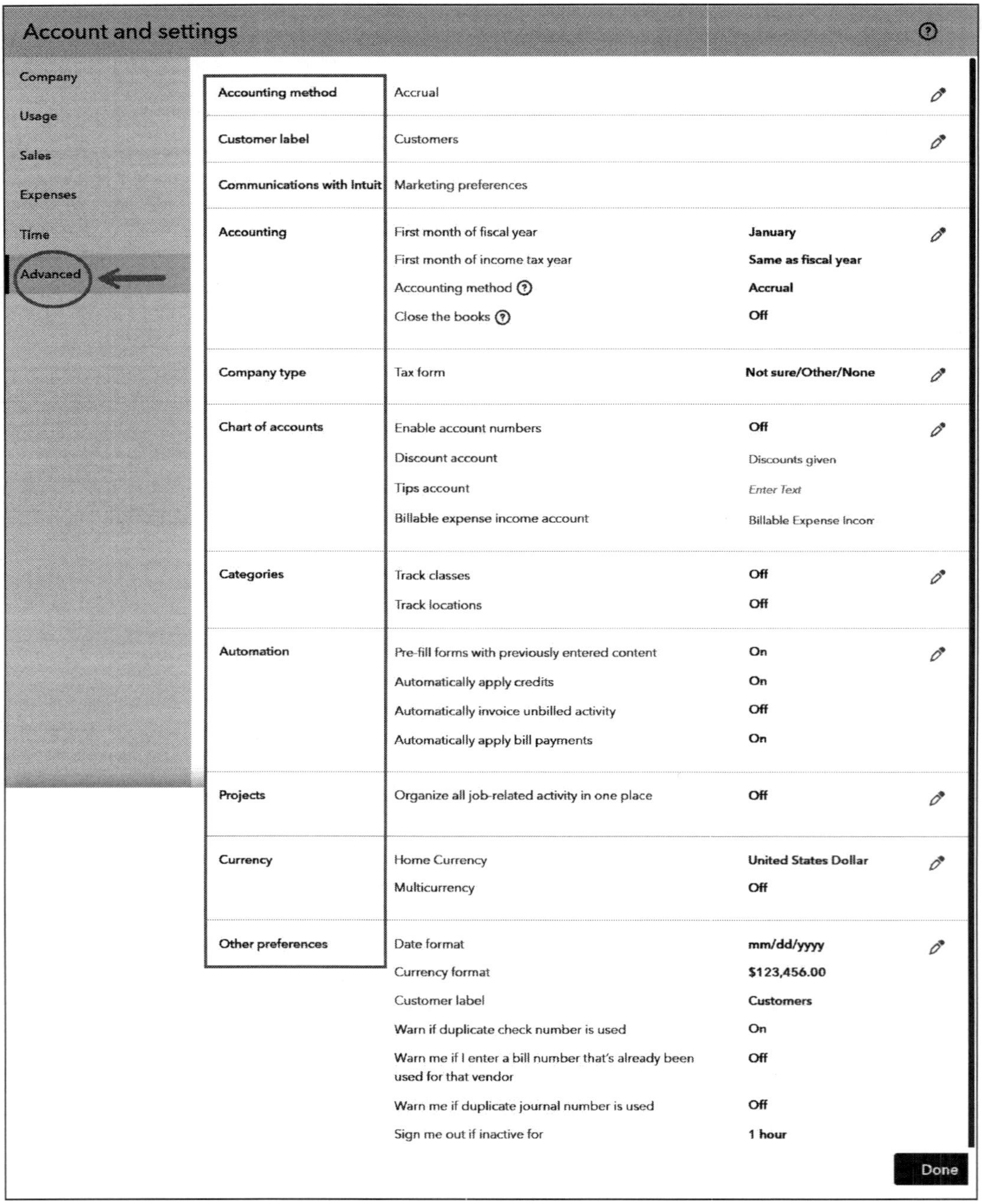

Figure 3.9: Advanced settings

A brief description of what information is included in the **Advanced** settings section is as follows:

- **Accounting method**: In the **Accounting method** settings, you will select whether you use cash basis or accrual basis accounting. If you're not sure, select cash basis for now and then follow up with your tax professional to obtain this information.
- **Accounting**: In the **Accounting** settings, you will select the first month of your fiscal year and income tax year, which may be the same. The accounting method will default from the **Accounting method** field, and there is an option to close the books. Closing the books allows you to prevent any changes from being made to your financial data after a certain date. For example, once you have filed your tax returns for the year, you should enter the last day of the previous year as your closing date (for example, 12/31/2026). This will ensure that information dated 12/31/2026 and prior cannot be changed. An optional password can be assigned to prevent changes to closed periods.
- **Company type**: In this field, you will select the structure of your business. The common business structures are sole proprietor, partnership, limited liability, C-Corp, and S-Corp. The company type is helpful in assigning your chart of accounts to specific line items on the tax return. This is beneficial for linking to tax software or for your tax preparer. For example, if you are a sole proprietor, then you will complete *Schedule C* to report your business income and expenses to the IRS.
- **Chart of accounts**: As we discussed in the previous chapter, the chart of accounts is a way to categorize your day-to-day business transactions. You have the option to assign account numbers to your chart of accounts list by turning on the **Enable account numbers** preference. If your business allows customers to leave tips, you can keep track of these tips in a separate account.
- **Categories**: There are two types of categories in QuickBooks—classes and locations. Classes are generally used to track income and expenses for departments or product lines. Locations are used to track income and expenses for multiple locations of your business. These preferences must be turned on for you to use them.
- **Automation**: You can save time by automating certain tasks. QuickBooks will automatically pre-fill forms based on the information you have provided in a previous transaction for a customer or vendor. You can also allow QuickBooks to automatically apply credit that's been received from vendor suppliers and bill payments. However, setting up your QBO file correctly is important before enabling any of the automated features.

- **Projects**: The **Projects** feature allows you to keep track of all income and expenses for jobs/projects that you are working on. To view all projects, click on the **Projects** tab, which is located on the left navigation bar.
- **Currency**: QuickBooks allows you to create invoices and pay bills in multiple currencies. You can do business with vendor suppliers and customers across the globe by providing invoices in their native currency. All of your financial reports can be generated in your home currency or any currency that you choose.

> Once you turn on the multi-currency feature, it cannot be turned off. This is because several conversion tables are activated in the background once you turn this feature on and start using it.

- **Other preferences**: The **Other preferences** section involves general formatting preferences for the dates and numbers that appear throughout the program. You can also select the type of label for your customers. For example, if you are a nonprofit organization, you can select **Donors**, and if you are a real estate investor, you can select **Tenants**. This nomenclature will appear throughout the program. This preference also includes a warning if you use a duplicate check number or vendor invoice number.

> You should turn both of these features on to help prevent duplicate payments. A similar warning is also included when recording journal entries. A journal entry is an adjustment made to the books for transactions that are only recorded prior to closing the books, such as depreciation. For security reasons, QBO will automatically sign you out after you have been inactive for 1 hour. However, you can change this setting to a maximum of 3 hours.

You now know that accounting settings affect several areas of QuickBooks. You can determine your chart of accounts structure, turn on time tracking, set your home currency, and turn on the multi-currency feature if you do business in other countries. In addition, you can turn on the projects and categories features for additional tracking of income and expenses.

To demonstrate some of the concepts taught in this chapter and to give you some additional insights not covered, check out my YouTube channel:

https://packt.link/du2BR

Summary

In this chapter, we covered key information and documents required to set up a QBO account. We also showed you how to customize the company settings, which include billing and subscription, usage limits, QuickBooks checking, sales, expenses, time, and advanced settings. Taking the time to set up your company file will help you save time in the long run because you won't have to do it later on. Plus, you won't have to worry about customer invoices or vendor bills missing key information because your company file wasn't set up properly.

Remember, you can always edit these settings whenever you need to. While it is ideal to complete this setup now so that when you are ready to start recording transactions in QBO, many of the fields on invoices and bills will automatically populate for you. At some point, if your contact information or business entity changes, you can always make any necessary updates.

In the next chapter, we will show you how to customize QuickBooks Online for your business. You will learn how to customize the chart of accounts list, how to connect your bank and credit card accounts to QBO, how to give other users access to your QBO file, and how to use apps with QBO.

Next steps

1. Download the key information and documents checklist and start compiling this information.
2. What is your business entity type? Contact your tax preparer if you are not sure.

3. How many people do you anticipate giving access to your books? (This will help you determine which QBO subscription plan to sign up for.)
4. Could you benefit from using classes? If so, how would you use them?
5. Could you benefit from using locations? If so, how would you use them?
6. Do you need to charge sales tax for the products or services that you sell? Contact your state or local government to find out.
7. Apply for a QuickBooks Payments account.

4

Customizing QuickBooks for Your Business

Whether you created your **QuickBooks Online** (**QBO**) account from scratch or transferred your details from another accounting software program, there are some additional areas that you need to set up to further customize QBO for your business.

In this chapter, we will show you how to add, edit, and delete accounts to customize the chart of accounts for your business. We will walk through the process of connecting your bank and credit card accounts to QBO so that transactions will automatically be downloaded. By connecting your bank accounts to QuickBooks, you will reduce, if not eliminate, the need to manually enter these transactions into QuickBooks. Please note that uploading bank and credit card transactions to QBO does not record them in your books. You will need to review and record these transactions after they are uploaded. In *Chapter 11, Managing Bank Feeds and Reconciling Bank and Credit Card Accounts*, we will cover this in detail. If you need to give other users access to your QuickBooks data, you can easily do so; we will show you how to give your bookkeeper, accountant, and other users access. A great way to help you streamline day-to-day tasks that can be time-consuming is by adding integrations. We will show you how to navigate the QuickBooks Integration Center. We will wrap up this chapter by showing you how to create customized sales templates that will not only show your customers how professional you are but will also allow you to make it easy for customers to pay you using a payment link via email or text message.

The following are the key topics that will be covered in this chapter:

- Customizing the chart of accounts list
- Connecting bank accounts to QBO
- Connecting credit card accounts to QBO
- Giving other users access to your QuickBooks data
- Using integrations in QBO
- Customizing sales templates

> The US edition of QBO was used to create this book. If you are using a version that is outside of the US, results may differ.

Customizing the chart of accounts list

As we saw in *Chapter 2, Getting Started with QuickBooks Online*, the chart of accounts is a list of accounts that is used to categorize your day-to-day business transactions. It is the backbone of every accounting system, and if it is not set up properly, it can result in inaccurate financial statements.

One of the benefits of using QuickBooks is that you don't have to create a chart of accounts from scratch. Based on the industry that you selected when you created your QBO account, QuickBooks will include a preset chart of accounts list. You can customize the chart of accounts by adding, editing, or deleting accounts to fit your business needs. In this section, we will show you how to add, edit, delete (inactivate), and merge accounts on the chart of accounts list.

Adding a new account to the chart of accounts list

The default chart of accounts list will include a generic list of accounts used by most businesses, with a few custom accounts related to your industry. However, you will most likely need to customize the list based on your accountant's preferences or your own. For example, if you sell products and services, you may want to create an income account for each, as opposed to lumping sales for both into one account.

Go through the following three steps to add a new account to the chart of accounts list:

1. Click on the **Accounting** app located on the left menu bar and select **Chart of accounts**, as shown in *Figure 4.1*:

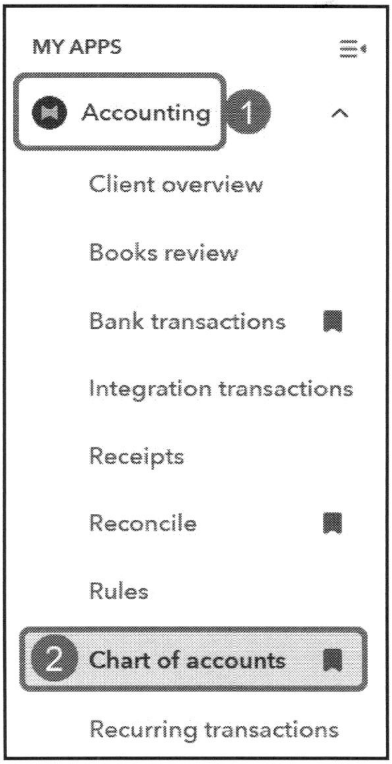

Figure 4.1: Navigating to Chart of accounts

2. Click on the **New account** button located in the upper-right corner of the screen, directly to the right of the **Run report** button, as shown in *Figure 4.2*:

Figure 4.2: The New account button

3. To create a new account, you will need to provide the account name, account type, detail type, and a description of the account, as shown in *Figure 4.3*:

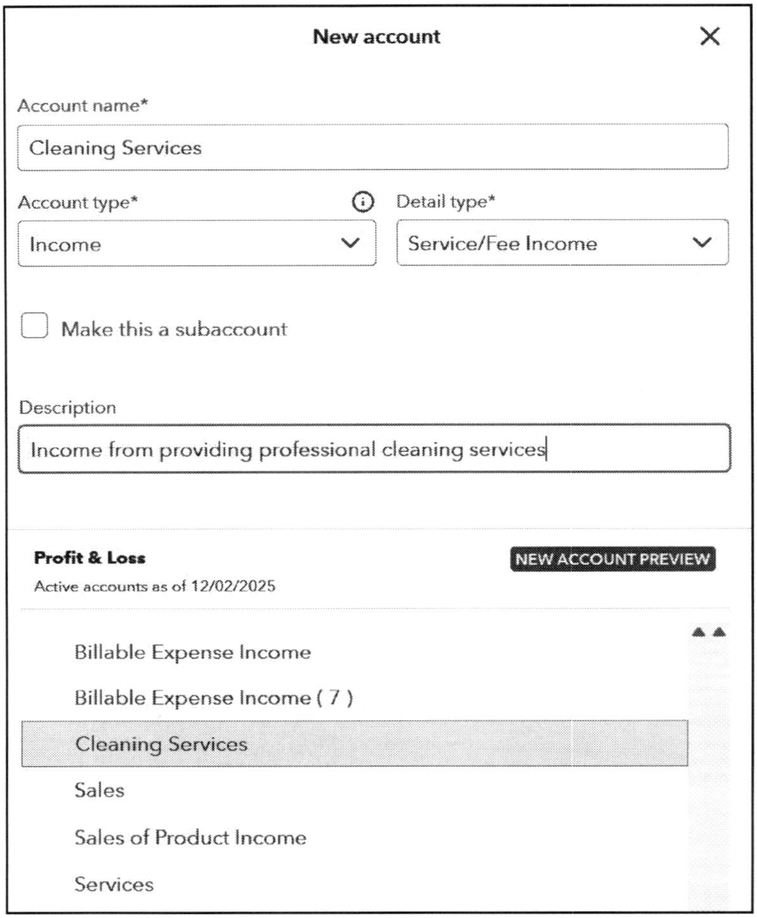

Figure 4.3: New account creation page

The following is a brief description of what information should be included in the fields that are labeled:

- **Account name (1)**: Type the name of the account in this field. In our example, it is **Cleaning Services**.
- **Account type (2)**: From the menu, select the account type that the new account should be categorized as. As we saw in *Chapter 2, Getting Started with QuickBooks Online*, the five main account types are assets, liabilities, equity, income, and ex-

penses. You will also find other account types in this list, such as fixed assets, banks, and credit cards, and they should be used when appropriate. In our example, it is **Income**.

- **Detail type (3)**: From the dropdown, select the description that is the closest match to the account that you are setting up. In our example, it is **Service/Fee Income**.
- **Description (4)**: This field is self-explanatory and should include a brief description of the types of transactions that should be posted to this account. In our example, it is **Income from providing professional cleaning services**.

> While you may be tempted to leave the **Description** field blank, we recommend that you don't. It can be useful to include a detailed description so that a bookkeeper or someone you have hired to manage your books will know what type of transactions belong in this account. If you don't think a description is needed, copy and paste the account name into this field. That way, this field will not appear blank on reports. You can also use this field to enter more details about the accounts, such as account numbers or other useful information.

- **NEW ACCOUNT PREVIEW (5)**: This section informs you of the financial report the account will show up on (**Profit & Loss**, in our example). In addition, it shows that **Cleaning Services** will be grouped with the **Income** accounts, in alphabetical order, on the profit and loss report.

4. Once you have completed all the fields for the new account and saved it, the new account will appear on your chart of accounts list, as shown in *Figure 4.4*:

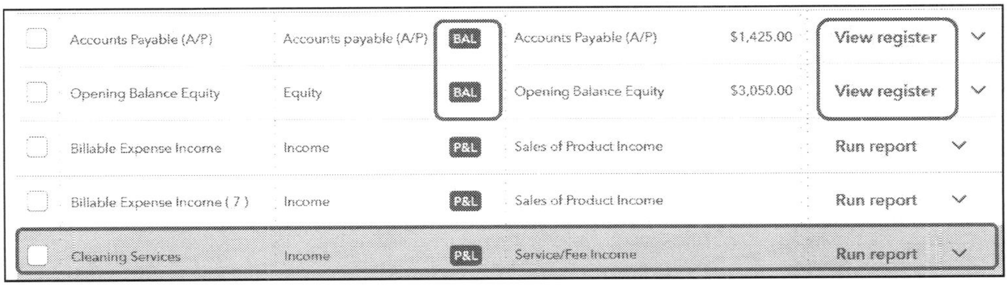

Figure 4.4: The chart of accounts list

Our new account, **Cleaning Services**, has been successfully added to the chart of accounts. Notice this account is labelled **P&L**. This means that you can find this account on the profit and loss (P&L)/income statement. By the same token, accounts that appear on the balance sheet report are labeled **BAL**. As discussed in *Chapter 1, Small-Business Bookkeeping 101,* income and expense accounts appear on the P&L report, and assets, liabilities, and equity accounts will appear on the balance sheet report.

As you can see, adding a new account to the chart of accounts list is pretty straightforward. If you need to add more than five accounts, you may want to consider importing new accounts instead of manually adding them. I recommend that you set up accounts that will be useful for you in managing your business.

> **Sub-accounts** are used to provide a more detailed breakdown of an account that is used for multiple types of transactions. For example, it is a good idea to create a main account for car expenses and sub-accounts for repairs, registration, and gasoline. Having a detailed breakdown of each type of expense will allow you to easily run a report to see how much you have spent on each account.

In the next section, we will show you how to import a chart of accounts list from an Excel file.

Importing a chart of accounts list

If your accountant has given you a chart of accounts list that they prefer you to use, you can import that list into QBO. Go through the following steps to import a chart of accounts list. The template can be found in the the following link: `https://github.com/PacktPublishing/Mastering-QuickBooks-2026-Seventh-Edition`.

1. Format your Excel spreadsheet to include the following columns (**Account Number**, **Account Name**, **Type**, and **Detail Type**) and save it in `.csv` or `.xls` format:

Account Number	Account Name	Type	Detail Type
112720	Checking Account - Bank of America	Bank	Checking
112721	Money Market - First National Bank	Bank	Money Market
410790	Product Sales Revenue	Income	Sales of Product Income
500780	Cost of materials	Cost of Goods Sold	Supplies & Materials

Figure 4.5: Chart of accounts import template

2. Navigate to **Accounting** | **Chart of accounts**, as indicated here:

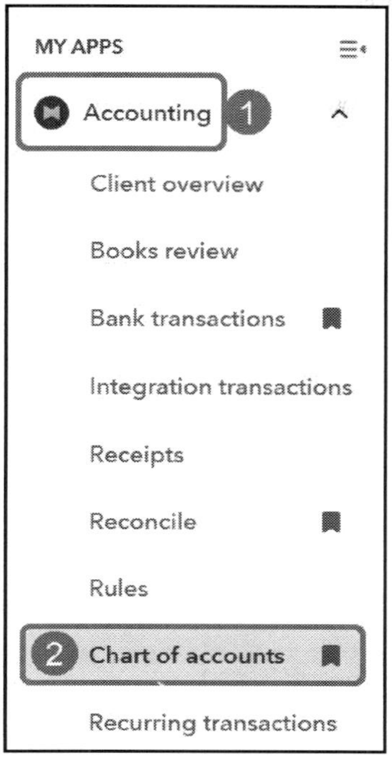

Figure 4.6: Navigating to Chart of accounts

3. Click on the arrow to the right of the **New account** button and select **Import**, as shown in *Figure 4.7*:

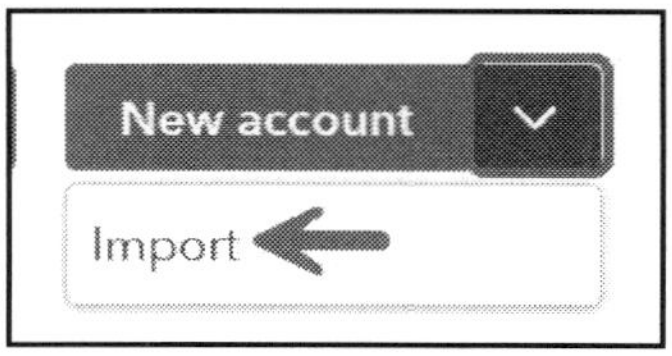

Figure 4.7: Clicking Import

4. The **Import Accounts** screen is displayed:

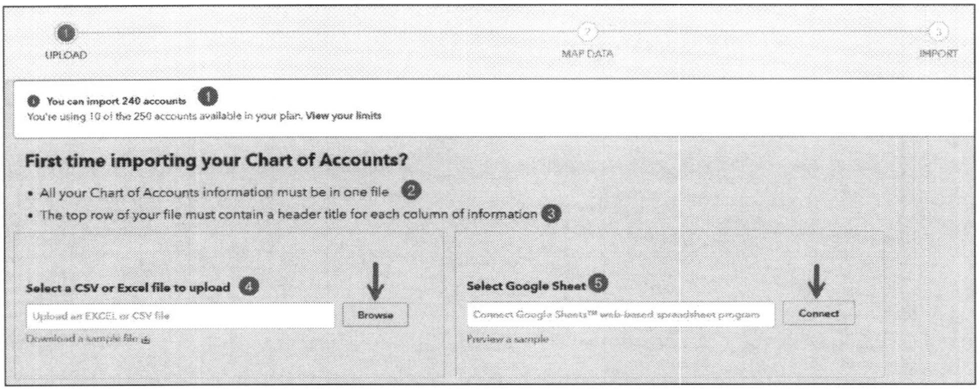

Figure 4.8: Import Accounts screen with highlighted items

A brief description of the highlighted items is as follows:

- **Import limit (1)**: Depending on the QBO plan you have purchased, you will be limited to a certain number of accounts you can import. In our example, the limit is 250, but we can only import 249 accounts after adding the **Cleaning Services** account in the previous example. If you have QBO Advanced, you won't see a limit since the number of accounts is *unlimited*.
- **All your Chart of Accounts information must be in one file (2)**: Be sure to organize all of your accounts in a single spreadsheet.
- **Include header information (3)**: When formatting your spreadsheet, be sure that the first row is a header row that contains a description of the info included in each column. Refer to *Figure 4.5*.
- **CSV or Excel file upload (4)**: You can upload a CSV or Excel (`.xls`) file format; no other file format is allowed.
- **Select Google Sheet (5)**: If you have your data in a Google Sheet, it is also compatible with QBO. Simply click the **Connect** button shown in the preceding screenshot and follow the onscreen instructions.

> *Download our sample Excel template and use it to import your accounts into QBO:* `https://github.com/PacktPublishing/Mastering-QuickBooks-2026-Seventh-Edition`.

Follow the onscreen prompts to complete the import. Next, we will show you how to edit the chart of accounts list.

Editing accounts on the Chart of accounts list

On occasion, you may want to make changes to an existing account on the **Chart of accounts** list. You can change the account name, description, and account type at any time; however, be careful with making a change to the account type if you have transactions that have already been posted. Changing the account type can impact the financial statements. Therefore, make sure you consult your accountant before doing so.

You can edit accounts on the **Chart of accounts** list by going through the following steps:

1. Click on **Accounting**, located on the left menu bar, and select **Chart of accounts**, as shown in *Figure 4.9*:

Figure 4.9: Selecting the Chart of accounts option

2. Scroll through the **Chart of accounts** list or use the search bar to find the account you want to edit. *Figure 4.10* shows the **ACTION** column on the far right. Click on the arrow located to the right of **Run report**:

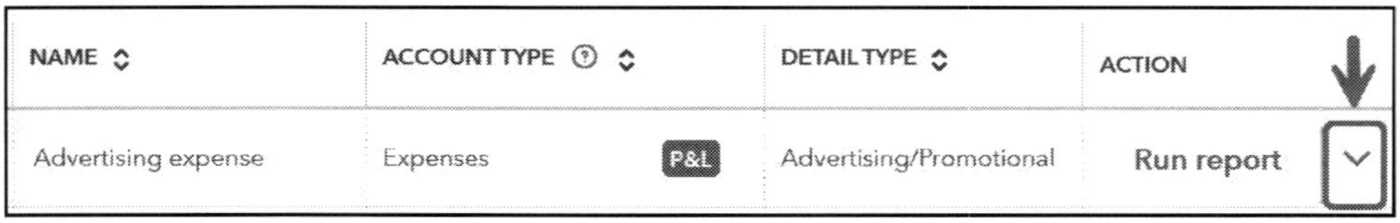

Figure 4.10: Editing an account

3. On the next screen, you will see two options: **Edit** and **Make inactive**, as shown in *Figure 4.11*:

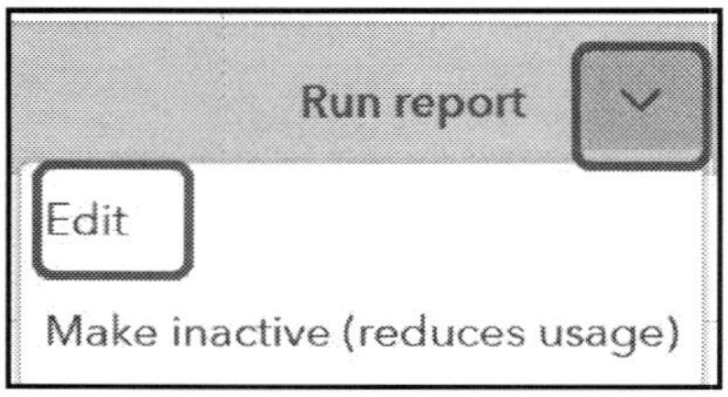

Figure 4.11: Choosing the Edit option

> All accounts that appear on the **Balance sheet** report will show a **View register** link in the **Action** column. This is because all balance sheet accounts keep a running balance from one period to the next, whereas income and expense accounts do not keep a running balance because they are closed at the end of each fiscal period (i.e., month). Therefore, income and expense accounts will show a **Run report** link in the **Action** column.

The following is a brief explanation of when you should edit an account and when you should make an account inactive:

- **Edit:** To make changes to the account name, account description, or sub-account, click on the **Edit** button.
- **Make inactive**: Once you have created an account in QuickBooks, there is no way to delete it. Instead, you will need to inactivate the account. When you inactivate an account in QuickBooks, it will still exist, but it will disappear from the **Chart of accounts** list and will not appear in any drop-down lists. The primary reason for this is that if you have recorded transactions to an account that you decide to stop

using, your transactions will still remain in QuickBooks. This is very important in order to maintain accurate financial records. If you need to review accounts that have been made inactive or reactivate an account, you can easily do so. We will cover this later, in the *Reactivating an account on the Chart of accounts list* section.

4. When you click **Edit**, the current account setup will be displayed. Make the necessary changes, as shown in *Figure 4.12*:

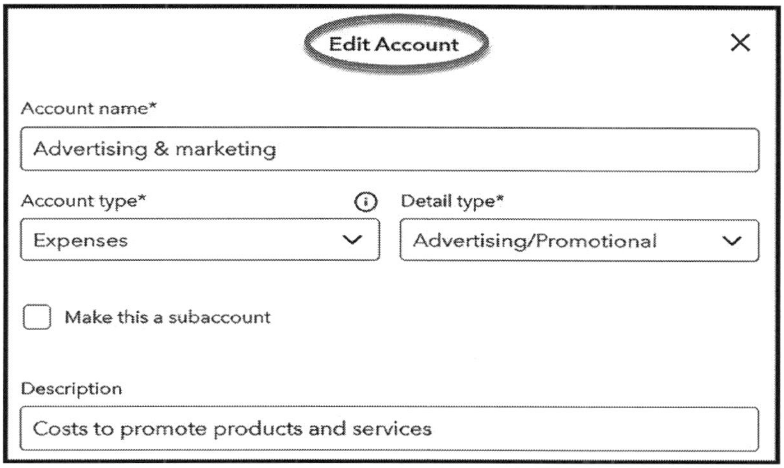

Figure 4.12: Editing the account details

If you have not used the account in a transaction, the **Account name** and **Account type** fields will be editable.

In this section, we covered how to make changes to an existing account on your **Chart of accounts** list. We also explained the difference between editing an account and making an account inactive. As previously mentioned, you cannot delete an account, but you can make it inactive. It's important to note that certain accounts, such as accounts receivable (A/R) and accounts payable (A/P) do not allow you to change the account type. In the next section, we will show you how to inactivate an existing account.

Inactivating an account on the Chart of accounts list

Once you add an account to the chart of accounts list, you cannot delete it; however, if you decide that you no longer want to use an account, you can inactivate the account. Inactivating an account will remove the account from the chart of accounts list and the drop-down menus, but it will still exist in the program. This will ensure that any transactions that have been recorded will remain intact, which will also ensure that you have accurate financial statements.

To inactivate an account, go through the following steps:

1. Click on **Accounting**, located on the left menu bar, and select **Chart of accounts**, as shown in *Figure 4.13*:

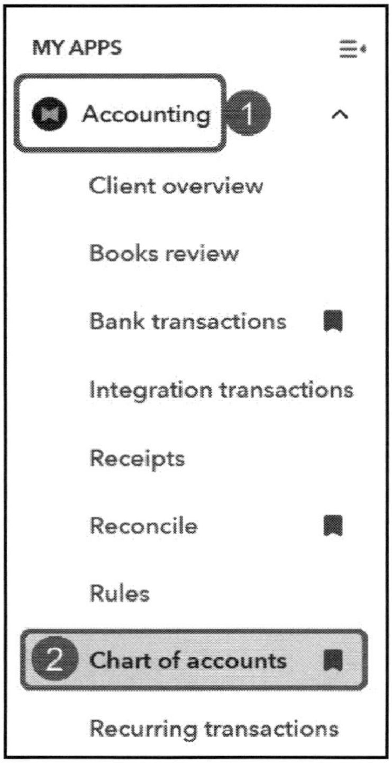

Figure 4.13: Navigating to the Chart of accounts option

2. Scroll through the **Chart of accounts** list to find the account you want to make inactive. In the **ACTION** column on the far right, click on the arrow located to the right of **Run Report**, as shown here:

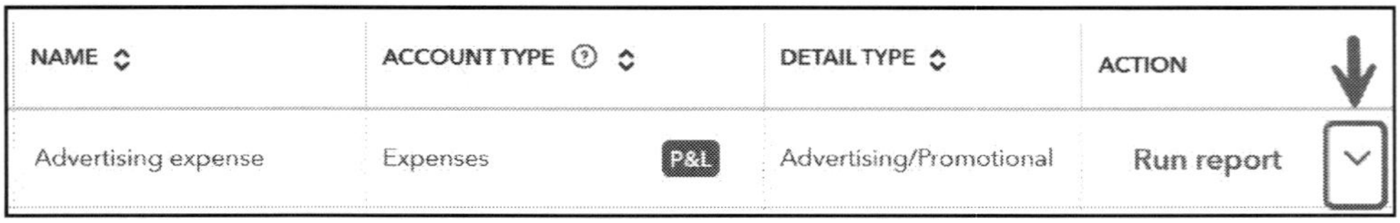

Figure 4.14: Editing an account

3. Select **Make inactive** from the drop-down arrow, as shown here:

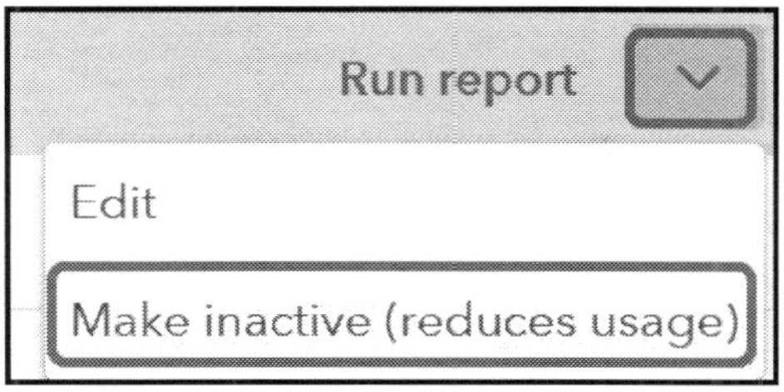

Figure 4.15: Making an account inactive

4. You will then receive a message similar to the one shown in the following screenshot, asking you to confirm that you would like to inactivate the account:

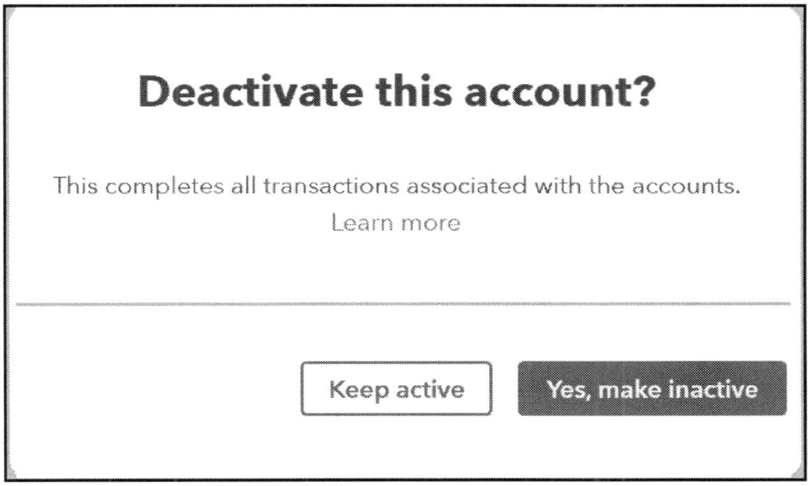

Figure 4.16: Inactivation confirmation message

5. Click **Yes, make inactive** to proceed with the inactivation, or **Keep active** to leave the account active.

Reactivating an account on the Chart of accounts list

If you decide to reactivate an account that was previously made inactive, you can easily do this:

1. From the chart of accounts list, click on the gear icon located directly above the **ACTION** column, as indicated here:

Figure 4.17: The gear icon

2. Put a checkmark in the box that says **Include inactive** so that all inactive accounts appear on the **Chart of accounts** list, as indicated here:

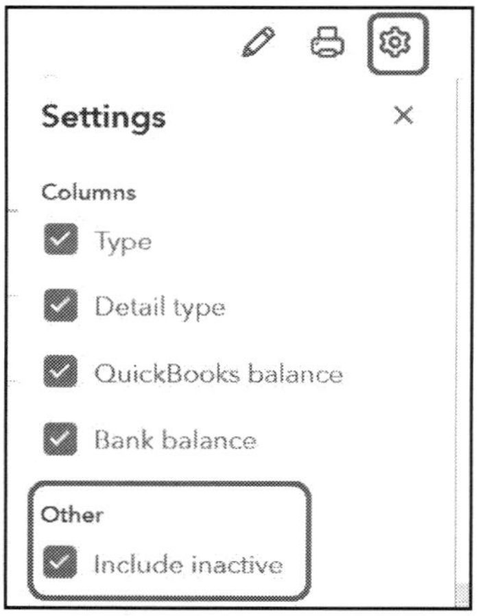

Figure 4.18: The Include inactive option

3. Next to the inactive accounts, click the link that says **Make active** to the right of the account, as shown here:

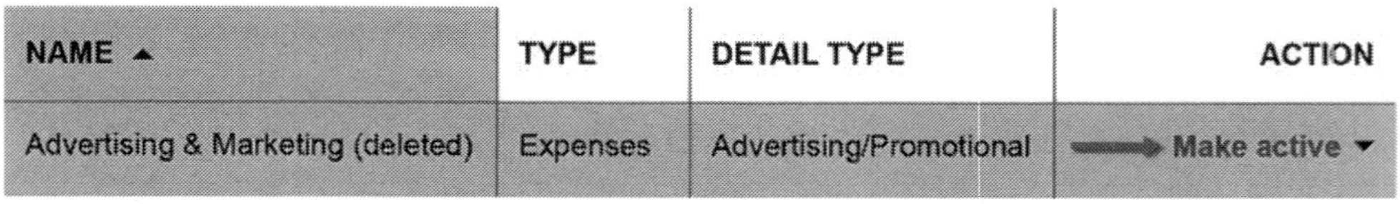

Figure 4.19: The Make active option

As mentioned previously, you cannot delete accounts in QBO. However, when an account is made inactive, you will see **deleted** in parentheses next to the account name. This may be confusing, but keep in mind that **deleted** does not mean the account has been deleted; it has actually been inactivated.

Merging accounts in QBO

An issue that you may encounter at some point is duplicate accounts. For example, you may end up having accounts with similar names, such as *office supplies* and *office supplies expense*. This can happen if you have more than one person adding accounts to the chart of accounts, or if you have not documented a procedure for creating new accounts. However, you can easily fix this issue by merging the accounts, which will combine all of the data from both accounts into one. Follow these steps to merge accounts:

1. Navigate to the account list and identify the duplicate accounts:

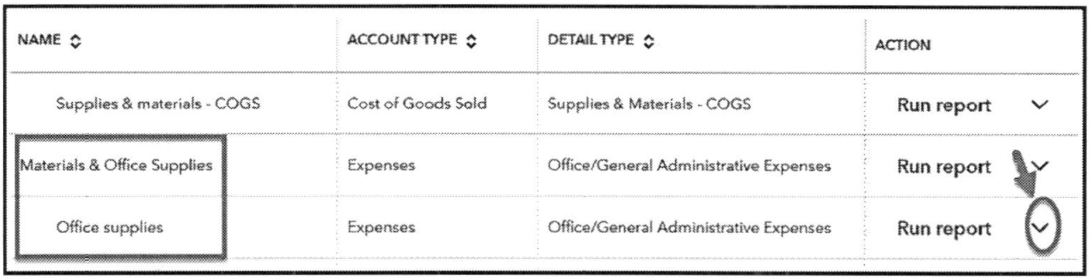

Figure 4.20: Identifying duplicate accounts in the Chart of accounts list

In the preceding screenshot, **Materials & Office Supplies** and **Office supplies** are the same accounts.

2. Click once on the account you plan to remove and choose **Edit** from the **Run report** drop-down in the far-right column. In our example, we will remove **Office supplies**.

The following account information will appear:

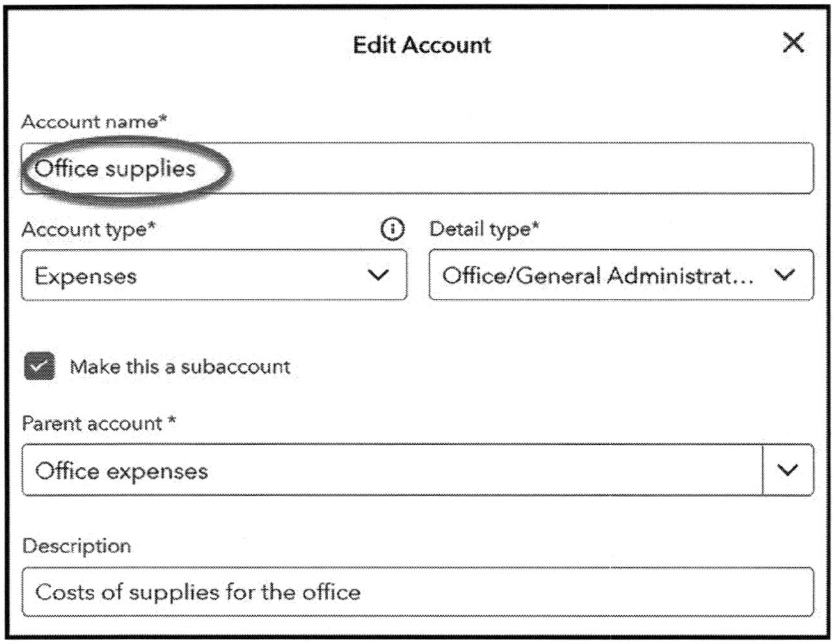

Figure 4.21: Displaying account information

3. Type the name of the account you wish to keep in the **Account name** field. In our example, this would be **Materials & Office supplies**.
4. Click the **Save** button.

   You must type the name of the account you would like to keep (in our case, **Materials & Office Supplies**) exactly as it appears in QuickBooks. To ensure accuracy, I recommend that you use your keyboard shortcuts to copy (*Ctrl* + *C*) and paste (*Ctrl* + *V*) the name so that it is correct. If you are a Mac user, it would be *Command* + *C* to copy and *Command* + *V* to paste.

> Please note that the account type and detail type must be the same for the accounts that you are merging. If they are not, QBO will not allow you to merge the accounts.

The following message will appear:

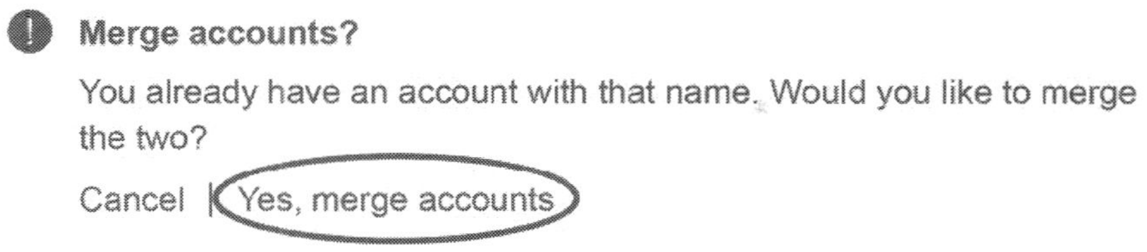

Figure 4.22: Confirm that you would like to merge the duplicate accounts

5. Choose **Yes, merge accounts** and then click the **Save** button, and the two accounts will be consolidated into one:

Materials & Office Supplies	Expenses	Office/General Administrative Expenses
Supplies	Expenses	Supplies & Materials

Figure 4.23: Chart of accounts list with the duplicate account removed

As you can see, the duplicate account (**Office supplies**) is no longer on the **Chart of accounts** list. All transactions recorded for this account have been transferred to the **Materials & Office Supplies** account.

You now know how to add an account, import a **Chart of accounts** list, edit an account, inactivate and reactivate an account, and merge accounts on the **Chart of accounts** list. The chart of accounts is, therefore, the backbone of the system, and now that you know how to manage your **Chart of accounts** list, you can be confident that your financial statements will be accurate.

In the next section, we will show you how to reduce the number of transactions entered manually by connecting your bank accounts to QuickBooks. In the long run, this will save you a lot of time.

Connecting bank accounts to QBO

One of the best features of using cloud accounting software such as QBO is the ability to connect your bank account to the software so that your books are always up to date with the most recent deposits and withdrawals that have been made to your bank accounts.

There are two ways in which you can update QuickBooks with your banking activity. You can connect your bank account to QuickBooks so that transactions are imported automatically into QuickBooks, or you can upload transactions from an Excel spreadsheet. We will walk you through each of these processes in more detail now.

Importing banking transactions automatically

There are several benefits to importing your banking transactions automatically. First, you will save a ton of time because you won't have to enter transactions manually. Second, QuickBooks will be updated on a *daily* basis with the most recent banking activity on your account. And finally, it will be a breeze to reconcile your bank account on a daily, weekly, or monthly basis.

Go through the following steps to import banking transactions automatically into QBO:

1. Select **Accounting** and then **Bank transactions** from the left menu bar, as shown in *Figure 4.24*:

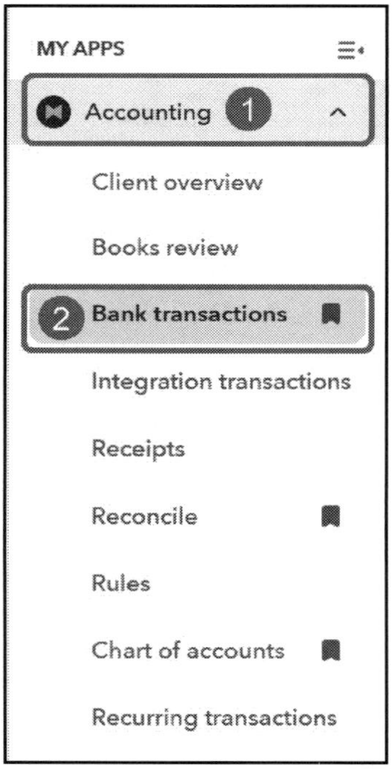

Figure 4.24: Selecting Bank transactions

2. If this is your first time connecting to a bank/credit card account, you will get the following screen. Click on the **Connect account** button, as shown here:

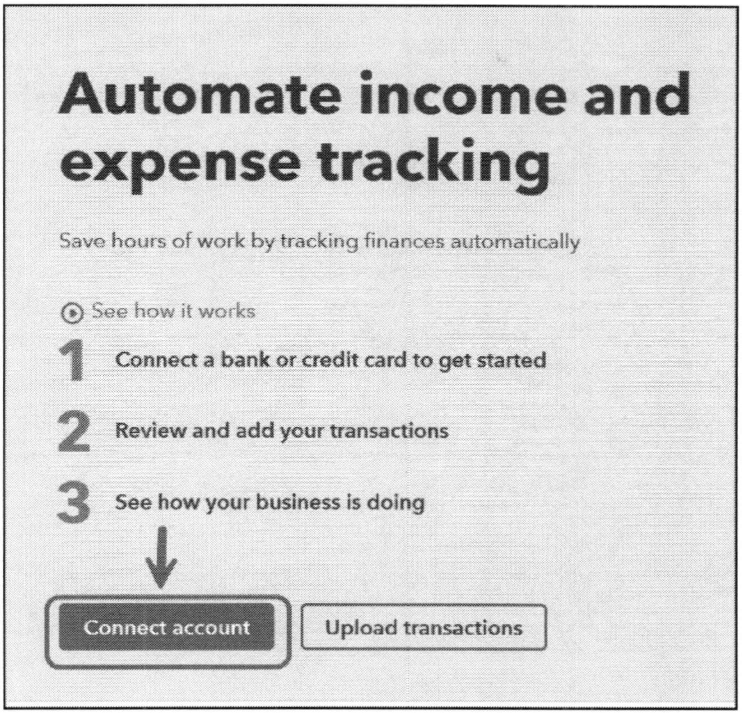

Figure 4.25: Clicking on Connect account

3. If you have connected to a bank/credit card account previously, you will see the **Link account** option. Click on it:

Figure 4.26: The Link account button

4. To connect your bank account, select your bank by clicking on the icon or typing the name of the bank in the search box, as shown here:

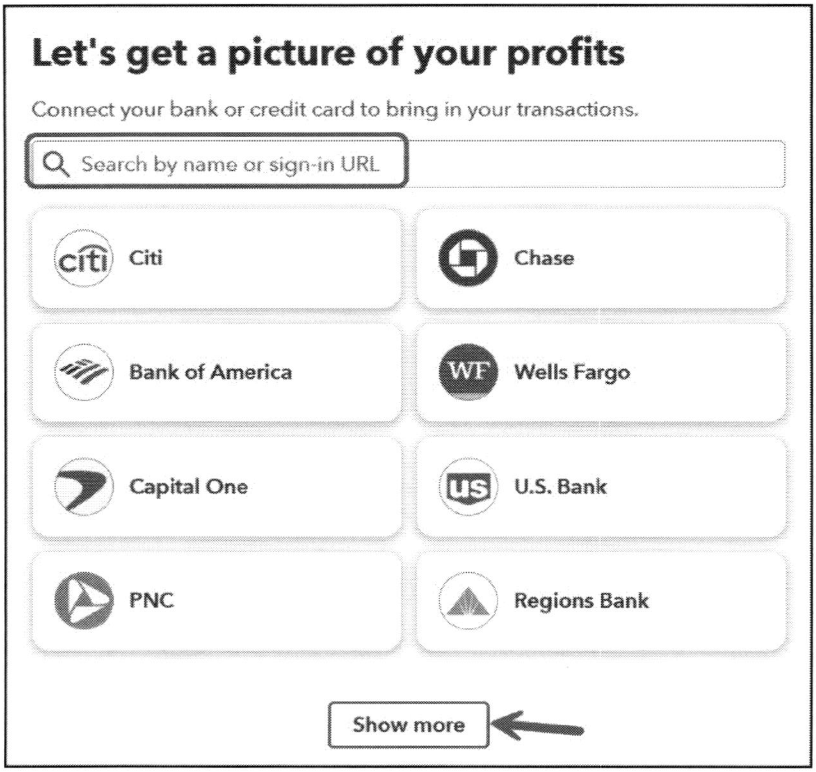

Figure 4.27: Selecting your bank

If you cannot locate your bank, you will not be able to connect your account to QuickBooks; however, you can still download your banking information into QuickBooks, which we will cover in the next section.

5. Sign in to your bank account using the secure user ID and password issued by your bank:

Figure 4.28: Signing into your bank account

6. Before connecting your bank account to QBO, you will be required to consent to the terms and conditions set by your bank. This consent confirmation is documentation that proves you agree to share your financial data with QuickBooks:

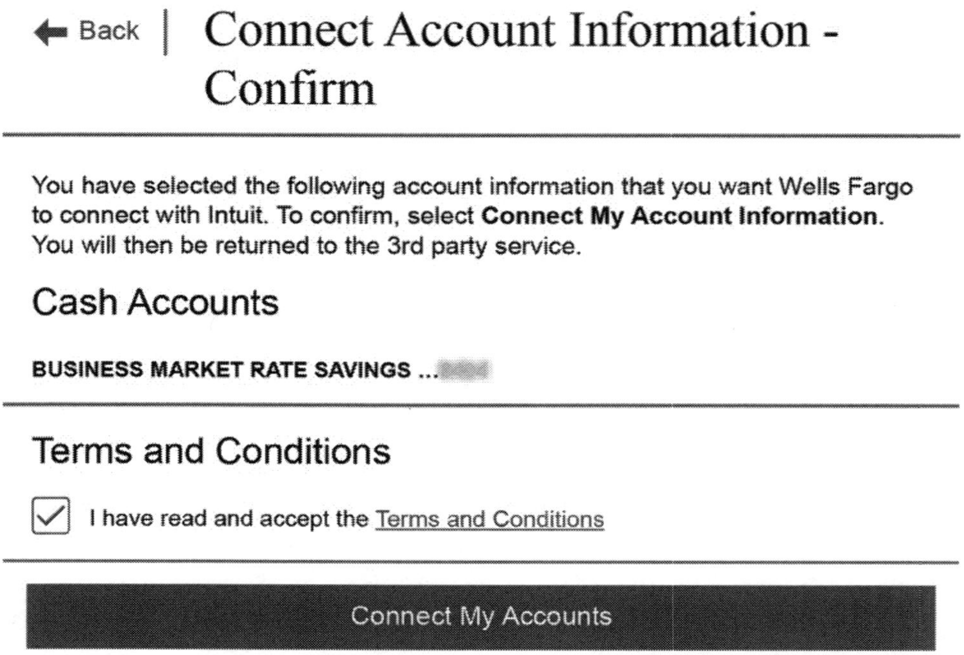

Figure 4.29: Consenting to your bank's terms and conditions

7. Follow the remaining onscreen instructions to connect your bank account to QuickBooks. If you have more than one account with the same financial institution, you will have the option to connect all bank accounts or select specific bank accounts to connect with QuickBooks.

> Make sure that you only connect *business* bank accounts to QuickBooks and not personal bank accounts; otherwise, you will have personal banking activity mingled with business transactions, which is not best practice.

Some financial institutions limit how far back in time you are able to pull data from. Let's say you need to import data for the last 12 months, but your bank only allows you to go back 90 days; go ahead and import those last 90 days. For the data that it did not allow you to access, you can either request a CSV (Excel) file from your online banking department so you can import it or enter the data manually from your bank statement.

You can save yourself a lot of time by connecting your bank account to QuickBooks so that your transactions automatically download. However, if your bank does not allow you to connect your account, you can still save time by obtaining an Excel (`.xls`) or CSV (`.csv`) file from your bank so that you can upload the transactions to your QuickBooks file.

A brand-new feature that has been released in QBO is the ability to import bank transactions using a PDF statement. If your financial institution does not allow you to download transactions in an Excel format, the PDF format will work.

Uploading banking transactions from an Excel, CSV, or PDF file

If your financial institution does not integrate with QuickBooks, then you need to upload your banking transactions from an Excel, CSV, or PDF file. Most banks allow you to download your transactions as a PDF or CSV file. Log in to your bank account and look for the **Download Transactions** option or other data download options. If you don't see this option, contact your bank and inform them that you need your banking transactions in a CSV file so that you can upload them into QuickBooks.

1. At the beginning of this chapter, we showed you how to add a new account to the **Chart of accounts** list. Follow those step-by-step instructions and add your bank account to QuickBooks.
2. Your bank account setup screen should resemble the one here:

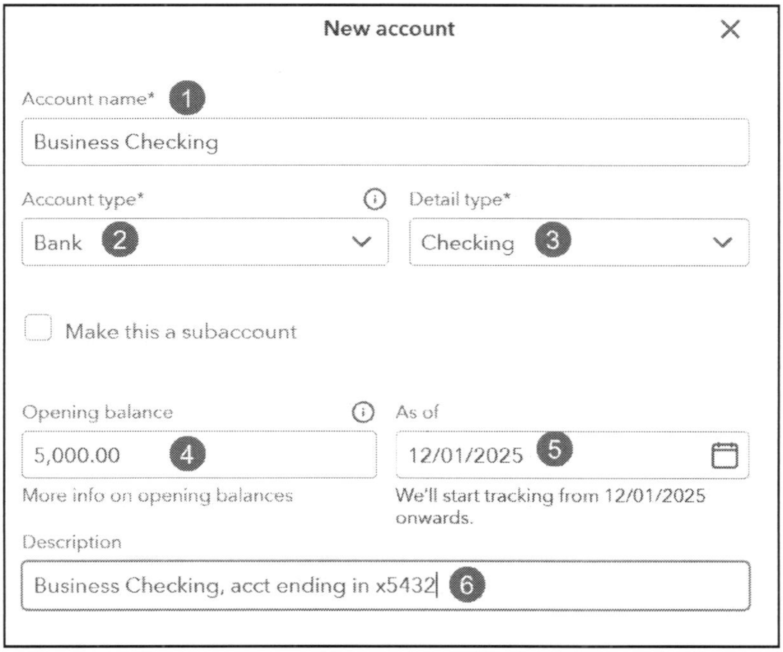

Figure 4.30: Bank account setup screen

3. Here is a brief explanation of how to fill in the new bank account fields:

    - **Account name (1)**: The name of the bank account belongs in this field. In our example, we have created a business checking account and named it accordingly. This will work if all of your bank accounts are at the same financial institution; however, if you have multiple bank accounts set up at different financial institutions, you should include the name of the bank along with the type of account in this field – for example, Wells Fargo Business Checking, Bank of America Business Savings, and so on.

    > If you have several accounts, it might be helpful to include the last four digits of each account number as part of the account name (such as Chase Business Checking, x5432). This will help you to quickly determine which account you are in.

    - **Account type (2)**: Select **Bank** from the drop-down menu.
    - **Detail type (3)**: Select the type of bank account you are setting up from the drop-down menu (**Savings**, **Checking**, etc.).
    - **Opening balance (4)**: Enter the current balance in your bank account as of your QuickBooks start date, which is the field next to it. For example, if you are starting to use QuickBooks as of January 1, enter the balance of your bank account as of the last day of the previous period, which would be December 31 of the previous year. If you have the January bank statement, the beginning balance can also be used since it should be the same as the ending balance on December 31. When connecting accounts to QBO, the beginning balance might get pulled in from the bank and post to the **Opening Balance Equity** account. At times, this balance might be incorrect, so it's important to verify it. If you are having issues with fixing this issue, be sure to reach out to your accountant or bookkeeper for assistance.
    - **As of (5)**: The **As of** date will be the last day of the previous period discussed in the preceding **Opening balance (4)**. In our example, December 1 will be the **As of** date.
    - **Description (6)**: You can include a brief description of the account that you are adding in this field, such as the name of the bank or financial institution and account number.

It's important to have your bank statements handy as you are adding bank accounts to QuickBooks. This is to ensure that you enter the correct balance and effective dates. It will also help you to balance later on when you are ready to reconcile the account.

4. From the gear icon, select **Import Data**, which is located in the **Tools** column, as shown here:

Figure 4.31: The Import Data option

5. The **Import Data** screen is where you can import bank data, charts of accounts, customers, invoices, journal entries, products and services, and vendors. Select the **Bank Data** option, as shown here:

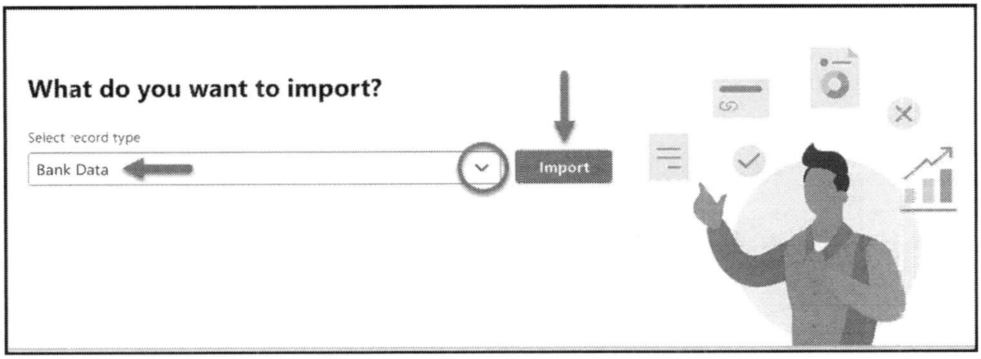

Figure 4.32: The Import Data screen

6. The following screen appears. Click on the arrow to select from the chart of accounts the bank account that you are importing data for, as indicated here:

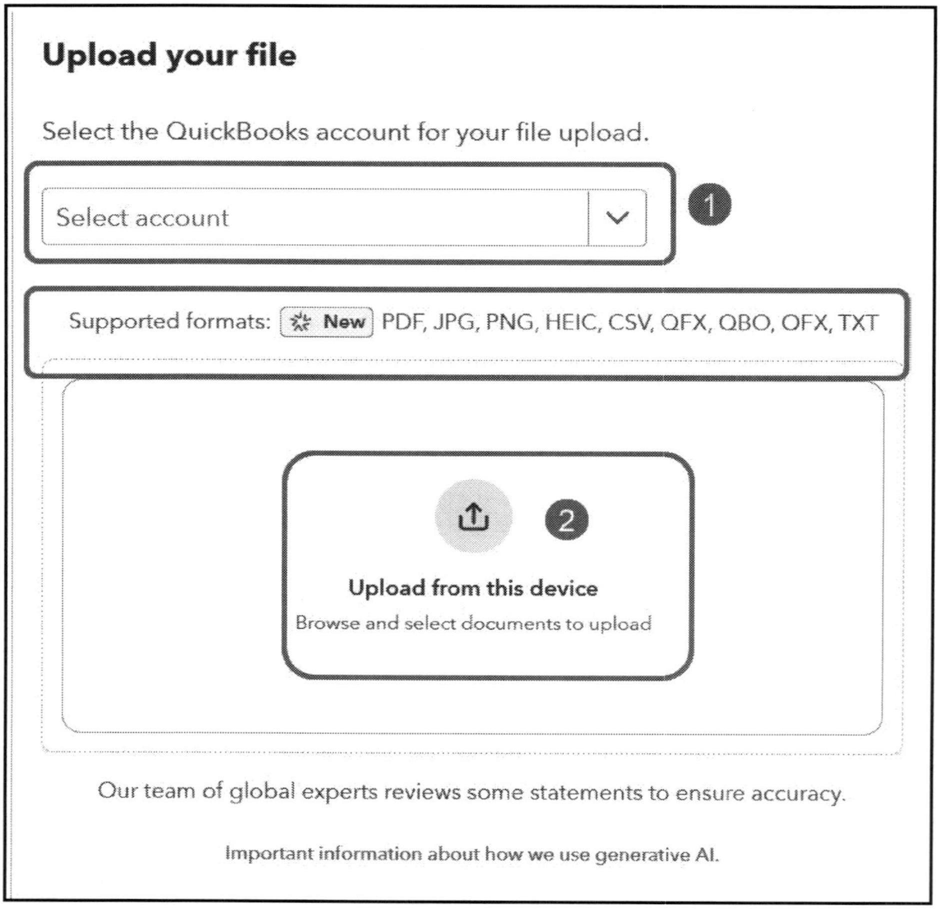

Figure 4.33: Selecting files to import

7. The selected filename will appear in the field, as shown here:

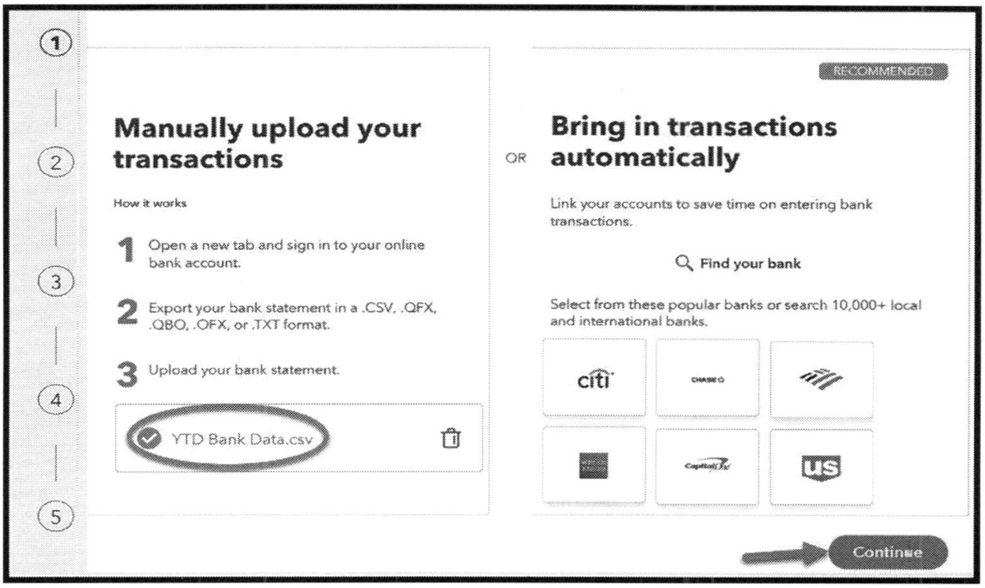

Figure 4.34: Checking the filename

8. Click the **Continue** button to proceed to the next step.
9. In this step, you will select the bank account from which you want the transactions to be uploaded to QuickBooks. Select the **Business Checking** account from the drop-down menu, as shown here:

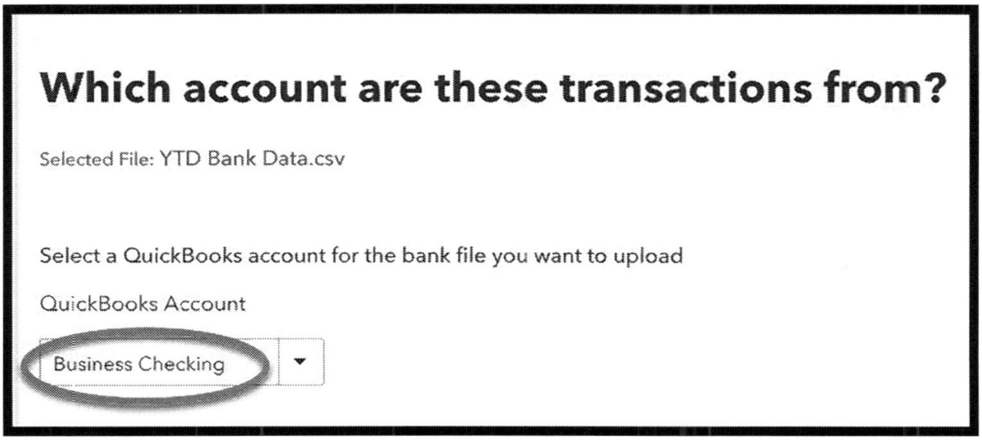

Figure 4.35: Selecting the bank account

10. Click **Continue**.

    If you have more than one bank account, you will need to set up an account on the chart of accounts for each bank account and link them.

    The following setup screen will appear:

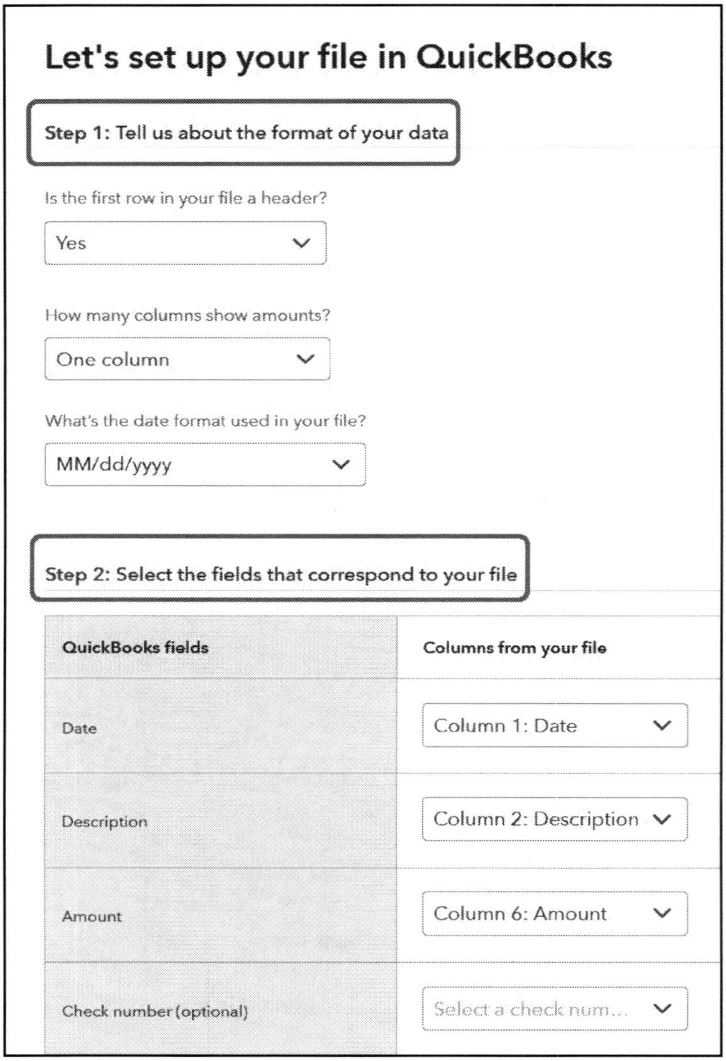

Figure 4.36: Setup screen

On this screen, you will provide responses to the three questions in step 1, and in step 2, you will map the columns in your CSV file to a field in QuickBooks. This is a very important step to ensure that the information is entered into the correct fields in QuickBooks.

For each QBO field located on the left, select the column from your import file that includes the corresponding data, as shown in *Figure 4.36*. There are three fields that need to be populated in QuickBooks: the transaction date, a brief description, and the transaction amount. A new field that is optional is the check number. You will need to indicate what column in your CSV file includes this information:

- **Date**: From the dropdown, select the column in the CSV file that includes the date of the banking transactions. You can also select the format that the date is in (for example, `mm/dd/yyyy`).
- **Description**: Select the column in the CSV file that includes descriptions of the transactions.
- **Amount**: From the dropdown, select the column in the CSV file that includes the transaction amounts. Amounts can be formatted into one column that includes both positive and negative numbers, or into two separate columns, one for positive numbers (deposits) and one for negative numbers (withdrawals). In our example, both positive and negative numbers are formatted into one column.
- **Check number**: If your data file includes check numbers, you can import that info or leave this field blank, since it is *optional*.

11. Click **Continue**.

A preview of how your data will be uploaded to QuickBooks will appear. It's important to review the data to ensure that the correct fields are populated:

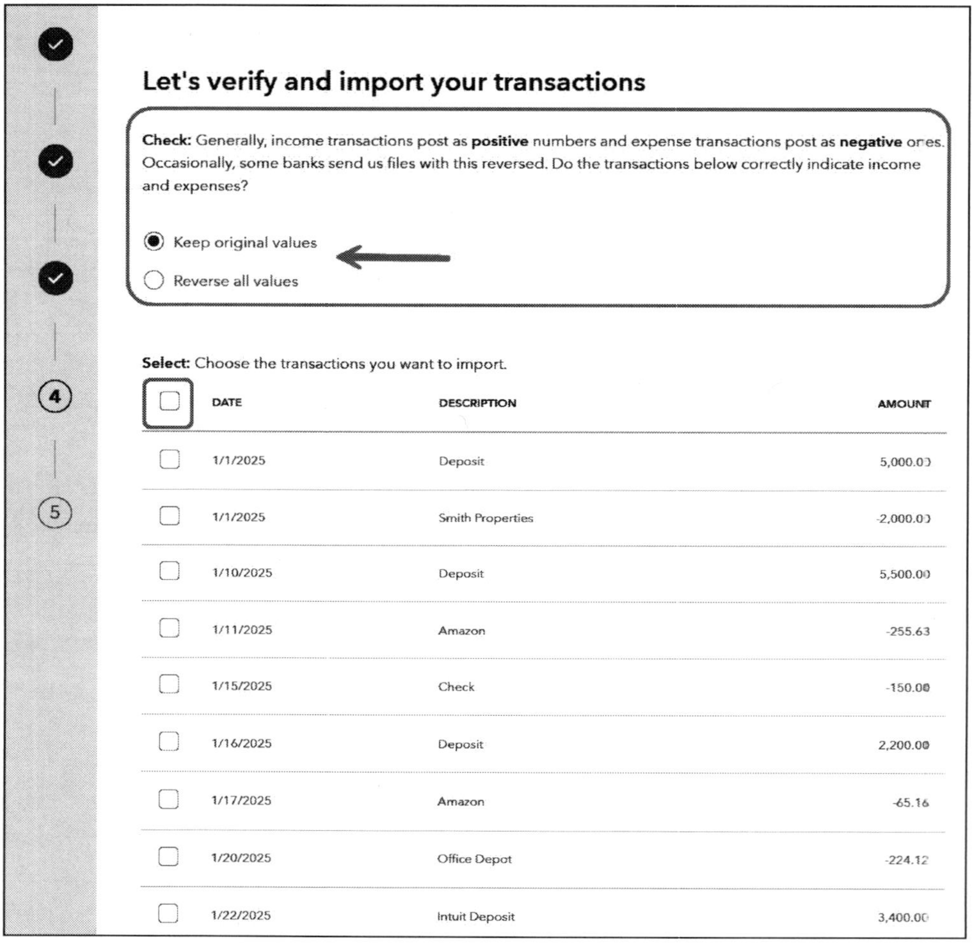

Figure 4.37: A preview of your data before importing to QBO

12. Double-check to make sure that the amount column has a positive number for deposits and a negative number for withdrawals. If this is not correct, select the **Reverse all values** option shown in *Figure 4.37* to fix it.
13. To select all transactions for import, put a checkmark in the box highlighted in the preceding screenshot. Alternatively, you can put a checkmark next to each individual transaction you wish to import into QBO.
14. Click the **Continue** button in the lower-right corner to proceed to the next screen.

15. On the next screen, QuickBooks will provide you with the number of transactions to be uploaded. This is your final opportunity to confirm that the data is correct. Once you confirm this, there will be no option to undo it. To proceed with the upload, click the **Yes** button, as shown here:

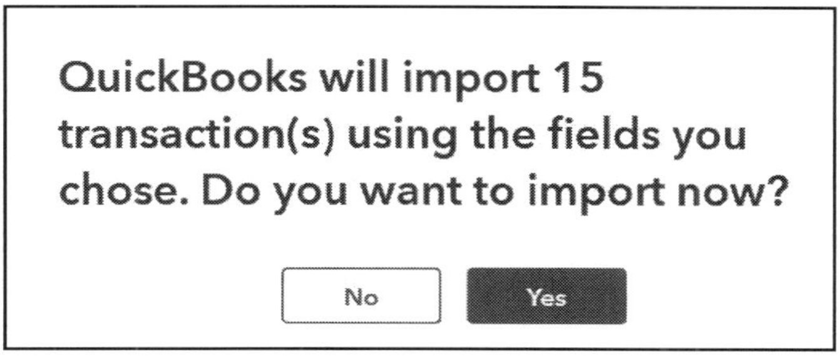

Figure 4.38: Confirming the import

16. After confirming the number of transactions to import, your transactions will be added to QuickBooks. To verify the data was imported correctly, head over to **Accounting > Bank Transactions**, where you can see the number of transactions that were successfully imported from your CSV file, along with their dates, descriptions, and dollar amounts. In *Chapter 11, Managing Bank Feeds and Reconciling Bank and Credit Card Accounts*, we will show you what to do with this data after it has been imported.

Now that we know how to import banking transactions, let's learn how to connect our credit card accounts in the next section.

Connecting credit card accounts to QBO

Similar to bank accounts, you can connect your credit card accounts to QBO. There are two ways that you can update QuickBooks with your credit card activity. You can connect your credit card account to QuickBooks so that transactions are imported automatically into QuickBooks. The other option is to upload transactions from an Excel spreadsheet. We will walk you through each process in more detail in the following sections.

Importing credit card transactions automatically

There are several benefits to importing your credit card transactions automatically. First, you will save a lot of time because you won't have to manually enter transactions. Second, QuickBooks will be updated daily with the most recent credit card activity on your account. Third, it will be much easier to reconcile your credit card accounts.

Listed here are the steps required to import credit card transactions automatically into QBO:

1. Select **Accounting** and **Bank transactions** from the left menu bar, as shown here:

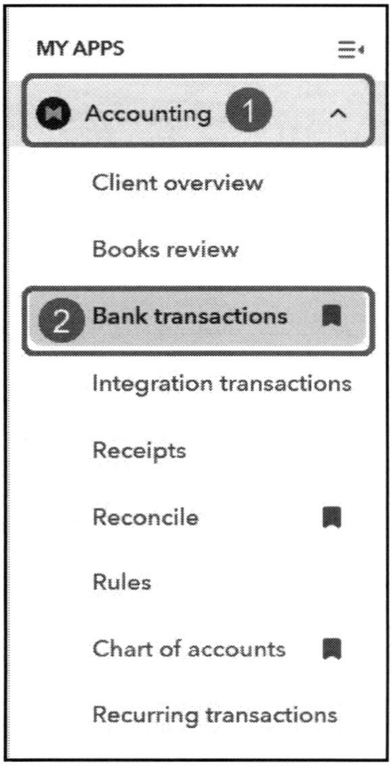

Figure 4.39: The Bank transactions option

2. On the following screen, you will see a link to a short video tutorial (**See how it works**), shown in *Figure 4.40*. This is a demo of how the banking center works. Click on the **Connect account** button, or the **Link account** button if you have previously connected a bank/credit card account:

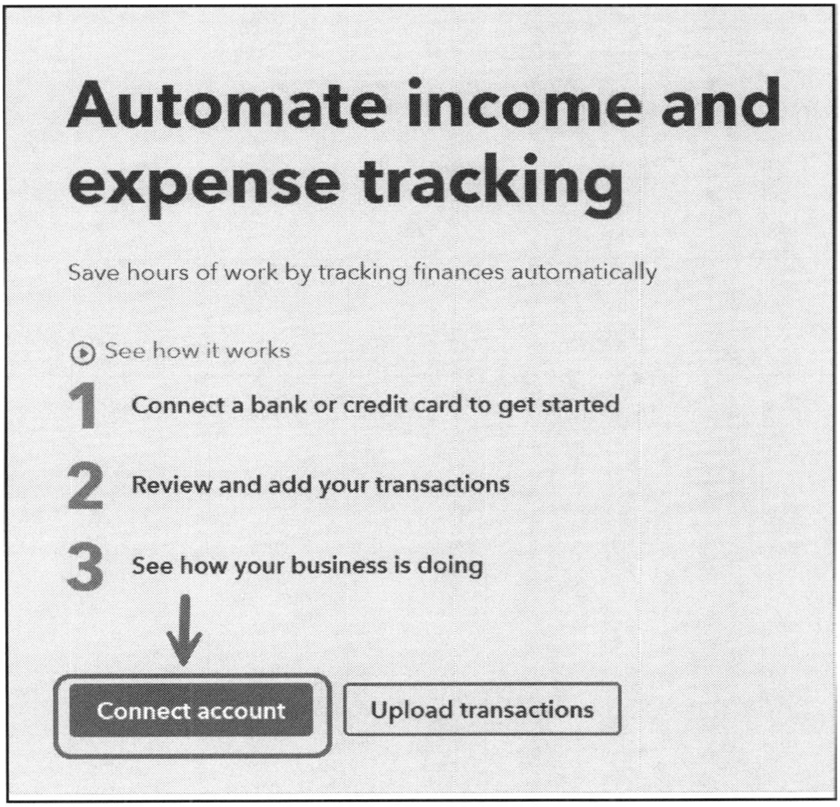

Figure 4.40: Connecting an account

3. To connect your credit card account, select your credit card company by clicking on the icon or typing the name of the financial institution in the search box, as shown here:

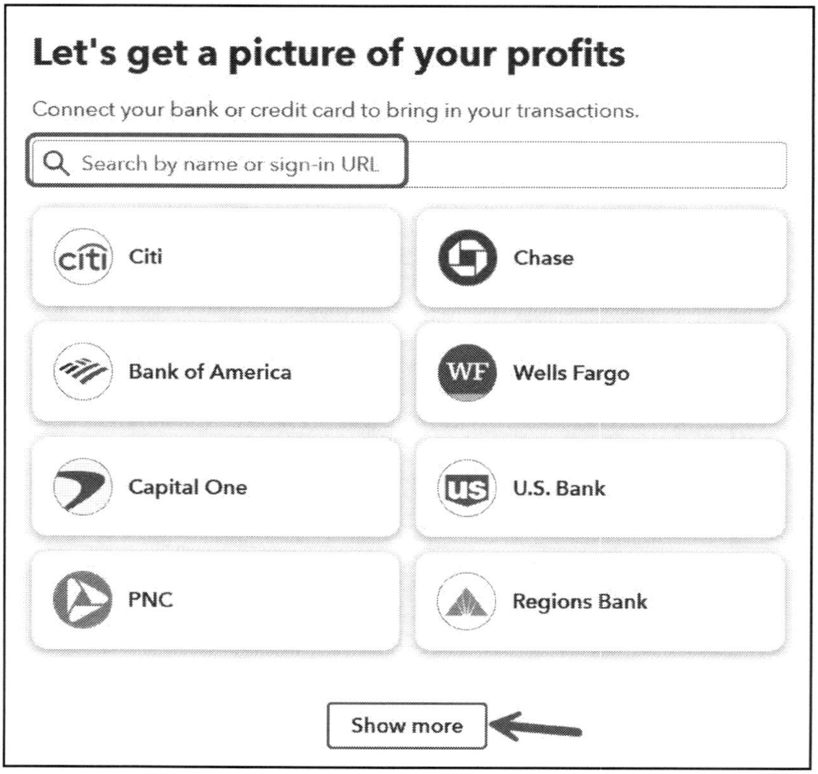

Figure 4.41: Selecting your bank

If you cannot locate your financial institution, you will not be able to connect your account to QuickBooks. Skip to the next section, *Uploading credit card transactions from an Excel or CSV file*.

4. Sign in to your credit card account using the secure user ID and password issued by your bank.
5. Before connecting your credit card account to QBO, you will be required to consent to the terms and conditions set by your bank. This consent is used as documentation, proving that you agree to share your financial data with QuickBooks.
6. Follow the remaining onscreen instructions to connect your credit card account to QuickBooks. If you have more than one account with the same financial institution, you will have the option to connect all credit card accounts or just select specific credit card accounts.

Make sure that you only connect *business* credit card accounts to QuickBooks and not personal credit card accounts; otherwise, you will have personal credit card activity mingled with business transactions, which is not ideal.

If you have multiple credit cards for one account, you will want to link the parent account only or the individual cards only, but not both. *The parent account is recommended as it makes reconciling much easier*. If you have linked the individual cards, you will need to have them listed as sub-accounts on your chart of accounts of a parent card, to be able to reconcile your monthly statement.

After connecting your credit card accounts to QuickBooks, they will appear in the banking center. From the banking center, you can see the date of the most recent download, along with a description and the amount of each transaction downloaded. If your financial institution does not allow you to connect your credit card account to QuickBooks, you will need to upload credit card transactions from an Excel or CSV file.

Uploading credit card transactions from an Excel or CSV file

If your financial institution does not integrate with QuickBooks, you will need to download your credit card transactions to an Excel or CSV file. Most banks allow you to download your transactions as a PDF or CSV file. Log in to your credit card account and look for a **Download Transactions** option. If you don't see this option, contact the credit card company and inform them that you need your transactions in a CSV file so you can upload them to QuickBooks.

As stated previously, you can now use a PDF file to upload transactions to QBO. In addition, there are programs that will extract transactions from bank and credit card PDF statements into QBO.

MoneyThumb is one of many programs that will do this:

`https://www.moneythumb.com/small-business-owners/`

To upload credit card transactions from an Excel or CSV file to QuickBooks, follow these instructions:

1. At the beginning of this chapter, we showed you how to add a new account to the chart of accounts list. Follow those step-by-step instructions and add your credit card account to QuickBooks.

2. Your credit card account setup screen should resemble the one in *Figure 4.42*:

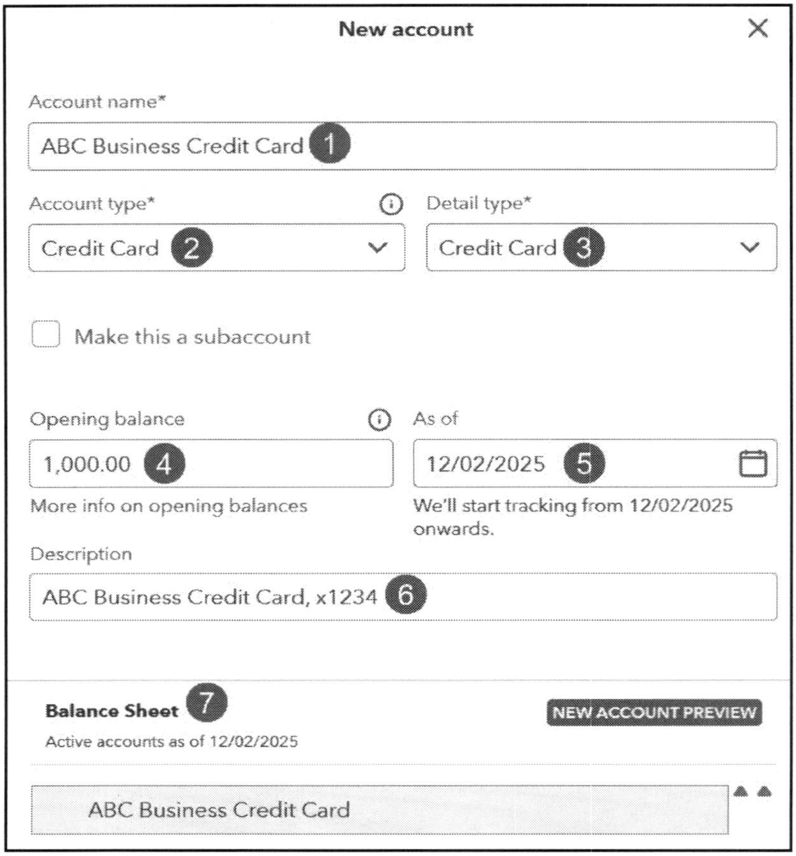

Figure 4.42: Adding account details for a credit card

The following is a brief explanation of the new credit card account fields:

- **Account name (1)**: The name of the credit card belongs in this field. If you have multiple credit card accounts at the same financial institution, you may want to consider entering the last four digits of each account in this field. This will make it easier when you are entering transactions and reconciling accounts. In our example, **ABC Business Credit Card** is the account name.
- **Account type (2)**: The account type will be **Credit Card**.
- **Detail type** (3): **Detail type** should default to the account type, **Credit Card**.

- **Opening balance (4)**: Enter the current outstanding balance due on your credit card account as of your QuickBooks start date (see *Step 5*). For example, if you began to use QuickBooks as of January 1, enter the balance owed on your credit card as of January 1. In our example, the opening balance is **$1,000.00**.
- **As of (5)**: From the dropdown, select the date you want to begin tracking your finances for this account. In our example, the **As of** date is **12/02/2025**.
- **Description (6)**: You can include a brief description of the account that you are adding in this field or enter the name of the account along with the last four digits of the account number. In our example, the description is **ABC Business Credit Card, x1234**.
- **NEW ACCOUNT PREVIEW (7)**: In this section, you will see a preview of where on the financial statements this account will appear. In our example, it will appear on the **Balance Sheet** report.

It's important to have your credit card statements handy as you are adding credit card accounts to QuickBooks. This is to ensure that you enter the correct balance and effective dates. If you leave this field blank, you will not be able to access this field later on; instead, you will have to make a balance adjustment directly in the credit card register.

3. From the gear icon, select **Import data** in the **Tools** column, as shown in *Figure 4.43*:

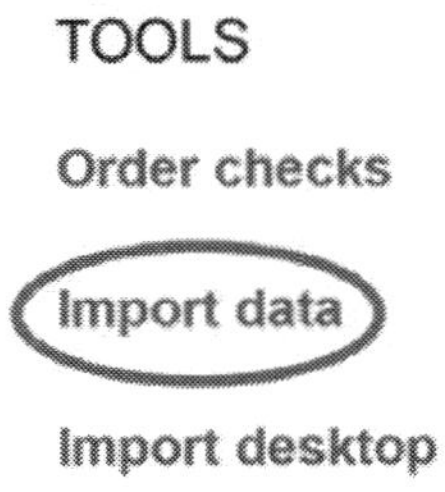

Figure 4.43: The Import data option

4. The **Import data** screen is where you can import bank and credit card transactions, customers, vendors, a chart of accounts list, a products and services list, and invoices. Select the **Bank Data** option to display the setup screen, as shown in *Figure 4.44*:

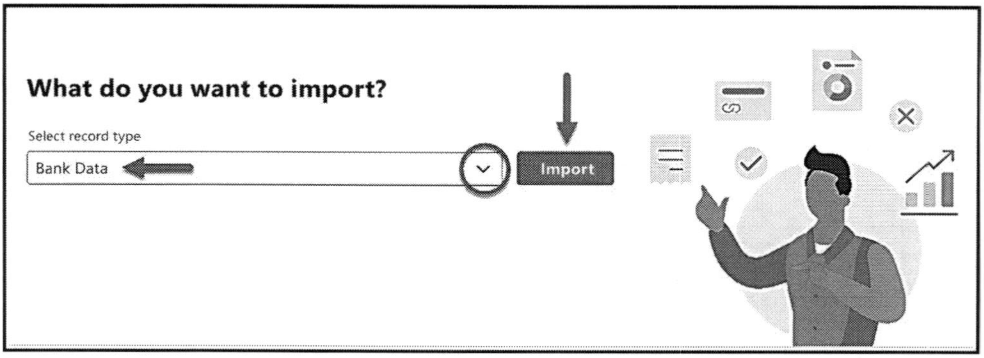

Figure 4.44: The Import data screen

The following screen appears. Click on **Upload from this device** to choose the file that includes your bank data, as indicated here:

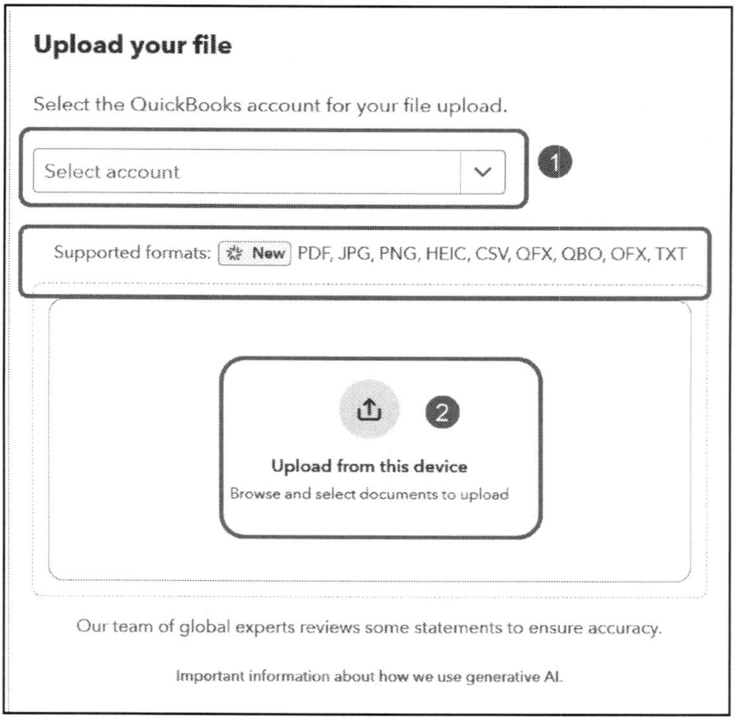

Figure 4.45: Clicking select files

The filename will appear in the field, as shown here:

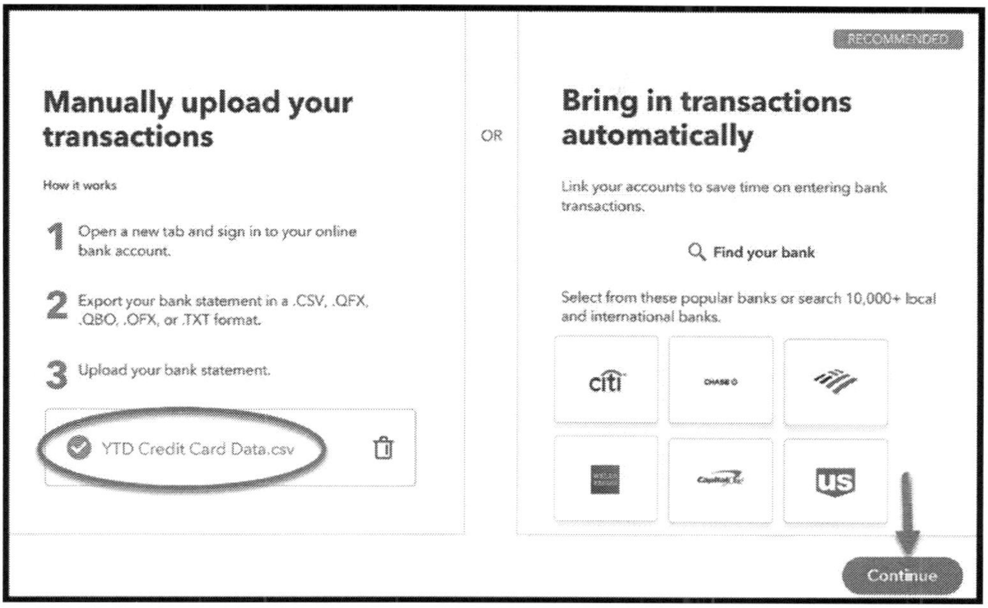

Figure 4.46: Checking the filename

5. Click the **Continue** button to proceed to the next step.
6. In this step, you will select the credit card account for which you want the transactions to be uploaded to QuickBooks. Select the **ABC Business Credit Card** account from the drop-down menu, as shown in *Figure 4.47*:

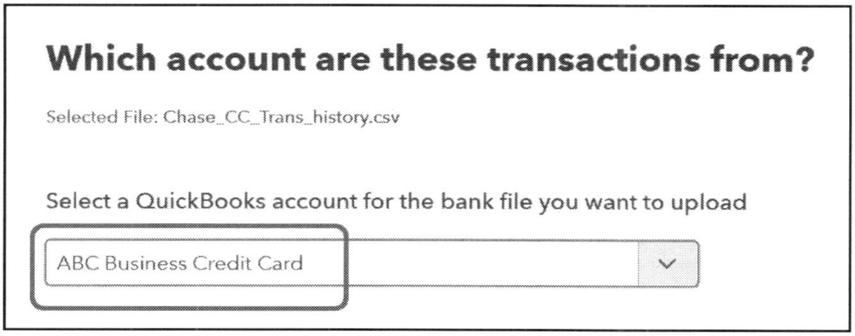

Figure 4.47: Selecting the account

7. Click **Continue** and the following screen appears:

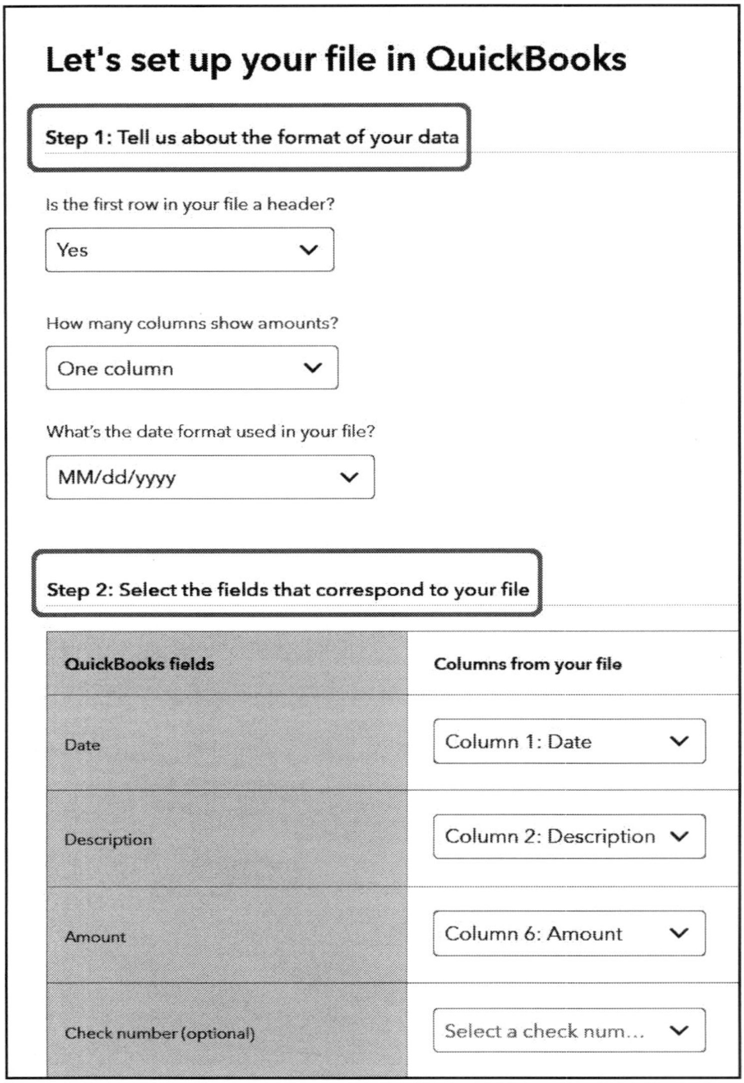

Figure 4.48: Setting up your file in QuickBooks

On this screen, you will respond to the three questions in **Step 1**, and in **Step 2**, you will map the columns in your CSV file to a field in QuickBooks. This is a very important step to ensure that the information is populated into the correct fields in QuickBooks.

If you have additional columns of information in your Excel or CSV file, that is OK. QuickBooks is only going to pick up the information in the three required fields: **Date**, **Description**, and **Amount**.

8. For each QBO field located on the left, select the column from your import file that includes the corresponding data, as shown in the preceding screenshot. There are three fields that need to be populated in QuickBooks: the transaction date, a brief description, and the transaction amount. You will need to indicate what column in your CSV file includes this information:

    - **Date**: From the dropdown, select the column in the CSV file that includes the dates of the credit card transactions. You can also select the format that the date is in (for example, mm/dd/yyyy).
    - **Description**: Select the column in the CSV file that includes descriptions of the transactions.
    - **Amount**: From the dropdown, select the column in the CSV file that includes the transaction amounts. Amounts can be formatted into one column that includes both positive and negative numbers or into two separate columns, one for positive numbers (credit card charges) and one for negative numbers (credit card payments and credits).

9. Click **Continue**. On the next screen, there appears a preview of how your data will be uploaded to QuickBooks. It's important to review the data to ensure that the correct fields are populated:

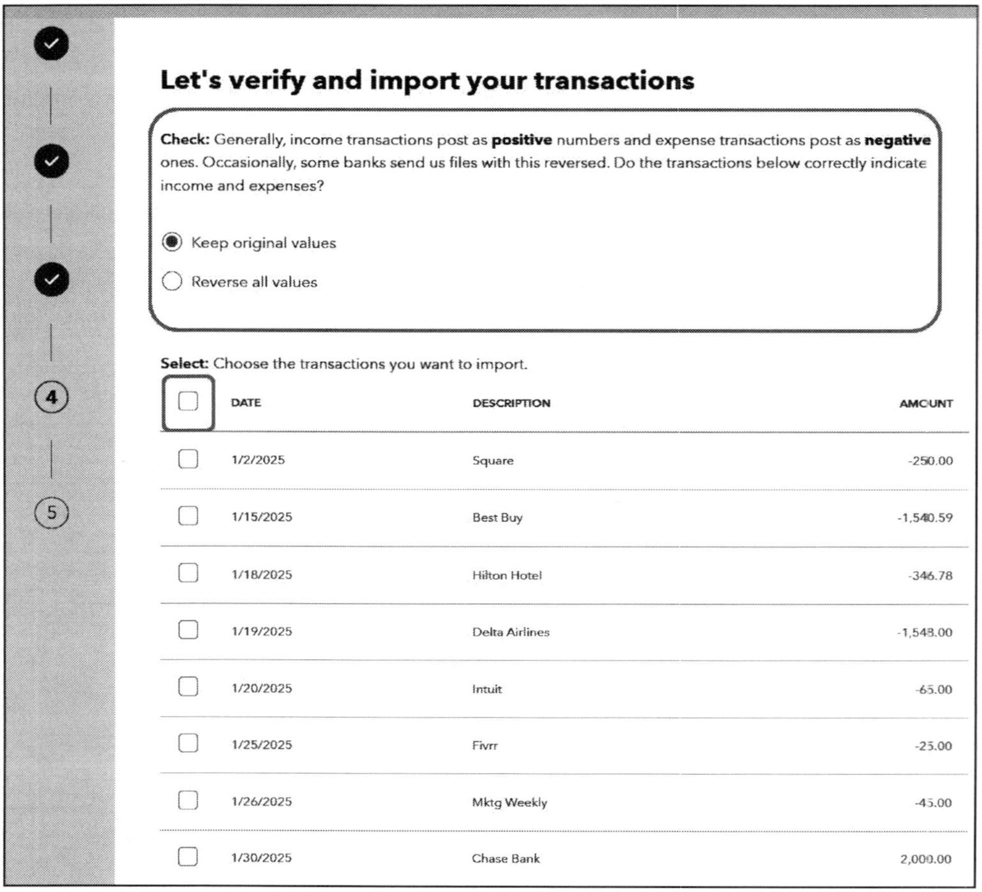

Figure 4.49: Checking your data

10. Click the **Next** button to proceed.
11. On the following screen, QuickBooks will provide you with the number of transactions to be uploaded. This is your final opportunity to confirm that the data is correct. Once you confirm this, there will be no option to undo it. To proceed with the upload, click the **Yes** button, as shown in the following screenshot:

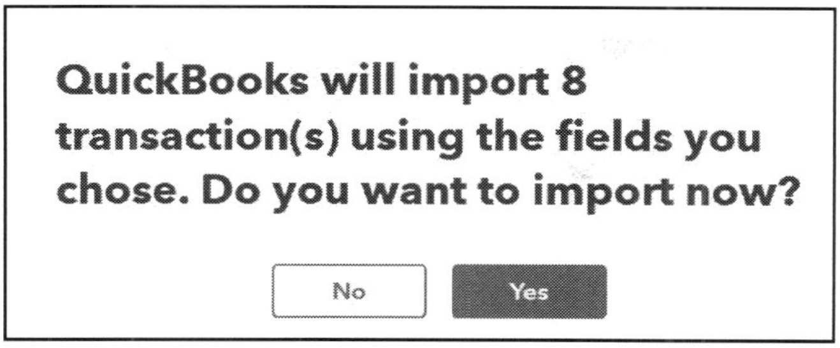

Figure 4.50: Confirming the import

After confirming the number of transactions to import, your transactions will be added to QuickBooks. To verify that the data was imported correctly, head over to the banking center, where you should see the dates, descriptions, and number of transactions that were successfully imported from your CSV file.

> Many financial institutions have different ways to connect your bank accounts to QuickBooks. I recommend that you contact the small business banking department at your bank and ask them what your options are for connecting your business bank accounts to QBO. By default, most banks allow you to import the last 90 days. However, if you need to go back further than that, be sure to inform them so that they can provide you with the best solution.

Giving other users access to your QuickBooks data

The ability to give other users access to your data is one of the many benefits of using QBO. Except for QBO Advanced, which includes three accountant users, the other QBO subscriptions include access for two accountant users and access for one or more additional users. There are two main groups that users fall into: **billable roles** and **non-billable roles**.

Billable roles count towards your user limit. For example, QBO Plus is limited to 5 users. Billable roles count toward this limit. There are nine *billable* roles that you can create in QBO:

- **Standard all access**
- **Standard no access**
- **Accounts receivable manager**
- **Accounts payable manager**
- **Standard limited customers and vendors**
- **In house accountant**
- **Company administrator**
- **HR manager**
- **Primary administrator**

Non-billable roles do not count toward your user limit. For example, if you give a contractor **Track time only** access, that access would *not* count toward your user limit because it is a non-billable role. There are two *non-billable* roles that you can create in QBO:

- **Track time only**
- **View company reports**

We will discuss each of these in more detail in the following subsections.

Standard all access user

The **Standard all access** user can access everything under customers and sales, as well as vendors and purchases. They also have full access to QBO without admin privileges, plus access to payroll, if QBO Payroll is enabled. This user has partial access to bills and company information. This user *does not* have the ability to change your QBO subscription, nor are they able to add, edit, or delete new users. Go through the following steps to assign the **Standard all access** role to a new user:

1. From the gear icon, select **Manage users** in the **YOUR COMPANY** column, as shown in *Figure 4.51*:

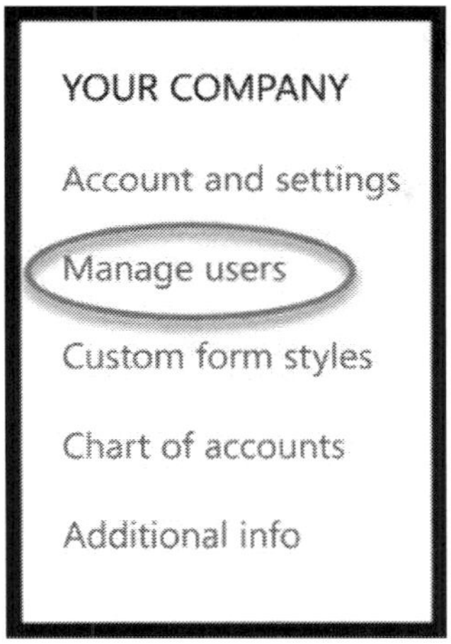

Figure 4.51: The Manage users option

2. Click on the **Add user** button:

Figure 4.52: The Add user button

3. Enter the first name, last name, and email address of the new user, as indicated in *Figure 4.53*:

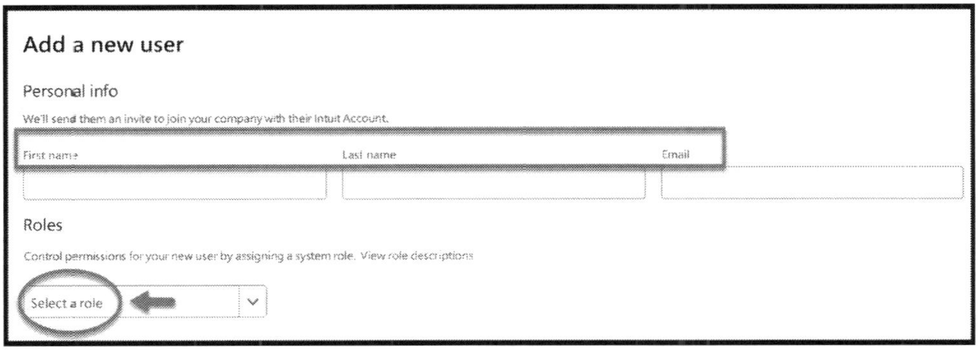

Figure 4.53: Choosing a user type

4. From the dropdown, select **Standard all access**, as indicated here:

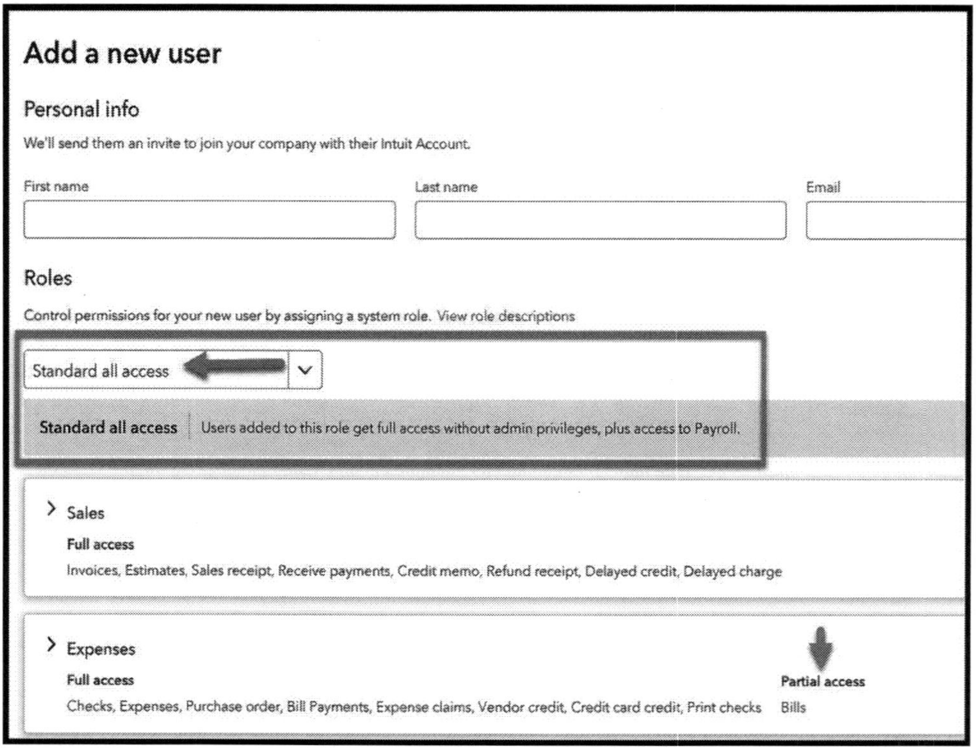

Figure 4.54: Selecting access rights for a new user

A **Standard all access** user will count toward the total number of users included in your QBO subscription. Once you have specified how much access you want the user to have, click the **Send invite** button in the lower-right corner of the screen to send the email invitation to the new user.

To recap, the following is a summary of the number of users that are included in each plan:

- QuickBooks Online Simple Start: 2 accountants and 1 user
- QuickBooks Online Essentials: 2 accountants and 3 users
- QuickBooks Online Plus: 2 accountants and 5 users
- QuickBooks Online Advanced: 3 accountants and 25 users

Standard no access user

The following is a snapshot of the access rights for **Standard no access**:

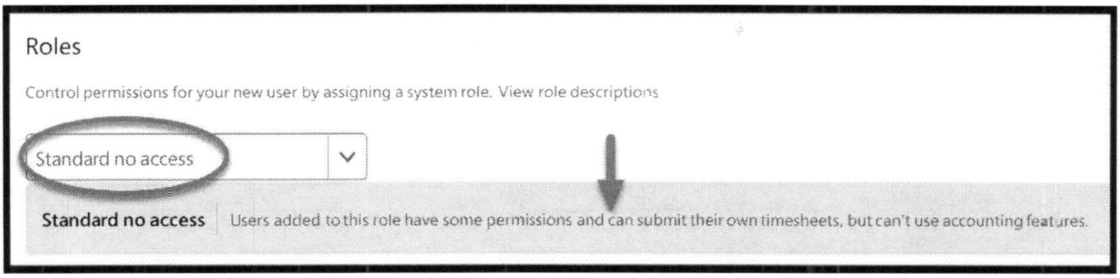

Figure 4.55: Access rights for the Standard no access role

Standard no access gives the user some permissions, such as submitting their own timesheet, but they have no access to accounting features.

Accounts receivable manager

The following snapshot shows the access rights for the **Accounts receivable manager** role:

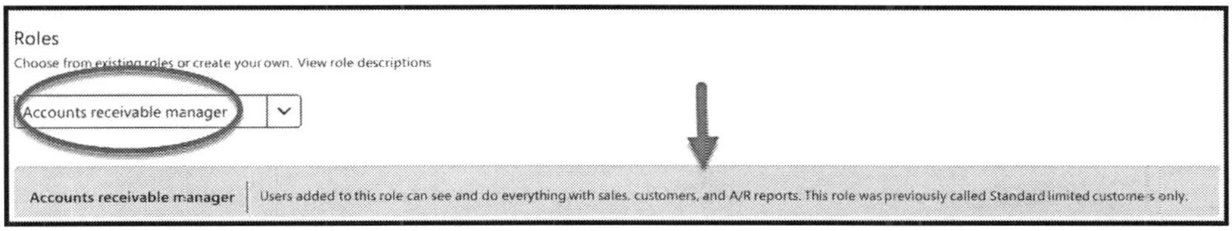

Figure 4.56: Access rights for the Accounts receivable manager role

The **Accounts receivable manager** role gives the user full access to sales, inventory, lists, and some bookkeeping tasks, such as bank deposits, but no access to employee and vendor lists, bank transactions, expense reports, or payroll reports. This role was previously called *Standard limited customers only*.

Accounts payable manager

Figure 4.57 shows the access rights for the **Accounts payable manager** role:

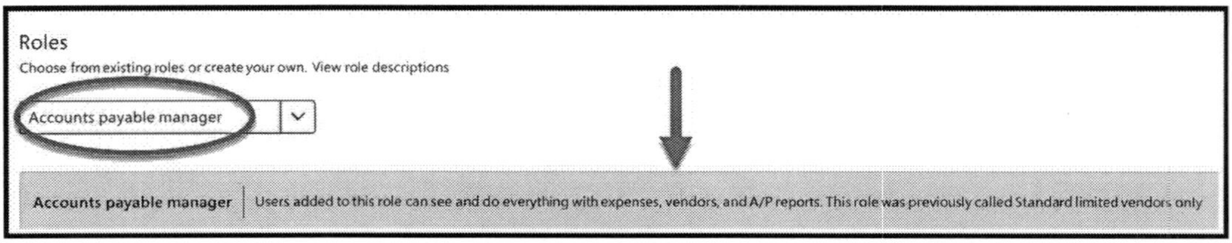

Figure 4.57: Access rights for the Accounts payable manager role

The **Accounts payable manager** role can access bill payments, vendor credits, expenses, checks, purchase orders, expense claims, vendors, and A/P reports. This role was previously called *Standard limited vendors only.*

Standard limited customers and vendors

The following is a snapshot of the access rights for **Standard limited customers and vendors**:

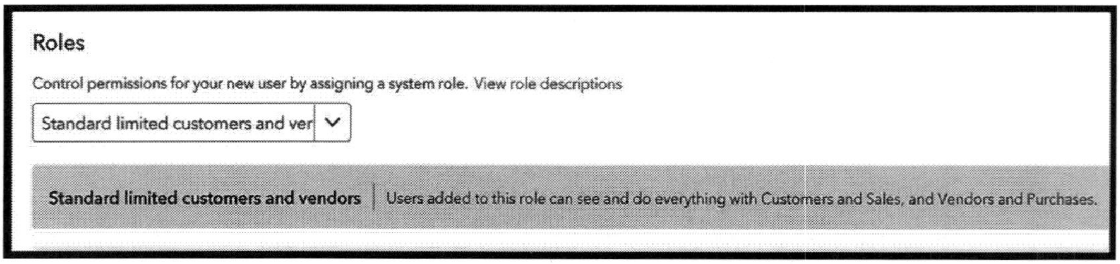

Figure 4.58: Access rights for Standard limited customers and vendors

The **Standard limited customers and vendors only** role gives the user the ability to manage all customers and sales transactions, vendors, and purchases. This level of access would be ideal for a bookkeeper who manages all aspects of **accounts receivable** (**A/R**) and **accounts payable** (**A/P**).

In house accountant

The following is a snapshot of the access rights for **In house accountant**:

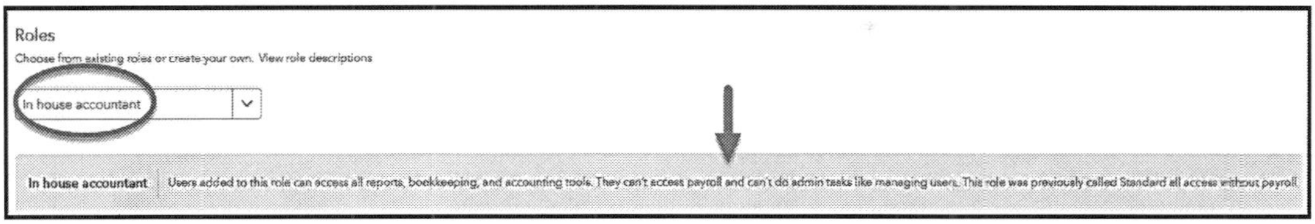

Figure 4.59: Access rights for the In house accountant role

The **In house accountant** role can access all reports, bookkeeping, and accounting tools. However, it can't access payroll and is not able to perform admin tasks such as managing users. This role was previously called *Standard all access without payroll.*

Company administrator

The **Company administrator** role includes access to every aspect of QuickBooks. This includes adding new users, changing passwords, and having control of your QBO subscription. Because there are no limitations to what this user can do, we recommend that you limit this role to owners of the business, IT personnel, or an officer of the company.

Since the company administrator has access to everything, you will just enter their name and email address to send them an invite to your QBO file. Once they accept, they will have full access to your QBO file.

Primary administrator

The **primary administrator** is the main user who has access to every part of QuickBooks. There can only be one primary admin user for a QBO account. They can manage all users and other admin tasks. By default, the person who sets up the QuickBooks account is automatically assigned as the primary admin. If you need to assign a new primary admin, you can always transfer the role to another user.

You cannot assign this role like the previous roles we have discussed. The only person who can transfer this role to someone is the existing primary administrator. If that person is no longer with the company, you will need to contact the QuickBooks tech support team for assistance.

> It is always advised to make the owner of the company the primary administrator since transferring the prior admin role from a former employee can be a hassle.

Reports-only user

The **View company reports only** role is very limited. This role can generate just about any report in QuickBooks except payroll or vendor and customer contact information; however, the reports-only user cannot add, edit, or change any QuickBooks data. They also do not have the ability to view anything outside of reports. This role is ideal for a business partner who wants to periodically review reports but has no day-to-day responsibilities. Unlike the standard and company admin roles, the reports-only role does not count toward your user limit, which means you can give reports-only access to an unlimited number of users, at no additional charge. To add a reports-only user, follow *Steps 1* and *2* in the *Standard all access user* section. In *Step 3*, select **View Company Reports** and follow the onscreen prompts to complete the setup.

Time tracking user

Similar to the **View company reports only** role, the **Track time only** role is also very limited. This role is limited to entering timesheets. It is ideal for employees and contractors who don't need access to any other areas of QuickBooks. Like the reports-only role, the time tracking user does not count toward your user limit. This means that you can add an unlimited number of time tracking users at no additional charge. To add a time tracking user, follow *Steps 1* and *2* in the *Standard all access user* section. In *Step 3*, select **Time tracking only** and follow the onscreen prompts to complete the setup.

Accountant user

Each QBO plan includes at least two accountant users, at no additional cost. The level of access the accountant user has is identical to that of the company administrator.

Accountant users can access all areas of QuickBooks. This includes adding users, editing passwords, and managing your QuickBooks subscription. You should be extremely careful who you give this level of access to; ideally, it should be limited to your **Certified Public Accountant** (**CPA**), tax preparer, or bookkeeper.

Go through the following steps to invite an accountant to access your QuickBooks data:

1. Click on the gear icon and select **Manage users** from the **YOUR COMPANY** column, as shown in *Figure 4.60*:

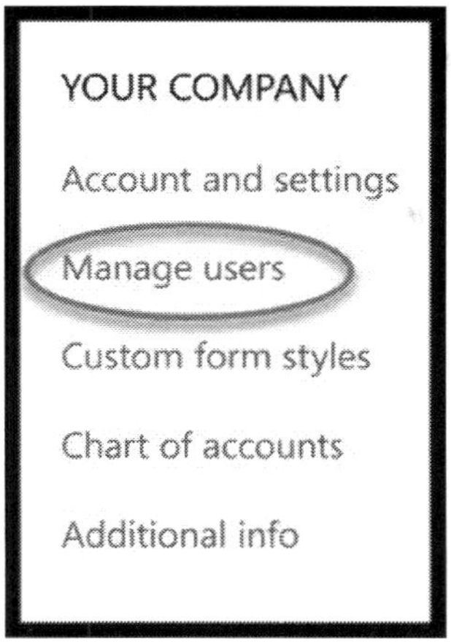

Figure 4.60: The Manage users option

2. On the **Manage users** page, click on **Accounting Firms**, as shown in *Figure 4.61*:

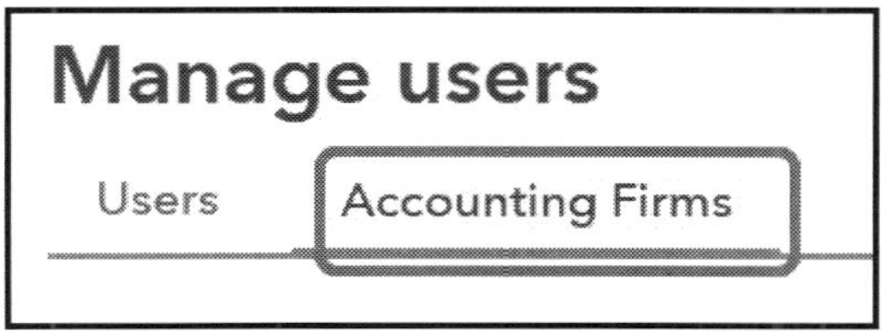

Figure 4.61: The Accountants access tab

3. The following screen appears.

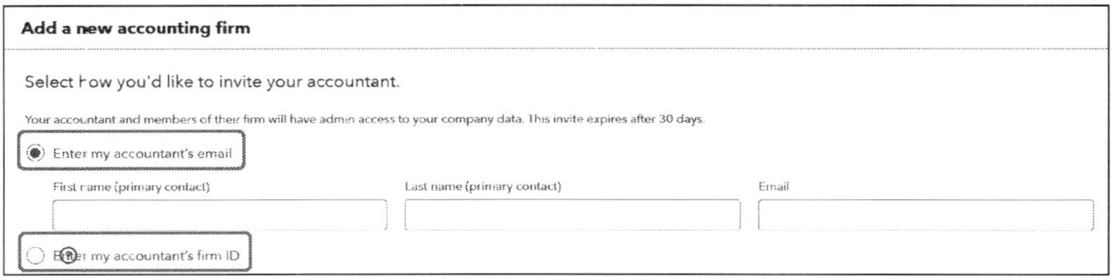

Figure 4.62: Inviting your accountant to your QBO account

You can invite your accountant using their email address or their firm ID. When using the email address, you will also need to provide their first and last name. If you select firm ID, you just need to ask your accountant for their firm ID (also known as the company ID). When inviting accountants using the firm ID, no additional information is required.

4. Click the **Invite** button to send the request to your accountant.

   Your accountant will then receive an email inviting them to access your QBO account. They will need to accept the invitation and create a secure user ID and password.

   While you won't need it for this exercise, you will typically need to provide the firm ID when contacting Intuit Support.

> You can obtain your firm ID (company ID) as follows:
>
> **PC users:** Press *Ctrl + Alt + ?*
>
> **Mac users:** Press *Command + Alt + ?*

Editing user privileges

You can remove or edit access for any user at any time. Follow these steps to edit a user's access to your QuickBooks file:

1. Navigate to the **Users** page, as shown in the upper left of *Figure 4.63*:

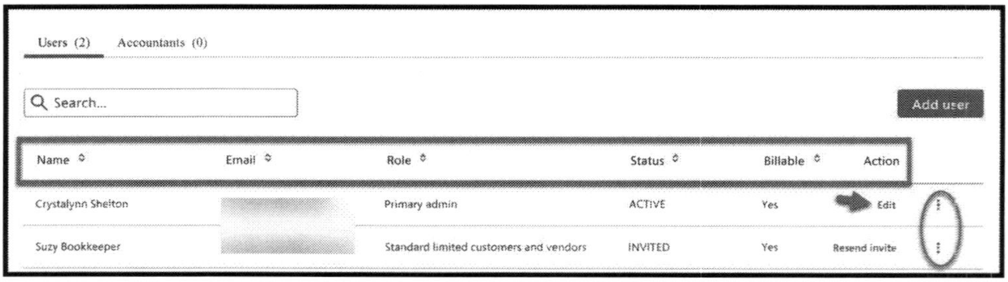

Figure 4.63: Users page in a QuickBooks file

2. Next to the appropriate user, click on **Edit** to change the user's role, or click on the three dots to the right of **Edit** and select **Delete** to remove the user's access altogether, as shown in *Figure 4.63*.

If a user has the **Primary admin** role (as *Crystalynn Shelton* does in *Figure 4.63*), you will not be able to delete that user. First, you will need to transfer the **Primary admin** access to another user. Once this is complete, you will be able to delete the previous **Primary admin** user.

You should now have a better understanding of the types of users you can set up in QuickBooks (standard – access, no access, limited customers and vendors, accounts receivable manager, accounts payable manager, in-house accountant, company admin, reports-only, time tracking, and accountant). Using the detailed information we have provided on the level of access each user has, you can start inviting your accountant, bookkeeper, and other users to access your QuickBooks data. For more details on the role descriptions and permissions for each role, head over to the online portal to access a complete list: `https://quickbooks.intuit.com/learn-support/en-us/help-article/access-permissions/user-roles-access-rights-quickbooks-online/L66POfRrI_US_en_US`.

We will wrap this chapter up by showing you how to navigate the QuickBooks Apps Center. Apps are a great way to help you streamline day-to-day business tasks that could otherwise be time-consuming.

Using apps in QBO

There are two types of apps that integrate seamlessly with QBO. First, is the QBO Mobile app, which is available for iPhones, iPads, Android phones, and Android tablets. It allows you to manage your day-to-day business functions on the go, which will transform how you do business.

Below, you will find step-by-step instructions on how to download the QBO Mobile app:

1. Open the App Store or Google Play on your device and search for `QuickBooks Online`. (It may not be available in some countries.)
2. Select **Free**, then **Install**.
3. If you are already signed up for QBO, use the same user ID and password to sign in to the app.
4. You may be asked to enter a one-time code to confirm your identity. Once confirmed, you can continue into your account.

> There are a number of functions that can be performed using the app. For a complete list by device, check out this Intuit article for the details: `https://quickbooks.intuit.com/learn-support/en-us/help-article/mobile-apps/compare-mobile-app-features/L97TKZ2ck_US_en_US?uid=m26j67uc`.

The second type of app that integrates seamlessly with QBO is third-party integrations. There are many benefits and a few risks of extending functionality through integrations. Some of the **benefits** of using integrations in QBO are as follows:

- The ability to expand the functionality of the software so you can have what you need to run all aspects of your business.
- Access to more than 800 third-party products that integrate seamlessly with QBO, allowing you to manage your inventory, accept online payments, pay your bills, and manage your e-commerce transactions. In *Chapter 17, Integrating E-Commerce Platforms with QuickBooks Online*, we show you how to see if your e-commerce store integrates with QBO.
- The companies featured in the QuickBooks Integrations Center have gone through an extensive vetting process and were approved by Intuit to create apps that will help you simplify tasks, streamline data entry, and sync with QuickBooks.

A couple of the **risks** involved with using third-party platforms are as follows:

- They are not free, which means the fees charged to use an integration will be in addition to what you pay for your monthly QBO subscription, so be sure to do a cost/benefit analysis to ensure you can take on the additional cost.
- You will need to give permission for your data in QBO to be shared with any company whose integration you wish to use. You can be confident that your data is secure, since that is also a requirement to become a partner with Intuit.

The integrations store is organized into categories based on app functionality. Customer reviews are included, along with short video demonstrations to show you how the software works and customer service information if you have additional questions. In this section, we will provide you with an overview of the Integrations Center, show you how to find platforms that are relevant to your business needs, and show you how to connect them to QBO.

Because of the large number of integrations that are available, it's impossible for ProAdvisors and accountants to be familiar with all platforms. Therefore, you will need to reach out to the technical support team for the integration that you choose for assistance with setup, implementation, and training needs. The data in your integrations must be maintained and accurate for it to transfer to QBO accurately.

Overview of the QuickBooks Integration Center

The layout of the Integration Center is very simple. You can easily search for integrations, see a list of the integrations you have added, and check out integrations that have been recommended based on the type of business you have. Let's take a closer look at the layout:

1. On the left menu bar, click on **Apps** to navigate to the App Center, as follows:

Figure 4.64: Navigating to the QuickBooks Integrations Center

The screen displays as shown in *Figure 4.65*:

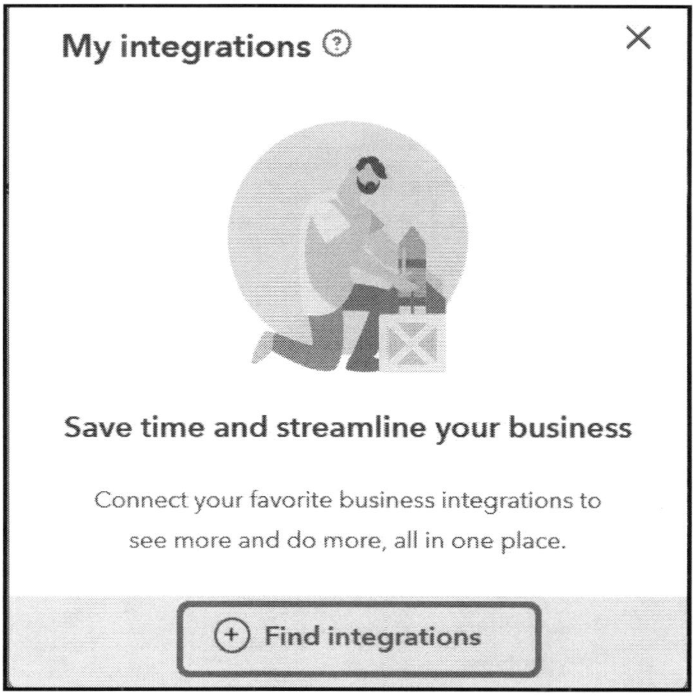

Figure 4.65: The My integrations and Find integrations window displays

2. To start your search, click on the **Find integrations** button shown at the bottom of the screen.
3. The Integrations Center will be displayed, as shown in *Figure 4.66*:

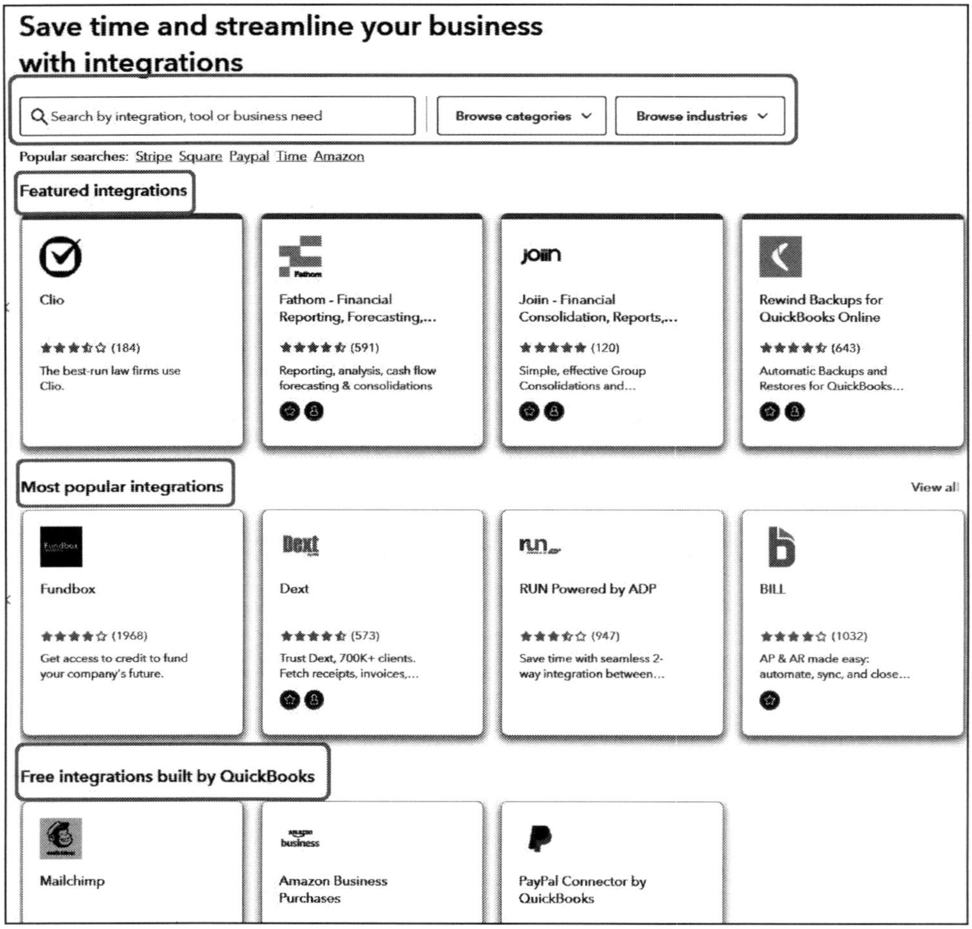

Figure 4.66: QuickBooks Integrations Center

The four key areas of the QuickBooks Integrations Center are as follows:

- **Search options:** If you know the name of the platform you are searching for, you can simply type the name of the integration into the search box shown in the preceding screenshot. However, if you don't know the name of the integration and simply want to search by category, you can do so by clicking on the **Browse categories** button.

- **Browse categories**: There are several categories you can search by, such as **Get customers**, **Get paid**, **Get capital**, **Manage workforce**, **Access advice**, **Be compliant and organized**, **Manage business**, **Manage sales**, and **Manage data**. This will help to narrow down the search so that you can quickly find the integrations that you are looking for.
- **Browse industries**: The ability to browse integrations by industry is a new one! I love this feature because it allows you to filter your results to the integrations that meet your specific industry needs. Some of the industries you will find on this list are accounting, entertainment, manufacturing, hospitality, technology, retail, and many more.
- **Free integrations built by QuickBooks**: In this section, you will find integrations that were created by QuickBooks.

If you're not sure which app to choose, I recommend that you schedule a live demo with the software company so that you can see how the integration works and get your questions answered. Many companies offer a trial period of 14 days or more so that you can try it before you buy it. Like QBO, there are no contracts, so you can cancel your subscription at any time. Let's now walk through an example of how to find integrations for your business.

Finding integrations for your business

As we mentioned previously, there are more than 800 integrations in the QuickBooks Integration Center. While it can be overwhelming at first, you should focus on the needs of your business. There is a lot of information in the center about each integration, which will save you the time you would have normally spent doing research. Let's take a look at an integration to see what kind of information you can expect to find here.

Scroll down to the **Most popular integrations** category and click on the **Fathom** app. You will be greeted with the following screen:

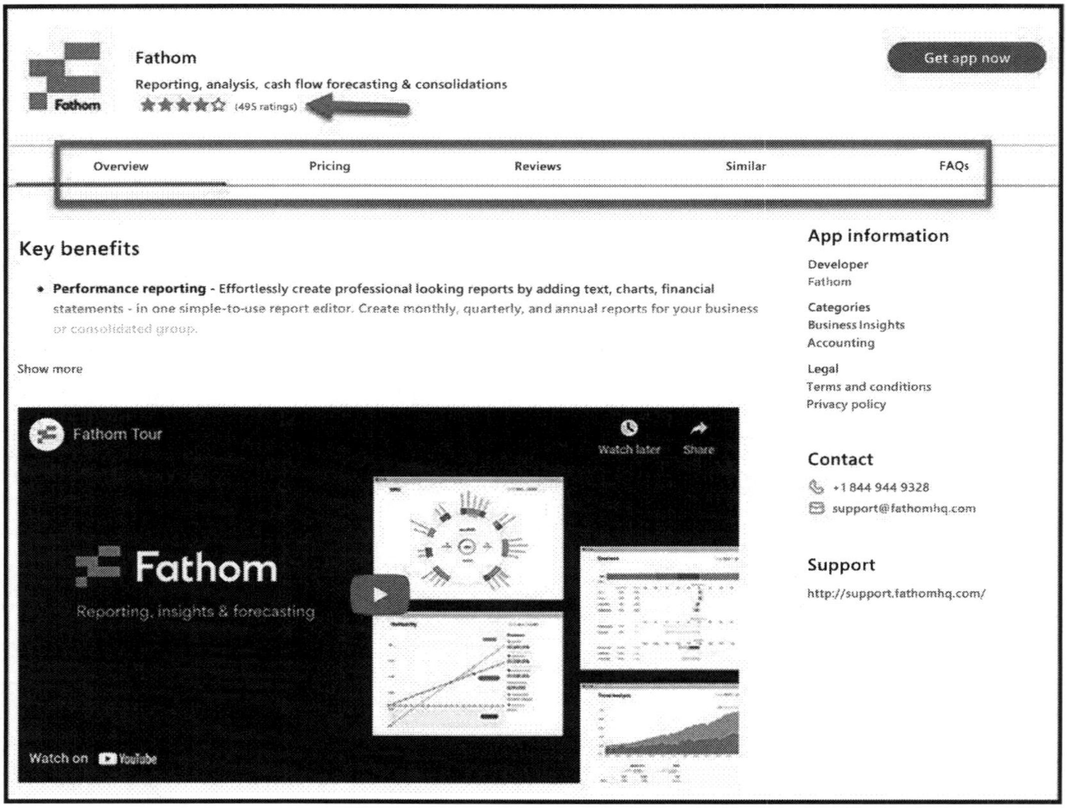

Figure 4.67: The profile for the Fathom integration

The following is a brief description of the information you will find in the app profile:

- **Overview**: The **Overview** tab includes a list of the key benefits the integration has, how the integration works with QBO, and additional details. Like Fathom, most integrations will include a short video to demonstrate how it works, along with additional screenshots of the user interface.
- **Pricing**: Unfortunately, these integrations are not free. Pricing will vary and is usually subscription-based, like QBO. However, you will be billed by the third-party company (in this case, Fathom), not QuickBooks. The good news is that most integrations will offer a free trial period of at least 14 days.

- **Reviews**: Like most products, you will see a rating of the integration based on customer reviews. Click on the link to see what customers are saying about the integration. The more reviews an integration has, the better the chance of getting a broad perspective.
- **Similar**: The **Similar** tab shows a list of integrations that have similar functionality to the one you are looking at.
- **FAQs**: A list of the most frequently asked questions and answers can be found on this tab.

Once you have decided which integration(s) to go with, it's easy to get started. Simply click on the **Get integration now** button located on each profile. Follow the onscreen instructions to complete the setup.

Reaching out to an industry-specific professional organization is a great way to find out the most popular integrations used for your industry. This may help narrow down your search for the right fit.

Customizing sales templates

QuickBooks allows you to create custom sales forms to match your brand and style. Taking the time to customize invoices and sales receipts will allow you to create professional-looking forms so your customers can easily see what they owe and make payments online in just a few minutes. You can customize invoices, estimates, and sales receipt templates.

Follow these steps to learn how to customize these sales templates:

1. Click on the gear icon and select **Custom form styles** from the **SETTINGS** column, as shown here:

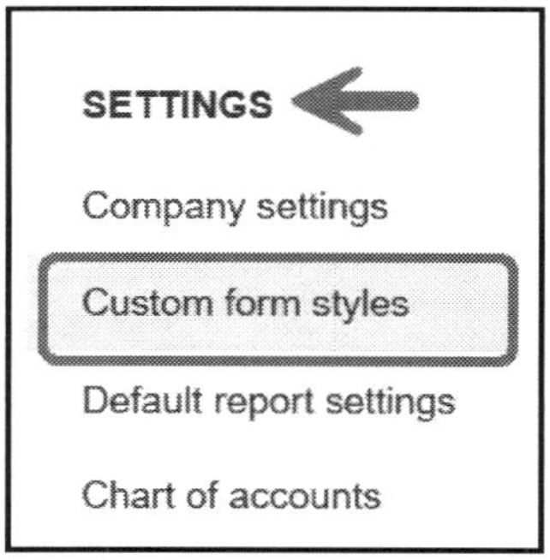

Figure 4.68: Navigating to Custom form styles

2. Click on the **New style** button and select a sales template to customize:

Figure 4.69: Clicking the New style button

3. The following window will display three areas you can customize for sales templates:

Figure 4.70: Three customization options for sales templates

The following is a brief explanation of the information you can customize in each of these areas:

- **Design**: The **Design** section allows you to create your template style and format. You will select a template design, add your company logo, add your brand colors, and choose the font size and style.
- **Content**: For **Content**, you can select what information you would like to appear on the sales template, including your basic contact information, such as a business telephone number and mailing address. You can also add your website and email address to the form. In the billing section, you can determine how much detail you would like to include in the sales form. For example, an invoice should include a list of each product or service you are billing the customer for.
- **Emails**: QuickBooks allows you to email a sales form directly to customers. In this section, you can decide whether you want to include full details or just summarized details of the invoice included in the body of the email. Also, you can choose to have a PDF document attached to the email. In *Figure 4.71*, you can see the standard email message customers will get with every invoice. You can choose to edit these fields to create a more customized message to your customers. At the very bottom, there is also a **Reminder email** template. This is used if you choose to send reminders to customers when invoices are coming due or past due.

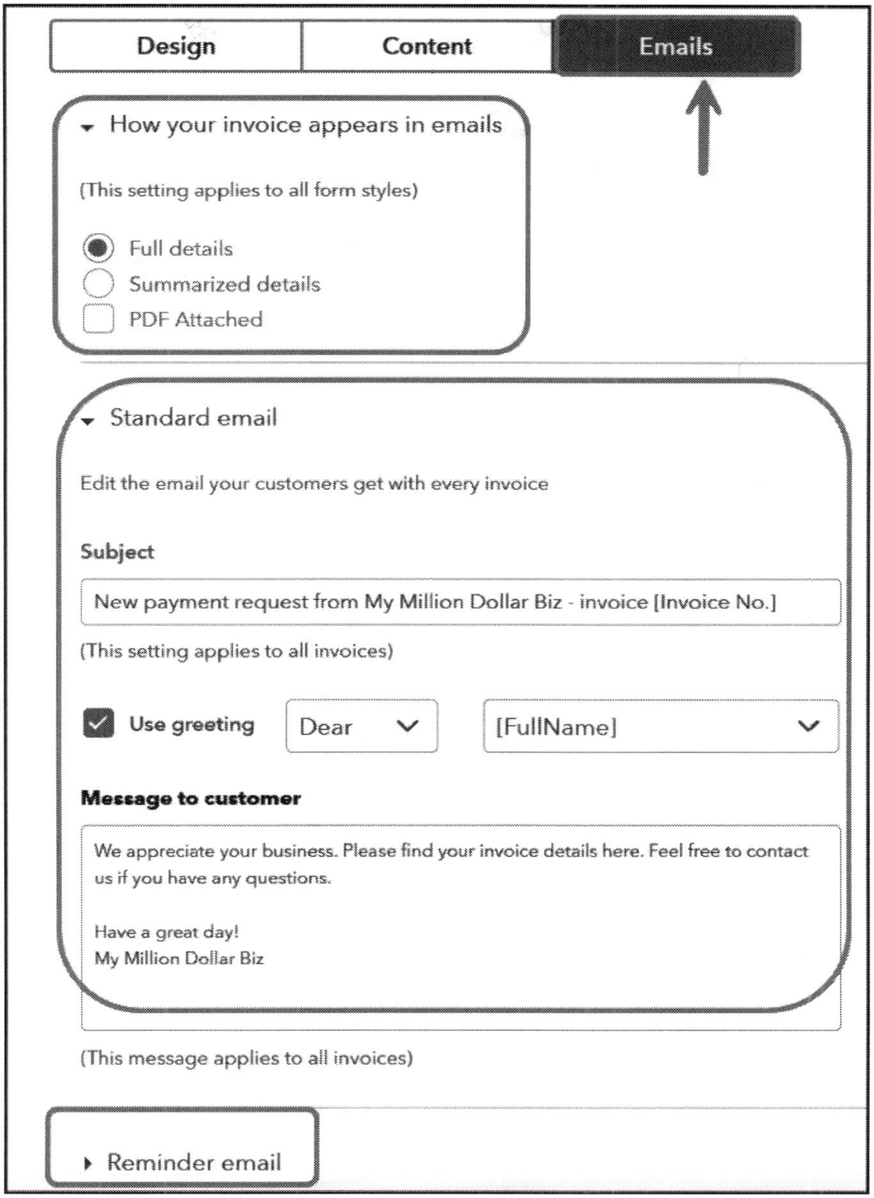

Figure 4.71: Review email options and print preview

4. After completing each section, click the **Preview PDF** button in the bottom-right corner of the screen to save your changes. A preview of your customized sales form should appear, as shown in *Figure 4.72*:

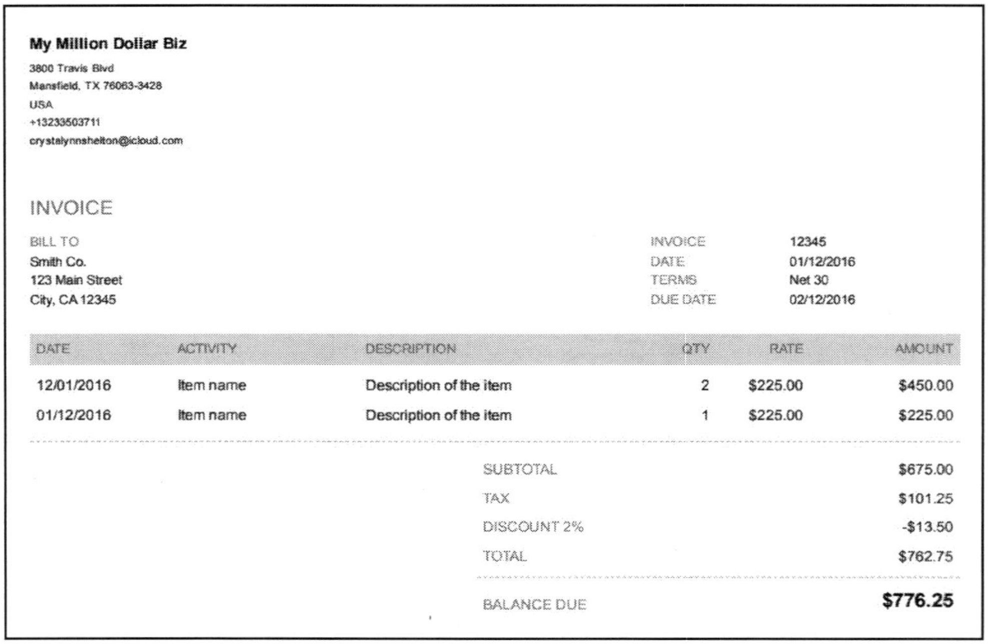
My Million Dollar Biz
3800 Travis Blvd
Mansfield, TX 76063-3428
USA
+13233503711
crystalynnshelton@icloud.com

INVOICE

BILL TO
Smith Co.
123 Main Street
City, CA 12345

INVOICE 12345
DATE 01/12/2016
TERMS Net 30
DUE DATE 02/12/2016

DATE	ACTIVITY	DESCRIPTION	QTY	RATE	AMOUNT
12/01/2016	Item name	Description of the item	2	$225.00	$450.00
01/12/2016	Item name	Description of the item	1	$225.00	$225.00

SUBTOTAL	$675.00
TAX	$101.25
DISCOUNT 2%	-$13.50
TOTAL	$762.75
BALANCE DUE	**$776.25**

Figure 4.72: Sample custom invoice for Small Business Builders, LLC

You can create an unlimited number of templates for various types of sales and customers. It is easy to make changes to them anytime. The best part is that you don't have to create any templates from scratch.

After completing the invoice form, you can click on the **Review and send** button in the bottom-right corner of the screen. This will display a screen that resembles the one in *Figure 4.73*. Within that screen, you can also select the option to text the invoice link to your customer. You'll also notice the option at the top of the screen to enter the customer's phone number and confirm that you have permission to send invoices via text.

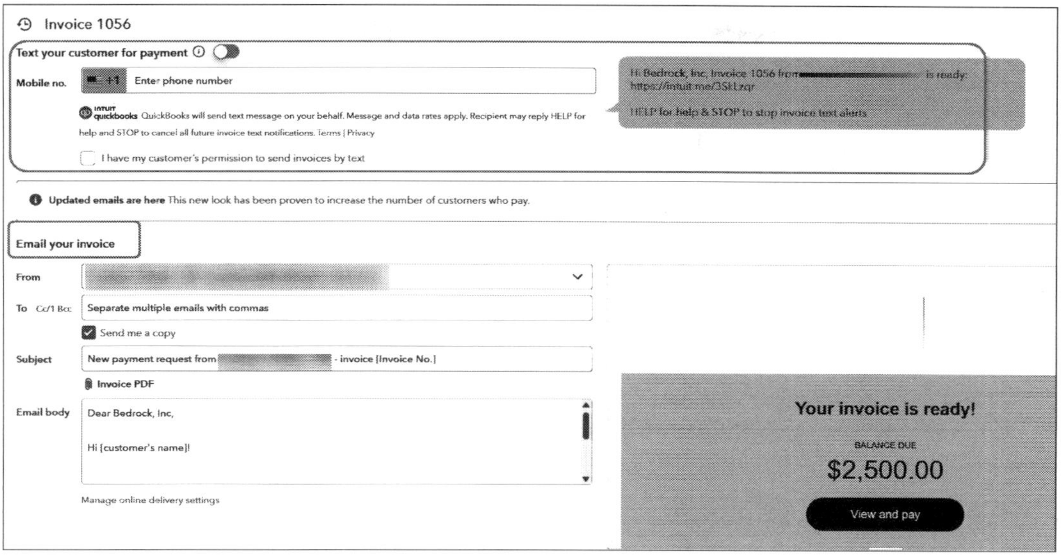

Figure 4.73: Text or invoices to customers in QBO

Learn how to customize sales forms and tips and tricks on customizing sales forms in QBO: `https://packt.link/du2BR`.

Since texting invoices to customers is a brand-new feature, you need to obtain your customer's permission to do this. Notice the box next to the statement **I have my customer's permission to send invoices by text** at the top of the page. In addition to sending invoices via text, I recommend that you also send your invoices via email over snail mail. Nowadays, people like to make online payments because they are much faster. Giving your customers the option to make online payments will help you get paid faster, which can help you maintain positive cash flow.

Summary

In this chapter, we showed you how to customize the chart of accounts by adding, editing, deleting, and merging accounts. We covered how to connect your bank and credit card accounts to QuickBooks so that transactions are automatically downloaded into QuickBooks. We also covered how to import banking transactions into QuickBooks from a CSV file. Keep in mind that the bank and credit card transactions are not yet recorded on your books.

After importing the transactions, they sit in the banking center and will require you to review and categorize them. In *Chapter 11, Managing Bank Feeds and Reconciling Bank and Credit Card Accounts*, we will show you how to do this.

We showed you how to give other users, such as a bookkeeper, business partner, or CPA, full or limited access to your QuickBooks data. Finally, we showed you how to search the QuickBooks App Center for apps that could help streamline your business processes. By now, you should know how to manage your chart of accounts and bank and credit card accounts, how to add additional users, as well as how to delete users, how to navigate the QBO Integration Center, and how to create customized sales templates.

In the next chapter, we will show you how to manage customers, and vendors in QBO. This will include how to add, edit, and inactivate customers, vendors, products, and services.

Next steps

1. Download the **Chart of accounts** import template: `https://github.com/PacktPublishing/Mastering-QuickBooks-2026-Seventh-Edition`.
2. Connect your *business* bank accounts to QBO.
3. Connect your *business* credit card accounts to QBO.
4. Invite other users to access QBO.

   Download the QBO app. You can find information regarding downloading the app here:

   `https://packt.link/25laf`.

5. If you have a bookkeeper or accountant that manages your books, schedule time to meet with that person each month. However, make sure that you have already reviewed your financial reports and made a list of your questions *prior to this meeting*. In other words, schedule your "money date" before you meet with your bookkeeper or accountant, if applicable.

6. Be sure to head over to my YouTube channel for step-by-step product demos in QBO. Use this link to access the channel:

   `https://packt.link/du2BR`

5

Managing Customer and Vendor Lists

Now that you've created your company files, it's time to add the people you do business with on a regular basis. This includes the customers to whom you sell your products and services and the vendors from whom you purchase services and supplies.

One of the benefits of adding customers and vendors to QBO is the ability to manage contact information, such as the mailing address, telephone number, and primary contact. This allows you to use QBO as your one-stop shop, not just for sales data but also when you need to make a quick call to your customer or vendor; all the pertinent information is just a few clicks away.

In this chapter, we will cover the following key concepts:

- Managing customer lists in QBO
- Managing vendor lists in QBO

By the end of this chapter, you will understand how to add, edit, delete, and merge customers and vendors.

The US edition of QBO was used to create this book. If you are using a version that is outside of the US, results may differ.

Managing customer lists in QBO

A customer is anyone that you sell products or services to. A customer can be an individual or a business.

Some of the information QBO allows you to keep track of related to customers includes contact information, such as their telephone number and email address, payment terms, invoicing, and payment history. You can enter customer information manually or import it from an Excel spreadsheet. If you need to make changes to the contact information for a customer, you can do so easily. If you stop doing business with a customer, you can make the customer inactive so that they no longer appear in the customer listings. You can also merge customers if you have duplicates. In this section, we will show you how each of these works, beginning with manually adding customers.

Manually adding customers in QBO

In order to add new customers to QBO, you need to have the basic contact details of your customers. This includes their company name, billing address, business telephone number, and the first and last name of the primary contact. You should also know what payment terms you will extend to customers (for example, net 30 days or net 60 days).

Follow these steps to add a new customer in QBO:

1. Navigate to **+ Create** from the left menu bar and then **Add customer**, as shown in *Figure 5.1*:

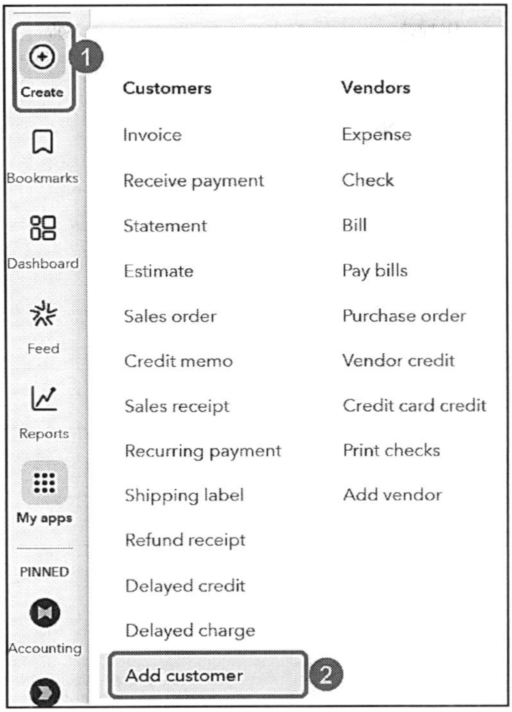

Figure 5.1: Navigating to Customers

The following screen will appear:

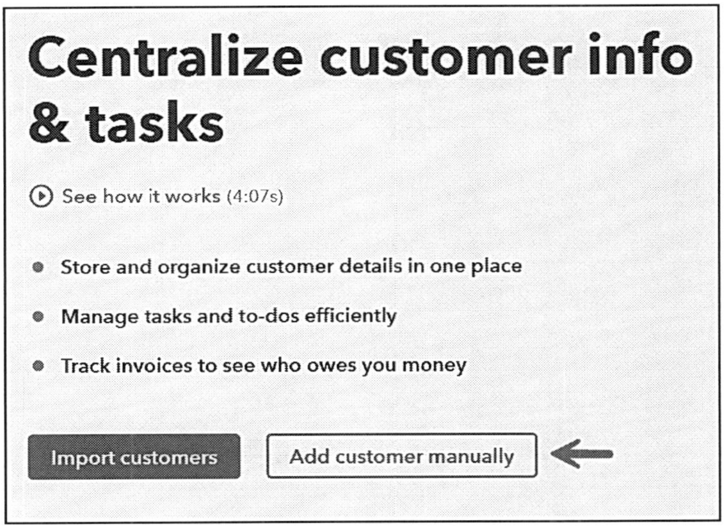

Figure 5.2: The Add customer manually button

2. Click on the **Add customer manually** button. Note that this button will not appear if you have added customers previously to QuickBooks.
3. Fill in the fields on the **Customer** information screen, as shown in *Figure 5.3*:

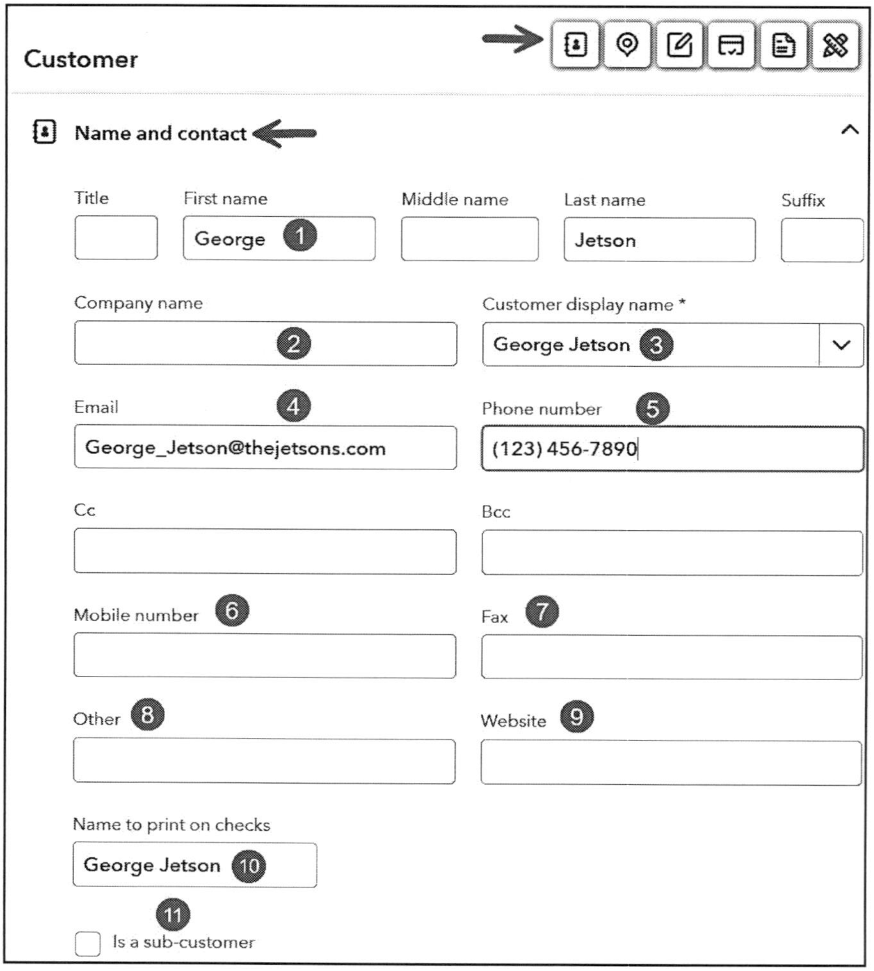

Figure 5.3: Filling in customer information

4. When adding a new customer, there are five key areas that need to be completed: **Name and contact**, **Addresses**, **Notes and attachments**, **Payments**, and **Additional information**. You can navigate to each area using the icons located in the top-right corner of the screen, as indicated in *Figure 5.3*.

The following is a brief description of the 11 fields of information you can enter in the **Name and contact** section. While the only required field is the **Customer display name** field, I recommend that you take the time to add as much information as you can about your customers:

- **First name** and **Last name** (1): If the customer is an individual, enter their first and last names in these fields. If the customer is a business, leave these fields blank. Note that if a business is a sole proprietorship or a single-member LLC and you want to keep track of the name of the business owner and the legal business name, complete both fields. Be sure to periodically review your customer list for duplicates. If you have more than one person adding customers, you want to make sure that they are consistent when adding customers using the **First name** and **Last name** fields and/or adding them using the **Company name** field. A good rule of thumb is to use the **First name** and **Last name** fields for customers who don't have a company name and use the **Company name** field for those who have a **doing business as (DBA)**.
- **Company name** (2): If the customer is a business, enter the business name in this field. If the customer is an individual, leave this field blank.
- **Customer display name** (3): There is no need to input anything in this field; it will automatically populate with the information you entered in the **Company name** or **First name** and **Last name** fields. This field is important because the information will be displayed in the customer list found in the customer center.
- **Email** (4): Enter the business email address for customers in this field.
- **Phone number** (5): Enter the business telephone number for customers in this field.
- **Mobile number** (6): Enter the mobile number for customers in this field.
- **Fax** (7): Enter the fax number (if applicable) for customers in this field.
- **Other** (8): Enter an additional contact phone number in the **Other** field.
- **Website** (9): Enter the website address for the business if you have one.
- **Name to print on checks** (10): Similar to the **Customer display name** field, this field will automatically populate with the information that you entered in the **Company name** or **First name** and **Last name** fields. If you need to change the payee name, enter the name you would like to appear on checks. Typically, you would issue a check to a customer in the case of a refund, so it is important to have the correct payee name in this field.

- **Is a sub-customer** (11): If you have more than one job or project you are working on for the same customer, you can create sub-customers to keep track of the income and expenses for each job separately. For example, if a contractor is working on a kitchen remodel and a bathroom remodel for the same customer, each of these jobs can be set up as a sub-customer so that you can track income and expenses for each job (sub-customer) separately. This will allow you to easily run reports by sub-customer (job, project) so that you can see the profitability of each one.

> Before you can create a sub-customer, the main customer must be added to QuickBooks first. Going back to our contractor example, the customer must be added to QuickBooks first before adding **kitchen remodel** and **bathroom remodel** as sub-customers.

Now you can go ahead and complete the following fields in the **Addresses** section:

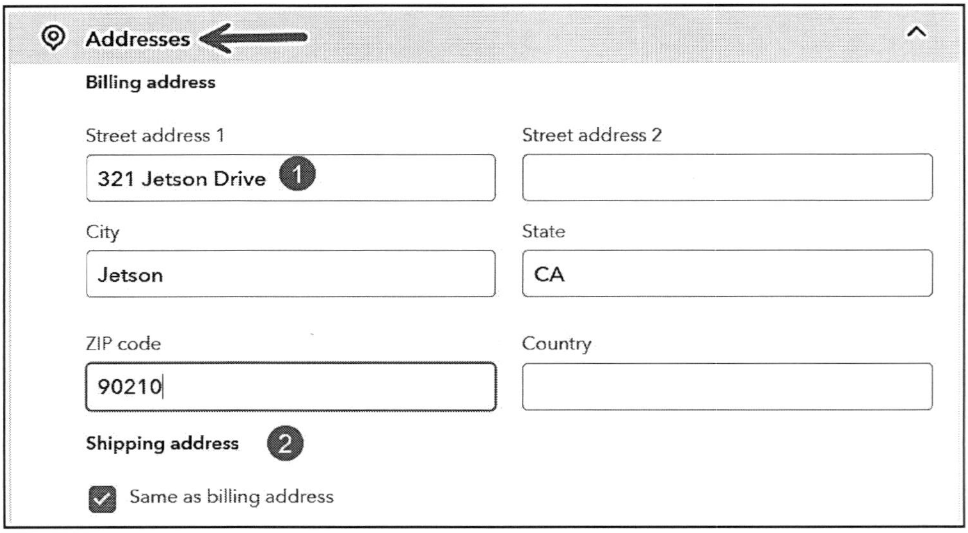

Figure 5.4: Addresses section of the customer information screen

The following is a brief description of the fields of information you can enter in the **Addresses** section:

- **Billing address** (1): Enter the address where your customers would like their invoices to be mailed to and/or where correspondence should be sent. Even if you plan to email all the invoices and other correspondence, we recommend that you keep an address on file for all customers.

- **Shipping address** (2): The address entered in the **Billing address** field will automatically be copied to the **Shipping address** field. This can be edited if necessary. The billing address will be used to mail invoices to customers, and the shipping address is where products are shipped, if applicable.

Complete the following fields in the **Notes and attachments** section:

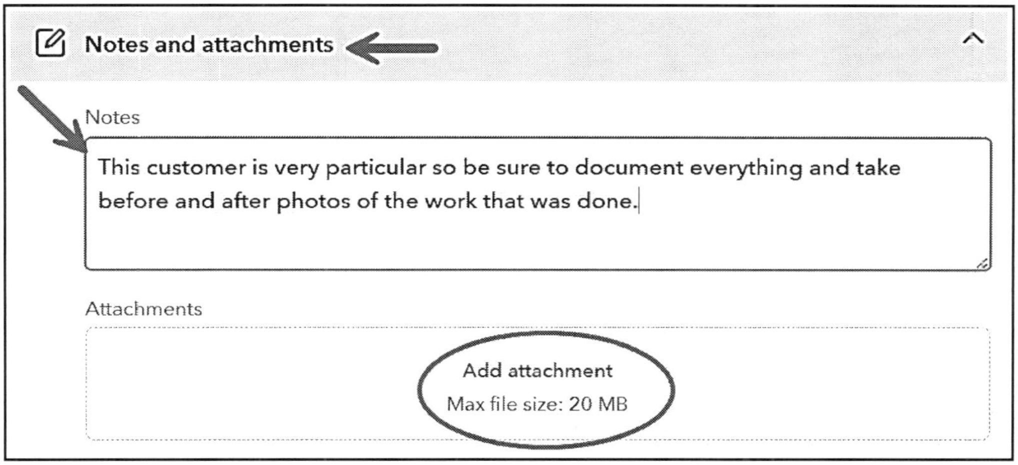

Figure 5.5: Descriptive note and button to add an attachment

Let's take a look at the following:

- **Notes**: This field is optional but can be used to enter additional information about your customers, such as any preferences they have, or even to document previous incidents or issues. This information is for internal use only and is not visible to the customer.
- **Attachments**: You can store important documents such as contracts, engagement letters, or proposals in QuickBooks. Simply scan the document to your computer and attach it to the customer with whom it is associated.

Complete the following five fields in the **Payments** section:

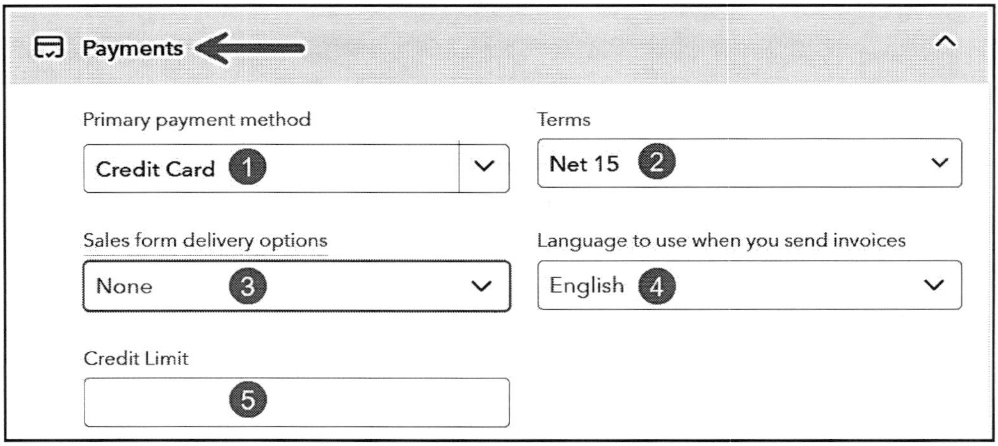

Figure 5.6: Payments section of the customer information screen

- **Primary payment method** (1): Choose from the drop-down list the payment method used most by the customer. **Cash**, **Check**, and **Credit card** are the options available, but you can also add new payment methods, such as **Cash App** or **Zelle**.
- **Terms** (2): Select the payment terms for customers in this field. For example, **Net 30** means the customer has 30 days from the invoice date to remit payment. If payment is not received by the due date, QuickBooks will flag the invoice as past due. You can set QuickBooks up to automatically send a reminder email to customers when invoices are coming due or past due. Refer to *Chapter 3*, *Company File Setup*, to learn how to do this.
- **Sales form delivery options** (3): From the dropdown, you can select the method with which you typically provide customers their invoices (**Email**, **Printed copy**, **Default method**, or **None** are the options).
- **Language to use when you send invoices** (4): From the dropdown, you can select the language you would like to invoice customers in. Currently, the choices are **English**, **French**, **Spanish**, **Italian**, **Chinese (Traditional)**, and **Portuguese (Brazil)**.
- **Credit limit** (5): Enter a credit limit for customers who you extend credit to. When an invoice is going to exceed the credit limit, QBO will notify you.

Complete the following fields in the **Additional info** section:

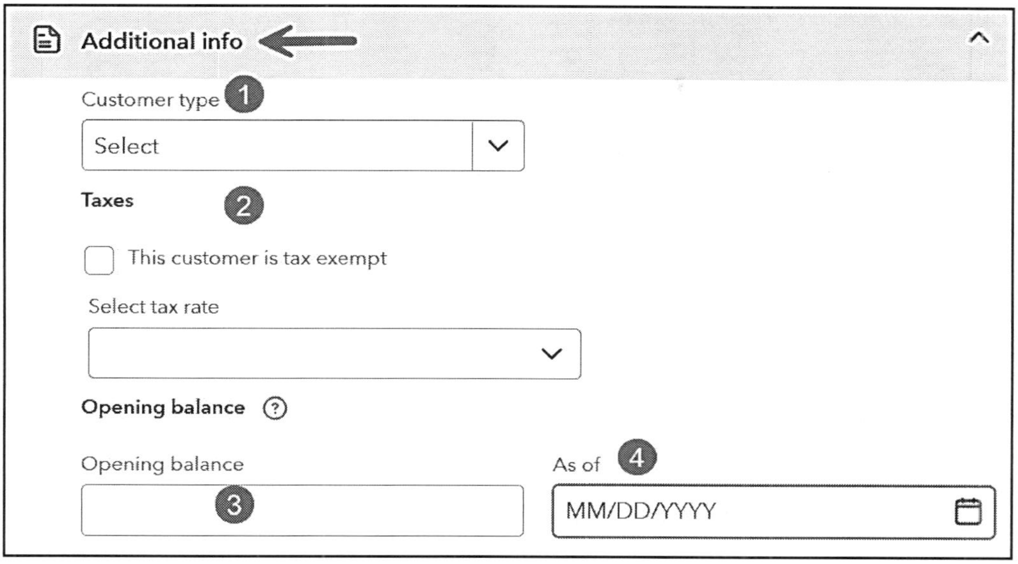

Figure 5.7: Additional info screen of the customer information screen

- **Customer type** (1): If you need to categorize your customers into different types (for example, wholesaler or retailer), you can create custom types and assign each customer to a type. This will allow you to run reports and filter by customer type to get detailed information, such as sales by customer type.
- **Taxes** (2): Enter the details for tax-exempt customers, such as their resale certificate number. In addition, you should request a copy of the certificate and attach it in the **Notes and Attachments** section. This will cover you if you ever have a sales tax audit and need to provide supporting information on why you did not charge a customer sales tax.
- **Opening balance** (3): Generally, you wouldn't use this field unless converting from other accounting software. This field is useful for recording the existing accounts receivable balance that customers have with you at the time of converting from your old accounting system to QuickBooks. However, if you plan to enter unpaid invoices into QuickBooks, leave this field blank.
- **As of** (4): If you entered an opening **accounts receivable** (**A/R**) balance as shown in *Figure 5.7*, enter the effective date in this field. This would typically be the date you start using QuickBooks to track your business finances.
- Be sure to click the **Save** button at the very bottom of the screen to save the customer information in QuickBooks.

If you have more than a handful of customers to add to QuickBooks, I recommend you put the customer information into an Excel spreadsheet and import the data into QuickBooks.

Importing customers into QBO

You can import all of your customer details from a CSV file into QuickBooks. A template can be found here: `https://github.com/PacktPublishing/Mastering-QuickBooks-2026-Seventh-Edition`.

Follow these steps to import customers into QBO:

1. Navigate to **Customers** by clicking on **+Create** from the left-hand menu bar and then **Add customer**, as shown in *Figure 5.8*:

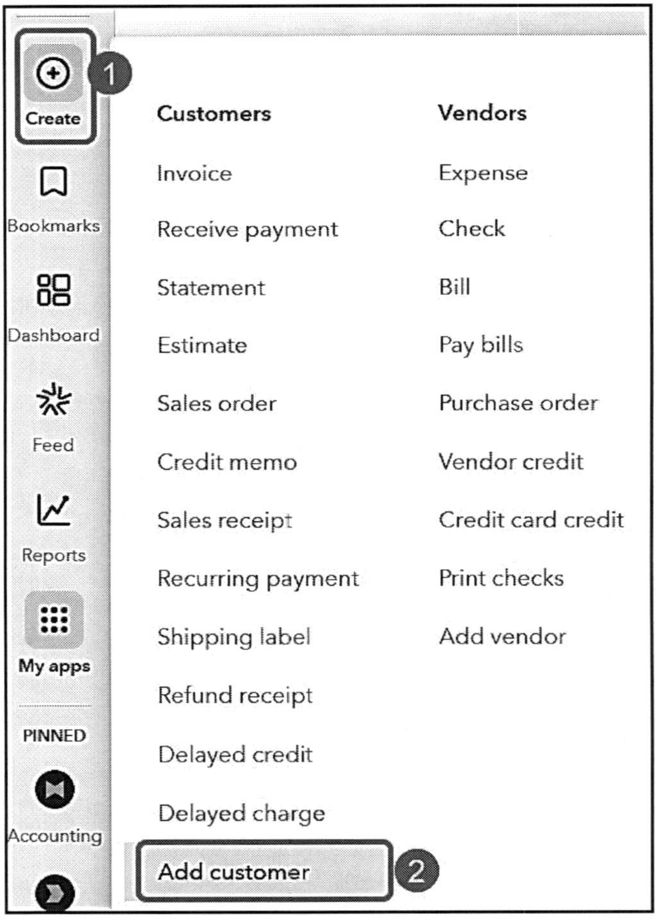

Figure 5.8: Navigating to Customers

2. Click the drop-down arrow next to the **New customer** button, located in the upper-right corner, and select **Import customers**, as shown in *Figure 5.9*:

Figure 5.9: The Import customers option

3. On the **Import customers** screen, click the **Browse** button to upload the Excel or CSV file from your computer, as shown in *Figure 5.10*:

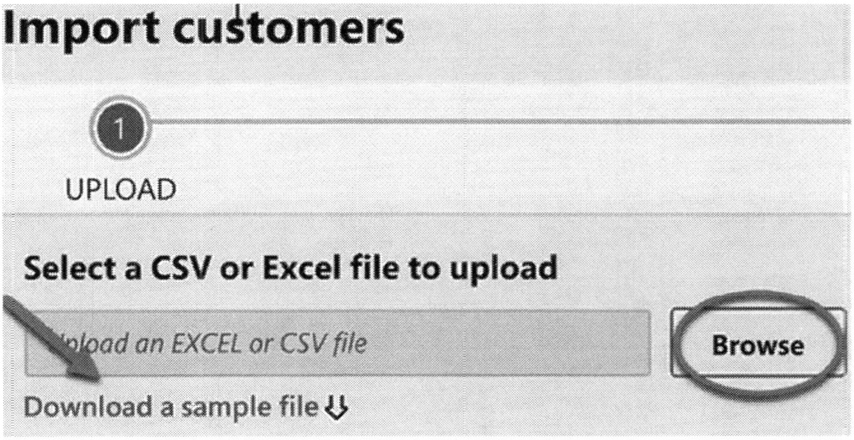

Figure 5.10: Uploading a CSV or Excel file

4. You can click on the blue hyperlink to download the sample file (shown in the preceding screenshot). This file includes all of the fields of information you can upload for customers. Save this file and use it as your template.
5. Follow the onscreen instructions to import your customer data into QBO.

A common error made when importing data is the use of special characters. QuickBooks will not accept the use of special characters (for example, `&`, `!`, and `$`), so be sure to avoid doing this. For additional tips on troubleshooting errors during importing, you can download the troubleshooting guide using this link: `https://github.com/PacktPublishing/Mastering-QuickBooks-2026-Seventh-Edition`.

Making changes to existing customers in QBO

There may be times when you need to correct or update a customer's information. For example, if a customer's address changes or their primary contact changes, you will need to update your records with the new information. Updating customer information is easy to do in QuickBooks – all you need to do is navigate to the Customer Center and select the customer that you need to make changes to.

Follow these steps to edit an existing customer in QBO:

1. Navigate to **Customers** by clicking on **+Create** from the left-hand menu bar and then **Add customer**, as shown in *Figure 5.11*:

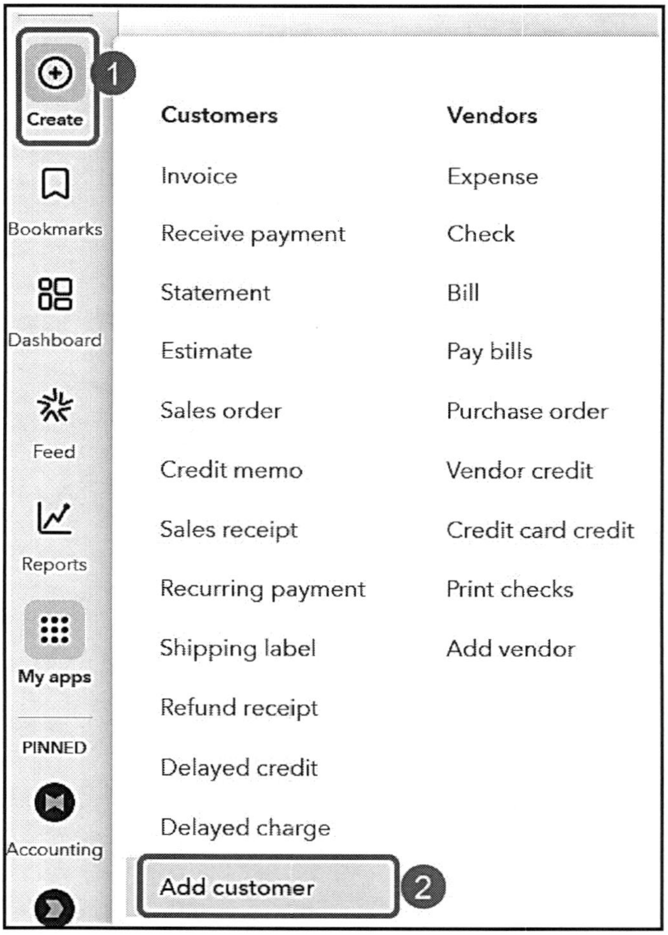

Figure 5.11: Navigating to Customers

2. The Customer Center will appear on the next screen. Click on the customer's name, as indicated in *Figure 5.12*:

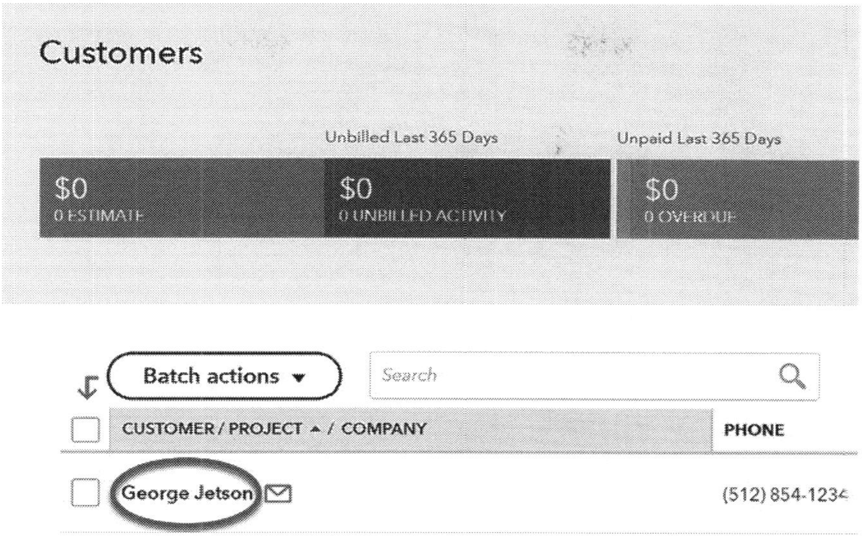

Figure 5.12: Editing customer details

3. The following screen appears. Click the **Edit** button (not shown) and make the necessary changes:

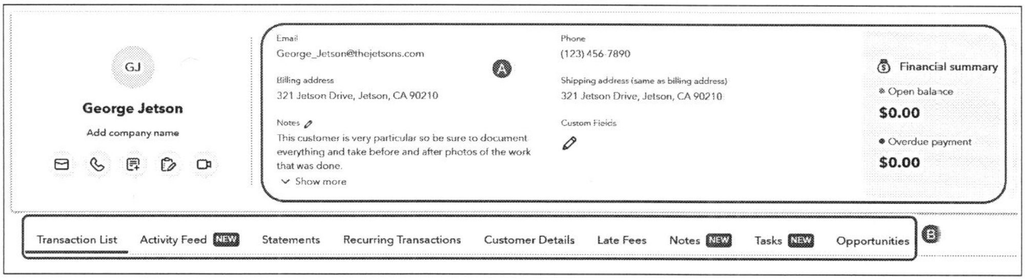

Figure 5.13: Edit button for a customer listed in the Customer Center

You can update the information you have on file for your customers at any time. Having up-to-date information will ensure that invoices, sales receipts, and other documents contain the most recent contact information, such as billing and shipping address information, on file.

Inactivating customers in QBO

You cannot delete customers, vendors, or products in QBO. However, similar to accounts on the chart of accounts (discussed in the previous chapter), you can inactivate customers, vendors, and products, which will keep the existing transactions recorded in QuickBooks but "hide" the customer, vendor, or item from the drop-down list.

Follow these steps to inactivate customers in QBO:

1. Navigate to **Customers** by clicking on **+Create** from the left-hand menu bar and then **Add Customer**, as shown in *Figure 5.14*:

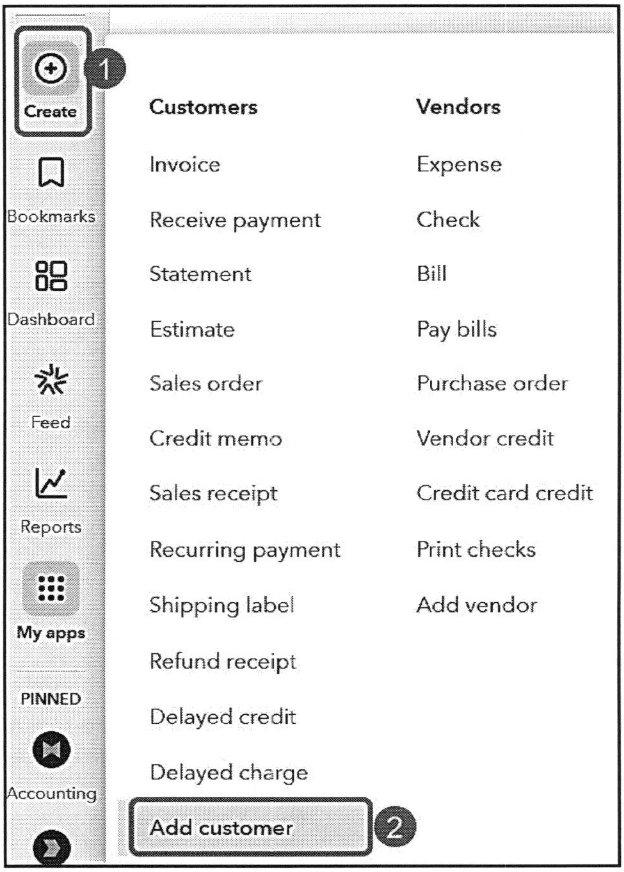

Figure 5.14: Navigating to Customers

2. Put a check mark next to the customer you want to inactivate, click the arrow next to **Batch actions**, and select **Make inactive**, as shown in *Figure 5.15*:

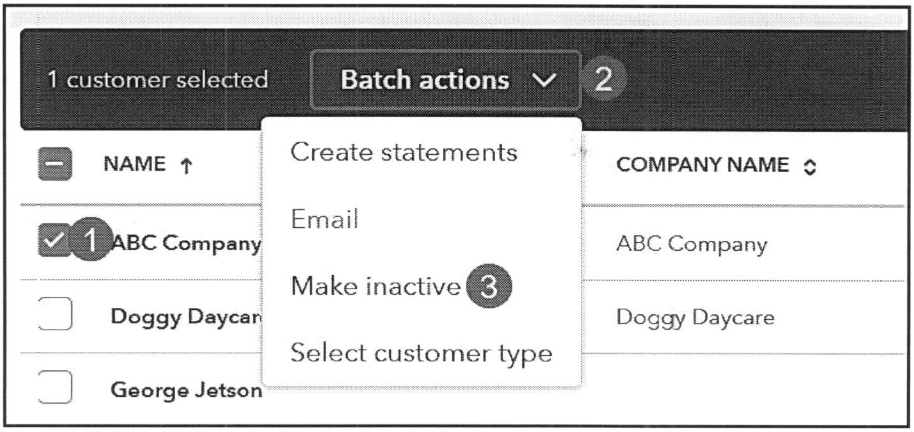

Figure 5.15: The Make inactive option

This **Make inactive** action will prevent someone from selecting customers you no longer wish to use, while preserving the historical transactions that have been recorded for each customer. We will cover how to make vendors and items inactive later on in this chapter.

Merging customers in QBO

A common issue that you may encounter is duplicate customers. If you have more than one person setting up customers in QuickBooks or you don't have an established way of adding new customers, you will run into this issue. The best way to avoid having duplicate customers is to establish a process to add new customers. For example, have only one person who is responsible for adding customers in QuickBooks, and establish whether you will enter customers by first name, last name or last name, first name.

If you do encounter duplicate customers, you can combine the information entered for the duplicate customers to create one customer profile.

Follow these steps to merge customers:

1. Navigate to the Customer Center and identify the duplicate customers:

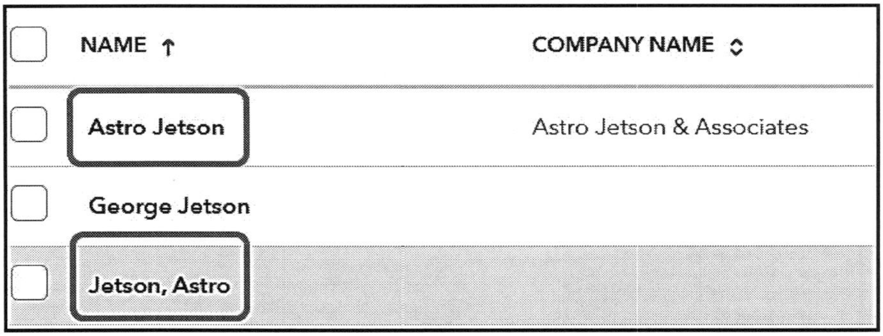

Figure 5.16: Identifying duplicate customers in the Customer Center

2. In *Figure 5.16*, **Astro Jetson** and **Jetson, Astro** are the same customer. Since the owner would like all customer information entered as "first name followed by last name," the customer profile we want to keep is the one at the top of the list, **Astro Jetson**.
3. Click once on the customer profile you plan to remove. In our example, this is **Jetson, Astro**. The following appears once we click on **Jetson, Astro**:

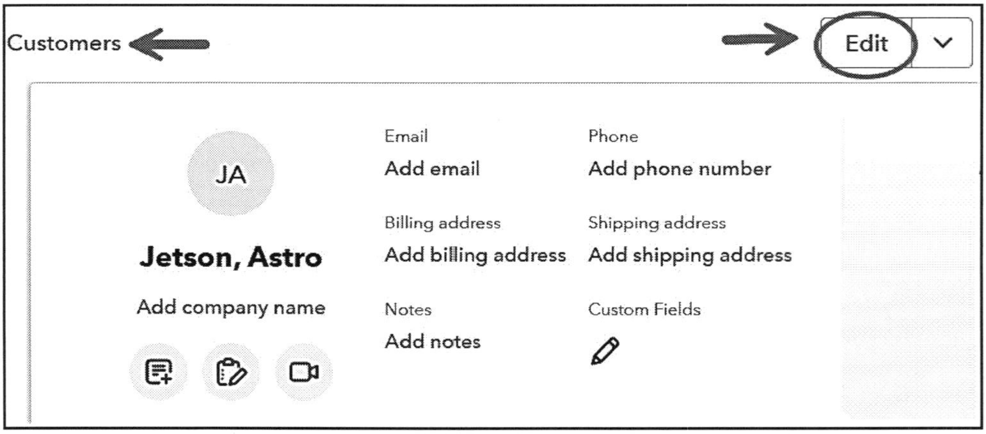

Figure 5.17: Viewing customer information

4. Click the **Edit** button and the customer information screen will appear:

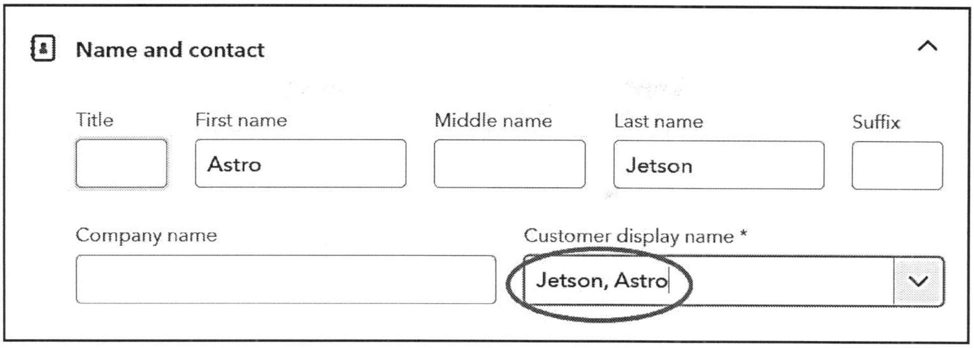

Figure 5.18: Editing information for an existing customer

5. Click once in the **Customer display name** field and type the name exactly as it appears in the customer profile that you wish to keep. In our example, this would be **Astro Jetson**, as shown:

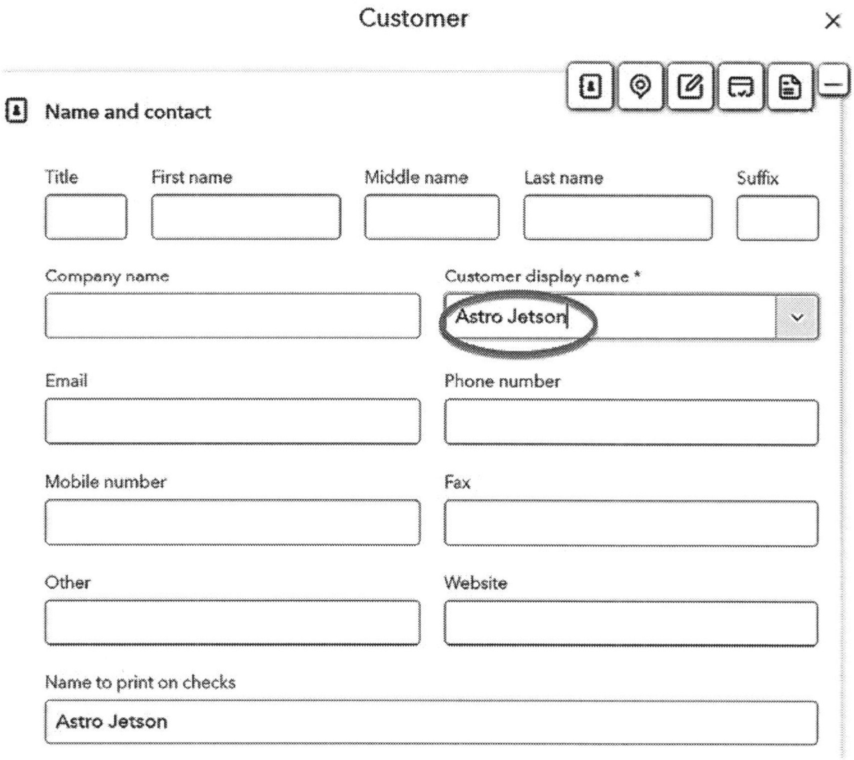

Figure 5.19: Editing the Customer display name field

6. Click the **Save** button in the lower-right corner.

   The following message will appear:

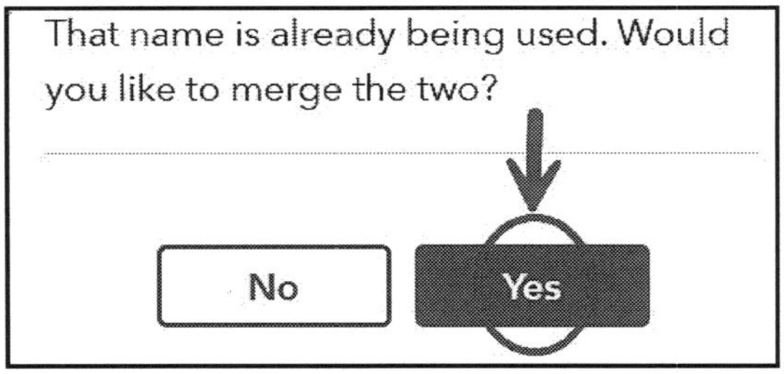

Figure 5.20: Confirming the merging of customers

7. Click **Yes** and the customer profiles will be combined into one, as shown in *Figure 5.21*:

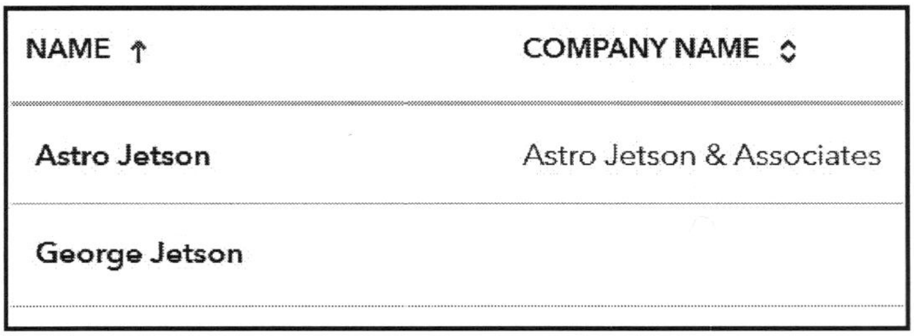

NAME ↑	COMPANY NAME ⬍
Astro Jetson	Astro Jetson & Associates
George Jetson	

Figure 5.21: The Customer Center with both profiles combined

As you can see, the duplicate profile (**Jetson, Astro**) is no longer on the customer list. All of the transactions recorded for that customer have been moved to the **Astro Jetson** profile. With that, we have shown you how to manually add, import, edit, inactivate, and merge customers. In the next section, we will show you how to add, import, edit, inactivate, and merge vendors.

> While you do not have to complete anything other than the customer's name to begin working, we recommend that you keep as much information as possible about your customer in QBO so that your records are complete and accurate.

Managing vendor lists in QBO

A **vendor** is an individual or a business that you pay. Vendors can be 1099 contractors, which are independent contractors whom you pay $600 or more in a calendar year, utility companies, or businesses you purchase products from. Similar to customers, you can keep track of all vendor information, such as the company's address, telephone number, email address, and federal tax ID number for 1099 reporting. 1099 reporting is required for contractors that you have paid $600 or more to within a calendar year.

In this section, we will show you how to add new vendors, edit existing vendors, inactivate vendors, and merge vendors in QuickBooks.

Manually adding vendors in QBO

To add new vendors to QBO, you need to have each vendor's contact details. This includes a business telephone number, remit to address, email address, and tax ID number (or social security number) for 1099 vendors. You can also enter the payment terms your vendor has extended to you. Entering these payment terms will allow QuickBooks to remind you when bills are due or past due.

Follow these steps to manually add vendors in QBO:

1. Navigate to **Vendors** by clicking on **+Create** on the left-hand menu bar and selecting **Add vendor**, as shown in *Figure 5.22*:

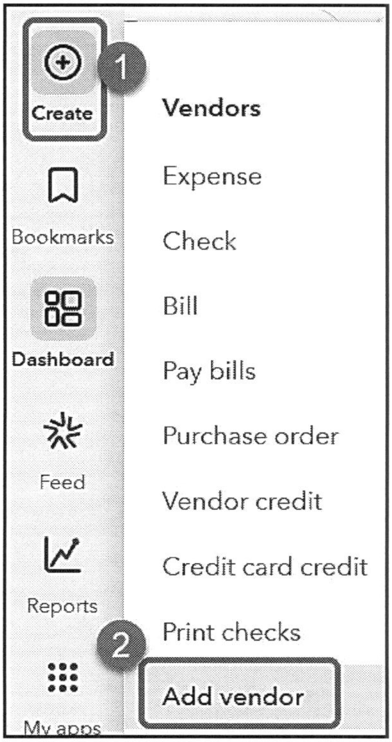

Figure 5.22: Selecting Vendors

2. Fill in the fields in the **Vendor** window, as shown here:

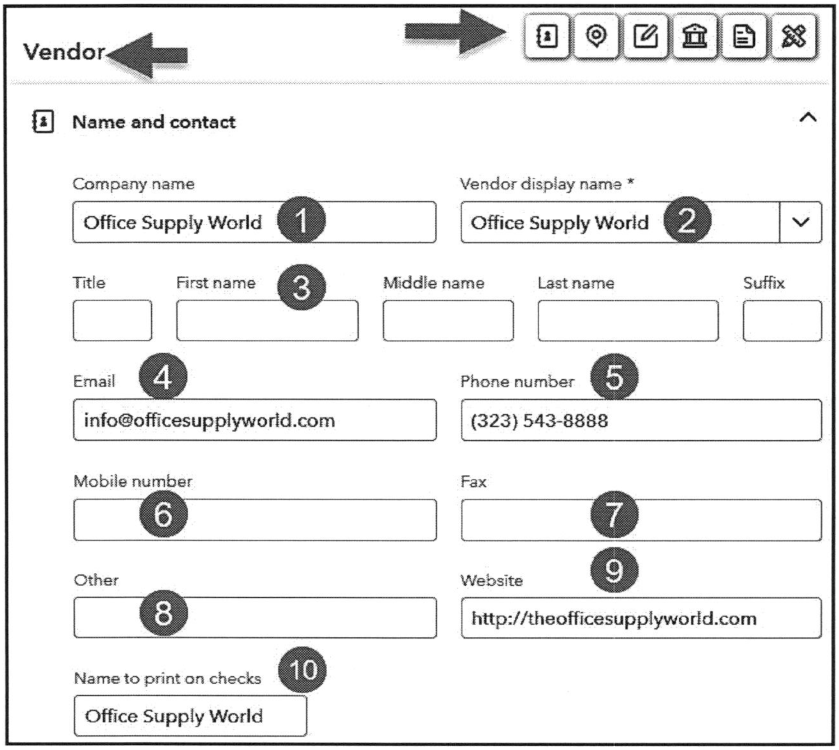

Figure 5.23: Filling in the Vendor window

The following is a brief description of the 10 fields of information you can enter for new vendors:

- **Company name** (1): Enter the name of the business that you are purchasing from. If the vendor is an individual, such as a 1099 contractor, leave this field blank and complete the **First name** and **Last name** fields instead.

> If you have an existing customer who is also a vendor, you will need to set them up as a vendor in QuickBooks. Since QuickBooks does not allow you to use duplicate names, we recommend you add additional verbiage after the name, such as "V" or "Vend," to differentiate between the customer profile and the vendor profile. For example, if Cameras-R-Us is already set up in QuickBooks, we would set it up as a vendor as Cameras-R-Us-V or Cameras-R-Us-Vend.

- **Vendor display name** (2): This field will automatically populate with the company name that was entered in *step 1*.
- **First name** and **Last name** (3): If purchasing from an individual and not a business, enter the name of the individual you are purchasing goods or services from. If the vendor is a sole proprietorship or LLC and you want to keep the name of the business owner, enter both.
- **Email** (4): Enter the primary email address for the vendor in this field. This email address will be used to send purchase orders and other vendor-related documents directly from QuickBooks.
- **Phone number** (5): Enter the vendor's telephone number in this field.
- **Mobile number** (6): Enter the vendor's cell phone number in this field.
- **Fax** (7): Enter the vendor's fax number in this field.
- **Other** (8): Enter any additional contact information in this field.
- **Website** (9): Enter the vendor's website information in this field.
- **Name to print on checks** (10): The information entered for the company name (1) or the first and last name (3) will automatically appear in this field. If necessary, you can edit this information.

1. Enter the address where you mail your payments. If you don't mail payments, you still want to complete these fields if you have the info:

Figure 5.24: Adding vendor address details

If you make your payments online or via credit card, it's still a good idea to keep an address on file for each vendor. This is especially important to do for 1099 contractors because you are required to mail a 1099 form to them at the end of the year for tax reporting purposes. It is important to keep up to date on rules for issuing 1099s. If you are unsure if a vendor should receive a 1099, please reach out to a tax professional for guidance.

2. Complete the **Notes and attachments** section, as shown in *Figure 5.25*:

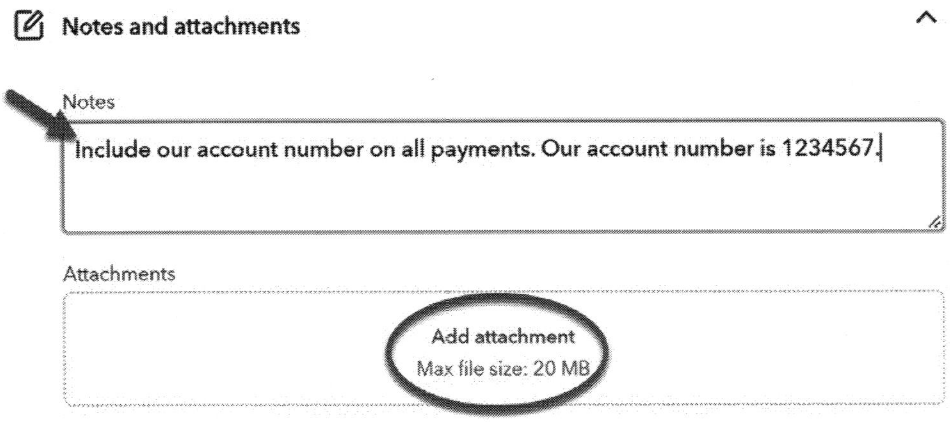

Figure 5.25: Notes and attachments section of the Vendor information screen

Like customers, you can add notes about your vendors and suppliers that are for *internal purposes only*. Any information added to this section is not visible to vendors. In addition, you can attach contracts, files, emails, and other pertinent documents in the section labeled **Add attachment**, as shown in *Figure 5.25*.

3. Complete the fields in the **Additional info** section:

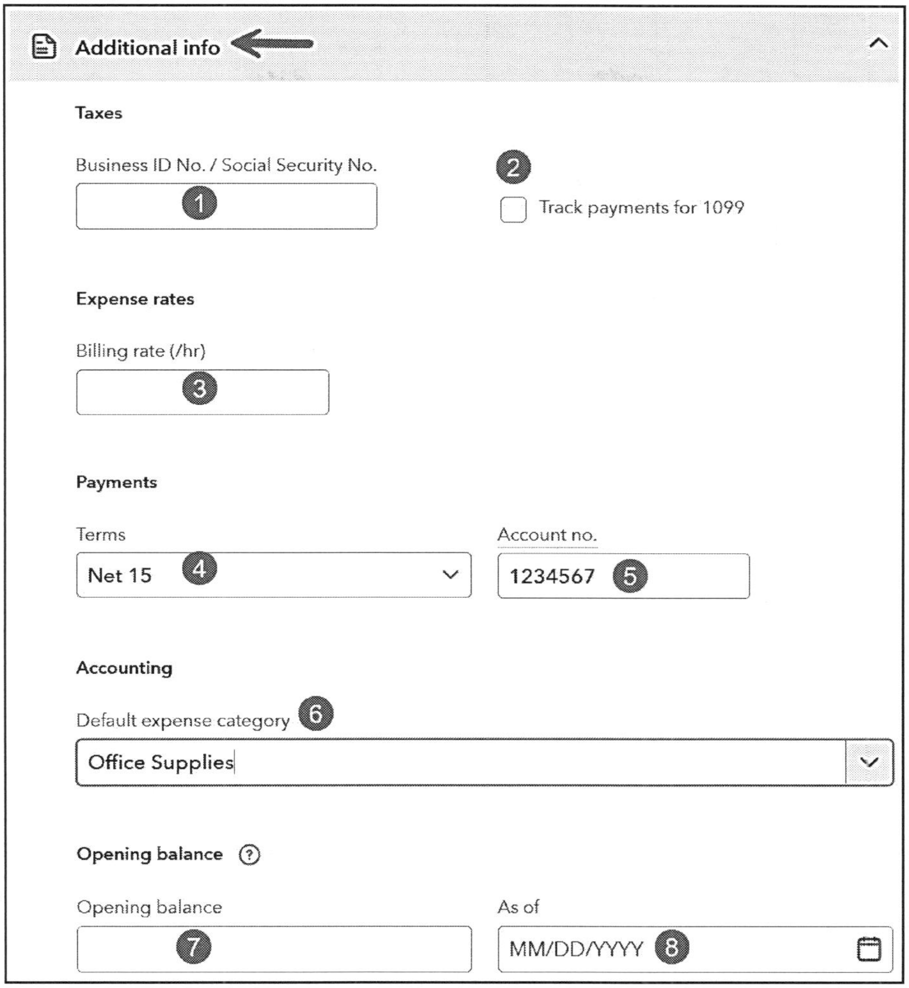

Figure 5.26: Additional info section of the Vendor information screen

- **Business ID No.** (1): Enter the social security number or federal tax ID number for all 1099 vendors in this field. If a business is incorporated, there is no need to obtain this information.

> It's good practice to request a W9 form from all 1099 contractors before you remit payment. A W9 form includes an individual's first and last names, **DBA** company name, mailing address, business entity (for example, sole proprietor or LLC), and social security or federal tax ID number. In *Chapter 14, Report Center Overview*, we cover how to invite a new contractor to complete an electronic W9 form.

- **Track payments for 1099** (2): Select this checkbox for any individuals you purchase goods and services from that are not incorporated. By marking this box, QuickBooks will flag these vendors so that they appear on the 1099 report at the end of the year.

> In the US, if you pay $600 or more to a 1099 contractor during the year, you are required to provide that contractor with a 1099 form at the end of the year. If total payments during the year do not equal $600 or more, you are not required to provide a 1099 form. In *Chapter 14, Report Center Overview*, we will introduce you to the Contractors Center. In the Contractors Center, you can add, edit, and pay 1099 contractors, as well as complete your annual 1099 report filings.

- **Billing rate** (3): If you have an agreed-upon billing rate that does not change, enter that information in this field. However, if the billing rate varies, leave this field blank.

- **Terms** (4): Select the payment terms the vendor has extended to you (for example, net 30 days, net 15 days, or due upon receipt). It's important to select payment terms so that QuickBooks can use this information to remind you when bills are due or past due.
- **Account no.** (5): If your vendor has given you an account number, enter it in this field. Otherwise, you can leave this field blank.
- **Default expense category** (6): If you use the same category for all payments to a vendor, you can select the category from the dropdown. This will allow QuickBooks to automatically populate the category field each time you record a new transaction for this vendor. If the category varies, leave this field blank.
- **Opening balance** (7): If you are converting from other accounting software to QuickBooks, you can enter the outstanding accounts payable balance for suppliers in this field. However, if you plan to manually enter unpaid bills into QuickBooks, leave this field blank.
- **As of** (8): If you entered an opening balance, enter an effective date in the **As of** field. In general, this date will be the same as the date you start tracking your income and expenses in QuickBooks.

Similar to customers, you can include a wealth of information in QuickBooks pertaining to your vendors. By including this information in QuickBooks, you can easily create purchase orders, bills, and other forms and documents without needing to enter this information over and over.

Importing vendors into QBO

If you have more than a few vendors to add to QuickBooks, you may want to consider importing the information instead of manually inputting it into QuickBooks. Similar to customers, you can import your vendor details from a CSV file. This template can be found here: `https://github.com/PacktPublishing/Mastering-QuickBooks-2026-Seventh-Edition`.

Follow these steps to import vendors into QBO:

1. Navigate to **Vendors** by clicking on **Expenses** on the left-hand menu bar and selecting **Vendors**, as shown in *Figure 5.27*:

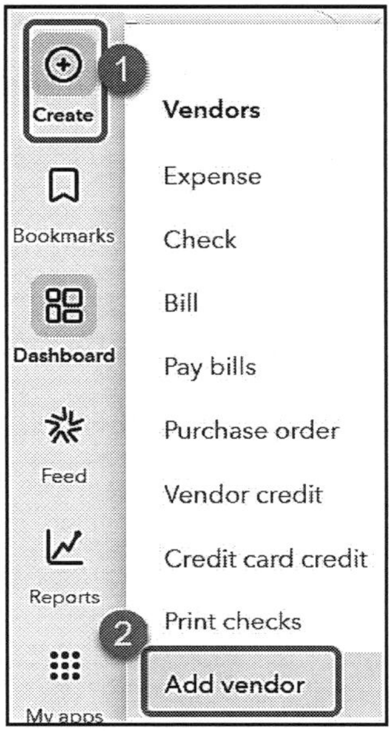

Figure 5.27: Selecting Vendors

2. Click on the arrow to the right of the **New vendor** button, located in the upper-right corner, and select **Import vendors**, as shown in *Figure 5.28*:

Figure 5.28: The Import vendors option

3. On the **Import vendors** screen, click the **Browse** button to upload the Excel or CSV file from your computer **or** click on the **Connect** button to upload a Google Sheet, as shown in *Figure 5.29*:

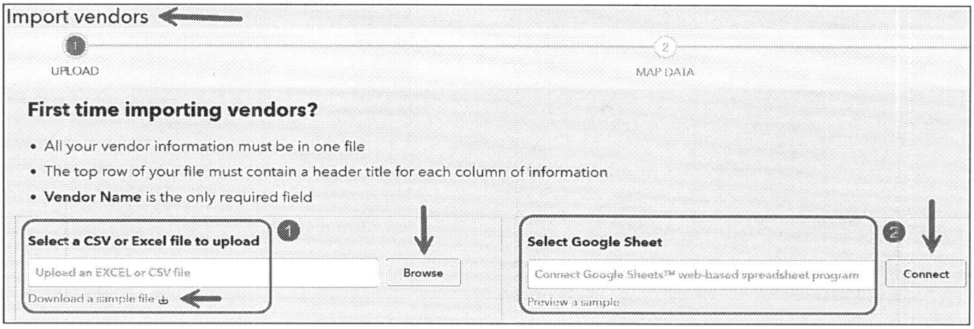

Figure 5.29: Uploading a CSV or Excel file

4. You can click on the blue link to download the sample file (shown in the preceding screenshot). This file includes all of the fields of information you can upload for vendors. Save this file and use it as your template.
5. Follow the onscreen prompts to import your vendors into QBO.

Review the vendor information to ensure accuracy. If you do find errors, you can easily fix them. Let's see how!

Making changes to existing vendors in QBO

Similar to customers, the information that you have on file for vendors can change. For example, the remit address where payments are mailed could change, or the telephone number may need to be updated. When it does, you can quickly update your records in QuickBooks. You will need to navigate to the Vendors Center and select the vendor that you need to make changes to.

Follow these steps to edit an existing vendor in QBO:

1. Navigate to **Vendors** by clicking on **Expenses** on the left-hand menu bar and selecting **Vendors**, as shown in *Figure 5.30*:

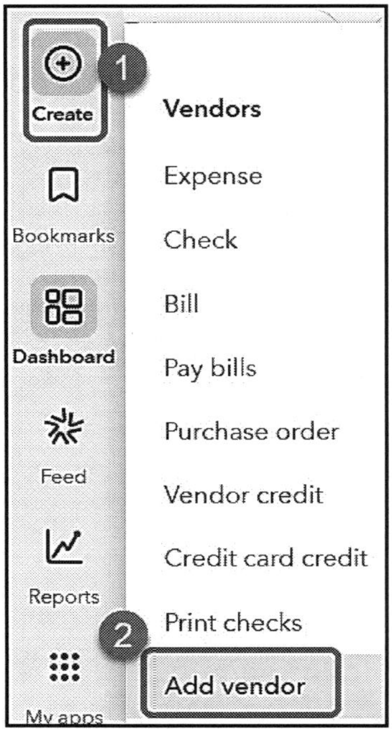

Figure 5.30: Selecting Vendors

2. Select the vendor you want to edit by clicking on the vendor's name, as shown in *Figure 5.31*:

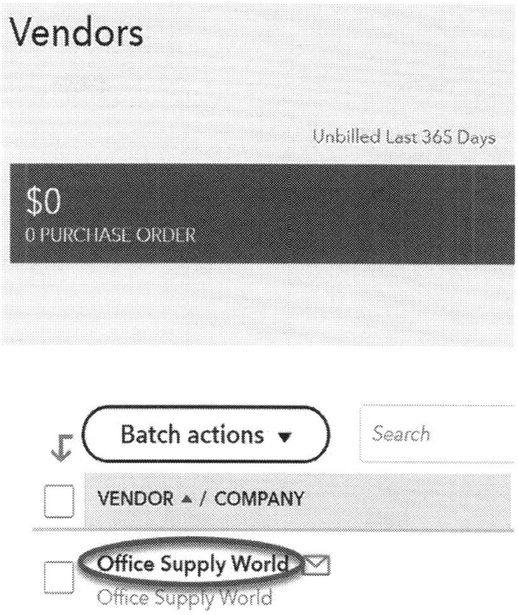

Figure 5.31: Clicking on a vendor name

3. The Vendors Center will be displayed on the next screen. Click on the **Edit** button to make changes:

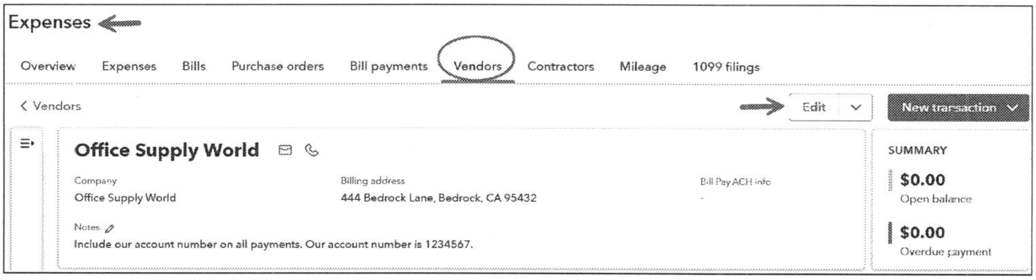

Figure 5.32: Editing a vendor

With the click of a button, QuickBooks makes it easy to update vendor contact information, such as email address, billing address, and more. This is critical when you are generating 1099 forms, for example, and need to get them in the mail before the deadline in January. Having up-to-date vendor information will ensure that all purchase orders, bills, and reports are accurate. If you decide you no longer want to do business with a vendor, but you have existing transactions in QuickBooks, you can inactivate vendors. Let's look at this next.

Inactivating vendors in QBO

Similar to customers, you cannot delete vendors, but you can inactivate any vendors you no longer do business with. As with inactivating accounts and customers, this **Make inactive** action will maintain your existing vendor transactions that were previously recorded but remove the vendor from the Vendors Center.

Follow these steps to inactivate vendors in QBO:

1. Click on **Expenses** on the left-hand menu bar, select **Expenses & Bills**, and choose **Vendors**, as shown in *Figure 5.33*:

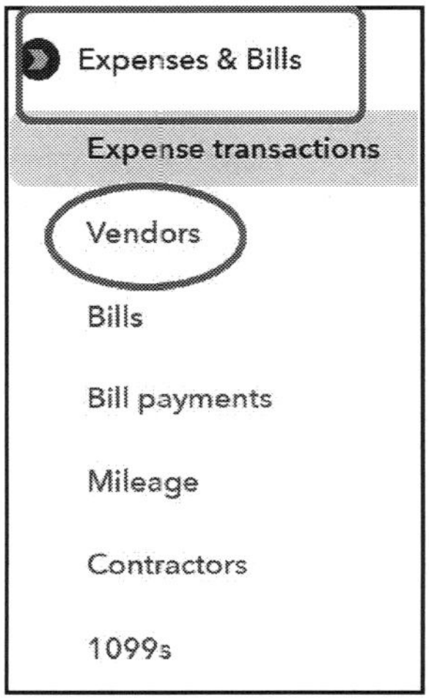

Figure 5.33: Selecting Vendors

2. Put a check mark in the box next to the vendor you want to inactivate and select **Make inactive**, as shown in *Figure 5.34*:

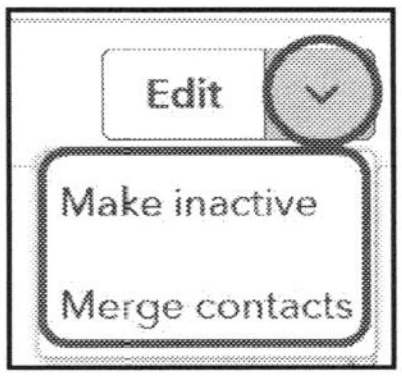

Figure 5.34: Making a vendor inactive

When you inactivate a vendor, QuickBooks will preserve the existing historical transactions but remove the vendor from the drop-down list so that it cannot be used in future transactions, such as purchase orders and bills.

Merging vendors in QBO

Similar to customers, you could run into an issue where you have inadvertently added a vendor twice. Like customers, you can easily merge duplicate vendors. Follow these steps to merge two vendor profiles:

1. Navigate to the Vendors Center and identify the duplicate vendors:

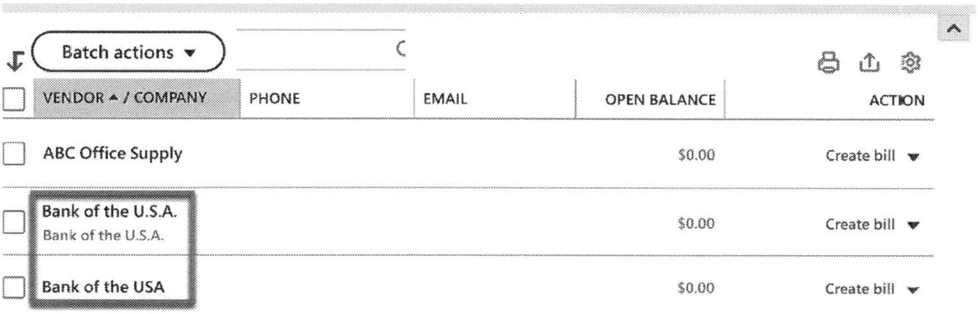

Figure 5.35: Duplicate vendors in the Vendors Center

2. Notice we have one vendor that includes a period after each letter in U.S.A. and another vendor without the periods in between. These are duplicate vendors, and we will keep the vendor that does not include the periods, **Bank of the USA**.
3. Click once on the vendor you do not wish to keep. In our example, that is the **Bank of the U.S.A**. The following screen appears after clicking once on **Bank of the U.S.A.**:

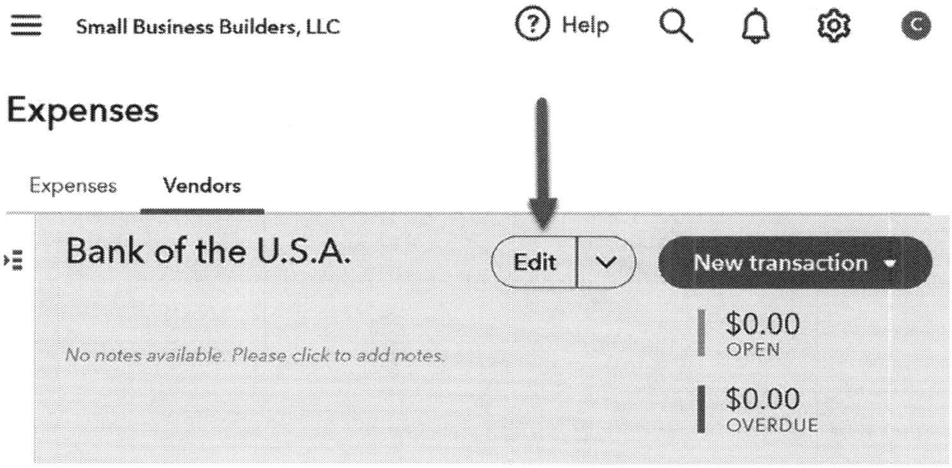

Figure 5.36: Viewing vendor information

4. Click on the **Edit** button, as indicated, and the **Vendor** information window will appear:

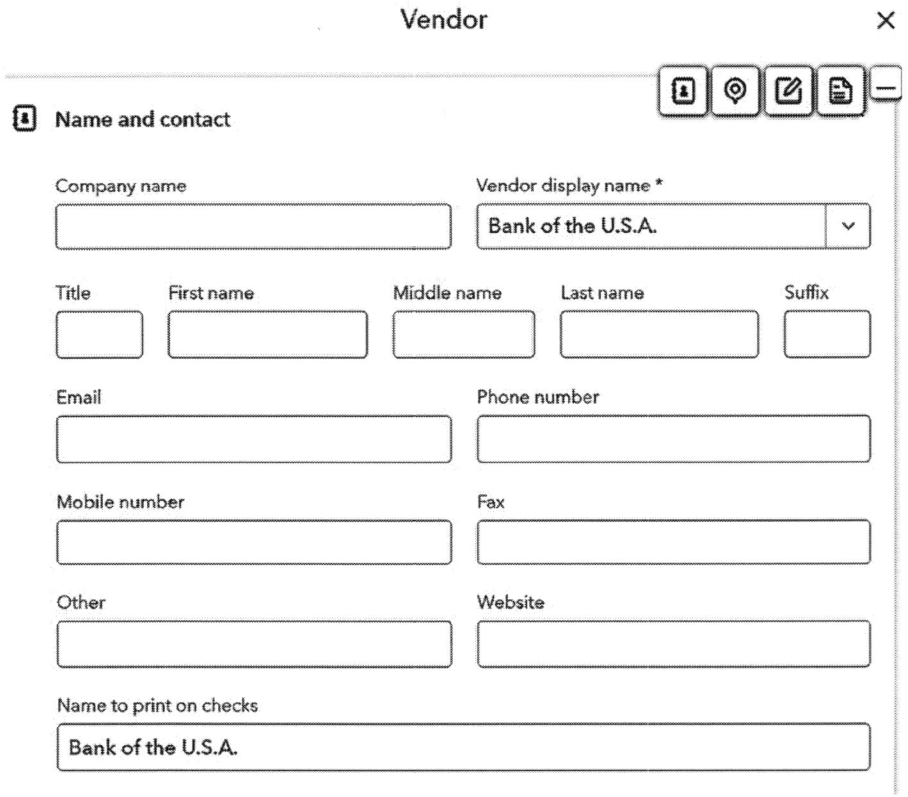

Figure 5.37: Editing information for an existing vendor

5. Click once in the **Company name** field and type the name exactly as it appears in the vendor profile that you wish to keep. In our example, this would be **Bank of the U.S.A.**. Repeat these steps for the **Vendor display name** field, as shown:

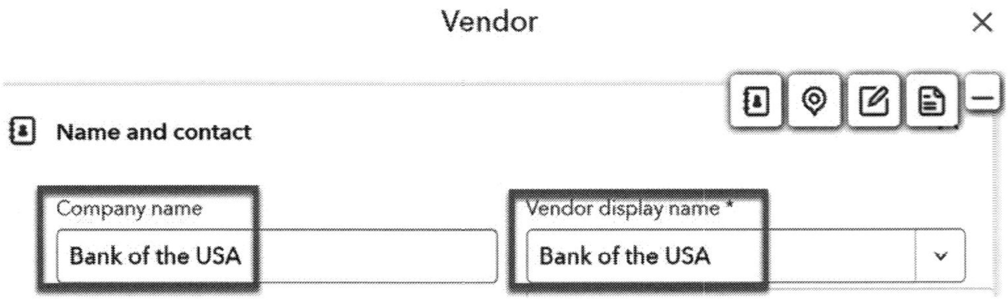

Figure 5.38: Editing the Company name and Vendor display name fields

6. Click the **Save** button in the lower-right corner. The following message will appear:

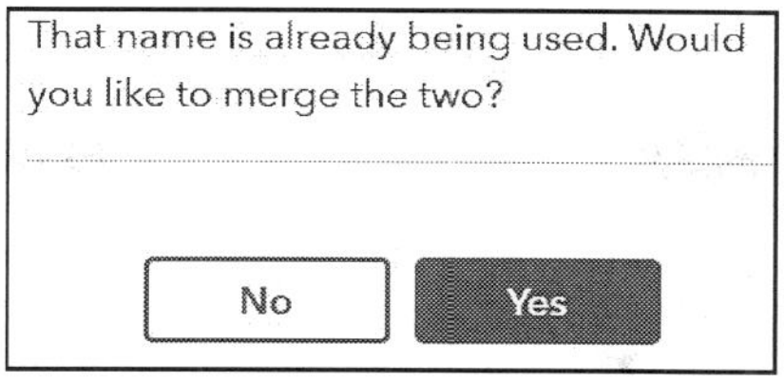

Figure 5.39: Confirming the merge of duplicate vendors

7. Click **Yes**, and the two vendor profiles will be combined into one:

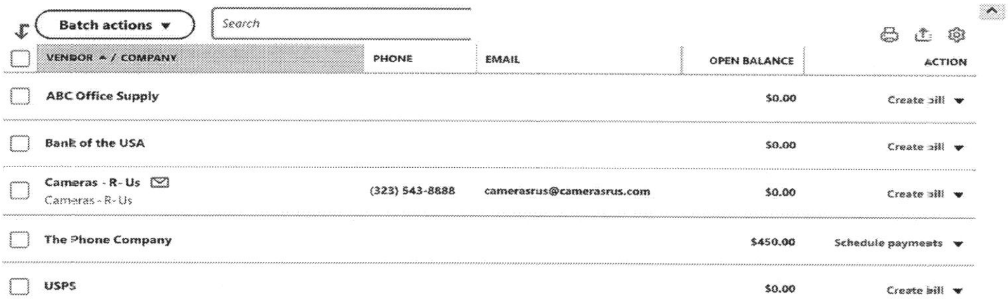

Figure 5.40: The Vendors Center with the vendors merged

As you can see, the duplicate profile (**Bank of the U.S.A.**) is no longer on the vendor list. All of the transactions recorded for that vendor have been moved to the **Bank of the USA** profile.

We have now covered how to manually add vendors, import vendors, make changes to existing vendors, inactivate vendors, and merge vendors.

> To demonstrate some of the concepts taught in this chapter and to give you some additional insights not covered, check out my YouTube channel at:
>
> `https://packt.link/du2BR`

Summary

In this chapter, we covered how to manage customer data by manually adding and importing information, editing existing customers, and inactivating customers you no longer do business with.

In addition, we covered how to manage vendor data by manually adding and importing information, editing existing vendors, inactivating vendors you no longer do business with, and merging duplicate customer and vendor records.

Keep in mind that you will need to update the customer and vendor lists when the information changes. For example, if customers and vendors move, you will need to update your records with their new mailing addresses.

Now that you understand how to manage your customers, it's time to learn how to set up and manage sales tax. In the next chapter, we will show you how to set up sales tax, create an invoice that includes sales tax, and run sales tax reports.

Next steps

1. Download the customer list template and enter the contact details for your existing customers.
2. Download the vendor list template and enter the contact details for your existing vendors.
3. Decide what the standard payment terms will be for all customers.

Part 2

Recording Transactions in QBO

This part is all about mastering the art of recording and tracking income and expenses in QuickBooks Online. You'll learn how to handle sales tax, create customized invoices, and record sales and expenses seamlessly. We'll also cover tips for managing recurring transactions. We will also introduce you to some of the great reports available in QBO. For example, the **A/R Aging** report will help you stay on top of unpaid customer invoices. The **A/P Aging** report will help you stay on top of what bills are coming due so that you can make timely payments to vendor suppliers. With practical examples and advice, you'll feel confident managing your business's finances.

This part comprises the following chapters:

- *Chapter 6, Managing Sales Tax*
- *Chapter 7, Recording Sales Transactions in QuickBooks Online*
- *Chapter 8, Customer Sales Reports in QuickBooks Online*
- *Chapter 9, Recording Expenses in QuickBooks Online*
- *Chapter 10, Vendor & Expense Reports in QuickBooks Online*

6

Managing Sales Tax

In the United States, sales tax is typically applied to the sale of products. However, some states and local tax jurisdictions also apply sales tax to certain types of services. The way sales tax works is that the tax is paid by customers who purchase your products. The business that collects the sales tax from its consumers is responsible for reporting the sales tax collected on a sales tax return and submitting it to the appropriate state and/or local tax authority. This tax is typically due on a monthly, quarterly, or annual basis, depending on the amount collected. If you fail to file and/or pay sales tax, you will incur penalties and interest until that tax is paid. Therefore, it's important to consult with your CPA or tax professional to determine which laws apply in your geographical location, as well as how often you need to file and when payment is due.

In this chapter, we will cover how to manage sales tax in **QuickBooks Online** (**QBO**).

One of the cons of the sales tax process in QBO is the inability to pay sales tax within the software itself; typically, you have to go to your state's website and make the payment. However, with the most recent version of QBO, you can file and pay sales and use taxes without leaving QBO if you are in one of six states: Minnesota, North Carolina, Rhode Island, Vermont, West Virginia, or Iowa. If you don't reside in one of these states, you cannot pay sales tax directly from QBO. Due to this, we will cover how to record the payment in QBO after you have paid your tax authority.

We will cover the following topics in this chapter:

- Setting up sales tax in QBO
- Creating an invoice that includes sales tax
- Sales tax reports
- Paying sales tax when it comes due

> The US edition of QBO was used to create this book. If you are using a version that is outside of the US, results may differ.

Do you need to charge sales tax?

Before we dive into the mechanics of setting up sales tax, you may be wondering whether you need to charge sales tax or not. The short answer is *yes* if you sell any type of product, such as T-shirts, books, coffee, and so on. If you don't sell a product but you do sell services, such as bookkeeping, legal, or consulting, then the answer is *maybe*. Because the answer is dependent on the rules and regulations of your state/local jurisdiction, it's important that you seek the advice of a CPA or tax preparer.

However, there are a couple of resources that we recommend you check out, the first of which is this article from the QuickBooks blog, *Do I need to charge sales tax?*: `https://quickbooks.intuit.com/r/taxes/need-collect-sales-tax-much/`.

Another great resource is **Avalara**, a company that specializes in sales tax compliance. Not only do they offer sales tax compliance services, but they are also a great resource for any questions you may have regarding whether you need to charge sales tax and how to go about making sure you are in compliance.

Setting up sales tax in QBO

If you are required to collect sales tax from customers, it is important that you complete the sales tax setup process in QuickBooks prior to invoicing customers. If you create an invoice without sales tax, you will ultimately underpay the sales tax you are required to submit to your local tax authority. This could lead to additional taxes and penalties, which can add up quickly. As the business owner, ultimately, you are responsible for collecting and remitting sales tax. Setting up sales tax in QuickBooks from the start allows QuickBooks to automatically calculate and keep track of the amount of sales tax that you owe.

Perform the following steps to set up sales tax:

1. Click **My apps**, then **Sales Tax**, and select **Overview**, as indicated in *Figure 6.1*, to navigate to the Sales Tax Center:

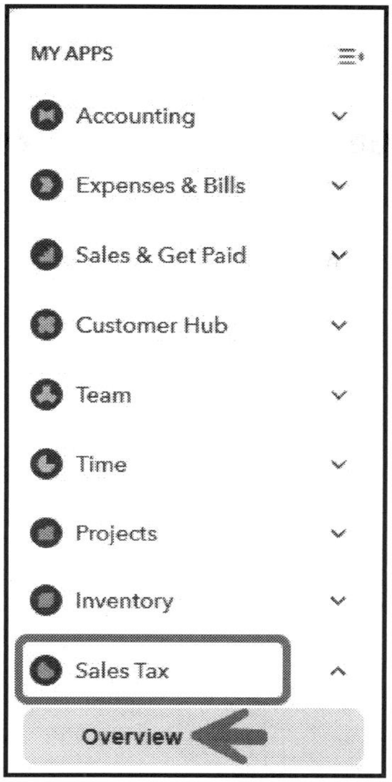

Figure 6.1: Navigating to the Sales Tax Center

2. The following message will appear. Click the **Get started** button, as indicated in *Figure 6.2*:

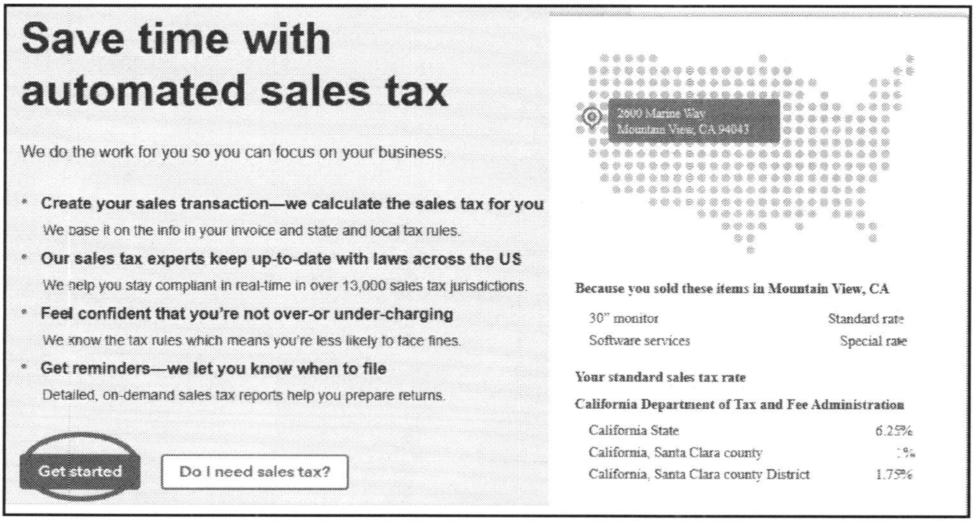

Figure 6.2: The Sales Tax Center welcome page

The following window will appear:

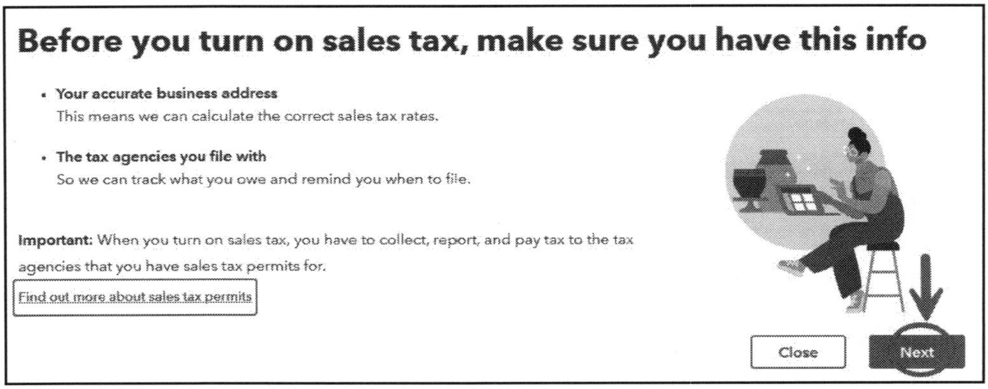

Figure 6.3: Info to have on hand before turning on sales tax

Before you turn on sales tax, you need to make sure that you have the following information at hand, as listed in *Figure 6.3*:

- Your business **address**
- The tax agencies you file with **so that QBO can track what you owe and when you need to file sales tax returns**
- Sales tax permits

3. Your business address should automatically populate the fields, as indicated in *Figure 6.4*. If it does not, fill in any missing fields and click **Next**:

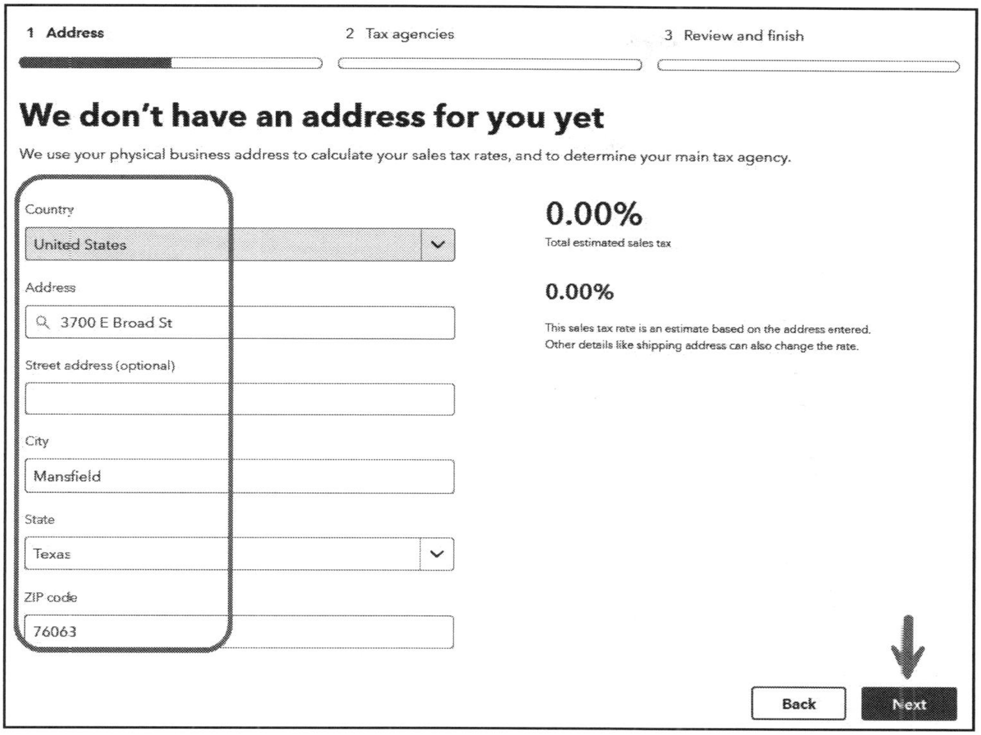

Figure 6.4: Entering a physical business address

4. The following screen will appear. Confirm that the business address is accurate; if it isn't, you can edit it as needed. Once it's accurate, the sales tax rate for each tax agency to which you should remit payment will be displayed, as indicated in *Figure 6.5*; click **Next**:

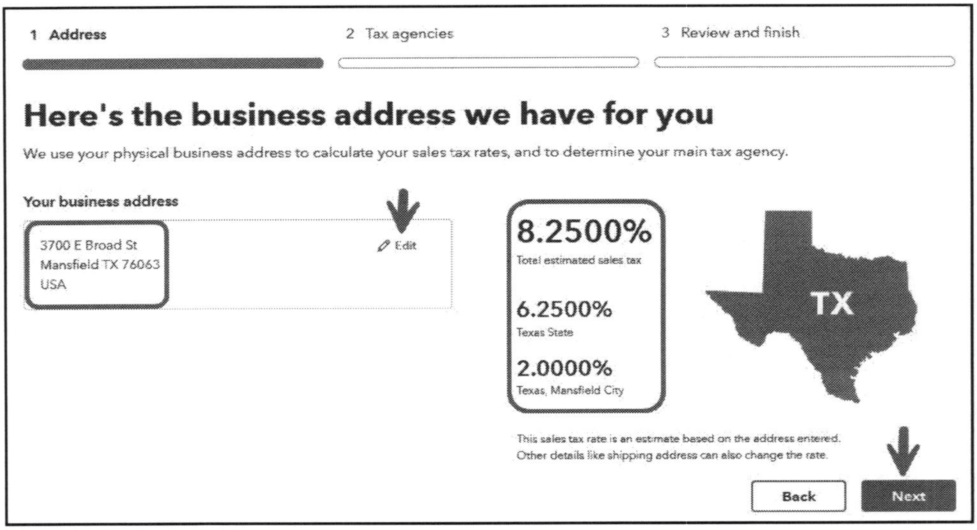

Figure 6.5: Confirming your business address and reviewing your sales tax rate

5. On the next screen, you will need to select your filing frequency from the drop-down menu; the options are **Annually**, **Semi-Annually**, **Quarterly**, and **Monthly**:

> If you are not sure what your filing frequency is, refer to your sales tax business registration documents.

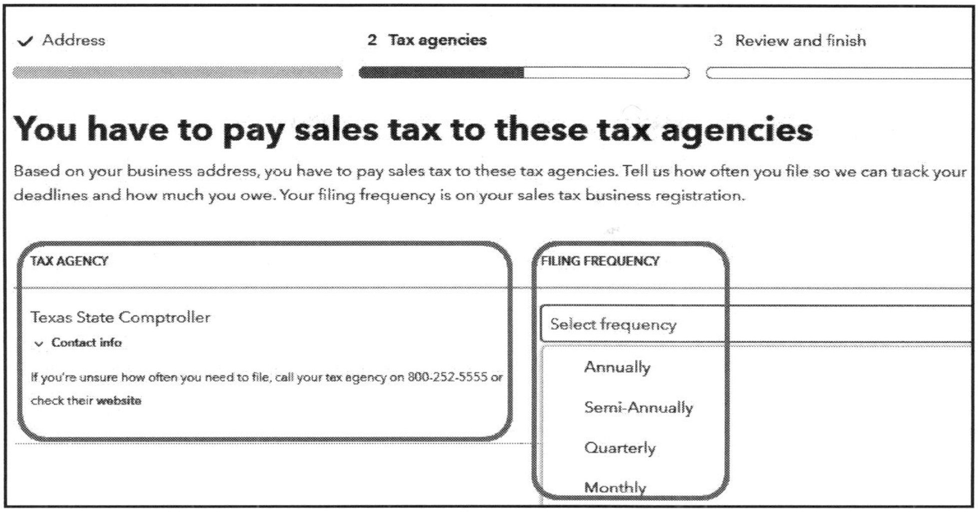

Figure 6.6: Reviewing tax agencies and selecting a tax filing frequency

6. If you are required to collect sales tax outside of your state, select **Yes** and click **Next** to select all of the jurisdictions you are required to collect sales tax from; otherwise, select **No**, as indicated in *Figure 6.7*:

Figure 6.7: Sales tax information outside of your state

Most businesses are *not* required to collect sales tax outside their state. If you are not sure, you need to consult with your tax professional or CPA on this matter.

7. Click **Next**. The following screen will appear, giving you one final opportunity to review the tax agency and filing frequency you've chosen:

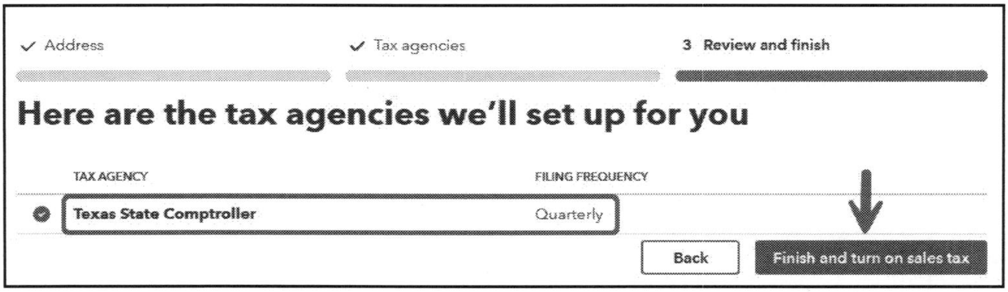

Figure 6.8: Final review of the tax agency and filing frequency

8. Click **Finish and turn on sales tax**; you will be taken to the following page:

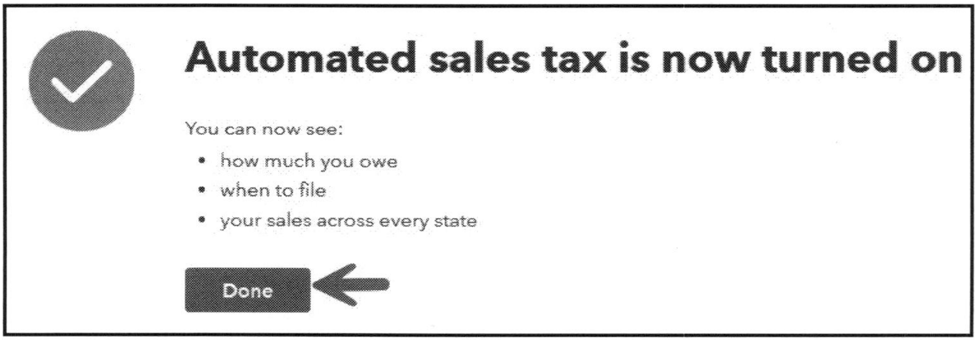

Figure 6.9: Automated sales tax setup is complete

9. Click the **Done** button; the Sales Tax Center will appear:

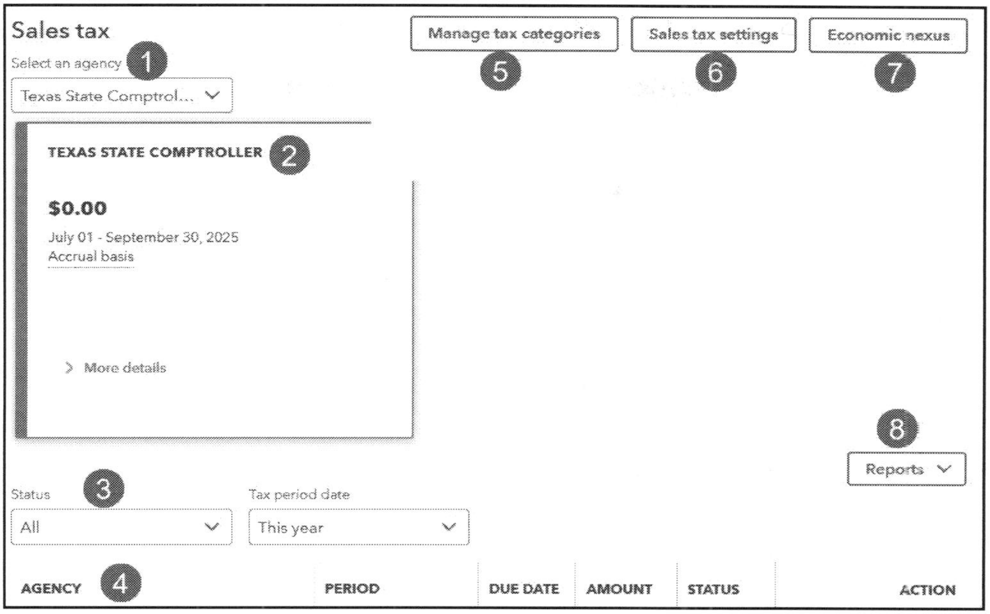

Figure 6.10: Sales Tax Center overview

10. Within the Sales Tax Center, you can see the amount of tax due for each agency you collect sales tax for. Let's take a closer look at what you can find here:

- (1) Select an agency from the drop-down menu, and it will appear, as shown in *Figure 6.10*.
- (2) The agency (**TEXAS STATE COMPTROLLER**, in our example) appears in this section, along with the tax period due and the accounting method.
- (3) Select the status and tax period date using the drop-down menus.
- (4) In this section, you will see a summary of your selections for the **AGENCY**, **PERIOD**, **DUE DATE**, **AMOUNT**, **STATUS**, and **ACTION** items.
- (5) Review **Manage tax categories** and make any necessary changes.
- (6) Review your sales tax settings and make any necessary changes.
- (7) Review your economic nexus. If you have a question about this standard, I recommend that you reach out to a tax professional or contact Avalara.
- (8) Generate sales tax reports. Since we don't currently have any taxable sales recorded, we will create an invoice with sales tax next.

Creating an invoice that includes sales tax

After completing the setup process for sales tax, you are ready to create invoices and sales receipts with sales tax. In this section, we will create an invoice and show you how to include sales tax. Perform the following steps:

1. From the left menu bar, click on **MY APPS** | **Sales & Get Paid** | **Invoices**, as indicated in *Figure 6.11*:

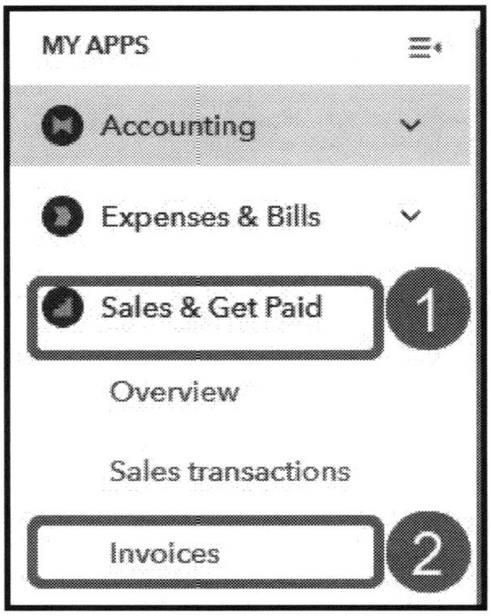

Figure 6.11: Navigating to Invoices

2. Click the **Create invoice** button, as indicated in *Figure 6.12*:

Figure 6.12: Creating an invoice

3. A blank invoice template will appear with seven key areas that need to be filled in:

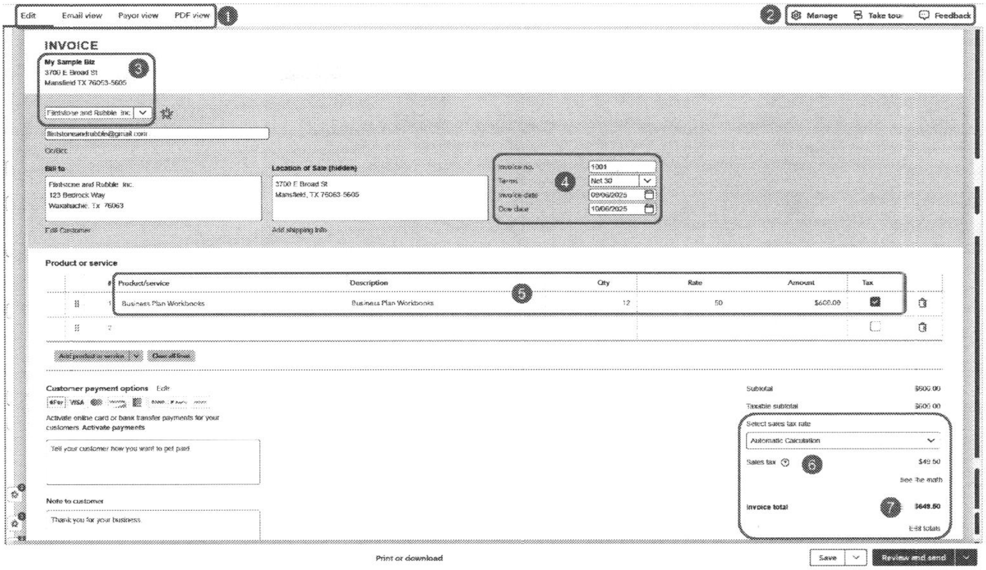

Figure 6.13: Completed invoice with sales tax

Let's take a closer look at the different areas you should get acquainted with:

- **Invoice view** (1): There are four different views for the invoice template. The default mode is **Edit**, which is the mode you want to be in when making changes to the invoice; **Email view** is the view that your customers will see when they receive the invoice via email; **Payor view** is the preview of the invoice when the customer receives it; and **PDF view** shows the invoice as a PDF document.
- **Other options** (2): In this section, you can manage invoice settings, take a tour of the features available for invoicing, and provide feedback to Intuit about your experience using the invoice template.
- **Your company information and customer information** (3): Your company mailing address, telephone number, and website information will appear in this section. This is the information that was entered when you set up your company preferences in *Chapter 3, Company File Setup*. Below this information is a drop-down field where you can select the customer you wish to create an invoice for.

- **Invoice details** (4): Within this section of the invoice, you will find the invoice number, which is automatically generated by QBO, and the payment terms, which you set up back in *Chapter 3, Company File Setup*. The invoice date and the due date will also appear in this section. All of these fields can be edited as needed.
- **Billing details** (5): From the drop-down menu, you can select the items you are billing your customer for. In *Chapter 5, Managing Customer and Vendor Lists*, we covered how to add products and services to QBO.
- **Sales tax** (6): Since we turned automatic sales tax on, the sales tax amount is automatically calculated as **$49.50** in our example. If you don't see sales tax here, return to the Sales Tax Center and review the settings for accuracy.
- **Invoice total** (7): The grand total of the invoice, including sales tax, will appear in this field. In our example, this is **$649.50**.

QuickBooks will automatically use your business address as the sales location. Be sure to confirm whether the location of the sale is correct. If necessary, you may need to charge a different sales tax based on the city/county/tax jurisdiction for each sale. You can even update your business address if needed within the account and settings. We showed you how to do this in *Chapter 3, Company File Setup*, but be sure to consult with your tax preparer or accountant for additional guidance.

4. Click the **Save** button to save the invoice and click **X** in the top-right corner to close the invoice.
5. Navigate back to the Sales Tax Center by clicking on **MY APPS | Sales Tax | Overview** from the left menu bar. The following window will appear:

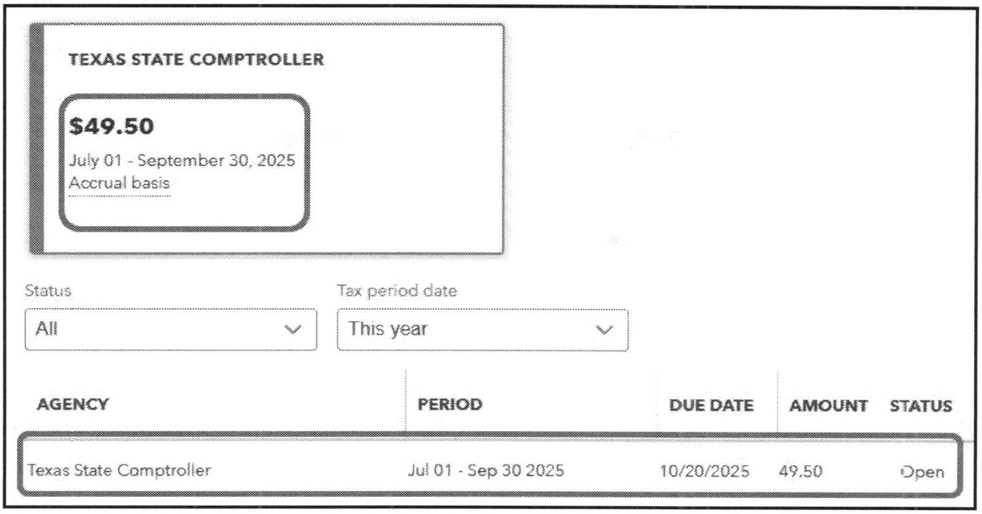

Figure 6.14: Sales Tax Center with the updated sales tax amount

As you can see, the tax of **$49.50** now shows up as an upcoming sales tax that will be due sometime in the future. Once the sales tax becomes due, its status will change to **Due**.

Next, we will cover the sales tax reports you can generate to determine how much sales tax you owe and when it's due. Sales tax reports are also used to complete the sales tax return.

Sales tax reports

QuickBooks makes it easy to stay on top of the sales tax that's been collected, which will ensure that you pay the correct amount when it's due. There are three reports available to help you stay on top of the sales tax you owe: a tax liability report, a taxable customer report, and a non-taxable transaction review report.

Within the Sales Tax Center, click on the **Reports** link to access the various sales tax reports, as indicated in *Figure 6.15*:

Figure 6.15: Sales tax reports

The first report is called **the Tax Liability Report**. This report will show you the sales tax that's been collected for a specific period of time. It will show gross sales, taxable sales, non-taxable sales, and the tax amount.

In the following report, there are four columns: **GROSS TOTAL**, **NON-TAXABLE**, **TAXABLE AMOUNT**, and **TAX AMOUNT**. The gross total amount is **$600.00**, the non-taxable amount is **$0**, the taxable amount is **$600.00**, and the total tax amount is **$49.50**:

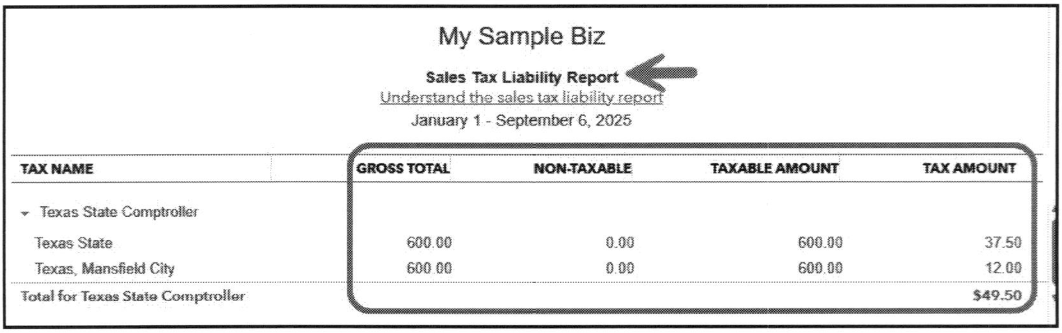
My Sample Biz
Sales Tax Liability Report
Understand the sales tax liability report
January 1 - September 6, 2025

TAX NAME	GROSS TOTAL	NON-TAXABLE	TAXABLE AMOUNT	TAX AMOUNT
Texas State Comptroller				
Texas State	600.00	0.00	600.00	37.50
Texas, Mansfield City	600.00	0.00	600.00	12.00
Total for Texas State Comptroller				$49.50

Figure 6.16: Sales tax liability report

The second option is **Taxable Customer Report**, which will list all customers who are subject to sales tax, along with their billing address, shipping address, taxable sales, and tax rate. Here is a snapshot of what this report looks like:

My Sample Biz

Customer Contact List

CUSTOMER	BILLING ADDRESS	SHIPPING ADDRESS	TAXABLE	TAX RATE
Flintstone and Rubble Inc.	123 Bedrock Way Waxahachie Tx 76063	123 Bedrock Way Waxahachie Tx 76063	Yes	TX-Mansfield (8.25%)

Figure 6.17: Taxable customer report

As you can see, it is easy to keep track of sales tax in QuickBooks. You can use the tax liability report and the taxable customer report to prepare your sales tax return. In addition, you can use these reports to determine the amount owed.

> Be sure to select the correct accounting method (cash or accrual) before running your reports. Refer to *Chapter 1, Small-Business Bookkeeping 101*, to learn the difference between cash and accrual accounting.

Paying sales tax when it comes due

As we mentioned at the beginning of this chapter, to pay your sales tax, you must visit the website of your state tax authority and submit payment online or mail a check before the due date.

Unfortunately, you cannot pay sales tax within QBO unless your business is located in Iowa, Minnesota, North Carolina, Rhode Island, Vermont, or West Virginia.

The ability to pay sales tax within QBO is a brand-new feature that includes the following benefits:

- Create sales tax returns automatically using QuickBooks data; these are formatted accurately for each of the six states this applies to
- File and pay sales and use taxes for $40 per filing, directly in QBO
- Track the status of a sales tax return with real-time updates
- Easily store and access past sales tax returns filed within QBO
- Receive reminders of upcoming sales tax deadlines to help you stay compliant and avoid penalties and interest

For businesses not located in one of the six states that can file their sales tax within QBO, you will need to manually record your sales tax payments within the software.

Follow these steps to record manual tax payments/adjustments in QBO:

1. Navigate to the Sales Tax Center (**MY APPS** | **Sales Tax** | **Overview**).
2. From the sales tax overview screen, click on the **Review sales tax** link, as shown in *Figure 6.18*:

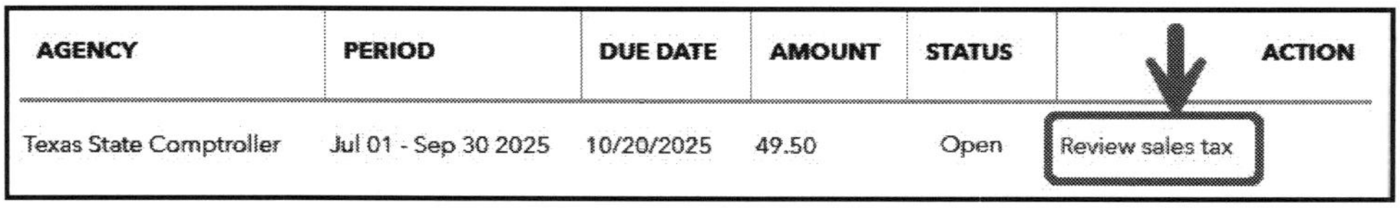

Figure 6.18: The Review sales tax link

3. The following screen will appear:

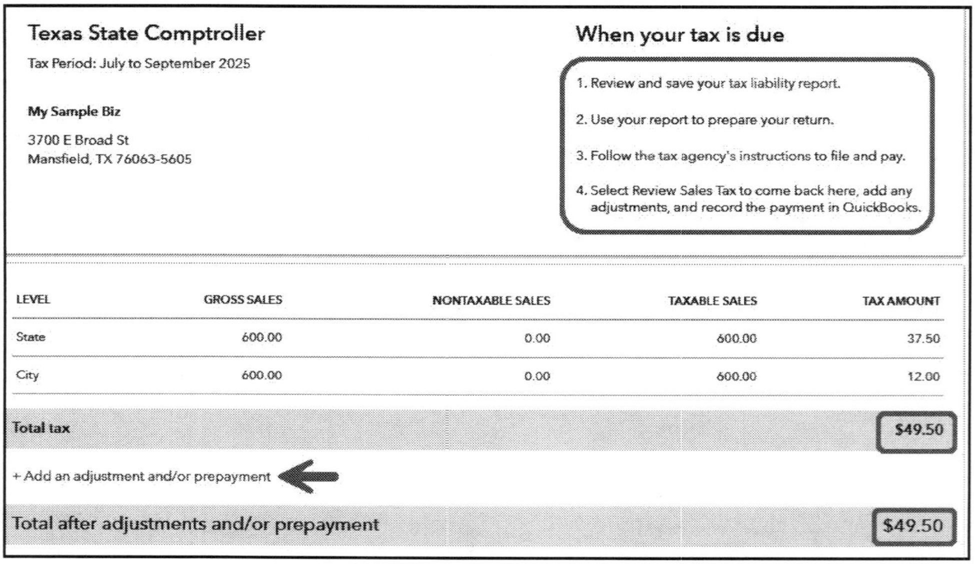

Figure 6.19: Reviewing and recording sales tax adjustments and payments

Follow the four steps highlighted in *Figure 6.19* once you are ready to make your sales tax payment. Once you've made the payment with your state tax authority, click on the **+Add an adjustment and/or prepayment** link indicated with the arrow in *Figure 6.19* to enter the details of the payment. Once you have entered the necessary payment information, **Total after adjustments and/or prepayment** should be zero.

To demonstrate some of the concepts taught in this chapter and to give you some additional insights not covered, check out my YouTube channel at:

`https://packt.link/du2BR`

Summary

In this chapter, we discussed the importance of setting up sales tax in QuickBooks so that it can automatically calculate sales tax for you. We showed you how to create an invoice and include sales tax, and we covered the key reports available to help you stay on top of your sales tax liability. The final step we covered is how to review and record your sales tax payments in QBO after you have made the actual payment with your state tax authority. As discussed, if you live in Iowa, Minnesota, North Carolina, Rhode Island, Vermont, or West Virginia, your instructions will vary because you will be able to make your sales tax payments within QBO.

It's important to make sure you set up sales tax and use the correct sales tax rate. This will help you avoid penalties or fees for under-reporting and underpaying sales tax to your state tax office. To ensure proper setup of sales tax, I recommend that you reach out to an accountant or tax professional who can review your setup for accuracy. Remember, you can only give them access to view company reports. That way, they can view your sales tax setup without being able to make changes without your permission. In *Chapter 4*, *Customizing QuickBooks for Your Business*, we showed you how to grant users access to your QBO data.

In the next chapter, we will cover how to record invoices and sales receipts in QBO.

7

Recording Sales Transactions in QuickBooks Online

In *Chapter 5, Managing Customer and Vendor Lists*, you learned how to customize QuickBooks by adding customers, vendors, and the products and services you sell to QuickBooks. In *Chapter 6, Managing Sales Tax*, you learned how to properly set up sales tax that you may need to collect from your customers. Now that you have completed your QuickBooks setup, it's time to dive into how to record sales and payments received from customers. Recording sales will allow you to keep track of how much money your business is making. This information is important and will help you determine whether or not your business is profitable.

In this chapter, we will focus on recording sales and customer payments in **QuickBooks Online** (**QBO**). There are several ways to record sales and payments in QBO. We will cover the various ways to record sales transactions, when you should use them, how to record each transaction, and the behind-the-scenes accounting that QuickBooks does for you. We will also show you how to record customer payments, how to issue credit memos and refunds to customers, and we will wrap up with how to create estimates.

In this chapter, we will cover the following key concepts, which you will find in the *Sales & Get Paid* app:

- Recording sales – invoices, sales receipts, recurring invoices, recurring payments, and creating payment links
- Recording customer payments manually
- Issuing credit memos and refunds to customers
- Creating estimates

> The US edition of QBO was used to create this book. If you are using a version that is outside of the US, results may differ.

Recording sales

Recording sales for a business can be accomplished in a variety of ways. There are two primary ways to record income in QBO. First, you can use a **sales invoice**, which allows you to bill a specific customer, who will pay you based on payment terms that are agreed upon upfront. Second, a **sales receipt** is used when you receive payment at the same time as you provide products/services to your customers. Three additional ways to record sales in QBO are recurring invoices, payment links, and a brand-new feature called recurring payments. A **recurring invoice** is used when you have a customer who pays the same amount on the same day (or date), such as a tenant who pays rent on the first of each month. A **payment link** allows you to send your customers a simple link that they can use to pay on the spot, wherever they are. **Recurring payments** are the newest payment method available in QBO. Recurring payments allow you to create an automatic payment and send it to your customer for approval in advance; no chasing down payments or sending reminders is required. We will start with recording income using a sales invoice.

Recording income using a sales invoice

A sales invoice is used to record income from customers who have been given extended payment terms. This means the customer does not pay at the time the product is sold or services are rendered; instead, they pay you sometime in the future. The most common payment term is **net 30**, which means the invoice is due 30 days from the sale date or the invoice date.

Unlike the sales receipt, which records both the sale and the receipt of payment in a single transaction, recording a sales invoice and payment is done in two steps. In this section, we will cover the first step: recording a sales invoice. We will cover recording customer payments later in the chapter.

To record a sales invoice in QBO, follow these steps:

1. Navigate to the **+ Create** menu and select **Invoice** under **CUSTOMERS**, as indicated here:

Figure 7.1: Navigating to the Invoice form

In *Figure 7.2*, we have an example of a complete sales invoice form:

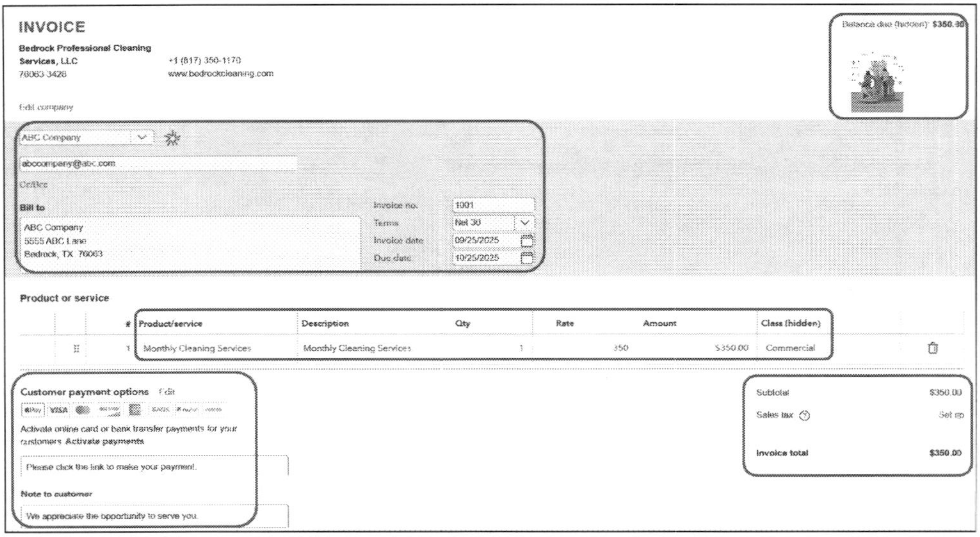

Figure 7.2: The Invoice form

2. Use the information in *Figure 7.2* to complete the invoice form, or use your own information to complete the form.

   Here are the fields that need to be completed in a sales invoice. All fields are required except for the **Description, Qty**, and **Note to customer** fields:

   - **Customer**: Select the customer from the drop-down menu. **ABC Company** is the customer selected in our example.
   - **Bill to**: This field will automatically be populated with the address information you have on file for your customer. If you have not set up the address information, you can type it directly in this field. The billing address in our example is **5555 ABC Lane, Bedrock, TX 76063.**
   - **Invoice no**: QuickBooks will automatically populate this field with the next available invoice number. In our example, the invoice number is **1001**.

   > You can start your invoice numbers with any number that you like, and then QBO will automatically generate future invoice numbers in numerical order. When creating your very first invoice, type the number that you would like to start with in this field. You must use numerical numbers only, no alphabetical characters.

- **Terms**: This field will automatically be populated with the payment terms you have set up for your customer. In our example, we have set payment terms of **Net 30**, which means the invoice is due 30 days from the invoice date. If you have not set up payment terms, you can select these from the drop-down menu.
- **Invoice date**: Enter the date of the sale in this field. The invoice date is **09/25/2025** in our example.
- **Due date**: This field is automatically calculated by QuickBooks. Since the payment terms are **Net 30**, it adds 30 days to the invoice date in order to compute the date payment is due. The due date is **10/25/2025** in our example.
- **Product/service**: From the drop-down menu, select the product and/or services provided to the customer. In our example, the product sold is **Monthly Cleaning Services**. Select **Add new** from the drop-down menu to add this service to the list if it has not been added previously.
- **Description**: This field will automatically be populated based on the product/service selected in the previous field. The description of the product sold in our example is **Monthly Cleaning Services**. You can edit this field as needed directly on the invoice.
- **Qty**: Enter the quantity of the product or the total hours to bill the customer. In our example, the fee is a flat amount, so the **Qty** field will automatically populate with **1**.
- **Rate**: This field will automatically be populated based on the product/service selected. However, if you don't have a rate set up, you can enter the price per unit or the hourly rate in this field. In our example, the rate for monthly cleaning services is **$350.00**.
- **Amount**: QuickBooks will automatically calculate the total invoice amount by taking the quantity and multiplying it by the rate. In our example, the total amount due is **$350.00**.
- **Class**: As discussed in *Chapter 3, Company File Setup*, a class can be used to represent a location, department, or business segment. In our example, Bedrock Professional Cleaning uses a class to represent the type of customer (**Commercial** or **Residential**). In our example, the class is **Commercial**. QBO has indicated "hidden," which means that this field is not visible to the customer.

- **Customer payment options**: When you sign up for a payment account, it allows you to offer a variety of ways for your customers to pay you. Currently, customers can use Apple Pay, Visa, Mastercard, Discover, AMEX, ACH, PayPal, or Venmo to remit payment. In *Chapter 3, Company File Setup*, we explained how to apply for a QuickBooks payment account.
- **Note to customer**: This field is optional. You can type a personal thank you message to your customer, and it will appear on the invoice. In our example, we have entered the following message: `We appreciate the opportunity to serve you.`
- **Subtotal**: QBO will automatically calculate the subtotal of the invoice prior to sales tax, if applicable. In our example, the subtotal is **$350.00**.
- **Sales tax**: In *Chapter 6*, we covered how to set up and manage sales tax in QBO. If you have set up sales tax, QBO will automatically calculate the appropriate sales tax in this field. If you have not set up sales tax but you need to, you can click on the **Set up** link in this field and walk through the steps to set up sales tax. In our example, we will leave sales tax turned off.
- **Invoice total**: QBO will automatically add the subtotal and the sales tax to get the invoice total. In our example, the invoice total is **$350.00**.

You have the option to print the sales invoice, email it, or save it as a PDF document. If you would like to allow customers to pay their invoices online, you will choose the email option so that they can receive a payment link.

> You can now send invoices in one of six languages: English, French, Spanish, Italian, Portuguese (Brazil), and Chinese (traditional). To select the preferred language for a customer, navigate to the customer profile and click on the **Language** tab. Refer to *Chapter 5, Managing Customer and Vendor Lists*, where we showed you how to select the language for customers.

When you create a sales invoice in QuickBooks, it has an impact on the balance sheet as well as the profit and loss statement. The accounts receivable account will increase, which will result in an increase in the total assets on the balance sheet report. Income will also increase on the profit and loss statement.

Figure 7.3 shows the transaction journal entry that will be recorded in QBO for our sample sales invoice shown in *Figure 7.2*:

Transaction Journal
Bedrock Professional Cleaning Services, LLC
All Dates

Transaction Date	Transaction Type	Num	Name	Memo/Description	Full Name	Debit	Credit
1 (2)							
09/25/2025	Invoice	1001	ABC Company	-	Accounts Receivable (A/R)	350.00	-
09/25/2025	Invoice	1001	ABC Company	Monthly Cleaning Services	Sales	-	350.00
Total for 1						$350.00	$350.00
TOTAL						$350.00	$350.00

Figure 7.3: Transaction journal entry recorded for invoice

The amount owed by customers—also known as accounts receivable—goes up by **$350.00**, and **Sales** is increased by **$350.00**.

Next, we will show you how to record income with a sales receipt.

Recording income using a sales receipt

A sales receipt is used when the sale of a product or service and the receipt of the customer payment take place simultaneously. For example, retail businesses, such as restaurants or clothing stores, will receive payment at the same time as they provide their service (for example, serving food to customers) or products (for example, clothing items for purchase). In general, you would record a sales receipt immediately upon making the sale so that you can either give a copy to your customer or send it via email. For a restaurant or coffee shop, you may only record sales receipts on a daily or weekly basis, especially if you have a **point of sale** (**POS**) system that you can use to keep track of your daily sales. You can record a sales receipt in QuickBooks by completing a couple of simple steps.

Follow these steps to record a sales receipt:

1. From the **+ Create** menu, select **Sales receipt**, as indicated in *Figure 7.4*:

Figure 7.4: Navigating to the sales receipt form

Figure 7.5 shows a completed sales receipt:

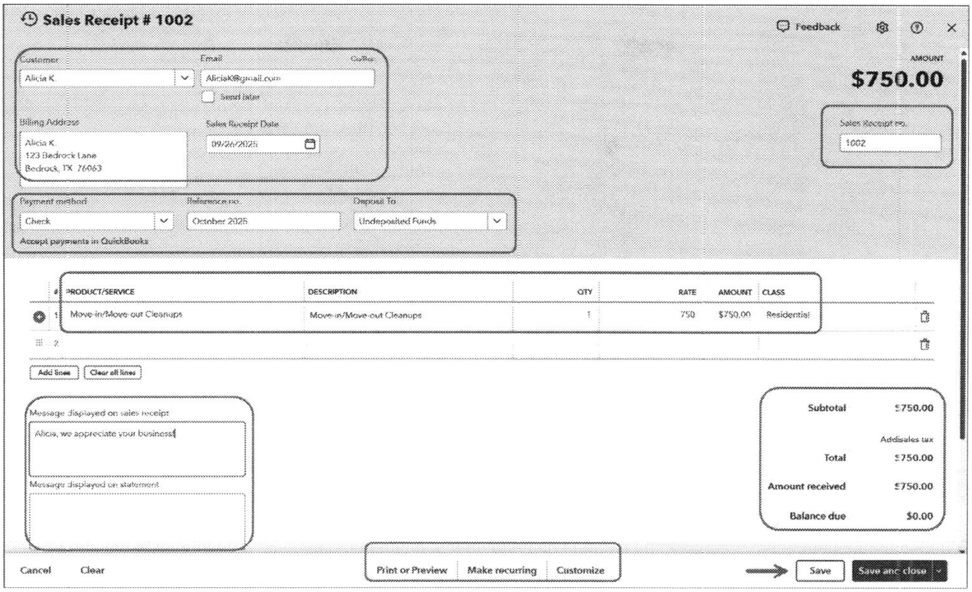

Figure 7.5: Completing the sales receipt form

2. You can complete the sales receipt using the information in *Figure 7.5* and the following list of fields, or enter the information that is relevant to your customer.

There are several fields of information that need to be completed on the **Sales Receipt** form. The following is a brief description of the information you need to include in each field:

- **Customer**: Select the customer you sold the product or service to by clicking on the drop-down arrow in this field. **Alicia K.** is the customer in our example. If you have not added any customers yet, you can add a new customer by typing the customer's name in this field.
- **Email**: This field will automatically be populated with the email address you have on file for the customer. The email address in our example is `AliciaK@gmail.com`. If the field is blank, you can type an email address directly in this field.

When you click the **Save and Send** button, QuickBooks will email the sales receipt to the email address you include in this field.

- **Billing Address**: This field will automatically be populated with the billing address you have on file for this customer. The billing address in our example is **123 Bedrock Lane, Bedrock, TX 76063**. If you don't have an address on file, you can enter one directly in this field.
- **Sales Receipt Date**: Enter the date of the sale in this field, which is **09/26/2025** in our example.
- **Payment method**: Select the payment method by clicking the drop-down arrow. We have selected **Check** in our example.
- **Reference no.**: If your customer paid by check, enter the check number in this field. If payment was made by cash or credit card, you can select it from the dropdown and enter a reference number, or leave this field blank. The reference number is **October 2025** in our example.
- **Deposit To**: From the drop-down menu, select the bank account to which you will deposit this payment. In our example, the funds will be deposited into the **Undeposited Funds** account.

> If you plan to deposit payments for multiple customers on the same day, select the **Undeposited funds** account instead of the **Business Checking** account as the **Deposit To** account. Later, you will be able to select the specific deposits made each day. This will make it much easier to reconcile the bank account.

- **Sales receipt no.**: QuickBooks will automatically generate this number, which is **1002** in our example.
- **PRODUCT/SERVICE**: From the drop-down menu, select the type of service (or product) sold to the customer. In our example, it is a **Move-in/Move-out Cleanup**. This service has **not** been added, so you will need to select **Add New** and complete the following fields to add it to the products/services list:
    - **Name**: `Move-in/Move-out Cleanup`
    - **DESCRIPTION**: Copy and paste the name in this field: `Move-in/Move-out Cleanup`
    - **Rate**: `$750.00`

- **QTY**: Enter the quantity of items sold or the total hours of service provided. In our example, the quantity is `1`.
- **RATE**: Enter the hourly rate for your services or the unit cost of the product sold. This field should automatically populate with the rate that was set. In our example, the rate is `$750.00`.
- **AMOUNT**: You don't need to enter anything in this field. QuickBooks will multiply the quantity by the rate to automatically calculate the total amount of the sales receipt. In our example, the total amount is **$750.00**.
- **CLASS**: As mentioned in the previous section, Bedrock Professional Cleaning groups its sales into one of two categories: **Residential** or **Commercial**. In our example, this customer is a **Residential** customer.
- **MESSAGE DISPLAYED ON SALES RECEIPT**: Similar to invoices, you can include a customized message to your customers in this field. In our example, the message is `Alicia, we appreciate your business!`.
- **TOTALS**: QBO will automatically calculate the subtotal, total, amount received, and balance due on the sales receipt.
- **SAVE**: You have four options to save your work. **Save** allows you to save your work, but keeps you in the current sales receipt form. **Save and close** allows you to save your work and close out of the sales receipt form. **Save and send** will send the sales receipt to the email address that appears at the very top of the form. **Save and new** will save the current sales receipt and open a new sales receipt form that you can create for another customer.

At the very bottom of the sales receipt screen, there are four actions to choose from—**Print or Preview**, **Make recurring**, **Customize**, and **More**—as shown here:

Figure 7.6: Menu options at the bottom of the sales receipt form

Here is a brief description of each of these action items:

- **Print or Preview**: This option allows you to print or display a preview of the sales receipt that your customer will receive when you send it via email or print a hard copy.

- **Make recurring**: After you create a customer sales receipt, you can save it as a recurring transaction if it will repeat on the same date or day. We will show you how to create a recurring sales receipt in the next section.
- **Customize**: Similar to invoices, you can customize the look and feel of a sales receipt by changing the color or font, adding a logo, or adding/removing fields on the form.
- **More**: This option allows you to choose from five different actions that you can take: **Copy**, **Void**, **Delete**, **Transaction journal**, and **Audit history**, as shown in *Figure 7.7*, and the list that follows:

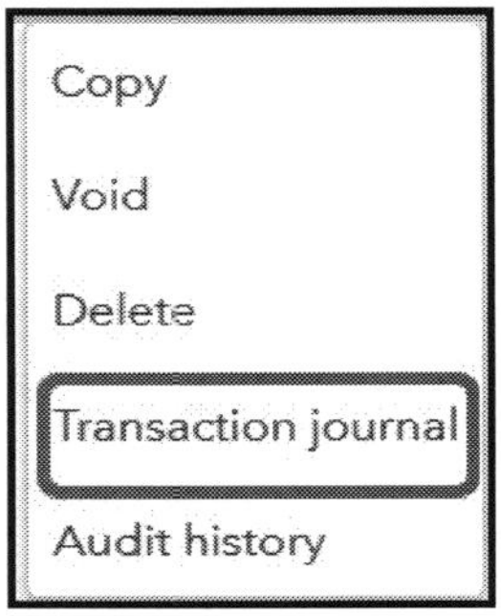

Figure 7.7: More menu options

  - **Copy**: This option allows you to create a duplicate of the sales receipt. This may come in handy when you need to create a sales receipt for the same product/service for multiple customers or the same customer.
  - **Void**: This option is used when you want to delete a transaction, but you want to keep a record of it. The transaction will zero out and remain on the books as a void.
  - **Delete**: This option is used when you want to completely remove a transaction from the books. Unlike the **Void** option, there will be no trace that it ever existed on the books.
  - **Transaction journal**: When you select this option, it provides you with the behind-the-scenes debits and credits that QBO recorded, as shown in *Figure 7.8*.
  - **Audit history**: This option will show you all of the changes that have been made to this transaction, along with the QBO users who made them. In *Chapter 15, Business Overview and Cash Management Tools and Reports*, we cover in detail the *Audit Log* report, which shows all the activity for every user that logs in to QuickBooks.

As mentioned in *Chapter 2, Getting Started with QuickBooks Online*, one of the benefits of using QuickBooks is that you don't need to have knowledge of debits and credits to use the software. QuickBooks will automatically debit and credit the appropriate accounts for you. However, it is important for you to understand the impact of recording transactions in QuickBooks.

The following figure shows the journal entry that is recorded behind the scenes in QuickBooks for the sales receipt displayed previously in *Figure 7.5*. As you can see, the **Undeposited Funds** account (a balance sheet account) is increased, and the **Cleaning Services Income** account (a profit and loss account) has been increased, which means that both the balance sheet and the profit and loss reports will be impacted.

Transaction Journal

Bedrock Professional Cleaning Services, LLC

All Dates

Transaction Date	Transaction Type	Num	Name	Memo/Description	Full Name	Debit	Credit
2 (2)							
09/26/2025	Sales Receipt	1002	Alicia K.	-	Undeposited Funds	750.00	-
09/26/2025	Sales Receipt	1002	Alicia K.	Move-in/Move-out Cleanups	Cleaning Services Income	-	750.00
Total for 2						$750.00	$750.00
TOTAL						**$750.00**	**$750.00**

Figure 7.8: Transaction journal entry recorded for a sales receipt

Now that you understand how to create a sales receipt and how it is recorded behind the scenes, we will show you how to automate sales receipts so that you not only save time but also get paid faster by creating a recurring sales receipt.

Recording income using a recurring sales receipt

One of the ways that you can improve cash flow is to make it easy for your customers to pay you. In addition to setting up a payments account so that you can receive payments via a number of payment methods (Apple Pay, Venmo, Credit Card, or ACH), you can also set up repeat customer payments on an automated recurring schedule. What this means is that you can set the payment up and forget about it. This type of payment is ideal for landlords who receive the same monthly rent from tenants, bookkeepers who bill a monthly fee for bookkeeping or payroll services, or, in our example, a weekly cleaning services fee.

Bedrock Professional Cleaning would like to create a recurring sales receipt for a client they provide cleaning services to on a weekly basis. They bill the client $150 each week for this service.

Follow these steps to create a recurring sales receipt:

1. Navigate to **+Create** > **Sales receipt**. Complete the sales receipt form as shown in *Figure 7.9* and described in the list that follows:

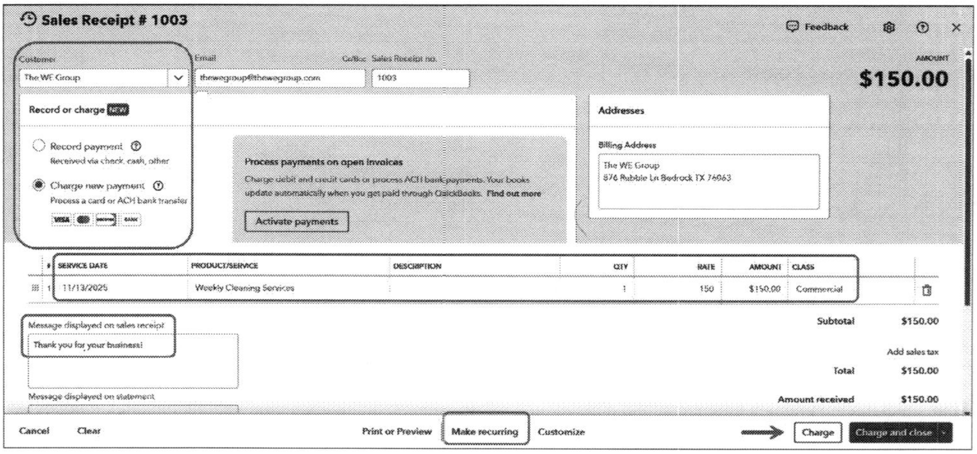

Figure 7.9: Creating a recurring sales receipt

- **Customer**: From the dropdown, select **The WE Group, Inc.**
- **Record payment**: Select this option to record a payment that you have already received via cash, check, or other payment method. Since the payment has not been received yet, we will select **Charge new payment**.
- **Charge new payment**: Select this option if you need to process a payment via debit/credit card or ACH. If you haven't done so, you will need to activate payments so that you are able to process online payments. Once payments are active, you will enter the credit card or bank details obtained from your client into the appropriate fields. After the first payment is processed, QBO will keep the payment details on file and automatically generate all future charges.
- **Reference no.**: This field will display once your payment account is active.
- **Deposit To**: This field will display once your payment account is active. It will automatically default to **Undeposited Funds (UDF)**. This account is the default account for all customer payments. In *Chapter 11, Managing Bank Feeds and Reconciling Bank and Credit Card Accounts,* I will explain in detail why this account is used to keep track of all payments received.
- **SERVICE DATE**: Enter the date that services were provided to the customer.

- **PRODUCT/SERVICE**: Select the appropriate product/service from the dropdown, and the **QTY**, **RATE**, and **AMOUNT** fields will populate. You can manually type or edit any field as needed. Select **Weekly Cleaning Services** for our example.
- **DESCRIPTION**: You can type a brief description in this field or leave it blank.
- **CLASS**: Select **Commercial** for our sample sales receipt.
- **Message displayed on sales receipt**: In our example, type the following message: `Thank you for your business!`

2. Once all the fields are completed, you can click **Charge** or **Charge and close** located in the lower-right corner, or **Charge and new** or **Charge and send** (click on the drop-down arrow to the right of **Charge and close**). Using the payment information that you entered, QBO will automatically process the payment. You (and your client) will receive email notifications once the payment process is completed.
3. To make the payment recurring, click on the **Make recurring** option at the bottom of the screen. If the sales receipt is no longer open on your computer, you will need to display it again to see the make recurring option, and the **Recurring Sales Receipt** screen will appear, as shown here:

Figure 7.10: Recurring Sales Receipt template

4. Complete the fields as follows:

- **Template name**: Each template is assigned a unique name; typically, this will be the customer's name or some variation of it. In our example, it is **The WE Group, Inc**.

- **Type**: There are three types to choose from: **Scheduled**, **Reminder**, and **Unscheduled. Scheduled** allows you to select a specific day, start date, and end date so the payments are automatically processed on the date specified. Select **Scheduled** in our example. If you choose **Reminder**, QBO will provide you with a notification when it's time to process a payment, and **Unscheduled** means that you will need to manually process the payment when you need to. Payments are not automatically processed, and you will not receive a reminder to make the payment if you choose the **Unscheduled** option.
- **Create**: You can choose to have QBO process the payment a certain number of days in advance of the actual due date. This field is optional, so you can also leave it blank, as shown in our example.
- **Customer**: Since we created this recurring payment from an existing sales receipt, this field has already been populated with our customer, **The WE Group, Inc.** If it were not, you can select the customer from the drop-down menu.
- **Email**: The customer's email will automatically populate in this field. If you don't have an email address on file, I recommend that you complete this field. By doing this, the customer will automatically receive an email with their sales receipt whenever a payment is processed.
- **Options**: You can choose to automatically send emails or print the sales receipt later on.
- **Interval**: Choose how often payments are processed (daily, weekly, monthly, or yearly); what day, day of the week, or date payments are processed, and the start and end date for automatic payments. In our example, we will schedule payments to process weekly on Mondays. The start date will be October 1, 2025, and we will not select an end date. We can always edit this template to make any necessary changes to upcoming payments or simply cancel the recurring payment if needed.
- **Save Template**: Click the **Save Template** button in the lower-right corner to save your changes. Your template should resemble the following:

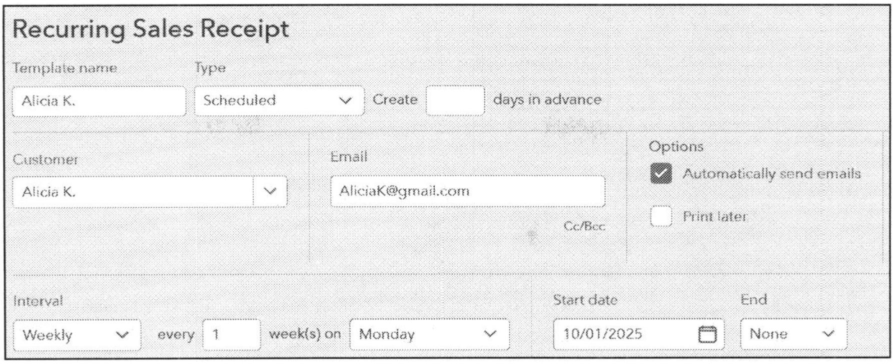

Figure 7.11: Completed Recurring Sales Receipt template

5. To review all recurring transactions, navigate to: **Gear** > **Recurring Transactions** (below the **LISTS** column), and the following screen will display:

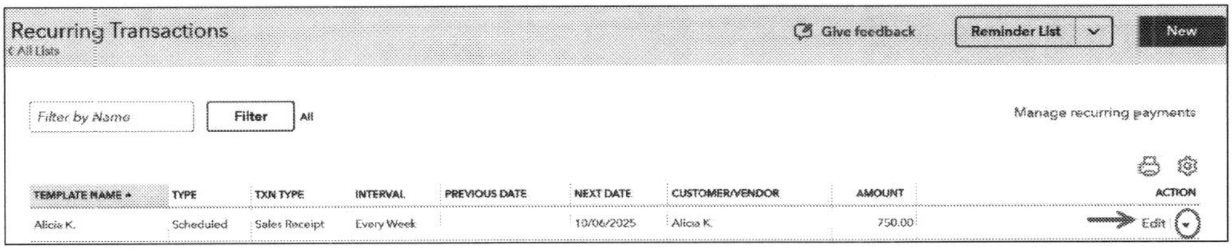

Figure 7.12: Viewing the Recurring Transactions list

6. You can make changes to the template by clicking on **Edit**, as shown in *Figure 7.12*. When you click on the drop-down arrow next to **Edit**, you have several options: **Use**, **Duplicate**, **Pause**, **Skip Next Date**, or **Delete**. A brief description of each of these options is next:

    - **Use**: If you did not schedule the recurring payment, you will select this option to create the payment manually. The template will display, and you will save it to process the payment immediately.
    - **Duplicate**: If you have multiple customers to create recurring sales receipts for, you can duplicate the existing sales receipt and select the client from the drop-down menu, and save it if the date and product/services are the same. If not, you can make any necessary changes and then save the template. For example, Bedrock Professional Cleaning Services has four other customers who receive the same type of service, and they would like to automate the payments.

- **Pause**: If you need to stop automatic payments temporarily, you can use this option. You can start automatic payments back up when you deem necessary.
- **Skip Next Date**: You can choose to skip an automatic payment if you need to. For example, if a client decides to skip service for a week or a month, you can simply select this option so that they are not charged. The recurring payments will resume automatically based on the scheduled interval.
- **Delete**: If you need to stop automatic payments, you can delete the recurring template. It will not delete any payments that have already been processed. It will just prevent any future payments from being processed automatically.

If you prefer to use invoices to record sales, you can also record income using a recurring sales invoice. It is very similar to what we just did when creating a recurring sales receipt. We will cover how to create a recurring sales invoice next.

> Before you set up a recurring sales receipt or recurring invoice payment, you should have your client complete a customer authorization form and keep that on file. You can download a copy of this form using this link: `https://github.com/PacktPublishing/Mastering-QuickBooks-2026-Seventh-Edition`.

Recording income using a recurring sales invoice

The steps to create a recurring sales invoice are very similar to a recurring sales receipt.

Follow these steps to create a recurring sales invoice:

1. Follow the steps outlined previously in this chapter to create a sales invoice. For the purposes of this exercise, you can display the invoice created for ABC Company. Navigate to **+Create** > **Invoice** and click on the clock in the upper-left corner to display recent transactions, as shown here:

Figure 7.13: Recent Transactions

2. Click on the invoice information to display the invoice for ABC Company.
3. On the far right, there will be several options that display. Click on the **Scheduling** box to display the recurring invoice option. There will be a radio button next to it that is grayed out. You will need to click on that button, and the recurring settings options identical to the recurring sales receipt will display. Follow the instructions in the previous section to complete the fields and create the recurring sales invoice. Make the following selections:
   - **Type: Scheduled**
   - **Template options**: Automatically send emails
   - **Start date**: `10/1/2025`
   - **Repeat**: Monthly on the 1st day
4. Save the template.
5. Navigate back to the recurring transactions list: **Gear** > **Recurring transactions**. The following screen will now show two recurring transactions: the sales receipt for Alicia K. and the recurring invoice for ABC Company:

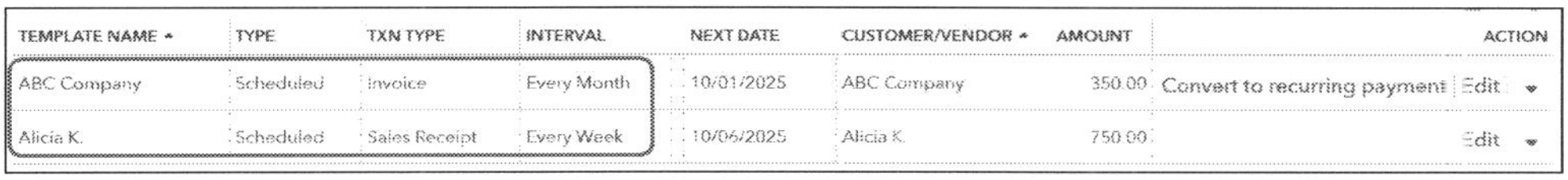

TEMPLATE NAME	TYPE	TXN TYPE	INTERVAL	NEXT DATE	CUSTOMER/VENDOR	AMOUNT		ACTION
ABC Company	Scheduled	Invoice	Every Month	10/01/2025	ABC Company	350.00	Convert to recurring payment	Edit
Alicia K.	Scheduled	Sales Receipt	Every Week	10/06/2025	Alicia K.	750.00		Edit

Figure 7.14: Reviewing the list of recurring transactions

While the steps to create a recurring sales invoice and a recurring sales receipt are very similar, they are very different. As discussed, a sales receipt allows you to automate payments so that you don't have to worry about chasing your customers down to get paid. However, the sales invoice allows you to automate sending invoices to your customers, but payment must be initiated by your customer. When your customer receives the invoice, it will include a link that they can click on to submit an online payment. However, if they do not submit the payment, you will need to follow up with them to do so. In *Chapter 3*, *Company File Setup*, we showed you how to create automatic reminders so that customers will receive email reminders when an invoice is coming due, due, or past due.

If you prefer to send invoices but don't want to chase your customers down for payment, a new feature called **recurring payments** is now available in QBO. We will cover this brand new payment option in detail next.

Creating recurring payments

Recurring payments combine the benefits of automating customer payments and utilizing a form similar to the sales invoice. In addition, you can create both a one-time payment and a recurring payment all at the same time! In our example, Bedrock Professional Cleaning Services has a new client who has just closed on their new home, and they want a one-time deep cleaning service prior to moving in, and then after that, they want weekly cleaning services. Instead of having to create a sales receipt for the one-time cleaning and then a recurring sales receipt for the ongoing weekly service, we can put both of these services on the same recurring payment template.

In *Figure 7.15*, we have created a recurring payment that includes both a one-time payment and a recurring payment. A brief description of each area follows.

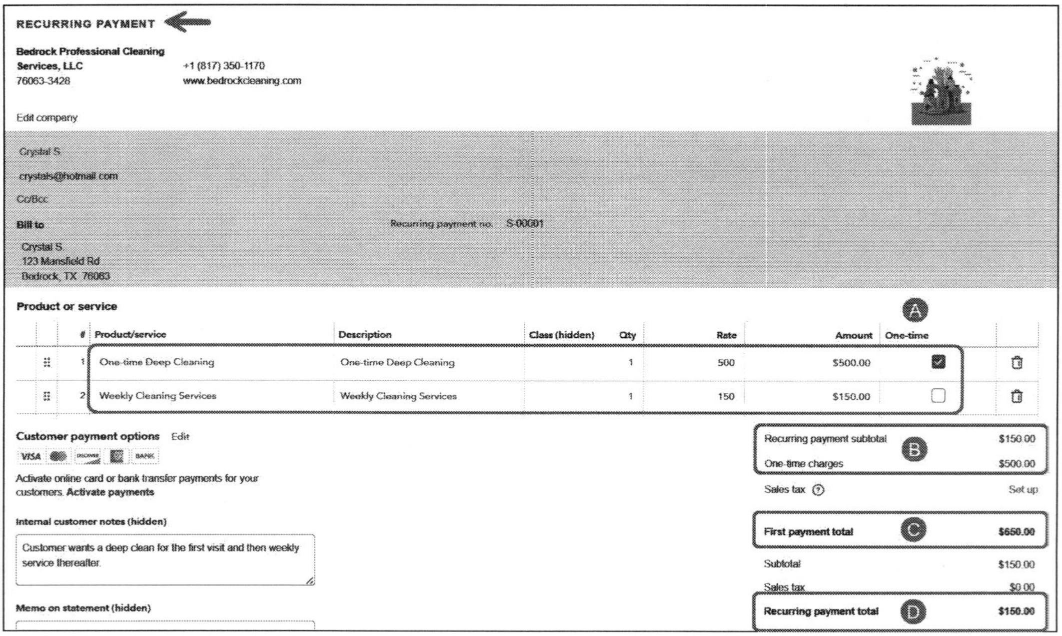

Figure 7.15: Recurring Payment template

- **Product/service**: In this section, you will select the product/service, just like an invoice or sales receipt. However, there is a **One-time** column where you can indicate with a check mark that a service is to be billed once, which means it will not be a part of the recurring payment schedule. In our example, there is a **One-time Deep Cleaning** fee of $500.00. In addition, there will be a **Weekly Cleaning Services** fee of $150.00 that will be processed automatically each week.

- **Recurring payment subtotal** and **On-time charges**: In this section, there is a breakdown of the recurring payment subtotal and the one-time charges. In our example, the recurring payment subtotal is $150.00, and the on-time charges are $500.00.
- **First payment total**: QBO combines the recurring payment and the one-time payment to calculate the first payment total. In our example, the first payment total is $650.00. This is the amount that the customer will be automatically charged once the customer has approved the recurring payment by entering their payment details.
- **Recurring payment total**: In this section, QBO provides the recurring payment amount, which is $150.00 in our example. This is the amount the customer will automatically be charged each week.

To schedule the recurring payment, you must complete the fields located to the right of the recurring template. Most of these fields you will recognize because they are the same as the recurring sales receipt and recurring invoice. In *Figure 7.16*, you will find a snapshot, which is followed by a brief description of each field:

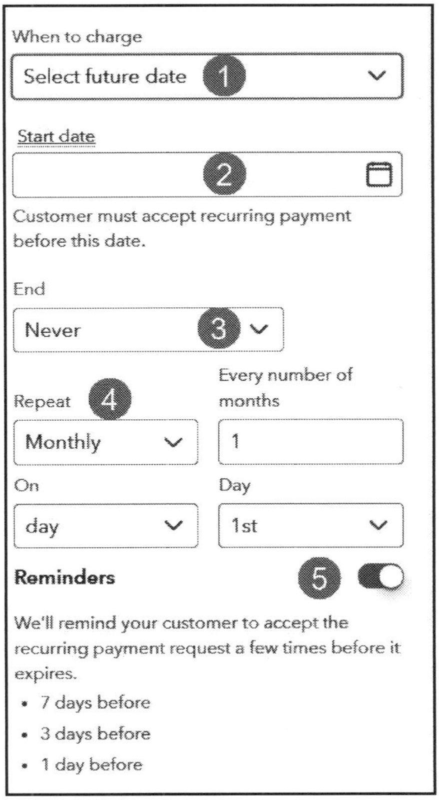

Figure 7.16: Recurring payment options

1. **When to charge**: From the dropdown, you can select a date in the future or immediately. Since the customer must accept the recurring payment first, the payment will be processed as soon as they submit their approval.
2. **Start date**: If you choose to select a future date in the first field, you will need to provide a start date in this field. As indicated in the screenshot, the customer must accept the recurring payment prior to this date.
3. **End**: You can provide an end date for the recurring payments or leave the default, which is **Never**. You can always delete or pause recurring payments as needed.
4. **Repeat**: From the dropdown, you can select monthly, daily, or annual, which will allow you to select a specific month, day, or date that you want the payment to be processed.
5. **Reminders**: This field is optional. You can turn it off by clicking on the radio button, and it will turn gray. If you leave reminders on, QBO will send a reminder to your customers to accept the recurring payment 7 days prior to the start date, 3 days prior, and the day before.

> Note: If your customer fails to accept the recurring payment prior to the start date, you will need to change the start date once your customer has approved the recurring payment.

> Customers only need to approve the recurring payment once. After that, all future payments will be processed automatically based on the payment schedule you have created.

Creating payment links

One of the quickest ways to get paid is to create a payment link that your customers can use to pay on the spot, wherever they are. If you have a QuickBooks Payments account, you can create a payment link. In *Chapter 3*, *Company File Setup*, we explained how to apply for a QuickBooks Payments account so that you can accept online payments from customers. If you don't have a QuickBooks Payments account, head over to *Chapter 3* for instructions on how to apply. Once you have the account set up, you can follow these steps to create and send a payment link to your customers:

1. Navigate to the **Sales & Get Paid** app and select **Payment links**. The following screen will display:

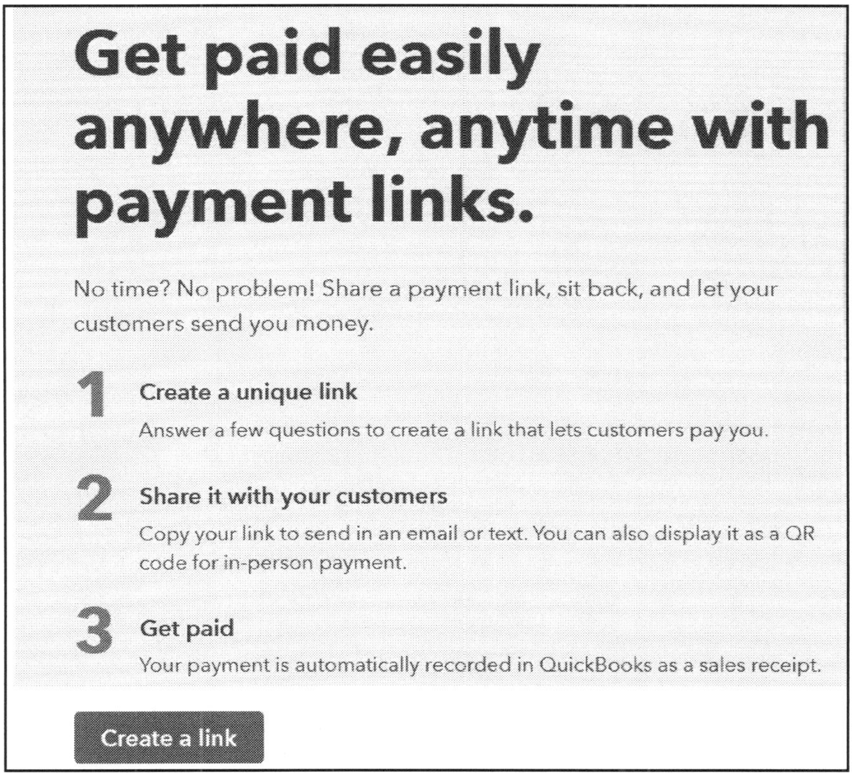

Figure 7.17: Creating a payment link

2. Click the **Create a link** button, and the following screen will display:

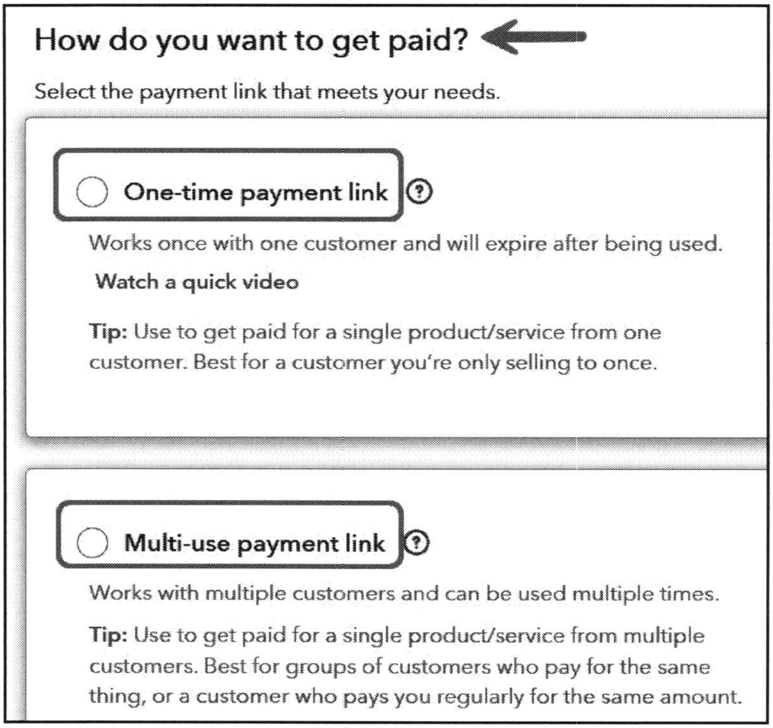

Figure 7.18: How do you want to get paid?

There are two types of payment links to choose from: a one-time payment link or a multi-use payment link. A brief description of both follows:

- **One-time payment link**: Use this link when you just want to send it to a specific customer to get paid for a single product/service. This link will expire after it is used. This kind of link would be ideal for a customer you're only selling to once.
- **Multi-use payment link**: Use this link for multiple customers to get paid for a single product/service. This is ideal for customers who pay for the same thing. For example, an author who has a book signing could provide this link or QR code so that customers can pay for their books on the spot before they get them signed. An example of a service would be if Bedrock Professional Cleaning had a booth at an event and they were offering a special promo of 50% off the first cleaning service, which comes to $75. They would create a payment link that they can share with anyone who visits their booth. Let's create that payment link.

3. Select **Multi-use payment link**, and the next screen will resemble the following:

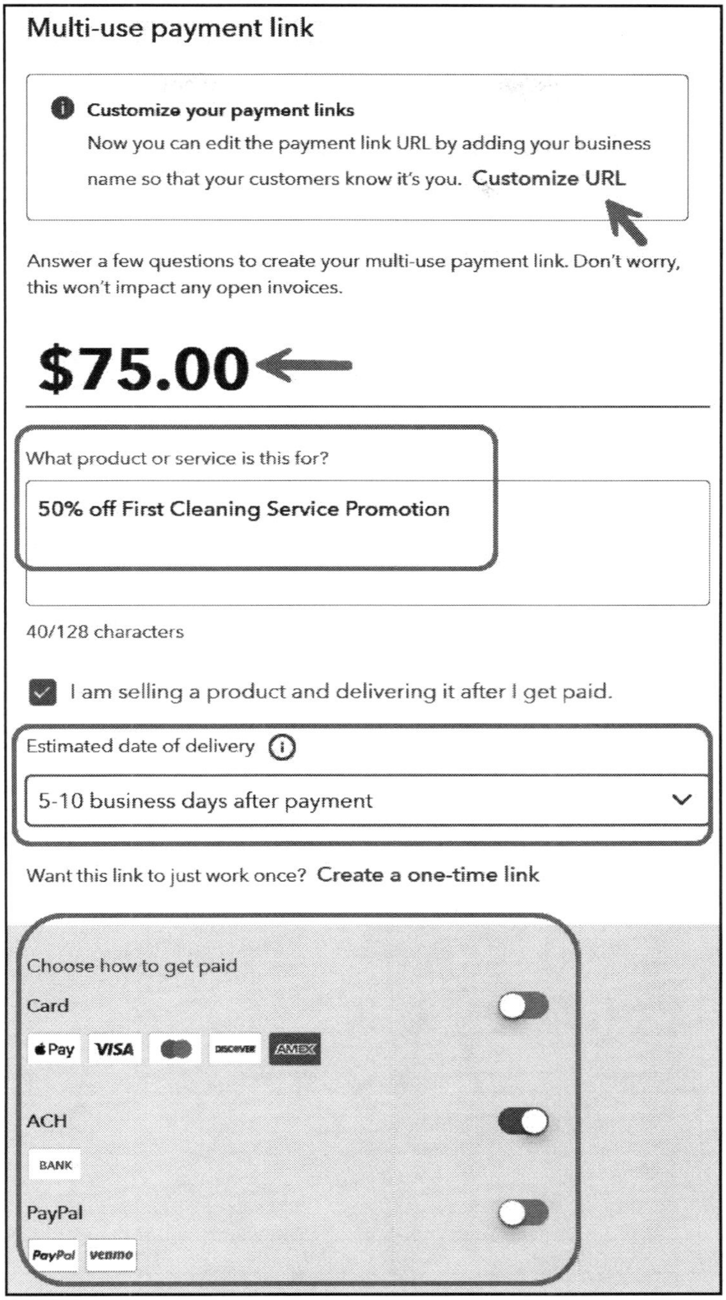

Figure 7.19: Completed multi-use payment link with payment methods

Here is a brief description of the fields to complete on this screen:

- **Customize your payment links**: QBO will create a unique payment link that you can edit to include your business name. If you choose not to customize the URL, QBO will create one for you.
- **Amount**: Type the payment amount in this field.
- **What product or service is this for?**: Type a brief description of the product or service sold.
- **I am selling a product and delivering it after I get paid**: Check this box if you are selling a product that you don't have with you, but will deliver to the customer some time in the near future.
- **Estimated date of delivery**: From the drop-down menu, select the approximate date you expect the product to be delivered. As shown in *Figure 7.19*, you can choose from 1 to 3 business days up to 20+ business days.
- **Payment method**: As a QuickBooks Payments customer, you can accept a variety of payment methods, as shown in *Figure 7.19*: ACH, PayPal, Venmo, and debit/credit card. You can turn all payment methods on or just turn on one. In our example, we have turned on **ACH** payments only.

4. Click **Create Link** in the bottom-right corner of the screen (not shown). Confirmation that the payment link has been created will display, as shown here:

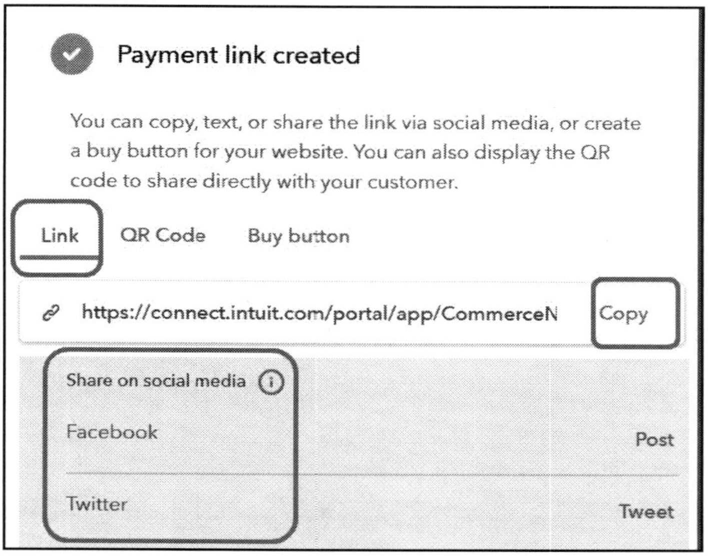

Figure 7.20: Payment link created

When a payment link is created, you can copy the link and email or text it to your customer, or you can share it on social media. If you click on the **QR Code** tab, you can choose to share that code with your customers via email or text message as well. Finally, you can create a customized **Buy** button and add it to your website, as shown in *Figure 7.21*.

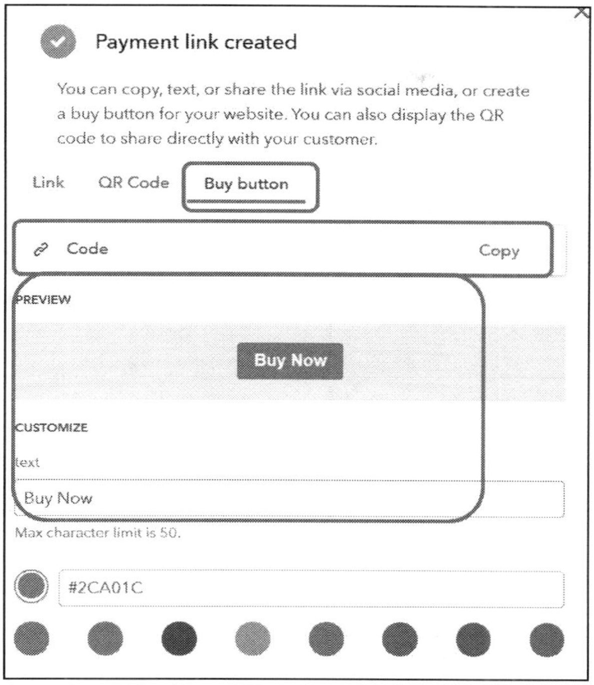

Figure 7.21: Customized Buy Now button (use the following link to view this image in color: https://packt.link/gbp/9781806386895)

You can customize the text and color of the button by simply typing in the text box to replace **Buy Now**. Choose a color that mirrors your brand right below the text box. Save your changes, and a page will display that allows you to manage both your one-time and multi-use payment links all in one place:

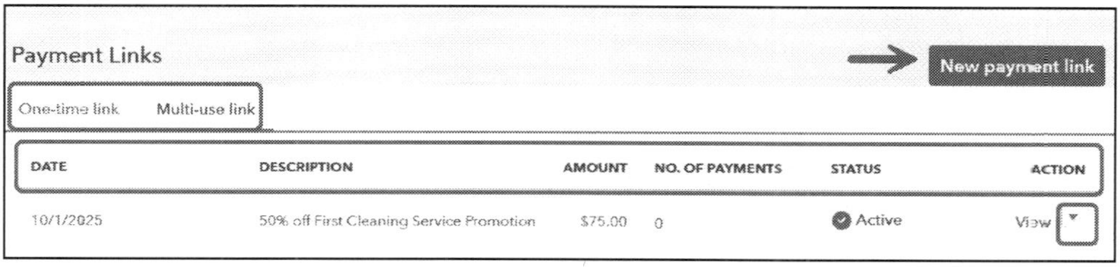

Figure 7.22: Payment Links page

A brief description of the information you will find on the **Payment Links** page follows:

- There is a tab that shows all one-time links and a tab that shows all multi-use links that you have created.
- The date the link was created, a brief description, the amount, the number of payments processed using that link, and the status of the link can also be found on this page.
- Below the **ACTION** column, you can view the details of the link, and if you click on the drop-down arrow, you have several options: **edit**, **delete**, **deactivate**, or **copy link**.
- Finally, you can add a new payment link by clicking on the **New payment link** button in the top-right corner of the page.

In conclusion, payment links are a great way to get paid faster by providing customers with a link or a QR code that they can use to pay you on the spot. When a customer pays you using a payment link, QBO will automatically record a sales receipt for you to keep your books in order.

In the next section, we will show you how to record customer payments manually for those customers who still prefer to pay using a check, Zelle, CashApp, or other forms of payment.

Recording customer payments manually

One of the key differences between recording a sales receipt versus a sales invoice is when and how payments are recorded. For recurring and non-recurring sales receipts, recurring invoices, recurring payments, and payment links, QBO automatically records the payment to your books. There is no manual intervention required to ensure that the payment is properly recorded.

However, if you record income using a sales invoice, you will receive payment based on the terms you have agreed with your customer. If the customer chooses to pay the invoice online, QBO will take care of recording the payment in the books and applying the payment to the open balance on the invoice. However, when a customer sends you a payment via check, Zelle, CashApp, or some other payment method that is outside of QuickBooks, you must manually record these payments so that they are applied correctly to the outstanding sales invoice.

Follow these steps to receive payment on an open invoice:

1. Click on the **+ Create** menu.
2. Navigate to **Receive payment**, located below **Customers**, as shown here:

Figure 7.23: Navigating to Receive payment

3. Complete the fields, as shown in *Figure 7.24*, to record the customer payment:

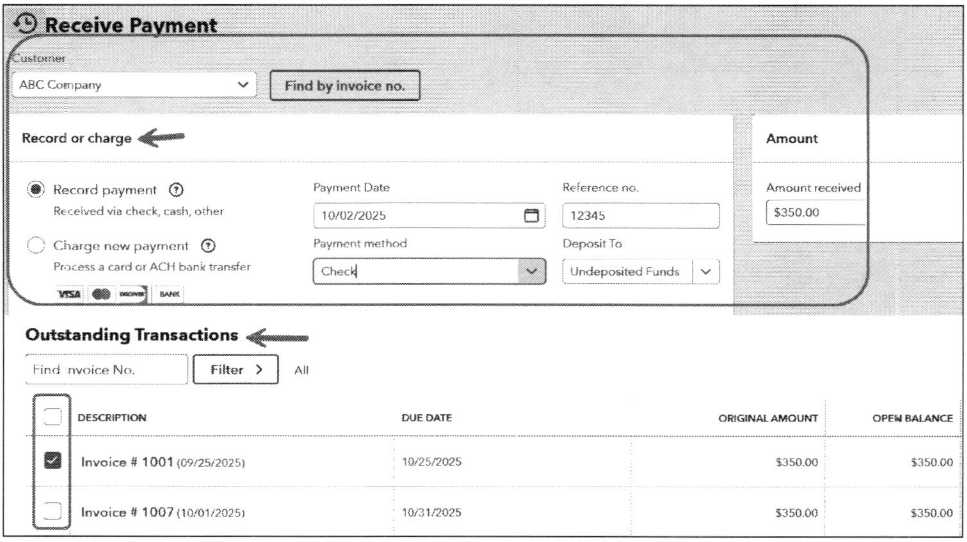

Figure 7.24: The Receive Payment window

The following are the key fields you need to complete to record customer payments:

- **Customer**: Select the customer by clicking the drop-down arrow. **ABC Company** is the customer selected in our example.

4. **Record payment**: Select this option if you have received a payment from your customer in the form of a check, cash, or other payment method.

    - **Payment date**: Enter the date payment was received. The payment date is **10/02/2025** in our example.
    - **Payment method**: From the drop-down menu, select the payment method received (that is, by check, cash, or another payment method). The payment method is **Check** in our example. If the payment method is not listed, you can type it in the field and select **Add**.
    - **Reference no.**: If payment was made by check, enter the check number in this field. If another payment method was used, you can leave this field blank. The reference number is **12345** in our example.
    - **Deposit To**: Select the bank account to which you will deposit this payment. **Undeposited Funds** is the **Deposit To** account in our example.
    - **Amount received**: Enter the amount of the payment received. The amount received in our example is **$350.00**.
    - **Outstanding Transactions**: A list of unpaid invoices will appear in this section. Based on the amount entered in the **Amount received** field, QuickBooks will select the invoice that matches that amount and is closest to the date of the transaction. In our example, **Invoice # 1001** for **$350.00** is the invoice for which payment has been received.

> By default, QBO will always apply payments to the oldest invoice, which is best practice. However, you can override QBO by removing the check mark and selecting the invoice you wish to apply the payment to. In addition, you can easily split the payment between the open invoices by typing the amount in the payment column.

5. Click the **Record** button in the bottom-right corner to save this payment.

6. Click the **More** button and select **Transaction journal** to see the journal entry QBO recorded behind the scenes, as shown in *Figure 7.25*:

Transaction Journal
Bedrock Professional Cleaning Services, LLC
All Dates

Transaction Date	Transaction Type	Num	Name	Memo/Description	Full Name	Debit	Credit
10 (2)							
10/02/2025	Payment	12345	ABC Company	-	Undeposited Funds	350.00	-
10/02/2025	Payment	12345	ABC Company	-	Accounts Receivable (A/R)	-	350.00
Total for 10						$350.00	$350.00
TOTAL						$350.00	$350.00

Figure 7.25: Automatic journal entry recorded for customer payment received

Recording customer payments affects the balance sheet report but not the income statement, if you are on an accrual basis. However, if you are on a cash basis, both the income statement and the balance sheet report will be affected. *Figure 7.25* shows the transaction journal entry that will automatically be recorded in QuickBooks for this customer payment of $350.00.

The **Undeposited Funds** account is increased by $350.00, which will result in an increase in the assets section of the balance sheet report. **Accounts Receivable** will decrease by $350.00, which will result in a decrease in the **Assets** section of the balance sheet report.

The **Receive payments** method should only be used when an invoice has previously been issued. Using **Receive payments** without an open invoice will result in a credit balance on the customer account, and it will show up as an unapplied payment on the balance sheet report. By the same token, do not record a customer payment using the deposits form if there is an open invoice that it should be applied to. This will cause you to double your income, and the open invoice will never be reconciled with the payment.

The **Accounts receivable aging summary** report shows all open invoices and credits for each customer. It should be reviewed periodically to capture any credits on customer accounts. We will review this report in the next chapter.

One of the newest features in QBO is **Charge new payment**, shown in *Figure 7.24*. This option gives you the ability to process a credit card or ACH payment in the **Receive Payment** window. This is ideal if your customer is having an issue with using the payment link in the invoice that you sent via email, or if you have a customer who has provided you with their payment information so that you can process the payment on their behalf. When you click the **Record and charge** button, it will not only apply the payment to the open invoice(s) selected, but the payment will be processed as a debit/credit card charge or ACH payment.

Let's record one more payment, this time using a payment method that was received outside of QBO. Follow these steps to record a $500 Zelle payment that Bedrock Professional Cleaning received from Crystal S:

1. Complete the fields as shown in *Figure 7.26*:

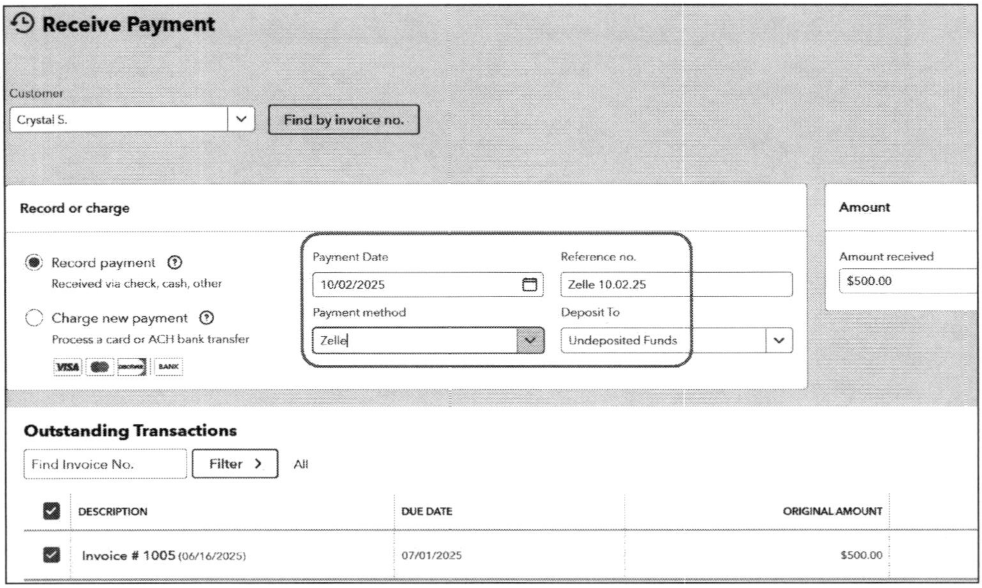

Figure 7.26: Recording a Zelle payment

A brief explanation of the two fields that differ when recording a payment method received outside of QBO follows:

- **Payment method**: From the dropdown, select the correct payment method. If it is not listed, choose **+Add New** to add the payment method. In our example, we have added **Zelle** as the payment method.
- **Reference no**: While this field is optional, I recommend that you enter something that reflects the payment type and date so that if you need to research this payment later, you have the payment method and the date that the payment was received in your business checking account.

2. After you save the transaction, the next step to complete the reconciliation will be to match the payment with the actual Zelle transaction that comes through the bank feed. In *Chapter 11, Managing Bank Feeds and Reconciling Bank and Credit Card Accounts*, we will cover how to match transactions like this one that have been previously recorded in QBO.

Issuing credit memos and refunds to customers

There may be times when a customer returns merchandise, or you need to refund a customer due to an issue with the services or products you have provided. When that happens, you can create a credit memo in QuickBooks that can be applied to a future invoice, or you can refund the customer instead. First, we will show you how to create a credit memo.

Follow these steps to create a credit memo for Alicia K. in QBO:

1. Click on the **Sales & Get Paid** app > **Invoices**, and a list of invoices similar to the following will display:

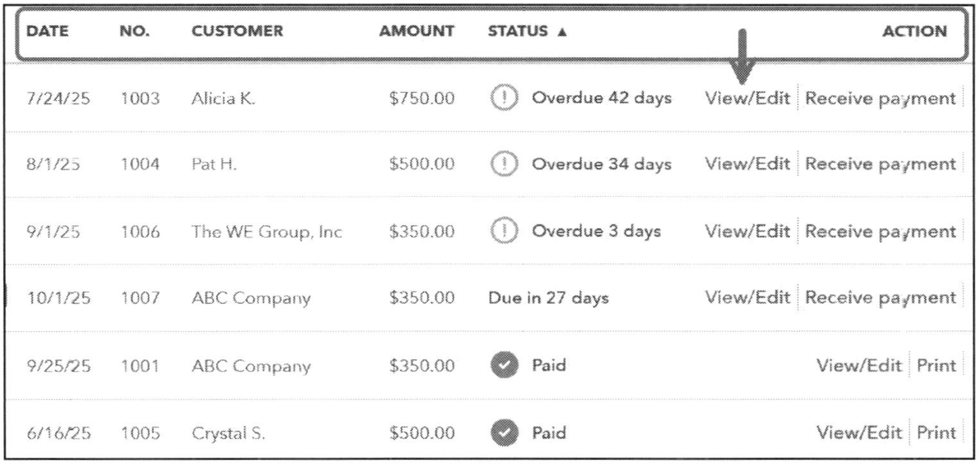

DATE	NO.	CUSTOMER	AMOUNT	STATUS ▲	ACTION
7/24/25	1003	Alicia K.	$750.00	Overdue 42 days	View/Edit | Receive payment
8/1/25	1004	Pat H.	$500.00	Overdue 34 days	View/Edit | Receive payment
9/1/25	1006	The WE Group, Inc	$350.00	Overdue 3 days	View/Edit | Receive payment
10/1/25	1007	ABC Company	$350.00	Due in 27 days	View/Edit | Receive payment
9/25/25	1001	ABC Company	$350.00	Paid	View/Edit | Print
6/16/25	1005	Crystal S.	$500.00	Paid	View/Edit | Print

Figure 7.27: Displaying open and paid invoices

2. Click **View/Edit** for the very first invoice, **1003**, billed to **Alicia K.**, and the invoice will display.
3. Scroll down to the very bottom of the page and click on the **More actions** link, select **Create a credit memo**, and QBO will copy all of the information on invoice 1003 for Alicia K. to a credit memo form, as shown in *Figure 7.28*:

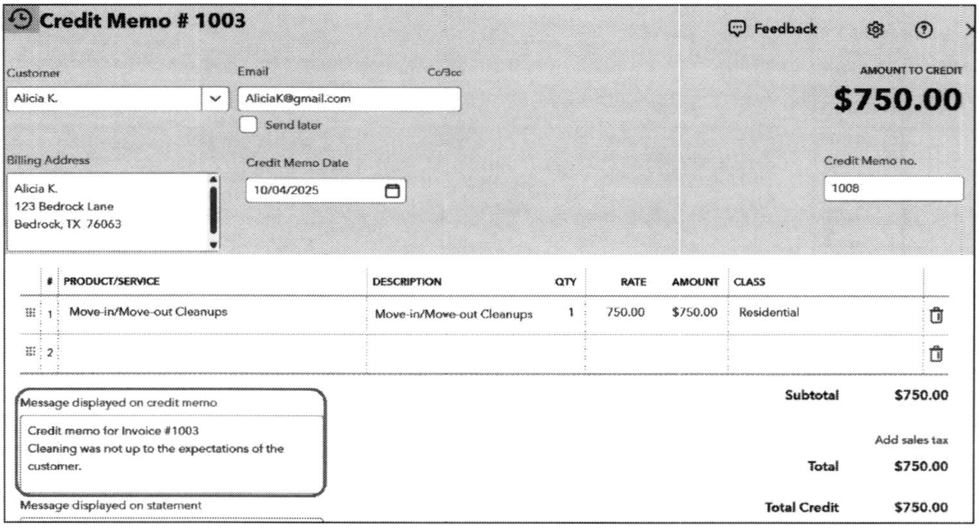

Figure 7.28: Complete Credit Memo form

4. Save and close the **Credit Memo** form if you want to credit the entire invoice amount. If not, you can change the amount to reflect the credit that you would like to issue.
5. Save and close, and the invoice list will appear showing the updated status of the invoice, as shown in *Figure 7.29*:

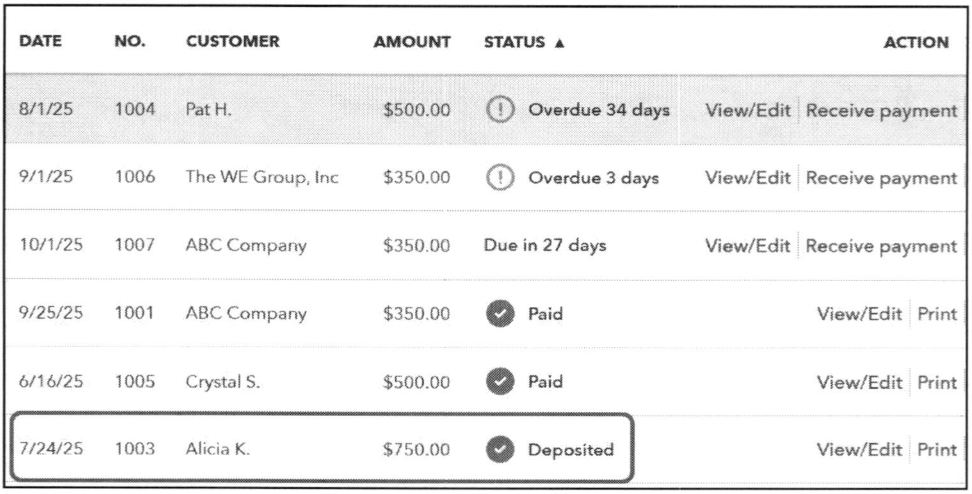

DATE	NO.	CUSTOMER	AMOUNT	STATUS ▲	ACTION
8/1/25	1004	Pat H.	$500.00	Overdue 34 days	View/Edit Receive payment
9/1/25	1006	The WE Group, Inc	$350.00	Overdue 3 days	View/Edit Receive payment
10/1/25	1007	ABC Company	$350.00	Due in 27 days	View/Edit Receive payment
9/25/25	1001	ABC Company	$350.00	Paid	View/Edit Print
6/16/25	1005	Crystal S.	$500.00	Paid	View/Edit Print
7/24/25	1003	Alicia K.	$750.00	Deposited	View/Edit Print

Figure 7.29 Credit memo auto-applied by QBO

Now that the credit memo has been recorded for the full amount of the invoice, the status of the invoice is **Deposited**. This is the same status that will show when a payment has been applied to an invoice, and it has been matched with the bank feed deposit. As mentioned previously, we will discuss matching transactions to bank feeds in *Chapter 11, Managing Bank Feeds and Reconciling Bank and Credit Card Accounts.*

6. Let's record a partial credit memo to invoice 1006 for The WE Group, Inc., for $50.00 and save it. The updated status is shown in *Figure 7.30*:

DATE ▼	NO.	CUSTOMER	AMOUNT	STATUS ▲
8/1/25	1004	Pat H.	$500.00	Overdue 34 days
9/1/25	1006	The WE Group, Inc	$350.00	Overdue 3 days Partially paid, $300.00 due
10/1/25	1007	ABC Company	$350.00	Due in 27 days
9/25/25	1001	ABC Company	$350.00	Paid
6/16/25	1005	Crystal S.	$500.00	Paid
7/24/25	1003	Alicia K.	$750.00	Deposited

Figure 7.30: Partial credit memo applied

Notice that the updated status is **Partially paid, $300.00 due**. Similar to the credit memo in full, a partial credit memo is automatically applied to the open invoice balance so that you don't have to manually apply it. This is one of the newest features in QBO, and it helps streamline the workflow and reduce errors that can occur when you have to manually apply credit memos. Next, we will walk through how to issue a refund to customers.

If your customer has already paid for a product/service and you agree to issue a refund, follow these steps:

7. Click on the **Sales & Get Paid** app > **Invoices**, and a list of customer invoices and payments similar to the following will display:

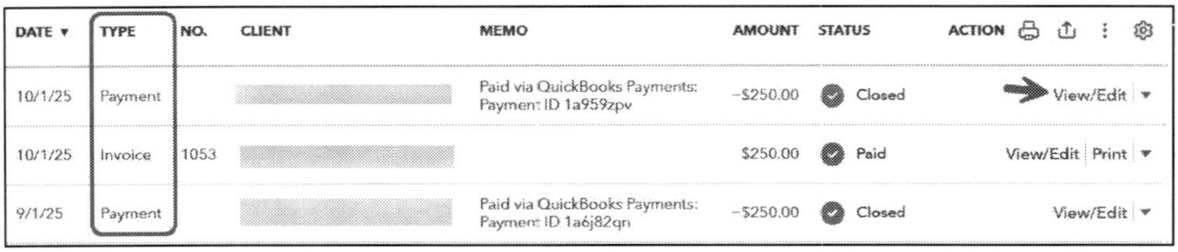

Figure 7.31: List of customer invoices and payments

8. Click **View/Edit** next to the payment that you want to issue a refund for, as shown in *Figure 7.31*.
9. The payment will display. Click the **More** button at the bottom of the page and select **Refund**, as shown in *Figure 7.32*:

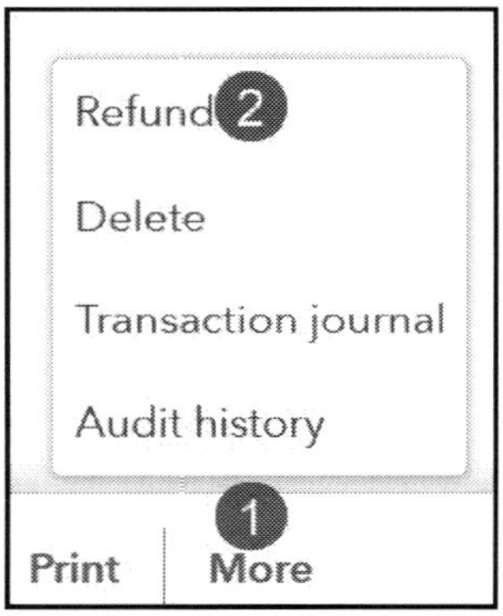

Figure 7.32: Clicking More and Refund

10. Follow the on-screen instructions to process the refund to the customer

If you need to create an estimate to send to a prospective customer for a product or service, you can create the estimate in QBO, send it via email directly from QBO, and track the status. In the next section, we will walk through how to create an estimate and turn it into an invoice with just a few clicks.

Creating estimates in QBO

QBO allows you to create an estimate, also known as a quote or proposal. In addition to being able to track the status of an estimate after it has been emailed to your customer, once they approve it, you can convert it to an invoice with just a few clicks.

Follow these steps to create an estimate for Pat H. in the amount of $350.00:

1. Click **+Create** and select **Estimate**, and the **ESTIMATE** template will display.
2. We have completed an **ESTIMATE** template in *Figure 7.33*:

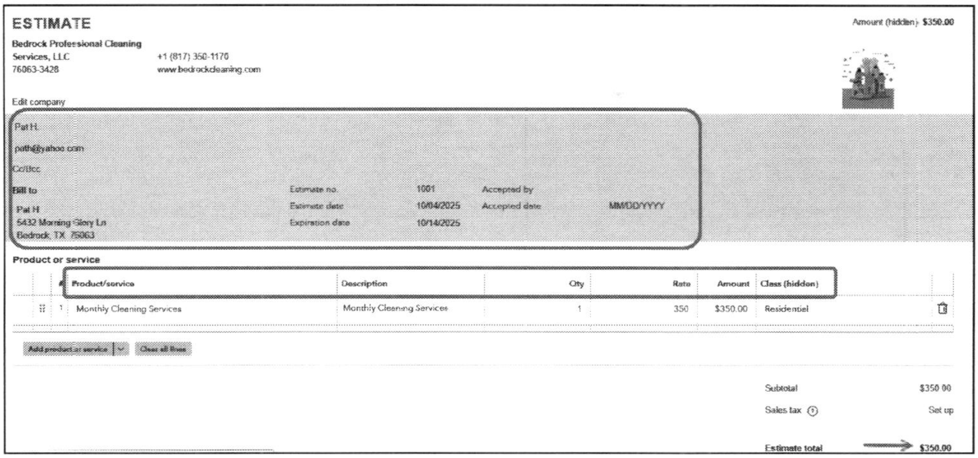

Figure 7.33: Completed ESTIMATE template

A brief description of the fields to complete for the estimate follows:

- **Customer name**: Select the customer from the drop-down menu. In our example, **Pat H.** is the customer.
- **Bill to**: The billing address on file for this customer will automatically populate in this field. If it does not, you can click the **Edit Customer** link to add the address details to the estimate. In our example, the address is **5432 Morning Glory Ln, Bedrock, TX 76063**.
- **Estimate no.**: This field will automatically populate with the next available number. In our example, the estimate number is **1001**. If you would like to customize this number, you can simply type directly in the field to make any changes.
- **Estimate date**: This date will automatically default to the day that you are creating the estimate. In our example, the estimate date is **10/04/2025**. However, you can edit this field by selecting a different date.
- **Expiration date**: If the estimate is only good for a specific period of time, you should include an expiration date. Bedrock Professional Cleaning's policy is that all estimates expire 10 days from the date of the estimate. In our example, the expiration date is **10/14/2025**.

- **Accepted by** and **Accepted date**: When a customer accepts the estimate, their name will appear in the **Accepted by** field along with the date that the estimate was accepted. You will be able to track the status so that you can see when an estimate has been accepted by your customer. We will cover tracking the status after we save this estimate.

The remainder of the estimate resembles the invoice form. Listed next is the information used to create the estimate in *Figure 7.33*:

- **Product/service**: Monthly Cleaning Services
- **Description**: Monthly Cleaning Services
- **Qty**: 1
- **Rate**: $350.00
- **Amount**: $350.00
- **Class**: Residential
- **Estimate total**: $350.00

3. Click the **Review and send** button in the bottom-right corner, and a preview of the email that will be sent to the customer will display, as shown in *Figure 7.34*:

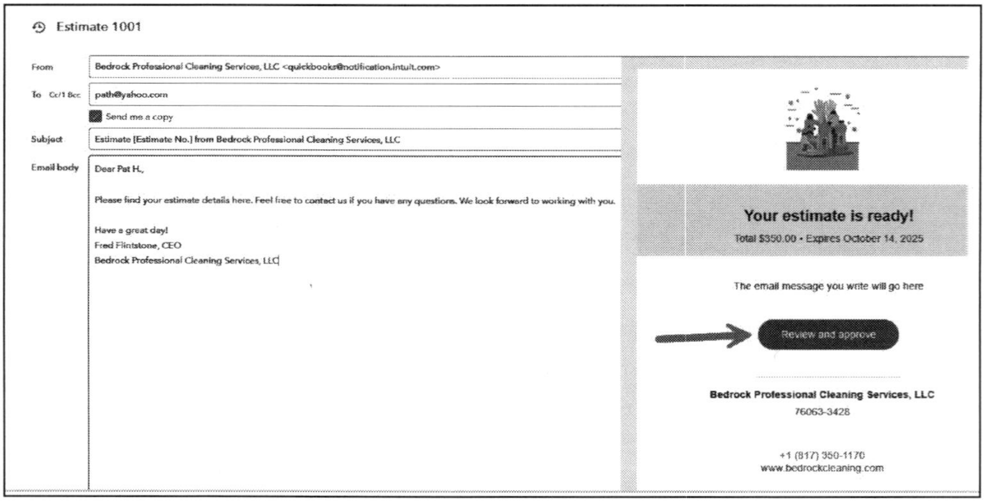

Figure 7.34: Preview of the email that customers will receive

On the left is a preview of the message included in the body of the email. You can type a custom message to your customer in this area. You can also select the **Send me a copy** checkbox right below the **To** field. On the right is what your customer will see when they receive the email. They can easily click on the **Review and approve** button to accept the estimate.

4. Once you are done with any changes, click the **Send estimate** button in the lower-right corner to send the email to your customer.
5. Navigate to **Sales & Get Paid** > **Customer Hub** > **Estimates**, and a list of all estimates will display, as shown here:

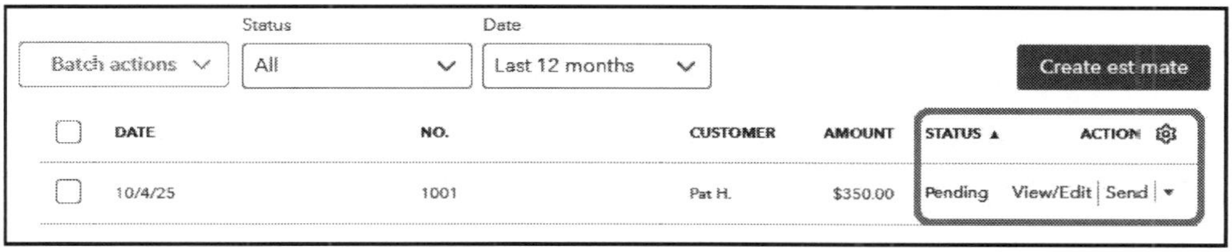

Figure 7.35: List of estimates created in QBO

In addition to the estimate date, number, customer, and amount, there are a **STATUS** column and an **ACTION** column. When you create and send the estimate to your customer, the status is **Pending**. Once a customer accepts the estimate, the status will change to **Accepted**. Like most forms, you can view/edit the form by clicking on the link shown in the preceding figure. You can click the **Send** link if you need to resend the estimate to your customer.

6. Click on the arrow to the right of **Send**, and you will see the following options:

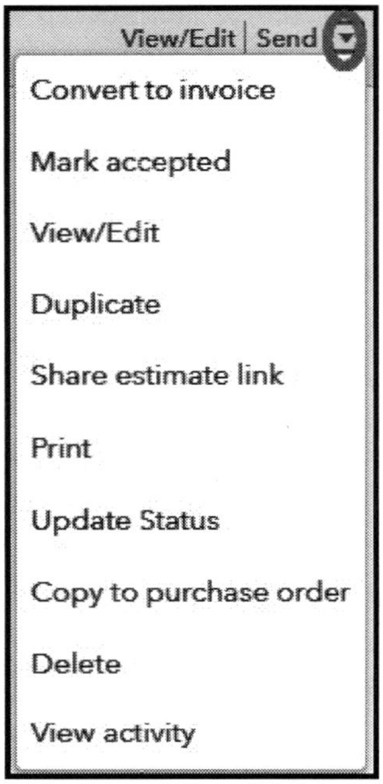

Figure 7.36: Options available for estimates

Here is a brief description of the options listed in *Figure 7.36* that are not self-explanatory:

- **Convert to invoice**: Select this option, and QBO will copy all the information from the estimate to an invoice form. You can make any necessary changes to the invoice and then send it via email to your customer for payment.
- **Mark accepted**: If your customer verbally accepts the estimate, you can manually mark the estimate as accepted on their behalf, which will update the status.
- **Duplicate**: Similar to invoices, you can duplicate an estimate if you need to create it for another customer with just a few tweaks.
- **Share estimate link**: QBO will create a link that you can share with your client. It allows the customer to download, print, or approve the estimate in an instant.
- **Update Status**: Click on this to see the most recent updates for an estimate.
- **Copy to purchase order**: QBO will copy the details of the estimate to a purchase order so that you can easily place an order with a vendor/supplier for products.

To recap, creating estimates provides you with the ability to provide customers with an estimate of products or services that they are considering purchasing from you. Once you have created an estimate, you can easily track the status to see when a customer accepts it, convert it to an invoice in a matter of clicks, easily share a link via email or text message, or copy it to a purchase order so that you can place an order for products needed to fulfill the customer's order. This concludes the final topic in this chapter; we will summarize what you have learned in this chapter and provide you with a peek into what is next.

Summary

In this chapter, you have learned how to record sales transactions for the sale of products and services using a sales invoice, a sales receipt, a recurring sales receipt, and a recurring sales invoice. We have introduced you to two new ways to accept payments from customers: recurring payments and payment links. We have also covered how to manually record payments made outside of QBO, such as via Zelle or a check. You now know when to use each sales transaction and how to record them in QBO. We have also covered the journal entry that is recorded behind the scenes by QuickBooks for each transaction. In addition, you have learned how to record customer payments so that they are correctly applied to open invoices. We showed you how to issue credit memos and refunds to customers and wrapped up by creating estimates. Recording sales transactions will allow you to keep track of how much money your business is making. This is important so that you can determine whether your business is profitable or not.

In the next chapter, we will look at the key reports you need to review to stay on top of your sales and accounts receivable balances.

8

Customer Sales Reports in QuickBooks Online

As a business owner, it's important that you understand where sales are coming from. QuickBooks has a number of reports that will give you insight into which customers are buying from you, which products your customers are buying, and which customers owe you money.

In this chapter, we will focus on five primary reports that will provide you with these details: the **accounts receivable** (**A/R**) aging report, the open invoices report, the sales by customer report, the sales by product/service report, and the sales by class summary report. In each section, we will discuss the information you will find on each report, how to customize the reports, and how to generate each report. Reviewing these reports consistently will let you know who owes you money, who your highest-paying customers are, which products and services are selling the most, and which business segment is generating the most revenue. Having access to this information will help you make informed business decisions.

The following topics will be covered in this chapter:

- Generating an accounts receivable aging report
- Generating an open invoices report
- Generating a sales by customer report
- Generating a sales by product/service report
- Generating a sales by class summary report

The US edition of QBO was used to create this book. If you are using a version that is outside of the United States, results may differ.)

Generating an accounts receivable aging report

To stay on top of unpaid customer invoices, you should generate and review the accounts receivable aging report on a *weekly* basis. If the payment terms for most of your customers are Net 30 and you see customers with balances that are 60 days or over, you need to send a payment reminder to customers or pick up the telephone and call them. In *Chapter 3, Company File Setup*, I showed you how to set up automatic payment reminders in QBO.

The **accounts receivable aging report**, also referred to as the **A/R aging report**, categorizes unpaid customer invoices into groups based on the number of days the invoice is past due. In general, there are five main categories: **Current**, **1-30 days**, **31-60 days**, **61-90 days**, and **91 and over**. QuickBooks calculates the number of days invoices are past due based on the invoice due date.

Follow these steps to generate an A/R aging report:

1. Navigate to **Reports>Standard reports** from the left menu bar, as indicated here:

Figure 8.1: Navigating to the Reports Center

2. Scroll down to the **Who owes you** section and select **Accounts receivable aging summary**, as indicated here:

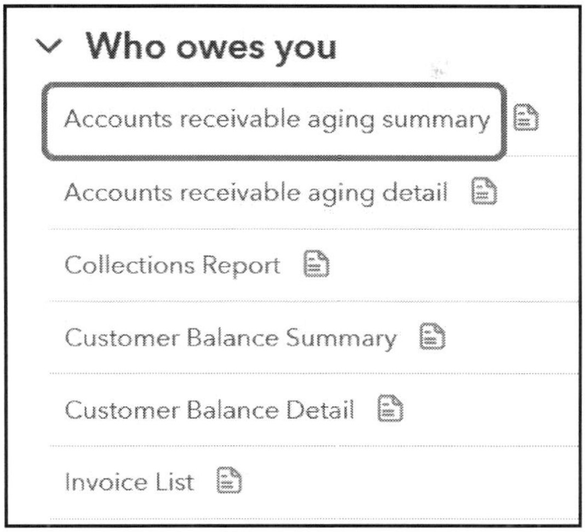

Figure 8.2: Selecting the Accounts receivable aging summary report

3. Notice that there is an **Accounts receivable aging summary** report and an **Accounts receivable aging detail** report. The detailed report includes information about each outstanding invoice for all customers. This includes the invoice number, invoice date, due date, and invoice amount.
4. While this report will show the details, when sorted by customer name, it will sort by customer in each date past due grouping.
5. The A/R aging summary report only includes one total for each customer for each of the applicable categories (for example, **Current**, **1-30 days**, and **31-60 days**). However, you can drill down to the details simply by clicking on a dollar amount in the report. If you click on the **Total** column for a customer, it will bring up the details for that customer regardless of the number of days past due.
6. Click on **Filter** to show only specific customers or click on **General options** to customize the format of numbers, aging method and period, header, and footer indicated here:

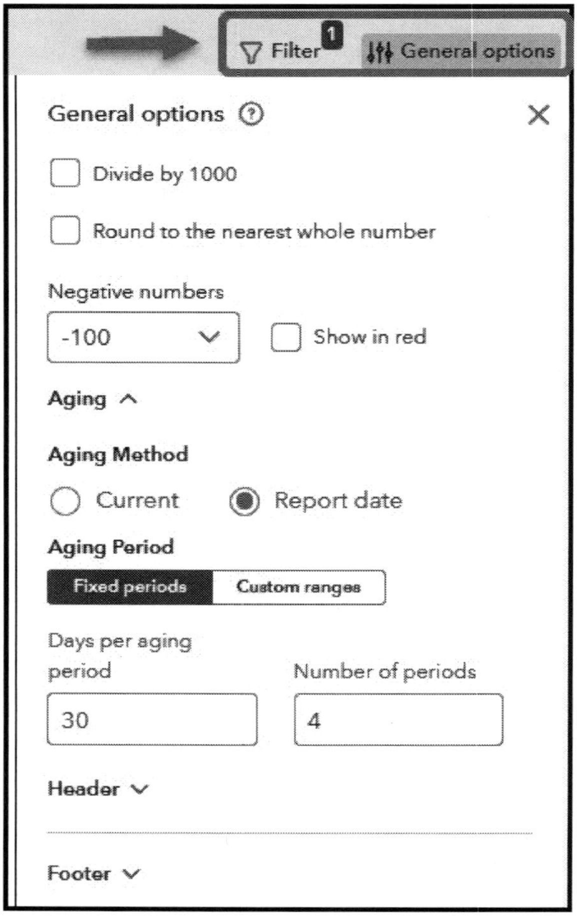

Figure 8.3: Choosing the parameters for the A/R aging summary report

The basic customization features available for the A/R aging report are as follows:

- **Report period**: Customize the date range as needed by selecting the reporting period from the drop-down menu. You can choose from more than 25 options, including the following: **Today**, **This Week**, **This Month**, **This Quarter**, or **This Year**. You can also enter a specific date range by selecting **Custom** from the drop-down menu.
- **Aging method**: You can select **Current**, which will calculate the age of the invoices as of today's date, or **Report date**, which will use the report period to calculate the number of days an invoice is past its due date.

- **Aging period**: The aging period is the number of days an invoice remains unpaid. You can choose a fixed period or a custom range.
- **Days per aging period**: You can determine the number of days per aging period. In our example, we have 30 days per aging period: **1-30**, **31-60**, **61-90**, and **91 and over**. You can also create custom ranges by selecting that option.
- **Number of periods**: You can determine the number of periods for your report. For example, in the A/R aging summary report that we will run next, there are four periods: **1-30**, **31-60**, **61-90**, and **91 and over**.
- **Header**: If you uploaded your company logo, you can select it so that it will show up on the report. The report period and company name are automatically selected for you. In *Chapter 3*, *Company File Setup*, we covered how to upload your company logo.
- **Footer**: The date and time prepared are automatically included on each report. If you would like to remove this info, you can do so in this section.
- After making your selections, you can click the **Save customization** button and enter a name for this report. Next time you want to run this report, simply click on **Custom reports** (not shown in the following screenshot) and click on the report you wish to run.
- Click the refresh button (not shown) to generate an accounts receivable aging summary report, similar to the one shown here:

A/R Aging Summary Report
Bedrock Professional Cleaning Services, LLC
As of October 4, 2025

Customer	CURRENT	1 - 30	31 - 60	61 - 90	91 AND OVER	Total
ABC Company	350.00	-	-	-	-	350.00
Alicia K.	-	-	750.00	-	-	750.00
Pat H.	-	-	500.00	-	-	500.00
The WE Group, Inc	-	350.00	-	-	-	350.00
TOTAL	**350.00**	**350.00**	**1,250.00**	-	-	**$1,950.00**

Figure 8.4: Sample A/R aging summary report

> Credits that appear in the report should be reviewed to determine whether the customer has prepaid or overpaid, or if a payment was recorded without an open invoice.

In this sample A/R aging summary report, **Bedrock Professional Cleaning Services, LLC** has outstanding invoices totaling **$1,950.00**. Of that total, **$350.00** is current; there are invoices that total **$350.00** in 1-30 days past due, **$1,250.00** is 31-60 days past due, and no invoices are more than 60 days past due. The business owner of Bedrock Professional Cleaning Services should follow up with the customers who have balances in the 31-60 days past due column. In our example, this would be Alicia K., since she has a past due balance of **$750.00**, and Pat H., who has a past due balance of **$500.00**.

If it becomes clear that a customer cannot afford to pay their outstanding balance, you will unfortunately need to write off a receivable as bad debt. To learn how to do this, refer to *Chapter 16, Closing the Books in QuickBooks Online*. To avoid incurring a bad debt or sending a customer to a collection agency (collection agencies will go after customers for outstanding amounts due on your behalf; in return, they collect a percentage of the debt as their fee), I recommend you follow up on past due invoices on a weekly basis.

Generating an open invoices report

The **open invoices report** is a list of unpaid customer invoices. It is very similar to the accounts receivable aging detail report, but it groups invoices by customer and not by the number of days they are past due. However, the open invoices report does include detailed information, such as customer name, invoice date, invoice number, invoice amount, transaction type, and payment terms. Like the A/R aging report, this report can help you to stay on top of the money owed to you. Next, we will walk through how to customize and generate the open invoices report.

Perform the following steps to customize and generate an open invoices report:

1. Navigate to **Reports** from the left menu bar, as indicated in *Figure 8.5*:

Figure 8.5: Navigating to the Reports Center

2. Scroll down to the **Who owes you** section and select **Open Invoices**.
3. Customize the report period and the aging method of the open invoices report, as indicated in *Figure 8.6*:

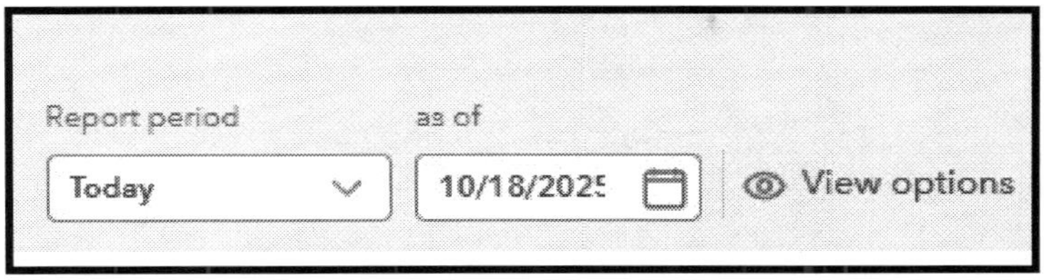

Figure 8.6: Selecting the parameters for the open invoices report

There are basic customizations available for an open invoices report, one of which is **Report period**. From the drop-down menu, select the date range you would like to run the report for. You can enter a specific date or choose from more than 25 options, including the following: **Today, This Week, This Month, This Quarter**, or **This Year**.

After making your selections, click the refresh button to generate the report. An open invoices report should look similar to the one here:

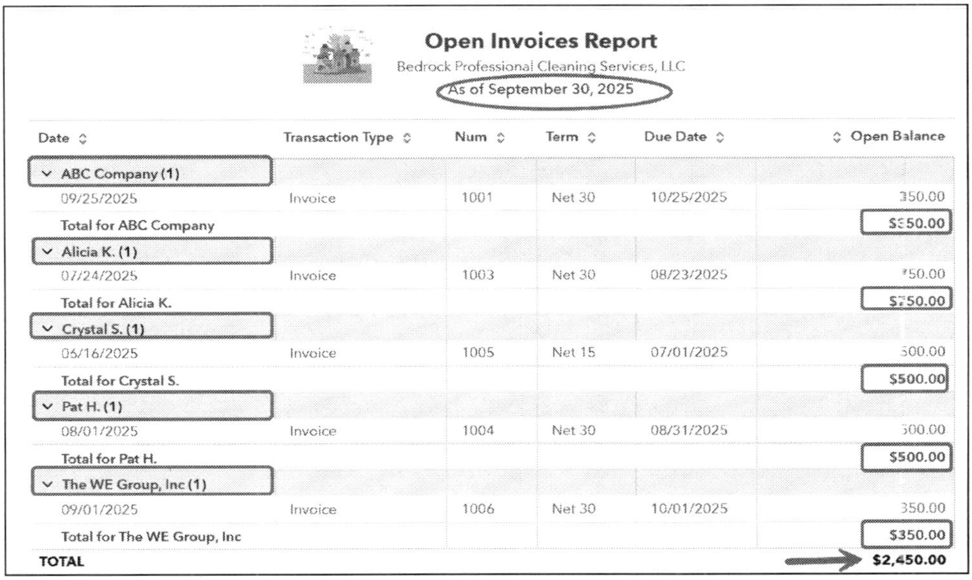

Open Invoices Report
Bedrock Professional Cleaning Services, LLC
As of September 30, 2025

Date	Transaction Type	Num	Term	Due Date	Open Balance
ABC Company (1)					
09/25/2025	Invoice	1001	Net 30	10/25/2025	350.00
Total for ABC Company					$350.00
Alicia K. (1)					
07/24/2025	Invoice	1003	Net 30	08/23/2025	750.00
Total for Alicia K.					$750.00
Crystal S. (1)					
06/16/2025	Invoice	1005	Net 15	07/01/2025	500.00
Total for Crystal S.					$500.00
Pat H. (1)					
08/01/2025	Invoice	1004	Net 30	08/31/2025	500.00
Total for Pat H.					$500.00
The WE Group, Inc (1)					
09/01/2025	Invoice	1006	Net 30	10/01/2025	350.00
Total for The WE Group, Inc					$350.00
TOTAL					$2,450.00

Figure 8.7: Sample open invoices report

In this sample open invoices report, Bedrock Professional Cleaning Services, LLC has several open invoices outstanding. All customers with open (unpaid) invoices are listed, along with the details of each invoice as of September 30, 2025. Open invoices total **$2,450.00**. This amount should equal the total of the A/R summary and detailed reports if they are generated for the same time period.

Review this report on a *weekly* basis and use it to follow up with customers whose invoices are becoming due or past due. If you notice invoices on this report that you have received a payment for, double-check that the payment was recorded in QBO. If it was not, record the payment and then generate this report again to update it. In *Chapter 7, Recording Sales Transactions in QuickBooks Online*, we covered how to apply customer payments to open invoices.

Generating a sales by customer report

The **sales by customer report** will give you, as a business owner, insight into who your highest-paying customers are. In addition, you will gain insight into customers who seldom make purchases, which can help you when creating a marketing campaign to increase customer sales. The sales by customer summary report includes a list of your customers and the total amount sold during the time period specified. We will show you how to customize and generate this report next.

Follow these steps to customize and generate a sales by client report:

1. Navigate to **Reports** in the left menu bar, as indicated here:

Figure 8.8: Navigating to the Reports Center

2. Scroll down to the **Sales and customer** section and select the **Sales by Customer Summary** option, as indicated here:

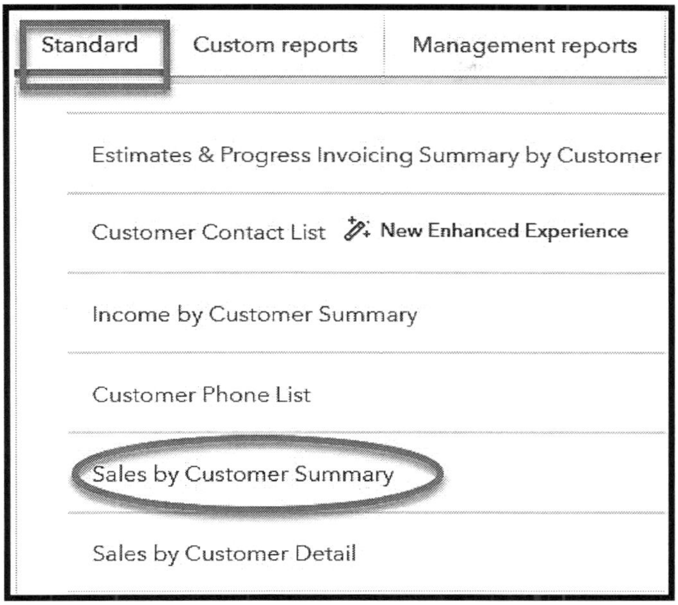

Figure 8.9: Running the Sales by Customer Summary report

Similar to the A/R aging report, the **Sales by Customer Summary** report also has a **Sales by Customer Detail** report. The primary difference between the two reports is that the detail report will display specific invoice information, such as the invoice date, invoice number, and invoice amount, while the summary report does not include this level of detail and is more pertinent for a high-level overview.

3. You can customize the report period and columns displayed, compare the current data to a previous period, filter the data by customer, payment method, or product/service, and select the number format, header, and footer for the **Sales by Customer Summary** report, as shown here:

Figure 8.10: Choosing the parameters for the Sales by Customer Summary report

The basic customizations available for the **Sales by Customer Summary** report are as follows:

- **Report period**: Select the time period to run the report for. You can enter a specific date range or choose from more than 25 options, including the following: **This Week**, **This Month**, **This Quarter**, or **This Year**.
- **Display columns by**: Choose how you want the columns to be displayed. From the dropdown, you can choose from the following: **Total Only**, **Days**, **Weeks**, **Months**, **Quarters**, **Years**, **By customer/client**, or **By product/service**.
- **Compare another period**: Compare the current period to a previous period by selecting one from the dropdown. The options available are **Previous Period**, **Previous Year**, or **Year to Date**.
- **Filter**: Filter the report by customer, payment method, or product/service to drill down to specific transactions.
- **General options**: Similar to the previous reports, you can change the number format, header, and footer information.
- You can click the **Save customization** button to save your report selections and follow the onscreen instructions to save the report as a custom report. The next time you want to run the report, click on the **Custom Reports** tab, and all your custom reports will appear in this tab.

After making your selections, click the refresh button to generate the report. A **Sales by Customer Summary** report, similar to the one shown in the following screenshot, should appear:

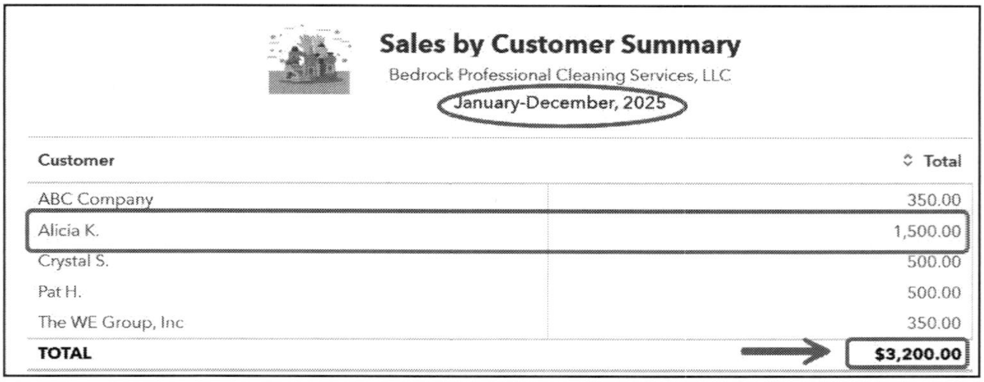

Figure 8.11: Sample Sales by Customer Summary report

In this sample **Sales by Customer Summary** report, the total sales for the period **All Dates** is **$3,200.00**. One way of interpreting this report is the following: according to this report, Alicia K. is the top customer with sales of **$1,500** for the year, and ABC Company and The WE Group, Inc are tied for the least amount of sales at **$350.00** for the year.

As a business owner, you could send Alicia K. a thank you for being a loyal customer, along with a coupon code to use for a future purchase. In addition, you could send ABC Company and The WE Group, Inc. an email that says "We've missed you" or "It's been a while," along with a coupon to use for a future purchase, to encourage them to make a purchase. This is just one of many ways you can use this information to make decisions in your business.

Generating a sales by product/service report

The **sales by product/service** report gives a business owner insight into which products and services are selling the most, as well as which products and services are not selling. Similar to the sales by customer report, you can use this information to create a marketing plan that will help you sell slow-moving products and services.

This information can also help you determine whether you should add new products and services or eliminate an existing product or service. The sales by product/service report includes the quantity sold (if applicable), the total sales amount, the percentage of sales, the average price, the cost of goods sold, and the gross margin of each item sold.

Follow these steps to generate and customize the sales by product/service report:

1. Navigate to **Reports** from the left menu bar, as indicated here:

Figure 8.12: Navigating to the Reports Center

2. Scroll down to the **Sales and Customer** section and select the **Sales by Product/Service Summary** option, as indicated here:

Figure 8.13: Running the Sales by Product/Service Summary report

3. Similar to the A/R aging report and the **Sales by Product/Service Summary** report, there is a detailed version of the sales by product/service report. It breaks down each product or service sold, along with the date and amount for each. The summary version is ideal for a high-level overview.
4. Customize the report period and the columns displayed, and select the accounting method to use for the sales by product/service report:

Figure 8.14: Choosing the parameters for the Sales by Product/Service Summary report

Here is a brief explanation of the fields to complete in order to generate a sales by product/service report:

- **Report period**: Select the time period to run the report for. You can enter a specific date range or choose from the following: **Today**, **This Week**, **This Month**, **This Quarter**, or **This Year**.
- **Accounting method**: Choose the accounting method to run the report for: **Cash** or **Accrual**. To learn more about cash versus accrual accounting, refer to *Chapter 1, Small Business Bookkeeping 101*.
- **Display|Filter|General options**: As with previous reports, you can choose which columns to display, filter the data, and make changes to the number font, header, and footer.

As previously mentioned, you can click the **Save customization** button to save your report selections and follow the onscreen instructions to save the report as a custom report. The next time you want to run the report, click on the **Custom Reports** tab, and all your custom reports will appear in this tab.

After making your selections, click the refresh button to generate the report.

A **Sales by Product/Service Summary** report similar to the one shown in the following screenshot should appear:

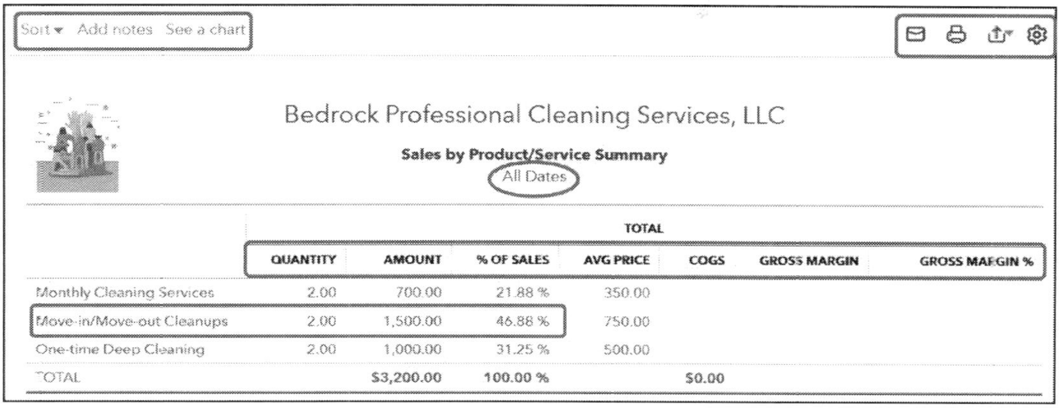

Bedrock Professional Cleaning Services, LLC

Sales by Product/Service Summary

All Dates

	TOTAL						
	QUANTITY	AMOUNT	% OF SALES	AVG PRICE	COGS	GROSS MARGIN	GROSS MARGIN %
Monthly Cleaning Services	2.00	700.00	21.88 %	350.00			
Move-in/Move-out Cleanups	2.00	1,500.00	46.88 %	750.00			
One-time Deep Cleaning	2.00	1,000.00	31.25 %	500.00			
TOTAL		$3,200.00	100.00 %		$0.00		

Figure 8.15: Sample sales by product/service summary report

In the preceding **Sales by Product/Service Summary** report, the total sales for the period January 1 to December 31, 2025 is **$3,200.00**.

> As a reminder, **cost of goods sold (COGS)** is the total cost a business has paid out of pocket to sell a product or service. It includes any direct costs that a business incurs in the manufacture, purchase, and sale or resale of products.

Move-in/Move-out Cleanups had the highest sales of **$1500.00**, or **46.88%** of total sales. Monthly Cleaning Services had the lowest sales of **$700.00**, which equates to **21.88%** of overall sales. The final report that we will cover in this chapter is the **Sales by Class Summary** report.

Generating a Sales by Class Summary report

The **Sales by Class Summary** report gives a business owner insight into which business segment is producing the most sales, as well as which business segment is not producing many sales. Similar to the sales by customer report, you can use this information to create a marketing plan that will help you to increase sales for the business segment that is lacking in sales. On the flip side, you can also reward those customers who fall into the business segment that is producing the most sales.

Follow these steps to generate and customize the **Sales by Class Summary** report:

1. Navigate to **Reports** from the left menu bar, as indicated here:

Figure 8.16: Navigating to the Reports Center

2. Scroll down to the **Sales and Customers** section and select the **Sales by Class Summary** report, as indicated here:

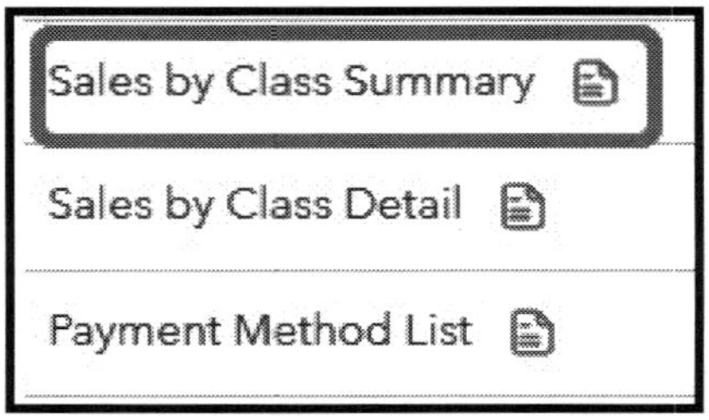

Figure 8.17: Selecting the Sales by Class Summary report

3. Similar to the A/R aging report and the **Sales by Product/Service Summary** report, there is a detailed version of the **Sales by Class Summary** report. It breaks down the sales for each business segment, including transaction type, transaction number, services, sales price, and invoice amount. The summary version is ideal for a high-level overview.
4. You can customize the report period and the accounting method by making the selections from the drop-down menus as shown here:

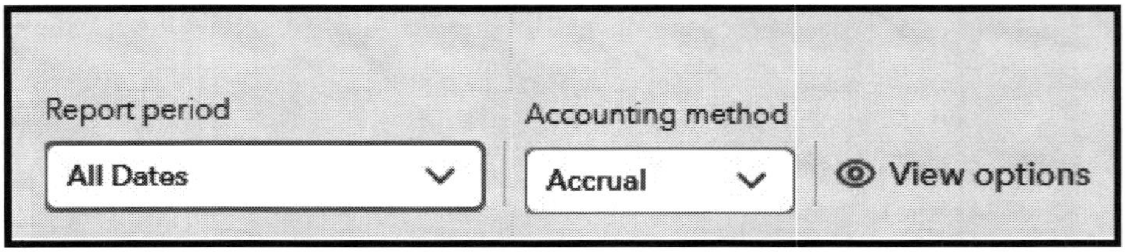

Figure 8.18: Choosing the report period and accounting method for reports

Here is a brief explanation of the fields to complete in order to generate a **Sales by Class Summary** report:

- **Report period:** Select the time period to run the report for. You can enter a specific date range or choose from the following: **Today**, **This Week**, **This Month**, **This Quarter**, or **This Year**.
- **Accounting method:** From the drop-down, select accrual or cash method, depending on the accounting method your business uses. In *Chapter 1, Small-Business Bookkeeping 101*, we explain the difference between cash and accrual accounting.
- **Display columns by:** Choose how you want the columns to be displayed. From the dropdown, you can choose from the following: **Total Only**, **Days**, **Weeks**, **Months**, **Quarters**, **Years**, **By customer/client**, or **By product/service**.
- **Compare another period:** Compare the current period to a previous period by selecting one from the dropdown. The options available are **Previous Period**, **Previous Year**, or **Year to Date**.
- **Filter|General options:** As with previous reports, you can filter the data and make changes to the number font, header, and footer.

5. As previously mentioned, you can click the **Save customization** button to save your report selections and follow the onscreen instructions to save the report as a custom report. The next time you want to run the report, click on the **Custom Reports** tab, and all your custom reports will appear in this tab.
6. After making your selections, click the refresh button to generate the report.
7. A **Sales by Class Summary** report similar to the one shown in the following screenshot should appear:

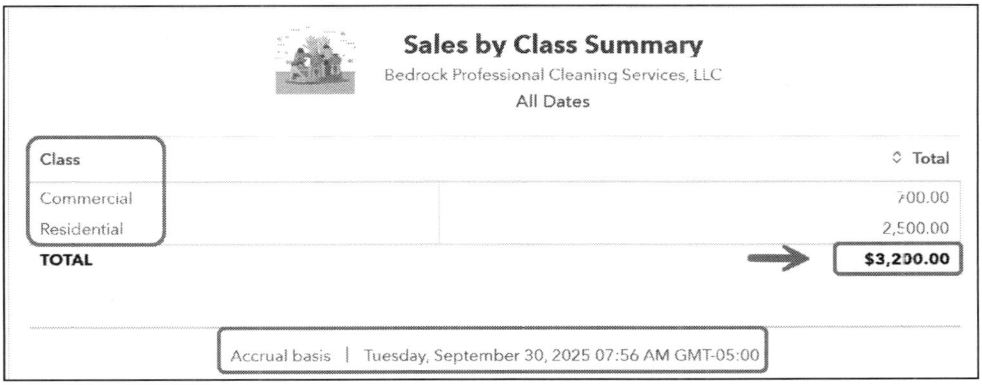

Figure 8.19: Generating a Sales by Class Summary report

In the preceding report, there are two business segments: **Commercial** and **Residential**. These segments represent the types of customers that Bedrock Professional Cleaning Services, LLC provides services to. Commercial customers have generated **$700.00** in **year-to-date (YTD)** sales, and residential customers have generated **$2,500.00** in YTD sales. The grand total of sales is **$3,200.00**. In the footer section of the report, you can see the date and the time the report was generated, as well as that the **Accrual basis** accounting method was selected. Using the information in this report, the business owner might want to send an email blast out to all commercial customers offering a promo code to boost sales for that business segment.

All reports can be saved in a group for easy access to use on a regular basis. We will show you how to do this in *Chapter 14, Report Center Overview*.

> To demonstrate some of the concepts taught in this chapter and give you some additional insights not covered, check out my YouTube channel at:
>
> `https://packt.link/du2BR`

Summary

Let's recap: we learned how to customize and generate five key reports that will give you insight into your customers and sales. We covered the A/R aging report, which provides you with the number of days for which customer invoices remain unpaid. We explained the open invoices report, which shows all unpaid customer invoices. The sales by customer report was covered, which includes key sales data for each of your customers, and the sales by product/service report was covered, which includes the products and services that are your top sellers. Finally, we showed you how to generate a sales by class summary report, which shows you sales by business segment. These reports are important in assisting you with determining where your sales are coming from and staying on top of unpaid customer invoices so that you can get paid faster. It is much easier to maintain a positive cash flow if payments are received on time. Now that we have shown you how to record money coming into your business and which reports provide you with insights into your sales, we are going to switch gears and focus on money going out of your business. In the next chapter, we will cover recording expenses and paying bills.

Next steps

1. Turn on automatic reminders for customers who have unpaid invoices. Refer to *Chapter 3, Company File Setup*, for instructions on how to do this.
2. Pick a day during the week to review the following key reports:
    - A/R Aging detail report
    - A/R Aging summary report
3. Make an action plan to address any unpaid customer invoices that are 60+ days overdue.
4. Schedule time on your calendar to review key reports on a *monthly* basis. Make it at least 45 minutes and plan to have your favorite caffeinated beverage or a nice breakfast or lunch. Call this **A Date with My Money** or something that you will look forward to.
    - A/R Aging detail report
    - A/P Aging detail report (refer to *Chapter 10, Vendor and Expense Reports in QuickBooks Online*)
    - Profit and Loss report (refer to *Chapter 15, Business Overview and Cash Management Tools and Reports*)
    - Balance sheet report (refer to *Chapter 15, Business Overview and Cash Management Tools and Reports*)

If you have a bookkeeper or accountant who manages your books, schedule time to meet with that person each month. However, make sure that you have already reviewed the reports and made a list of your questions *prior to this meeting*. In other words, schedule your "date" before you meet with your bookkeeper or accountant, if applicable.

9

Recording Expenses in QuickBooks Online

Managing expenses and bills incurred by a business is one of the primary reasons why many businesses decide to use QuickBooks. Most businesses know when they are generating income, but when it comes to where their money is going, it's a whole different story. For a business to be profitable, it must be able to control expenses that directly affect the bottom line.

In this chapter, we will show you four ways to record expenses, also known as **money-out** transactions: entering and paying bills, managing recurring expenses, writing and printing checks, and capturing and categorizing receipts and bills.

Entering a bill is ideal for suppliers who have extended credit to you. You receive your purchases immediately, and payment is due sometime in the future. However, expenses that require immediate payment should be paid via check, debit card, or credit card. In *Chapter 11, Managing Bank Feeds and Reconciling Bank and Credit Card Accounts*, we will show you how to record payments made with a debit or credit card. Writing a check allows you to record both the expense and the payment at the same time.

Using one or more of these methods will give you access to detailed reports that will give you insight into all of your money-out transactions. This is a key component in having the ability to control expenses.

In this chapter, we will cover the following topics:

- Adding and paying bills
- Managing recurring expenses

- Writing checks
- Printing checks
- Editing, voiding, and deleting expenses
- Capturing and categorizing receipts and bills

By the end of this chapter, you will know how to add and pay your bills, as well as how to create recurring expenses for rent, utilities, and other recurring costs. Plus, you will understand how to write a check and print it directly from QuickBooks, all while becoming familiar with the various ways in which you can upload receipts and bills in QuickBooks.

> The US edition of QBO was used to create this book. If you are using a version that is outside of the US, results may differ.

Adding and paying bills

For purchases made on account, adding bills to QuickBooks and paying them a few days before they become due is the best way to manage your cash flow. If you add bills to QuickBooks as you receive them, you can run reports that will show you which bills are due or nearly due so that you can plan ahead and ensure you have sufficient cash on hand to pay them. Unpaid bills are also referred to as **accounts payable**, or **A/P** for short. In the following sections, we will cover how to add bills, after which we will discuss how to pay bills in QBO.

> There are a number of apps available to help automate the bill entry process. From the left navigation bar, select **Apps**. In the search box, type `bill pay`; several options, such as **Bill Pay for QuickBooks Online** and **bill.com**, will appear. To learn more about the Intuit Apps marketplace, please refer to *Chapter 4, Customizing QuickBooks for Your Business*.

Entering bills into QuickBooks Online

As advised earlier, adding your bills to QuickBooks before they come due will help you manage your cash flow. You can easily run reports, such as the **Unpaid Bills** report or the **A/P Aging** report, to see which bills are coming due or are past due. There are a couple of ways you can add your bills to QuickBooks: you can upload a bill that you have saved on your computer, or you can manually create the bill. First, we will cover how to manually create a bill.

Follow these steps to create a bill in QBO:

1. Click on the **Expenses & Pay Bills** app located at the very top of your dashboard, as indicated in *Figure 9.1*:

Figure 9.1: Navigating to Expenses & Pay Bills from the left menu bar

2. On the screen that appears, you will see **Upload multiple bills**, **Create bill**, **Schedule online payment**, **Pay bills**, and **Record expense**. Click on **Create bill**, as shown here:

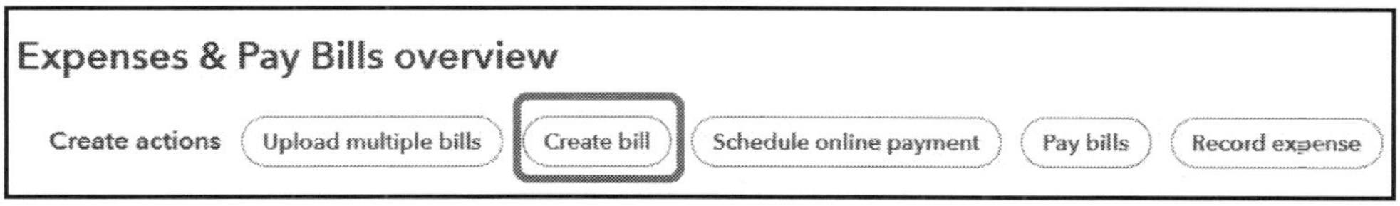

Figure 9.2: The Expenses & Pay Bills overview window

3. Fill in the fields in the **Bill** template form, as indicated:

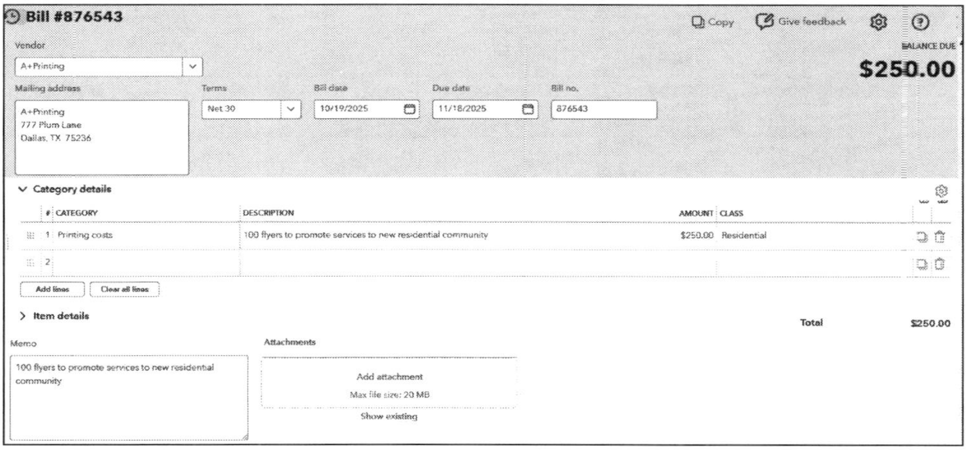

Figure 9.3: Filling in the Bill form for a vendor

The following is a brief description of the key fields in the **Bill** form. All fields must be completed:

- **Vendor**: Select a vendor from the drop-down menu, or add a new vendor if they have not been previously set up in QuickBooks. You can do this by selecting **Add New** from the drop-down menu. In our example, **A+Printing** is the vendor.

- **Mailing address**: This field will automatically populate for vendors you have previously created in QuickBooks. If this is a new vendor, you can enter the address in this field. In our example, the address is **777 Plum Lane, Dallas, TX 75236**.
- **Terms**: This field will automatically populate with the vendor terms you have set up. If you have not previously set up vendor terms, you can select the appropriate payment terms from the drop-down menu. The payment terms should be **Net 30** for **A+Printing**.
- **Bill date**: Enter the date that appears on the vendor bill. Our bill date is **10/19/2025**.
- **Due date**: The due date will be calculated automatically based on the payment terms selected. If payment terms were not selected, you can also enter the due date directly in this field. The due date in our example is **11/18/2025**.
- **Bill no.**: The bill number is the invoice number assigned by the vendor supplier. If the bill does not include a unique number, create one. Having a unique bill number is very important so that QuickBooks can track bills and alert you if there is a duplicate bill number being used. If a bill does not include a bill number, utilize the bill date, or something unique, for each bill. The bill number in our example is **876543**.
- **Category details**: Complete this section if you have purchased services from the vendor. In our example, Bedrock Professional Cleaning Services has had 100 flyers printed.
- **Item details**: Complete this section if you have purchased a product that you need to keep in inventory so that you can track the quantity and/or costs. If the items purchased are not put into inventory, use the **Category details** tab. From the drop-down menu, select the product/service purchased. If the item has not been added to QuickBooks, you can do so on this screen by selecting the **Add new** option. The **New item** window will appear, where you can complete the item setup process. For more information on adding a new item to the products and services list, see *Chapter 18, Managing Products and Services.*
- **DESCRIPTION**: Enter a brief description of what was purchased in this field. For this example, the description is **100 flyers to promote services to new residential community**.
- **AMOUNT**: Enter the total amount of the bill in this field. In our example, the total amount calculated is **$250.00**.
- **CLASS**: If applicable, select a class from the dropdown. In our example, the class is **Residential**.
- **Memo**: Completing this field is *optional*. You can simply copy and paste the description into this field, or you can type it directly in this field. In our example, we copied and pasted `100 flyers to promote services to new residential community` into this field.

- **Save** or **Save and schedule payment**: You have the option to save the bill and schedule payment at a later date, or schedule the payment now. We will save the bill for now and cover how to schedule payment later in this chapter.

In our example, this bill impacts both the Profit and Loss and Balance Sheet reports. A/P has increased by $250.00, which increases liabilities on the Balance Sheet report. Printing costs have also increased by $250.00, which increases expenses on the Profit and Loss report.

The journal entry that is recorded in QuickBooks for the preceding bill is shown in *Figure 9.4*:

Transaction Journal
Bedrock Professional Cleaning Services, LLC
All Dates

Transaction Date	Transaction Type	Num	Name	Memo/Description	Full Name	Debit	Credit	Adj
˅ 3 (2)								
10/19/2025	Bill	876543	A+Printing	100 flyers to promote services t...	Accounts Payable (A/P)	-	250.00	No
10/19/2025	Bill	876543	A+Printing	100 flyers to promote services t...	Printing costs	250.00	-	No
Total for 3						$250.00	$250.00	
TOTAL						$250.00	$250.00	

Figure 9.4: Journal entry to record a vendor bill

In our example, we used the **Category details** section because services were purchased. If you are recording the purchase of a product that you were going to put into inventory (such as T-shirts, workbooks, or other items for resale), instead of services, you would select the item from the drop-down field of the **Item details** section. This would increase inventory, which is an asset on the balance sheet. A/P would still increase by the amount that was purchased. To stay on top of your bills, it's a good idea to enter them as soon as you receive them. Be sure to enter the date of the bill and the due date; this will ensure that QuickBooks calculates the correct due date and alerts you when a bill is coming due. At the bottom of the bill form, you can even attach a copy of the bill to this transaction by clicking on **Add attachment**.

Uploading bills to QuickBooks

The second way you can add bills to QBO is by uploading them from your computer. You will need to follow *Steps 1* and *2*, as indicated previously, to manually create a bill. For the remaining steps, you will need to select **Upload multiple bills**. The following screen will appear:

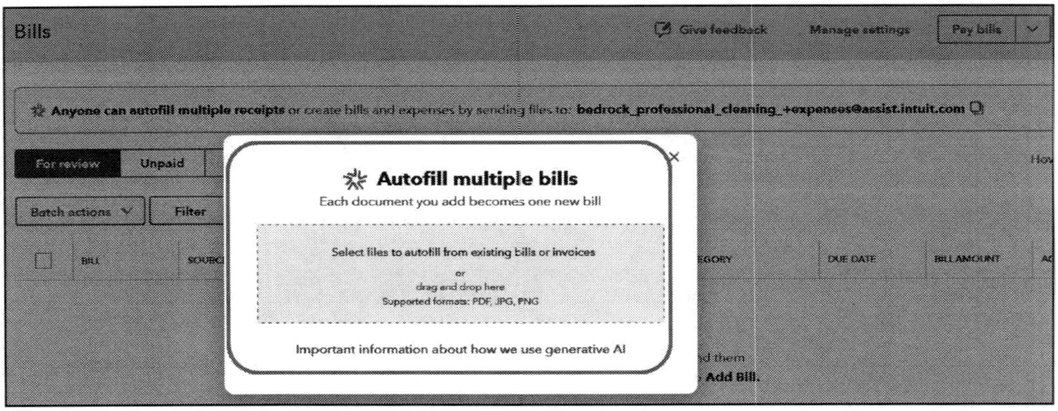

Figure 9.5: Uploading bills from a computer to QBO

You can now follow these steps:

1. On the screen that appears, you can drag or drop bills that you have saved on your computer. Bills can be in one of three formats: PDF, JPG, or PNG.
2. You can close the **Autofill multiple bills** window by clicking on the **X** icon in the top-right corner, shown in *Figure 9.5*. Once you've done this, the **Bills** center will appear:

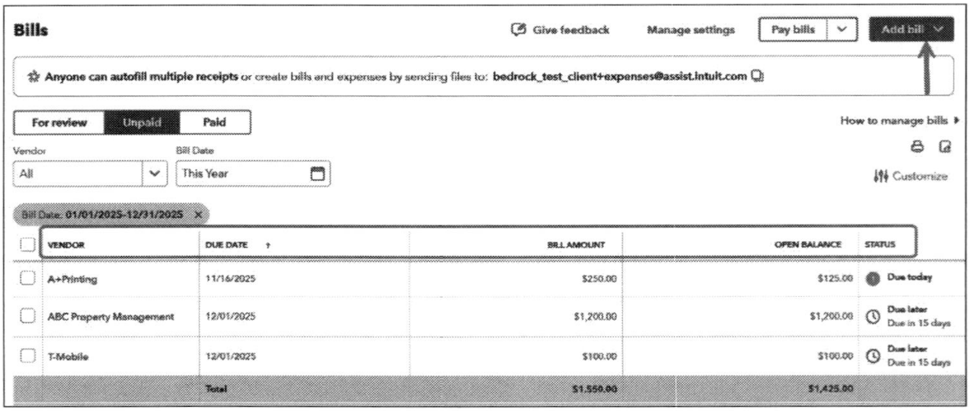

Figure 9.6: Uploading bills from your computer

If the bill is not saved on your computer, do that first and then return to this step.

3. Upon clicking the **Unpaid** tab, you will see several details about your open bills: **VENDOR**, **DUE DATE**, **BILL AMOUNT**, **OPEN BALANCE**, and **STATUS**.

4. You can also click on the **Add bill** button in the top-right corner to upload single or multiple bills at once.
5. Once the upload is complete, your screen should resemble the one shown in *Figure 9.7*. Bills that have been uploaded can be found on the **For review** tab, which provides you with a summary of the information QBO has captured for the bill. Bills on the **For review** tab have not been recorded on the books. Once you've reviewed this information, make any necessary changes; then you can save the bill, which will record it on the books. The **Unpaid** tab lists bills that are recorded on the books but haven't been paid yet. Finally, the **Paid** tab includes bills that have been recorded on the books and paid.

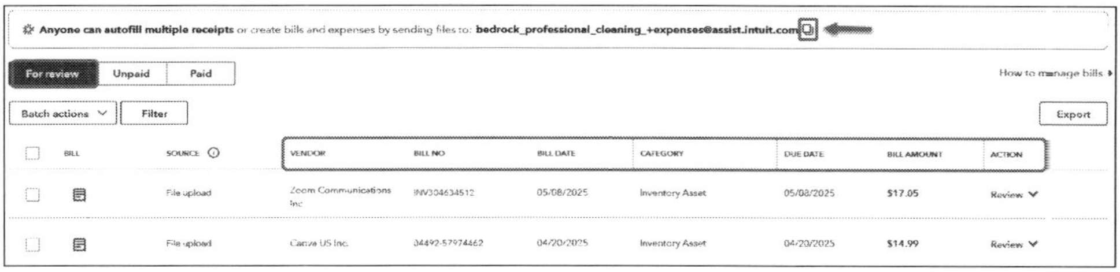

Figure 9.7: Bills for review

6. Click on the **Review** link located to the far right, below the **Action** column (shown in *Figure 9.7*); a snapshot of the bill, along with the fields to be completed, will appear:

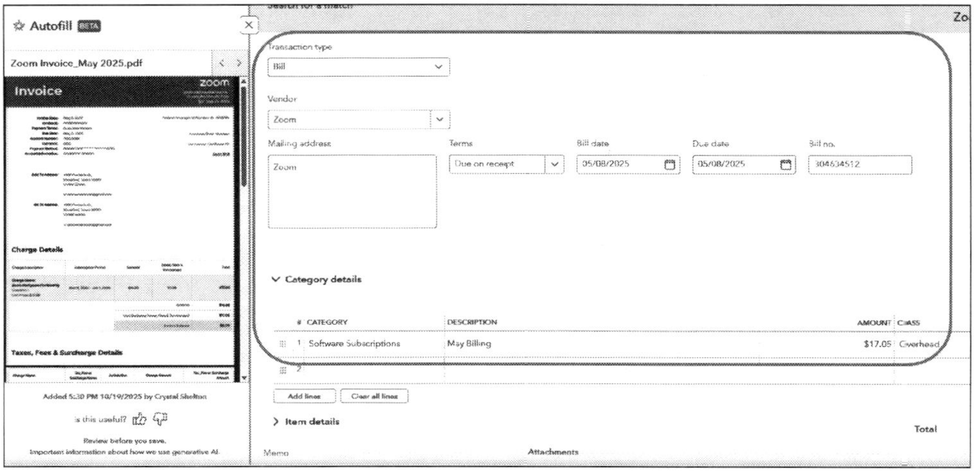

Figure 9.8: Reviewing details of the bill that's been uploaded to QBO

Fill in the following fields:

- **Transaction type**: This field will automatically populate with **Bill**, which is correct for an expense that has not been paid. However, if you have uploaded a receipt or an invoice that has already been paid, click the drop-down arrow and select **Receipt**.
- **Vendor**: This field indicates the vendor or supplier whom you need to pay. In our example, this would be **Zoom**. If Zoom is not already set up in QBO, you can easily click on the drop-down menu and select **Add Vendor** to add Zoom to the vendor list.
- **Terms**: Select the correct payment terms from the drop-down menu. In our example, the terms are **Due on receipt**.
- **Bill date**: The date of the bill is reflected in this field. Notice that QBO has completed this field for us. In our example, the bill date is **05/08/2025**.
- **Due date**: This field has also been completed by QBO. In our example, the due date is the same as the bill date, **05/08/2025**, since our terms are due upon receipt.
- **Bill no.**: The invoice or bill number belongs in this field. As shown, QBO has automatically populated this field. In our example, the bill number is **304634512**.
- **Category details**: This field has been populated by QBO based on the account previously used to pay this type of bill. Similar to the due date, you can edit this field if needed. In our example, the category is **Software Subscriptions**.
- **DESCRIPTION**: This field is *optional*. In our example, the description is **May Billing**.
- **AMOUNT**: This field has been automatically populated by QBO. In our example, the amount is **$17.05**.
- **CLASS**: Select the appropriate business segment this expense is related to. If an expense is not directly related to one business segment, you can create an **Overhead** class, as we have done in our example.
- **Memo**: Any additional information you would like to add can be added in this field. This field is for internal purposes only, so your vendor/supplier will not be able to view this information.
- **Attachments**: Similar to the sales transactions we covered in *Chapter 7, Recording Sales Transactions in QuickBooks Online*, you can attach supporting documents such as receipts, contracts, and expense transactions. Since we uploaded a bill, that bill will automatically be included as an attachment when we save this transaction.

7. In the bottom-right corner of the screen, you have the option to save as a draft, which will save the changes that you have made but not record the bill on the books. The other option is **Save and close**, which will save your changes and record the bill on the books. Click the arrow to the right of the **Save and close** button; you will have the option to save and schedule the bill for payment.
8. Select **Save and close**; when you return to the bill center, you will see that this bill has moved from the **For Review** tab to the **Unpaid Bills** tab.

> If this purchase was made on behalf of a customer, you can turn on the **Track expenses and items by customer** setting. This will add a customer column to the bill form, allowing you to select the customer. If you would like to bill the customer back for this purchase, this feature will allow you to select a billable option. When you create a new invoice for the customer, QBO will automatically ask you whether you would like to add the unbilled expense item to the invoice.

Now that you know how to add your bills to QBO, we will discuss how to pay bills.

Paying bills in QuickBooks

Once you've entered a bill into QuickBooks, you will need to pay it before the due date. Paying bills in QuickBooks will ensure that the A/P balance is always up to date. It will also allow you to run reports and see which bills have been paid or need to be paid.

Follow these steps to pay bills in QBO:

1. From the dashboard, click on **Expenses & Pay Bills** and select **Pay bills**, as shown here:

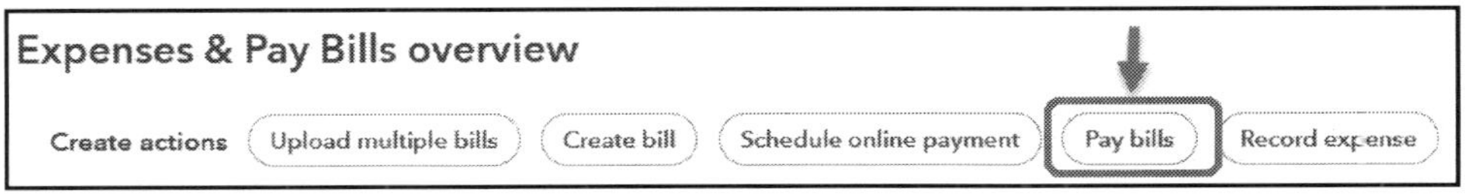

Figure 9.9: Navigating to Pay bills from the Vendors menu

2. The **Pay Bills** window will appear:

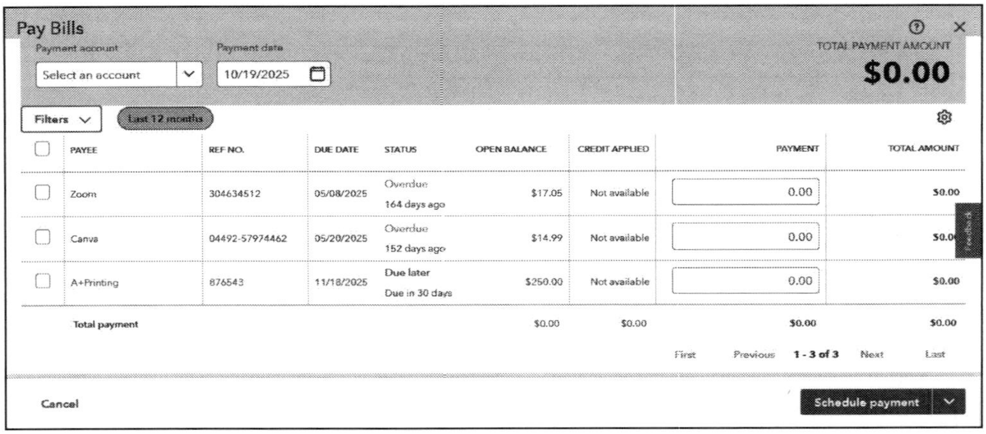

Figure 9.10: The Pay Bills window appears

3. Fill in the fields indicated in the following figure to record the bill payment:

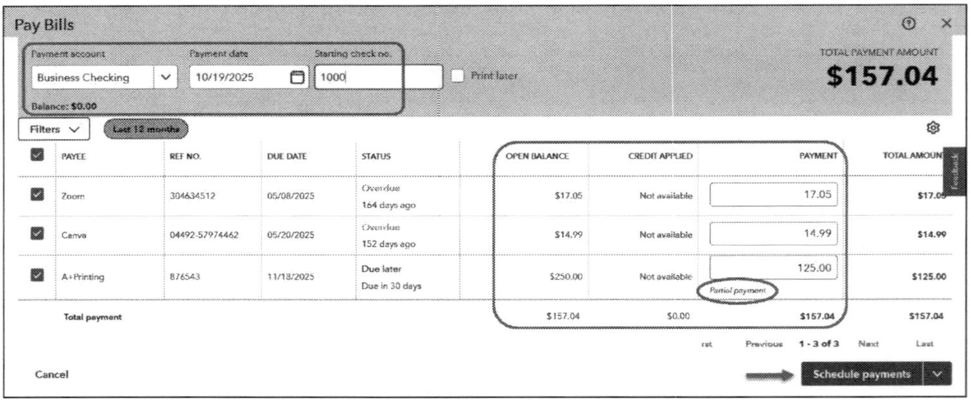

Figure 9.11: Completing the Pay Bills form

The following is a brief description of the fields in the **Pay Bills** form; all fields must be completed:

- **Payment account**: Select the bank or credit card account from which you want to deduct this bill payment. **Business Checking** is the account that's been selected in our example.
- **Balance**: The amount below the payment account is the current balance per QuickBooks. In our example, the available amount is **$0.00**.

> Please note that if you have banking transactions that have not been reviewed and added to QuickBooks, this balance will not match your actual bank account. Be sure to double-check your actual bank balance before making payments.

- **Payment date**: Select the date on which you will pay this bill. If you're writing a check, this will be the check date. The payment date is **10/19/2025** in our example.
- **Starting check no.**: If you are writing a check, make sure the check number is the next available number. The starting check number is `1000` in our example.
- **Print later**: Put a checkmark in this box if you don't plan to print the check now, but will print it later. We will show you how to print checks later in this chapter.
- **PAYEE**: This field will include a list of the payees with open bills. To select a bill for payment, put a checkmark in the box to the left of the **PAYEE** field. In our example, we have three payees with open bills: **Zoom**, **Canva**, and **A+Printing**.

> If you have more than one bill for a vendor and your vendor prefers separate checks for each invoice, select the first bill and save it, and then select each bill one at a time, clicking **Save** in between each. Then, when you print checks, there will be separate checks for each bill. An example where this might be useful is paying utility bills. Many utility companies prefer separate checks per account for which you are paying a bill.

- **REF NO.**: This field will include the invoice number (or bill number) that was entered when the bill was saved in QuickBooks. In our example, **304634512** is the reference number for the Zoom bill, **04492-57974462** is the reference number for the Canva bill, and **876543** is the reference number for the A+Printing bill.
- **DUE DATE**: This field will automatically populate with the due date that was entered when the bill was saved in QuickBooks. In our example, the due date for the Zoom bill is **05/08/2025**, the due date for the Canva bill is **05/20/2025**, and the due date for the A+Printing bill is **11/18/2025**.

- **OPEN BALANCE**: This field will automatically be populated with the unpaid amount of the bill. The open balance for the Zoom bill is **$17.05**, the open balance for the Canva bill is **$14.99**, and the open balance for the A+Printing bill is **$25.00**.
- **CREDIT APPLIED**: If you have any open credits for a vendor, you will see them listed in this column. You can choose to use the credit or leave it and use it later on. In our example, none of the bills have an open credit at this time. You can manually edit the amount of the credit that you want to apply to a bill, or allow the full credit to be applied.
- **PAYMENT**: Enter the amount you would like to pay in this field. You can pay the bill in full or make a partial payment. If you make a partial payment, QuickBooks will keep track of the remaining balance due for you to pay in the future. We are going to pay the Zoom and Canva bills in full since they are overdue. We will make a partial payment for the A+Printing bill of **$125.00**.
- **TOTAL AMOUNT**: This column is automatically calculated for you. You cannot edit this field. The total amount in our example is **$157.04**.

4. You have the option to pay your bills online using your bank account (**Automated Clearing House**, or **ACH**) or debit/credit card information. There is a basic plan, which is free, and two paid plans starting at $15.00/month, plus transaction fees. To learn more about bill payment services, select the **Schedule Payments Online** button. However, if you prefer to manually write checks or print them from QuickBooks, click on the arrow to the right of **Schedule Payments Online** and select **Save**. We will cover how to write checks in QuickBooks later in this chapter.
5. Let's look at the transaction journal entry that is recorded behind the scenes when a bill payment is made. From the dashboard, navigate to your bill payments by going to **Expenses & Pay Bills | Expense transactions**. The list of expenses recorded in QBO will appear:

☐	DATE	TYPE	NO.	PAYEE	CATEGORY	TOTAL	ACTION
☐	10/19/2025	Bill Payment	1002	A+Printing		-$125.00	View/Edit
☐	10/19/2025	Bill Payment	1001	Canva		-$14.99	View/Edit
☐	10/19/2025	Bill Payment	1000	Zoom		-$17.05	View/Edit
☐	10/19/2025	Bill	876543	A+Printing	Printing costs	$250.00	Schedule payment
☐	05/08/2025	Bill	304634512	Zoom	Software Subscriptions	$17.05	View/Edit
☐	04/20/2025	Bill	04492-57974462	Canva	Software Subscriptions	$14.99	View/Edit
		Total				$125.00	

Figure 9.12: Navigating to bill payments

Figure 9.12 includes a list of all expenses that were previously recorded. As you can see, the date, transaction type, bill number, check number, payee, category, and total amount of the expense are listed. In the **Action** column located to the far right, you can view/edit a transaction, schedule a payment, or click on the drop-down arrow and choose **Delete** or **Void**.

6. Click on **View/Edit** for the **A+Printing** bill payment. The following window will appear

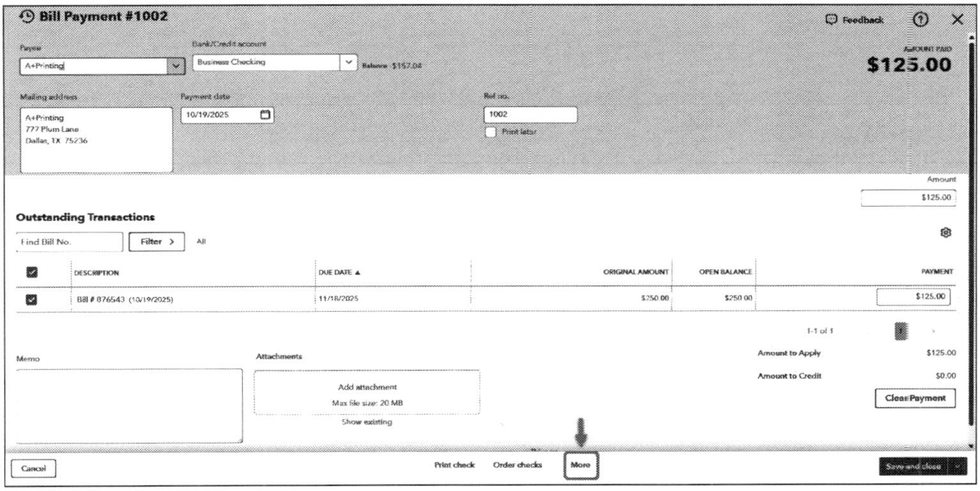

Figure 9.13: Viewing the Bill Payment transaction

7. Select **More** at the very bottom of the screen, as shown in *Figure 9.13*; the transaction journal shown in *Figure 9.14* will appear.

The following report shows the journal entry that's recorded for the A+Printing bill payment if you are on an accrual basis:

Transaction Journal
Bedrock Professional Cleaning Services, LLC
All Dates

Transaction date	Transaction type	Num	Name	Memo/Description	Full name	Debit	Credit
2 (2)							
11/16/2025	Bill Payment (Check)	1	A+Printing	-	Business Checking	-	125.00
11/16/2025	Bill Payment (Check)	1	A+Printing	-	Accounts Payable (A/P)	125.00	-
Total for 2						$125.00	$125.00
TOTAL						$125.00	$125.00

Figure 9.14: Journal entry to pay bills

When you pay a bill in QuickBooks, it only has an impact on the Balance Sheet report. The A/P balance goes down because you no longer owe your vendor for the bill, and the business checking account goes down because a payment has been made. If you pay the bill with a credit card, the credit card balance goes up, which increases liabilities.

In our example, the debit to A/P decreases total liabilities on the Balance Sheet report by **$125.00**. In addition, the credit to the business checking account decreases the total assets on the Balance Sheet report by **$125.00**. If you are on a cash basis, the debit would be to an expense account, such as printing, and reproduction costs and the credit would be to the business checking account.

In this way, paying bills in QuickBooks will give you access to detailed information about your expenses. You can run reports to show how much you are spending, which vendors you purchase from, and how often you purchase from them. These reports will help you control what you are spending your money on, which allows you to properly manage your expenses. In *Chapter 10, Vendor and Expenses Reports in QuickBooks Online*, we'll cover the key reports you will need to stay on top of vendor bills and expenses.

There may be times when you need to request a credit from a vendor who did not deliver as promised. We'll cover how to enter vendor credits next.

Entering vendor credits into QuickBooks

If you overpay a vendor or receive a credit for canceling an order or services, you can enter the credit memo into QuickBooks. By entering the credit memo into QBO, you can easily apply it to an unpaid bill or a bill for future purchases from the vendor. However, if you don't plan to order from that vendor again, you should request a refund. In our example, Bedrock Professional Cleaning Services decided that they did not need 100 flyers after all, and that 50 was enough. If you recall, they paid 50% of the bill received from A+Printing, and there is an outstanding balance of $125.00. We are going to apply the credit memo received to the open balance on the books for A+Printing.

To enter vendor credits into QBO, you will need to complete the following steps:

1. Navigate to the Vendors Center from the dashboard by going to **Expenses & Bills | Vendors** and the following will display:

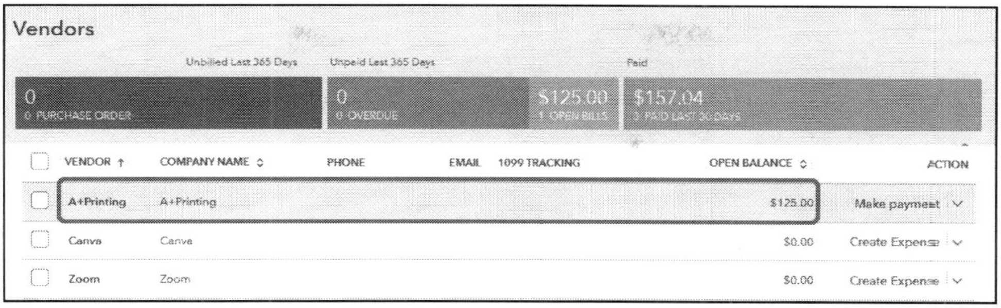

Figure 9.15: Navigating to the Vendors Center

As shown in *Figure 9.15*, A+Printing has an open balance of $125.00. We will enter a credit memo to offset this amount.

2. From the **+Create** menu, select **Vendor credit** (located below the **Vendors** column), as shown here:

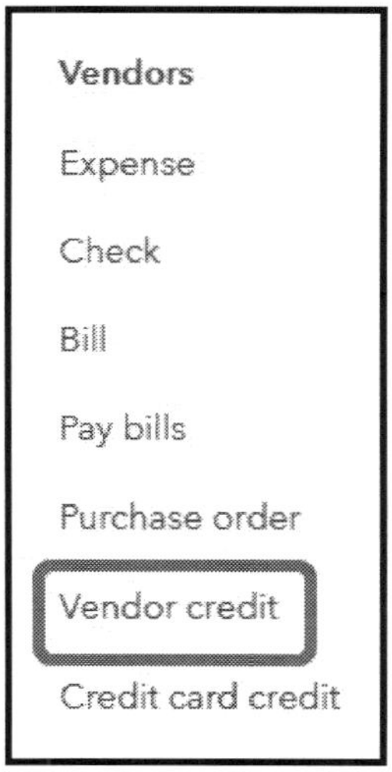

Figure 9.16: Navigating to the Vendor Credit form

3. The **Vendor Credit** form will appear. Fill in the fields in this form, as shown here:

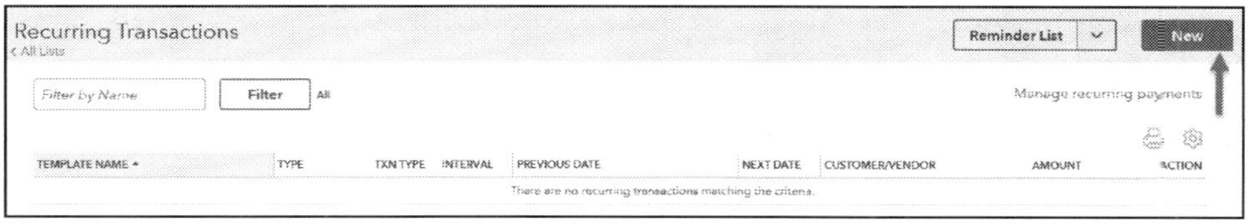

Figure 9.17: Clicking New to create a new Recurring Transactions template

The following is a brief description of the key fields in the **Vendor Credit** form. All fields must be completed, except for the **DESCRIPTION** field, which is optional but recommended:

- **Vendor**: Select a vendor from the drop-down menu. In our example, **A+Printing** is the vendor.
- **Mailing address**: This field will automatically populate for vendors you have previously created in QuickBooks. If this is a new vendor, you can enter the address in this field. In our example, the address is **777 Plum Lane, Dallas, TX 75236**.
- **Payment date**: Enter the date that appears on the vendor credit memo. Our payment date is `10/20/2025`.
- **Ref no.**: The reference number is the vendor credit memo number assigned by the vendor supplier. If the vendor credit memo does not include a unique number, create one. Having a unique vendor credit memo number allows QuickBooks to track vendor credits and alert you if a duplicate number is being used. If a vendor credit memo does not include a number, I typically use the letters `CM`, short for credit memo, and the original bill number paid. The vendor credit memo number in our example is **CM876543**.
- **Category details**: Complete this section if you have purchased services or non-inventory expenses from the vendor. In our example, we have selected **Printing costs**, which is what was on the original bill.
- **Item details**: Complete this section if you have purchased an item added to QuickBooks that you need to keep track of quantity and/or costs for. From the drop-down menu, select the product/service purchased. If the item has not been added to QuickBooks, you can do so on this screen by selecting the **Add new** option. The new item window will appear so that you can complete the item setup. For more information on adding a new item to the products and services list, see *Chapter 5, Managing Customer and Vendor Lists.*
- **DESCRIPTION**: Enter a brief description of why the credit memo was issued. In our example, the description is `To reverse remainder of bill #876543 due to cancellation of 50 flyers`.
- **AMOUNT**: In our example, the total amount of the credit is **$125.00**.
- **MEMO**: Include a brief description of why the credit memo was issued and which bill it will be applied to. In our example, the memo is `Credit to apply to bill #876543, we reduced order from 100 flyers to 50 flyers`.

- **ATTACHMENT**: For documentation purposes, it's a good idea to attach a copy of the vendor credit document received from the vendor. I also recommend keeping a copy of all documents in a cloud-based storage software such as Dropbox or Google Drive for safekeeping.

If you receive the credit before paying the original bill in full (as we have done), when you record the vendor credit into QBO, the A/P account will be reduced by the credit, and the expense account will be reduced by the same amount. The A/P account will impact the total liabilities on the Balance Sheet report, and the expense account will reduce expenses on the profit and loss report.

The journal entry that will be recorded in QuickBooks for the preceding vendor credit is shown here:

Transaction Journal
Bedrock Professional Cleaning Services, LLC
All Dates

Transaction Date	Transaction Type	Num	Name	Memo/Description	Full Name	Debit	Credit
9 (2)							
10/20/2025	Vendor Credit	CM876543	A+Printing	Credit to apply to bill #876543, ...	Accounts Payable (A/P)	125.00	-
10/20/2025	Vendor Credit	CM876543	A+Printing	To reverse remainder of bill #87...	Printing costs	-	125.00
Total for 9						$125.00	$125.00
TOTAL						**$125.00**	**$125.00**

Figure 9.18: Journal entry to record a vendor credit

In our example, the debit to **Accounts Payable** decreases the current liabilities on the Balance Sheet report by **$125.00**, and the credit to **Printing Costs** decreases the total expenses on the profit and loss report by **$125.00**. Creating recurring expenses can save you a lot of time, so let's cover this next.

Managing recurring expenses

In this section, we will show you how to create a template for recurring (repeat) expenses. Most businesses purchase goods and services from the same vendors. For example, rent and utilities are examples of recurring expenses that are generally paid monthly. Instead of creating these expenses from scratch each month, you can create a recurring expense, which is a template you can save with the vendor, amount, account, and other pertinent information.

When you are ready to pay a recurring expense, you can schedule the expense to be recorded automatically on a certain day. You can manually generate the expense when you need to pay it, or you can have QuickBooks send you an alert when it's time to make a payment. Using recurring expense templates will save you time and will reduce the amount of manual data entry required.

Follow these steps to create a recurring expense in QuickBooks:

1. Navigate to the gear icon and select **Recurring Transactions** from the **Lists** column, as indicated here:

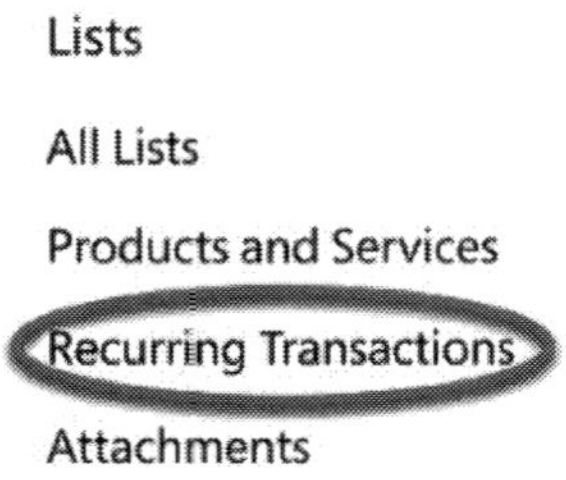

Figure 9.19: Selecting Recurring Transactions from the Lists menu

2. Click the **New** button in the top-right corner:

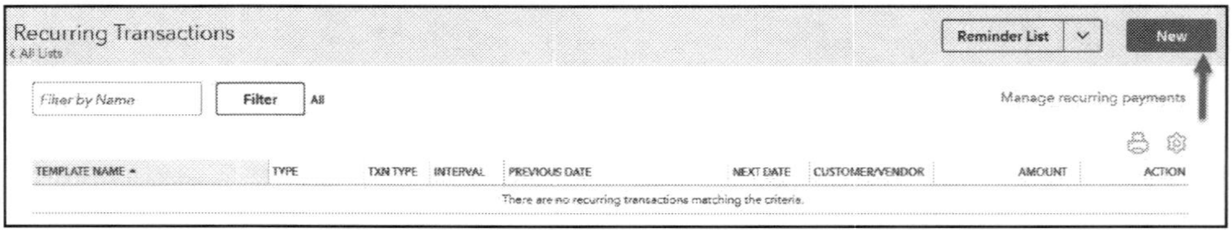

Figure 9.20: Clicking New to create a new Recurring Transactions template

3. Select the transaction type from the drop-down menu, as indicated in *Figure 9.21*, and click the **OK** button:

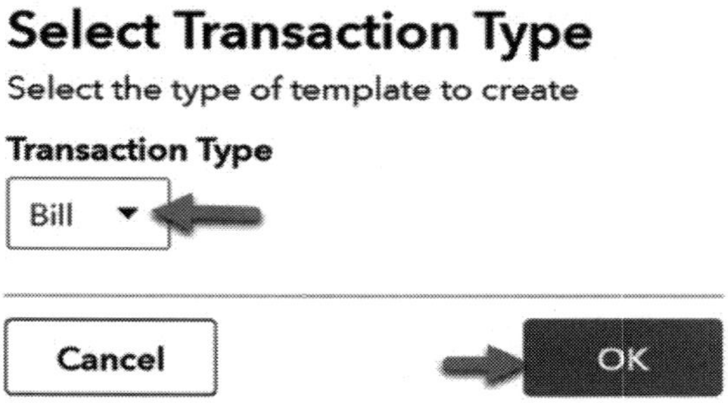

Figure 9.21: Selecting the transaction type for a Recurring Transactions template

You can create a recurring transaction for several different types of transactions. The options available from the drop-down include **Bill**, **Check**, **Credit card credit**, **Credit memo**, **Deposit**, **Estimate**, **Expense**, **Invoice**, **Journal entry**, and a few others. While the screens may differ slightly, they will be very similar to what you can see in this example.

Bedrock Professional Cleaning Services would like to create a recurring template for their monthly rent expense.

4. From the dropdown, select **Expense**. A blank **Recurring Transactions** template will appear, called **Recurring Expense**. Fill in the fields like so:

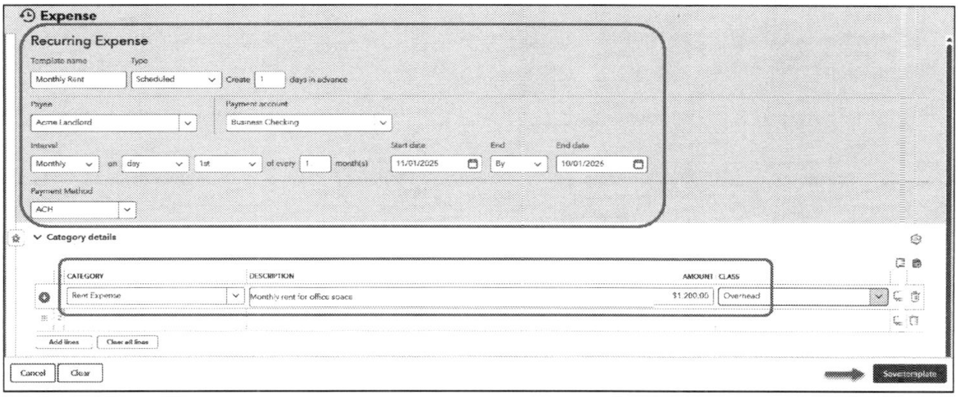

Figure 9.22: Filling in the Recurring Expense template

The following is a brief description of the information required to complete the **Recurring Expense** template:

- **Template name**: This field should include the type of expense or the payee's name. **Monthly Rent** is the template name in our example.
- **Type**: From the drop-down menu, you can select **Scheduled**, **Reminder**, or **Unscheduled**. **Scheduled** is the type of template we are setting up.
- **Create X days in advance**: QuickBooks will create the transaction in advance of the due date. 1 day in advance has been selected in our example.
- **Vendor**: Select the payee from the drop-down menu. If you have not added vendors to QuickBooks, you can add a new vendor by selecting **Add new** from the drop-down field. **Acme Landlord** is the vendor in our example.
- **Interval**: This field refers to how often you would like to create this recurring transaction. The options are **Daily**, **Weekly**, **Monthly**, or **Yearly**. **Monthly** is the interval that's been selected in our example.
- **Start date/End**: Select the date on which you would like to start using the recurring transaction. If applicable, you can select an end date or select **None**. The start date is **10/01/2025**, and the end date is **10/01/2026** in our example.

- **Payment Method**: From the drop-down, select the payment method used to pay this expense. In our example, the monthly rent is automatically deducted from the bank account, so **ACH** is the payment method in our example.
- **CATEGORY**: From the drop-down menu, select the account that accurately describes the type of purchase made. The category is **Rent Expense** for our example.
- **DESCRIPTION**: Include a brief description of the expense in this field. `Monthly rent for office space` is the description in our case.
- **AMOUNT**: Enter the amount of the expense in this field. The amount is `$1200.00` in our example.

5. Be sure to click **Save template** when you are done. After saving the template, the **Recurring Transactions** template list will appear, as indicated here:

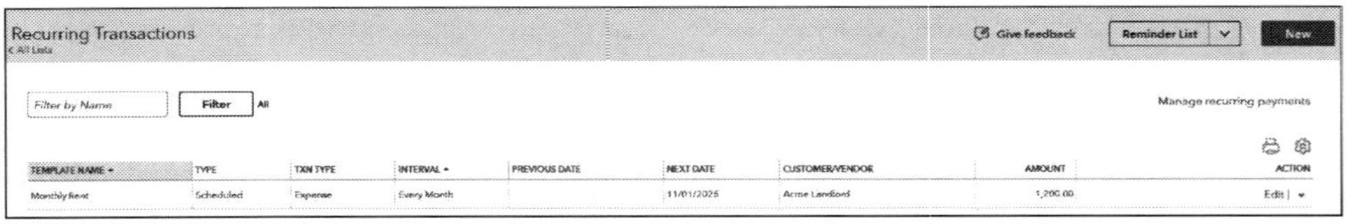

Figure 9.23: The Recurring Transactions template (Recurring Expense)

6. In the **Recurring Transactions** template list, you will see the information previously entered in the template. The following information appears in *Figure 9.23*:

- **TEMPLATE NAME: Monthly Rent.**
- **TYPE: Scheduled.**
- **TXN TYPE: Expense.**
- **INTERVAL: Every Month.**
- **NEXT DATE: 11/01/2025.**
- **CUSTOMER/VENDOR: Acme Landlord.**
- **AMOUNT: 1,200.00.**
- **ACTION**: From the drop-down menu in this column, you can choose **Edit**, **Use** (record), **Duplicate**, **Pause**, **Skip**, or **Delete**. **Edit** simply allows you to make changes to the template; **Duplicate** allows you to create a template with the same information; **Pause** allows you to stop the recurring transaction temporarily; **Skip** allows you to skip a recurring transaction; and **Delete** allows you to delete the template.

- In addition to creating recurring transactions such as expenses, you can also create the following types of recurring transactions:
- **Bill: Schedule payment for purchases made on credit with specific payment terms (Net 30, Net 60, etc.).**
- **Check**: This is for payments made via check for products or services purchased.
- **Credit card credit**: This is money that was refunded to you from a previous credit card charge. It could also be a cashback rebate given to you by your credit card merchant for meeting a certain spending threshold.
- **Credit memo**: A credit memo is issued to customers for a product they have returned or for services that were not provided.
- **Deposit**: A deposit is money received from customers, which is then deposited into your bank account. If you have customers who pay via wire transfer or ACH bank transfer periodically, you could set these deposits up as recurring.
- **Estimate**: An estimate is a bid or quote, created to provide customers with an approximate cost of your products or services.
- **Invoice**: An invoice is a sales form, used to record the sale of products or services provided on credit.
- **Journal entry**: A journal entry form is used to make adjustments to the financial statements before closing the books.
- **Refund**: A product returned by you or your customer will result in a refund of the payment that was made for the returned goods or unfulfilled services.
- **Sales receipt**: A sales receipt is used to record sales whereby payment is made immediately by the customer (for example, businesses such as clothing stores or restaurants).
- **Transfer**: A transfer is used to move money between bank accounts, such as business checking and savings accounts.
- **Vendor credit**: A vendor credit is a refund issued to you by a vendor supplier for a product you have returned or for services that were not performed.

> Recurring transactions are ideal for loan payments or other cash disbursements for which you may not receive a monthly bill.

If you need to pay a bill that was unexpected or past due, *you don't need to enter it as a bill and then pay it*. Instead, you can pay it with a debit or credit card and categorize it when it comes into the banking center, *or* you can go directly to the check register and write a check. We will cover writing checks in the next section.

Writing checks

So far, we have discussed how to pay expenses by entering them as bills and paying them at a later date, and how to set up recurring expenses. A third way in which you can record expenses for your business is by writing checks. The benefit of writing checks directly in QuickBooks is that you don't have to waste time manually writing a check.

Instead, you can create checks and print them directly from QuickBooks. This is ideal for vendors that typically don't accept debit or credit card payments, such as the storage facility that Bedrock Professional Cleaning Services uses to store its supplies. Let's write a check to pay the monthly storage fee of $250.00.

Follow these steps to write checks in QBO:

1. Click on the **+ New** button and select **Check** in the **Vendors** column, as indicated here:

Figure 9.24: Navigating to Check

2. The following screenshot shows the fields of the **Check** form that need to be filled in:

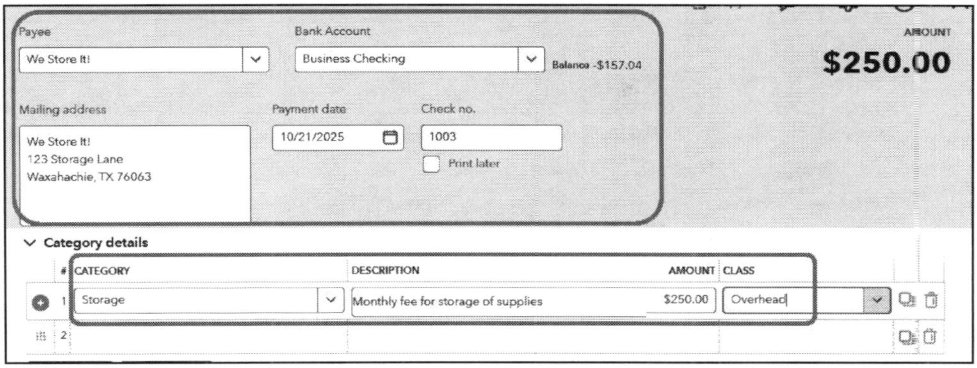

Figure 9.25: Completing the Check form

The following is a brief description of what information you will see in the **Check** form, as well as what to include (if applicable):

- **Payee**: From the drop-down menu, select the vendor to whom you are making a payment. If you haven't added vendors, you can do so by selecting **Add new** from the drop-down menu. **We Store It!** is the payee in our example.
- **Bank Account**: This field will automatically populate with your business checking account. However, if you have more than one checking account, be sure to select the correct account from the drop-down menu. **Business Checking** is the bank account in our example.
- **Balance**: Based on the bank account selected, you will see the current balance (per QuickBooks) of the business checking account you have selected. The current balance in the business checking account is **-$157.04** in our case.
- **Mailing address**: This field will automatically be populated with the information on file for the payee. In our case, the mailing address is **123 Storage Lane, Waxahachie, TX 76063.**
- **Payment date**: This date should reflect the check date. In our example, the payment date is **10/21/2025**.

- **Check no.**: The check number will automatically be populated with the next available check number. The check number is **1003** in our example.

> You can also use the **Check** form to record expenses paid with a debit card. Instead of entering a check number in the **Check no.** field, you would use **DB** or **Debit**, indicating the expense was paid with a debit card. To record ACH transactions, you would put **ACH** in the **Check no.** field.

- **Category details:**
    - **CATEGORY**: Select the category (account) that best describes the items purchased. In our example, the category is **Storage**.
    - **DESCRIPTION**: Enter a detailed description of the items purchased. **Monthly fee for storage of supplies** is the description in our example.
    - **AMOUNT**: Enter the amount of the purchase. The amount in our example is **$250.00**.
    - **CLASS**: If applicable, enter the business segment this purchase applies to. In our example, the class is **Overhead**.

When entering a check into QuickBooks, it can have an impact on accounts that appear on both the balance sheet and the profit and loss (income statement). The balance sheet will always be affected because the bank account is included in the assets section of the balance sheet. However, the profit and loss will only be affected if you are buying services or purchasing items that you can expense, such as office supplies. Otherwise, if you purchase a product for resale (inventory), it will only have an impact on the balance sheet.

The following screenshot shows the journal entry that was recorded for the check in *Figure 9.25*:

Transaction Journal
Bedrock Professional Cleaning Services, LLC
All Dates

Transaction Date	Transaction Type	Num	Name	Memo/Description	Full Name	Debit	Credit
11 (2)							
10/21/2025	Check	1003	We Store It!	-	Business Checking	-	250.00
10/21/2025	Check	1003	We Store It!	Monthly fee for storage of supp...	Storage	250.00	-
Total for 11						$250.00	$250.00
TOTAL						$250.00	$250.00

Figure 9.26: Journal entry to record payment of a bill by check

In our example, the **Storage** expense increased by **$250.00**, which increases expenses on the profit and loss (income statement). The **Business Checking** account decreased by **$250.00**, which means assets have gone down on the Balance Sheet report.

After entering a check, you can choose to print the check immediately or wait and print a batch of checks later on. In the next section, we will show you how to print checks.

Printing checks

To print checks, you must purchase check stock that is compatible with QBO. You can order checks from a variety of places, such as your financial institution or directly from Intuit. Visit the *Intuit Checks and Supplies* (`https://intuitmarket.intuit.com/checks`) website to learn more.

Follow these steps to print checks:

1. Click on the **+ New** button and select **Print Checks** in the **Vendors** column, as indicated here:

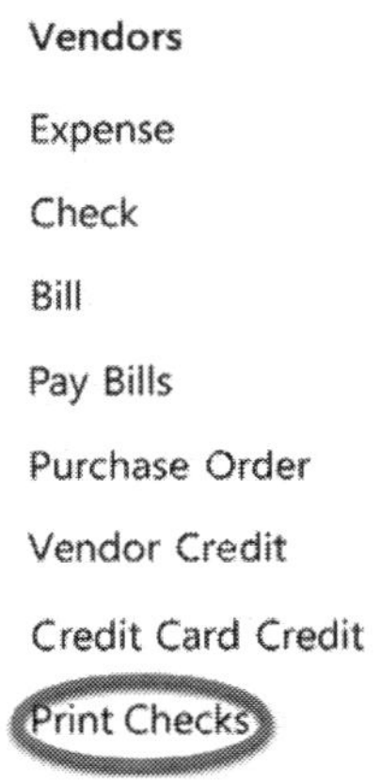

Figure 9.27: Navigating to Print Checks

2. Follow the steps on the next screen to ensure that your printer is set up properly:

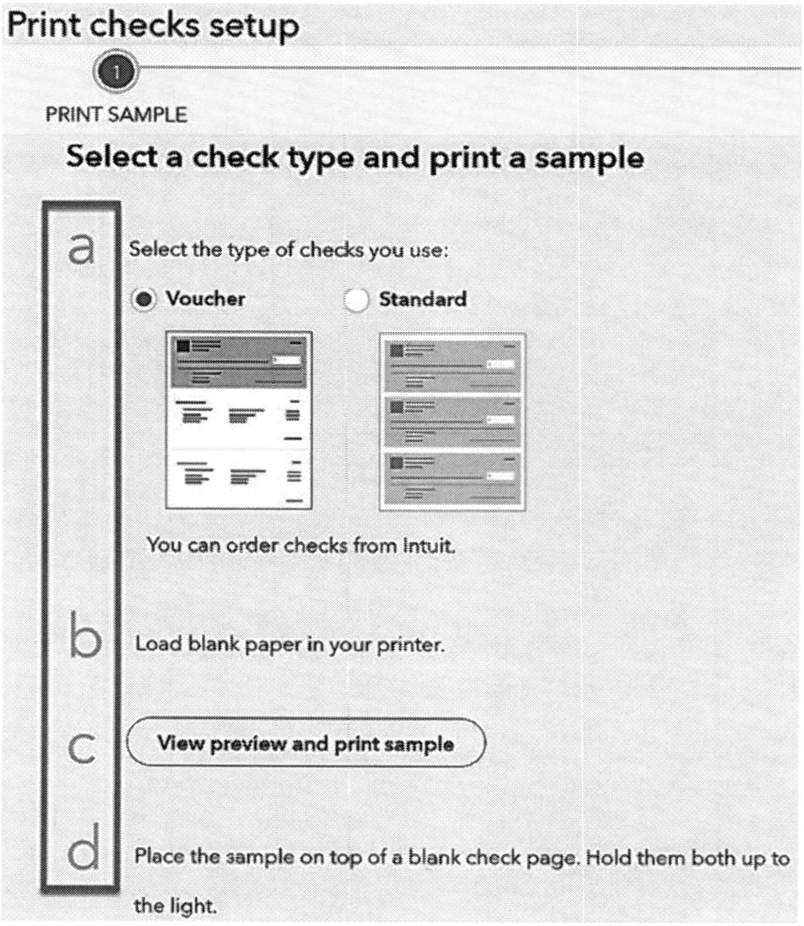

Figure 9.28: Selecting a check type for printing checks

We can choose from the following options:

a. **Select the type of checks you use**: There are two types of checks: **Voucher** and **Standard.** The **Voucher** check includes one check per page and two printed vouchers (one for you and one for the payee). The **Standard** check includes three checks per page and no voucher.

> A voucher is a printout of the payment details, including the bill number, amount, and check number.

b. **Load blank paper in your printer**: Before loading real check stock, run a test using a blank piece of paper. Draw an arrow on the top of the first sheet of paper to see how the information will print; this will show you how to load the check stock in your printer.

c. **View preview and print sample**: You can preview a sample check to see whether it is aligned properly. If not, follow the on-screen instructions to fix any issues before using real check stock. Checks will print to a preview screen where you can select your printer.

As discussed, printing checks directly from QuickBooks will save you time when you reconcile your bank account. Since expenses paid with a check are automatically recorded in QuickBooks when you save the check, you won't have to worry about manually entering them later on. One way to have quick access to source documents is to attach receipts and bills to transactions by using the capture and categorize receipts feature. We will discuss this shortly.

Let's say you have pizza delivered to the office and you need to quickly print one check. Click the **+ New** button, select **Check**, enter the payment details, and select **Print check** at the bottom of the screen.

> To eliminate the need for paper checks, envelopes, and postage, QBO Bill Pay or a bill payment app is recommended. This also eliminates your bank account and routing number from being sent out in paper form. Using a bill pay service or paying via ACH is a safeguard for your account information.

Editing, voiding, and deleting expenses

Like most transactions in QuickBooks, you can edit bills up until they are paid. However, after you have paid a bill, you will need to either record a credit memo if you overpaid or request a new bill if you have underpaid. You can still make changes to a paid bill if the changes do not affect the amount. To edit a bill, you need to go to the Vendor Center, select the vendor, and then click on the bill you wish to make changes to. After making the necessary changes, save the bill and close it.

You can also edit checks similarly. So long as you haven't printed the check, you can make any changes necessary. Navigate to the check register, locate the check, and make the necessary changes. After you have printed a check, you will need to void it if it is incorrect. From the check register, select the check that needs to be voided. Click the **Edit** option; the check will display on your screen.

At the very bottom of the page, you will see a tab that says **More**. Click on it; the following menu will appear:

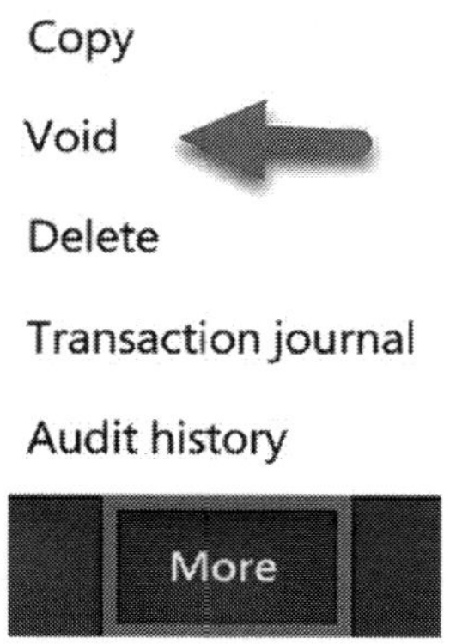

Figure 9.29: Reaching the option to void an expense via the More button

For expenses in general, if you have not closed the books or reconciled the bank account for the period, you can make changes to expenses that were previously recorded.

> If you have closed the books or reconciled the bank account for the period, you *cannot* make changes to the transaction date or amount. If a correction to the books is required, you will need to consult with your accountant to discuss recording a journal entry. See *Chapter 16, Closing the Books in QuickBooks Online*, to learn more about journal entries.

Capturing and categorizing receipts and bills

Receipt capture allows you to attach receipts and bills to transactions in QuickBooks. As a result, you will be able to quickly access source documents when needed. This feature works in two different ways. First, you can attach receipts and bills to transactions previously entered into QBO. Second, you can use receipt capture to record a transaction for the first time. Of course, you can use both methods interchangeably.

Perform the following steps to capture a receipt or bill:

1. Navigate to **Accounting** and select **Receipts**.
2. The following screen will appear:

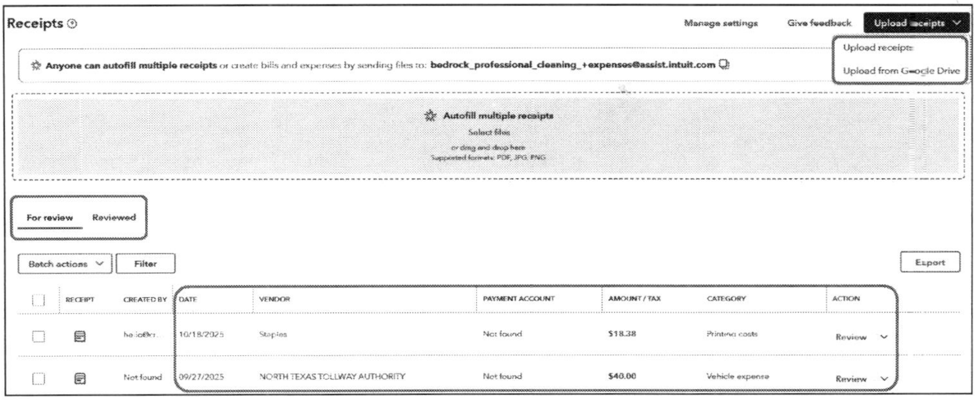

Figure 9.30: Reviewing and uploading receipts to QBO

3. There are three options available for capturing receipts:

   - **Upload from computer**: If a receipt is saved to your computer, select this option and navigate to where the receipt is located on your computer.
   - **Upload from Google Drive**: If the receipt is located in your Google Drive account, you can access it by clicking on the **Upload receipts** button and selecting **Upload from Google Drive**, as shown in *Figure 9.30*. Follow the on-screen instructions to connect Google Drive to QBO.
   - **Forward from email**: At the top of this page, you will have a custom email address that is assigned to your business. You can give this email address to anyone you would like to have the ability to forward bills, receipts, and expenses to QBO. To the far right of the email address is the copy symbol, which allows you to easily copy and paste it into an email or document so that it can be shared with authorized users.

> Keep in mind that for each of the receipt capture options, there should only be *one receipt per file*. If you try to include more than one receipt in a file, QuickBooks will not be able to process the receipt capture.

4. Once you've added receipts to QuickBooks, they will show up in the **For review** section, just below the receipt capture options, as shown in *Figure 9.30*.
5. Click on the **Review** link in the **ACTION** column located on the far right; the following information will be displayed:

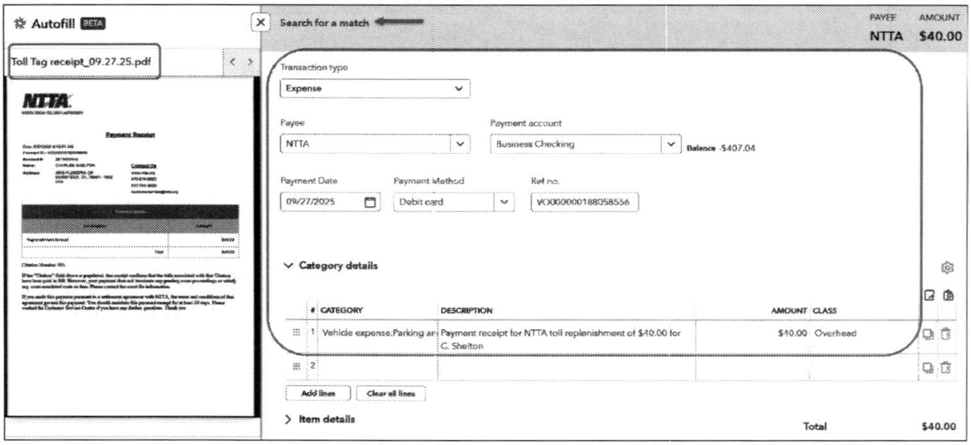

Figure 9.31: Reviewing an uploaded receipt in QBO

6. QBO will read the information from the receipt and complete the fields for you. However, you should review all fields for accuracy and edit any fields that are blank or incorrect. Once you are satisfied with the information, you have the following options:
   - **Save as draft**: This option will allow you to save any changes you have made, but it will not record the expense in your books. Choose this option if you are not ready to save the transaction and plan to return to do so.
   - **Save and close**: This option will save your changes and record the expense on the books. QBO will automatically attach a copy of this receipt to the transaction for future reference.

> When reviewing receipts, keep in mind that if the expense was paid with a business checking account, or a business debit or credit card that is linked to QBO in the bank feed, you do not want to save this transaction; instead, you must choose the **Search for a match** option at the very top of the screen. This will allow you to search for the matching bank feed transaction. If you do not search for a match but you save the transaction, QBO will record this expense twice: both here in the receipt capture and in the bank feed. This will cause expenses to be overstated on the profit and loss statement.

To summarize, we have covered how to capture and categorize receipts and bills, which allows you to attach source documents, such as bills, to existing transactions. In addition, you can create new transactions using this feature, which will save you the time you normally would have spent entering the data manually. *Please note that bills and receipts MUST be reviewed by someone for them to be cleared out of this area. They will remain in this section until someone reviews them and takes action.*

Tracking mileage

If you need to keep track of mileage for business, you can do so using the QBO app. The QBO app will automatically track all mileage and upload it to QBO. From there, you can designate which miles are for business versus personal use. In addition, if you forget to use the app, you can also manually add trips to QBO.

Follow these steps to navigate to mileage tracking:

1. From the dashboard, click on **Expenses & bills**.
2. Select **Mileage**; the following screen will appear:

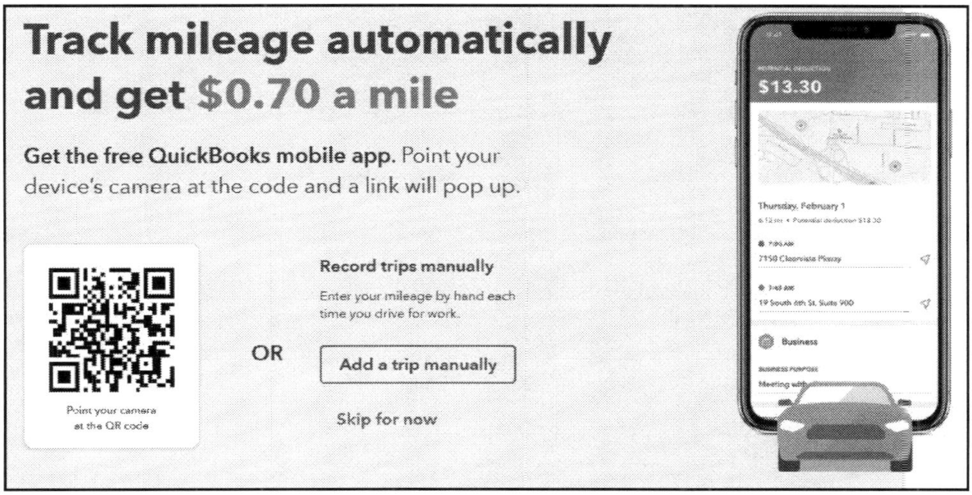

Figure 9.32: Navigating to mileage tracking

3. Point your cellphone camera at the QR code to download the QBO app.

That wraps up how to download the QBO app so that you can start tracking your business mileage automatically, manually, or both.

To demonstrate some of the concepts taught in this chapter and to give you some additional insights not covered, check out my YouTube channel at:

`https://packt.link/du2BR`

Summary

In this chapter, we showed you how to enter and pay your bills, how to enter vendor credits, how to manage recurring expenses, how to write checks, and how to print checks. We also covered the three ways in which you can upload bills and receipts to QuickBooks. Then, we introduced you to an easy way to keep track of mileage to/from business events and your client's offices. Having a good understanding of the various options you have to record your expenses will ensure that they are recorded properly. By recording your expenses promptly, you have a good idea of what your obligations are, which helps you stay on top of your cash outflow.

In the next chapter, we will cover the key reports you need to review to stay on top of the money you owe to vendor suppliers (A/P), as well as have a better understanding of where your money is going.

Next steps

1. Download the QBO app and start uploading your receipts ASAP! You can use the following QR code or the link given here.

   `https://packt.link/25laf`

2. Set up the mileage tracker located within the QBO app.
3. Give your custom email address to all vendors/suppliers so that all bills and receipts of payment can go directly to QBO. Within QBO, navigate to **Expenses & Bills** | **Bills** and copy your custom email address located at the top of the page.
4. Apply for a QBO Bill Pay account so that you can pay your bills directly within QBO. To do so, navigate to **Expenses & Bills** | **Bills**.
5. Make a list of vendors/suppliers that you could set up as recurring and set them up in QBO.
6. If you have a bookkeeper or accountant who manages your books, schedule time to meet with that person each month. However, make sure that you have already reviewed the reports and made a list of your questions *before this meeting*. In other words, schedule your "date" before you meet with your bookkeeper or accountant, if applicable.

10

Vendor and Expenses Reports in QuickBooks Online

Having access to reports that give you detailed insight into what your expenses are, who you are paying, and the amount paid to each vendor will help you control expenses and maintain a profitable business. There are a number of reports in **QuickBooks Online** (**QBO**) that will help you understand what you owe to vendor suppliers and other creditors.

We will dive into the information you can expect to find in each report, how to customize the report, and how to generate reports. We will also discuss ways you can use reports to help you manage your expenses and cash flow. I recommend you run these reports and review them on a weekly basis. Having access to this information will help you manage your cash flow and stay on top of the money that goes out of your business.

All the reports we will cover in this chapter can be sorted in multiple ways by clicking on column headings that contain arrows. You can also export these reports to Excel for additional personalized formatting.

In this chapter, we will focus on the following key reports:

- Understanding the **accounts payable** (A/P) aging report
- Utilizing the unpaid bills report
- Understanding the expense-by-vendor summary report
- Utilizing a bill payments report

The US edition of QBO was used to create this book. If you are using a version that is outside of the US, results may differ.

Understanding the accounts payable (A/P) aging report

An **A/P aging report** groups unpaid bills based on the number of days by which they are outstanding or by which they will be due. In *Chapter 9, Recording Expenses in QuickBooks Online*, we covered how to record expenses. Similar to the A/R aging report that we saw in *Chapter 8, Customer Sales Reports in QuickBooks Online*, there are five main groups of bills: **Current, 1-30 days, 31-60 days, 61-90 days**, and **91 days and over**. QuickBooks calculates the age of a bill by using the bill's due date. To stay on top of bills, business owners should review this report on a weekly basis and take the necessary steps to pay bills that are nearly due. For bills coming due, you should go ahead and process the payment online with your financial institution or write a check directly from QuickBooks to ensure they arrive by the due date. In *Chapter 9, Recording Expenses in QuickBooks Online*, we showed you how to pay bills.

Follow these steps to generate an A/P aging report:

1. Navigate to **Reports** from the left menu bar, as indicated in *Figure 10.1*:

Figure 10.1: Navigating to the Reports Center

2. Scroll down to the **What you owe** section and select **Accounts payable aging summary**, as indicated in *Figure 10.2*:

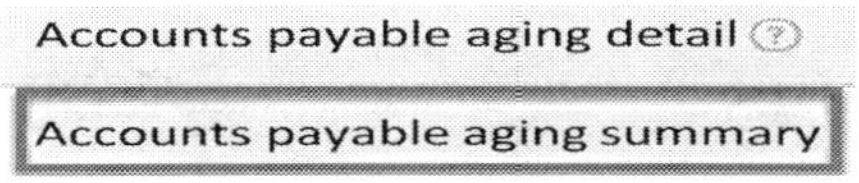

Figure 10.2: Selecting the Accounts payable aging summary report

3. In addition to the **Accounts payable aging summary** report, there is an **Accounts payable aging detail** report. The detailed report includes information about each bill for the vendor. This includes the bill date, bill number, due date, and amount due. The summary report, on the other hand, includes the open balance for each vendor, grouped by the age of the bill (**Current, 1-30 days, 31-60 days, 61-90 days**, and **91 days and over**).
4. Click on the **General options** button, and you can customize the number format, aging method, days per aging period, and number of periods for the A/P aging summary report, header and footer, and the columns to display. You can also filter by vendor and configure other general customizations, as indicated in *Figure 10.3*:

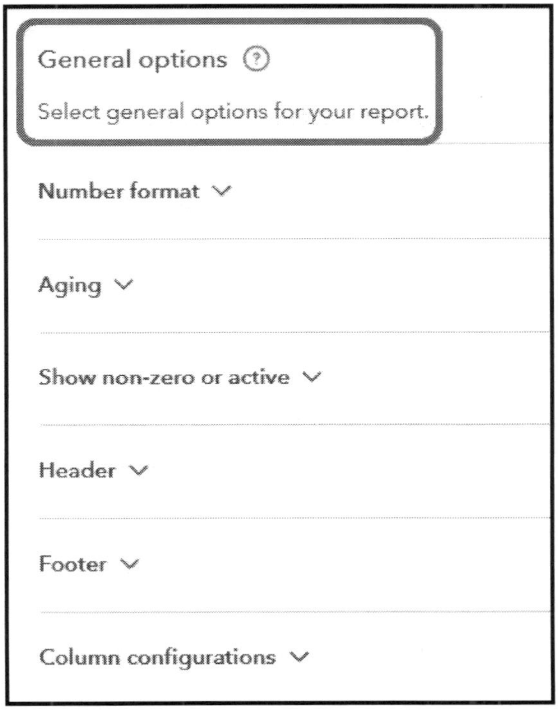

Figure 10.3: Report customization options

The following are brief descriptions of the customizable fields available for an A/P aging summary report:

- **Report period**: You can select preset dates from the drop-down menu, which include **Today, This week, This month, This quarter**, and **This year**. If you prefer a custom date range, select **Custom** from the dropdown and manually enter the dates.
- **Number format**: When it comes to formatting numbers on this report, you can choose to divide the numbers by 1,000 or remove the cents so that only whole numbers show up on the report. You can also show negative numbers in red.
- **Aging**: You can choose an aging method of **Current** or **Report date**. **Current** will calculate the age of each bill as of today's date, whereas **Report date** will use the report period to calculate the number of days a bill has remained outstanding (unpaid).
- **Show non-zero or active only**: You can choose to display non-zero only, which means only accounts with activity for the report period specified will be displayed in the report. You can also choose to show active accounts only, which means any account that was made inactive will not be shown on the report. You can learn more about how to make accounts inactive by reviewing *Chapter 4, Customizing QuickBooks for Your Business.*
- **Days per aging period** (not shown): Customize the number of days per aging period or use the standard 30 days per aging period.
- **Number of periods** (not shown): Similar to **Days per aging period**, you can also customize the number of periods in which to group bills. In the preceding example, we have chosen four periods (**1-30**, **31-60**, **61-90**, and **91 days and over**).
- **Header/Footer**: You can customize the header information, such as the report title, and the footer information, such as the date/time prepared.
- **Filter** (not shown): You can filter the A/P aging report for a specific vendor by selecting the vendor from the dropdown. If you want to review unpaid bills for just a few vendors, you can also choose more than one vendor from the drop-down menu.
- **Column configurations**: For multi-entities, you can turn this feature on to show entity names in the columns.

> Having the ability to customize the report title comes in handy if this is a report you would like to generate on a regular basis without having to recreate it. Change the title to represent the changes made (i.e., **A/P Aging for Office Supply Vendors**) and click the **Save as** button to save the report to your **Custom Reports** list.

After making your selections, click the **Refresh** button to update the report. An A/P aging summary report—similar to the following one—will appear:

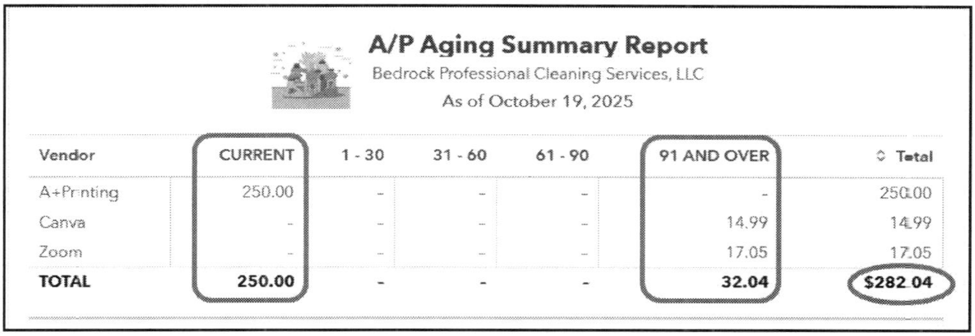

A/P Aging Summary Report
Bedrock Professional Cleaning Services, LLC
As of October 19, 2025

Vendor	CURRENT	1 - 30	31 - 60	61 - 90	91 AND OVER	Total
A+Printing	250.00	-	-	-	-	250.00
Canva	-	-	-	-	14.99	14.99
Zoom	-	-	-	-	17.05	17.05
TOTAL	**250.00**	**-**	**-**	**-**	**32.04**	**$282.04**

Figure 10.4: Sample A/P aging summary report

In this sample A/P aging summary report, **Bedrock Professional Cleaning Services, LLC** has outstanding bills that total **$282.04** with three vendors: **A+ Printing, Canva, and Zoom.** Of this amount, **$250.00** is current, and **$32.04** is 91 or more days past due**.** You can click on any dollar amount or the **TOTAL** column to see the details of the bill. To maintain favorable credit terms with vendor suppliers, the business owner needs to make a payment or make arrangements to pay the past due amount.

Before contacting vendor suppliers, you need to run an unpaid bills report to see the details behind the open balances on this A/P aging summary report. We will show you how to generate an unpaid bills report next.

Utilizing the unpaid bills report

An **unpaid bills report** is a list of all bills that have not been paid, as of the date range for the report. It is very similar to an A/P aging detail report, with the exception that it does not group invoices based on the number of days outstanding. The report includes details such as the vendor's name and a list of all unpaid bills, including amount, due date, number of days past due, and open balance. You can use this report to quickly identify bills that are coming due or past due. This will allow you to follow up with vendors to make payment arrangements for any bills that are past due or coming due.

Follow these steps to generate and customize an unpaid bills report:

1. Navigate to **Reports** from the left menu bar, as indicated in *Figure 10.5*:

Figure 10.5: Navigating to Reports

2. Scroll down to the **What you owe** section and select **Unpaid Bills**, as indicated in *Figure 10.6*:

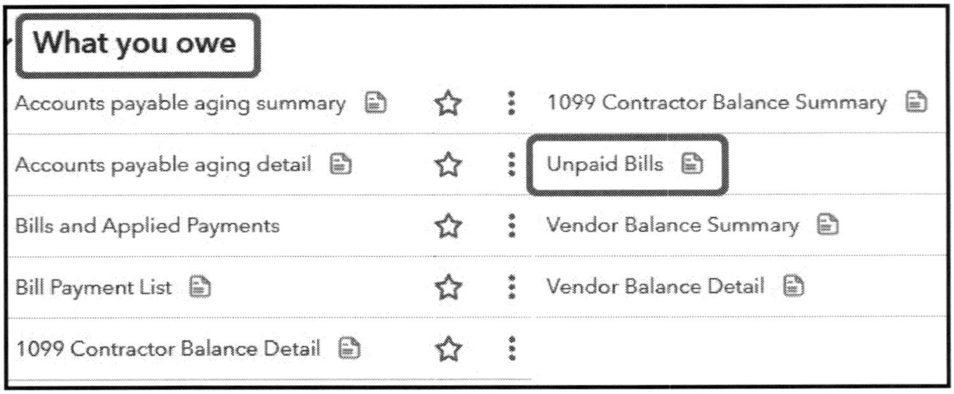

Figure 10.6: Running the unpaid bills report

3. Customize the unpaid bills report by clicking on the **General options** button and selecting a report period (not shown), number format, aging method, header/footer info, and column configurations, as indicated in *Figure 10.7*:

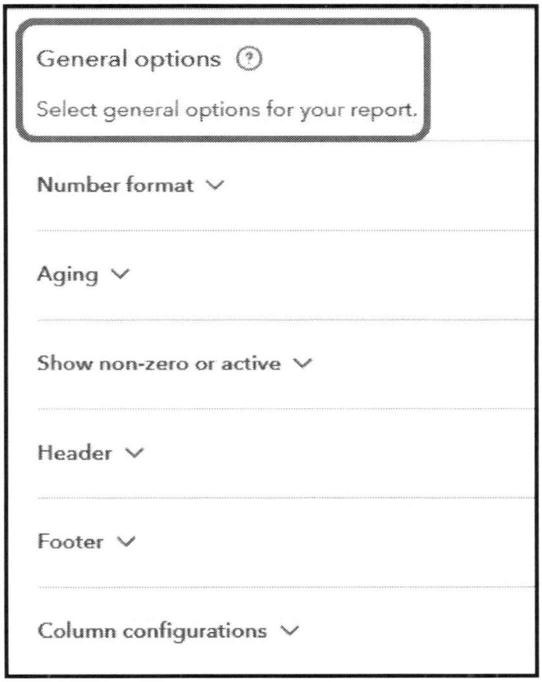

Figure 10.7: Report customization options

The following are brief descriptions of the customizable fields available for an unpaid bills report:

- **Report period**: Select the date range for which to run the report. You can manually enter a date range or choose from the following: **Today**, **This Week**, **This Month**, **This Quarter**, or **This Year**.
- **Number format**: When it comes to formatting numbers on this report, you can choose to divide the numbers by 1,000 or remove the cents so that only whole numbers show up on the report. You can also show negative numbers in red (not shown).
- **Aging**: The aging method is used to calculate the number of days a bill is past its due date. You can select the **Current** option, which will use today's date, or you can select the **Report date** option. The **Report date** option will use the report period to calculate the number of days the bill remains unpaid.

- **Min. Days Past Due (not shown)**: If applicable, you can enter a minimum number of days a bill is past due, or you can leave this field blank.
- **Filter** (not shown): You can filter the unpaid bills report by selecting a specific vendor, payment terms, and due date for the bill.
- **Header/Footer**: Similar to the A/P aging report, you can show your company logo and company name, as well as customize the report title and period, in the **Header** section. You can also choose whether to show the date and time prepared in the **Footer** section of the report.

After making your selections, click the **Refresh** button to generate the unpaid bills report. An unpaid bills report, similar to the following one, should appear:

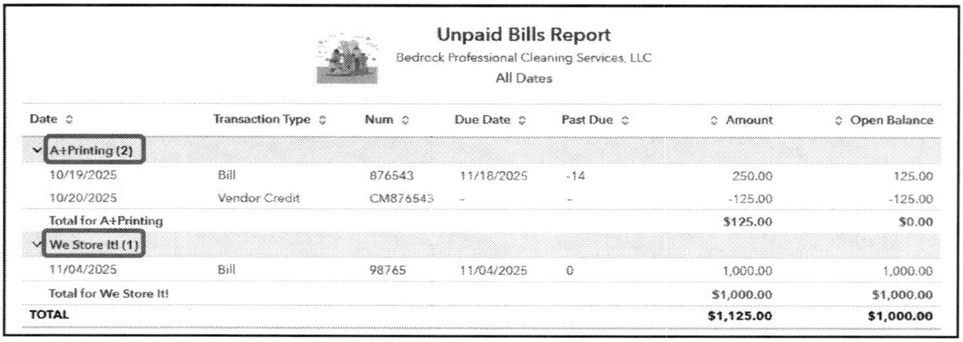
Unpaid Bills Report
Bedrock Professional Cleaning Services, LLC
All Dates

Date	Transaction Type	Num	Due Date	Past Due	Amount	Open Balance
A+Printing (2)						
10/19/2025	Bill	876543	11/18/2025	-14	250.00	125.00
10/20/2025	Vendor Credit	CM876543	-	-	-125.00	-125.00
Total for A+Printing					$125.00	$0.00
We Store It! (1)						
11/04/2025	Bill	98765	11/04/2025	0	1,000.00	1,000.00
Total for We Store It!					$1,000.00	$1,000.00
TOTAL					$1,125.00	$1,000.00

Figure 10.8: Sample unpaid bills report

In this sample unpaid bills report, **Bedrock Professional Cleaning Services, LLC** has unpaid bills totaling **$1,125.00**. There is also a credit memo for $125.00 for A+ Printing, which brings the total amount owed to $1,000.00. The bills pertain to two vendors: **A+ Printing** and **We Store It!**. The oldest bill has been past due for **14** days in the amount of **$250.00**.

This report lists the vendors in alphabetical order and includes the vendor name, contact phone number (not shown), bill date, transaction type, transaction number, due date, number of days past due, and outstanding amount. To maintain good credit with your vendor suppliers, you should review this report on a weekly basis and contact vendors to make payment arrangements.

To help you stay on top of what you are spending your money on, you need to review the expenses-by-vendor report. The expenses-by-vendor summary report focuses on your expenses. Unlike the unpaid bills report, you can gain insight into the types of expenses your business has, such as cellphone bills, office supplies, and rent. We will show you how to run this report next.

Understanding the expenses-by-vendor summary report

In order to maintain a healthy and positive bottom line, you need to be aware of what your business expenses are. An **expenses-by-vendor summary report** provides detailed information about the vendors with whom you are spending your money. This report includes a list of vendors and the total amount you have paid for a specific time period. You can use this report to gauge what your largest expenses are. Plus, you can also use the information in this report to negotiate better pricing with those suppliers from whom you purchase the most.

Follow these steps to generate an expenses-by-vendor summary report:

1. Navigate to **Reports** from the left menu bar, as indicated in *Figure 10.9*:

Figure 10.9: Navigating to the Reports Center

2. Scroll down to the **Expenses and vendors** section and select **Expenses by Vendor Summary**, as indicated in *Figure 10.10*:

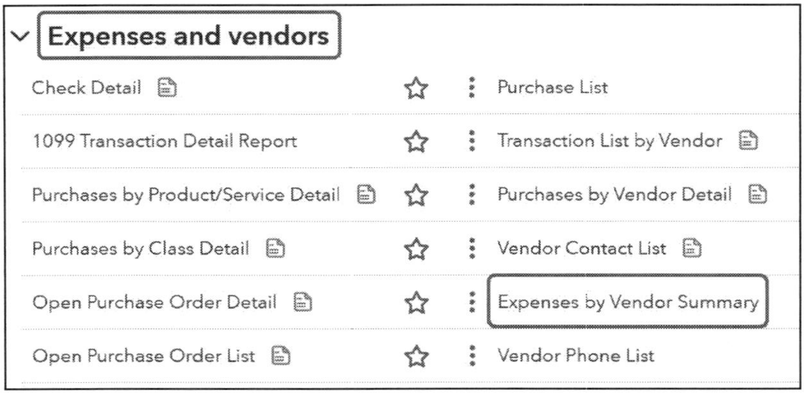

Figure 10.10: Selecting the Expenses by Vendor Summary report

3. You can customize the report by clicking on the **General options** button and selecting the reporting period, accounting method, number format, columns to display, and period comparison, as indicated in *Figure 10.11*:

Figure 10.11: Report customization options

The following are brief descriptions of the customizable fields available for an expenses-by-vendor summary report:

- **Report period**: From the drop-down menu, select a reporting period or manually enter the date range for which to run the report.
- **Accounting method**: Select the accounting method (**Cash** or **Accrual**) for which you would like to run the report. If you are not sure of which method to choose, refer to *Chapter 2, Getting Started with QuickBooks Online*. In that chapter, we explain how to choose the right accounting method for your business.
- **Number format**: Format numbers by dividing by 1,000, displaying them with or without cents, and making negative numbers red. You have three formatting options for negative numbers: **-100**, **(100)**, or **100-**.
- **Show non-zero or active only**: You can choose to display non-zero only, which means only accounts with activity for the period will show up on the report. You can also show active accounts only, which means any account that was made inactive will not be shown on the report.
- **Header/Footer**: You can show your company logo and company name, as well as customizing the report title and period in the **Header** section. You can also choose whether to show the date and time prepared in the **Footer** section of the report.
- You can learn more about how to make accounts inactive in *Chapter 4, Customizing QuickBooks for Your Business*.
- **Column configurations**: For multi-entities, you can turn this feature on to show entity names in the columns.
- **Compare (not shown)**: You can compare the current period to a **previous period** (**PP**), the current year to the **previous year** (**PY**), or view the period as a percentage of the **year-to-date** (**YTD**).

> By comparing a current period to a PP, you are able to gauge whether your expenses are about the same as the previous month, quarter, or year, or whether they are up or down from the previous month, quarter, or year. This can be a good way to identify a potential issue with expense categorization and/or overspending in some areas.

After making your selections, click the **Refresh** button to update the report. An expenses-by-vendor summary report, similar to the following one, should display:

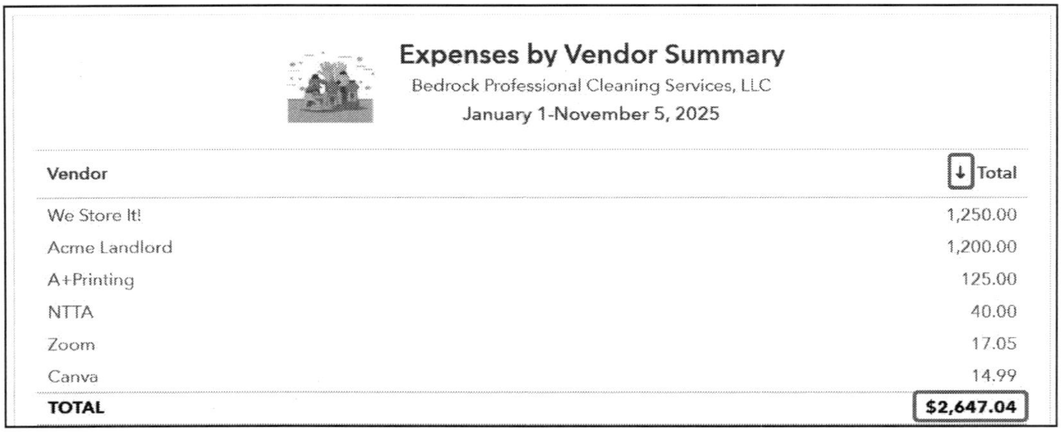

Expenses by Vendor Summary

Bedrock Professional Cleaning Services, LLC

January 1-November 5, 2025

Vendor	Total
We Store It!	1,250.00
Acme Landlord	1,200.00
A+Printing	125.00
NTTA	40.00
Zoom	17.05
Canva	14.99
TOTAL	$2,647.04

Figure 10.12: Sample expenses-by-vendor summary report

In the sample **Expenses by Vendor Summary** report, the total expenses for **Bedrock Professional Cleaning Services, LLC** are **$2,647.04**. To easily identify which vendors they are spending the most on, we have sorted the **Total** column so that the amounts are in descending order (from largest to smallest). You can click on the arrow next to the **Total** column, shown in *Figure 10.12*, to sort the amounts. **We Store It!** received the highest payment of **$1,250.00, and Canva received the least amount at $14.99**. The report gives business owners insight into where they are spending their money. As discussed, this can be helpful when it comes to negotiating a better price for goods and services.

> If you see an amount listed under **Unspecified vendor** on the report, be sure to click on the amount to verify it is made up of journal entries for items such as payroll. In some cases, it is correct, but it's important to review any amount listed as unspecified vendors. If the vendor's name was inadvertently not selected, it's important to go ahead and add it. You can click on any amount to drill down to the transaction, which will allow you to make the necessary changes.

To drill down to specific payments made to vendors, you can run a bill payments report. We will show you how to generate this report next.

> The vendor summary report is great for reviewing what you have paid vendors for the year to determine who may be subject to 1099s. You can quickly review the report to see whom you have paid $600 or more to, which is the threshold for generating a 1099 form. You can learn more about how to process 1099s in *Chapter 12, Managing 1099 Contractors and Introducing QuickBooks Time in QBO.*

Utilizing the bill payments report

A **bill payments report** includes detailed payment information about the bills you have paid. The report is broken down by the method of payment (for example, cash, credit card, or check). It includes the payment date, check number (if applicable), vendor, and amount paid. If you want to determine the payments made for a specific time period, this report will give you the information you need.

To generate a bill payments report, follow these steps:

1. Navigate to **Reports** from the left menu bar, as indicated in *Figure 10.13*:

Figure 10.13: Navigating to the Reports Center

2. Scroll down to the **What you owe** section and select **Bill Payment List**, as indicated in *Figure 10.14*:

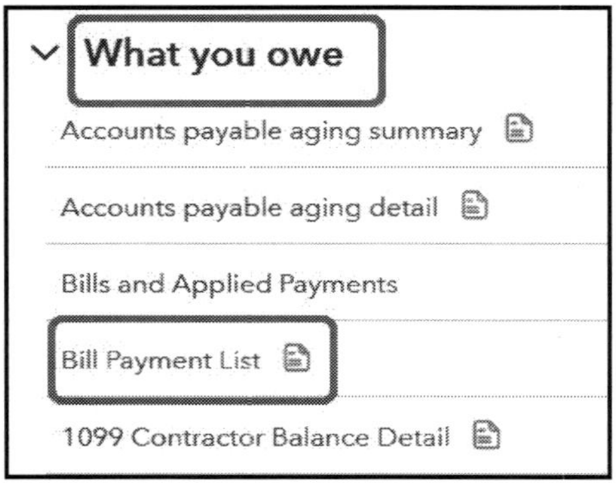

Figure 10.14: Running the bill payment list report

3. On the next screen, you can customize the report period and determine how the report is grouped, as indicated in *Figure 10.15*:

Figure 10.15: Customizing the bill payment list report

The following are brief descriptions of the customizable fields available for an expenses-by-vendor summary report:

- **Report period**: From the drop-down menu, select a reporting period or manually enter the date range for which to run the report.
- **Accounting method**: Select the accounting method (**Cash** or **Accrual**) for which you would like to run the report. If you are not sure of which method to choose, refer to *Chapter 2, Getting Started with QuickBooks Online*. In that chapter, we explain how to choose the right accounting method for your business.
- **Number format**: Format numbers by dividing by 1,000, displaying them with or without cents, and making negative numbers red. You have three formatting options for negative numbers: **-100**, **(100)**, or **100-**.
- **Show non-zero or active only**: You can choose to display non-zero only, which means only accounts with activity for the period will show up on the report. You can also show active accounts only, which means any account that was made inactive will not be shown on the report.
- **Header/Footer**: You can show your company logo and company name, as well as customize the report title and period, in the **Header** section. You can also choose whether to show the date and time prepared in the **Footer** section of the report.
- **Column configurations**: For multi-entities, you can turn this feature on to show entity names in the columns.

After making your selections, click the **Refresh** button to update the bill payment list report. A bill payment list report, similar to the following one, should be displayed:

Bill Payment List
Bedrock Professional Cleaning Services, LLC
All Dates

Date	Num	Vendor	Amount
Business Checking (3)			
10/19/2025	1000	Zoom	-17.05
10/19/2025	1001	Canva	-14.99
10/19/2025	1002	A+Printing	-125.00
Total for Business Checking			-$157.04
TOTAL			-$157.04

Figure 10.16: Sample bill payment list report

This report includes the payment date, check number (or payment reference number), vendor, and amount paid. In the sample bill payment list report, **Bedrock Professional Cleaning Services, LLC** has paid a total of **$157.0** to its vendors from the checking account. When funds are withdrawn from the checking account, a negative amount reduces the balance in the checking account. This is the reason why the total for checks is **-$157.04**.

You can run this report for any time period to gain insight into payments made to all vendors. This information can help you to forecast the amount of cash you need to have available to meet your obligations to vendors.

> Don't forget to click **Save customizations** for reports that you will use on a regular basis. As mentioned previously, this will save your reports to the **Custom** report list so that you don't have to waste time searching for reports and reformatting them each time you need to review them. You can also create custom groups, such as closing reports or tax preparation reports, so that you can easily generate a group of reports for a particular person or purpose. To understand how to group reports, review *Chapter 14, Reports Center Overview.*

> To demonstrate some of the concepts taught in this chapter and to give you some additional insights not covered, check out my YouTube channel at:
>
> `https://packt.link/du2BR`

Summary

In this chapter, we learned about four key reports that will help you to control your business expenses and stay on top of payments to your vendors. We learned about the A/P aging report, the unpaid bills report, the expenses by vendor report, and the bill payments report. We accomplished this goal by following instructions on how to customize and generate each of these reports. In addition, we explained how these reports will help you to stay on top of unpaid bills so that you can maintain a good credit history with your vendors.

While all of the reports that we covered in this chapter are important, I recommend that you review the A/P aging report and the unpaid bills report on a weekly basis. Reviewing unpaid bills and their corresponding due dates will assist you in calculating how much cash you need on hand to meet your current obligations. If you know that you will not be able to make a payment on time, you can proactively reach out to your vendor/supplier to inform them and work out a payment plan. On a monthly basis, I recommend that you review the expenses by vendor report so that you can keep tabs on your spending from month to month and make necessary adjustments as needed. In *Chapter 11, Managing Bank Feeds and Reconciling Bank and Credit Card Accounts*, we will cover one of the tasks that you will spend the majority of your time doing: reviewing deposits and withdrawals that come in from your bank or credit card accounts and making sure that they are properly recorded.

In *Next steps*, we have listed a few action items that you should do in order to stay on top of your expenses and bills.

Next steps

1. Go through your vendor list and make sure that you have set payment terms for each one. This will ensure that when a bill is on the verge of being due, QBO will notify you of upcoming bills that are due when you log into your account. Refer to *Chapter 3, Company File Setup*, for instructions on how to do this.
2. Pick a day during the week to review the following key reports:
    - A/P Aging detail report
    - A/P Aging summary report
3. Make an action plan to address any unpaid bills that are 60+ days overdue. Contact vendor suppliers to make payment arrangements, if needed.

4. Schedule time on your calendar to review key reports on a *monthly* basis. Make it at least 45 minutes and plan to have your favorite caffeinated beverage or a nice breakfast or lunch. Call this **A Date with My Money** or something that you will look forward to.
    - A/R Aging detail report (refer to *Chapter 8, Customer Sales Reports in QuickBooks Online*)
    - A/P Aging detail report (refer to *Chapter 10, Vendor and Expense Reports in QuickBooks Online*)
5. Profit and loss report (refer to *Chapter 15, Business Overview and Cash Management Tools and Reports*)
6. Balance sheet report (refer to *Chapter 15, Business Overview and Cash Management Tools and Reports*)
7. If you have a bookkeeper or accountant who manages your books, schedule time to meet with that person each month. However, make sure that you have already reviewed the reports and made a list of your questions *prior to this meeting*. In other words, schedule your "date" before you meet with your bookkeeper or accountant, if applicable.

Part 3

Managing Bank Feeds, EE's, and Contractors in QBO

We begin this section by introducing you to the new and improved bank feeds center. You will learn how the **Accountant** Agent can help to streamline the review of bank transactions.

Managing employees and contractors can feel overwhelming, but QuickBooks Online simplifies the process. In this section, I'll guide you through setting up payroll, filing tax forms, and generating reports. You'll also learn how to work with 1099 contractors, including what forms you'll need and how to make payments. This part should give you the tools to easily reconcile your bank and credit card accounts, as well as to manage your workforce efficiently and stay compliant with ease.

This part comprises the following chapters:

11

Managing Bank Feeds and Reconciling Bank and Credit Card Accounts

In *Chapter 4*, *Customizing QuickBooks for Your Business*, we showed you how to connect bank and credit card accounts to **QuickBooks Online** (**QBO**) to reduce the amount of time you spend manually entering data. Reviewing these transactions will give you important insight into where you are spending your money. While many business owners can tell you who their top five customers are, they typically don't know what their top five expenses are.

In this chapter, we will show you how to manage bank and credit card transactions that have been uploaded to QuickBooks. Dealing with fraudulent transactions has become a reality for many people. On more than one occasion, I received a call from my financial institution asking me to verify purchases that, for one reason or another, sent a red flag to my bank because they were "out of the norm" for me or made internationally. Reconciling your bank and credit card accounts often will help you identify unauthorized purchases that your financial institution does not catch. Since there is a time limit on when you can dispute these charges, it's important to be aware of them as soon as possible.

When bank and credit card transactions are uploaded, they are organized in the **Bank Transactions Center**. This area serves as a holding place where transactions can be reviewed before they are recorded in your books. Before these transactions can be recorded in QuickBooks, you must review them. This includes matching them with transactions that have already been entered into QuickBooks, adding payee or category information, and providing any additional details to help identify each transaction. With the most recent edition of QBO, you will have the assistance of the accounting agent, who will review transactions and make suggestions on how to categorize them, match them with existing transactions already recorded in QBO, and make vendor/customer recommendations based on previously recorded transactions. If you have QBO Essentials, Plus, or Advanced, the accounting agent is included with your subscription. We will also show you how bank rules can help to reduce the number of transactions requiring manual review. Last but not least, we will show you how to reconcile your accounts.

Reconciling is the process of making sure your QuickBooks data matches the monthly statements provided by your financial institution. By reconciling often, you can catch errors made by the bank or credit card company and catch fraudulent transactions a lot sooner. Another exciting new feature in QBO is auto-reconciliation. AI-powered reconciliation provides a summary outlining potential discrepancies between QBO and our bank/credit card statements. The tool is in Beta currently, but as soon as it is ready, I will post a video on my YouTube channel (`https://packt.link/du2BR`) to show you how it works!

In this chapter, we will cover the following topics:

- Overview of the Bank Transactions Center
- Matching bank transactions
- Editing bank transactions
- Creating and using bank rules
- Reconciling accounts
- Troubleshooting tips

By the end of this chapter, you will have a solid understanding of how the Bank Transactions Center works. You will know how to match transactions and how to edit transactions by adding a memo or changing the category. You will be more efficient with managing bank transactions by using the suggestions made by the accounting agent and implementing bank rules. Finally, you will be confident in reconciling your accounts with the statements received from your financial institution using the new auto-reconciliation tool. We will start by giving you an overview of the Bank Transactions Center, which is where you will find uploaded bank and credit card transactions.

> The US edition of QBO was used to create this book. If you are using a version that is outside of the United States, results may differ.

Overview of the Banking Center

The Banking Center is where you can manage bank and credit card transactions that have been uploaded into QuickBooks from your financial institution. These transactions require your review before they are recorded in your books.

Follow these steps to navigate to the Bank Transactions Center:

1. Click on the **Accounting** tab, located on the left menu bar, and select **Bank transactions**, as indicated in *Figure 11.1*:

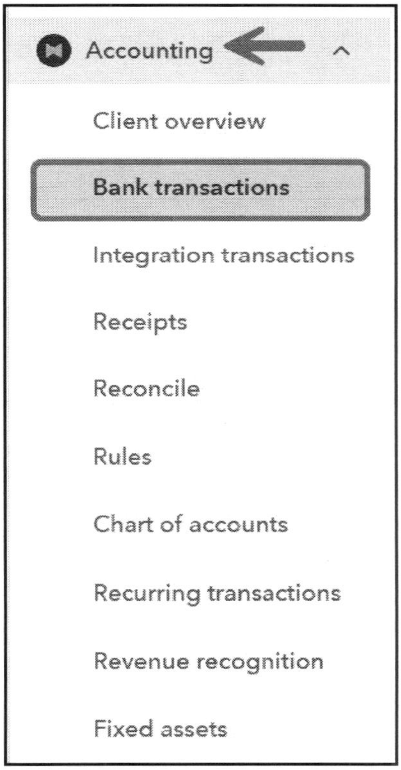

Figure 11.1: Navigating to the Bank Transactions Center

2. The Bank Transactions Center will appear, as indicated in *Figure 11.2*:

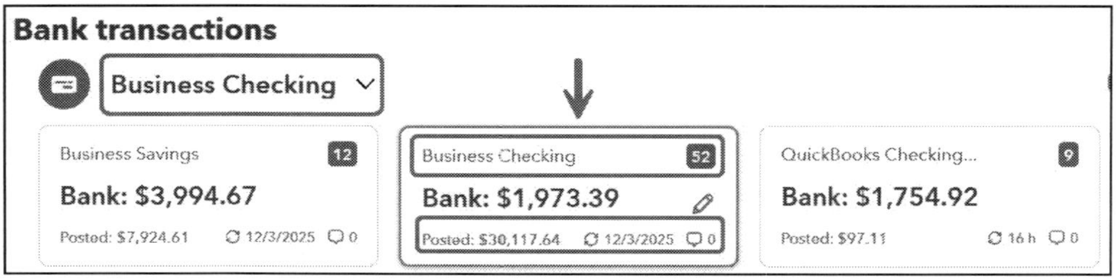

Figure 11.2: Bank and credit card accounts in the Bank Transactions Center

3. At the very top of the page, you will see tiles that represent bank and credit card accounts you have added to QuickBooks. On each tile, you will find the name of the account, the current balance (per the bank), the current balance (per QuickBooks), and the number of transactions that require review before they can be recorded in a QuickBooks account register. The following is a brief description of the information you will find in the Bank Transactions Center:

    - **Bank account name**: At the very top of each tile, you will find the name of the account (in our example, **Business Checking**, **Business Savings**, and **QuickBooks Checking**).
    - **Bank balance**: The balance of the account, per your financial institution, will be displayed below the bank account name. In our example, **Business Savings** has a bank balance of **$3,994.67**, **Business Checking** has a bank balance of **$1,973.39**, and the **QuickBooks Checking** has a balance of **$1,754.92**.
    - **In QuickBooks**: The balance of the account, per QuickBooks, will be displayed right below the bank balance and is labelled as **Posted**. In our example, **Business Savings** has a posted balance of **$7,924.61**, **Business Checking** is **$30,117.64**, and **QuickBooks Checking** is **$97.11**. If you need to edit the account information or update your banking login info, you can do so by clicking on the pencil icon shown on the **Business Checking** tile.
    - **Pending transactions**: Transactions that have been uploaded from your financial institution and require your review will be indicated in the upper-right corner of each tile. In the screenshot in *Figure 11.2*, these numbers are **12**, **52**, and **9**.

If you have not connected a bank or credit card account to QuickBooks, your screen will not appear as it does in *Figure 11.2*. Instead, you will be given the **Connect account** or **Upload transactions** options, as shown in *Figure 11.3*:

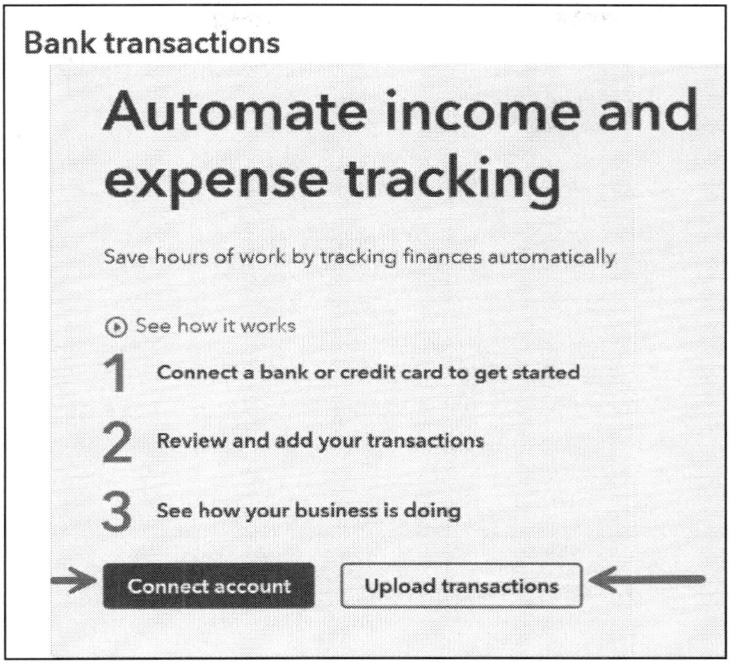

Figure 11.3: Option to connect accounts in the Banking Center

In *Chapter 4, Customizing QuickBooks for Your Business*, we covered the step-by-step process of connecting your bank and credit card accounts to QBO.

Below the bank and credit card tiles, the transactions that have been uploaded to QBO are categorized into three groups: **Pending**, **Posted**, and **Excluded**, as shown in *Figure 11.4*.

Figure 11.4: Pending, Posted, and Excluded groups

A brief description of each of these follows:

- **Pending**: The transactions that appear in this group are waiting for you to categorize or match them so that you can post them to your books.
- **Posted**: The transactions that appear in this group have been matched or categorized and recorded in your books. This is the tab that pending transactions will move to once you have posted them.
- **Excluded**: The transactions that appear in this group have been manually added here because they should not be posted to your books. There may be times when duplicate transactions are downloaded to the Banking Center or a personal bank or credit card account has been connected to QBO in error. Don't worry if you accidentally exclude a transaction and then realize that you need it. You can easily undo the move to **Excluded**, and the transaction will move back to the **Pending** tab.

If the bank balance and the posted balance in QuickBooks match, this means all uploaded transactions have been recorded. As a result, you will not see a number in the upper-right corner of the tile. If the balances do not match and you don't have any transactions in the **Pending** tab, that does not necessarily mean that you are missing something. A difference in the two balances can be from outstanding items that have not yet cleared the bank due to timing differences, or transactions that have not yet been uploaded to QBO.

If you imported your transactions into QuickBooks from a CSV file instead of connecting your bank and credit card accounts to QuickBooks, you will only see a posted balance in QuickBooks; you will not have a bank balance for each account. I recommend reviewing transactions on a daily or weekly basis so that you don't get too far behind.

Before we dive into the mechanics of how to review and take action on pending bank transactions, I think it's important to give you an overview of the layout first. *Figure 11.5* shows the layout of pending bank transactions.

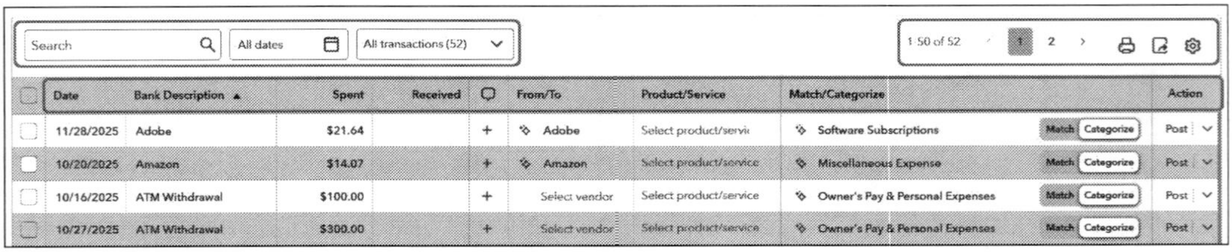

Figure 11.5: Pending bank transactions layout

Here is a brief description of what information you can expect to see here:

- **Search** and **Filter**: At the top, in the search box, you can type text or a number to locate a specific transaction(s). You can also select specific dates in the box next to the **Search** field, and the last field allows you to filter transactions to show: money in, money out, ready to post, suggested matches, transfers, and several other options.
- **Date**: This is the date that the transaction occurred, per the financial institution
- **Bank Description**: This field will include the name of the payee (i.e., **Adobe** or **Amazon**) or a brief description of the transaction type (i.e., **ATM Withdrawal**).
- **Spent**: This column will reflect money that was withdrawn (for bank accounts) or charged (for credit card accounts). These amounts are also referred to as **money out**.
- **Received**: This column will reflect money that was deposited into your bank account or payments made to your credit card accounts. These amounts are also referred to as **money in** transactions.
- **Request more information**: The icon that looks like a chat box allows you to request information from your clients (or team) about a specific transaction. For example, in *Figure 11.5*, we have an Amazon transaction for $14.07 but no other information to help us determine what was purchased. You can click on the + symbol, and a box will display so that you can type a question and request a receipt or other supporting documentation, if needed. Later in this chapter, I will show you how to manage these requests.
- **From/To**: In this column, select from the dropdown the payee (money out) or customer (money in) transactions. In order to be able to locate transactions later on and to have complete financial reports, I recommend you complete this field for all transactions.
- **Product/Service**: If you use products/services, you can select the product/service that is appropriate for the transaction.
- **Match/Categorize**: In this column, you will see the option to match or categorize the transaction. This is where you will start to reap the benefits of the accounting agent (AI). The accounting agent will go through the transactions, and if it finds a corresponding transaction (match) in QBO, the **Match** option will show up in this column and in the **Action** column. If it does not find a matching transaction in QBO, the **Categorize** option will be highlighted with the option to post in the **Action** column. In the next section, we will go through a few examples so that you can have a better understanding of when to match versus when to categorize transactions.

- **Action**: This column will either say **Match** (as explained previously) or **Post. Post** means that the transaction is ready to be recorded on the books. This means you have reviewed and completed the **From/To** field and the **Product/Service** field (if applicable), and you have attached all supporting documents, if applicable.

  Once you select or click on **Match** or **Post**, the transaction will move from the **Pending** tab to the **Posted** tab. In addition to **Match** and **Post**, you can take additional action by clicking on the arrow to the right of **Post/Match**. When you do so, the following options will display:

- **Split**: If you need to allocate a transaction to more than one category, product/service, you can split the transaction to accomplish this.
- **Create rule**: As mentioned briefly, rules allow you to set up a set of conditions so that QBO can automatically categorize transactions that occur on a regular basis (i.e., monthly cellphone expense or monthly rent).
- **Categorization history**: Using AI, QBO will display how transactions with the same vendor/customer name were previously categorized so that you can be consistent with what has been done in the past. If there is no historical information, then the accounting agent will learn based on the selections you make.
- **Exclude**: You can choose to exclude a transaction that you do not wish to record in QBO, such as duplicates, as previously mentioned. Any transaction that is moved to the **Excluded** tab can be deleted from there.

A brief explanation of the icons shown in the upper-right corner of *Figure 11.5* follows:

- **Number of transactions**: The number of transactions shows up here as well as at the very bottom of the page. In our example, there are a total of 52 transactions, and page 1 displays 1–50.
- **Pages**: The number of pages is right after the number of transactions. In our example, there are two pages. You can click directly on a page number or click the arrow to advance to the next page.
- **Printer**: You can print the transactions out. Keep in mind that it will only print the current page.
- **Export**: The *export* button allows you to export the transactions to an Excel file.

- **Settings**: Here, you can control the columns that display automation, other preferences, and page size, as shown in *Figure 11.6*:

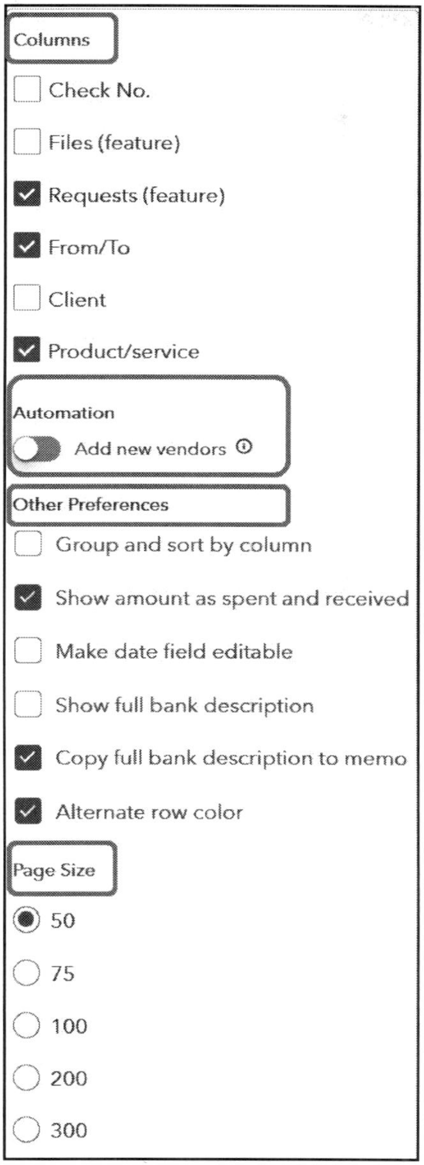

Figure 11.6: Settings in Bank Transactions Center

A brief explanation of the options shown in *Figure 11.6* follows:

- **Columns**: You can choose to add/remove columns as needed, depending on what your business requires.
- **Automation**: You can toggle this feature on, and QBO will automatically add new vendors to your vendor list as they come through the bank transactions. I do not recommend that you turn this feature on. See the following highlighted box for clarification.
- **Other Preferences**: You have several preferences that you can add/remove, such as making the **Date** field editable, showing the full bank description, as well as other options.
- **Page Size**: You can expand the number of transactions that appear on each page. In our example, we have it set to **50**, but you can go as high as **300** on one page at a time.

> Do not allow QBO to automatically add new vendors to the vendor list. The reason why you don't want to do this is that it will just clutter your QBO file with unnecessary information. For example, if you purchase gasoline at 4–5 different gas stations (Shell, Texaco, Costco, etc.), QBO will add each of these merchants to your vendor list. Instead, what you should do is create a vendor called `Fuel purchases` and put all gas purchases under this one vendor. You can even create a bank rule that will do this for you! Bank rules will be covered later on in this chapter.

Now that we have shown you how to navigate the layout of the Bank Transactions Center, you are ready to take action on the uploaded transactions. In the next section, we will show you how QuickBooks can save you time by matching uploaded transactions with transactions previously entered into QuickBooks.

Matching transactions

In this section, we will cover a process called **matching transactions**. The accounting agent will automatically attempt to match transactions that have been uploaded into QuickBooks with transactions that have already been recorded in QuickBooks. This process can help you save the time you would normally have spent trying to match transactions manually. We will show you how this process works by going through examples.

In the **Pending** tab, you can filter the bank transactions to show suggested matches. Click on the drop-down arrow and select **Suggested matches**, as shown in *Figure 11.7*:

Figure 11.7: Filtering bank transactions for suggested matches

We can see the accounting agent has attempted to match three transactions that were previously entered into QuickBooks:

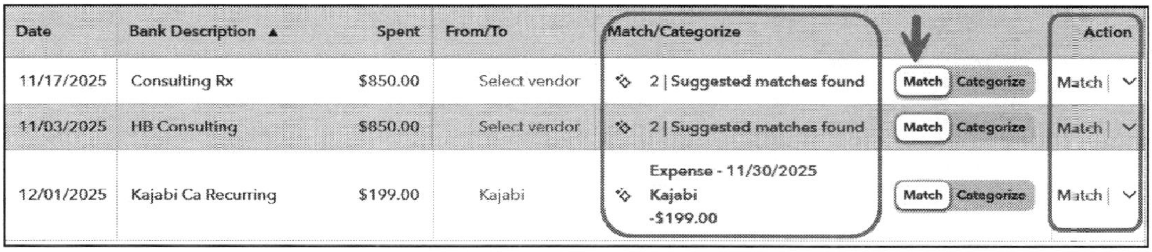

Figure 11.8: Match Bank transactions in the Pending tab

The following is a brief explanation of the preceding three transactions for which QuickBooks has found a match:

- **11/17/2025 payment of $850.00**: The accounting agent has found an expense transaction on or around **11/17/25** that matches a payment for **$850.00** with a bank description of **Consulting Rx**. If this is correct, you can simply click the **Match** button that is below the **Match/Categorize** column or the **Match** link below the **Action** column. Both will record the transaction in your books. If you are not sure whether the two transactions are a match, click on the **Suggested matches found** link to review the transaction details. If you determine that it is incorrect, click on the **Categorize** button located to the right of **Match** and proceed to categorize the transaction. After selecting the category and completing the **From/To** field, click **Post** to record the transaction, and it will move from the **Pending** tab to the **Posted** tab.
- **11/03/2025 payment of $850.00**: Take the same action that we took for the preceding **11/17/20255** payment.
- **12/01/2025 payment of $199.00**: The accounting agent has found a matching expense transaction dated **11/30/2025** for **$199.00** that has been recorded in QBO. You can click on the description (**Expense - 11/30/2025**) to view the details of the transaction and confirm whether or not the accounting agent is right. In our example, the transaction is a receipt that was uploaded to QBO, and it is a correct match to this payment. Therefore, we will click the **Match** link below the **Action** column to record the transaction in the books.

Keep in mind that if you don't match transactions that have already been recorded in QBO, you will duplicate them in your books by categorizing them here. In the three preceding examples, if we did not match these transactions and instead categorized and posted them, they would be recorded in QBO twice. This would result in overstated expenses on the *Profit and Loss* report, and the bank account balance would be understated on the *Balance Sheet* report. This would prevent us from reconciling the accounts to the bank/credit card statements.

As mentioned previously, when you click **Match**, these items will move from the **Pending** tab to the **Posted** tab. These items will also be marked as cleared in QuickBooks, which will be important when we get ready to reconcile these accounts later on. If QuickBooks has not found the right match, you can replace it with the correct match.

To change the match recommended by QuickBooks, click on the **Suggested matches found** link below the **Match/Categorize** column, and then click on **Find other matches**, as indicated in *Figure 11.9*:

Figure 11.9: Matching transactions in the Banking Center

In addition to matching transactions, you will need to provide additional information, such as the payee and category (the account), before the transaction can be recorded in QuickBooks. While the **payee** field is optional, it's important that you complete that field for detailed reports, 1099s, and many other accounting functions. Bank transactions that have not been matched will remain in the Banking Center to be categorized and posted to your books. Some examples are debit card and **Automated Clearing House** (**ACH**) transactions, and manual or handwritten checks.

Now that we have shown you how matching transactions work and how you can post a matching transaction with just a few clicks, we will cover how to make any necessary changes to recorded transactions. In the next section, we will cover how to edit banking transactions.

Editing banking transactions

When you first start adding bank transactions to QuickBooks, you will need to review each transaction to ensure it has a proper payee (vendor) or customer and account category assigned to it. As you begin to repeat transactions, QuickBooks will remember how a transaction was recorded previously, and it will automatically assign the payee (vendor) and account category for expenses. Be sure to verify that everything is correct before recording the transaction in QuickBooks.

Follow these steps to edit bank transactions in the Banking Center:

1. From the left menu bar, select **All apps** > **Accounting** > **Bank transactions**, as indicated in *Figure 11.10*:

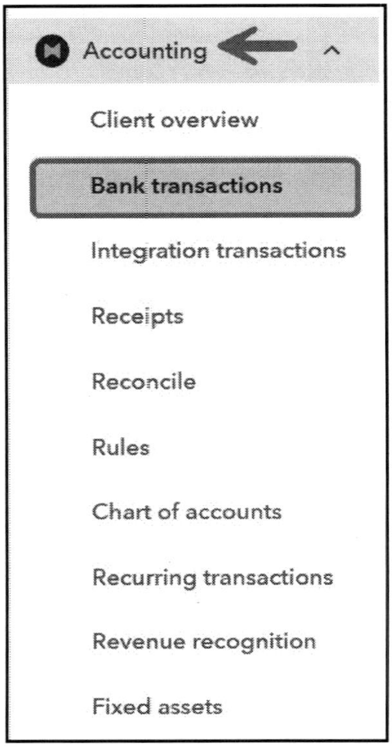

Figure 11.10: Navigating to the Banking Center

2. Click on the **Pending** tab, as indicated in *Figure 11.11*:

Figure 11.11: The Pending tab in the Banking Center

3. Click anywhere within any of the banking transactions listed to make any necessary changes, as indicated in *Figure 11.12*:

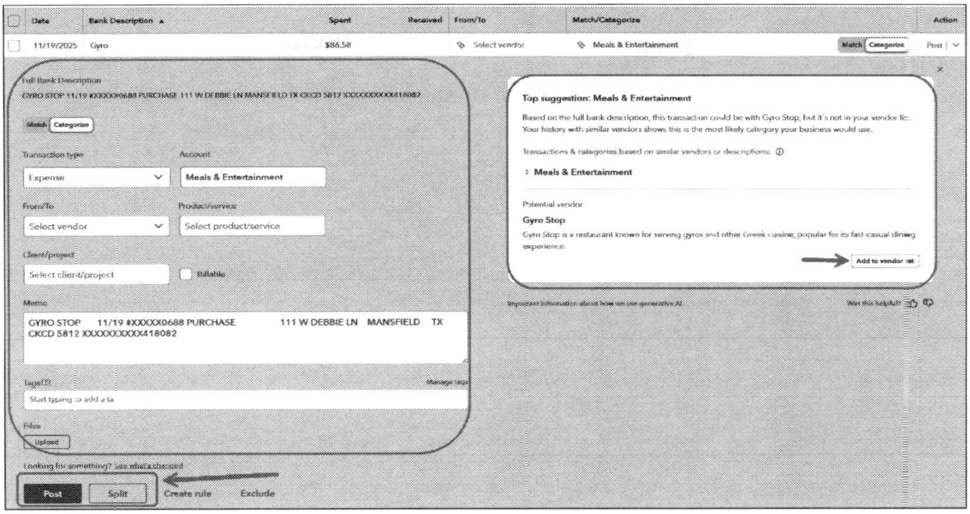

Figure 11.12: Editing a transaction in the Banking Center

You will find the following information in the banking transaction editing window:

- **Full Bank Description**: This information comes directly from the financial institution. It is used to help you identify what the transaction is for. You will not be able to edit this information.
- **Transaction type**: Select the transaction type from the drop-down menu; the options are **Expense**, **Check**, **Transfer**, and **Credit Card Payment**.
- **Account**: Select the appropriate account from the drop-down menu, based on the type of purchase that was made or income that was received.
- **From/To**: For withdrawals, select the payee (vendor) from the drop-down menu. For deposits/receipt of customer payments, select the customer from the drop-down menu. If it is a new vendor or customer, you can click **Add new** from the drop-down menu and add them here. It is important to complete this field for reporting purposes, such as 1099 preparation.
- **Product/service**: This is a relatively new option; you can categorize bank transactions as a product/service from your items list. Keep in mind that if you select a product/service, the **Account** field will be grayed out. You cannot assign both an account and a product/service to a bank transaction.

- **Client/project**: From the drop-down menu, select a client/project that the transaction is associated with, if applicable. To the right of this field is a box to mark the transaction as billable. If this is something you need to bill a client back for, be sure to click the **Billable** box.
- **Memo**: The bank details will generally appear in this field. This will generally include the merchant, date of purchase, and the credit/debit card used to make the purchase. You can edit this information as needed.
- **Tags**: Use tags to earmark or flag specific types of income or expenses you choose to keep an eye on. While tags have been discontinued for brand-new users, existing users are still able to use them for now.
- **Files**: Select the **Upload** button to attach receipts and any other supporting documentation for the transaction. It is a good idea to attach a receipt for expenses that are $75.00 or more. There is a chance that a receipt may already be attached to a transaction along with a notification like this: **We found a receipt that matches this transaction and attached it for you**. If you use the **receipt capture** feature, when the corresponding transaction is uploaded from the bank, it will match the two together. This will allow you to link the actual receipt to the transaction. To ensure that QBO has correctly identified a match, click on the attachment to view the receipt. If it is **not** a match, you can remove the receipt by clicking the **X** button at the end of the filename. You can learn more about how receipt capture works in *Chapter 9, Recording Expenses in QuickBooks Online*.
- **Split**: To the right of the **Post** button is a **Split** button. A split transaction allows you to assign more than one category (account) to a transaction. For example, let's say you purchased an office chair that cost $300. The total bill was $325, which includes a shipping charge. You can split this bill by putting `$300` into the **Office expenses** category and $25 into the **Shipping/freight expenses** category.
- **Post**: Once all fields are complete, click on the **Post** button to record this transaction in the check or credit card register in QuickBooks. When you post this transaction in QBO, it will move over to the **Posted** tab within the Banking Center.

As discussed, QuickBooks will automatically recall the vendor or customer and category (account) that was previously used.

If you realize that a transaction that you previously accepted and moved over to the **Posted** tab needs to be fixed, you can easily edit this transaction as follows.

Click on the **Posted** tab, locate the transaction, and click on the **Undo** option in the far-right column, as indicated in *Figure 11.13*:

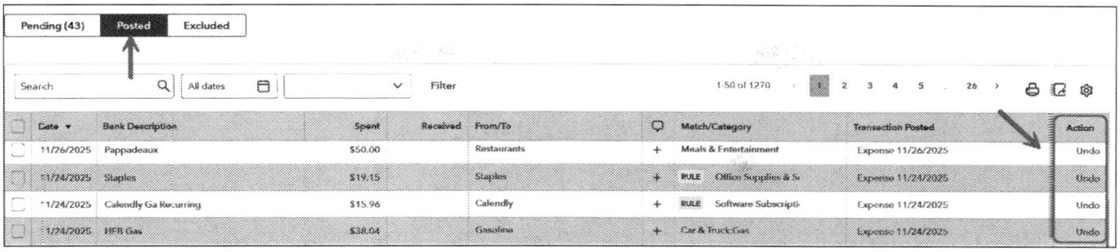

Figure 11.13: Undoing a transaction previously posted in the Banking Center

The transaction will move back to the **Pending** tab.

> Next to the **Posted** tab is the **Excluded** tab. This tab is used to handle transactions you do not want posted in QuickBooks. For example, if a duplicate transaction was uploaded into QuickBooks (which is rare but does happen), you would only want to post one of the transactions that were uploaded. Since you are not able to delete uploaded transactions, simply mark the transaction as *Excluded*, and it will move from the **Pending** tab to the **Excluded** tab. Please note that transactions that appear in the **Excluded** tab are *not recorded* in your books and, therefore, have no impact on the financial statements. Transactions on the **Excluded** tab can be deleted.

Now that we have shown you how to modify banking transactions, we will introduce you to bank rules in the next section. Using bank rules is the best way to ensure the accuracy of transactions recorded. We will discuss how to create and use bank rules in the next section.

Understanding bank rules

Bank rules are a list of conditions that must be met in order for QuickBooks to automatically assign a payee, account (category), class, and location to upload banking transactions to. Bank rules will apply only to bank or credit card transactions in the **Pending** tab of the Banking Center. Since most businesses have the same transactions that take place month after month, using bank rules can save you the time you would have spent reviewing transactions in the Banking Center before they can be recorded in QuickBooks.

Follow these steps to create a bank rule:

1. Click on **All apps** > **Accounting** > **Rules**, as indicated in *Figure 11.14*:

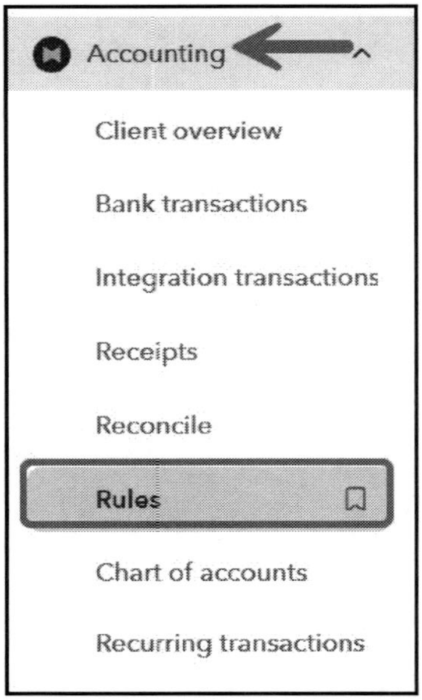

Figure 11.14: Navigating to bank rules

2. Click on the **New rule** button, as indicated in *Figure 11.15*:

Figure 11.15: Creating a new bank rule

3. The **Create rule** template displays. Complete the fields as follows:

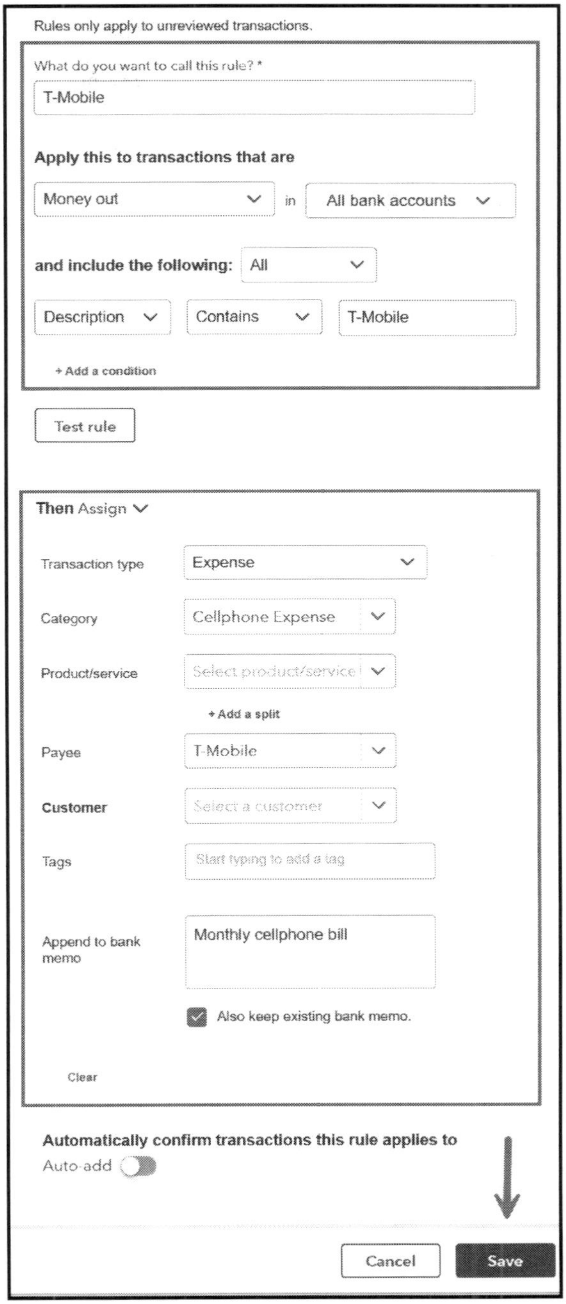

Figure 11.16: Completing the fields required to create a new bank rule

The following is a brief explanation of the fields to complete for a new bank rule:

- **What do you want to call this rule?**: The first field allows you to assign a name to the rule. In our example, we are using `Monthly Cellphone Expense`.
- **Apply this to transactions that are**: You can apply rules based on **Money out** or **Money in**, and choose to apply this to all bank accounts or a specific bank account. If you have multiple accounts, you can set up rules that are specific to a bank account, even when a vendor is paid using multiple bank accounts.
- **Conditions**: You can create several conditions based on **Bank text**, **Description**, or **Amount**. In our example, we have selected **Bank text**.
- **Contains/Doesn't contain/Is exactly**: You can select whether the transaction contains, doesn't contain, or is exactly the information that you enter into the next field.
- **Text box**: This field contains text that will appear either in the **Bank text** or **Description** field when the transaction is uploaded into QuickBooks. If you selected the amount as part of your criteria, then you will enter an amount in this field. In our text box, we have entered `T-Mobile`, which is the name of the payee.
- You can click the **Add a condition** link to add multiple conditions. Based on the conditions you have set, QuickBooks will automatically assign a category to the transaction using the information in the next section.
- **Transaction type**: From the drop-down menu, select the type of transaction for which you are creating this rule. In our example, this is **Expense**.
- **Category**: From the drop-down menu, select the category (account) that best describes the purchase. In our example, we have selected **Utilities: Telephone**.
- **Product/service**: From the drop-down menu, select a product or service this transaction is related to, if applicable. For example, if this were a printing expense you incur to produce workbooks that you sell to customers, you would select **Workbooks** in this field.

> As previously mentioned, if you select a product/service, you will not be able to select a category. This is because when you select a product/service, it is already linked to a category on your items list.

- **Add a split**: If the transaction should be split between two or more accounts (categories), you can click the **Add a split** link and indicate the accounts that should be used.
- **Payee**: From the drop-down menu, select the payee for this rule. In our example, the payee is **T-Mobile**.
- **Customer**: From the dropdown, select a customer that this expense is related to. For example, if this is an expense that you pay on behalf of a customer, then you would select the customer's name from the dropdown. This information will allow you to bill the customer back or simply review a summarized report.
- **Tags**: If you use tags, you can indicate a tag here if it is related to this transaction.
- **Replace bank memo**: This field is optional but can be used to provide additional details about the transaction. In our example, we have used `Monthly cellphone bill`. It will replace the bank memo unless you mark the box right below that says **Also keep existing bank memo**.

If you have multiple bank and credit card accounts that use the same vendor, and you need to record the transactions to different office locations, then you will need to set up rules specific to that bank or credit card account. For example, while the category might be the same, such as **Telephone Expense**, you would still need to set up a rule to categorize one bill to the Texas office and one bill to the California office.

Now that you have a better idea of how bank rules work and how to create them, in the next section, we will show you how to apply these bank rules to bank transactions.

How do you want to apply this rule?

At the bottom of this page is the **Automatically confirm transactions this rule applies to** option. As of the time of writing this book, this feature is automatically turned on, which means QuickBooks will automatically assign the category (account) based on your selections at the top of the page and will automatically record the transaction in QuickBooks without the need to review it first. If you would prefer to review all transactions before they are recorded, turn this feature off.

I recommend that you review all bank transactions before they are recorded in QuickBooks. After reviewing transactions for the first couple of months, once you are comfortable that they are being categorized correctly, you can always change the bank rules to auto-categorize and auto-add later on.

If set up properly, bank rules can automatically categorize and record 85% or more of your bank and credit card transactions. If you have a lot of transactions coming through, this will save you hours, which you can spend on other aspects of your business.

Start with one bank rule to see how it works, and then add more as you get comfortable with using them. For example, you could set up a bank rule for your monthly cellphone expenses to start. This type of expense typically is for the same amount and payee and occurs monthly.

> Similar to suggested matches, you can filter bank transactions to show only the ones where a rule has been applied. In addition, you can sort the transactions by column (**Date**, **Description**, **Spent**, **Received**, **From/To**, and **Match/Categorize**). It can be beneficial to sort by **Description** or **From/To** in order to group similar transactions and categorize and post them in a batch. Be sure to check out our YouTube channel, where we demonstrate tips and tricks to manage your bank transactions efficiently: `https://packt.link/du2BR`.

Using bank rules will also help to expedite the reconciliation of bank and credit card accounts. We will discuss this in more detail in the following section.

Reconciling accounts

Reconciling is the process of making sure your QuickBooks records agree with your bank and credit card statements. At a minimum, reconciling should take place on a monthly basis, if not more often. One of the benefits of using cloud-based accounting software such as QBO is that your banking information is uploaded on a daily basis. This means that you could reconcile as often as weekly, or even daily. There is no need to wait until the bank statement arrives at the end of the month to reconcile your accounts.

Follow these steps to reconcile a bank or credit card account:

1. From the gear icon, select **Reconcile**, as indicated in *Figure 11.17*:

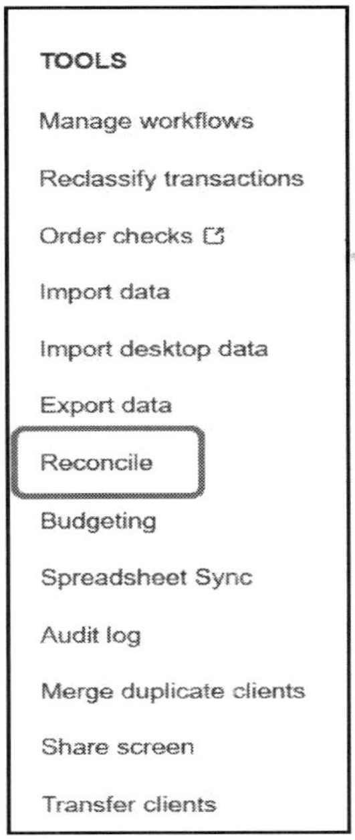

Figure 11.17: Navigating to Reconcile in QBO

The **Reconcile** window will appear, as indicated in *Figure 11.18*:

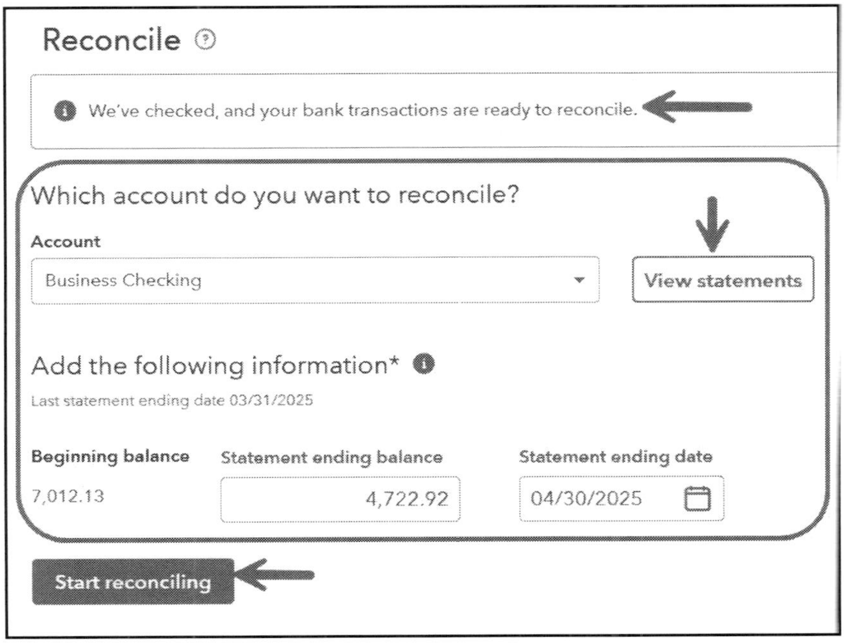

Figure 11.18: Initial reconciliation window

2. If a transaction that was previously reconciled has been changed, QuickBooks will include a message on this screen. Be sure to follow the on-screen instructions to troubleshoot the imbalanced transaction.

> This issue must be addressed before proceeding with the current reconciliation.

3. The fields that need to be completed in the reconciliation window shown in *Figure 11.18* are as follows:

    - **Account**: From the drop-down menu, select the bank or credit card account you want to reconcile. In our example, the account is **Business Checking**.
    - **Beginning balance**: This field will automatically populate with the ending balance of the previous month. If you have never reconciled the account before, the balance in this field will be the opening balance entered when you created the account in QuickBooks. In our example, the beginning balance is **$7,012.13**.
    - **Statement ending balance**: Enter the ending balance of the bank or credit card statement you are reconciling. In most cases, if you are receiving bank statements in QBO, this field will automatically populate with the statement's ending balance. In our example, the statement ending balance is **$4,722.92**.
    - **Statement ending date**: Enter the ending date on the bank or credit card statement you are reconciling. Similar to the ending balance, if you are receiving statements in QBO, this field will automatically populate for you. In our example, the ending date is **04/30/2025**.

4. A brand-new feature since the last QBO edition is the ability to request PDF statements to automatically download into QBO. In *Figure 11.18*, there is an option to view statements. Clicking on this link will open a window that will include all of the statements for the bank account in PDF format. As shown in *Figure 11.19*, statements will be grouped by **Unreconciled** and **Reconciled**:

Figure 11.19: Viewing bank statements in QBO

5. If you want to receive statements in QBO, click on the **Request statements** option, which will be visible if you have not requested statements yet. Keep in mind that your financial institution must participate in this program for you to access your statements in this manner.
6. Click the **Start reconciling** button once all the fields have been completed.
7. On the next screen, the following information will appear, which is the header information when reconciling accounts:

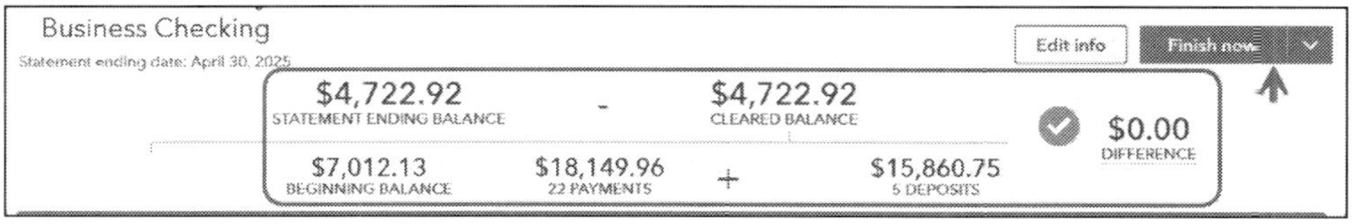

Figure 11.20: Header information in the reconciliation window

A brief description of the information found in the header window is as follows:

- **STATEMENT ENDING BALANCE**: This field will automatically be populated with the statement ending balance entered on the preceding start reconciliation screen.
- **CLEARED BALANCE**: This field will summarize all the transactions that have cleared on your bank or credit card statement.
- **BEGINNING BALANCE**: This field will automatically be populated from the prior month's reconciliation. If you have not reconciled this account previously, it will display the beginning balance entered when the account was created in QuickBooks.
- **PAYMENTS**: This field will summarize all of the payments/withdrawals that have cleared on your bank or credit card statement.
- **DEPOSITS**: This field will summarize all of the deposits that have cleared on your bank or credit card statement.
- **DIFFERENCE**: The difference between the statement ending balance and the cleared balance will appear in this field. The goal is to reach a difference of $0.00. Zero indicates that all items that have cleared your bank or credit card statement have been recorded in QuickBooks. The goal is to never click **Finish now** until the difference is zero.

8. The following is a snapshot of the bank and credit card information that appears after the header information:

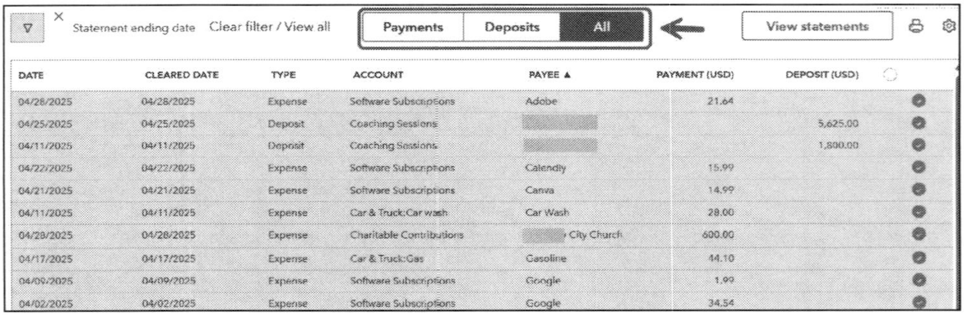

Figure 11.21: Bank and credit card details listed in the reconciliation window

Here's a brief explanation of the details in the reconciliation window shown in the preceding screenshot:

- **Transaction type**: At the top of the screen, there are three tabs: **Payments, Deposits,** and **All**. You can click on one of the first two tabs to filter by a specific transaction type, or you can select **All**.
- **Transaction details**: The transaction date, cleared date, transaction type, reference number (not shown), category (account), payee, memo (not shown), and amount of each transaction that has been recorded in QuickBooks are listed in this section.

9. If a transaction appears on your bank or credit card statement, you need to put a check mark in the radio button (located in the far-right column) to mark it as cleared in QuickBooks. Each time you mark a transaction as cleared, it will be included in the cleared balance in the header section shown previously. As discussed, after marking all items that have cleared your bank or credit card statement, you should have a difference of zero, as shown in *Figure 11.20*. If you do not, you are either missing a transaction in QuickBooks, or you may have marked a transaction as cleared that does not appear on your statement.
10. Once your difference equals zero, you can click the **Finish now** button to generate the bank reconciliation reports. If you are having an issue with balancing to zero, you can save your work and pick up where you left off. Click on the drop-down arrow next to the **Finish now** button, and you can choose to save for later or close without saving, as indicated in *Figure 12.22*:

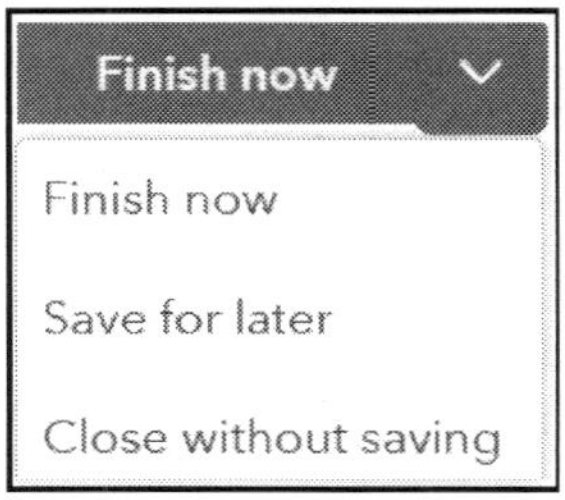

Figure 11.22: Options for saving bank reconciliation in QBO

If you are having trouble reconciling to a difference of zero, compare the deposit total in the header window to the deposit total on your bank statement. If it matches, then you know there is an issue with withdrawals. If it doesn't match, then you know there is an issue with deposits. Do the same comparison on the withdrawal side. You could be out of balance with both or with just one transaction type. In addition, if your difference is divisible by nine, it could be a transposition error.

> Do not click the **Finish now** button if you don't have a difference of zero. Instead, click the **Save for later** option. You can always come back and resume the reconciliation from where you left off.

11. After successfully reconciling accounts, be sure to save the summary and detail bank reconciliation reports. They will be made available after you complete the bank reconciliation. Bank reconciliation reports are one of several reports that auditors will request during an audit, so it is very important to save these reports to your computer. If you forget to save the reports, you can always access them from within the Banking Center. You can also keep copies of your monthly statements saved in QBO.
12. After reconciling an account, you may discover that you need to edit a transaction that was previously reconciled. Be sure that you don't change the amount; otherwise, your account will be out of balance. However, you can edit the **Category** (account) and **Description** fields easily.
13. Navigate to the chart of accounts and click on the **View register** link next to the bank account, as indicated in *Figure 11.23*:

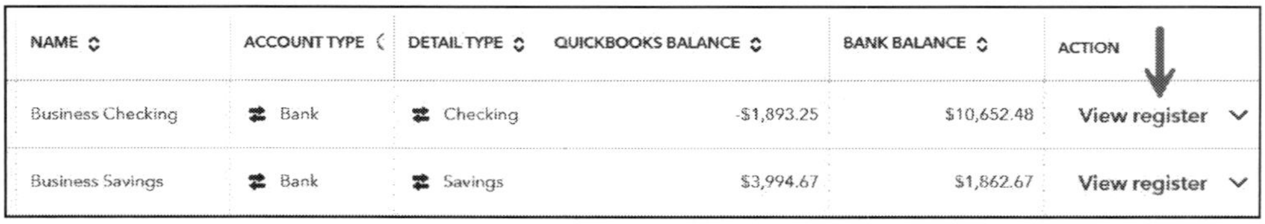

Figure 11.23: Editing a transaction that was previously reconciled

14. Make the necessary edits and save your changes.

As discussed, reconciling your accounts will help to ensure you haven't accidentally omitted recording any transactions. Plus, it will help you ensure that your books agree with your financial institution's records. It's important to reconcile all of your bank and credit card accounts on a monthly basis (or more frequently, if possible), in order to catch errors made by the bank or to identify fraudulent transactions.

Troubleshooting tips for reconciling bank and credit card accounts

There will be times when you might encounter an issue with reconciling your bank or credit card statements to QBO. If you are having trouble getting to a **$0.00** difference, as shown in *Step 7* previously, here are a few troubleshooting tips you can try:

1. Narrow the search down to the transaction type. To do this, compare the total withdrawals on the bank/credit card statement to the total payments in the reconciliation window, as shown here:

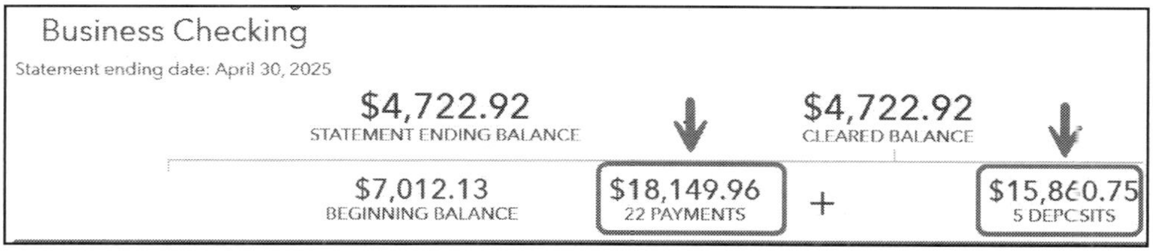

Figure 11.24: Reviewing total payments and total deposits

2. If they do not match, there is an issue with a payment (withdrawal). Do the same comparison for the deposits. Compare the total deposits on the bank statement to the deposits shown in the reconciliation window. If they do not match, you have an issue with deposits.
3. If you discover that you are out of balance for both the payments (withdrawals) and the deposits, tackle them separately. In other words, balance the withdrawals first and then move on to deposits, or vice versa.
4. Look for the exact dollar amount that you are out of balance by. For example, in *Figure 11.25*, the difference is **-$3,800.00**:

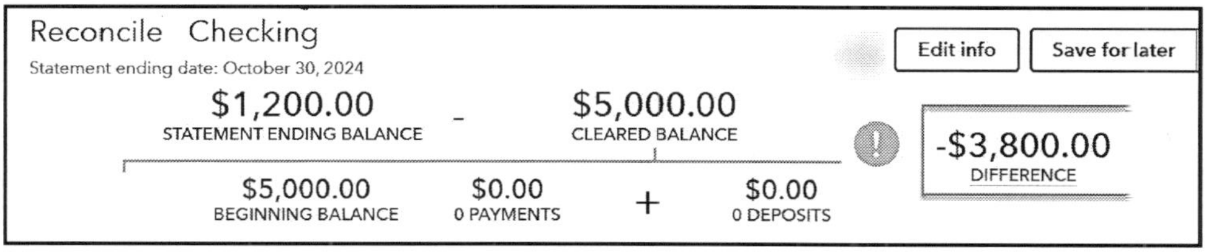

Figure 11.25: Reviewing the difference in the reconciling window

In our example, we would look for this amount on the bank statement and within the reconciling window for payments and deposits.

5. Double-check that the statement ending balance, beginning balance, and statement ending date are correct. If you need to make any corrections, click on the **Edit info** button shown in *Figure 11.25* to make the necessary changes.
6. Verify that all of the transactions you have selected in the reconciliation window are actually on the bank/credit card statement. If not, you need to deselect them. It is possible that there is a timing difference, which means they will appear on the statement in the following month.
7. If you find that there is a transaction listed on the bank statement but it is not showing up in QuickBooks, you will need to go to the Banking Center to see whether it is listed there. If so, complete the necessary fields (**Payee** and **Category**) and post the transaction. When you return to the reconciliation window, it should be listed there, but you will need to select it by putting a check mark in the radio button to update the totals.
8. If you have been at it for a while, I recommend that you take a break. You can click the **Save for later** option, and it will save your work so that you can pick up where you left off. Sometimes, taking a breather and coming back can help you spot what's causing the difference.

> After reconciliation is complete, this is a good time to look at outstanding items on both the check side and the deposit side. Research and determine whether additional cleanup work is needed so that your cash balance on your books is accurate.

Summary

In this chapter, we have discussed how to manage uploaded bank and credit card transactions. You have learned how to match uploaded transactions with transactions previously recorded in QuickBooks. You now know how to make changes to transactions so that the correct payee and category (account) are recorded. You have also learned how to create bank rules in order to reduce the number of transactions you need to review in the Banking Center, which will save you time. Finally, you understand the importance of reconciling bank and credit card accounts on a frequent basis to ensure your records are in sync with your financial institution.

We have met our goal of giving you the knowledge to successfully manage your uploaded bank and credit card transactions. Having this knowledge will help you save the time you would normally have spent manually entering bank and credit card transactions into QuickBooks.

Reconciling your accounts will also help you become familiar with how much money you are spending, as well as what you are spending it on. Remember, having the ability to control your expenses will help to improve your bottom line. In the next chapter, we will show you how to manage payments to 1099 contractors, including annual 1099 reporting. We will also introduce you to QuickBooks Time.

Next steps

1. If you have not done so already, connect all of your business bank and credit card accounts to QBO.
2. Reconcile all business bank and credit card accounts.
3. Generate financial reports, such as *Profit and Loss* and *Balance Sheet* reports, for accuracy.
4. If you have a bookkeeper or accountant who manages your books, schedule time to meet with that person each month. However, make sure that you have already reviewed your financial reports and made a list of your questions prior to this meeting. In other words, schedule your "money date" before you meet with your bookkeeper or accountant, if applicable.
5. Be sure to head over to my YouTube channel for step-by-step product demos in QBO. Use this link to access the channel:

`https://packt.link/du2BR`

12

Managing 1099 Contractors and Introducing QuickBooks Time in QBO

As a small business owner, there will be times when you need to have someone design your website, manage your social media, or just assist you with administrative tasks. Unfortunately, many small businesses cannot afford to hire full-time employees to carry out these tasks. Instead, they will hire an individual or an agency.

These individuals or agencies are considered to be independent contractors, also known as **1099 contractors**. Payments to 1099 contractors must be tracked so that you can report this information to the IRS at the end of the year.

To ensure payments are tracked properly, you will need to set up contractors in QuickBooks, add an account to post all payments to, pay contractors with a paper check (or an **electronic fund transfer** (**EFT**), or debit/credit card), and provide a 1099 form to all the contractors who meet the threshold at the end of the year. If the total payments to a contractor equal $600 or more, you must issue a 1099 form and report this information to the IRS. Failure to track and report payments to 1099 contractors could lead to penalties and fines.

> To determine what constitutes a 1099 vendor versus an employee, be sure to visit `http://irs.gov` for more information. The laws around this are updated each year, so check out the IRS website to stay up to date on changes made each year.

We will introduce you to the **Contractors Center**, a one-stop shop for all things related to contractors. From setup to 1099 processing, you can manage all aspects of independent contractors within the Contractors Center. We will show you how the Contractors Center automates this process, which will save you the time you normally would have spent tracking down key information so that you can provide 1099 reports to both contractors and the IRS each year.

In this chapter, we will cover the following topics:

- Setting up 1099 contractors
- Tracking and paying 1099 contractors
- 1099 year-end reporting
- Introducing QuickBooks Time

> The US edition of QBO was used in this book. If you are using a version that is outside of the US, results may differ.

Let's get started with setting up 1099 contractors in QBO.

Setting up 1099 contractors

It's important to set up 1099 contractors correctly in QuickBooks to ensure payments are tracked for 1099 reporting purposes. In the most recent version of QBO, there is now a way to collect the information normally provided on a paper W-9 form electronically. A W-9 form is similar to a W-4 form for an employee. It includes the contractor's name, mailing address, business entity type (sole proprietor, partnership, S-Corp, or C-Corp), tax ID number, and signature.

To set up a new contractor, you simply send an invitation to them, which requires them to create a user ID and password. Once they do so, they can complete the W-9 form online. Once the form is completed, you will be notified and can go into QBO and view the electronic W-9 form.

Within the Contractors Center, you can also process contractor payments and generate reports as needed.

> It is best practice to obtain a complete W-9 form from each contractor before you make your first payment to them. Having this information is important because you will need it to create a 1099 form, if applicable.

Follow these steps to set up a 1099 contractor in QuickBooks:

1. Navigate to **Expenses & Bills** and then **Contractors**, as shown in *Figure 12.1*:

Figure 12.1: Navigating to the Contractors Center

2. Click **Add your first contractor**. If you already have contractors in QBO, your screen will look slightly different, and you will see the option to add a contractor:

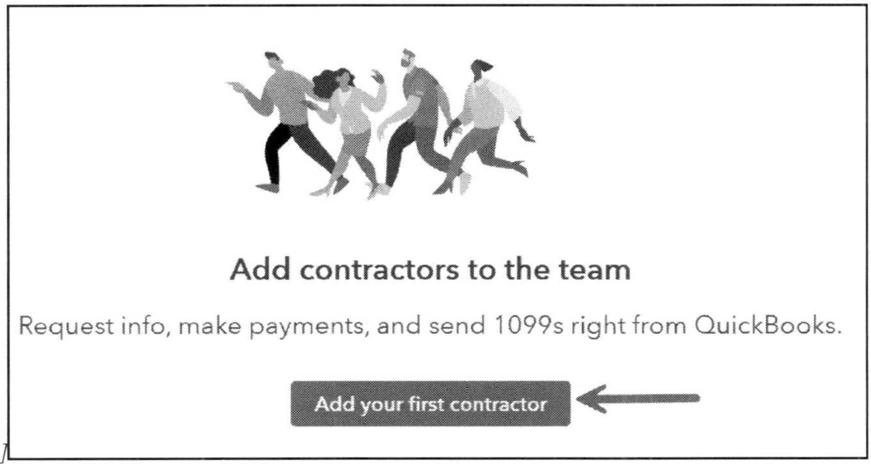

Figure 12.2: Clicking on Add your first contractor

3. The following screen will display. Complete the fields and click on the **Add contractor** button, as shown in *Figure 12.3*:

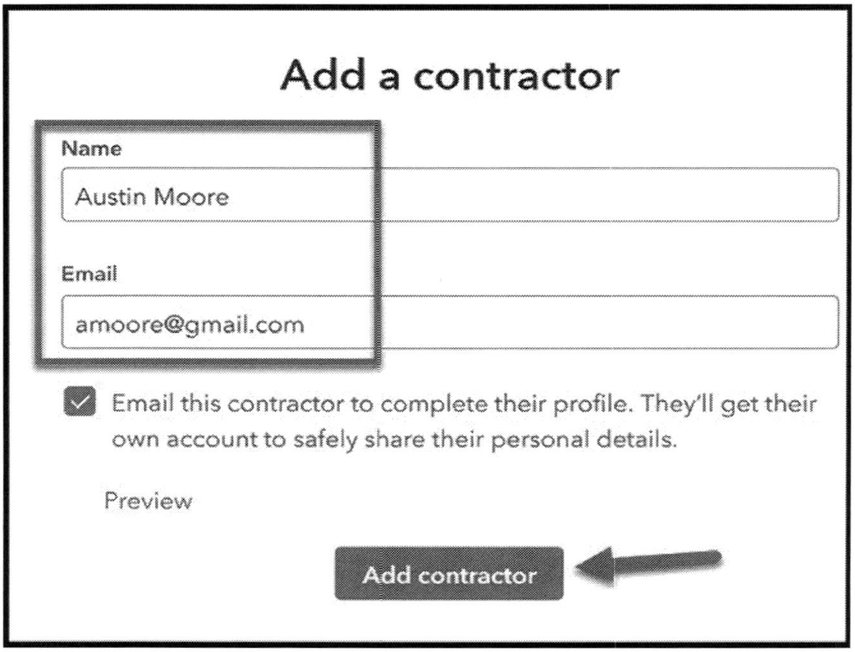

Figure 12.3: Completing the fields to add a new contractor

Before QBO allows you to add a contractor, you will see a pop-up that requires you to enter a security code that will be sent to you via text message or email. You will not be allowed to proceed until you enter this code. This level of security is to ensure that the person who is adding a contractor is authorized to do so. Once the code is entered, the email invitation will be sent to the contractor, per the note right below the **Email** field shown in *Figure 12.3*.

> If you already have a W-9 form and you want to enter the information manually, remove the check mark next to **Email this contractor to complete their profile. They'll get their own account to safely share their personal details.** an click **Add contractor**. You can add the pertinent information on the next screen.

4. Contractors will receive an email similar to the one shown in the following screenshot. They will need to click on **Get started** to gain access to a portal where they can manage W-9 information, banking information if they would like to be paid via direct deposit, and 1099 information:

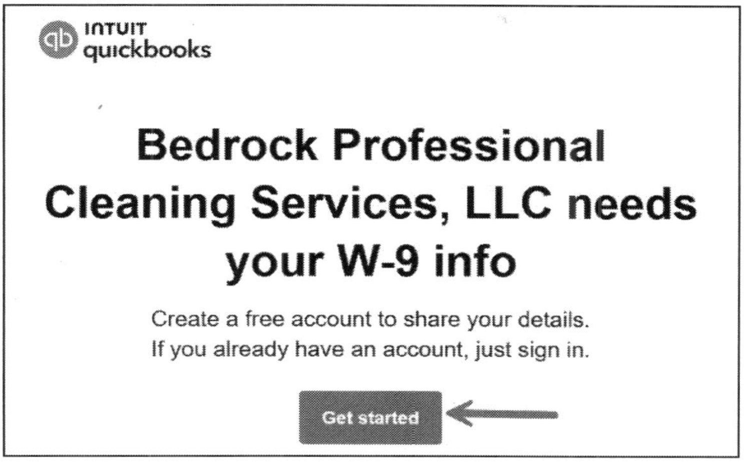

Figure 12.4: Sample email contractors will receive

5. After completing the necessary fields, you will see the new contractor listed in the **Contractors Center**, as shown in *Figure 12.5*:

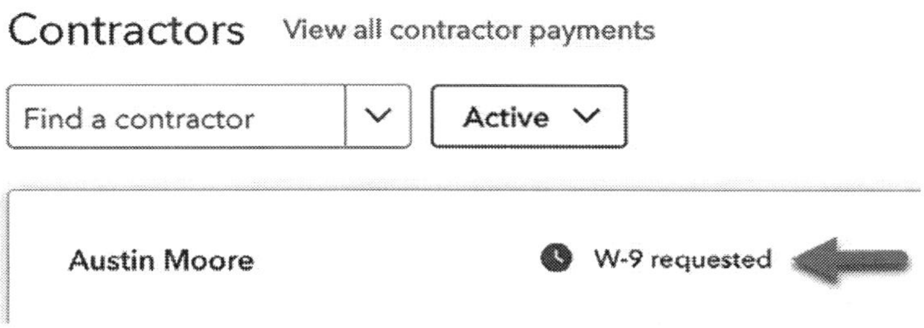

Figure 12.5: Status of the new contractors listed in the Contractors Center

After adding a new contractor, you will see them listed within the Contractors Center along with a note indicating that the current status is **W-9 form has been requested**.

6. Once the W-9 form has been completed, the status will change to **W-9 ready**, as shown in *Figure 12.6*:

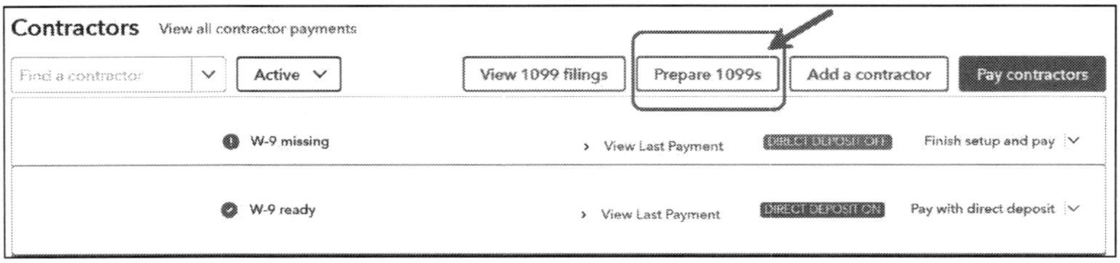

Figure 12.6: Reviewing the W-9 status for contractors

Repeat these steps for each 1099 contractor you pay throughout the year. Once you have added all your contractors to QuickBooks, you are ready to make payments. We will discuss how to track and pay 1099 contractors next.

Tracking and paying 1099 contractors

The simplest way to keep track of payments to 1099 vendors is to create an account called `Contractor labor expense`. This account should be added to your chart of accounts list and used to post all 1099 payments. For more information on adding accounts to the chart of accounts, refer to *Chapter 4, Customizing QuickBooks for Your Business.*

You can pay 1099 contractors within the Contractors Center. Follow these steps to set up a payment to a contractor:

1. Navigate to the Contractors Center (**Expense & Bills** | **Contractors**).

   The following screen will display:

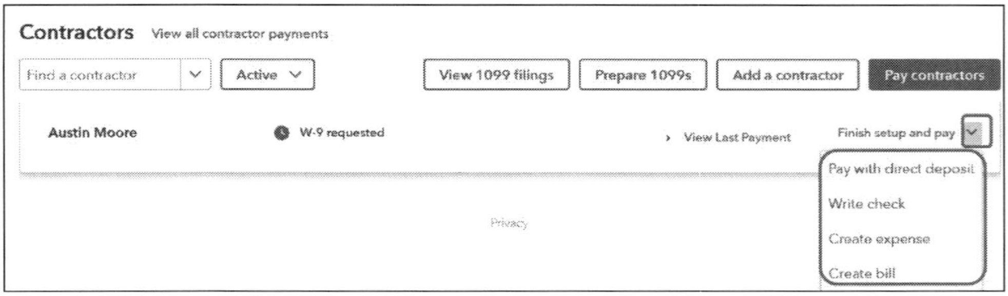

Figure 12.7: Paying contractors within the Contractors Center

2. In the far-right column, click on the arrow to select the payment method (**Pay with direct deposit**, **Write check**, **Create expense**, or **Create bill**). Please note that if you would like to pay contractors with direct deposit, you will need to enter their payment details (bank account and bank routing number) before you can do so. This information can be entered by selecting the **Finish setup and pay** link that is shown in *Figure 12.7*.
3. If you select **Pay with direct deposit**, you will see the screen shown here:

Figure 12.8: Paying a contractor via direct deposit in QBO

Complete the fields indicated in *Figure 12.8* as follows:

- **Enter payment** (1): Enter the total amount of the payment.
- **Corresponding account in QuickBooks** (2): From the dropdown, select the expense account (e.g., contractors' expenses, website design, etc.).
- **Description** (3): Enter a brief description of the type of services provided by the contractor (e.g., monthly social media marketing). This field can also indicate the time period the payment is for (e.g., services for 11/01 to 11/15).
- **Customer** (4): If you do have customers that you bill back for time worked by contractors, you can select the customer from the dropdown. This payment will also be included in the unbilled expenses account, which you can add to a customer's invoice in order to be reimbursed.
- **Paid from** (5): You will see the bank account that the payment will be deducted from. This will typically be the business checking account or your payroll account if you have a separate account for employee and contractor payments.
- **Corresponding account in QuickBooks** (6): From the dropdown, select the bank account in QuickBooks that corresponds to the actual bank account the payment will be deducted from in the **Paid from** field.
- **Pay date** (7): Select the date you would like the payment to be made. QBO allows you to set a date in the future. Typically, this will be the next business day as long as you submit it before 5 P.M. PT, as indicated in *Figure 12.8*.
- **Pay** (8): Click on the **Pay** button to submit the payment.

> After the payment is submitted, you will receive an email indicating that this payment is in process. If you have added their email address in QBO, the contractor will also receive an email to let them know that the payment is in process. The email will include the payment amount and the date the payment has been scheduled for.

Now that you know how to add independent contractors to QuickBooks, set up an account to track payments, and make payments, it's time to discuss what you will do with this information.

1099 year-end reporting

1099 year-end reporting consists of printing and mailing 1099 forms to contractors who meet the $600 threshold and reporting this information to the IRS by January 31st each year. This date is subject to change, so be sure to visit `http://irs.gov` each year to confirm the due date.

Similar to a **W-2 form** or **Wage and Tax Statement** for an employee that includes the amount paid in wages for a calendar year, the 1099 form includes the amount you have paid to a contractor within the calendar year.

This form is used by independent contractors to report their earnings for the year on their tax returns. Failure to provide this information to the IRS and the contractors could result in fines and penalties.

When you are ready to generate 1099 forms, the process is very simple. First, you review the accuracy of your information and the basic contact information for each contractor. Then, you review the payments that have been flagged as 1099 payments. If this information is correct, you can have Intuit process your 1099 forms electronically for a fee. Another option is to manually print and mail the 1099 forms yourself.

There are various types of 1099 forms. The most common are Form 1099-DIV, which is issued for dividends and distributions, Form 1099-INT, which is issued for interest income, and Form 1099-MISC, which is issued for miscellaneous income.

> Currently, the IRS requires you to exclude payments made to a 1099 vendor via debit card, credit card, or gift card from Form 1099-MISC. In addition, payments made through third-party payment networks, such as PayPal and QuickBooks Payments, should also be excluded. Instead, these payments are reported by the card issuers and third-party networks on Form 1099-K. The 1099 vendor will receive a copy of Form 1099-K directly from the card issuers.

Follow these steps to learn how to do 1099 reporting:

1. Navigate to the **Contractors Center**, as shown in *Figure 12.9*:

Figure 12.9: Navigating to the Contractors Center

2. Click on **Prepare 1099s**, as shown in *Figure 12.10*:

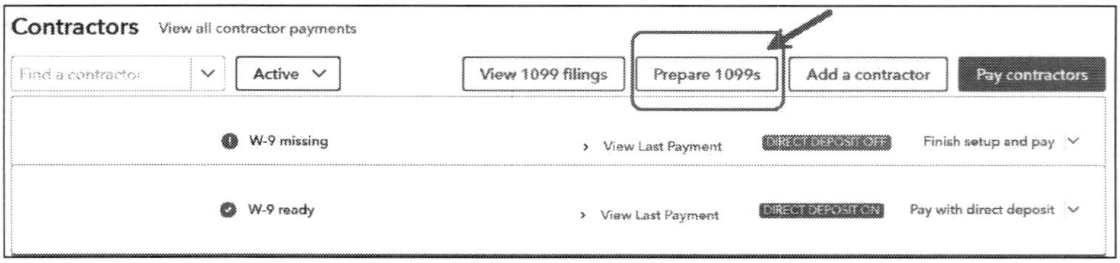

Figure 12.10: Clicking the Prepare 1099s button

3. If this is your first time preparing 1099s, the following screen will appear. Click the button for the plan you wish to choose:

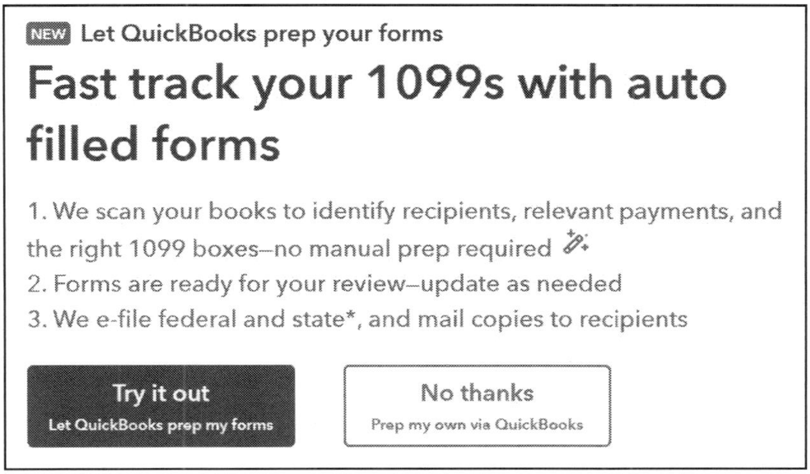

Figure 12.11: Choosing your 1099 processing plan

The following is a comparison of the two plans available for 1099 processing:

Feature	**Let QuickBooks prep your forms**	**Prep with QuickBooks' help**
E-filing and tracking	✓	✓
Combined federal and state e-filing (CFSF)	✓	✓
Recommended list of vendors who appear to need a 1099	✓	
Scanned and filtered list of payments to report on 1099s	✓	
Pre-filled, editable 1099 forms	✓	
Printed and mailed copies to recipients	Included	Included

Table 12.1: Comparing 1099 processing plans

A brief description of what is included in each plan is provided here:

- **E-filing and tracking**: Intuit will submit your forms to the IRS electronically and track their status.
- **Combined federal and state e-filing (CFSF)**: An IRS program that allows for simpler federal and state filings. Click the link to find out whether your state is supported: `https://packt.link/EFteI`.
- **Recommended list of vendors who appear to need a 1099**: QBO automatically scans all vendors and flags those that meet the 1099 criteria, removing corporations. You can edit the list as needed.
- **Scanned and filtered list of payments to report on 1099s**: QBO scans all transactions in your QBO file to identify payments that should be reported on 1099 forms, excluding credit card payments.
- **Pre-filled, editable 1099 forms**: QBO will determine the correct 1099 form for each vendor and allocate payment totals to the correct fields on the form. You can always make edits.
- **Printed and mailed copies to recipients**: QBO will send the forms on your behalf via snail mail and email.

If you have QBO Payroll Elite, 1099 processing is included with your subscription plan. If you don't have the Elite payroll plan, the pricing is as follows:

1099 Plan	First 3 forms	Forms 4-20	Forms 21+
Let QBO prep your forms	$17.99/form	$13.99/form	$9.99/form
Prep my own via QBO	$5.99/form	$4.99/form	$2.99/form

Table 12.2: E-filing price per form

Please note that this is the pricing as of the time of writing this book and is subject to change.

If you have prepared 1099s in QBO before, you will see the deadline for e-filing 1099s and the deadline for printing and mailing 1099s for the upcoming tax season.

4. On the next screen, you can review your company information and make any necessary corrections:

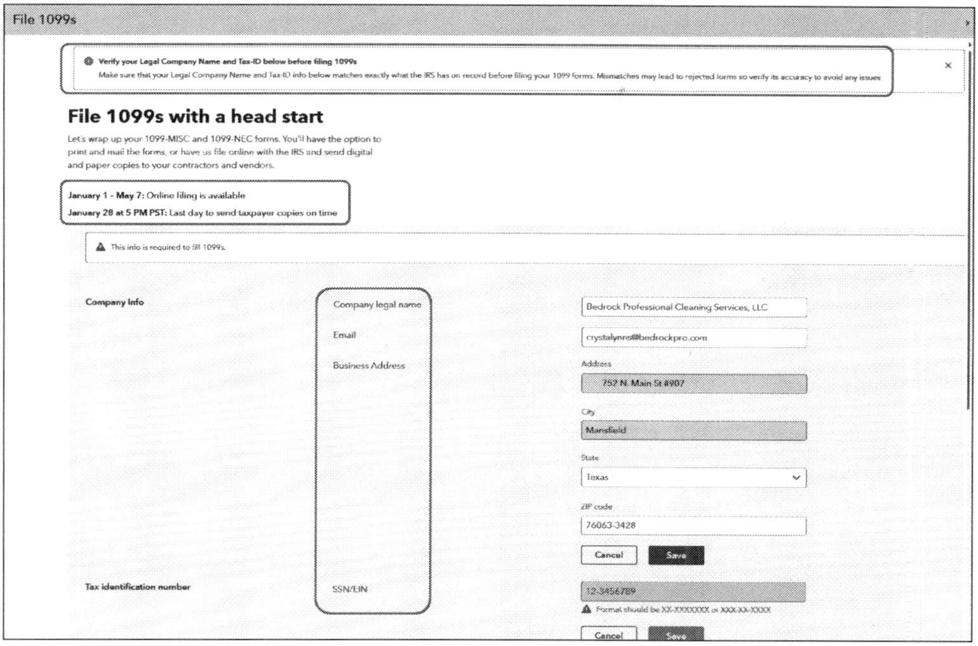

Figure 12.12: Reviewing your company info for accuracy

5. Click the **Save** button when you are done.

6. Click **Next** at the bottom of the screen. Then, select the box and the account you have categorized 1099 payments to, from the list shown in *Figure 12.13*:

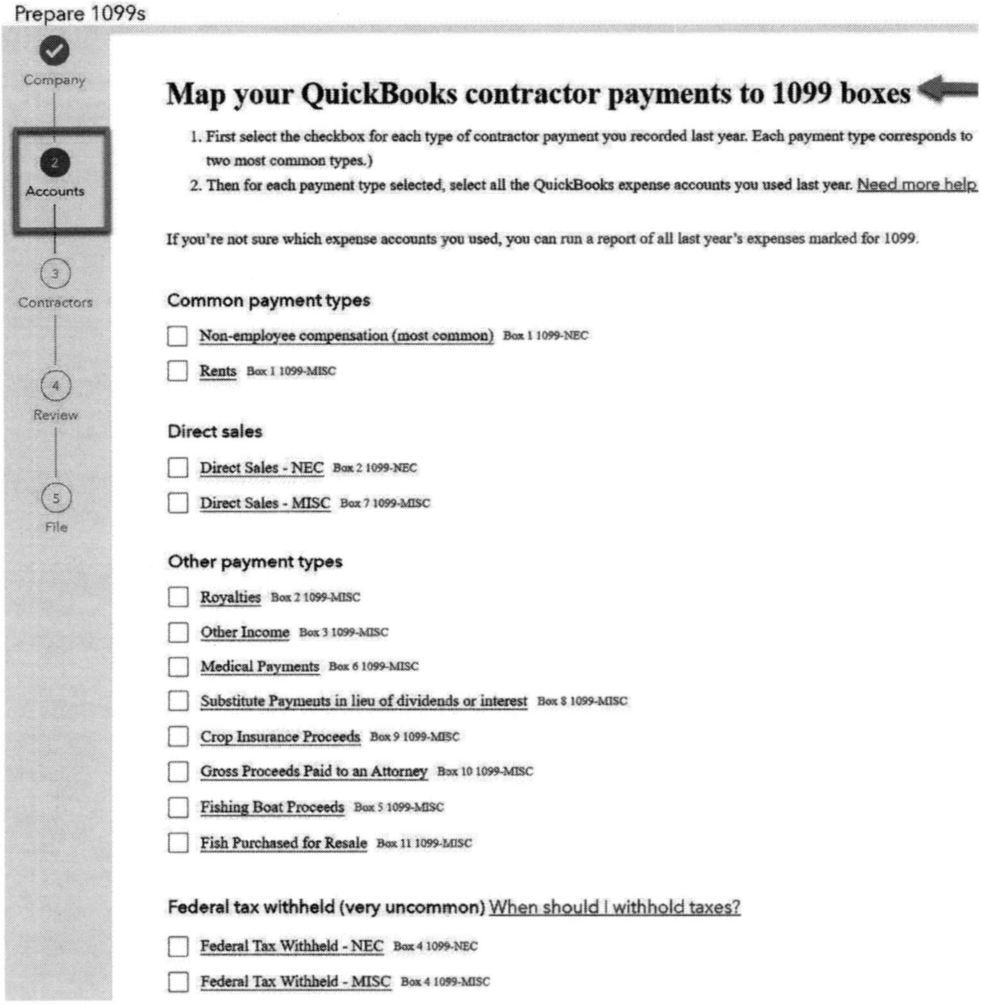

Figure 12.13: Mapping QuickBooks contractor payments to 1099 boxes

In general, you will select the first box, **Non-employee compensation (most common)**, on the 1099 forms you generate for the contractors you have paid. In the dropdown below this box, select the account (category) these payments were posted to (e.g., **Contract labor**). To learn more about which box to select, refer to the IRS instructions for Form 1099. You can find this information at `http://irs.gov`.

7. On the next screen, review your contractors' information to ensure that it is accurate:

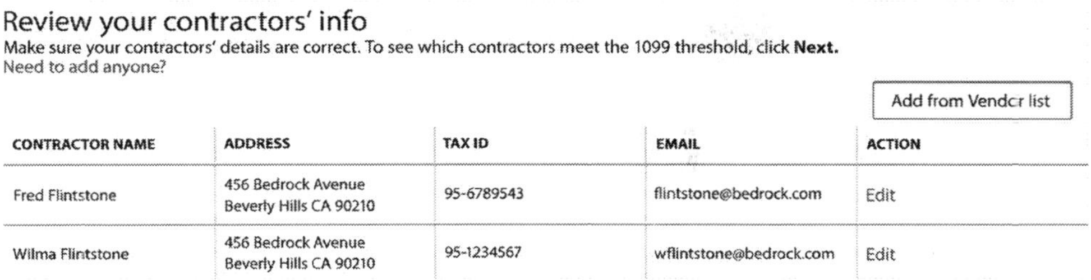

Figure 12.14: Reviewing contractors' info for accuracy

Note that you cannot print 1099 forms if your contractor's mailing address or tax ID (or Social Security number) is missing. You must obtain this information prior to printing the 1099 forms.

8. A list of contractors that meet the 1099 threshold will be displayed on the next screen:

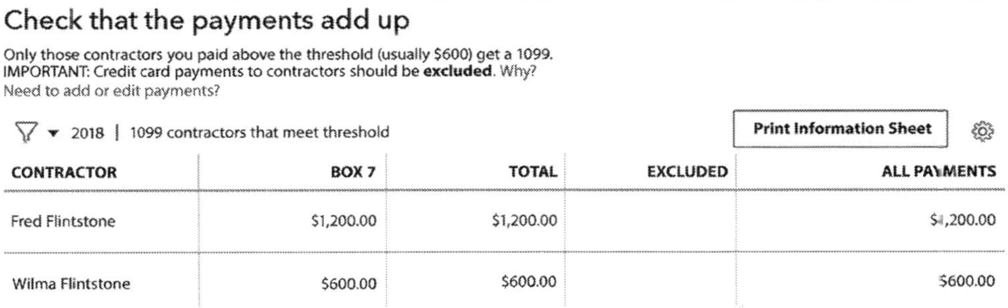

Figure 12.15: Reviewing 1099 payments for accuracy

To meet the 1099 threshold, contractors must have received payments totaling $600 or more within the calendar year. If a contractor was paid less than $600, you are not required to issue a 1099 form, and the contractor won't show up in the preceding list.

9. On the next screen, select the 1099 plan that works best for you:

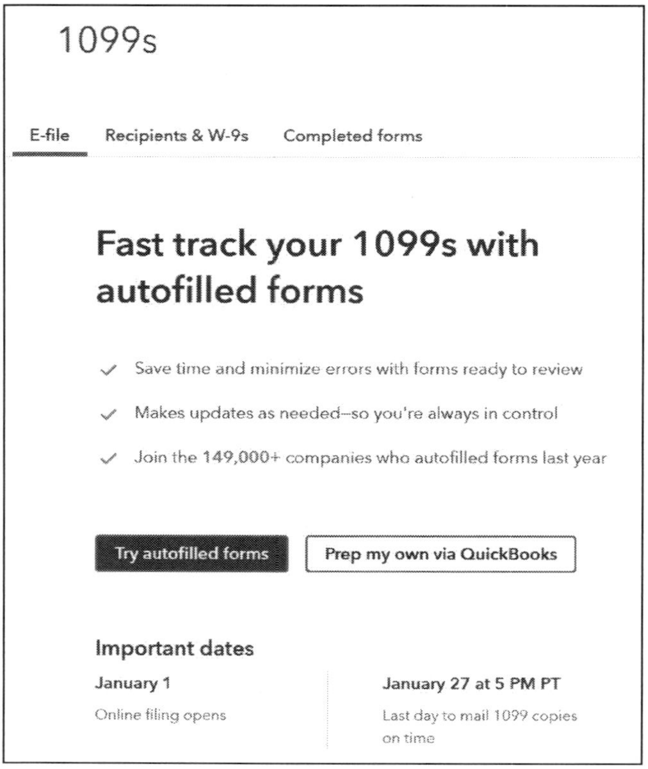

Figure 12.16: Choosing the method you wish to use to file 1099 forms

The two 1099 plans available are the following:

- **Let QuickBooks prep your forms**: QBO does all of the heavy lifting with this plan. QBO will scan your books to identify 1099 contractors with relevant payments and automatically select the right 1099 boxes, no manual prep required. You will have the opportunity to review the forms and make any updates or changes as needed. After you review the forms, Intuit will e-file both the federal and state forms and mail copies to the recipients or send an email notification to those whose email address you have on file. This plan starts at $17.99/form for the first three forms; if you have between 4 and 20 forms, there is a slight discount of $13.99/form, and for 21 or more forms, it is $9.99/form. This is the most efficient way to process your 1099 forms. They will be sent to contractors as well as the IRS. You will also have a copy to keep on file for your records. While printing and mailing is an option, it is recommended to file electronically if possible.

- **Prep my own via QuickBooks:** Instead of QBO doing the work, you will need to determine which contractors need to receive a 1099 form, along with which 1099 form they need to receive. However, this plan does include the ability to e-file and track your forms submitted to the IRS and applicable state filings. This plan starts at $5.99/form for the first three forms, $4.99/form if you have anywhere between 4 and 20 forms, and $2.99/form for 21 or more forms that need to be filed.

Please note that the prices of these plans may differ. Visit `https://www.intuit.com/` for the most up-to-date pricing plans available. To select a plan, just click on the plan you want to choose and follow the onscreen prompts to complete filing your 1099 forms.

Another way that you can track the hours worked by employees and contractors is to use the QuickBooks Time feature. QuickBooks Time allows you to ensure that all billable hours are accounted for so that your customer invoices are accurate.

Introducing QuickBooks Time

If you have a service-based business that relies on the ability to keep track of billable hours, **QuickBooks Time** is a great solution. Similar to QBO Payroll, there are three QuickBooks Time plans: Basic, Premium, and Elite. The Basic plan is included in all QBO subscriptions at no additional cost. However, you (or your employees/contractors) will have to enter time manually with the basic plan.

The following is a comparison chart of the features included in the Premium and Elite plans:

	Premium	**Elite**
Cost	$20/month + $8 per user per month	$40/month + $10 per user per month
Seamless QuickBooks integration	✓	✓
Streamlined payroll and invoicing	✓	✓
Workforce mobile app	✓	✓
Mobile crew time entry	✓	✓
Attach photos	✓	✓

	Premium	**Elite**
See who's working	✓	✓
Track time to jobs and customers	✓	✓
Customize reports	✓	✓
Create schedules	✓	✓
Calculate billable hours	✓	✓
Unlimited live customer support	✓	✓
Manage time off	✓	✓
Time kiosk	✓	✓
Assign jobs and projects to employees		✓
Track mileage		✓
Track time to projects		✓
Track project progress to plan		✓
Project estimates versus actuals reporting		✓
Project activity feed and messaging		✓
Timesheet signatures		✓
Geofencing		✓

Table 12.3: Comparing Premium and Elite QuickBooks Time plans

As you can see in the preceding table, both the Premium and Elite plans include the following features:

- **Seamless QuickBooks integration**: One of the benefits of using QuickBooks Time over a third-party company is that you can manage time tracking directly in QuickBooks. There are no spreadsheets to import or journal entries to record to get the data into QBO; it's automatically there!
- **Streamlined payroll and invoicing**: When you add employees and/or contractors to QuickBooks Time, their hours can be added to payroll to pay hourly employees, contractor payments, or customers whose invoices are based on billable hours for a job or project.
- **Workforce mobile app**: With the Workforce app, employees can clock in and out and access their pay stubs, W-2s, time off, and much more. As an employer, you can review and approve timesheets, verify who is on-site at a job or on the road, and so much more.
- **Mobile crew time entry**: Users have a variety of options for clocking in and out. For example, mobile workers can use their smartphone app.
- **Web- and cloud-based time tracking**: In addition to mobile workers using their smartphone app, office-based employees can use their web browsers, and shift-based workers can use an on-site tablet-based digital punch card called Time Clock Kiosk.
- **See who's working**: Using GPS technology, you can see where your team is working and when they clocked in/out so that you can schedule new jobs anytime from anywhere.
- **Track time to jobs and customers**: To ensure accurate customer billing, you can easily track the time for all jobs and customers so those hours can be included on the invoice.
- **Customize reports**: QuickBooks Time includes a library of customizable reports to help you manage all employee and contractor hours. You won't have to create reports from scratch; these reports are automatically included with your subscription to a QuickBooks Time plan.
- **Calculate billable hours**: As mentioned previously, QuickBooks Time will automatically keep track of billable hours. Whether you are an attorney who needs to bill clients back for hours worked or a plumber, QuickBooks Time allows you to ensure that you are paid for all hours worked on a project or job.
- **Unlimited live customer support**: Similar to all QBO subscription plans, there is a dedicated support team available to answer your questions. Unlimited support is available at no additional charge.

- **Manage time off**: Your team can enter time off; you can enter holiday time off for one or multiple employees at once.
- **Time Kiosk**: Set up a digital clock on a tablet, desktop, or laptop so your team can easily click in and out. Employees can also submit timesheets from the Time Kiosk.

As you can see in *Table 12.3*, the Elite plan is double the monthly cost of the Premium plan: $40/month versus $20/month. In addition, the cost per user is $8/user for Premium and $10/user for Elite. If you are not tracking time by project or job, the Premium plan should work for you. However, if you do need to keep track of billable hours by job/project, you should choose the Elite plan.

Summary

To recap, you now know what information is required to set up 1099 contractors in QuickBooks, how to track payments that have been made to 1099 contractors, the various ways you can pay 1099 contractors, and how to report and file 1099 forms at the end of the year. If you hire individuals such as an attorney or a bookkeeper to provide services to your business, you now know how to set them up in QuickBooks and track payments that are made to them throughout the year. You also know that the threshold for reporting 1099 payments is $600 in payments within a calendar year. We have also shown you how to sign up for the 1099 service provided by Intuit so that you can e-file your forms with the IRS and applicable states. Finally, we introduced you to QuickBooks Time, which helps you to keep track of billable hours for employees and contractors.

1099 reporting is just one of the many tasks that must be performed at the end of the year. In the next chapter, we will cover how to set up payroll for employees, the key reports needed to stay on top of payroll expenses, and what payroll tax forms need to be filed, as well as their respective due dates.

Next steps

1. Use this link to head over to our YouTube channel to watch a video on the ins and outs of 1099 processing:

`https://packt.link/du2BR`

2. Generate a 1099 Transaction Detail report and review it to ensure all contractors that you have paid so far appear in the report.
3. Generate an Expenses by Vendor Summary report as a backup to ensure all contractors have been identified as such.

> If you see a line item called **Unidentified Vendor**, that means you have recorded transactions that have not been assigned to a vendor. Review those transactions and update the vendor field so that they are properly reported.

4. For any contractors that are missing from the report, send them an invitation to complete an online W-9 form or request a paper copy and update QBO with this information.
5. Implement a process going forward that ensures you collect the W-9 information from all contractors prior to making any payments.
6. Before the end of the year, head over to the 1099 reporting center and begin the process of reviewing the 1099 forms to ensure that you have all of the required information for each contractor (mailing address, entity type, and email address). Request any missing information and update QBO once you receive it.

13

Managing Employees in QuickBooks Online

Managing payroll is one of the most important aspects of your business. If not done right, it could negatively impact your employees since they may not be paid the right amount. It could also result in interest and penalties if payroll taxes are not filed and paid on time.

There are four main aspects of managing payroll: setting up your employees with the proper deductions and benefit elections, processing payroll by ensuring that the hours paid are correct and on time, generating payroll reports to gain insight into total payroll costs, and filing payroll tax forms and making payments on time. In this chapter, we will cover the information required to properly set up payroll and how to subscribe to an Intuit payroll subscription. We will walk through adding new employees to the payroll, cover the key payroll reports that will provide you with insight into payroll costs, and wrap up with the importance of filing payroll tax forms and making payments on time.

If you do not understand how payroll works or you do not wish to do your own payroll, it is highly recommended that you subscribe to the QBO Elite payroll plan, which is the full-service payroll option. QBO Elite is equivalent to third-party payroll services such as ADP and Paychex. We will provide additional details about the QBO Payroll Elite plan later on in this chapter.

One of the features included in all payroll plans at no additional cost is access to an HR Advisor platform called Mineral. You can chat or speak with an HR professional to ask questions you may have concerning hiring or firing employees. They also provide templates such as offer letters and employee handbooks, and other pertinent information to ensure that you remain compliant with how you manage both employees and contractors. To learn more about this amazing tool, you can log into QBO, click on the Payroll app, and select **HR Advisor**.

In this chapter, we will cover the following topics:

- Setting up payroll
- Adding new employees to payroll
- Generating payroll reports
- Filing payroll tax forms and payments

> The US edition of QBO was used in this book. If you are using a version that is outside of the US, results may differ.

Setting up payroll

The most important aspect of ensuring an accurate payroll is to set up the payroll properly before you run your first payroll. Setting up payroll involves gathering information about your employees, such as their names, mailing addresses, and social security numbers. As an employer, you will need a federal tax ID number and a business bank account for payroll checks and payroll taxes. You will need to determine what benefits you will offer employees, how often you will pay employees (for example, weekly, bi-weekly, or monthly), and the payment method you will use (for example, paper check or direct deposit).

> It is best practice to manage payroll out of a separate checking account from all other operating expenses. That way, you ensure that the funds for the payroll taxes remain in the account until you remit payment to the state and federal government.

In the following sections, we will provide you with a checklist of information you need to have handy to complete your employer profile and set up employees. This chapter provides the basic information needed to set up payroll. However, business owners should consult with a **Certified Public Accountant** (**CPA**) or payroll specialist to ensure their payroll taxes, insurance, 401 (k) plans, and other payroll-related items are in compliance with both federal and state regulations.

You can download a payroll setup checklist, a new employee checklist, and an *Employee Direct Deposit Authorization* form, along with other pertinent information, using this link: `https://github.com/PacktPublishing/Mastering-QuickBooks-2026-Seventh-Edition`.

Payroll setup checklist and key documents

As discussed, the key to ensuring the accuracy of payroll checks, payroll tax forms, and payments is to ensure that your payroll is set up properly. To set up payroll, you will need to gather information from your employees. Also, you will need to have certain documents and information handy to complete the employer information section. This information may vary state by state, so it is important, while following this guide, that you refer to your local employment development office for specific requirements.

The following table shows a summarized checklist of the information required to set up your payroll:

Employee info	**Employer info**
Hire date and birth date	**Federal employer identification number (FEIN)**
Form W-4: Employee withholding info (Federal and State) Form I-9: Employment Eligibility Verification	State agency ID number (if applicable) **State Unemployment Insurance (SUI)** Contribution rate State assessment, surcharge, administrative, or training tax rates
Salary or hourly rate	Business bank account information
Sick leave or vacation policy	Types of employee compensation
Payroll deductions and contributions	Types of employee benefits
Payment method	Employee travel reimbursement policy
Direct deposit authorization form (if applicable)	Other deductions: wage garnishment Remote or work-from-home employees

Table 13.1: Checklist of employee and employer info needed to set up payroll

The following is a brief explanation of the *employee* information required to set up payroll:

- **Hire date**: This is the official start date for an employee. This information will be used to determine benefits eligibility, as well as vacation and sick pay, if that is something you offer to your employees.
- **Birth date**: The employee's birthdate is used to determine eligibility for retirement benefits, 401K contributions, and other benefits.
- **Form W-4**: This is an official form issued by the **Internal Revenue Service (IRS)** to gather employee withholding information, which determines the amount of federal tax withheld from paychecks. You can download this form from `http://irs.gov` and include it in your employee new hire packet. Be sure to check your state's Department of Revenue website for any withholding forms that are needed.
- **Form I-9**: This form is called **Employment Eligibility Verification**, and it is used to verify the identity and employment authorization of individuals hired to work in the US.
- **Salary or hourly rate**: This is the agreed-upon salary or hourly rate for an employee.
- **Sick leave or vacation policy**: If you plan to offer sick or vacation leave, you will need to determine the number of hours an employee can earn toward sick or vacation leave. This is called an accrual rate.
- **Payroll deductions and contributions**: These are the deductions, such as wage garnishment or contributions for health care, 401(k), or other benefits that an employee has agreed to participate in. Deductions can be post-tax or pre-tax. Please check with your accountant if you are unsure of the taxability of any deductions.
- **Payment method**: Most employers will pay their employees in the form of a check or direct deposit. If the employee signs up for direct deposit, they will need to complete a direct deposit authorization form.
- **Direct deposit authorization**: If an employee would like their paycheck to be electronically deposited into their bank account, this form gives the employer the authority to do so. Employers must save this form on file along with other payroll information. You can find a sample direct deposit form here: `https://github.com/PacktPublishing/Mastering-QuickBooks-2026-Seventh-Edition`.

  Employee files are important for all businesses and should comply with all federal, state, and local requirements. When in doubt, seek guidance from a **CPA** or HR professional. New hire packets should be part of your normal business practices. These packets will generally include all of the necessary paperwork required under the employment law.

The following is a brief explanation of the *employer information* required to set up payroll:

- **FEIN**: Employers are required to have a federal tax ID number before they can process payroll for employees. This number is used by the IRS to keep track of employee and employer payroll tax payments and filings. If you don't have an FEIN, you can apply for one at `http://irs.gov`.
- **State agency ID number**: If you live in one of the states that are subject to income tax, you will need to apply for a state employer identification number. Similar to the FEIN, the state employer ID number is used to keep track of payroll tax payments and filings.
- **SUI contribution rate**: The percentage employers must pay on employee wages to fund their state's unemployment insurance programs. Contact your state's unemployment insurance office to obtain your rate.
- **State assessment, surcharge, administrative, or training tax rates**: These are additional taxes that could be applicable at the state level. You can contact your state agency directly to inquire about whether or not these taxes are applicable.

  Most states have a website where business owners can apply for their state agency ID number. It is important to know which taxes apply to your state and to consult an advisor regarding payroll tax withholding requirements for remote employees.

- **Business bank account information**: As discussed, I recommend that you set up a separate bank account to keep track of payments made to employees in the form of payroll checks or direct deposits. Also, all payroll tax payments made to the IRS or your state need to be made out of this account. Since most payments are made electronically, you will need the routing number of your financial institution and the full account number.

  Similar to your business checking account, you will need to add the payroll bank account to your chart of accounts list in QuickBooks. Refer to *Chapter 4, Customizing QuickBooks for Your Business*, where we cover how to add an account to the chart of accounts list.

- **Types of employee compensation**: This includes how you plan to compensate employees: hourly rates, salaried wages, bonuses, commission, and tips.
- **Types of employee benefits**: Details regarding benefits provided to employees will need to be entered into QuickBooks. This includes the employee and employer portions of health care, 401(k) plans, and sick leave and vacation pay.
- **Employee travel reimbursement policy**: If employees travel on behalf of your business and incur expenses, such as business meals, airfare, and hotel costs, you need to set up your payroll to reimburse employees for these.

A simpler way to handle employee reimbursements is to process the payments outside of payroll. This would involve setting up an employee as a vendor and writing a check to reimburse them for business expenses paid with personal funds. Refer to *Chapter 5, Managing Customer and Vendor Lists*, for instructions on how to add an employee as a vendor.

- **Other deductions**: On occasion, you may receive wage garnishments for employees who owe back taxes or child support. These are court-ordered requests that you cannot ignore. Instead, you must set up the garnishment amount as a deduction for the employee. These requests will typically have an end date that is based on the total outstanding amount. Be sure to set these payments up exactly as they are outlined in the letter. If you don't, you could be subject to penalties as a result. Please also note that some states limit the number of garnishments that can be withheld simultaneously. Please refer to your state guidelines if this issue arises.
- **Remote or work-from-home policy**: Nowadays, many employers have employees who work from home either 100% of the time or part of the time. It's important to establish what the policy is for these remote employees and ensure that it is communicated across the board. This policy should be included in your new employee handbook and communicated when onboarding new employees.

If you plan to manage payroll within QBO, an Intuit payroll subscription is required. With a payroll subscription, you are able to manage payroll from setup to payroll tax and forms filing. Payroll checks are automatically calculated based on the most recent payroll tax tables, which are automatically downloaded for you so that you don't have to calculate payroll manually. Now that you have a good understanding of the key documents and information required to properly set up payroll, you are ready to sign up for an Intuit payroll subscription.

Signing up for an Intuit payroll subscription

Setting up payroll in QBO can be done in six easy steps:

1. Click on the **Payroll** app located on the dashboard toward the end of the carousel of QBO apps, as shown here:

Figure 13.1: Navigating to the Payroll app

2. Click on the payroll features that you would like to have, and QBO will recommend a subscription plan that includes those features, as shown in *Figure 13.2*:

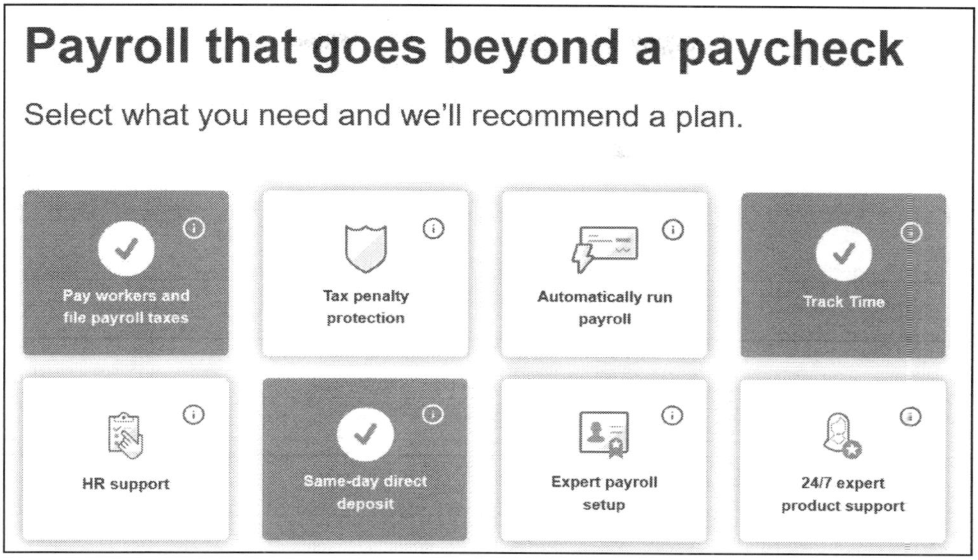

Figure 13.2: Making payroll selections

Based on the selections made in the previous screen, QBO recommends the Elite plan for Bedrock Professional Cleaning Services LLC, as shown in *Figure 13.3*:

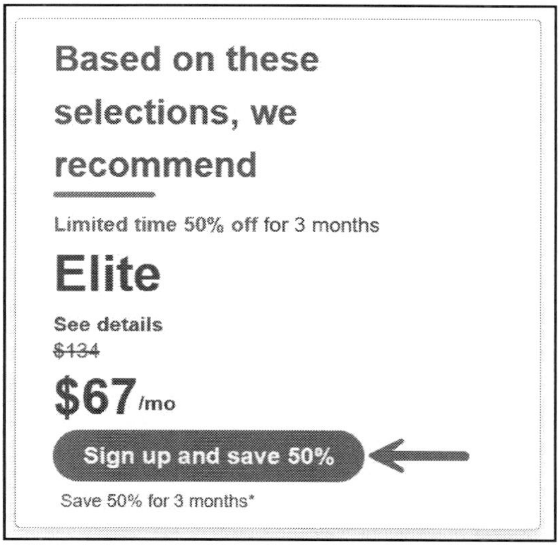

Figure 13.3: Payroll plan QBO recommends

3. To choose the recommended plan, click the **Sign up and save 50%** button, as shown in *Figure 13.3*.

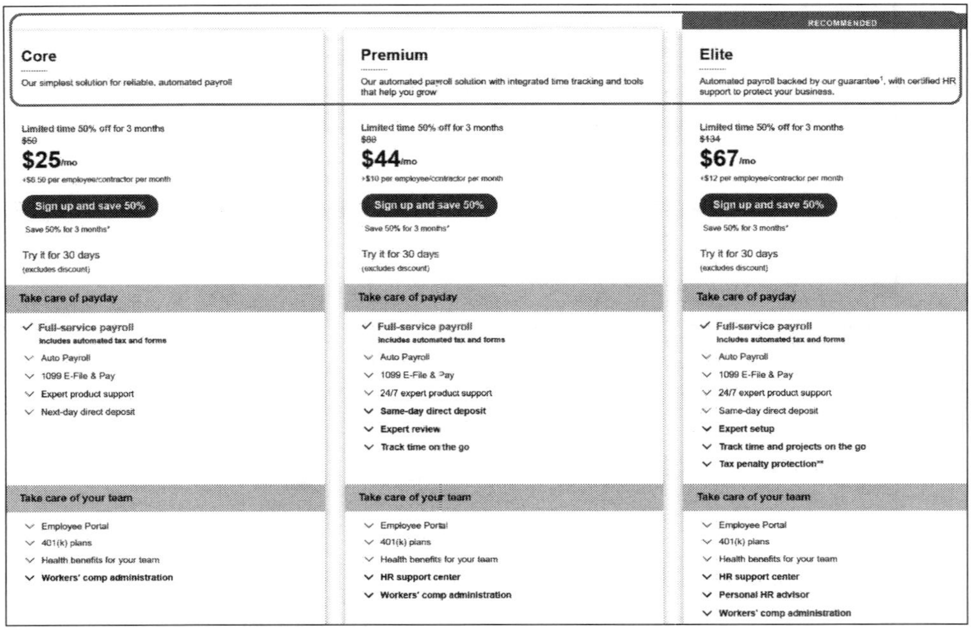

Figure 13.4: Reviewing features included in QBO payroll plans

Pricing is based on the current rates and is subject to change. Please visit `https://www.intuit.com/` (click on **Products** and select **QuickBooks**) for the most up-to-date information.

> Intuit no longer provides printing and mailing of W-2s and 1099s as part of subscriptions. These processes will incur an additional fee. Be sure to visit the website for the most up-to-date information on this.

The following is a brief explanation of each QBO payroll plan currently available:

- **Core**: This plan is ideal for employers who prefer to manage their payroll in-house. The subscription fee includes updated payroll tax tables that are used to automatically calculate payroll taxes and payroll checks for you—no manual calculation is required! With this plan, you can process payroll checks, electronically make payroll tax payments for state and federal taxes, and file payroll tax forms for state and federal taxes only. This plan does not offer local tax payments and filings. You will need to print the forms and upload them to the necessary local sites as required. This plan also includes next-day direct deposit.

The Core plan is recommended for small payrolls and someone with payroll experience. This is due to the fact that the responsibility for local payroll tax filings and payments will remain with the business owner.

- **Premium**: This plan includes all of the features outlined in the Core plan, plus automated local tax filings, same-day direct deposit, workers' comp administration, an HR support center, a QuickBooks expert who will review your payroll setup, and the ability to allow employees to track time using their mobile device. When setting up payroll, links will be available for applying for certain state ID numbers that are required.
- **Elite**: This plan includes customized setup by a QBO payroll expert, payroll processing, completion of tax forms, and automated payroll tax payments for federal, state, and local governments. Unlike the Core and Premium plans, it includes multi-state payroll filings, the ability to track projects from any mobile device, time tracking, tax penalty protection up to $25,000, access to a personal HR advisor, and 24/7 product support, which can be beneficial if there is an issue with payroll or an individual paycheck. Voids and corrections must be made by the payroll service.

QuickBooks Payroll is available in all 50 states, and all payroll plans include the following key features:

- Unlimited payroll runs
- Calculated paychecks and taxes
- Automated taxes and forms
- Workforce portal
- Custom user access by setting permission levels
- Garnishment and deductions management
- Payroll reports
- Unlimited chat and telephone support at no additional cost

It is advised to check local payroll tax filing requirements to confirm that the payroll subscription you have chosen can handle all necessary filings.

Adding new employees to payroll

Depending on your business needs, setting up payroll and running payroll will vary based on the benefits offered and the applicable taxes. Therefore, we recommend you follow the step-by-step instructions within QuickBooks to learn how to set up and run payroll. In this section, we will provide you with a sample demonstration of what you can expect when adding new employees to payroll:

1. After selecting the QBO payroll subscription, the following screen will appear:

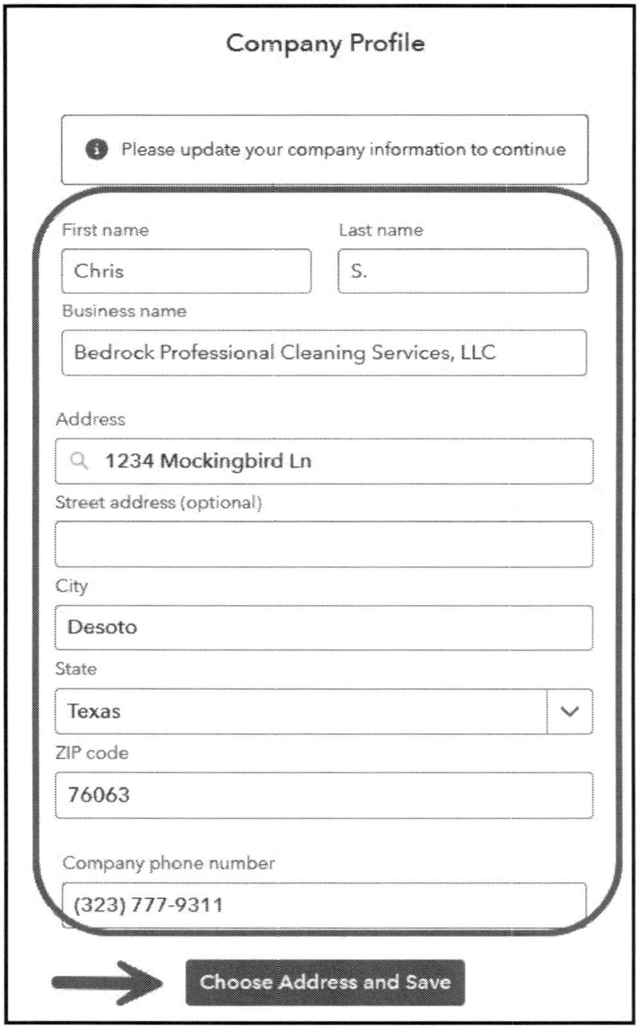

Figure 13.5: Entering company information for payroll

Complete any fields that are missing information and click the **Choose Address and Save** button at the bottom of the screen.

2. From the dashboard, navigate to the **Team** menu and click on the **Add an employee** button, as shown in *Figure 13.6*:

Figure 13.6: Adding a new employee

3. Complete the fields for the new employee and click the **Add employee** button at the bottom, as shown in *Figure 13.7*:

Figure 13.7: Completing the fields to add a new employee

The information for the new employee that Bedrock Professional Cleaning Services has hired is as follows:

- **First name**: `Ashley`
- **Last name**: `Brown`
- **Email**: `abrown@bedrockcleaningllc.com`
- **Hire date: 11/01/2025**

> An email address is important for providing access to your employee, where they can make updates and access pay stubs and W-2s.

4. The following screen displays three key areas in the employee profile—**Personal info**, **Employment details**, and **Emergency contact**—as well as a profile picture:

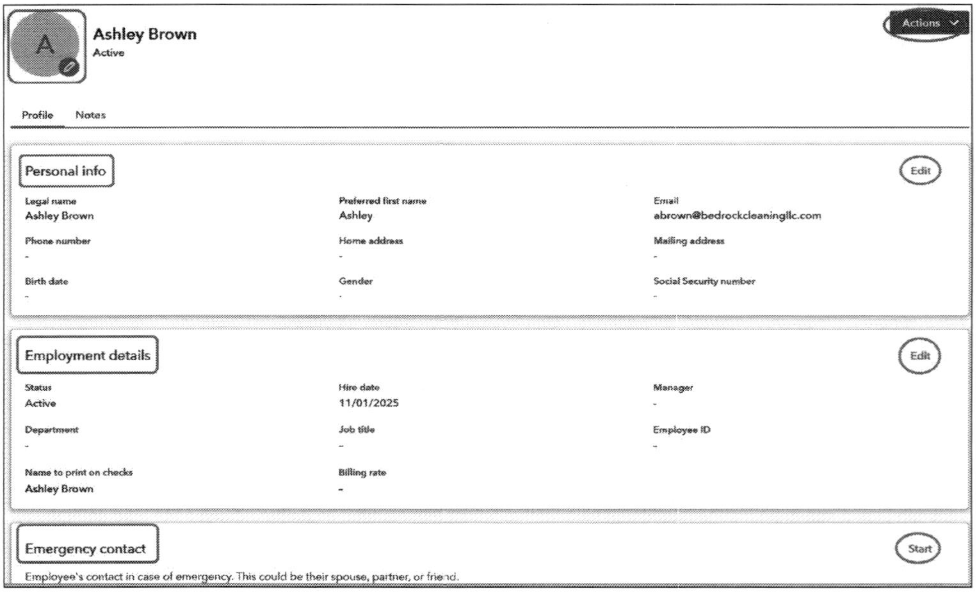

Figure 13.8: Displaying the employee profile

- **Profile picture**: At the very top of the screen, you can upload a picture of the employee to the left of their name. Click on the pencil and follow the on-screen instructions to upload the picture from your computer.

- **Personal info**: In this section, you can edit the employee's name, email address, home address, mailing address, birth date, gender, and social security number. Please note that the address plays an important role in determining state and local payroll tax obligations.
- **Employment details**: In this section, you can edit the employee's status (**Active** or **Inactive**), hire date, manager/supervisor, department, job title, employee ID, the name to print on paychecks, and their billing rate.
- **Emergency contact**: Enter the employee's emergency contact in this section. This could be a spouse, partner, friend, or family member.
- **Notes**: Right below the profile picture, there is a tab to the right of the **Profile** tab where you can type any notes that you would like to keep on file for internal purposes only.
- **Actions**: In the upper-right corner of the screen, there is an **Actions** button. When you click on the drop-down arrow, you have the option to change the status of an employee to **Inactive**. This would be ideal if an employee is terminated.

5. After completing all the necessary fields, click on the **Employee List** link in the upper-left corner, and the following will display:

Figure 13.9: Employee list

Within the employee list center, you can add new employees, complete payroll setup, create paychecks, and process payroll taxes.

6. From the **Payroll** app, click on **Payroll overview**, and the following screen will display:

Figure 13.10: Payroll overview

Depending on the payroll subscription plan you have, your overview screen will differ slightly. Bedrock Professional Cleaning Services LLC signed up for the Payroll Elite subscription plan, which includes access to a payroll expert who will set up the payroll for them. All they have to do is click on the **Request a call** button to schedule their appointment. It is ideal to have access to all of the information for both the employee and the employer that we discussed at the beginning of the chapter. There is a short video that shows how payroll works. In addition, you can start onboarding right away and contact support when you need them.

I recommend that you sign up for Payroll Elite for the first 30 days to gain access to the Intuit Payroll experts who can ensure that your payroll is set up and smooth out any kinks during the first couple of payroll runs. After that, you can downgrade to the Premium plan if you don't need all the bells and whistles that Elite comes with.

Unfortunately, we cannot walk you through the employer information setup or the payroll processing setup since it requires real data. However, you now know how to properly set up your new employees in payroll. All payroll subscription plans include unlimited tech support 24/7, so do not hesitate to reach out if you have any questions or run into any issues. Next, we will cover the key reports you can generate to stay on top of payroll costs.

Generating payroll reports

By now, you know that QBO includes a library of preset reports that provide business owners with insights into every aspect of their business. There are several summary and detailed reports you can generate to gain insight into your payroll costs, payroll deductions and contributions, vacation and sick leave, and payroll taxes. If you have the Core plan, these reports will help you complete payroll tax forms and make payroll tax payments to the local tax authorities.

> It's important to note that if you have not signed up for a payroll subscription plan, you will *not* see the payroll reports covered in this chapter. These reports are only available to payroll subscribers.

Follow these steps to generate payroll reports:

1. Click on **Reports** on the left navigation bar, as indicated in *Figure 13.11*:

Figure 13.11: Navigating to the Reports center

2. Scroll down to the **Payroll** section, and you will see several reports, as shown in *Figure 13.12*:

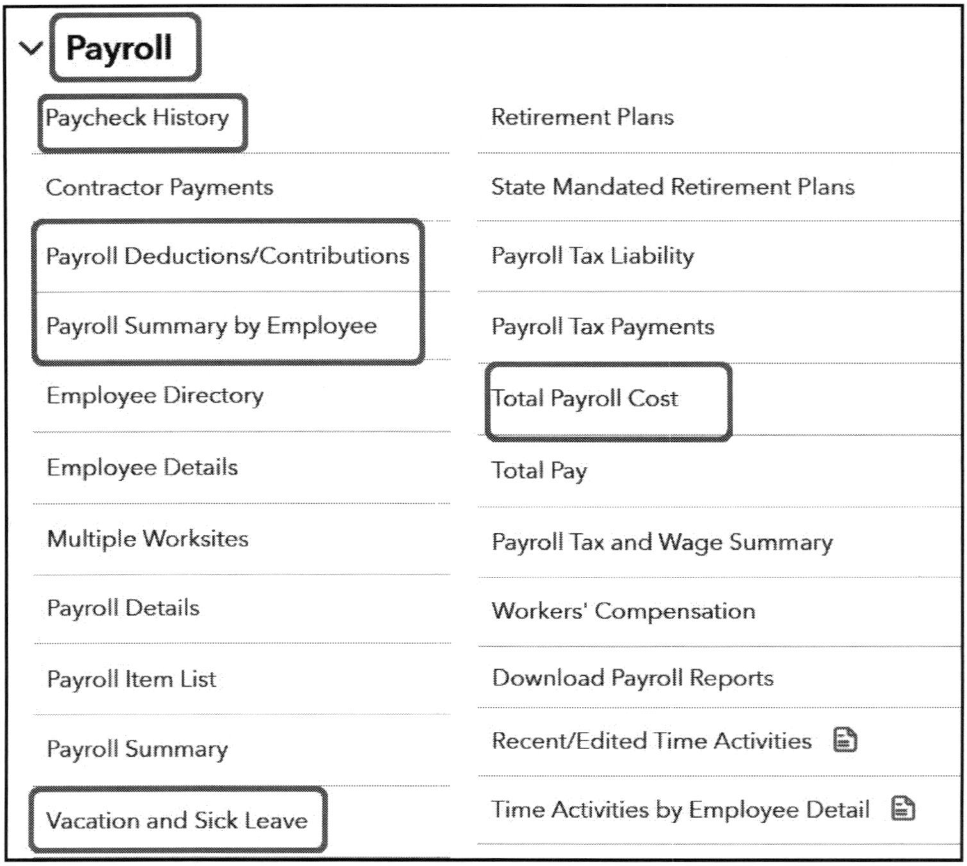

Figure 13.12: Payroll reports available for QBO Payroll subscribers

While you will find several great reports to help manage your payroll, I have found that there are five key reports that will help you stay on top of your payroll costs:

- **Paycheck History**: This report includes a list of paychecks that have been issued. You can use this report to edit check numbers, print pay stubs, and more.
- **Payroll Deductions/Contributions**: This report details payroll deductions by employee as well as employer contributions made for each pay period.
- **Payroll Summary by Employee**: This is a comprehensive report that includes wages, deductions, and taxes totaled by the employee or payroll period.

- **Vacation and Sick Leave**: This report details the total vacation and sick pay that has been used, as well as the remaining balance.
- **Total Payroll Cost**: This report includes all costs associated with paying employees, such as total pay, net pay, deductions, company contributions, and taxes.

3. To generate a report, simply click on the report and select the pay period you would like to see data for. Similar to other QBO reports, you can save payroll reports as PDF files or export them to Excel. In the next chapter, we will show you how to do this.

One of the key benefits of generating reports is that they include the information you need in order to file payroll tax forms and make payroll tax payments. In the next section, we will discuss your options for filing and making payroll tax payments.

Filing payroll tax forms and payments

Employers are required to file payroll tax forms and make payroll tax payments at the federal, state, and sometimes local levels. The due dates will vary by employer and are generally based on the dollar amount of the payroll and other factors specific to your business. The good news is that all QBO Payroll plans will take care of calculating, paying, and filing payroll taxes at the state and federal levels. As discussed, the Core plan is the only one that does not automatically take care of the local tax authority.

There are a few key reports that you should generate to help you understand the total cost of payroll to your business. These reports are also shown in *Figure 13.12*:

- **Payroll Tax Liability**: This report provides you with the details of how much payroll tax you are required to pay and how much you have already paid to state and federal tax authorities for a specified period of time.
- **Payroll Tax Payments**: This report provides you with the details of all tax payments you have made for a specific period of time.
- **Payroll Tax and Wage Summary**: This report shows total and taxable wages that are subject to federal and provincial/regional/state withholding for a specific period of time.

While QBO Payroll handles the tax payments and filings on your behalf, it is still your responsibility to make sure that the tax forms and payments are submitted to the proper tax authorities on time. Otherwise, you could be subject to hefty penalties and fines. All payroll plans include unlimited tech support. Therefore, be sure to contact the Intuit payroll support team with any questions or concerns you may have regarding taxes.

It is recommended that you keep a checklist of when your payroll taxes are due and when the related filings must be submitted.

To demonstrate some of the concepts taught in this chapter and to give you some additional insights not covered, check out my YouTube channel:

https://packt.link/du2BR

Summary

To recap, you now know what information is required to set up employees. We showed you how to onboard new employees in payroll and what payroll reports are available so that you can gain insight into your total payroll costs. Finally, we discussed the importance of filing payroll tax forms and submitting payroll tax payments on time. Be sure to consult with a CPA, HR professional, or payroll expert to ensure that payroll is set up properly. Otherwise, you run the risk of encountering errors, which could result in steep penalties.

Payroll tax returns and W-2s are just a few of the many tasks that must be performed at the end of the year. In *Chapter 16*, *Closing the Books in QuickBooks Online*, we will cover, in detail, all of the year-end tasks that you will need to do. Making sure that you complete all of these tasks in a timely manner will ensure that your financial reports are up to date, so that you can file your taxes in a timely manner. In the next chapter, we will introduce you to the Reports center and show you how to locate key reports when you need them.

Next steps

If you do not currently have employees, you can bookmark this chapter and return to it when you decide to hire your first employee. However, if you do have employees that you need to onboard to payroll, take the following next steps to get the ball rolling:

1. Download the *Payroll Setup Checklist*, *New Employee Checklist*, and the *Direct Deposit Authorization Form* using this link: `https://github.com/PacktPublishing/Mastering-QuickBooks-2026-Seventh-Edition`.
2. If you need assistance on how to go about hiring employees, check out a free resource called Mineral. It is included within QBO, and it is located within your payroll menu as follows: **Payroll** | **HR Advisor**. You can chat with an HR expert or schedule a call. Mineral offers advice on how to set company policies, follow HR laws, manage conflict within the workplace, and onboard and terminate employees.
3. Gather all of the information outlined in the *Payroll Setups Checklist* and *Key Documents* section for each employee.
4. Schedule an appointment with the QBO Payroll Support team to get someone to walk you through setting up your payroll (Elite subscribers only).
5. If you don't have the Elite payroll subscription, follow the on-screen instructions to add employees to payroll. If you run into an issue or have any questions, give the Intuit payroll team a call for assistance.

Part 4

Closing the Books and Generating Reports in QBO

Closing the books might sound daunting, but it doesn't have to be. In this part, I'll share a simple checklist that will ensure you don't miss anything, whether you close the books on a monthly basis or once a year. From reconciling accounts to recording year-end adjustments, you'll know exactly what to do. While we introduced you to the report center in *Part 3*, we will take a deeper dive into each report group and demonstrate how to filter reports and customize them to meet your business needs.

This part comprises the following chapters:

- *Chapter 14, Report Center Overview*
- *Chapter 15, Business Overview and Cash Management Tools and Reports*
- *Chapter 16, Closing the Books in QuickBooks Online*

14

Report Center Overview

Now that you know how to enter income and expenses into QuickBooks, it's time to learn how to generate reports to gain insights into the overall health of your business. In *Chapter 8, Customer Sales Reports in QuickBooks Online*, we showed you how to run key reports to track and stay on top of your income and accounts receivable. In *Chapter 10, Vendor and Expense Reports in QuickBooks Online*, we showed you how to generate reports that will help you analyze your expenses so that you can make informed decisions. In this chapter, we are going to introduce you to other key reports that are available in QuickBooks Online to help you stay on top of your business finances.

Financial reporting allows you to take a step back from day-to-day bookkeeping tasks and look at your business from a different perspective. By taking the time to generate reports such as a profit and loss (income statement) or the balance sheet report, you can see whether your business has been profitable and, if so, what has made it profitable. On the flip side, you can also dig into why your business has not been profitable and determine what the resolutions are for that.

In this chapter, we will show you how to navigate through the Reports Center and give you an overview of the reports available. We'll show you how to customize reports to meet your business needs. We will also cover how to share reports with your accountant and business stakeholders.

Understanding how to run reports will help you gain insights into all aspects of your business. Having access to your income, expenses, and other key performance indicators will help you make good business decisions in the short and long term.

The following topics will be covered in this chapter:

- Navigating the Reports Center
- Reports available in the Reports Center

- Customizing reports
- Exporting reports
- Sending reports via email

By the end of this chapter, you will be able to navigate the Reports Center and know which reports you have access to and how to customize reports to meet your needs. You will also be able to export reports in Excel or PDF format and email them to stakeholders.

> The US edition of QBO was used to create this book. If you are using a version that is outside of the United States, results may differ.

Navigating the Reports Center

Before we dive into how to navigate the Reports Center, let's cover the five key reports that business owners like yourself should be looking at on a regular basis:

- The **profit and loss (P&L) report**, also known as the **income statement**
- The **balance sheet report**, which provides you with your net equity for the business
- The **accounts receivable (A/R) aging report**, which shows you the total amount owed by your customers
- The **accounts payable (A/P) aging report**, which shows what you owe creditors and suppliers
- The **statement of cash flows**, which shows your cash flow activities

These reports will help you evaluate your business finances and help you make informed decisions. As previously mentioned, we have already covered the A/R aging report and the A/P aging report. In the next few chapters, we will explore generating, customizing, and using P&L, balance sheet, and statement of cash flows reports. As you will see, there are a lot more reports available within the Reports Center, which allow you to dig into the details of every aspect of your business.

> Financial statements should be reviewed on a monthly basis at a minimum after all bank and credit card accounts have been reconciled. This will allow you to identify any issues so that you can correct them before filing your tax returns.

In this section, we will cover how the Reports Center is organized so that you can easily locate the report you need. The Reports Center includes several prebuilt reports that can give you summarized or detailed information about various aspects of your business. It is organized into five main sections: **Standard reports**, **Custom reports**, **Management reports**, **Budgets**, and **Financial planning**. The reports that you will review on a regular basis are located in the **Standard reports** section.

To access the Reports Center, follow these steps:

1. Click on **Reports** located on the left menu bar, select **Standard reports**, and the reporting groups will display:

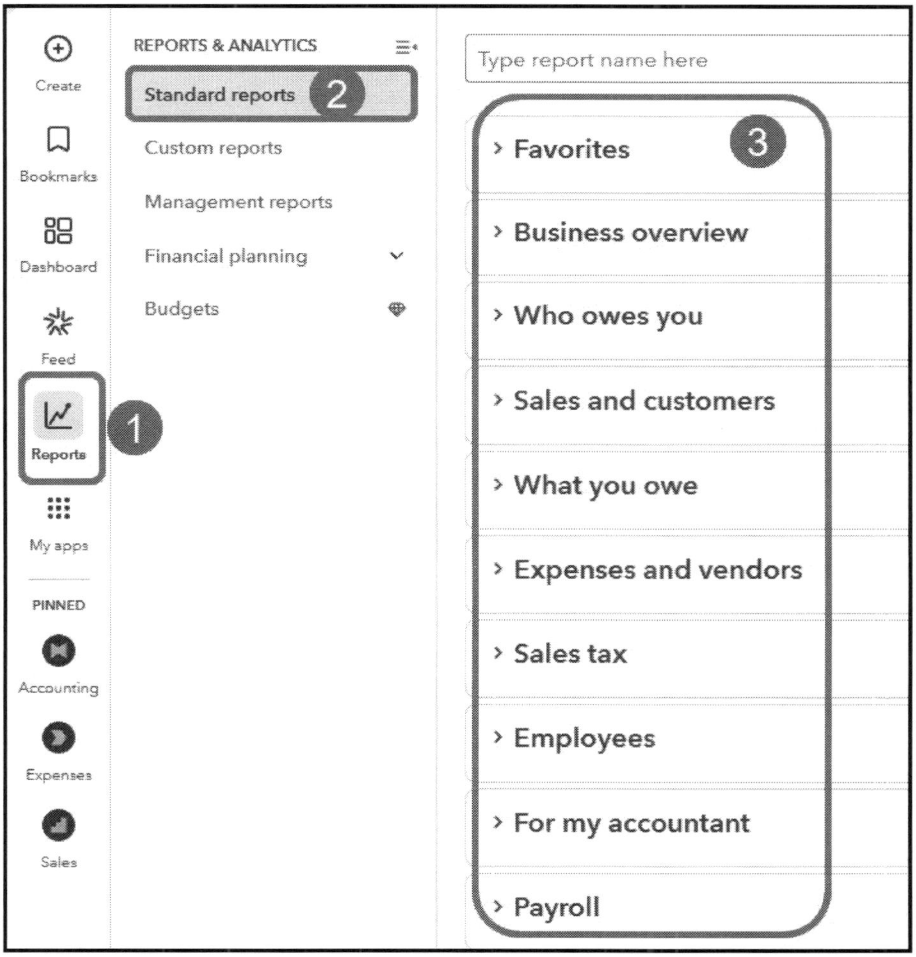

Figure 14.1: Navigating to the Reports Center

Standard reports are categorized into the following reporting groups:

- **Favorites**: You can mark your most frequently used reports as favorites, and they will be listed here. To add a report to your **Favorites** list, simply click the star icon located to the right of each report (not shown).
- **Business overview**: This group includes reports that provide insight into the overall health of your business. You will find both a detailed report and a summary overview of P&L, the balance sheet, and a statement of cash flow reports in this group.
- **Who owes you**: Money owed to you by your customers is also known as A/R. In this group, you will find reports to help you stay on top of your A/R balances. The A/R aging detail and summary, open invoices, and collections reports can be found in this group.
- **Sales and customers**: This group includes detailed and summary reports that provide insights into who your top customers are and what products and services they are buying. Income by customer, products and services lists, and sales by customer are just a few of the reports you will find in this group.
- **What you owe**: Money you owe to others is also known as A/P. In this group, you will find reports to help you stay on top of your A/P balances. A/P aging, bill payment list, and unpaid bills are just a few of the reports you will find in this group.
- **Expenses and vendors**: This group includes reports that provide insights into who and what you are spending your money on. Some examples of reports you will find in this group are check detail, expenses by vendor, 1099 detail reports, and open purchase orders.
- **Sales tax**: If you have the sales tax feature turned on, this group includes reports that provide details on the sales tax your business has collected. Examples of reports found here include the sales tax liability report and the sales tax detail report. In *Chapter 6, Managing Sales Tax*, we covered how to generate these sales tax reports. Note: If you do not have the sales tax feature turned on, you will not see this group of reports.
- **Employees**: If you have employees, this group includes reports that will provide you with employee information. A couple of reports you can find in this group include employee contact lists and time activities. If you manage payroll in QuickBooks, head over to the **Payroll** reports group for more detailed payroll reports.

- **For my accountant**: Reports that assist your accountant in preparing your taxes can be found in this group. In this group, you will find profit and loss, balance sheet reports, and a list of the chart of accounts, along with many other reports. In *Chapter 15, Business Overview and Cash Management Tools and Reports*, we will cover how to generate these reports.
- **Payroll**: If you have the **Payroll** feature turned on, you will have access to several detailed and summary payroll reports by employee, location, and class. Note: If you do not have a payroll subscription, you will not see this group of reports.

2. Click on the **Custom reports** tab located below **Standard reports**, as indicated here:

Figure 14.2: Selecting Custom reports

Custom reports will include any report you have customized and saved. We will discuss how to customize reports later in this chapter.

3. Click on the **Management reports** tab located below **Custom reports**, as indicated here:

Figure 14.3: Selecting Management reports

Management reports include professional report packages that you can download and customize with items such as a cover page and a table of contents. These reports can be used when presenting financial statements to a board of directors or a financial institution when seeking financing. The number of reports you can access depends on your QBO subscription level. In the *Customizing reports* section of this chapter, we will cover how to customize management reports to fit your specific needs.

4. Click on the **Performance center** tab located below **Management reports**, as shown here:

Figure 14.4: Selecting Performance center reports

Performance reports allow you to view your data in the format of a chart. You can see trends in revenue, A/R aging, A/P, and expenses, among other options. You can add up to 25 charts, using the filters you choose.

5. Click on the **Financial planning** tab located below **Performance center**, as shown here:

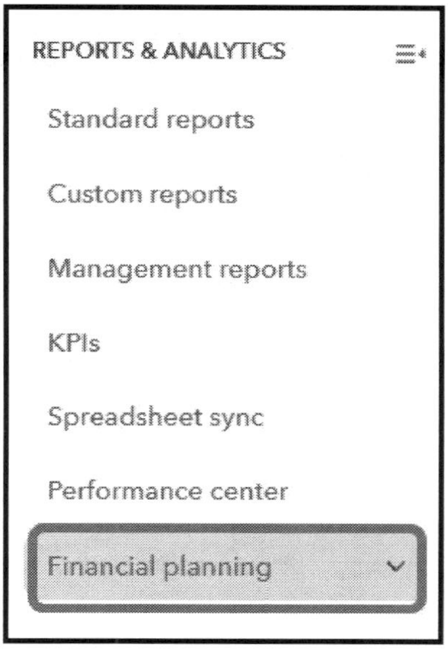

Figure 14.5: Selecting Financial planning reports

Financial planning reports include reports that give you insights into your cash flow. You will find reports and charts for trends in your cash flow, a cash flow planner, as well as budgeting and forecasting tools.

Now that you understand how to navigate the Reports Center and have an idea of the variety of reports you can run, we will cover what reports are available to you based on your QuickBooks Online subscription in the following section.

Reports available in the Reports Center

In *Chapter 2, Getting Started with QuickBooks Online*, we discussed the four subscription levels you can purchase for QBO: Simple Start, Essentials, Plus, and Advanced. Depending on the subscription level you have purchased, you could have access to anywhere between 20 and 100 or more reports. Simple Start includes more than 20 reports, Essentials includes more than 40 reports, Plus includes more than 65 reports, and Advanced includes more than 100 reports. The following is a breakdown of some of the reports you will find in each QBO subscription.

QBO Simple Start includes more than 20 reports, some of which are listed here:

Profit & Loss	Sales by Customer
Balance Sheet	Sales by Product/Services
Statement of Cash Flows	Transaction List by Vendor
Customer Balance Summary	Check Detail
A/R Aging Summary	Payroll Reports (if **Payroll** is on)
Taxable Sales	Customized Reports
Transaction List by Date	Product/Service List
Reconciliation Reports	Deposit Detail

Table 14.1: A list of reports included in the QBO Simple Start plan

In addition to the reports included in Simple Start, QBO Essentials includes over 40 reports, including the following:

A/P Aging	Profit & Loss Detail
Bill Payment List	Sales by Customer Detail
Company Snapshot	Terms Listing
Customer Balance Detail	Trial Balance
Expenses by Vendor	Unbilled Charges
General Ledger	Unpaid Bills
Income by Customer Summary	Vendor Balance

Table 14.2: A list of reports included in the QBO Essentials plan

In addition to the reports included in Simple Start and Essentials, QBO Plus is where the reporting gets even better, with more than 65 reports, including budgeting and reporting by class:

Budget Overview	Purchases by Product/Service
Budget vs. Actuals	Purchases by Location/Class
Class Listing	Sales by Location or Class
Profit & Loss by Class	Time Activities by Customer
Profit & Loss by Location	Time Activities by Employee
Open Purchase Orders	Transaction Detail by Account

Table 14.3: A list of reports included in the QBO Plus plan

In addition to the reports included in Simple Start, Essentials, and Plus, QBO Advanced has more than 100 reports. It also includes business analytics with an Excel reporting tool.

Now that you have a better idea of all the reports you have access to with your QBO subscription, you are ready to learn how to customize the reports. In the next section, we will show you how to customize reports to meet your business requirements.

Customizing reports

As discussed, you don't have to create a report from scratch in QuickBooks Online; you can customize an existing report to get the data you need. You can save any changes you make to a report so you don't have to recreate it each time.

The following are the steps we need to follow to customize an existing report:

1. Navigate to the Reports Center, as indicated in *Figure 14.1*.
2. Select the report you want to customize. In this case, we will customize the Profit and Loss report, which is located in the Business overview report group, as indicated:

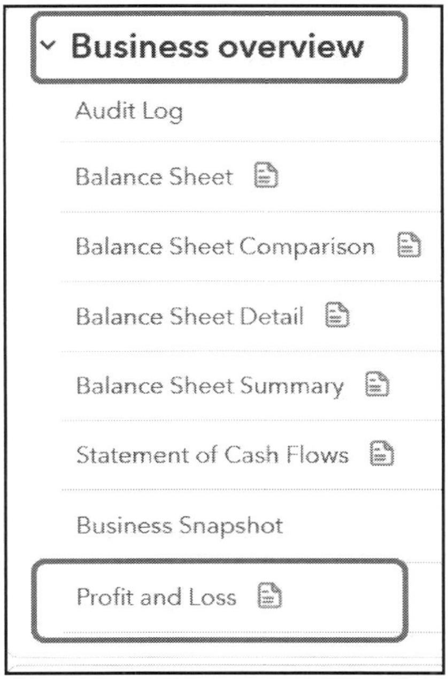

Figure 14.6: Running the Profit and Loss report

The **Profit and Loss** report will display, but let's discuss the reports toolbar first, shown here:

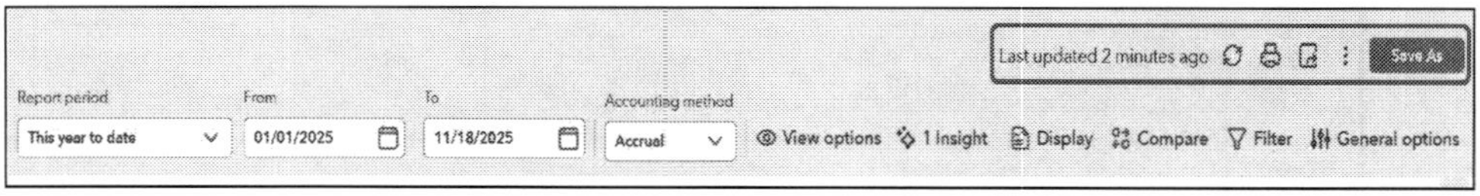

Figure 14.7: The Report Center Tool Bar

The Report Center toolbar consists of the following selections:

- **Refresh**: In the upper-right corner, you will always see a notification about the last time a report was updated. To the right of that notification is the **Refresh** button. You can click on that button anytime to update the report for any recent changes that you have made.
- **Print**: The **Print** button is located to the right of the **Refresh** button. You can print a hard copy of any report that you generate in QBO.
- **Export**: The **Export** button is located to the right of the **Print** button. You can export reports to an Excel spreadsheet or a PDF.
- **Save As**: To save customizations that you have made to a report so that you don't have to recreate them, click the **Save As** button and customize the name of the report, such as `Bedrock Prof Cleaning P&L by Class Report`.
- **Report period**: Choose the timeframe you would like to use to create the report. You can choose a report period from the dropdown or type in specific **From** and **To** dates.
- **Accounting method**: Choose the accounting method: **Accrual** or **Cash**. We covered accounting methods in *Chapter 1, Bookkeeping 101*.
- **View options**: You have the ability to view all accounts and subaccounts on a report, which would be the **Expand all** view, or to see a more summarized report that just shows only the parent accounts, which is the **Collapse all** view.

Next, I have included the remaining options on the reports toolbar along with a snapshot of each one:

- **Insights**: The accounting agent automatically analyzes the data in each report and provides its findings. For example, if there is a significant increase or decrease in income, it will point that out so that you are aware and can investigate, if necessary. Here is an example of what you can expect to see:

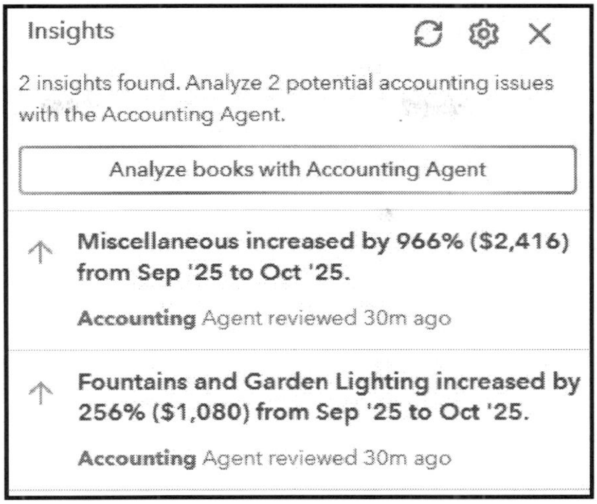

Figure 14.8: Reviewing Insights by the accounting agent

- **Display**: You can choose how you want to display columns on reports. You can choose from five options: **Customer**, **Employee**, **Product/Service**, **Transaction date**, and **Vendor**, as shown here:

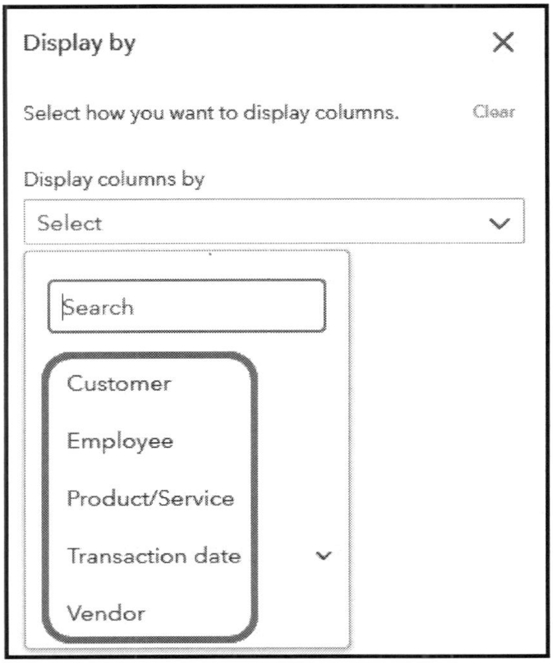

Figure 14.9: Choosing how data displays on reports

- **Compare**: You can do a side-by-side comparison of the **previous year (PY)**, **previous period (PP)**, **year-to-date (YTD)**, **previous-year-to-date (PY YTD)**, or a **custom period (CP)**. You can also choose to calculate variances between the reports; your options for this are **% of Row**, **% of Column**, **% of Expense**, and **% of Income**, as shown here:

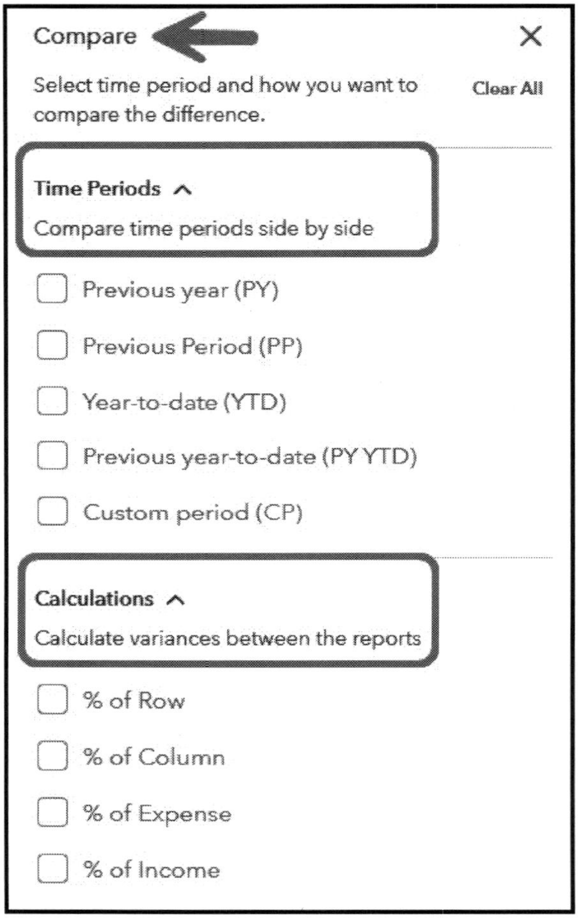

Figure 14.10: Comparing data side by side

- **Filter**: Report data can also be filtered by distribution account, account type, customer, vendor, employee, or product/service, as shown in this figure:

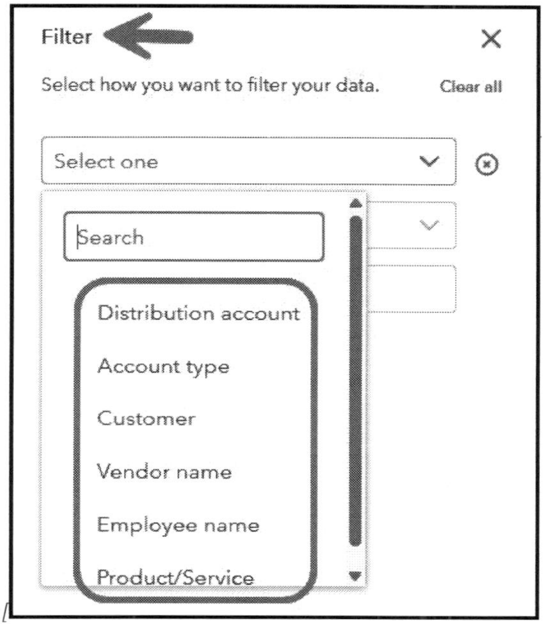

Figure 14.11: Filtering data on reports

- **General options**: General options affect the look and feel of the report and include **Number format**, **Header**, **Footer**, and **Edit section titles**.

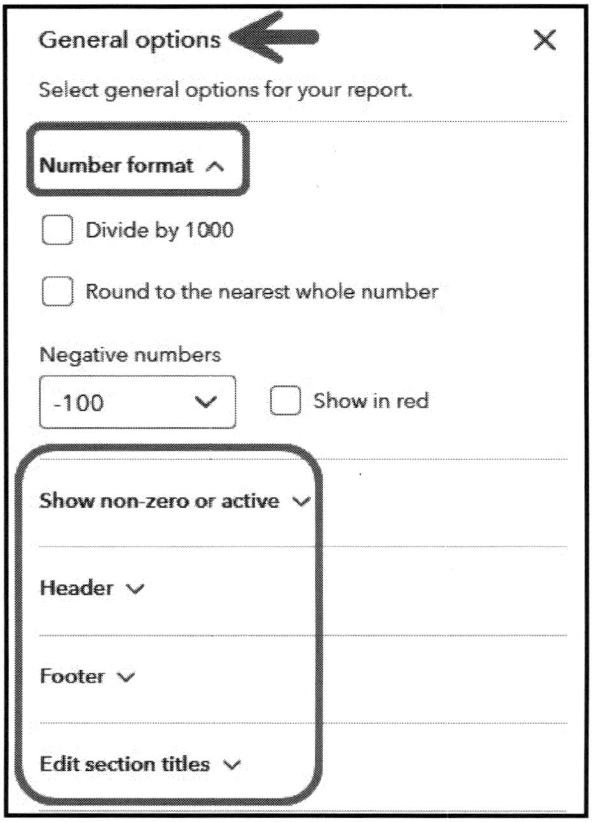

Figure 14.12: General options for reports

Saving a customized report

After you finish making all of your report selections, you can save your changes so they will remain each time you run the report. Click on the **Save As** button located in the upper-right corner of the screen, as shown here:

Figure 14.13: Saving customized report settings

The window that appears is shown here, followed by a brief explanation of each field:

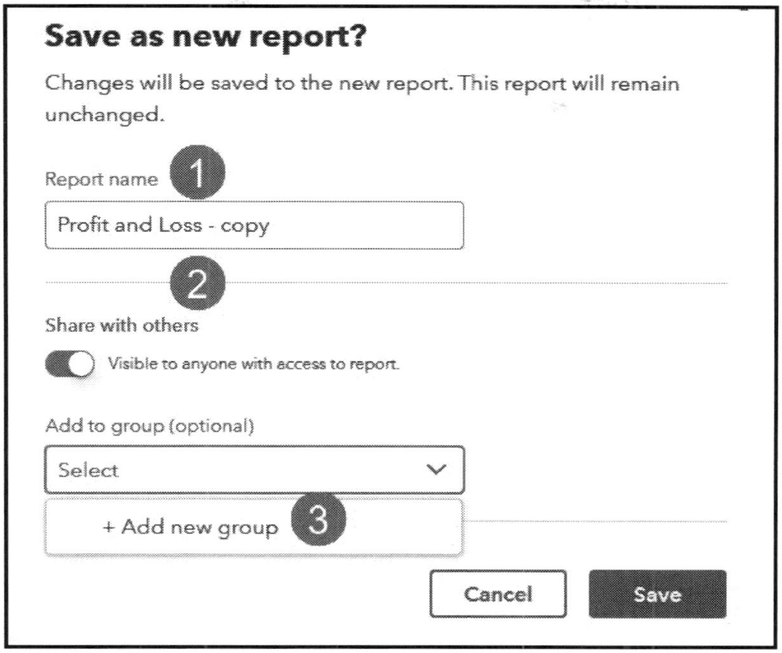

Figure 14.14: Saving a custom report

- **Report name** (**1**): The default report name will appear in this field. You can customize the name of the report by adding your business name, for example, `Profit and Loss - Bedrock Professional Cleaning Services, LLC`.
- **Share with others** (**2**): This field allows you to share the report with other users within your company. Click the drop-down arrow and select specific users or **All**.
- **Add to group** (**3**): Report groups are used to run multiple reports at once. For example, if you typically run the same five reports when closing the books, you can put all five reports in a group and generate them at the same time. Click **Add new group** directly below the field to create a group.

> Groups are great to use for recurring reports or reports that you share with others. This will help you be more efficient and save you some time.

Customizing management reports

If you would like to produce a set of financials to present to a board of directors or a prospective investor, management reports are ideal for these stakeholders. As previously mentioned, management reports can be accessed just below **Custom reports**, as shown here:

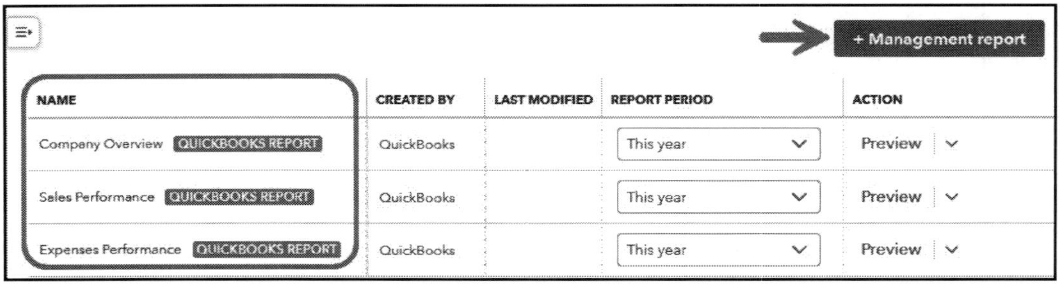

Figure 14.15: Viewing the Management reports tab

As you can see, there are three packages of management reports to choose from. Here is a brief description of what is included in each one:

- **Company Overview**: In addition to a cover page and a table of contents, this package includes a P&L report and a balance sheet report. You can choose a report period by selecting it from the drop-down menu, as shown in *Figure 14.15*.
- **Sales Performance**: In addition to a cover page and a table of contents, this package includes a P&L report, A/R aging details, and a sales-by-customer summary report.
- **Expenses Performance**: In addition to a cover page and a table of contents, this package includes a P&L report, an A/P aging detail report, and an expenses-by-vendor summary report.

To see the reports included in a report package, click on the **Preview** link listed below the **ACTION** column shown in *Figure 14.15*. If you would like to edit the report package, send it via email, or export it as a PDF or Word document, click on the arrow to the right of **Preview** and make your selections.

If you would like to create a custom management report package, follow these instructions:

1. Click on the **+ Management report** button shown in *Figure 14.15*, and the following screen displays:

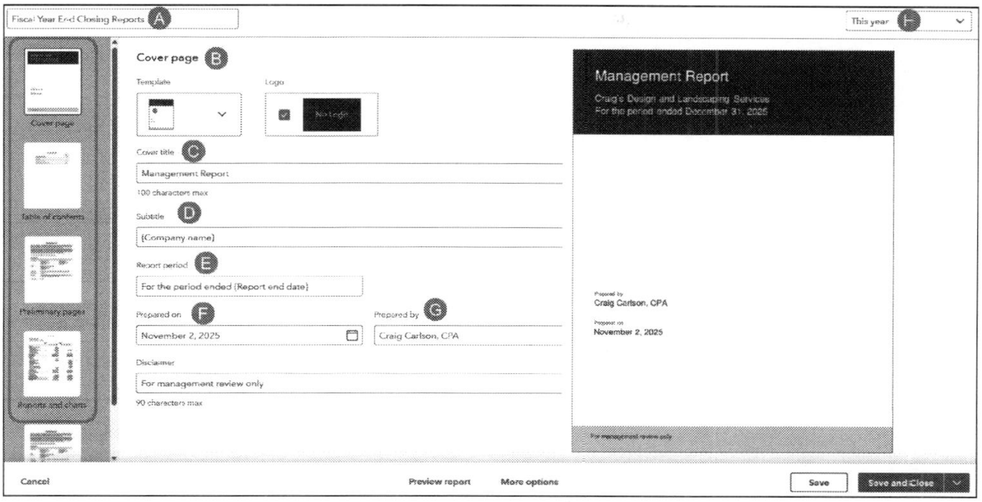

Figure 14.16: Customizing management reports

Complete the fields as follows:

- **Template name** (**A**): Create a title for the management report package (i.e., `Fiscal Year End Closing Reports`).
- **Cover page** (**B**): Click on **Template** to choose a cover page. You can also click on **Logo** to include your logo, or you can exclude it. Complete the fields marked **C**–**G** or leave the default.
- **Table of contents**: On the left side of the screen, you can choose to include (or exclude) a table of contents.
- **Preliminary pages**: Below **Table of contents**, you can add more preliminary pages, for example, a letter to the recipient of the package (i.e., accountant, tax preparer, or board of directors).
- **Reports**: Below **Preliminary pages**, you can choose the reports you want to include in the report package. Select from any of the reports that are available in the Reports Center.

- **End notes**: Below **Reports**, you can add any footnotes or additional information you would like to include with the financial statements can be added in this section.
- **Report period (H)**: In the upper right corner, choose the time period to run the report package for from the drop-down menu.

After making your selections, save your new management report package, and it will be available on the **Management reports** tab to generate at any time you need it.

Now that you know how to customize reports to fit your business needs, you are ready to learn how to share reports. You can export reports to Excel, PDF, or a printer, or email them directly from QuickBooks.

Exporting reports

You have several options to choose from when it comes to exporting your QuickBooks data. Like most programs, you can print a hard copy of any report. If you need to manipulate the data or add additional information, exporting the data to Excel might be a good option. If you need to share your data with your accountant, a board member, or anyone who does not have access to QuickBooks, you can save any report as a PDF document and email the report. Finally, you can email a report directly from QuickBooks.

When you select the **Email** option, you can send it to multiple people and copy in anyone you need. When sending a report via email, the report will be attached as a PDF document.

When you run a report in QuickBooks, the **Export** menu will automatically appear in the upper-right corner, as indicated here:

Figure 14.17: Multiple ways to export a report from QBO

The following is a brief explanation of each icon:

- **Printer**: The *printer* icon is used if you would like to print a hard copy of a report.
- **Paper**: The icon that resembles a sheet of paper with an arrow going through it is used to export reports to Excel or PDF.

- **Three dots**: The three dots located between the *paper* icon and the **Save As** button allow you to add a note to the report, email the report, schedule the report to be sent via email, run the report and sync the data in an Excel spreadsheet, and add a report to the **Management reports** package.

We will discuss exporting reports to Excel first, followed by PDF. Lastly, we will show you the step-by-step process of emailing reports directly from QuickBooks.

Exporting reports to Excel

As discussed in the previous section, if you need the ability to manipulate the data on a report or add additional columns and rows, you can export reports to Excel. Follow these steps:

1. Display the report you wish to export, as indicated here:

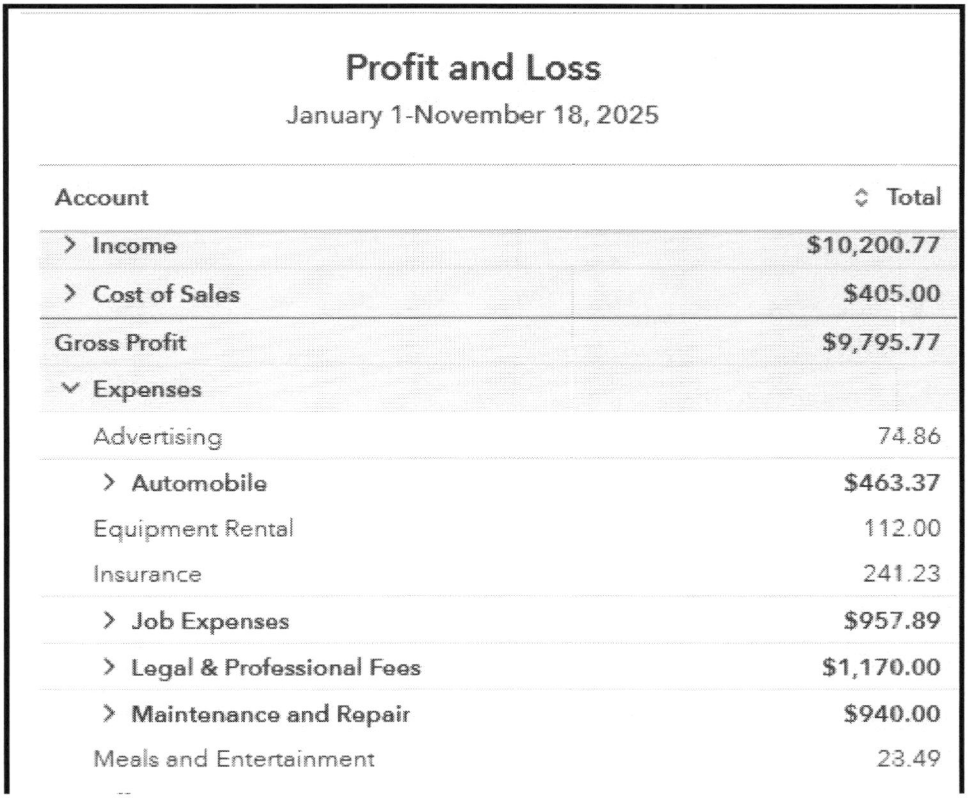

Figure 14.18: Reviewing a sample Profit and Loss report

2. Click on the icon that resembles a sheet of paper with an arrow going through it and choose to export to Excel. The report displays in an Excel spreadsheet, as follows:

	A	B
1	**Profit and Loss**	
2	**January 1-November 18, 2025**	
3		
4	**Distribution account**	**Total**
5	Income	
6	Design income	2,250.00
7	Discounts given	-89.50
8	Landscaping Services	1,477.50
18	**Total for Landscaping Services**	**$6,513.97**
19	Pest Control Services	110.00
20	Sales of Product Income	912.75
21	Services	503.55
22	**Total for Income**	**$10,200.77**
23	Cost of Sales	
24	Cost of Goods Sold	405.00
25	**Total for Cost of Sales**	**$405.00**
26	**Gross Profit**	**$9,795.77**
27	Expenses	
28	Advertising	74.86
29	Automobile	113.96
31	**Total for Automobile**	**$463.37**
32	Equipment Rental	112.00
33	Insurance	241.23
34	Job Expenses	155.07
40	**Total for Job Expenses**	**$957.89**
41	Legal & Professional Fees	75.00
45	**Total for Legal & Professional Fees**	**$1,170.00**
46	Maintenance and Repair	185.00
48	**Total for Maintenance and Repair**	**$940.00**
49	Meals and Entertainment	28.49
50	Office Expenses	18.08
51	Rent or Lease	900.00
52	Utilities	
55	**Total for Utilities**	**$331.39**
56	**Total for Expenses**	**$5,237.31**
57	**Net Operating Income**	**$4,558.46**
58	Other Expenses	
59	Miscellaneous	2,916.00
60	**Total for Other Expenses**	**$2,916.00**
61	**Net Other Income**	**$(2,916.00)**
62	**Net Income**	**$1,642.46**

Figure 14.19: Profit and Loss report exported to Excel

3. At this point, you can save the report to your computer and make any necessary changes.

> If the report is not immediately displayed on your screen, look at the very bottom (or top) of the screen, and there should be an **Excel** icon. Click on it to display the report in Excel. If the report shows all zeros, click on the **Enable** message that appears at the top of the spreadsheet. That should allow the numbers to populate as expected.
>
> After exporting a report to Excel, any changes you make in QBO will *not* update the report that was exported. You will need to follow the steps to generate the report and export it to Excel again to see any revisions made. In QBO Advanced, there is a tool called **Spreadsheet sync** that will automatically update an Excel spreadsheet for changes made in QBO.

If you need to send reports to anyone outside of the company, I recommend you export the reports to PDF instead of Excel. This is what we will cover next.

Exporting reports to PDF

If you need to share reports with your accountant, members of your board of directors, or a financial institution, exporting the reports to a PDF file is a great option. The initial steps for exporting reports to PDF are identical to those for exporting reports to Excel (in the previous section):

1. Click on the paper icon and choose **Export to PDF**, and the report will appear on your screen, as shown here:

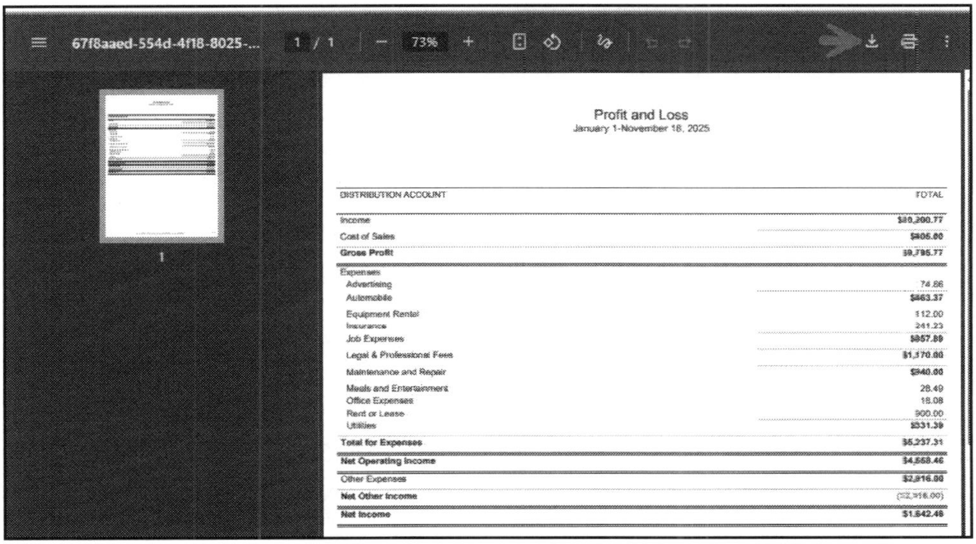

Figure 14.20: Profit and loss report exported to PDF

You can save the report to your computer by clicking on the arrow pointing down in the upper-right corner, or you can print a hard copy of the report by clicking on the **Print** button next to it.

That wraps up two of the three primary ways you can export your data out of QuickBooks so that you can share it with your business stakeholders. In the next section, we will cover one final way of sharing reports: by sending them via email directly from QuickBooks.

Sending reports via email

Sending reports via email involves the same steps required to export reports to Excel and PDF format:

1. Display the report you wish to send via email, click on the three dots, and select **Email report** from the drop-down list.

   The following window will appear:

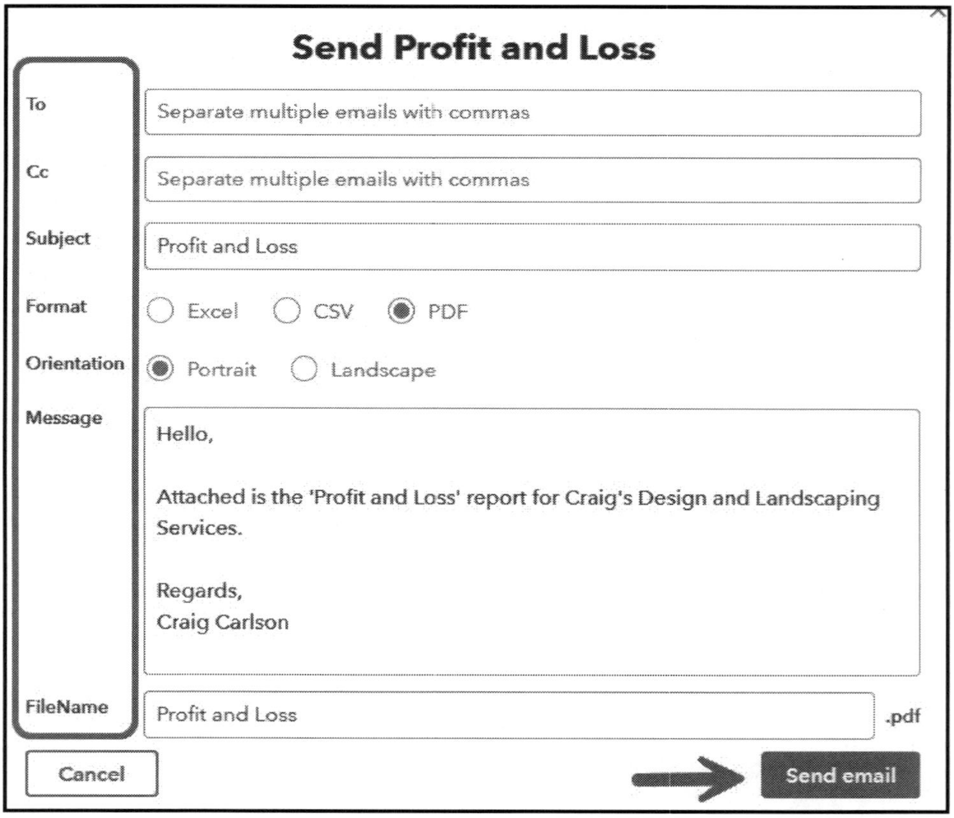

Figure 14.21: Completing the required fields to email the report directly from QBO

The following is a brief description of the fields that need to be completed:

- **To**: Enter the email address of each recipient in this field. You can enter multiple email addresses by putting a comma in between each one.
- **CC**: Enter the email address for each recipient that needs to receive a carbon copy of the report. To enter multiple email addresses, put a comma in between each email address.
- **Subject**: This field will automatically be populated with the name of the report. You can make changes to this field.
- **Body**: This field will automatically be populated with a standard message. You can customize the email message to fit your needs.
- **FileName**: The report you are emailing will be attached as a PDF document.

2. After completing all the fields, click the **Send email** button to email the report, as shown in *Figure 14.21*.

Emailing reports can be an easy and secure way to share data with your accountant and stakeholders in your business. The reports are attached in PDF format so they cannot be manipulated.

Summary

We have introduced you to the Reports Center and covered all the different types of reports available at your fingertips. You have learned how to run reports, edit the data on reports, and save your changes. We have shown you how to share your data by printing a hard copy, exporting the information to Excel, saving it in PDF format, and emailing it directly from QuickBooks. This will help you share information safely and securely on a need-to-know basis instead of giving access to your company data.

In the next chapter, we will dive into the reports available in the *Business Overview & Cash Flow* report group. We will cover reports such as the P&L statement, the balance sheet report, and the cash flow statement.

Next steps

1. Before you generate financial statements, make sure all bank, credit card, and loan accounts have been reconciled.
2. Review your balance sheet, income statement, and statement of cash flows, and jot down any questions that you have prior to meeting with your bookkeeper/accountant.
3. If you have a bookkeeper or accountant who manages your books, schedule time to meet with that person each month. However, make sure that you have already reviewed the reports and made a list of your questions prior to this meeting. In other words, schedule your "date" before you meet with your bookkeeper or accountant, if applicable.
4. Be sure to subscribe to my YouTube channel to learn more tips and tricks on how to customize reports in QBO. You can access the channel here:

`https://packt.link/du2BR`

15

Business Overview and Cash Management Tools and Reports

In *Chapter 14, Report Center Overview*, we explained how to navigate the Report Center, what reports are available based on your **QuickBooks Online** (**QBO**) subscription level, how to customize reports to meet your business needs, and how to export reports using Excel, PDFs, and email. In this chapter, we will discuss the three primary reports that provide a good overview of your business: **profit and loss statements**, **balance sheet reports**, and **statements of cash flows**. We will explain what information is included in each report, how to customize it, and how to generate the report. In addition, you will learn how to create a budget from scratch so that you can keep track of your income and expenses in relation to the set budget for the year. This information will go a long way in helping you make decisions about your business.

Finally, we will introduce you to the **Cash Flow Planner**. One of the biggest issues many small businesses face is managing their cash flow. The Cash Flow Planner can help you predict when you might encounter a cash shortfall so that you can take the necessary remedial steps before it happens. The Cash Flow Planner allows you to create real or hypothetical cash flow scenarios without affecting your actual data in QBO. Additionally, the audit log report provides you with the activity of all QBO users. You can see how long a user was logged in, when they logged out, and the changes (if any) that were made by each user.

By the end of this chapter, you will have a better understanding of what information you will find in the balance sheet, profit and loss statement, and statement of cash flow reports. In addition, you will know how to generate each report, as well as how to create an income and expense budget from scratch.

The following topics will be covered in this chapter:

- Understanding profit and loss statements
- Generating balance sheet reports
- Understanding the statement of cash flows
- Creating a budget
- Using the Cash Flow Center
- Generating the audit log report

The US edition of QBO was used to create this book. If you are using a version that is outside of the United States, results may differ.

Understanding profit and loss statements

In this section, we will show you how to customize and generate a profit and loss statement. The **profit and loss statement**, also referred to as the **income statement**, or **statement of activities** in the non-profit sector, shows you how profitable a business is over a period of time. This report summarizes all the income accrued and expenses incurred by a business over a specific period of time. The difference between income and expenses is shown on the report as either net profit (when income exceeds expenses) or net loss (when expenses exceed income). Like most reports, you can customize the profit and loss statement to meet your business needs.

Reports can be run on an accrual or cash basis by simply selecting the option you want directly on the report. In *Chapter 14, Report Center Overview*, we showed you how to select the accounting method for reports.

Additionally, before preparing any reports, it is important to confirm that your books are reconciled for the reporting period. In *Chapter 11, Managing Bank Feeds and Reconciling Bank and Credit Card Accounts*, we covered how to reconcile your accounts in QBO.

Follow these steps to generate and customize a profit and loss statement:

1. Navigate to **Reports > Standard reports** in the left menu bar, as shown here:

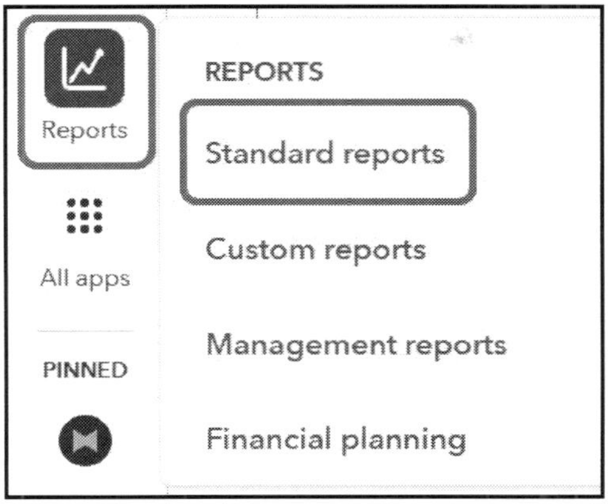

Figure 15.1: Navigating to the Report Center from the left menu bar

2. Scroll down to the **Business Overview** section and select **Profit and Loss**, as shown here:

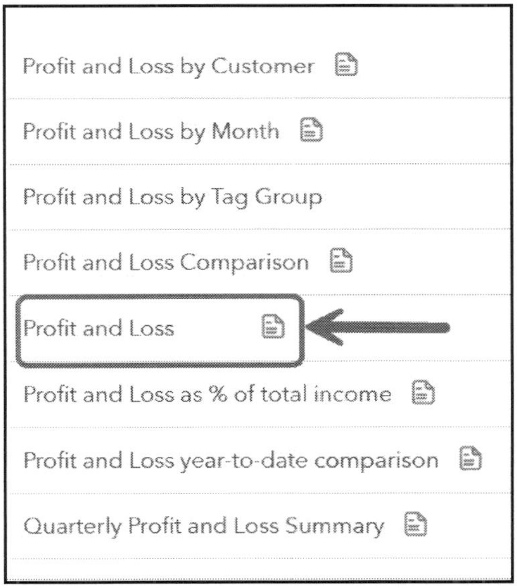

Figure 15.2: Selecting the profit and loss report

3. As you can see, there are several different types of profit and loss reports that you can run in QuickBooks Online: **Profit and Loss by Customer**, **Profit and Loss by Month**, **Profit and Loss by Tag Group**, **Profit and Loss Comparison**, **Profit and Loss**, **Profit and Loss as % of total income**, **Profit and Loss year-to-date comparison**, and **Quarterly Profit and Loss Summary** are preset custom reports.
4. You can customize the report period, accounting method, which columns to display, comparison period, how to filter the data, and change the look and feel of the report within the general settings:

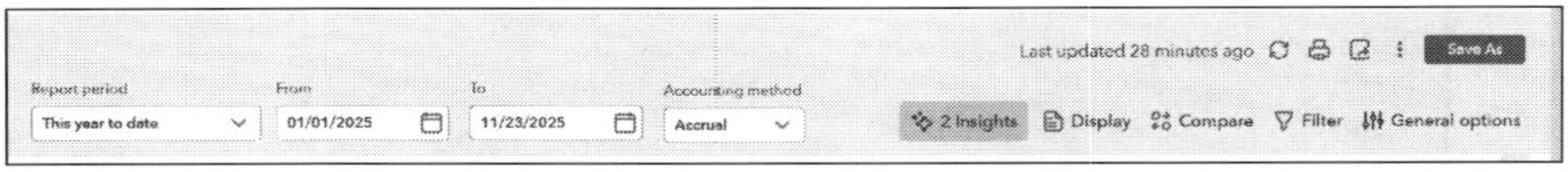

Figure 15.3: Choosing the report's parameters

Brief descriptions of the basic customization options for a profit and loss report are as follows:

- **Report period**: From the drop-down menu, you can choose a preset time period (such as **This year to date**), and the **From/To** date fields will be populated automatically for you. The other option is to type directly into the **From/To** date fields.
- **Accounting method**: You can choose the accounting method you would like to run the report for, cash or accrual. You can learn more about the cash and accrual methods in *Chapter 1, Bookkeeping 101*.
- **Insights (AI)**: With the introduction of AI agents to QBO, throughout QBO, you will see recommendations, reminders, and insights on reports based on an analysis of the data by the Accounting Agent. In *Chapter 2, Getting Started with QuickBooks Online*, we discussed the agents available in each of the QBO subscription plans.
- **Display**: There are a number of options you can choose from when it comes to how to display columns on a report. From the dropdown, you can select days, weeks, months, quarters, years, customers, vendors, employees, and products or services.
- **Compare**: You can compare your data to a previous period by making a selection from the dropdown.
- **Filter**: For a more focused review, you can filter the profit and loss report by distribution account, account type, customer, vendor, employee, or product/service.

- **General options:** You can make changes to number formatting, show non-zero or active accounts, and add a header or footer. In *Chapter 14, Report Center Overview*, we covered in detail how to customize reports.

The following is a snapshot of a sample profit and loss report that has been generated in QBO:

Profit and Loss

Craig's Design and Landscaping Services

January-December, 2025

Account	Total
Income	
Design income	2,250.00
Discounts given	(89.50)
Landscaping Services	$1,477.50
Job Materials	$4,736.47
Labor	$300.00
Total for Landscaping Services	$6,513.97
Pest Control Services	110.00
Sales of Product Income	912.75
Services	503.55
Total for Income	$10,200.77
Cost of Sales	
Cost of Goods Sold	405.00
Total for Cost of Sales	$405.00
Gross Profit	$9,795.77
Expenses	
Advertising	74.86
Automobile	$113.96
Fuel	349.41
Total for Automobile	$463.37
Equipment Rental	112.00
Insurance	241.23
Job Expenses	$155.07
Job Materials	$802.82
Total for Job Expenses	$957.89
Legal & Professional Fees	$75.00
Accounting	640.00
Bookkeeper	55.00
Lawyer	400.00
Total for Legal & Professional Fees	$1,170.00
Maintenance and Repair	$185.00
Equipment Repairs	755.00
Total for Maintenance and Repair	$940.00
Meals and Entertainment	28.49
Office Expenses	18.08
Rent or Lease	900.00
Utilities	$331.39
Total for Expenses	$5,237.31
Net Operating Income	$4,558.46
Other Expenses	
Miscellaneous	2,916.00
Total for Other Expenses	$2,916.00
Net Other Income	($2,916.00)
Net Income	$1,642.46

Figure 15.4: Example profit and loss report

In this profit and loss report, Craig's Design and Landscaping Services' total income of **$10,200.77** and expenses totaling **$5,237.31** yield a net profit of **$1,642.46** for the period January 1 to December 31, 2025.

> If an income or expense account has a negative balance, it is a good idea to click and check the individual transactions to see whether an item has been categorized to the wrong account. You can drill down to the detailed transactions by clicking on an amount in the report.

Now that you understand the information you will find in a profit and loss statement, as well as how to generate a customized profit and loss statement, we will cover the balance sheet report next. We will show you how to customize a balance sheet report to meet your specific business requirements.

Generating balance sheet reports

A **balance sheet report** summarizes the assets, liabilities, and owner's equity for a business at any point in time. This report allows you to assess the **liquidity** (access to cash or assets that can be quickly turned into cash) of a business, which is important for potential investors and creditors. As with most reports, you can customize the balance sheet report to meet your business needs. We will show you how to generate the report and customize it in this section.

Follow these steps to generate and customize a balance sheet report:

1. Navigate to **Reports>Standard reports** in the left menu bar, as shown here:

Figure 15.5: Navigating to the Report Center from the left menu bar

2. Scroll down to the business overview section and select **Balance Sheet**, as shown here:

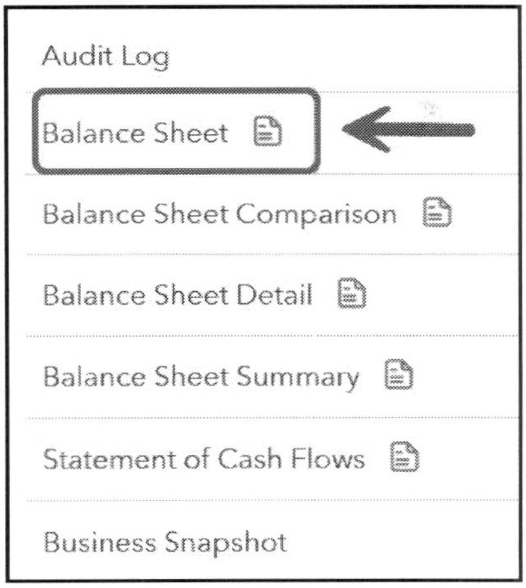

Figure 15.6: Choosing the balance sheet report

As you can see, there are several different types of balance sheet reports you can run in QBO. The **Balance Sheet Comparison** report, the **Balance Sheet Detail** report, and the **Balance Sheet Summary** report are preset custom reports.

3. You can customize the report period, accounting method, which columns to display, comparison period, how to filter the data, and change the look and feel of the report within the general settings:

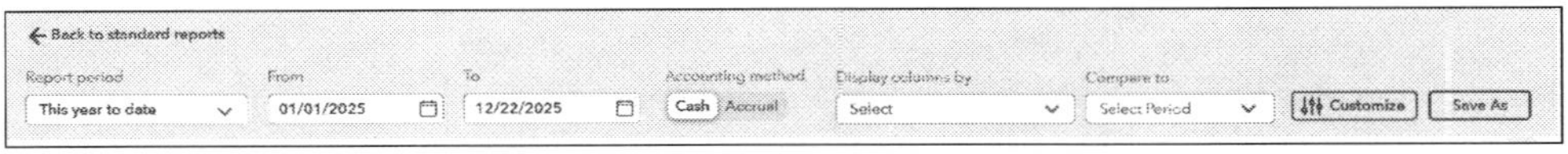

Figure 15.7: Selecting the parameters for the balance sheet report

A brief description of the basic customization options for a balance sheet report is as follows:

- **Report period**: From the drop-down menu, you can choose a preset time period (such as **This year to date**), and the **From/To** date fields will be populated automatically for you. The other option is to type directly into the **From/To** date fields.
- **Accounting method**: You can choose the accounting method you would like to run the report for, cash or accrual. You can learn more about the cash and accrual methods in *Chapter 1, Bookkeeping 101.*
- **Insights (AI)**: With the introduction of AI agents to QBO, throughout QBO, you will see recommendations, reminders, and insights on reports based on an analysis of the data by the Accounting Agent. In *Chapter 2, Getting Started with QuickBooks Online*, we discussed the agents available in each of the QBO subscription plans.
- **Display**: There are a number of options you can choose from when it comes to how to display columns on a report. From the dropdown, you can select days, weeks, months, quarters, years, customers, vendors, employees, and products or services.
- **Compare**: You can compare your data to a previous period by making a selection from the dropdown.
- **Filter**: For a more focused review, you can filter the profit and loss report by distribution account, account type, customer, vendor, employee, or product/service.
- **General options**: You can make changes to number formatting, show non-zero or active accounts, and add a header or footer. In *Chapter 14, Report Center Overview*, we covered in detail how to customize reports.

The following is a snapshot of a sample balance sheet report that has been generated in QBO:

Balance Sheet

Craig's Design and Landscaping Services

As of December 31, 2025

Account	Total
Assets	
Current Assets	
Bank Accounts	
Checking	1,201.00
Savings	800.00
Total for Bank Accounts	**$2,001.00**
Accounts Receivable	
Accounts Receivable (A/R)	5,281.52
Total for Accounts Receivable	**$5,281.52**
Other Current Assets	
Inventory Asset	596.25
Undeposited Funds	2,062.52
Total for Other Current Assets	**$2,658.77**
Total for Current Assets	**$9,941.29**
Fixed Assets	
Truck	
Original Cost	13,495.00
Total for Truck	**$13,495.00**
Total for Fixed Assets	**$13,495.00**
Total for Assets	**$23,436.29**
Liabilities and Equity	
Liabilities	
Current Liabilities	
Accounts Payable	
Accounts Payable (A/P)	1,602.67
Total for Accounts Payable	**$1,602.67**
Credit Cards	
Mastercard	157.72
Total for Credit Cards	**$157.72**
Other Current Liabilities	
Arizona Dept. of Revenue Payable	0.00
Board of Equalization Payable	370.94
Loan Payable	4,000.00
Total for Other Current Liabilities	**$4,370.94**
Total for Current Liabilities	**$6,131.33**
Long-term Liabilities	
Notes Payable	25,000.00
Total for Long-term Liabilities	**$25,000.00**
Total for Liabilities	**$31,131.33**
Equity	
Opening Balance Equity	(9,337.50)
Retained Earnings	-
Net Income	1,642.46
Total for Equity	**($7,695.04)**
Total for Liabilities and Equity	**$23,436.29**

Figure 15.8: Sample balance sheet report

In this balance sheet report, Craig's Design and Landscaping Services' has total assets of **$23,436.29**, liabilities totaling **$31,131.33**, and total equity of **$-7,695.04** for the period January 1 to December 31, 2025.

Now that you understand the information you will find in a balance sheet report, as well as how to generate a customized balance sheet, we will cover the statement of cash flows next. We will show you how to customize the statement of cash flows, which gives you insights into the cash flow of a business.

Understanding the statement of cash flows

The **statement of cash flows** is a detailed report that shows the cash coming in and going out of your business over a period of time. It groups cash flow into three categories: operating, investing, and financing activities. **Operating** activities include items that are part of the day-to-day business operations, such as cash due from customers (accounts receivable) or money due to vendors (accounts payable). **Investing** activities include the purchase of assets for the business, such as a computer. **Financing** activities include money coming in from a business loan or line of credit.

Similar to the profit and loss and balance sheet reports, you can customize the statement of cash flows to meet your business needs. We will show you how to generate the report and customize it in this section.

Follow these steps to customize and generate a statement of cash flows report:

1. Navigate to **Reports > Standard reports** in the left menu bar, as shown here:

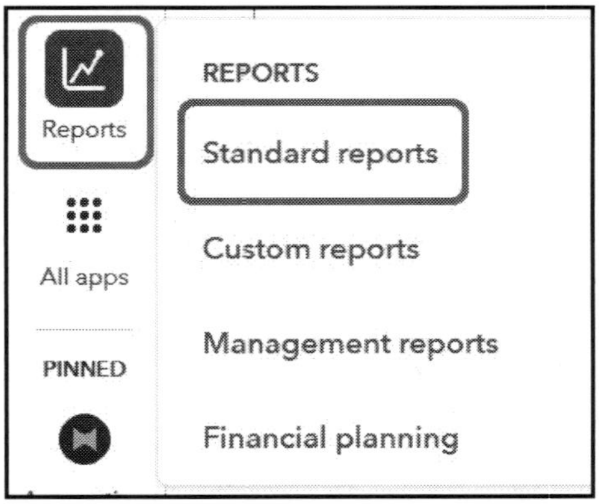

Figure 15.9: Navigate to the Report Center from the left navigation bar

2. Scroll down to the **Business Overview** section and select **Statement of Cash Flows**, as shown here:

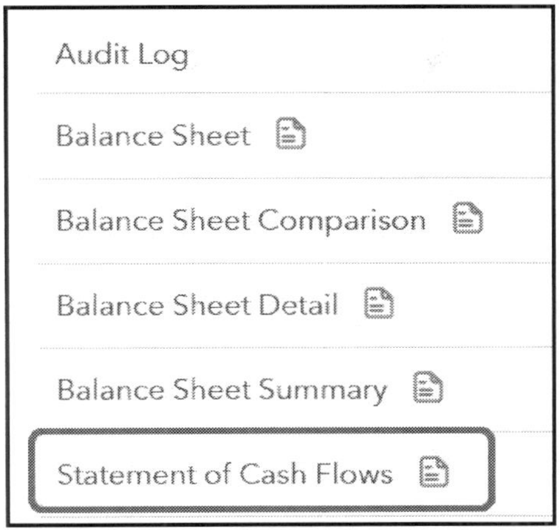

Figure 15.10: Selecting the statement of cash flows report

3. You can customize the date range and columns to display, as shown here:

Figure 15.11: Choosing the parameters of the statement of cash flows report

Brief descriptions of the basic customization options for a statement of cash flows report are as follows:

- **Report period**: From the drop-down menu, you can choose a preset time period (such as **This year to date**) and the **From/To** date fields will be populated automatically for you. The other option is to type directly into the **From/To** date fields.
- **Insights (AI)**: With the introduction of AI agents to QBO, throughout QBO, you will see recommendations, reminders, and insights on reports based on an analysis of the data by the Accounting Agent. In *Chapter 2, Getting Started with QuickBooks Online*, we discussed the agents available in each of the QBO subscription plans.
- **Display**: There are a number of options you can choose from when it comes to how to display columns on a report. From the dropdown, you can select days, weeks, months, quarters, years, customers, vendors, employees, and products or services.
- **Filter**: For a more focused review, you can filter the profit and loss report by distribution account, account type, customer, vendor, employee, or product/service.

- **General options**: You can make changes to number formatting, show non-zero or active accounts, and add a header or footer. In *Chapter 14*, *Report Center Overview*, we covered in detail how to customize reports.

4. After making your selections, click the **Refresh report** button.

   A statement of cash flows similar to the following will appear on your screen:

Statement of Cash Flows

Craig's Design and Landscaping Services

January-December, 2025

Full name	Total
Cash flows from operating activities	
Net Income	1,642.46
Adjustments for non-cash income and expenses:	
Accounts Payable (A/P)	1,602.67
Accounts Receivable (A/R)	(5,281.52)
Arizona Dept. of Revenue Payable	0.00
Board of Equalization Payable	370.94
Inventory Asset	(596.25)
Loan Payable	4,000.00
Mastercard	157.72
Total for Adjustments for non-cash income and expenses:	**$253.56**
Net cash from operating activities	**$1,896.02**
Cash flows from investing activities	
Truck:Original Cost	(13,495.00)
Net cash used in investing activities	**($13,495.00)**
Cash flows from financing activities	
Notes Payable	25,000.00
Opening Balance Equity	(9,337.50)
Net cash used in financing activities	**$15,662.50**
NET INCREASE (DECREASE) IN CASH AND CASH EQUIVALENTS	**$4,063.52**
Cash and cash equivalents at beginning of year	**$0.00**
CASH AND CASH EQUIVALENTS AT END OF YEAR	**$4,063.52**

Figure 15.12: Sample statement of cash flows

In this statement of cash flows report, Craig's Design and Landscaping Services' has a net cash provided by operating activities amount of **$1,896.02**, cash used in investing activities is **($13,495.00)**, and cash used in financing activities is **$15,662.50** for the period January 1 to December 31, 2025. The cash at the end of the period is **$4,063.52**.

> Financial statements should be reviewed on a monthly basis at a minimum after all bank and credit card accounts have been reconciled. This will allow you to identify any issues so that you can correct them before filing your tax returns. It is ideal to review and verify that the balance sheet report is accurate before you review the profit and loss statement. If all accounts have been reconciled and the balances tie out to the balance sheet report, then most likely your profit and loss statement will be accurate.

Now that you understand the information you will find in a statement of cash flows, as well as how to generate a customized report, we will show you how to create a budget from scratch.

Creating a budget

After you've been in business for a year or two, you may want to take advantage of tools that will help you strategize and plan for the future. You can create a budget in QBO from scratch or use existing data from the previous year. When you create a budget, you can keep track of your actual income and expenses to see whether you are coming in over or under budget.

QuickBooks allows you to create budgets for all income and expense accounts. You can also create a budget for specific customers. We will show you how to create a budget from scratch in this section. To access the budgeting feature, you must be subscribed to QBO Plus or QBO Advanced.

Follow these steps to create a budget:

1. Click on the gear icon and select **Budgeting**, as shown here:

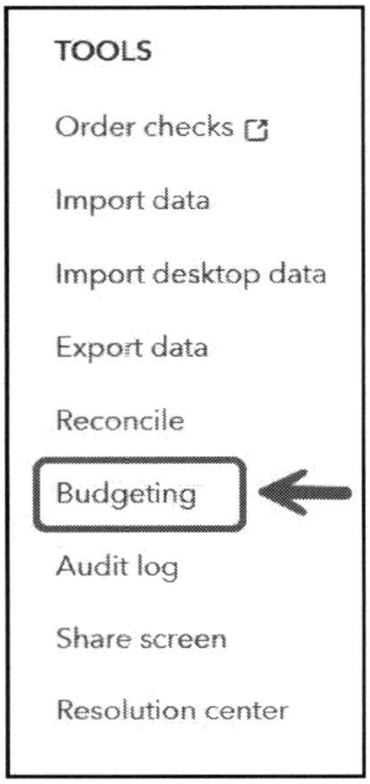

Figure 15.13: Navigating to Budgeting from the TOOLS menu

The following screen will appear:

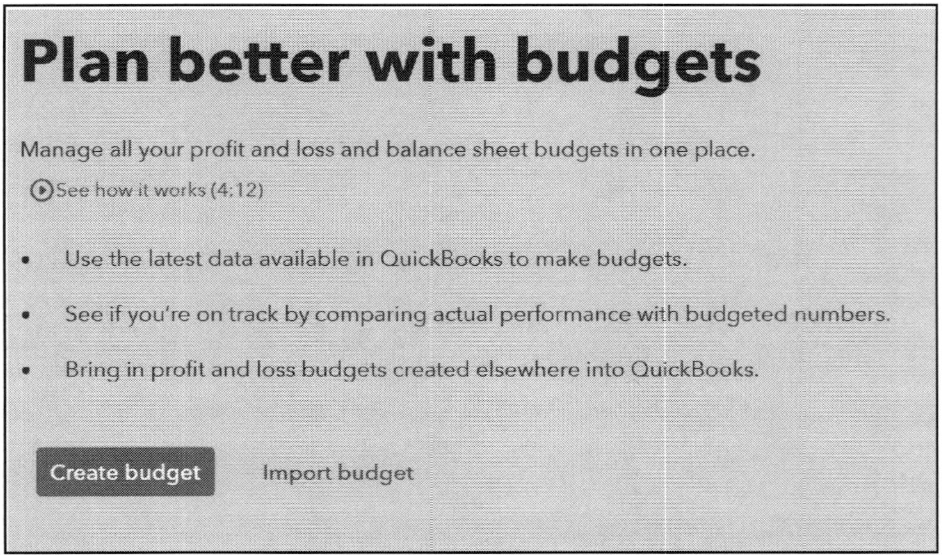

Figure 15.14: The Create budget button

2. Click on the **Create budget** button.
3. On the next screen, you will need to select a budget type, time period, and budget format you want to create:

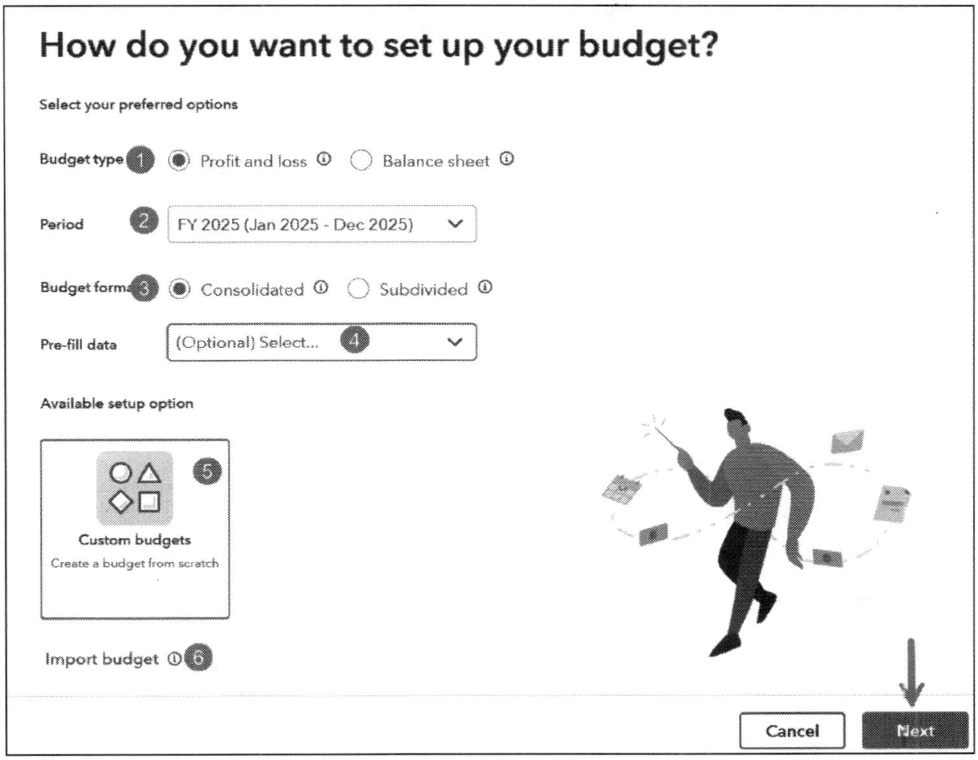

Figure 15.15: Choosing the parameters of the budget

Brief explanations of the information included on the preceding screen are as follows:

- **Budget type (1)**: There are two budget types available: **Profit and loss** and **Balance sheet**. In our example, we have selected **Profit and loss**. This option will allow you to create your budget based on expected income and expenses so that you can project your expected profit/loss for the time period specified.
- **Period (2)**: Select the fiscal year the budget is for (for example, **FY 2025 (Jan 2025 – Dec 2025)**). Besides the current year, the other options available from the dropdown are to go back two years or to go forward four years.

- **Budget format** (3): There are two formats available: **Consolidated** or **Subdivided**. A consolidated budget allows you to create a plan at the organizational level. A subdivided budget allows you to create individual budgets based on location, class, department, or customers.
- **Pre-fill data** (4): Instead of creating a budget from scratch, you can choose to have QBO pre-fill the budget template using the actuals from the current year or go back as far as four years. From the dropdown, select the year you would like to use.
- **Custom budgets** (5): After completing fields 1-4, click this box to display the budget template.
- **Import budget** (6): A tool called Spreadsheet sync allows you to securely send your budget information between QuickBooks Online Advanced and your spreadsheet for up-to-date company insights.

4. After completing the fields, click **Next.** A screen that resembles the following will appear:

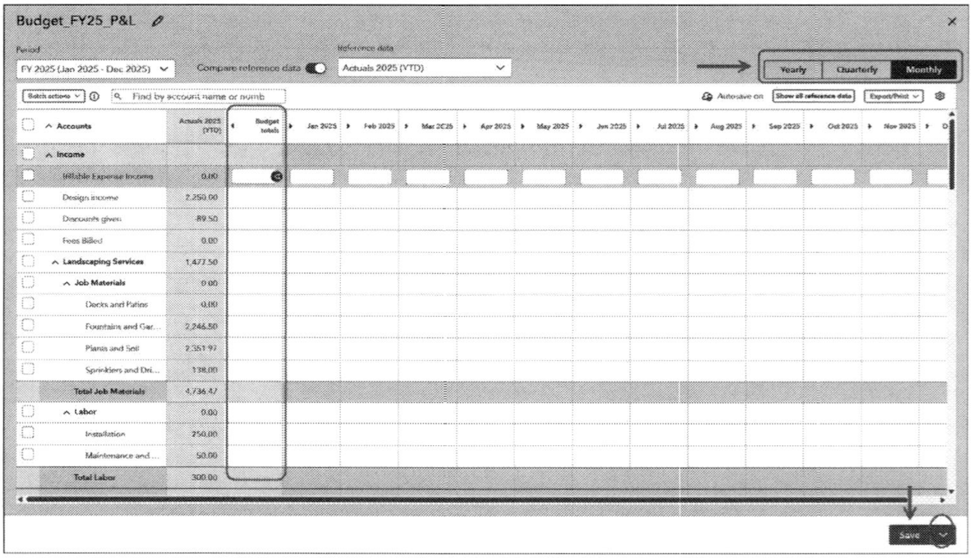

Figure 15.16: Complete budget template

5. Enter an amount in each cell and press *Tab*. If the budgeted amount for each month is the same, enter the total budget amount in the **Budget totals** column and then click the blue arrow that appears to split the total across all 12 months evenly. Be sure to repeat this step until you have completed all the income and expense items.

   QuickBooks will automatically total each month, along with each income and expense item. Be sure to click the **Save** button located in the bottom-right corner to save your work.

> For certain entities, such as non-profits that need to use up a certain budgeted amount each year, you can put the total budgeted amount in the first month of the fiscal year. Then, your profit and loss budget versus actuals report will show the amount you have remaining in each line item as the year progresses.

6. To close out of the budget, click the dropdown to the right of **Save** and select **Save and close**. The following screen will appear:

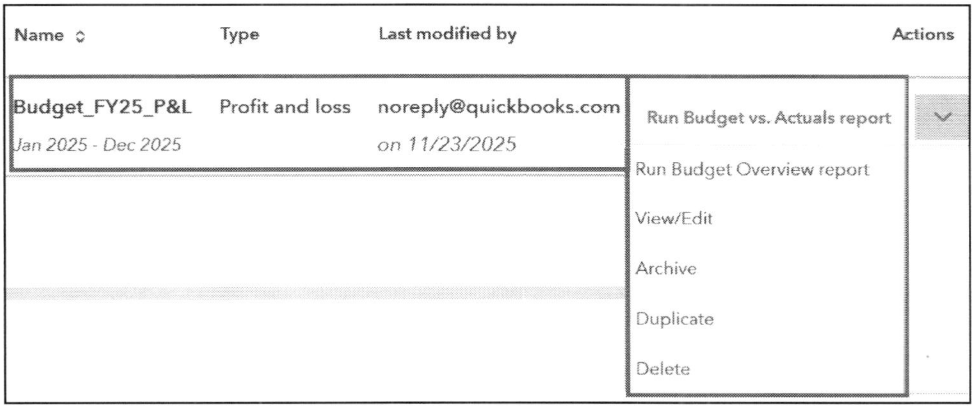

Figure 15.17: Editing an existing budget

This screen will show a list of budgets that have been created, including the budget name, type, and the last modification. In addition, you can access your budget reports by clicking on the **View/Edit** button. You can archive, duplicate, or delete budgets from this menu, as well as generating reports. There are two reports that you can run to review and manage your budget: a **budget versus actuals** report and a **budget overview** report, as shown in the preceding screenshot. A brief description of the information you will find in both reports is as follows:

- **Budget versus actuals report**: The budget versus actuals report includes side-by-side columns, one for the budgeted amount and one for the actuals as of a specific time period. The difference between the budget and the actuals will appear in a variance column. This information can help you determine the areas where you are within your budget or over budget so that you can make any necessary adjustments.
- Like the budget overview report, you can export the budget versus actuals report to Excel or PDF, or you can email the report directly from QuickBooks.
- **Budget overview report**: After entering your budget, you can run this report to review the budget to ensure that it is accurate. If changes are required, you can go back into the budget template to make the necessary changes. Like most reports in QBO, you can export the budget overview report to Excel or PDF. You can also email the budget overview report directly from QuickBooks.

You now know how to create a budget from scratch for income and expenses, as well as how to generate the budget overview report and the budget versus actuals report.

Using the Cash Flow Center

One of the challenges many small businesses face is staying on top of their cash flow. Within QBO, you can access several tools that will help you to stay on top of your cash flow:

1. To access the Cash Flow Center, click on **Reports > Financial planning > Cash flow overview** as shown here:

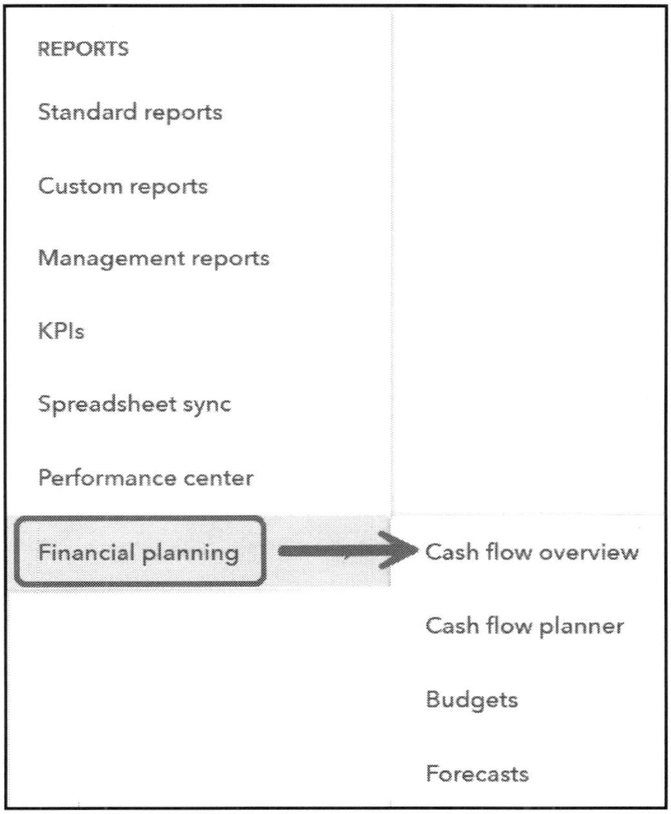

Figure 15.18: Navigating to the Cash Flow Center

The Cash Flow Center will appear, as shown here:

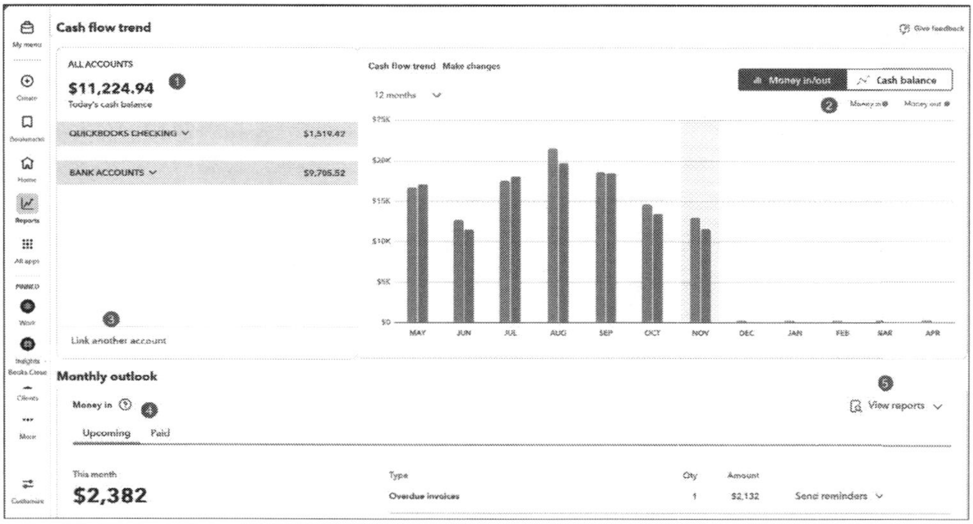

Figure 15.19: Cash Flow Center window

Here is a brief explanation of how this tool works:

- In the upper-left corner is a list of all bank accounts and their current balances. In our example, the total cash balance is $11,224.94. This amount is broken down between a QuickBooks Checking account that has a balance of $1,519.42 and other bank accounts with a balance of $9,705.52.
- In the middle of the screen is the cash flow trend in the form of a graph. The green bar indicates money that has come into the business, and the blue bar represents money that has gone out.

Link another account As discussed in *Chapter 4, Customizing QuickBooks for Your Business*, you can connect accounts to QuickBooks so transactions will automatically import. You can link another bank account directly within this screen. Directly below the cash flow trend is the monthly outlook, as shown here:

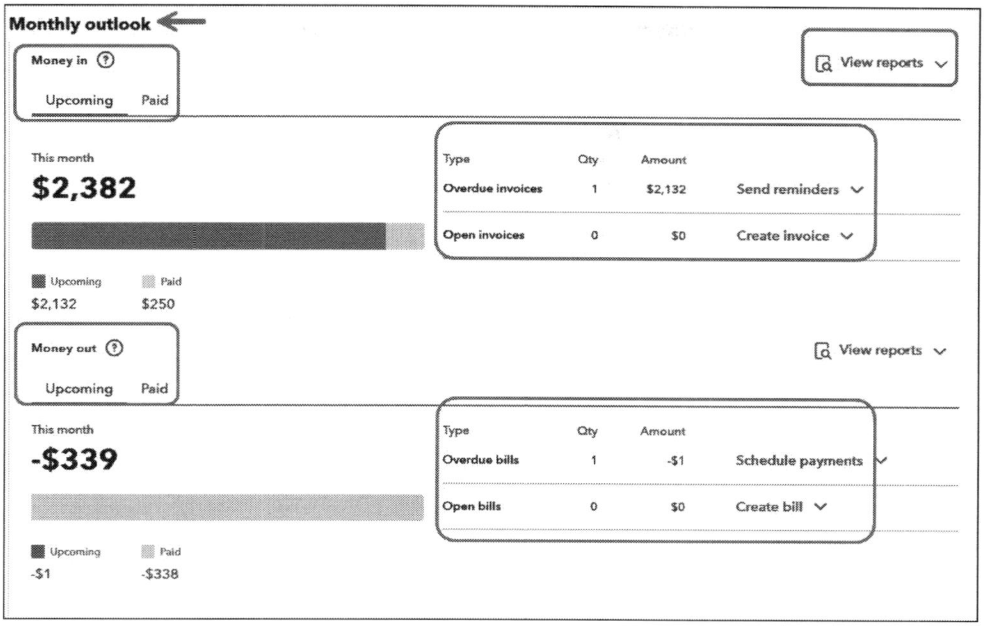

Figure 15.20: Reviewing the monthly outlook for cash flow

In the preceding screenshot, the top of the screen refers to the **Money in** activities:

- There are two tabs: One is for **Upcoming** payments from customers ($2,132 in our example). The **Paid** tab shows the total of payments received from customers for services and/or products provided ($250 in our example).
- In the section below that, customer invoices are categorized as overdue and open. You can send reminders for the overdue invoices or create an invoice within this section. In the upper-right corner, there is a **View reports** link. From here, you can generate the open invoices report, the invoice list, and the sales by customer details report.

2. Below the **Money in** section is an overview of the **Money out** activities:

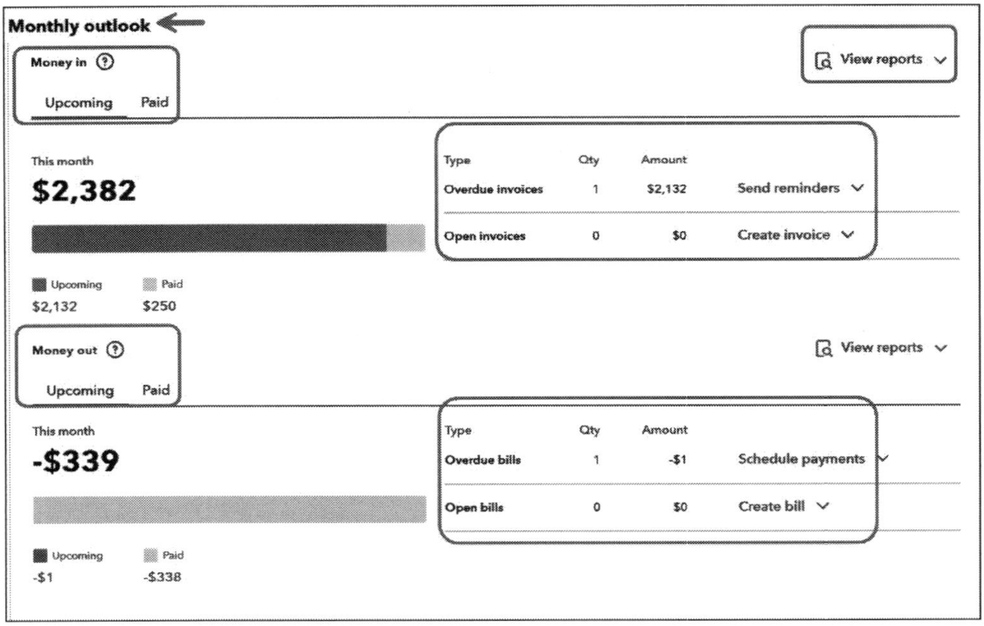

Figure 15.21: Highlighted areas for the Money in and Money out sections

As we did in the **Money in** section, we have highlighted the following areas in **Money out**:

- In this section, you will see two tabs: **Upcoming** payments to be made to suppliers ($-1 in our example) and payments made to vendor suppliers within the last month (-$338 in our example).
- In this section, you will see the quantity and total amount of overdue bills and open bills. You can **schedule payments** or **create bills** within this section.
- When you click on the **View reports** link, you can generate the unpaid bills, bill payment list, and expenses by vendor summary reports for more details.

Cash Flow Planner

Within the Cash Flow Center, you will find a new and improved **Cash Flow Planner**. The Cash Flow Planner allows you to create real or hypothetical cash flow scenarios without affecting your QuickBooks data. To get the most out of the Cash Flow Planner, be sure to connect all of your business debit and credit card accounts. In addition, add any real or hypothetical scenarios to get an idea of how your cash flow will be impacted. Best of all, you don't have to worry about it affecting your actual QuickBooks data.

Follow these steps to access the Cash Flow Planner:

1. Click on the **Planner** tab and the following will display:

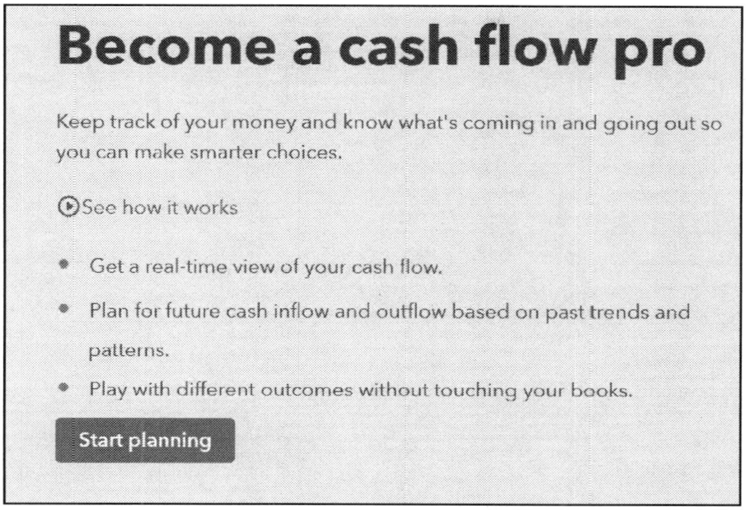

Figure 15.22: Accessing the Cash Flow Planner

Click on the **Start planning** button, shown in the preceding screenshot, and the following message will be displayed:

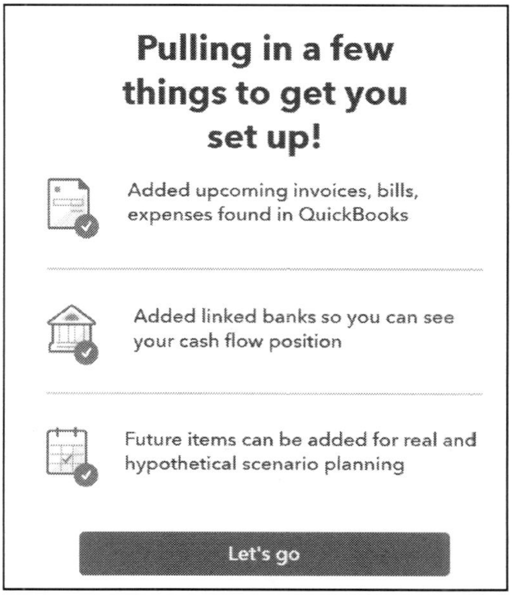

Figure 15.23: Overview of Cash Flow Planner

After you click the **Let's go** button shown in the preceding screenshot, the following will appear:

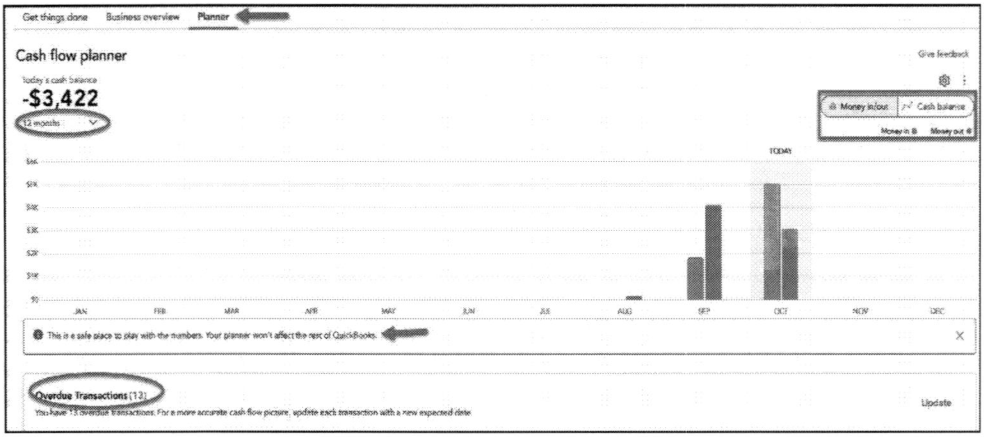

Figure 15.24: Reviewing the Cash Flow Planner

Based on the income and expenses you have recorded in QBO, the Cash Flow Planner will display money in (green bar) versus money out (blue bar) transactions for the time period you have selected. In the preceding screenshot, we have it set for 12 months. However, you can choose this month, 3 months, 6 months, or 24 months. In the upper-right corner, you can switch the planner to **Cash balance**, and you will see the expected cash balance for the time period specified.

2. Scroll down to see the **Upcoming** section:

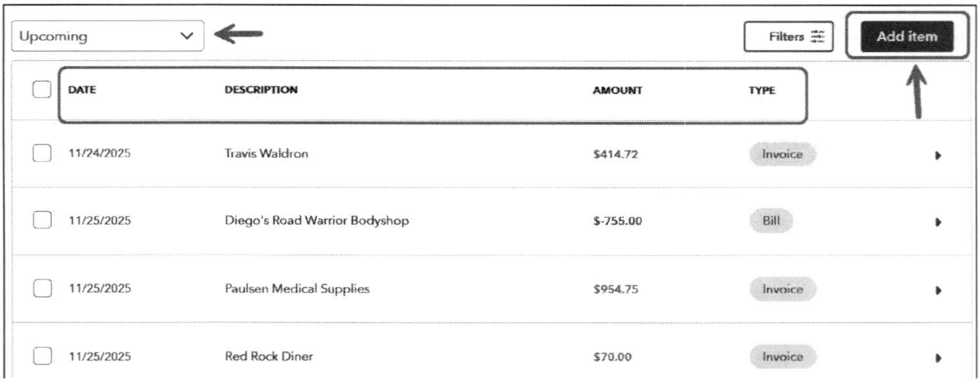

Figure 15.25: Upcoming activity in the Cash Flow Planner tool

This section includes details of how QBO arrived at the money in/money out information shown in the preceding screenshot. You can click the **Add item** button to add any additional income or expense items that you are aware of (and that are not yet recorded in QBO) to see the impact on your cash flow.

> Remember, nothing that you do in this area of QBO will affect your books. This is where you get to run hypothetical scenarios to help predict your future cash flow, which will help you to make informed decisions about your business.

Generating the audit log report

The audit log report shows you everything that has happened in your company file, so you can keep track of who has been in QuickBooks and what they have been doing. It shows you the date a change was made, the user who made the change, what the change (event) was, and the history if there is more than one change that was made.

Follow these steps to generate the audit log report:

1. Navigate to **Reports > Standard reports** in the left menu bar, as shown here:

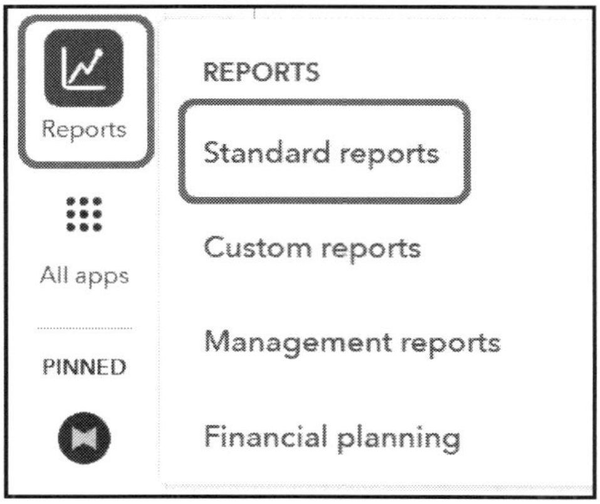

Figure 15.26: Navigating to the Report Center from the left navigation bar

2. Scroll down to the **Business overview** section and select **Audit Log**, as shown here:

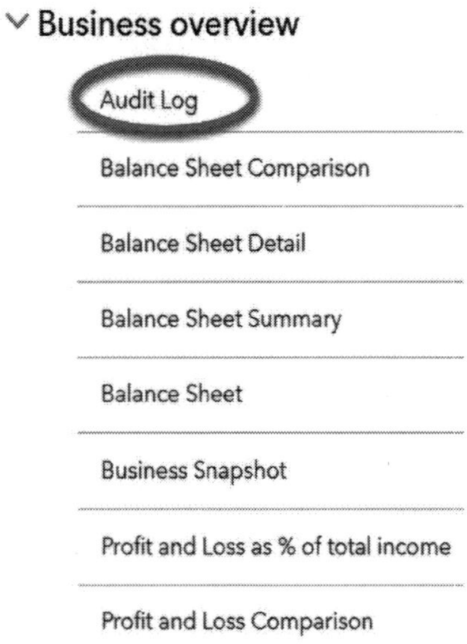

Figure 15.27: Clicking on Audit Log in the Business overview group

3. The audit log report will appear:

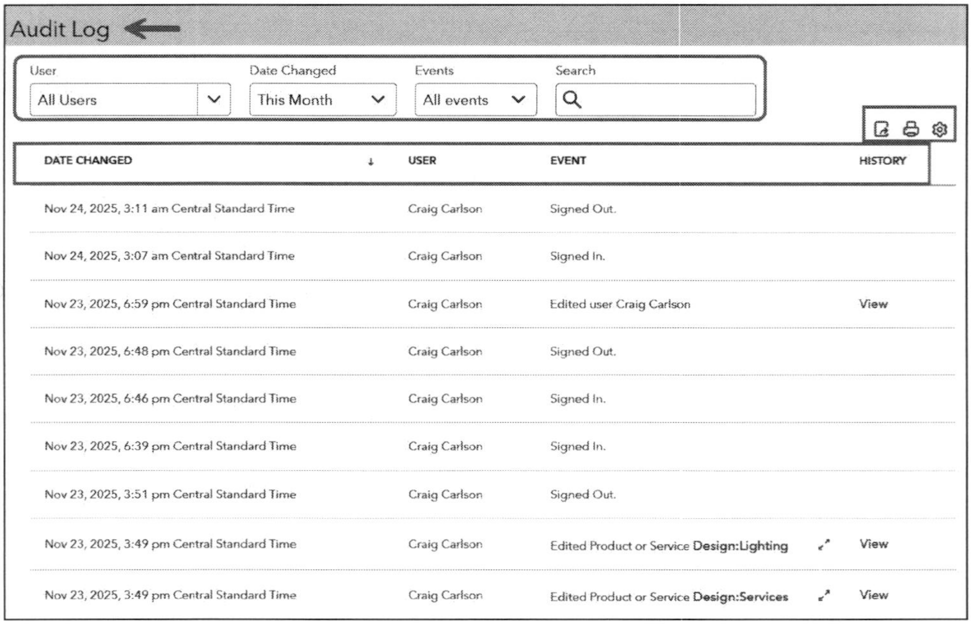

Figure 15.28: Sample audit log report

At the top of the report, there are four fields you can use to filter the report by: **User**, **Date Changed**, **Events**, and **Search**.

This report will come in handy if there is ever a question as to who changed what in your data file. With the latest edition of QBO, not only can you print a hard copy of the report but now you can email it and export this report to Excel or as a PDF.

Summary

As discussed in *Chapter 14*, *Report Center Overview*, once you have customized the reports you plan to use on a regular basis, it is a good idea to memorize them and/or create a group of reports that will appear in your **Custom reports** tab. In this chapter, we explained the information you can find in the three primary financial reports: profit and loss statements, balance sheet reports, and statements of cash flows.

We also showed you how to customize the reports and generate them. In addition, we showed you how to create a budget from scratch and run budget reports. Finally, we touched on what you can do with the tools available in the QuickBooks Cash Flow Center and showed you how to generate the audit log report to view the history of changes to your company file.

In the next chapter, we will show you how to properly close the books in 10 steps.

Next steps

1. Be sure to head over to my YouTube channel for step-by-step product demos in QBO. Use this link to access the channel:

   `https://packt.link/du2BR`

2. Before reviewing reports, preparing budgets, or examining cash flow projections, the first step is to confirm that all bank accounts, credits cards, and loan balances are reconciled.

3. If you have a bookkeeper or accountant who manages your books, schedule time to meet with that person each month. However, make sure that you have already reviewed your financial reports and made a list of your questions *prior to this meeting*. In other words, schedule your "money date" before you meet with your bookkeeper or accountant, if applicable.

16

Closing the Books in QuickBooks Online

After you have entered all of your business transactions into QuickBooks for the year, you will need to finalize your financial statements so that you can hand them off to your accountant to file your taxes. To ensure you have recorded all business transactions for the financial period, we have included a checklist that you can follow to close your books. Closing your books will ensure that no additional transactions are entered into QuickBooks once you have finalized your financial statements. If you have a bookkeeper or an accountant who manages your books, they should ensure that all of the steps have been completed.

In this chapter, we will cover each item on the checklist. This includes reconciling all bank and credit card accounts; making year-end accrual adjustments (if applicable); recording open invoices, bad debt expenses (if applicable), unpaid bills, fixed asset purchases made throughout the year, and depreciation; taking a physical inventory; adjusting retained earnings; and preparing financial statements.

> Many of the tasks in this section are typically performed by an accountant. Adding your tax preparer or **Certified Public Accountant (CPA)** as a user will allow them to access your QuickBooks data—this will allow the accountants to run reports and review the items that are needed so that they can perform these tasks in preparation for your tax return. Later in this chapter, I will show you how to give your accountant access to your data.

The topics covered in this chapter are as follows:

- Recording journal entries
- Reviewing a checklist to close your books
- Reconciling all bank and credit card accounts
- Making year-end accrual adjustments
- Recording all accounts receivable
- Recording bad debt expenses
- Recording all accounts payable
- Reviewing new fixed asset purchases and adding them to the chart of accounts
- Making depreciation journal entries
- Taking a physical inventory and recording inventory adjustments
- Adjusting retained earnings for owner/partner distributions
- Setting a closing date and password
- Preparing key financial reports
- Giving your accountant or tax preparer access to your data

By the end of this chapter, you will know all of the tasks that you need to complete in order to close your books for the year. While most small businesses close their books annually, if you close your books on a monthly or quarterly basis, you will still need to follow the steps outlined in this chapter.

> The US edition of QBO was used for this book. If you are using a version that is outside the US, the results may differ.

Recording journal entries

Before we dive into the details of the checklist, let's discuss recording journal entries. Since many of the items on the checklist will require a journal entry, we will cover the details of what a journal entry is and how to create one.

A **journal entry** is used to adjust your books for transactions that have not been recorded throughout the year. Depreciation expenses for fixed assets, income and expense accruals, and adjustments to retained earnings are three examples we have already mentioned in this chapter. Journal entries are used to record items that cannot be recorded at the transactional level (through checks, deposits, transfers, etc.).

Follow these steps to record a journal entry in QuickBooks:

1. Click the **+ Create** button and select **Journal entry**, as indicated in *Figure 16.1*:

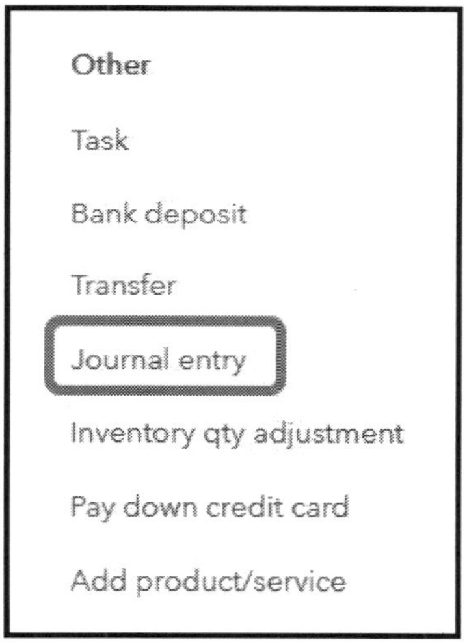

Figure 16.1: Selecting Journal entry in the Other column

2. A screen will appear, similar to the one shown in the following screenshot:

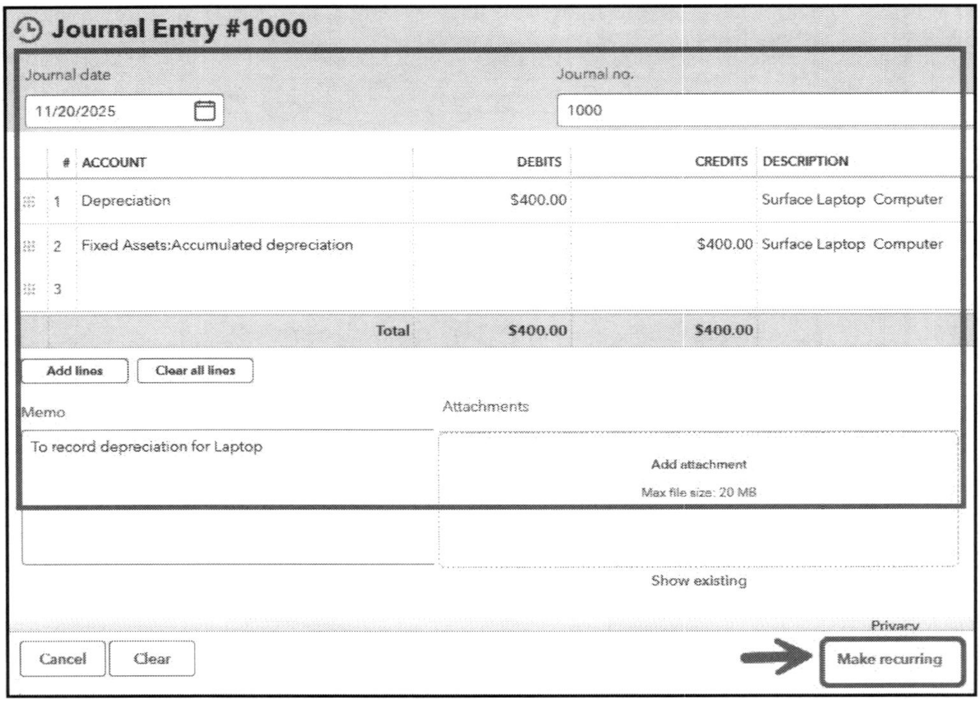

Figure 16.2: Journal Entry template

The following is a brief explanation of the fields that need to be completed in order to record a journal entry:

- **Journal date**: Enter the effective date of the journal in this field.
- **Journal no.**: QuickBooks will automatically populate this field with the next available journal number. If this is the first journal entry you have recorded, you can enter a starting number (such as **1000**), as shown in *Figure 16.2*, and QuickBooks will increment each journal entry number thereafter. Otherwise, QBO will start with 1.
- **ACCOUNT**: Select the account from the drop-down menu.
- **DEBITS**: Enter the debit amount in this field.
- **CREDITS**: Enter the credit amount in this field.

- **DESCRIPTION**: Type a detailed description of the purpose of the journal entry in this field. Adding a detailed description is recommended; it is helpful when referring to a journal entry to have an explanation of why it was made.
- **NAME (not shown)**: If this journal entry is associated with a customer, you can select that customer from the drop-down list in this field.
- **Memo**: Include a brief description of the purpose of the journal entry, as indicated in *Figure 16.2*.
- **Attachments**: If you have any source documentation you would like to include, you can attach those documents directly to this transaction.
- **Make recurring**: To help you stay on top of these types of adjustments, you can make this journal entry recurring. This means you can set up this journal entry to automatically record on the date you specify. If you don't want QBO to automatically record the journal entry for you, you can also just receive a reminder to record the journal entry. To learn more about how to set up recurring transactions, refer to *Chapter 9, Recording Expenses in QuickBooks Online*.

Be sure to record all journal entries prior to generating financial statements. If you give your CPA or accountant access to your data, they can record all of the necessary journal entries and then generate the financial reports required to file your tax returns. We are now ready to dive into our checklist.

Reviewing a checklist for closing your books

As discussed, there are several steps you will need to take in order to close your books for the financial period. How often you close your books (for example, monthly, quarterly, or annually) will determine how often you need to complete these steps. Remember the importance of closing your books, as this will ensure that all transactions for the financial period have been recorded and that your financial statements are accurate, which is important because your accountant will use them to file your business tax return.

The following is a checklist of the steps you need to complete in order to close your books. You should complete them in the order presented:

1. Reconcile all bank and credit card accounts.
2. Make year-end accrual adjustments.
3. Record all accounts receivable.
4. Record bad debt expenses.

5. Record all accounts payable.
6. Review new fixed asset purchases and add them to the chart of accounts.
7. Make depreciation journal entries
8. Take a physical inventory and record inventory adjustments.
9. Adjust retained earnings for owner/partner distributions.
10. Set a closing date and password.
11. Prepare key financial reports.
12. Give your accountant or tax preparer access to your books.

The purpose of closing the books is to ensure that the elements that impact the financial statements are reviewed and deemed accurate before finalizing the financial statements, which will, in turn, be used to file your business tax return. We will discuss each of these steps in detail, starting with reconciling all bank and credit card accounts.

1. Reconciling all bank and credit card accounts, loans, and lines of credit

In *Chapter 11, Managing Bank Feeds and Reconciling Bank and Credit Card Accounts,* you learned how to reconcile your bank and credit card accounts. We also covered loans and lines of credit in *Chapter 11,* and how these accounts should also be reconciled. It's important that you reconcile these accounts before closing the books so that you can ensure that all income and expenses for the period have been recorded in QuickBooks.

This will ensure that your financial statements are accurate and that you don't miss out on any tax deductions.

2. Making year-end accrual adjustments

If you are on the **accrual** basis of accounting, you need to make sure that all income and expenses that have been incurred for the period are recorded. In *Chapter 1, Bookkeeping 101,* we discussed what accrual basis accounting versus cash basis accounting is. Some examples of accruals that may be required are inventory purchases where you have received the product but not the bill and employee wages. Be sure to consult with your accountant for the proper recording of these transactions. We will discuss journal entries in more detail later in this chapter.

3. Recording all accounts receivable for the end of the period

Review the A/R Aging Detail report to make sure that it reflects all outstanding invoices as of the end of the year. Whether you are on an accrual or cash basis, you should invoice any customers for whom you have performed work prior to the end of the year. This will ensure that all income is properly recorded on the books and will show up on your Profit and Loss report (income statement). If there are delinquent invoices on the A/R Aging report that you don't think you will be able to collect payment on, you should write those invoices off as bad debt expense.

4. Recording bad debt expenses

If you're in business long enough, there will come a time when a customer is unable or unwilling to pay you. If you use cash-based accounting, you don't need to record bad debt expenses because you don't have accounts receivable. However, if you do extend credit to your customers and, after attempting to collect the payment, you become aware that you will not be able to do so, you should write off the bad debt. This will ensure that your financial statements remain accurate and that revenue is not overstated.

There are three steps you need to follow in order to write off bad debt: first, you need to add a bad debt item to the products and services list; next, you need to create a credit memo; and finally, you need to apply the credit memo to the unpaid customer invoice. We will walk you through these steps in this section.

Creating a bad debt item

As established, the first step of recording bad debt expenses is to add an item to the products and services list for tracking. Follow these steps to create a bad debt item:

1. Click on the gear icon and select **Products and Services**, as shown in *Figure 16.3*:

Figure 16.3: Completing the fields to add bad debt to the products and services list

As you can see in *Figure 16.4*, there are four item types to choose from. **Service** is the item type we will use for bad debt expenses:

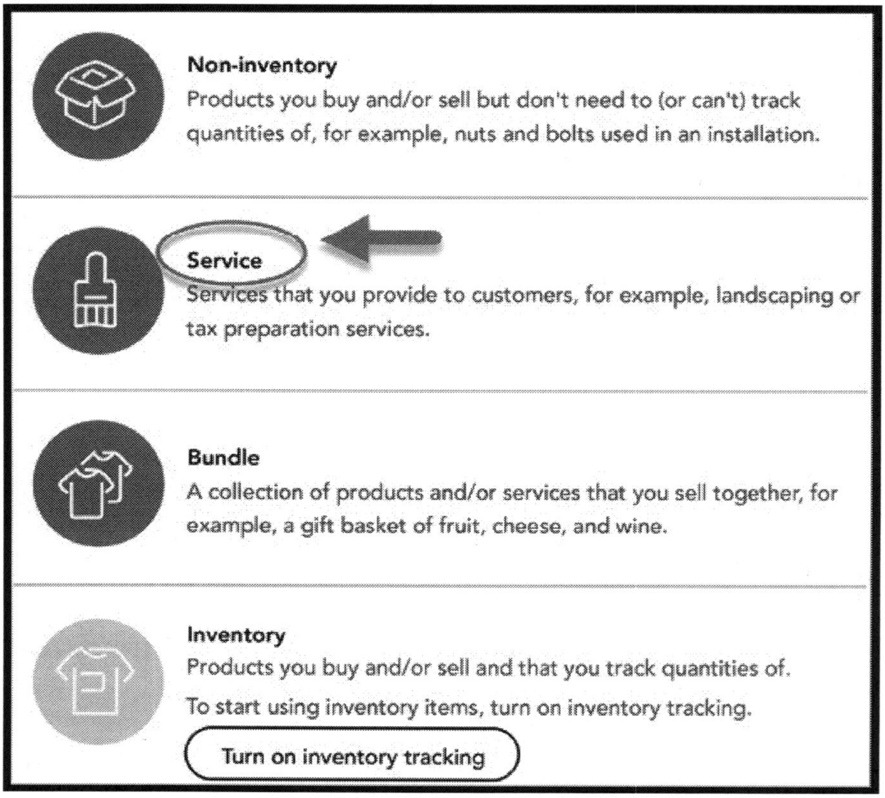

Figure 16.4: Selecting the item type

2. Fill in the following fields to add **Bad Debt Expense** to the items list:

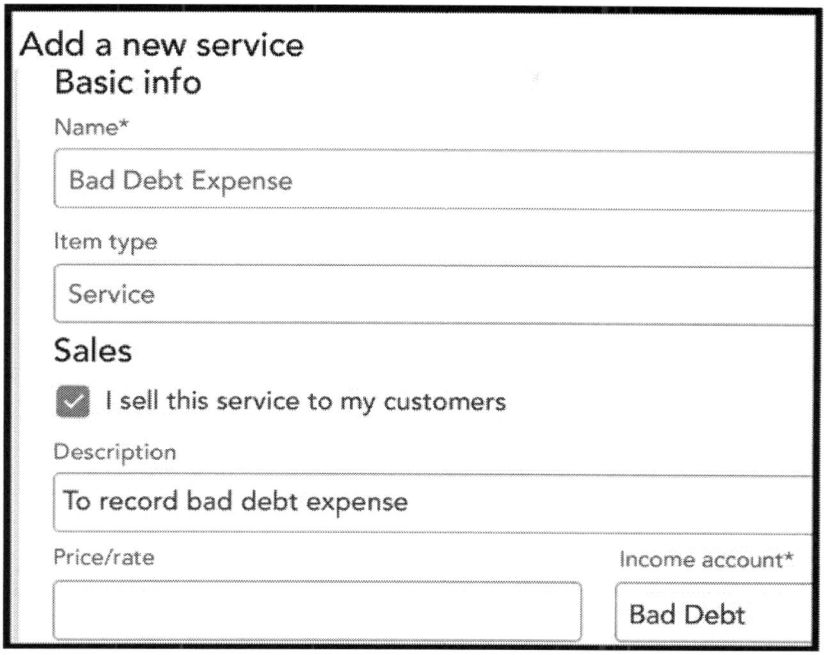

Figure 16.5: Complete the fields for adding a new service item

3. Brief descriptions of the fields to fill in are as follows:

   - **Name**: Enter `Bad Debt` or `Bad Debt Expense` in the item's **Name** field.
   - **Description**: Enter a brief description of the types of transactions that will be recorded using this item.
   - **Price/rate**: You would normally enter the price/rate that you charge your customers for the service item that you are setting up. However, since this amount will vary, we will leave this field blank.
   - **Income account**: From the drop-down menu, select **Bad Debt**. This should be an expense account on the chart of accounts list. If you did not create this account, click on the drop-down arrow, scroll up, and select **Add new** to create the bad debt expense account.

Now that you've set up the new **Bad Debt** expense item, you can use this item to record the bad debt on a credit memo form.

Creating a credit memo

In previous versions of QBO, we had to create a credit memo first, then manually apply the credit memo to the open invoice. In the latest version of QBO, you can open the unpaid invoice first and then create the credit memo, which will copy the info from the original invoice to the credit memo form for you!

Since QBO copies the product/services information over, you will need to change the product/service item to the **Bad Debt** expense item that we set up in the previous step, as shown in *Figure 16.6*:

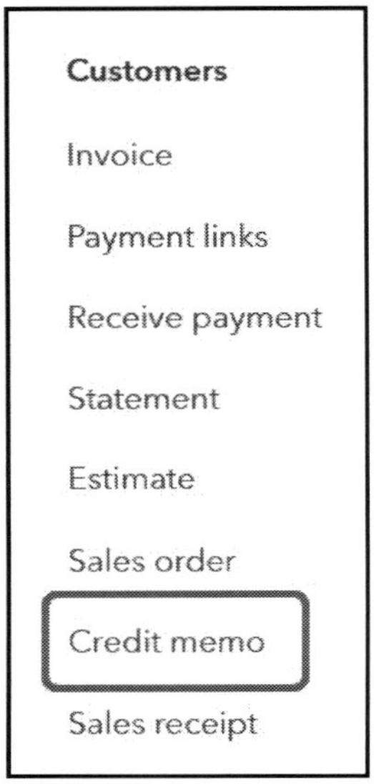

Figure 16.6: Navigating to Credit memo

After saving the credit memo, you can view the status of the unpaid invoice and the credit memo in the customer center, as follows:

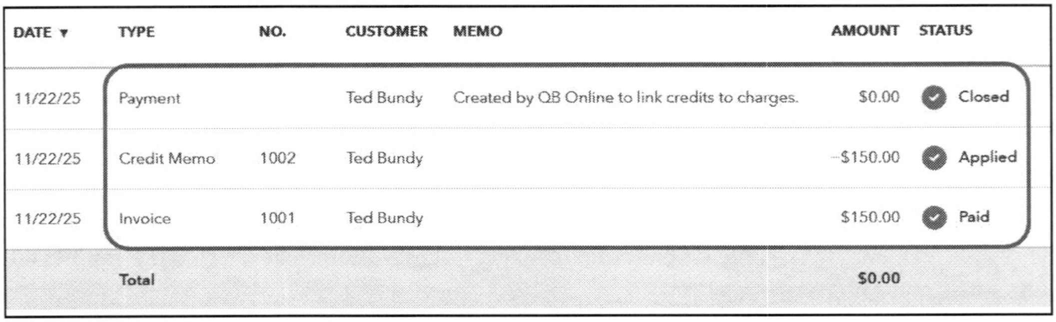

DATE ▼	TYPE	NO.	CUSTOMER	MEMO	AMOUNT	STATUS
11/22/25	Payment		Ted Bundy	Created by QB Online to link credits to charges.	$0.00	Closed
11/22/25	Credit Memo	1002	Ted Bundy		-$150.00	Applied
11/22/25	Invoice	1001	Ted Bundy		$150.00	Paid
	Total				$0.00	

Figure 16.7: Credit memo automatically applied by QBO

As you can see in *Figure 16.7*, the credit memo has been applied to the unpaid invoice. The status of the invoice is now paid, and the status of the credit memo is applied. QBO also created a payment transaction type to reflect that the credit has been linked to the open invoice and the transactions are closed.

5. Recording all accounts payable for the end of the period

Review the A/P Aging Detail report to make sure that it reflects all unpaid bills as of the end of the year. If it does not, you should record any missing bills that you have received from contractors, vendors, and suppliers for services provided and/or goods delivered prior to the end of the year. This will ensure that all expenses show up on the Profit and Loss report.

6. Reviewing new fixed asset purchases and adding them to the chart of accounts

If you purchased any fixed assets during the year, you should add these to QuickBooks. As mentioned in *Chapter 1, Bookkeeping 101*, fixed assets can be equipment purchased for your business, such as computers or printers. Furniture such as desks and chairs is also considered fixed assets.

Fixed assets are subject to **depreciation**, which is a **tax-deductible expense**. Depreciation is the reduction of the value of a fixed asset due to wear and tear. Tax-deductible expenses can reduce your tax bill, so you want to make sure that you take all of the deductions to which you are entitled. If you have not recorded new fixed-asset purchases, then you will not have depreciation expenses recorded, which means you will miss out on what could be a significant tax deduction.

Your tax preparer should have a detailed list of fixed assets that have been reported on previous tax returns. It is a good idea to review this list annually to ensure it includes new purchases and/or disposal of assets. It's also important to conduct a physical check to ensure that all of the assets on the books still exist and have not been disposed of.

One of the newest features available in QBO is the ability to manage fixed assets. If you are using the QBO Advanced plan, QBO will automatically calculate depreciation and record monthly depreciation expenses for you. For immediate access to the fixed-asset management tool, you can upgrade your QBO subscription. Click on the gear icon, select **Subscriptions and billing**, click on the **Upgrade** button, and follow the on-screen instructions.

For those of you who are not on the QBO Advanced plan and don't wish to upgrade, follow the next steps to add your fixed assets to QBO.

Please note that if you have already entered the fixed asset as an expense into QBO, you should not record it as a fixed asset. For businesses located in the US, the IRS recommends that you record purchases as expenses if they are $2,500 or less. Anything that is more than $2,500 should be entered as a fixed asset.

To add fixed assets to QuickBooks, you will need to have the following information on hand since it will be used to calculate depreciation:

- Date of purchase
- Purchase price
- Type of asset
- Make and model (if applicable)
- Year (for vehicle purchases)

Follow these steps to add a fixed asset to QuickBooks:

1. From the left menu bar, click on **Accounting**, as indicated in *Figure 16.8*:

Figure 16.8: Navigating to Chart of accounts

2. Select **Chart of accounts,** and then click the **New** button, as indicated in *Figure 16.9*:

Figure 16.9: Clicking the New button

3. For a new fixed asset, complete the fields, as shown in *Figure 16.10*:

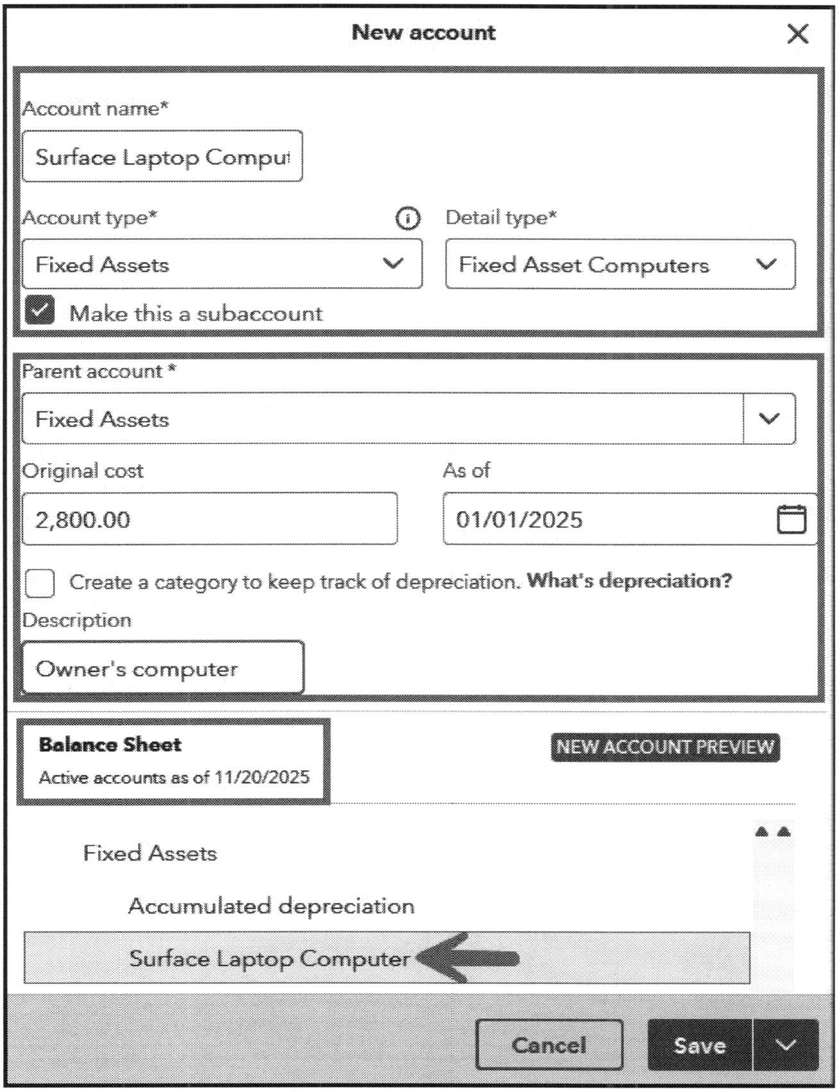

Figure 16.10: Entering details for a fixed asset

The following is a brief explanation of the fields that need to be completed for a new fixed asset:

- **Account name**: Type the name of the fixed asset in this field. In our example, this is `Surface Laptop Computer`.
- **Account type**: Select **Fixed Assets**, as shown in *Figure 16.10*.
- **Original cost**: The original cost is what you actually paid for the item. In our example, the original cost is $2,800.00. This amount will be used to calculate depreciation.
- **As of**: Enter the date the asset was purchased in this field. In our example, the purchase date was **01/01/2025**.
- **Description**: Type a more detailed description of the fixed asset in this field, or you can enter the account name again. In our example, we have entered `Owner's computer`.

> It's important to keep track of who is in possession of all fixed assets. For larger businesses with several employees who are issued laptop computers, you need to have the make, model, and serial number of each computer on file. If you don't use QBO Advanced, which has the fixed-asset manager, I recommend you create an Excel or Google Sheet to log this information.

- **NEW ACCOUNT PREVIEW**: In this section, you will see the financial statement this account will appear in. In our example, the balance sheet is the report that all assets will show up in.

4. Click the **Save** button to add the asset to your chart of accounts list.

Be sure to complete these steps for each fixed asset you have purchased during the accounting period, provided that you have not already entered the items as an expense. Please be sure to consult with your tax professional to ensure fixed-asset purchases are recorded properly on your books. Remember, fixed assets include items that cost more than $2,500 as per the latest IRS standards. After adding fixed assets to QuickBooks, you need to record depreciation expenses for the period.

7. Making depreciation journal entries

After adding fixed assets to QuickBooks, you need to record depreciation expenses for the period. As established earlier, **depreciation** is the reduction in the value of an asset due to wear and tear after it has been in service for a period of time. To reflect the reduced value, you must record the depreciation expense in your books. Depreciation is also a tax-deductible expense, which can help to reduce your overall tax liability.

As mentioned previously, if you subscribe to the QBO Advanced plan, QuickBooks will automatically compute and record depreciation for you. However, if you don't have QBO Advanced, you will need to calculate depreciation manually or have your accountant do this for you.

8. Taking a physical inventory and recording inventory adjustments

Reconciling inventory involves making sure that the products you have on your shelf match what your books reflect as on-hand inventory. You should take a physical inventory count at least once a year, if not more often. After taking a physical count, any discrepancies between the books and the physical count should be recorded in QuickBooks as inventory adjustments. After recording these inventory adjustments, your books and your warehouse will be in sync.

Follow these steps to record inventory adjustments in QuickBooks:

1. Click on the **+ Create** button, and select **Inventory qty adjustment** in the **Other** column, as shown in *Figure 16.11*:

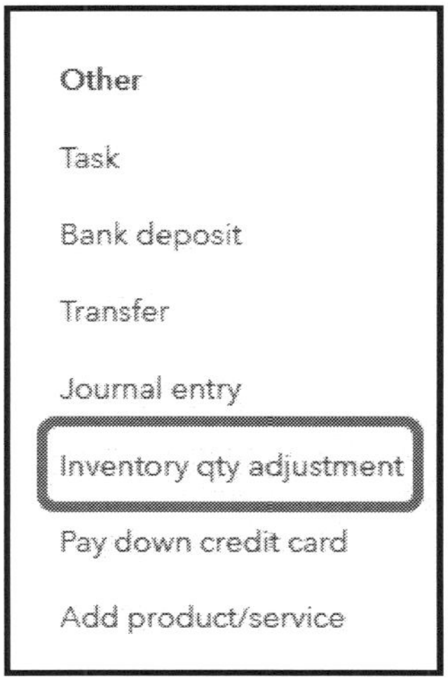

Figure 16.11: Choosing Inventory qty adjustment

2. Complete the fields for the inventory adjustment, as indicated in *Figure 16.12*:

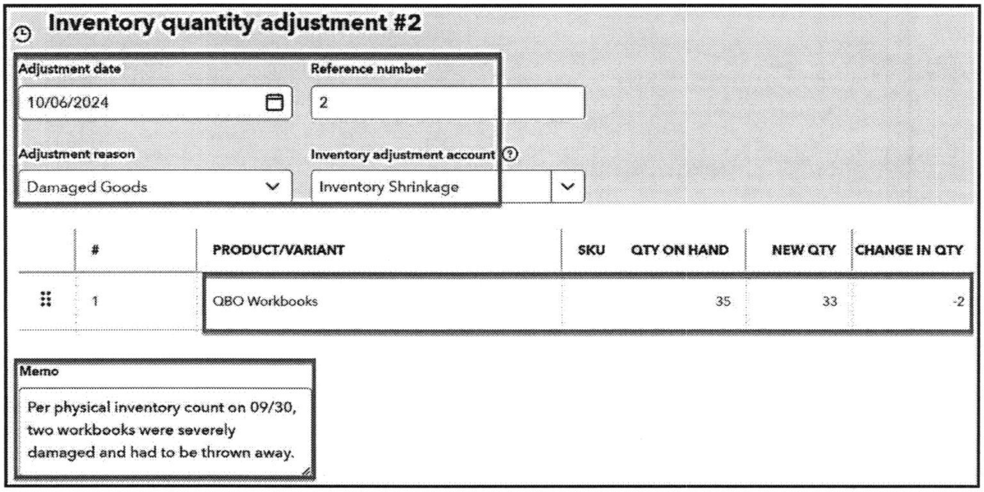

Figure 16.12: Completing the fields to record the inventory adjustment

The following is a brief explanation of the fields that need to be completed in order to record an inventory adjustment:

- **Adjustment date**: Enter the effective date of the adjustment. This date should be on or before the last day of the closing period. In our example, the inventory count was taken on `10/06/2024`.
- **Reference number**: This field will automatically populate with a number. If you prefer to customize the reference number, you can do so by typing directly into this field. In our example, the reference number is `1000`.
- **Adjustment reason**: From the drop-down menu, select the reason for the adjustment. The options available are **Damaged Goods**, **Stock write-off**, **Inventory count**, **Shrinkage**, **Inventory Revaluation**, **Stolen Goods**, **Expired**, **Returned Goods**, and **Marketing/Promotion**.
- **Inventory adjustment account**: **Inventory Shrinkage** is the default account that will appear in this field. However, you can click the drop-down arrow and select a different account, or add a new one.
- **PRODUCT/VARIANT**: From the drop-down menu, select the item for which you are making an adjustment. In our example, **QBO Workbooks** has been selected.
- **SKU**: If your products have an SKU, this information will automatically populate once you select the product.

- **QTY ON HAND**: This field will automatically be populated with what you currently have recorded in QuickBooks. This field cannot be adjusted.
- **NEW QTY**: Enter the quantity, based on the physical count that was taken in this field.
- **CHANGE IN QTY**: QuickBooks automatically computes the adjustment required by taking the difference between the **QTY ON HAND** and **NEW QTY** values entered.
- **Memo**: Enter a brief explanation of why the adjustment was made.

If you have extensive inventory-tracking requirements that go beyond what's available in QBO, visit the Intuit app marketplace, where there are over 700 add-on programs that integrate seamlessly with QBO. In *Chapter 4, Customizing QuickBooks for Your Business*, we covered how to navigate the QuickBooks App Center.

9. Adjusting retained earnings for owner/partner distributions

Retained earnings are the cumulative amount of your income and expenses for the prior period(s). This amount will be posted to the retained earnings account at the end of your fiscal/calendar year. QuickBooks will automatically make this entry for you. Depending on the type of organization (corporation, partnership, LLC, sole proprietorship, or non-profit), you may need to move this balance to other equity accounts.

To distribute profits to the owners, you will need to create a journal entry to an equity account entitled *owner's draw* or *owner distributions* and offset it with retained earnings. Be sure to consult with your CPA or tax preparer if you are not familiar with this process.

To summarize what we have covered so far: many of the steps in the closing process are designed for you to review the transactions that have been recorded throughout the fiscal year, as well as make adjustments as needed for accruals such as wages, depreciation of fixed assets, and retained earnings of owner/partner distributions. The primary way these closing adjustments are recorded is through journal entries.

10. Setting a closing date and password

In an effort to maintain the integrity of your data, you should set a closing date and password after you have entered all transactions for the closing period. By setting a closing date, users will receive a warning message if they attempt to enter transactions that affect the closing period. For example, if you set a closing date of **12/31/25**, users will receive a warning message if they attempt to enter any transactions dated **12/31/25** or earlier.

Follow these steps to set a closing date and password in QBO:

1. Click on the gear icon, and then select **Account and settings** in the **YOUR COMPANY** column, as indicated in *Figure 16.13*:

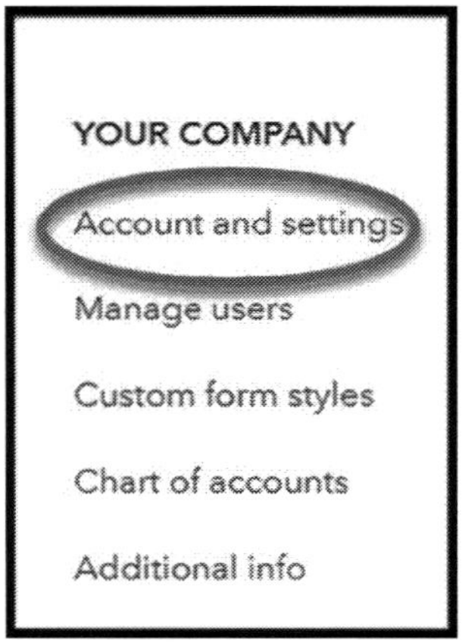

Figure 16.13: Selecting Account and settings in the YOUR COMPANY column

2. Click on the **Advanced** tab, as indicated in *Figure 16.14*:

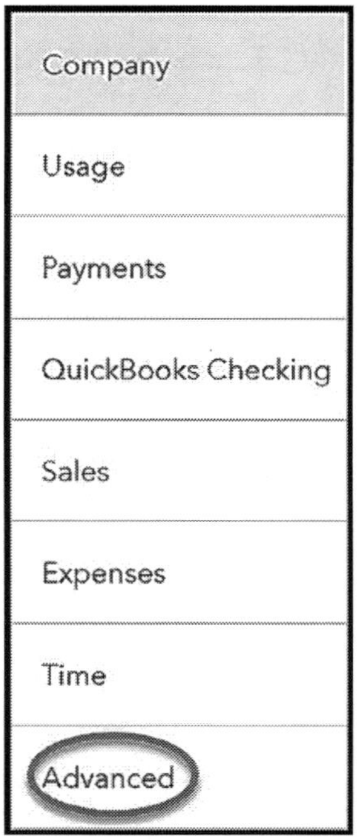

Figure 16.14: Clicking the Advanced option

3. The **Accounting** preferences are located toward the middle of the next screen, as indicated in *Figure 16.15*:

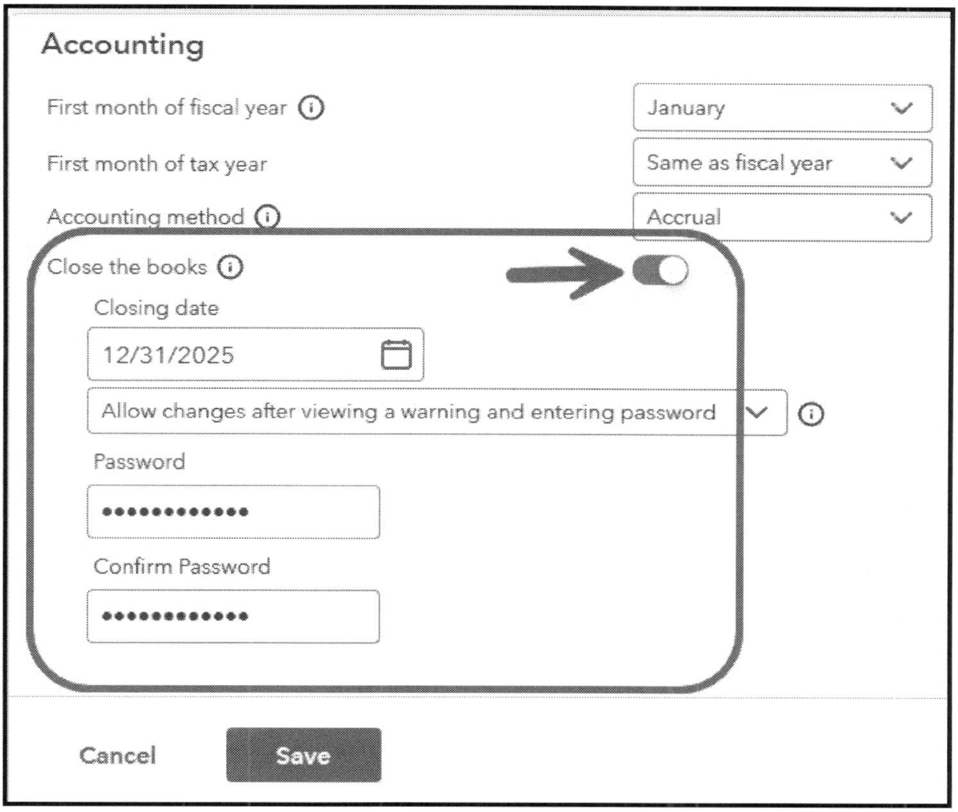

Figure 16.15: Reviewing the Accounting preferences

In the **Close the books** section, you can enter the closing date (that is, **12/31/2025**), which will give users a warning if they attempt to enter transactions dated on the closing date or prior to it. There are two types of warning messages. The first is **Allow changes after viewing a warning**. This message will allow users to proceed with entering the transaction after they close the warning message. The second is **Allow changes after viewing a warning and entering password**, as shown in *Figure 16.15*. This message requires users to enter a password to proceed with entering transactions. To choose this option, select it from the drop-down field, as shown in *Figure 16.15*, and enter the password you would like to use.

Since QuickBooks does not have a formal closing process, choosing the option that requires a password to make changes is highly recommended, keeping users from making changes to prior years where tax returns have already been filed. *Don't give the closing password to anyone who is not authorized to enter transactions after the closing date.* It is recommended that you set the closing date as the last day of the tax year you are filing for. For example, if following a calendar year, it would be December 31.

11. Preparing key financial reports

After you have completed the first 10 steps in the closing checklist, you are ready to prepare financial statements. There are three primary financial statements you will need to prepare:

- The trial balance
- The balance sheet
- The income statement (Profit and Loss report)

In *Chapter 15, Business Overview and Cash Management Tools and Reports,* we covered what the balance sheet and income statement reports are, how to interpret the data, and how to generate these reports in QuickBooks. Your accountant, or CPA, will also request a Trial Balance report. A Trial Balance report lists all the debits and credits recorded in QuickBooks for the period. If everything has been recorded properly, debits will always equal credits on this report.

Follow these steps to run a Trial Balance report in QuickBooks:

1. Navigate to **Reports**, as indicated in *Figure 16.16*:

Figure 16.16: Clicking Reports to navigate to the Reports Center

2. In the **For my accountant** section, click on **Trial Balance**, as indicated in *Figure 16.17*:

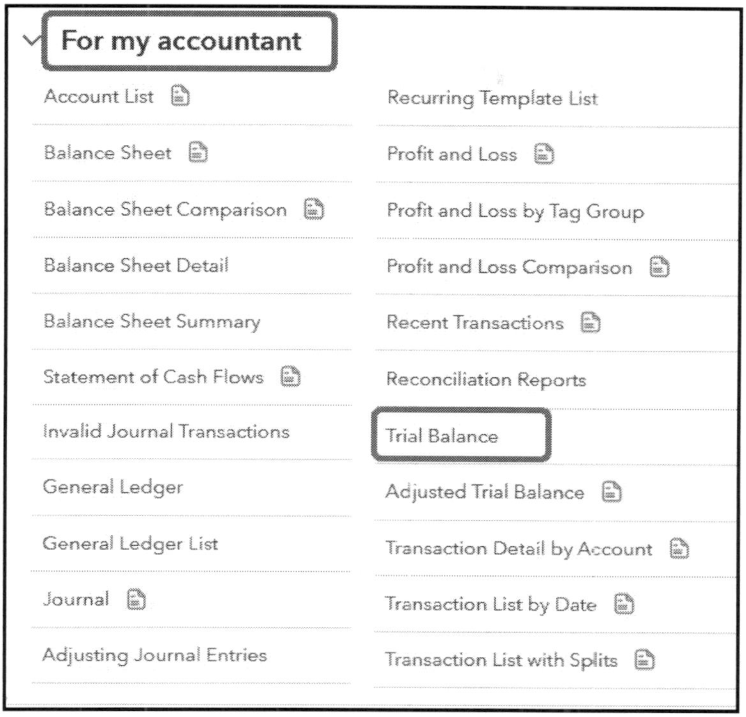

Figure 16.17: Running the Trial Balance report

3. The Trial Balance report will appear. Click the **Customize** button:

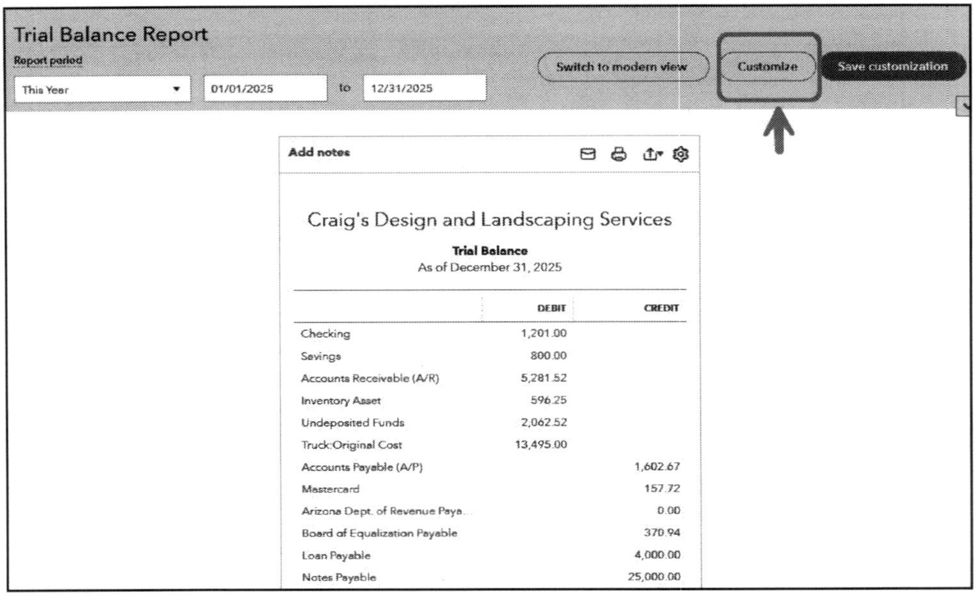

Figure 16.18: Customizing the Trial Balance report

The following report customization options will appear:

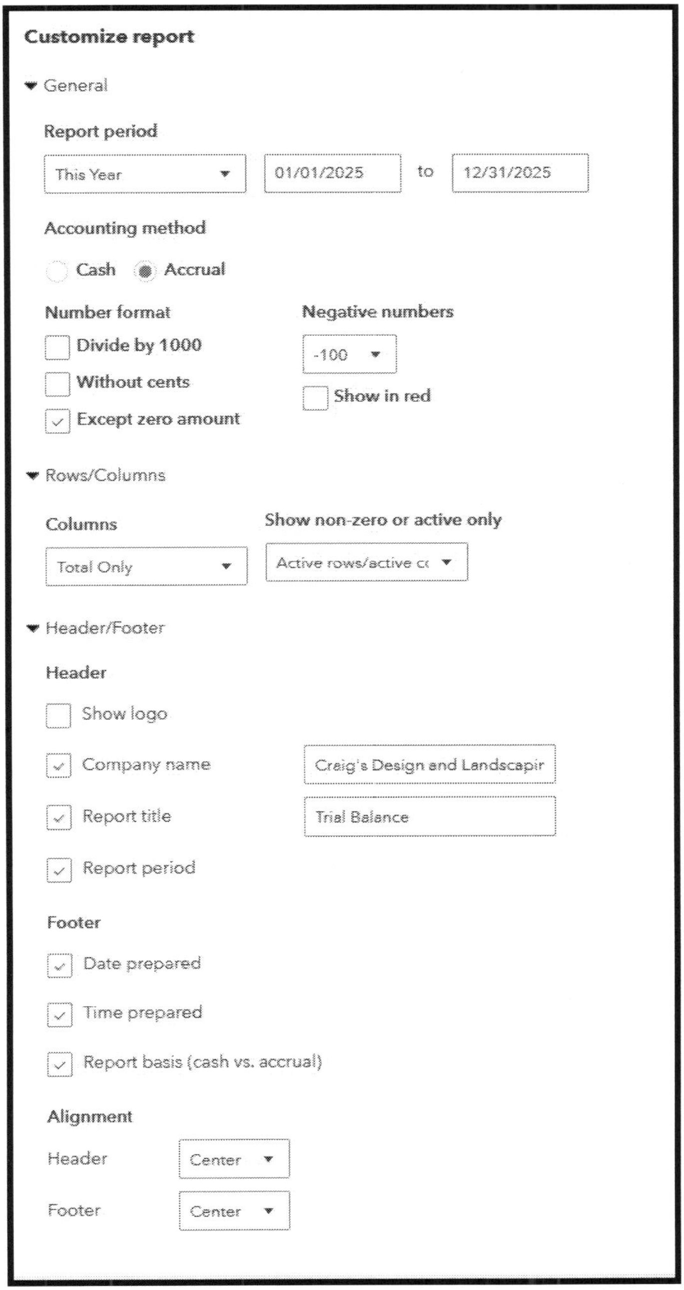

Figure 16.19: Reviewing the report customization options

There are a number of options available to customize the trial balance report. The following is a brief description of some of the information that can be customized:

- **Report period**: You can select a preset report period, such as **Last Year**, from the drop-down menu, or type a date range in the fields to the right of the preset field.
- **Accounting method**: As previously discussed in this book, you can choose the accounting method you want to be applied to the report—**Cash** or **Accrual**.
- **Number format**: There are a variety of options to format the numbers on a report. Omitting the cents and excluding accounts with a zero balance are just a couple of the options, as shown in the preceding screenshot.
- **Rows/Columns**: Choose which rows/columns are visible on the report.
- **Header**: You can edit the company name and the title of the report in the header section.
- **Footer**: You can choose to show the date/time when the report was prepared.
- **Alignment**: You can decide how best to align the information that appears in the header and footer sections of the report.

4. When you are done with your customizations, click the **Run report** button in the bottom-right corner (not shown).

A report similar to the one in *Figure 16.20* will appear:

Craig's Design and Landscaping Services

Trial Balance

As of December 31, 2025

	DEBIT	CREDIT
Checking	1,201.00	
Savings	800.00	
Accounts Receivable (A/R)	5,281.52	
Inventory Asset	596.25	
Undeposited Funds	2,062.52	
Truck:Original Cost	13,495.00	
Accounts Payable (A/P)		1,602.67
Mastercard		157.72
Arizona Dept. of Revenue Payable		0.00
Board of Equalization Payable		370.94
Loan Payable		4,000.00
Notes Payable		25,000.00
Opening Balance Equity	9,337.50	
Design income		2,250.00
Discounts given	89.50	
Landscaping Services		1,477.50
Landscaping Services:Job Materials:Fountains and Garden Lighting		2,246.50
Landscaping Services:Job Materials:Plants and Soil		2,351.87
Landscaping Services:Job Materials:Sprinklers and Drip Systems		138.00
Landscaping Services:Labor:Installation		250.00
Landscaping Services:Labor:Maintenance and Repair		50.00
Pest Control Services		110.00
Sales of Product Income		912.75
Services		503.55
Cost of Goods Sold	405.00	
Advertising	74.86	
Automobile	113.96	
Automobile:Fuel	349.41	
Equipment Rental	112.00	
Insurance	241.23	
Job Expenses	155.07	
Job Expenses:Job Materials:Decks and Patios	234.04	
Job Expenses:Job Materials:Plants and Soil	353.12	
Job Expenses:Job Materials:Sprinklers and Drip Systems	215.66	
Legal & Professional Fees	75.00	
Legal & Professional Fees:Accounting	640.00	
Legal & Professional Fees:Bookkeeper	55.00	
Legal & Professional Fees:Lawyer	400.00	
Maintenance and Repair	185.00	
Maintenance and Repair:Equipment Repairs	755.00	
Meals and Entertainment	28.49	
Office Expenses	18.08	
Rent or Lease	900.00	
Utilities:Gas and Electric	200.53	
Utilities:Telephone	130.86	

Craig's Design and Landscaping Services

Trial Balance

As of December 31, 2025

	DEBIT	CREDIT
Miscellaneous	2,916.00	
TOTAL	**$41,421.60**	**$41,421.60**

Figure 16.20: Example trial balance report

As discussed, the total debits value ($41,421.60 in the preceding example) should always equal the total credits ($41,421.60), as it does in the preceding report. If it does not, you will need to look into any discrepancies. The good news is, 99.99% of the time, this report will balance (debits equal credits) because QuickBooks does not allow you to post one-sided journals, which means that for every debit, there is always an offsetting credit to keep things in balance.

> If you do have a trial balance that does not balance (debits don't equal credits), you should calculate the difference between the debits and credits and then look for that amount on the report. Most likely, there is an amount in one of the columns (debit or credit) that does not appear in the other column.

To summarize, you will need to review three key financial reports before closing your books: the balance sheet, the income statement, and the Trial Balance report. If you have a CPA or an accountant who reviews your financials and prepares your tax return, you can give that person access to your books so that they can run these reports without having to bother you. We will discuss giving your accountant access to your data next.

Always review the information on your reports one last time before sharing them with any third party outside of your organization. You can add these reports to a report group and send them out instead of running them individually. Refer to *Chapter 14, Report Center Overview*, for details.

12. Giving your accountant access to your data

If you have an accountant or tax preparer to whom you need to grant access to your data, you can invite them to access your QBO file. All you need to do is request their email address so that you can send them an email invitation to access your data.

Follow these steps to invite an accountant to access your QuickBooks data:

1. Click on the gear icon and select **Manage users** in the **YOUR COMPANY** column, as shown in *Figure 16.21*:

Figure 16.21: Selecting Manage users from the YOUR COMPANY column

2. On the **Manage users** page, click on **Accounting Firms**, as indicated in *Figure 16.22*:

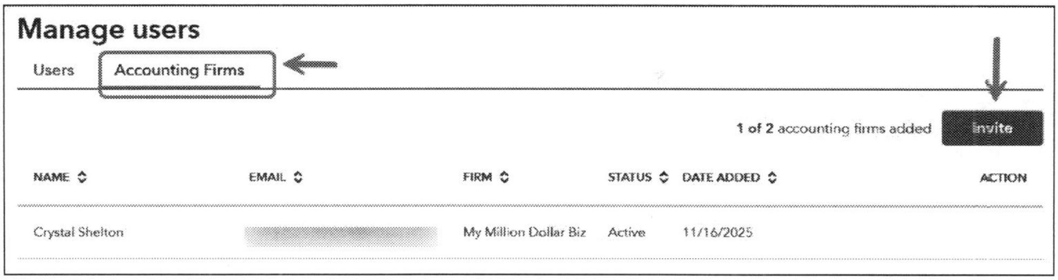

Figure 16.22: Clicking on Accounting Firms and Invite

3. Enter your accountant or tax professional's first name, last name, and email address, as shown in *Figure 16.23*, and click on **Invite** to invite your accountant to access your QuickBooks data:

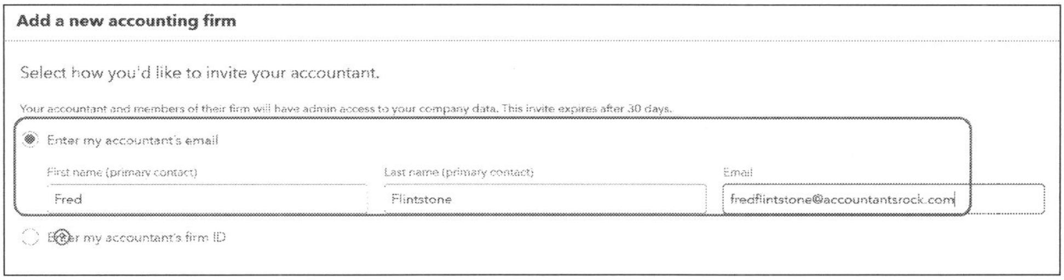

Figure 16.23: Entering the accountant's details

4. If your accountant/tax professional has QBO, you can add them using their firm ID, as shown here:

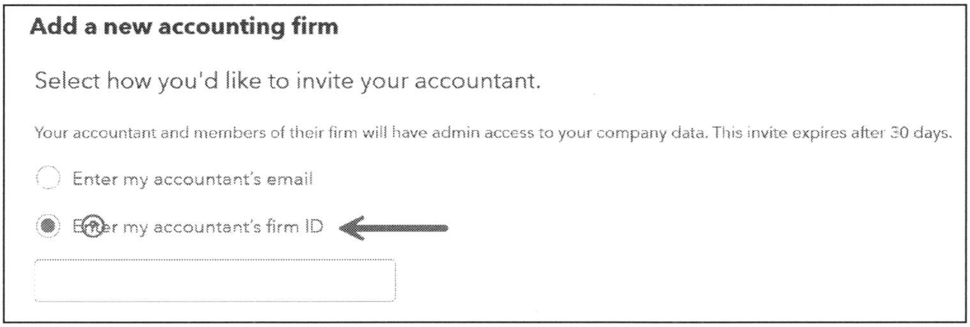

Figure 16.24: Entering the accountant's firm ID

Your accountant will receive an email, inviting them to access your QBO account. They will need to accept the invitation and create a secure password, or enter their existing password if they have a QBO account. Their user ID will be the email address that you entered in the form (shown in *Figure 16.23*).

To obtain your company ID, press *Ctrl + Alt + ? or Command + Alt + ?* and a window similar to this one will display:

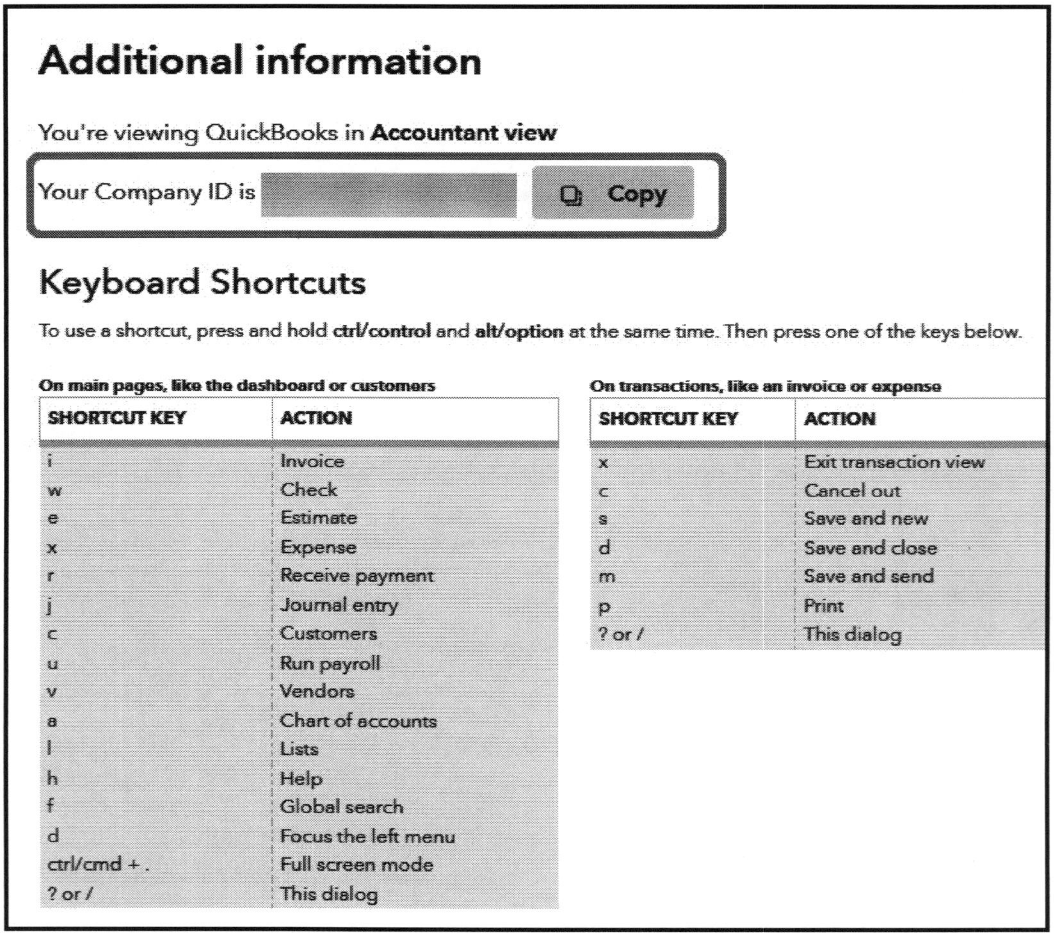

Figure 16.25: Displaying the company ID

Once you have given your accountant access to your books, they can simply log in to QuickBooks to get the information they need to prepare your taxes. This is highly recommended if your accountant needs to make any year-end adjustments. You can add/remove permissions access as needed if you prefer them only to have access at tax time. To resend an invite or delete access, go back to the **Accounting firms** tab and click the **Resend invite** button or click the drop-down arrow and select **Delete** to remove the access.

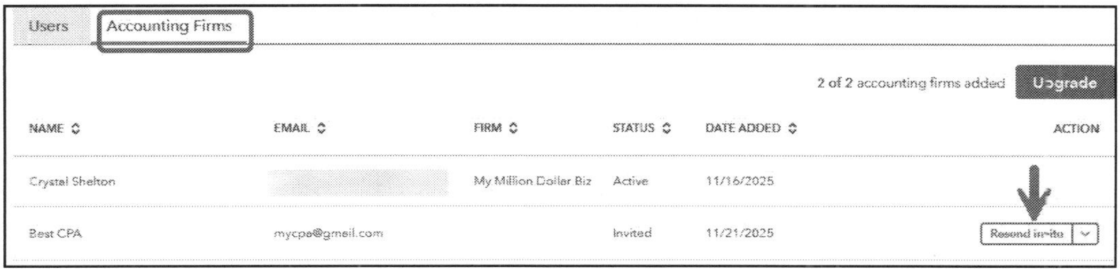

Figure 16.26: Option to resend an invite from the accountant user page

Inviting your tax preparer or accountant to access your books is the last step on our closing-the-books checklist. Giving a user accountant access is equivalent to giving someone admin access. The accountant can do 95% of what the admin can do, except for upgrading or canceling your QBO account. With that said, be thoughtful about whether someone needs this level of access. In most cases, you can give them access to view reports only, and they can consult with you if there are any changes that they would recommend.

Summary

In this chapter, you have learned about the key tasks that need to be completed to close your books for the accounting period. As discussed, you need to reconcile all bank and credit card accounts; record year-end accrual adjustments (if your accounting is accrual-based), open customer invoices, bad debt expenses (if applicable), and any unpaid bills; add fixed-asset purchases; record depreciation expenses; take a physical inventory and make the necessary adjustments; adjust retained earnings for distributions made to the business owners; set a closing date and password; and prepare key financial statements. You can perform these tasks yourself, or you can give your accountant access to your QuickBooks data to take care of this for you.

If you have an online store that uses a platform such as Etsy or Shopify, you can connect those sales channels to QBO. In the next chapter, we will discuss the pros and cons of connecting a sales channel to QBO and show you how to do so.

Next steps

1. Be sure to head over to my YouTube channel for step-by-step product demos in QBO. Use this link to access the channel:

   `https://packt.link/25laf`.

2. You can download a closing checklist here: `https://github.com/PacktPublishing/Mastering-QuickBooks-2026-Seventh-Edition`.
3. If you have a bookkeeper or accountant who manages your books, schedule time to meet with that person each month. However, make sure that you have already reviewed your financial reports and made a list of your questions *prior to this meeting*. In other words, schedule a "money date" before you meet with your bookkeeper or accountant, if applicable.

Part 5

Integrating E-Commerce Platforms and Advanced Inventory

If your business involves an online store or complex inventory needs, this part is for you. We'll start by integrating your online store within QBO, covering everything from connecting sales channels to evaluating the pros and cons of integrations. Then, we'll dive into advanced inventory management – showing you how to track products, manage purchase orders, and generate reports to keep your business running smoothly.

This part comprises the following chapters:

- *Chapter 17, Integrating E-Commerce Platforms with QuickBooks Online*
- *Chapter 18, Managing Products and Services*

17

Integrating E-Commerce Platforms with QuickBooks Online

If you sell products on a sales channel such as Etsy, Shopify, Amazon, or another online store, your business falls into the e-commerce industry. Like other small businesses, it's important that you stay on top of your bookkeeping. It doesn't take long before an e-commerce business owner realizes that putting their products on an e-commerce platform isn't enough. Why? Because most of these platforms only capture one aspect of your business – sales. They will typically keep track of customer orders, shipping, order fulfillment, and credit card processing. They do not keep track of indirect expenses such as utilities, rent, monthly telephone bills, monthly internet bills, payroll, and so on. In order to have a complete set of financial statements, all aspects of your business need to reside in one system – **QuickBooks Online** (**QBO**).

In *Chapter 4*, *Customizing QuickBooks for Your Business*, we introduced you to the QuickBooks Integrations Center. There are more than 45 sales channels that allow you to manage your e-commerce business. Some of the sales channels that seamlessly integrate with QBO are WooCommerce, Shopify, Etsy, Amazon, eBay, and Square, to name a few.

> Throughout this chapter, the terms e-commerce, sales channel, integration, and online store are used interchangeably.

In this chapter, we will cover the following topics:

- Reviewing integrations to decide whether connecting them to QBO is right for you
- Pros of connecting a sales channel to QuickBooks
- Cons of connecting a sales channel to QuickBooks
- How to connect your sales channel to QuickBooks

To see the full list of e-commerce integrations that are available with QBO, navigate to the **Integrations** menu located in the top-right corner of the dashboard, as shown here:

Figure 17.1: Navigating to the Integrations Center

1. The following screen will display:

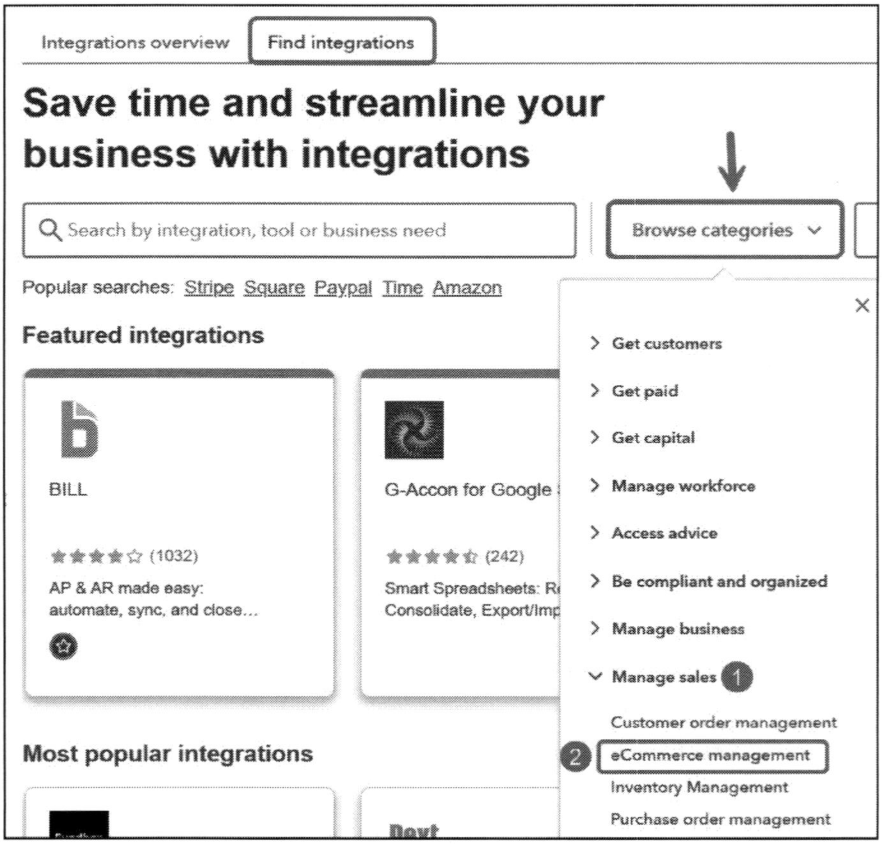

Figure 17.2: Finding e-commerce management integrations

2. As shown in *Figure 17.2*, click on **Browse categories>Manage sales>eCommerce management** to see more than 45 e-commerce apps that integrate with QBO:

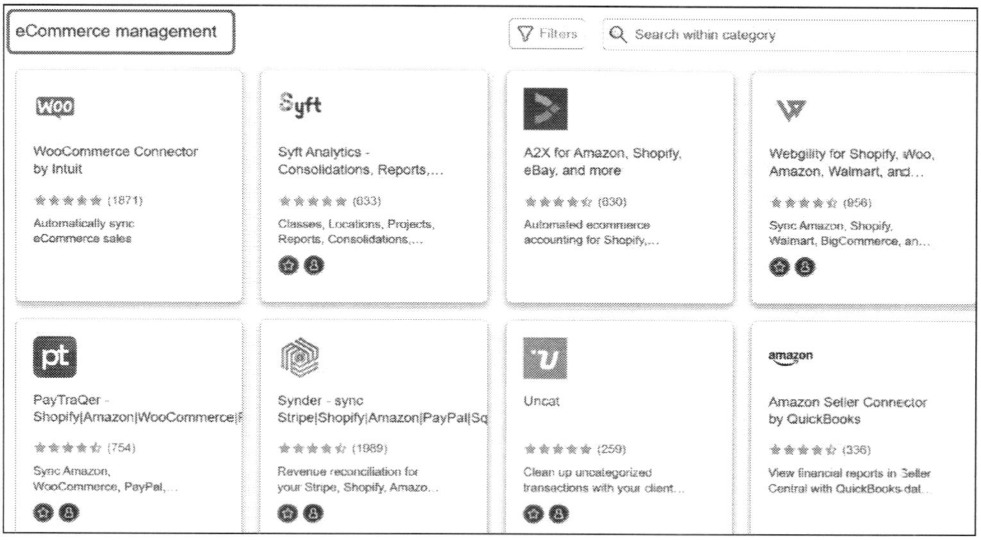

Figure 17.3: Displaying e-commerce integrations available

Do not proceed to connect an integration without fully understanding how it works. You must *find out* how the integration app works and set up a few things before connecting it to QBO. Otherwise, you will run the risk of importing duplicate transactions that will cause your financial statements to be incorrect. Once you connect an integration, there is no undo button.

> The US edition of QBO was used to create this book. If you are using a version that is outside of the United States, results may differ.

Reviewing integrations before connecting them to QBO

Intuit has done most of the legwork so that you don't have to start your research from scratch. For example, when you select an integration, you will find an overview of what the integration does, how much it costs, customer reviews, similar integrations to the one you have chosen, and FAQs, as shown here:

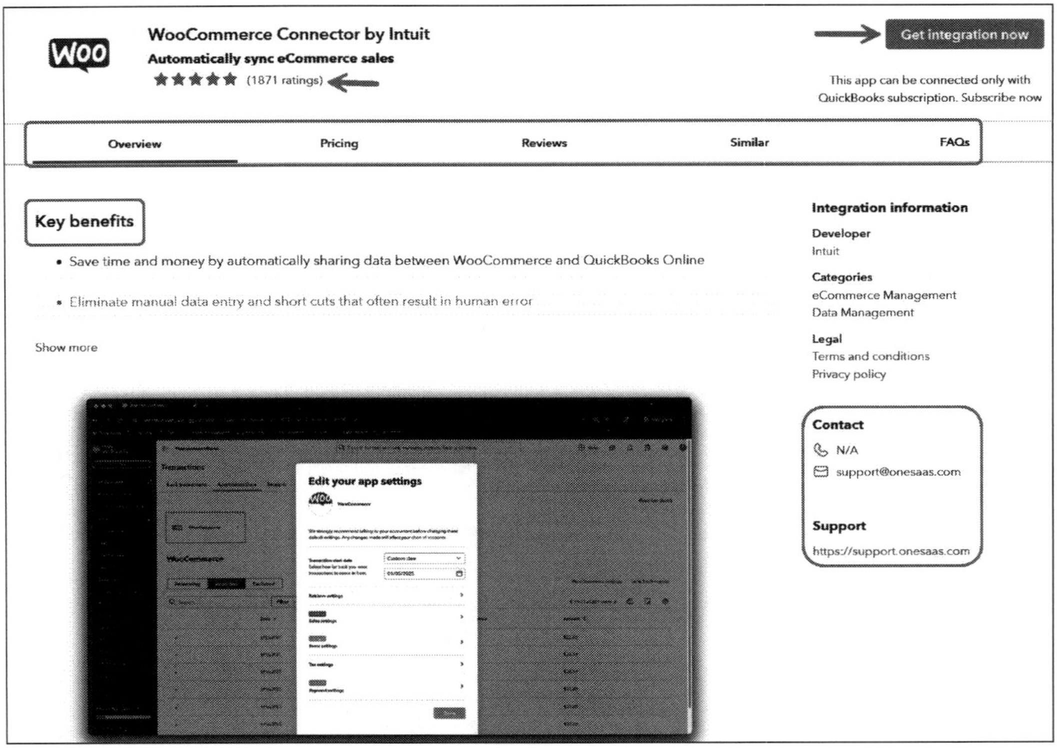

Figure 17.4: Integration overview in QBO

Additional information you will find here are the key benefits of using the app, how it works with QBO, and the contact information for the company. Unfortunately, this information isn't going to be enough for you to make a decision. If the integration sounds like it will work for you, contact the company to schedule a demo. Most of these companies will either point you to their website where they have a pre-recorded video you can watch, or they will contact you to schedule a live demo. I suggest you do both, if the option is available.

If you watch a pre-recorded demo, it will spark questions that are related to how things would work with your particular business; write these questions down. These questions can be answered during the live demonstration.

In case you are not comfortable with making this decision on your own, be sure to have your accountant or bookkeeper attend the demo with you. They will know precisely what questions to ask.

There are both pros and cons to connecting a sales channel to QBO. We will cover the pros first.

Pros of connecting a sales channel to QuickBooks

There are several pros to integrating your e-commerce platform with QBO. Following is a list of pros that I've found invaluable when integrating e-commerce integrations:

- **Access to complete financial statements**: When you integrate your e-commerce platform with QBO, all aspects of your business finances – the money coming in (sales) and the money going out (expenses) – are in one centralized location. This allows you to generate reports such as your profit and loss, balance sheet report, and statement of cash flows that include everything. Without this integration, you will need to generate reports from QBO and from your e-commerce system and then manually enter the numbers into an Excel spreadsheet to combine them.
- **Eliminates manual data entry**: E-commerce integration allows you to eliminate the need to manually record sales in QBO using an invoice or sales form. Instead, this data will automatically import from the e-commerce integration into QBO on a daily or hourly basis – and in some cases, a few minutes!
- **Accurate and reliable data**: One of the benefits of eliminating manual data entry is to minimize errors that occur when data has to be entered manually. Importing the data takes the human element out of the equation, which improves the accuracy of the data, making it very reliable.
- **No expensive equipment or IT department required**: Like all the integrations you will find in the Intuit Integration Center, e-commerce apps do not require you to purchase any expensive servers or IT personnel. The monthly cost of the integration includes unlimited tech support. While the days/times when the support team is available might vary depending on the company, you can be assured that if you run into an issue, there will be a team that is available to assist you.
- **Access to new features/upgrades**: Similar to QBO, there are always improvements made to these integrations, as well as new features that you will gain access to as a subscriber.
- **Cloud-based**: All e-commerce integrations are cloud-based. You can either access your information by logging into QBO or you can go directly to the integration's website in most cases. For both, you just need a mobile device with an internet connection.

Cons of connecting a sales channel to QuickBooks

While there are many pros to integrating e-commerce platforms with QBO, there are a few cons that you need to be aware of:

- **Additional costs**: The cost of the e-commerce integrations is *not* included in your QBO subscription. You will have to pay a monthly fee that will typically be based on the number of users who need access to the integration. As mentioned previously, pricing can be found in the Intuit Integration Center.
- QuickBooks Certified ProAdvisors (like myself) may be able to get you a discount on the pricing of certain integrations. If you need assistance with managing your books or researching apps, I recommend you check out the **Find A ProAdvisor** directory to locate a qualified QuickBooks Pro: `https://quickbooks.intuit.com/find-an-accountant/`.
- **Initial investment of time and/or money**: In my experience, many small business owners do not have the time or expertise to go about selecting the right integration. This means you will need to hire an accounting professional who can do the research and manage the integration for you. Be sure to build this into your costs when considering integrating e-commerce integrations. If the integration setup is not correct and the information in your app is not monitored, it will not flow into QBO correctly.
- **Security risk**: One of the requirements of connecting QBO with any integration is that you will have to agree to share information with the integrations. This is part of having the ability for the data in both QBO and the e-commerce integration to sync. There will always be a risk in doing this, but you can rest assured that Intuit has taken the steps to properly vet each product that has been granted access to the Intuit Integration Center. There are strict requirements that the integrations must meet in order to be included. To learn more about this process and how Intuit protects your data, check out Intuit's privacy statement at `https://www.intuit.com/privacy/statement/`.
- **Email/chat support only**: To minimize costs, many of the customer service/support teams are only available via email or chat. It is rare that you will have access to a support person via telephone. Make sure that you read the reviews for the integrations you are considering and find out what customers say about the quality of the support.
- **Access to support**: One other note regarding tech support for integrations: Many of the support teams work overseas and may not offer 24/7/365 support. When reviewing integrations to determine which will work best for you, find out the hours of operation for tech support. If they offer a subscription that includes 24/7/365 support, you may want to consider it.

How to connect a sales channel to QuickBooks

While I highly recommend you consult an accountant or QuickBooks Certified ProAdvisor to assist you with connecting your sales channels to QBO, you can do it yourself. Please note that the instructions in this section only apply to businesses that meet the following criteria:

- You sell only in the US and get paid in USD
- You don't need to bring in customers, products, or inventory from your sales channels

If you *don't* meet one or both criteria, consult with a QuickBooks Certified ProAdvisor who can assist you with other options. If you *do* meet *both* criteria, then follow these instructions to connect your sales channel to QBO:

1. Sign in to QBO as the **company admin**. The only user who has the authority to connect sales channels is someone with **company admin** access. In *Chapter 4, Customizing QuickBooks for Your Business*, we covered how to give other users access to QBO.
2. On the left navigation bar, select **All Apps>Sales & Get Paid>Sales Channels**, then select **Connect sales channel**, as shown here:

Figure 17.5: Navigate to Connect sales channel

3. On the next screen, select the sales channel you want to connect and click on the **Next** button:

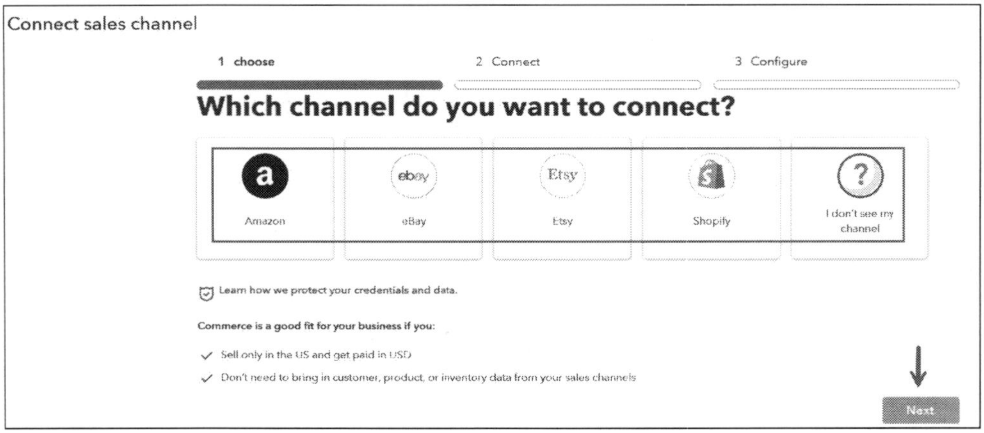

Figure 17.6: Select a sales channel to connect

If you don't see your sales channel listed, select the **I don't see my sales channel** option for a complete list of sales channels that integrate with QBO.

For demonstration purposes, we are going to walk through how to connect to Shopify. Please keep in mind that the screenshots you see may differ if you are connecting to a different sales channel.

4. Select **Shopify** and you will see the following screen, where you'll be offered the option of bringing in past orders and payouts:

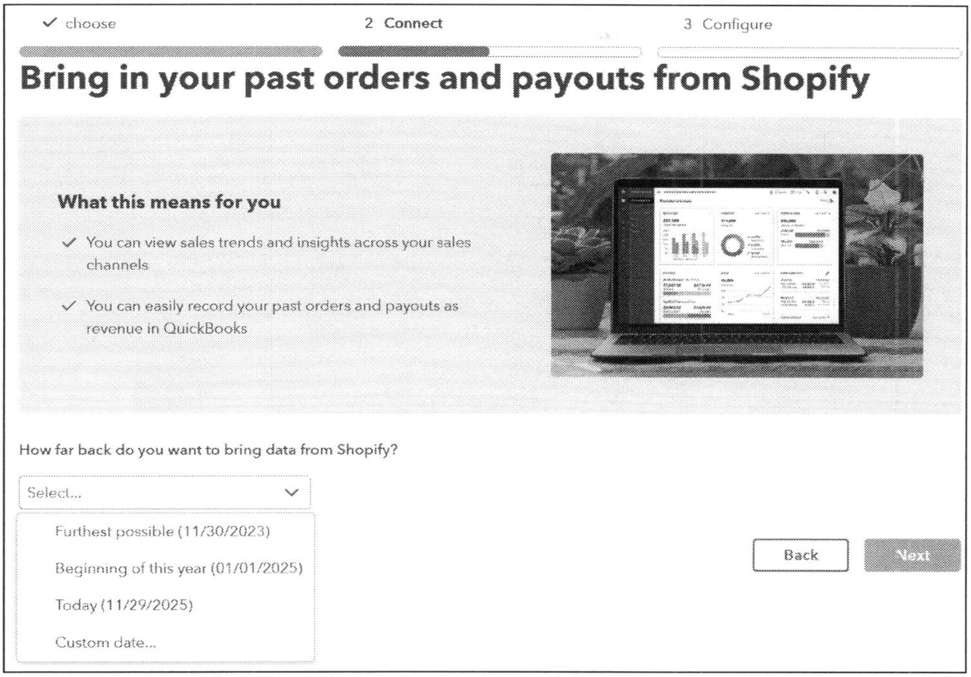

Figure 17.7: Choosing how far back to bring in data from Shopify

Shopify allows you to bring historical data into QBO so that you can record past orders and payouts as revenue, as well as viewing sales trends and insights. As shown in *Figure 17.7*, you can choose one of the following options:

- Two years prior to today
- Beginning of the year
- Today's date
- Choose a custom date range, not to exceed two years prior

When making this decision, be sure that you do not bring in data for any year that you have already filed taxes for. In addition, do not bring in data for a time period that you have already recorded the revenue for. For example, let's say it is November and you have already recorded revenue in QBO for the first 10 months of the year. The start date should be November 1.

Caution

Be sure you select the correct date range. Once you click the **Next** button, you will not be able to change this. If you are not sure what date range to use, please consult with your CPA or ProAdvisor for assistance.

1. Click the **Next** button, and the following screen displays:

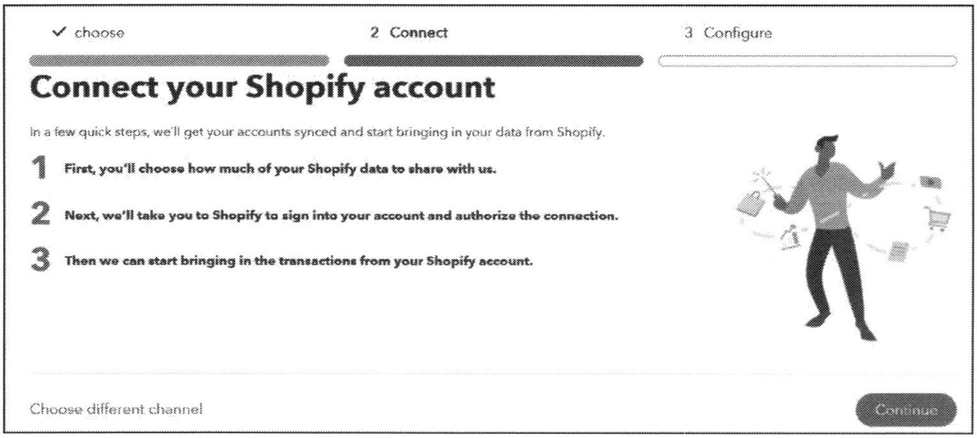

Figure 17.8: Next steps to connect your Shopify account

In *Figure 17.8*, you will find a summary of the next few steps that will take place:

- Choose how much of your Shopify data to share with QBO
- Sign in to your Shopify account and authorize the connection
- Transactions from Shopify will start to import into QuickBooks automatically

2. Click **Continue** and the **Need consent to connect** screen displays:

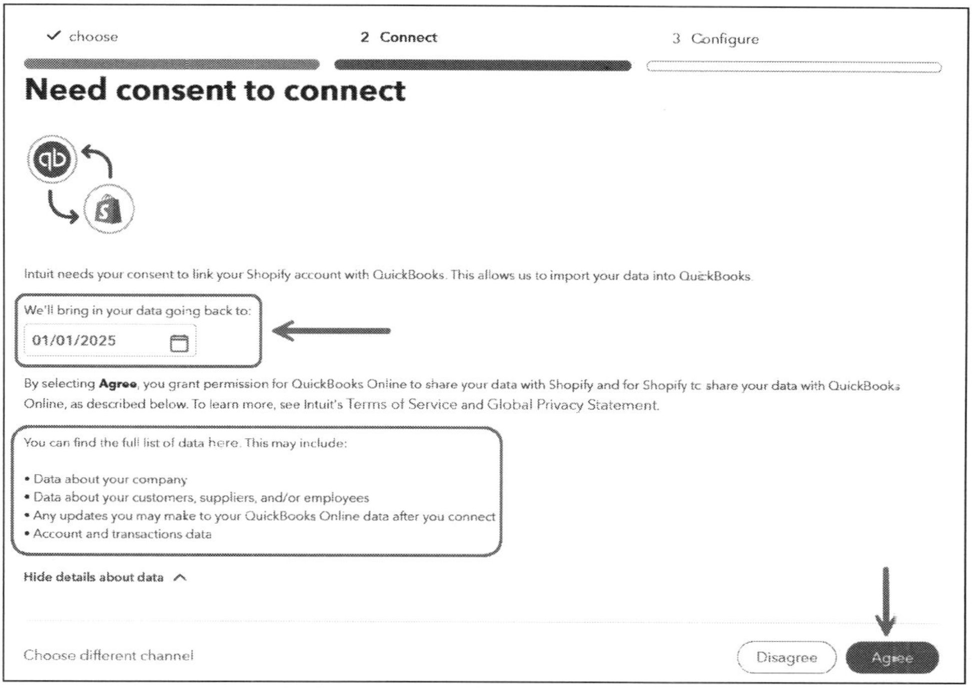

Figure 17.9: Consent to connect QuickBooks to a Sales channel account

On this screen, you will need to perform the following actions:

- Confirm the start date that you want to bring sales data from Shopify into QBO for

> *Note that this will be your last opportunity to verify this date before the data imports; you cannot undo this action once it is complete.*

- Click the **Agree** button to move on to the next step.

- Enter your Shopify store address to get started, as shown here:

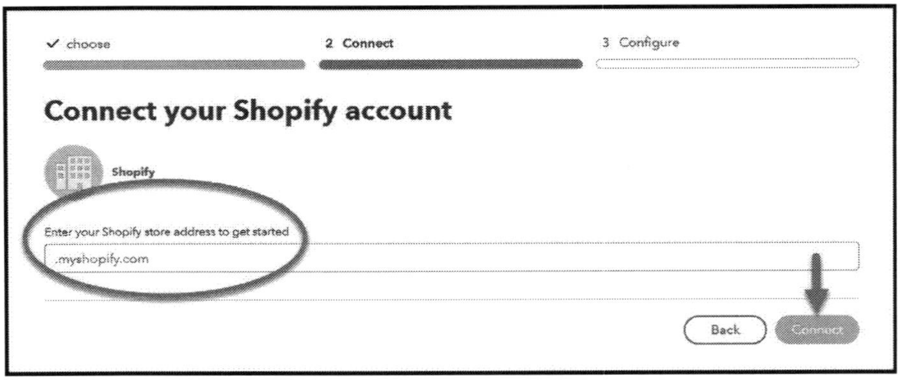

Figure 17.10: Final step to connect your Shopify account

3. Select the **Connect** button and follow the onscreen instructions to sign in to your Shopify account and complete the integration.

> After you successfully connect your sales channel to QBO, you will need to ensure that payouts are mapped to the correct bank accounts. Your deposits must be mapped to the correct bank account so that they can be recorded in QBO in the same manner that they are deposited into your bank account. Skipping this step could result in duplicate entries from your bank, which will prevent you from being able to reconcile your accounts with the bank statements. Be sure to consult your accountant or bookkeeper on the best way to do this.

Now that you have a better understanding of the importance of connecting your online store to QuickBooks Online, many of you may also need to know how to manage the complexities that often come with inventory. We will cover this topic in the next chapter.

Summary

In this chapter, we explained the importance of not only managing your sales for your online store but also having everything in one central location so that you can generate reports that include sales, expenses, assets, and liabilities for your business. We showed you how to navigate to the QBO Integrations Center, where you can find information on all the sales channels that help manage e-commerce businesses, such as pricing, demos, and customer reviews. Having this information at your fingertips will help you determine whether connecting the integration to QBO is right for you. We covered several pros of connecting your sales channels to QBO, as well as a few cons. Finally, we covered in detail the steps you would take to connect a sales channel, such as Shopify, to QBO.

In the next chapter, we will cover how to properly manage the complexities that often come with purchasing and selling products.

Next steps

1. Be sure to head over to my YouTube channel for step-by-step product demos in QBO. Use this link to access the channel:

   `https://packt.link/du2BR`

2. If you have a bookkeeper or accountant that manages your books, schedule time to meet with that person each month. However, make sure that you have already reviewed your financial reports and made a list of your questions *prior to this meeting*. In other words, schedule your "money date" before you meet with your bookkeeper or accountant, if applicable.

18

Managing Products and Services

In the previous chapter, we discussed how Etsy, Square, Shopify, and other platforms allow you to easily manage sales and inventory for your online store, but don't take into account all of the expenses that you incur, such as rent, payroll, and utilities. If you sell products in a brick-and-mortar store or out of your garage, you can easily keep track of these expenses as well as product orders, on-hand stock, and product sales to customers in QBO. While QBO is not ideal for the complex needs of a manufacturing and wholesale business, it has the capability to manage simple, straightforward inventory.

In *Chapter 1, Bookkeeping 101*, we discussed three inventory methods: **last-in, first-out** (**LIFO**), **first-in, first-out** (**FIFO**), and **average cost**. In the past, QBO only used the FIFO method to track inventory. However, in the most recent updates, you can now choose **moving average cost** (**MAC**) to keep track of inventory cost and quantities. If you are not familiar with inventory methods, consult with an accountant to understand which method is right for your business. In this chapter, we will walk you through each step of the inventory management process, starting with turning on the **inventory** feature, all the way to generating key reports that help you manage inventory. As discussed in *Chapter 2, Getting Started with QuickBooks Online*, the two plans that include inventory tracking are Plus and Advanced.

In this chapter, we will cover the following topics:

- Turning on inventory tracking in QuickBooks
- Adding products to QuickBooks
- Recording product sales in QuickBooks

- Ordering products from vendors/suppliers
- Receiving products into the inventory
- Generating inventory reports

> The US edition of QBO was used to create this book. If you are using a version that is outside of the United States, results may differ.

Turning on inventory tracking in QuickBooks

If you have QBO Plus or Advanced, one of the questions you will encounter as you go through the initial setup is whether you need to track inventory. If you select **Yes**, the inventory feature will automatically turn on for you. However, if you select **No**, you will need to go into the account settings to turn inventory tracking on before you can add your products to QBO.

Follow these steps to turn on inventory tracking:

1. Click on the gear icon and select **Account and settings**, as shown here:

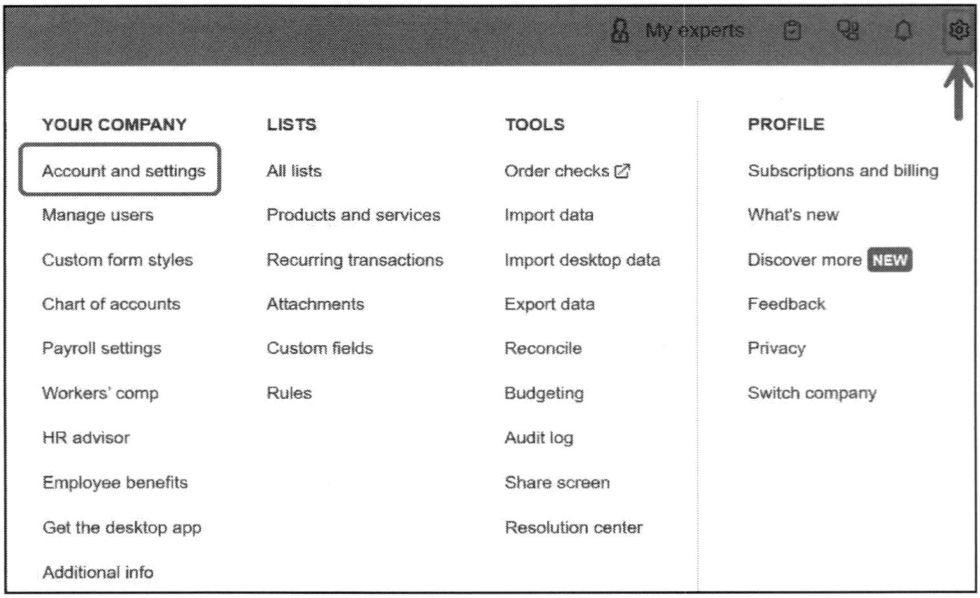

Figure 18.1: Navigating to Account and settings

The following screen displays:

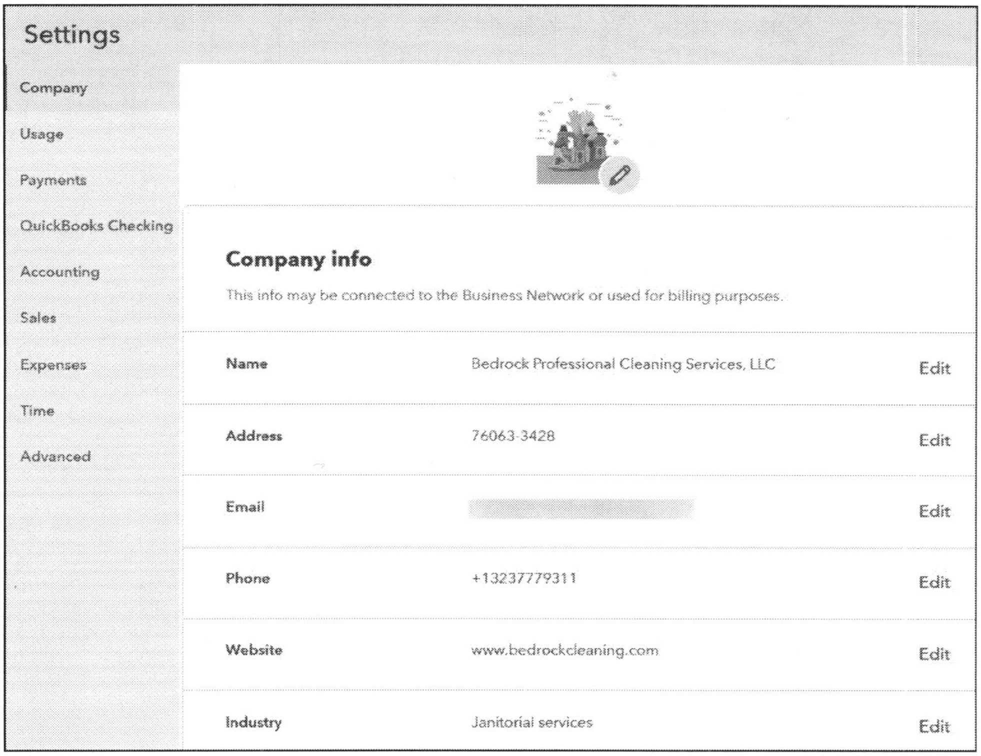

Figure 18.2: Displaying Account and settings

2. Select **Sales** on the left menu bar. The **Products and services** section is where the inventory tracking options are:

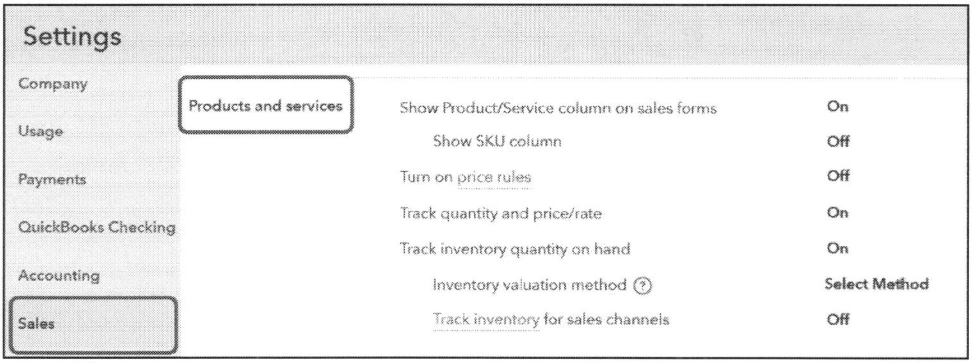

Figure 18.3: Reviewing inventory tracking options

Here is a brief description of the inventory tracking options available:

- **Show Product/Service column on sales forms**: This option is typically automatically turned on. It ensures that there is a column on your sales forms that shows what products the customer has purchased.
- **Show SKU column**: If you use an SKU to identify your products, turning this feature on ensures that there is a column on your sales forms that displays the SKU. An SKU is a unique number used to identify a retail product for inventory purposes. This option is normally turned off, so you will need to click on the radio button to turn it on.
- **Turn on price rules**: Price rules allow you to set up special pricing for specific customers for a specified timeframe. For example, you can create a price rule that allows for a 50% discount on all Christmas decorations that begins on December 26th. By default, this feature is off, so you will need to turn it on to start using it.
- **Track quantity and price/rate**: This option is typically automatically turned on. It ensures that there is a column on your sales forms that shows the quantity and price of products.
- **Track inventory quantity on hand**: This option allows you to track inventory quantities and cost. As mentioned previously, it will automatically turn on if you indicated that you need to track inventory during the setup process. If you did not, you will need to turn it on here.
- **Track inventory for sales channels**: If you have an online store, turning this feature on will automatically bring in your inventory from the sales channel you are using (e.g., Etsy, Shopify, etc.).
- **Inventory valuation method**: There are now two inventory methods to choose from: FIFO or MAC. As mentioned previously, you can learn more about each of these methods in *Chapter 1, Bookkeeping 101*.
- **Revenue recognition**: This feature allows you to record a payment for a product or service you'll deliver in the future and recognize the revenue over time. This feature is only available in QBO Advanced subscriptions. It is recommended that you consult with an accounting professional before turning on this feature to ensure that you need it and that you understand how it works.

3. Turn on the following features for basic inventory tracking:
    - **Show Product/Service column on sales**
    - **Track quantity and price/rate**
    - **Track inventory quantity on hand**
    - **Choose your inventory valuation method**
4. Save your changes and click **Done** in the bottom-right corner of the screen to close the **Account and settings** window.

Adding products in QuickBooks Online

After you have turned on inventory tracking, you are ready to add the products that you sell in QuickBooks. You can choose to add products manually or import them from an Excel (`.xls`) or CSV (`.csv`) file. If you've got more than five products, I recommend using the *import* option. In this chapter, I will cover how to add products manually. To learn how to import from a spreadsheet, refer to *Chapter 5, Managing Customer and Vendor Lists*, for step-by-step instructions.

Follow these steps to add products to QuickBooks Online:

1. Click on the gear icon and select **Products and services** in the **LISTS** column, as shown here:

Figure 18.4: Navigating to Products and services

The **Products & services** center displays:

Figure 18.5: Displaying the Products & services center

2. Click on the **New** button, as shown in the preceding screenshot, and the item types display:

Figure 18.6: Selecting the Inventory item type

3. Select **Inventory item** and complete the fields as shown here:

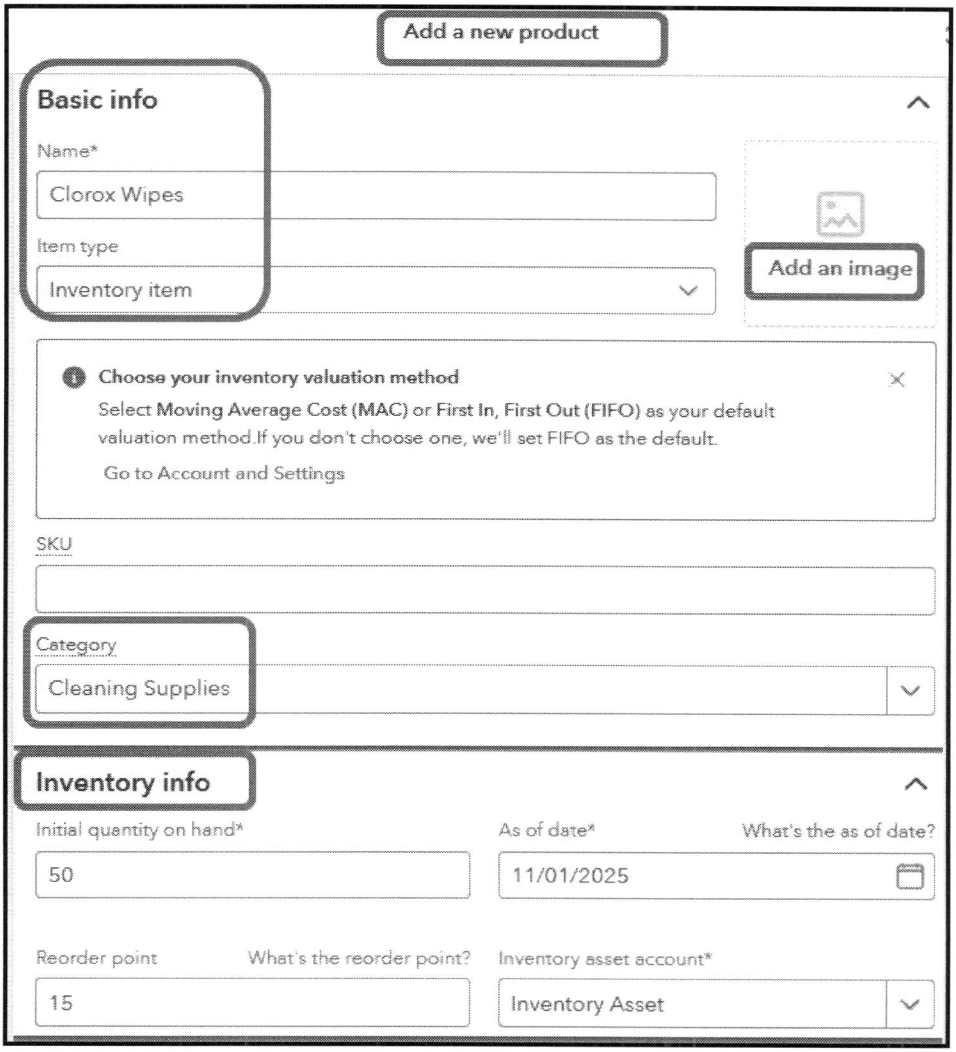

Figure 18.7: Completing the basic and inventory fields to add a new product to QBO

Here is a brief description of the fields to complete in the **Basic info** and **Inventory info** sections to add a new product:

- **Name**: Type the name of the product in this field (`Clorox Wipes`).
- **Item type**: This field will automatically populate with the selection made in step 2 (**Inventory item**).

- **Choose your inventory valuation method**: If you have not selected an inventory valuation method, you will see a notification similar to the one in *Figure 18.7*. As stated, if you do not choose an inventory valuation method, QBO will default to **FIFO**.

> **Important!**
>
> Once the inventory valuation method has been set, it cannot be changed.

- **KU**: Type the SKU in this field, if applicable.
- **Category**: Categories allow you to group products that are similar. For example, Small Business Builders has created a category for workbooks and one for the services that they sell. To create a new category, just click in the field and select **Add New** (**Cleaning Supplies**).
- **Initial quantity on hand**: You will need to know what your current inventory is for each product that you add to QBO. This is a required field, so you will not be able to leave it blank (`50`).
- **As of date**: This is the date that you start tracking inventory in QBO; ideally, this will be the date that you set up the product in QBO (`11/01/2025`).
- **Reorder point**: A reorder point is the threshold when you should reorder more of a stock item. QuickBooks uses reorder points to let you know what's running low and what's out of stock (`15`).
- **Inventory asset account**: This field will automatically populate with **Inventory Asset**.

> Do not change the inventory asset account without consulting your accountant!

The following screenshot displays the **Sales** and **Purchasing** fields required when adding a new product:

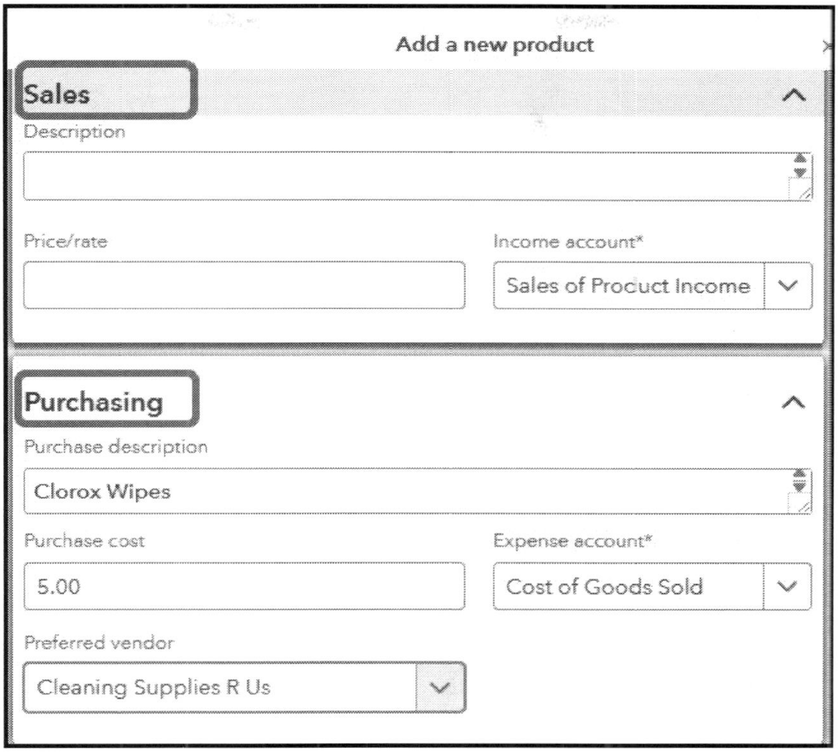

Figure 18.8: Completing the Sales and Purchasing fields to add a new product to QBO

The following **Sales** fields will appear on sales forms such as invoices, sales receipts, and estimates. Since the product that we are setting up is not sold to customers, these fields are blank in *Figure 18.8*:

- **Description**: Enter a brief description of the product for sale.
- **Price/rate**: Enter the sales price per unit in this field.
- **Income account**: When setting up a product, this field will typically default to **Sales of Product Income**. However, if you would like to select a different account or set up a new account, you can do so. Simply click the drop-down menu and select the preferred account, or choose **Add new** to create a new income account.
- **Sales tax category**: In most cases, products for resale are taxable. If you are not sure whether you should charge sales tax, please consult a tax professional or contact the state/local tax authority to find out (`Taxable-standard rate`).

The following purchasing fields will appear on forms such as purchase orders, bills, expenses, and checks. Since this product is ordered from a supplier, these fields are completed in *Figure 18.8*:

- **Purchase description:** Enter a brief description of the product that you are purchasing from the vendors/suppliers. This description may vary from the sales description in *Figure 18.8* because you will need to use the description that your supplier has created to place your order (`Clorox Wipes`).
- **Purchase cost:** Enter what you pay your vendor/supplier for the product. Note that when calculating the cost of goods sold, QuickBooks will use what you actually paid to your vendor/supplier (`5.00`).
- **Expense account:** This field will automatically populate with the account. (**Cost of Goods Sold**).

> Similar to the inventory asset account, please do not change the expense account without consulting with an accountant. It could *significantly* affect your financial statements.

- **Preferred vendor:** This field is optional. You can designate the vendor/supplier from whom you typically order this product. If you cannot locate the vendor when you click the drop-down menu, choose **Add new** to add the vendor to QBO (**Cleaning Supplies R Us**).

Recording product sales in QuickBooks Online

After adding your products to QBO, you are ready to record sales to your customers. Recording sales for products is very similar to recording services. In *Chapter 7, Recording Sales Transactions in QuickBooks Online*, we covered how to record sales for services, and we touched on how this would work for product sales. In this section, we will cover how to record an invoice for product sales as well as the impact that would have on the financial statements.

Important!

Since Bedrock Professional Cleaning Services does not sell products, we will use a fictitious company called Small Business Builders for the remaining topics we will cover in this chapter.

Follow these steps to record product sales on an invoice:

1. Navigate to the **+Create** button **(1)** and select **Invoice (2)**, as indicated here:

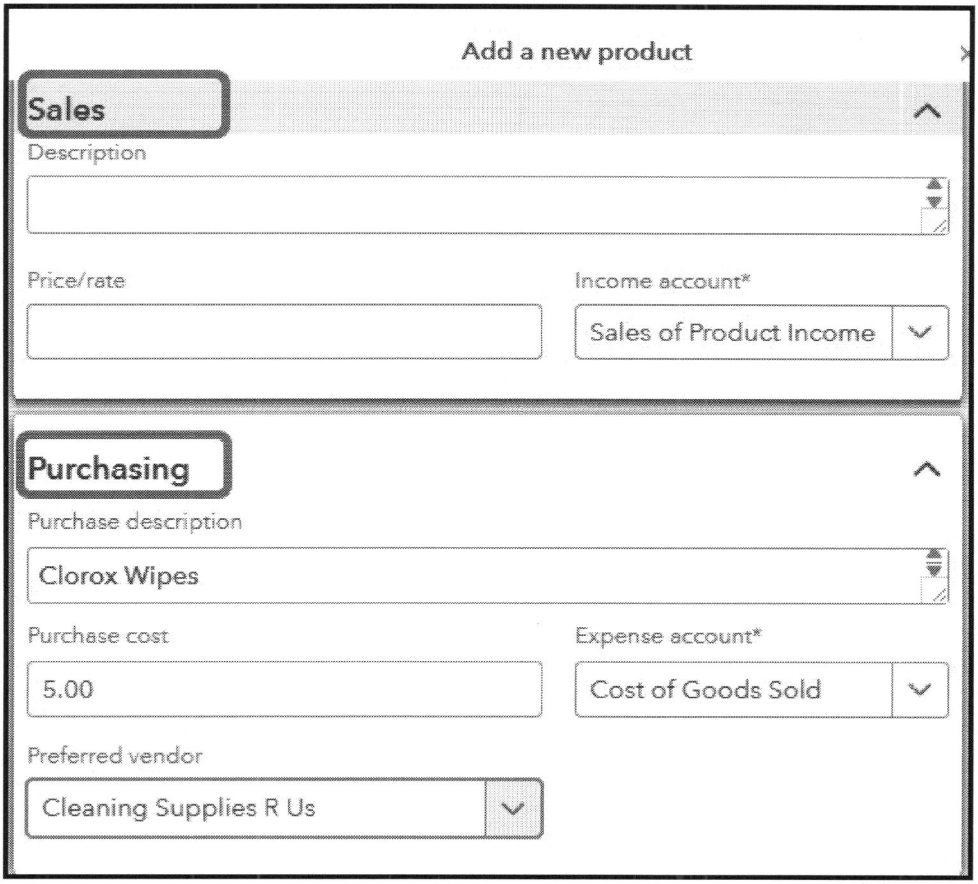

Figure 18.9: Navigating to the Invoice form

2. A blank invoice form will be displayed. Complete the form as shown:

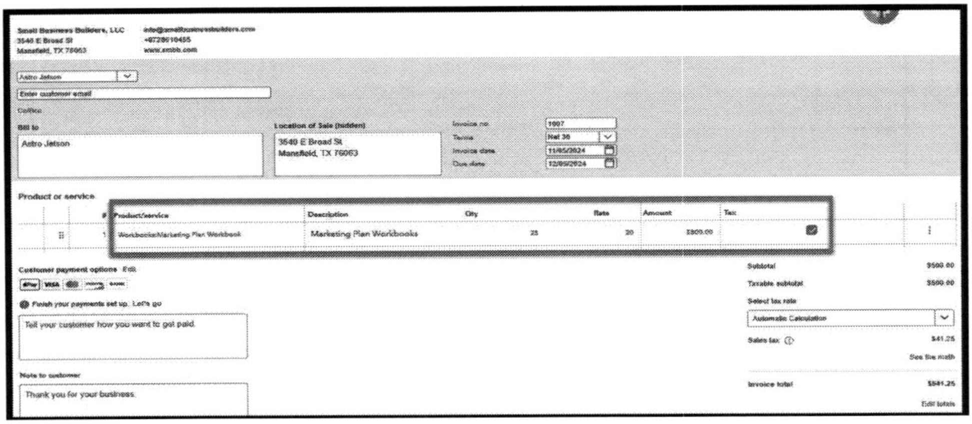

Figure 18.10: Completing an invoice form for a product sale

As you can observe, 25 marketing plan workbooks were sold to Astro Jetson. Since we added this product to QBO prior to creating the invoice, we simply selected **Marketing Plan Workbooks** from the drop-down menu in the **Product/service** column, and all of the other fields were automatically populated as follows:

- **Description: Marketing Plan Workbooks**
- **Qty: 25**
- **Rate: 20**
- **Amount: $500.00**
- **Tax:** Green checkmark indicates that the item is taxable
- **Sales tax: $41.25**
- **Invoice total: $541.25**

When this invoice is saved, the following journal entry is recorded behind the scenes:

Transaction Journal
Small Business Builders, LLC
All Dates

Refresh report
Last updated a few seconds ago

Transaction id	Date	Transaction type	Num	Name	Memo/Description	Account full name	Debit	Credit
27 (6)								
27	11/05/2024	Invoice	1007	Astro Jetson	-	Accounts Receivable (A/R)	$541.25	-
27	11/05/2024	Invoice	1007	Astro Jetson	Marketing Plan Workbooks	Sales of Product Income	-	$500.00
27	11/05/2024	Invoice	1007	Astro Jetson	Marketing Plan Workbooks	Inventory Asset	-	$125.00
27	11/05/2024	Invoice	1007	Astro Jetson	Marketing Plan Workbooks	Cost of goods sold	$125.00	-
27	11/05/2024	Invoice	1007	Astro Jetson	-	Texas State Comptroller Payable	-	$31.25
27	11/05/2024	Invoice	1007	Astro Jetson	-	Texas State Comptroller Payable	-	$10.00
Total for 27							$666.25	$666.25
							$666.25	**$666.25**

Figure 18.11: Transaction journal entry recorded on invoice for product sales

The *Balance Sheet* report was impacted by the increase of $541.25 to the **Accounts Receivable (A/R)** account, the decrease of $125.00 to the **Inventory Asset** account, and the increase of the two **Texas State Comptroller Payable** accounts for $31.25 and $10.00, respectively, for sales tax.

On the *Profit & Loss* report, the **Sales of Product Income** account increased by $500.00, and the **Cost of goods sold** account increased by $125.00.

To see the transaction journal in QBO, display the invoice (after saving it), click on **More actions** located at the very bottom of the screen, and select **Transaction journal**.

Ordering products from vendor suppliers in QuickBooks

When you are running low on products and need to place an order with a vendor/supplier, you should complete a purchase order form in QBO. The purchase order includes the contact details of the vendor/supplier, a description of the product, the quantity, and the total amount. After completing this form, you can email it directly to your vendor/supplier to place your order.

Follow these steps to create a purchase order:

1. Click on the **+Create** button and select **Purchase order** listed in the **Vendors** column, as shown here:

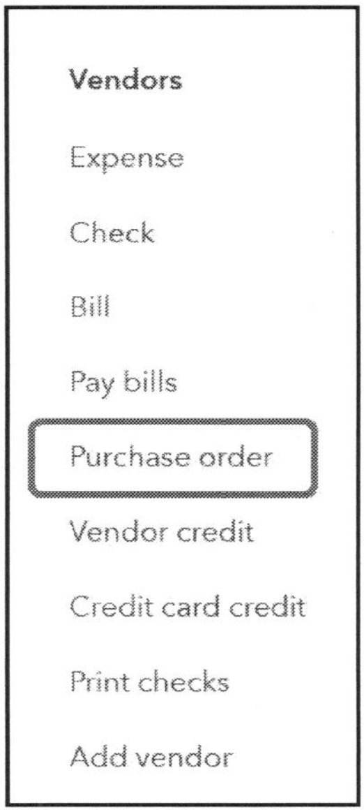

Figure 18.12: Navigating to Purchase order

2. A blank purchase order form displays. Complete the fields as follows:

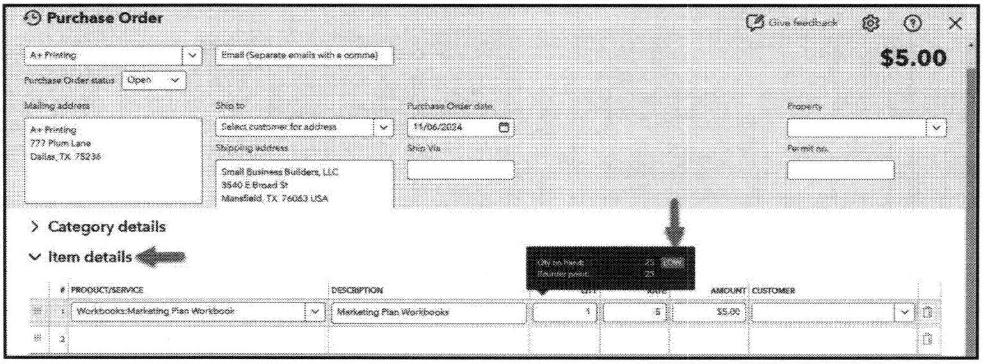

Figure 18.13: Complete purchase order form

- **Vendor name**: Select the vendor supplier from the drop-down menu.
- **Mailing address**: This field will automatically populate with the address you have on file.
- **Purchase Order date**: This field will default to today's date, but you can edit it if needed.
- **Shipping address**: This field will automatically populate with the address you have on file.
- **Ship Via**: Type the shipping method in this field (UPS, FedEx, USPS, etc.).
- **Category details**: This section is to be completed if you need to place an order for items that are not going into inventory (i.e., office supplies). This section is collapsed in *Figure 18.13*, but you can click the arrow to the left of **Category details** to display the fields to complete. Since we are ordering products that will be put into inventory, we will complete the **Item details** section.
- **Item details**: In this section, you will select the product/service from the drop-down menu, and the **DESCRIPTION** field and the **RATE** field will automatically populate with the information you have on file for the product. You just need to type the quantity you would like to order, and QBO will calculate the amount for you.

Hover your mouse over the **QTY** field, and you will see a pop-up that shows the current quantity on hand and the reorder point, as shown in *Figure 18.13*. Since the quantity on hand is the same as the reorder point, there is a **LOW** alert because once your inventory levels are less than or equal to the reorder point, it's time to place an order.

After you complete the *Purchase Order* form, you can save it and print it out or email it directly from QBO to your vendor supplier. The purchase order does not have any financial impact on your books. It is simply a record of products ordered. Once you receive your products into inventory, that will create a financial record. We will cover receiving products into inventory next.

Receiving products into the inventory

When your order arrives from your vendor supplier, you need to verify that everything you ordered has been received. If there are any discrepancies, you should notify your vendor supplier via email immediately. To record the inventory received into QBO, you will complete a bill form. The vendor supplier might put your bill in the box with the products, or they might send it to you via email or snail mail. Whether you have received the actual bill or not, you still want to record the inventory received.

Follow these steps to record inventory received from a vendor supplier:

1. Click on the **+Create** button and select **Bill**, which is listed in the **Vendors** column:

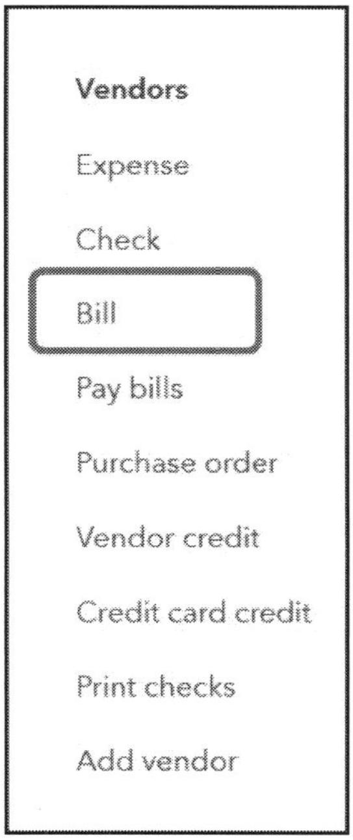

Figure 18.14: Navigating to the Bill form

2. A blank **Bill** form displays, as shown here:

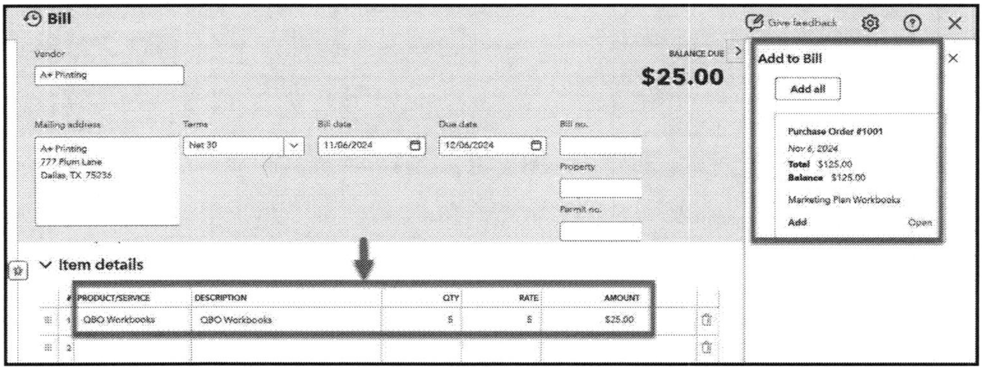

Figure 18.15: Completing the Bill form

3. To the far right, you will see a window open and the option to add the items on the purchase order to the bill. Click the **Add all** button at the top of that window to confirm the transfer of the information on the purchase order to the **Bill** form.
4. The purchase order information will appear in the **Item details** section. If all the items were received, you don't need to edit anything in this section. However, if you did not receive all the items, you will need to edit the **QTY** field to reflect the number of items that were received. For example, let's say that all five items were in the box, but two of them were damaged. You don't want to receive damaged items in your inventory because they are not sellable. In our example, you would change the quantity from 5 to 3 to accept the products that were not damaged.

As mentioned previously, you would need to contact the vendor supplier to inform them of the issue so that they can either replace the damaged items or issue a credit memo to you. In *Chapter 7, Recording Sales Transactions in QuickBooks Online*, we covered how to process a credit memo.

After completing the **Bill** form, you can save it and pay it prior to the due date. To pay the bill, navigate to the **+Create** button and select **Pay bills** located in the **Vendors** column. For step-by-step instructions on how to pay bills, refer to *Chapter 9, Recording Expenses in QuickBooks Online.*

So far, we have covered how to turn on inventory tracking, add your products to QBO, record product sales, order products from vendor suppliers, and receive those products into the inventory. Now, we will share key reports that will help you stay on top of managing your inventory.

Generating inventory reports

As you know by now, the Reports Center in QBO includes several reports that you can generate with just a few clicks. While you can build your own reports, there is no need to. There are six reports that small businesses use regularly to manage their inventory: **Open Purchase Order List**, **Purchases by Product/Service Detail**, **Inventory Valuation Detail**, **Sales by Product/Service Detail**, **Purchases by Vendor Detail**, and **Physical Inventory Worksheet**. Each of these reports can be exported to Excel, PDF, or emailed directly out of QBO. Once you generate a report, the icons in the upper-right corner allow you to export the data into the format you need. For more information on reports, refer to *Chapter 14*, *Report Center Overview*.

Brief descriptions and screenshots of each report are included next.

Open Purchase Order List report

The **Open Purchase Order List** report is a standard report that you will find in the **Expenses and Vendors** report group. This report will show you a list of open purchase orders, grouped by vendor. You can use this report to determine which orders have not been received from vendor suppliers. In addition, if an order has been received but the purchase order form is listed on the report, the goods were not received against the purchase order. In that situation, you can simply click on the purchase order on the report to drill down to the purchase order and change the status to **Closed**.

Figure 18.16 is a screenshot of an **Open Purchase Order List** report:

Open Purchase Order List by Vendor
Small Business Builders, LLC
All Dates

Refresh report
Last updated a few seconds ago

Vendor	Date	Num	Memo/Description	Ship via	Amount	Open Balance
A+ Printing (2)						
A+ Printing	11/06/2024	1002	-	-	$900.00	$900.00
A+ Printing	11/06/2024	1003	-	-	$50.00	$50.00
Total for A+ Printing					$950.00	$950.00
					$950.00	**$950.00**

Figure 18.16: Generating an Open Purchase Order List report

The **Open Purchase Order List** report includes the following information:

- Vendor name
- Purchase order date
- Purchase order number
- Memo/description included on the purchase order

- Ship via method
- Purchase order amount
- Open balance

In our example, there are two open purchase orders for **A+ Printing**. Since the open balance for both purchase orders is the same as the total amount, that means that no items have been received for either order. To obtain additional details about these orders, hover your mouse over any field that has data (date, number, or amount) and double-click. The purchase order form will display all of the details.

Purchases by Product/Service Detail report

The **Purchases by Product/Service Detail** report is a standard report that you will find in the **Expenses and Vendors** report group. This report includes a list of the purchases made for both products and services, grouped by product or service. You can use this report to get an overall view of how much you have spent on all products/services or a specific product/service for the time period you specify.

Figure 18.17 shows a screenshot of a **Purchases by Product/Service Detail** report:

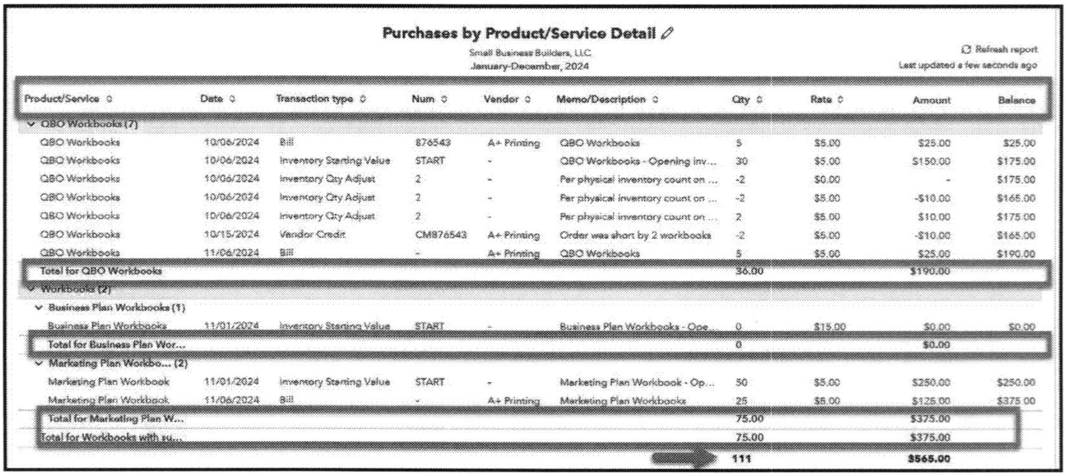

Purchases by Product/Service Detail
Small Business Builders, LLC
January-December, 2024
Refresh report
Last updated a few seconds ago

Product/Service	Date	Transaction type	Num	Vendor	Memo/Description	Qty	Rate	Amount	Balance
QBO Workbooks (7)									
QBO Workbooks	10/06/2024	Bill	876543	A+ Printing	QBO Workbooks	5	$5.00	$25.00	$25.00
QBO Workbooks	10/06/2024	Inventory Starting Value	START	-	QBO Workbooks - Opening inv…	30	$5.00	$150.00	$175.00
QBO Workbooks	10/06/2024	Inventory Qty Adjust	2	-	Per physical inventory count on …	-2	$0.00	-	$175.00
QBO Workbooks	10/06/2024	Inventory Qty Adjust	2	-	Per physical inventory count on …	-2	$5.00	-$10.00	$165.00
QBO Workbooks	10/06/2024	Inventory Qty Adjust	2	-	Per physical inventory count on …	2	$5.00	$10.00	$175.00
QBO Workbooks	10/15/2024	Vendor Credit	CM876543	A+ Printing	Order was short by 2 workbooks	-2	$5.00	-$10.00	$165.00
QBO Workbooks	11/06/2024	Bill	-	A+ Printing	QBO Workbooks	5	$5.00	$25.00	$190.00
Total for QBO Workbooks						36.00		$190.00	
Workbooks (2)									
Business Plan Workbooks (1)									
Business Plan Workbooks	11/01/2024	Inventory Starting Value	START	-	Business Plan Workbooks - Ope…	0	$15.00	$0.00	$0.00
Total for Business Plan Wor…						0		$0.00	
Marketing Plan Workbo… (2)									
Marketing Plan Workbook	11/01/2024	Inventory Starting Value	START	-	Marketing Plan Workbook - Op…	50	$5.00	$250.00	$250.00
Marketing Plan Workbook	11/06/2024	Bill	-	A+ Printing	Marketing Plan Workbooks	25	$5.00	$125.00	$375.00
Total for Marketing Plan W…						75.00		$375.00	
Total for Workbooks with su…						75.00		$375.00	
						111		$565.00	

Figure 18.17: Generating a Purchases by Product/Service Detail report

The **Purchases by Product/Services Detail** report is grouped by product/service and includes the following information:

- Product/service
- Date of purchase

- Transaction type: bill, inventory adjustments, or vendor credit
- Reference number
- Vendor name
- Memo/description
- Quantity
- Rate/cost per unit
- Total amount of purchase
- Balance

In our example, there are three products that were purchased between January and December 2024. There were 36 QBO workbooks purchased for $190.00; no purchases were made for business plan workbooks, and 75 marketing plan workbooks were purchased for $375.00.

Inventory Valuation Detail report

The **Inventory Valuation Detail** report is a standard report that you will find in the **Sales and Customers** report group. This report shows the quantity on hand, the value of the inventory, and the average cost for each inventory item.

Figure 18.18 shows a screenshot of an **Inventory Valuation Detail** report:

Small Business Builders, LLC

Inventory Valuation Detail

January - December 2024

DATE	TRANSACTION TYPE	NUM	NAME	QTY	RATE	FIFO COST	QTY ON HAND	ASSET VALUE
QBO Workbooks								
10/06/2024	Bill	876543	A+ Printing	5.00	5.00	25.00	5.00	25.00
10/06/2024	Inventory Starting Value	START		30.00	5.00	150.00	35.00	175.00
10/06/2024	Inventory Qty Adjust	2		-2.00	5.00	-10.00	33.00	165.00
10/15/2024	Vendor Credit	CM876543	A+ Printing	-2.00	5.00	-10.00	31.00	155.00
11/06/2024	Bill		A+ Printing	5.00	5.00	25.00	36.00	180.00
Total for QBO Workbooks				**36.00**		**$180.00**	**36.00**	**$180.00**
Workbooks								
Business Plan Workbooks								
11/01/2024	Inventory Starting Value	START		0.00	15.00	0.00	0.00	0.00
Total for Business Plan Workbooks				**0.00**		**$0.00**	**0.00**	**$0.00**
Marketing Plan Workbook								
11/01/2024	Inventory Starting Value	START		50.00	5.00	250.00	50.00	250.00
11/05/2024	Invoice	1007	Astro Jetson	-25.00	5.00	-125.00	25.00	125.00
11/06/2024	Bill		A+ Printing	25.00	5.00	125.00	50.00	250.00
Total for Marketing Plan Workbook				**50.00**		**$250.00**	**50.00**	**$250.00**
Total for Workbooks				**50.00**		**$250.00**	**50.00**	**$250.00**

Figure 18.18: Generating an Inventory Valuation Detail report

The **Inventory Valuation Detail** report is grouped by product/service and includes the following information:

- Transaction date
- Transaction type: bill, inventory adjustment, or vendor credit
- Transaction number
- Vendor name
- Quantity
- Cost per unit
- FIFO cost
- On-hand quantity
- Asset value

There is also a summarized version of this report available within the **Sales and Customers** report group. In our example, there are three items: **QBO Workbooks**, **Business Plan Workbooks**, and **Marketing Plan Workbooks**. The QBO workbooks and the marketing plan workbooks have an on-hand inventory of 36 units and 50 units, respectively. The FIFO cost is $180.00 for the QBO workbooks and $250.00 for the marketing plan workbooks. You can hover your mouse over any field on the report and double-click to drill down to additional details.

Sales by Product/Service Detail report

The **Sales by Product/Service Detail** report is a standard report you will find within the **Sales and Customers** report group. It includes a breakdown of all your sales for the time period specified.

Figure 18.19 shows a screenshot of a **Sales by Product/Service Detail** report:

Small Business Builders, LLC

Sales by Product/Service Detail

January - December 2024

DATE	TRANSACTION TYPE	NUM	CUSTOMER	MEMO/DESCRIPTION	QTY	SALES PRICE	AMOUNT
▾ Business Plan Workbook							
09/22/2024	Invoice	1001	Tina Turner	Business Plan Workbook	12.00	50.00	600.00
Total for Business Plan Workbook					**12.00**		**$600.00**
▾ Workbooks							
▾ Marketing Plan Workbook							
11/05/2024	Invoice	1007	Astro Jetson	Marketing Plan Workbooks	25.00	20.00	500.00
Total for Marketing Plan Workbook					**25.00**		**$500.00**
Total for Workbooks					**25.00**		**$500.00**
TOTAL					**37.00**		**$1,100.00**

Figure 18.19: Generating a Sales by Product/Service Detail report

The **Sales by Product/Service Detail** report is grouped by product/service and includes the following information:

- Date of sale
- Transaction type (invoice, sales receipt, or credit memo)
- Transaction number
- Customer
- Memo/description of product sold
- Quantity sold
- Sales price per unit
- Total sales amount

Purchases by Vendor Detail report

The **Purchases by Vendor Detail** report is a standard report you will find within the **Expenses and Vendors** report group. It lists all the products you have purchased by vendor over the time period specified.

Figure 18.20 shows a screenshot of a **Purchases by Vendor Detail** report:

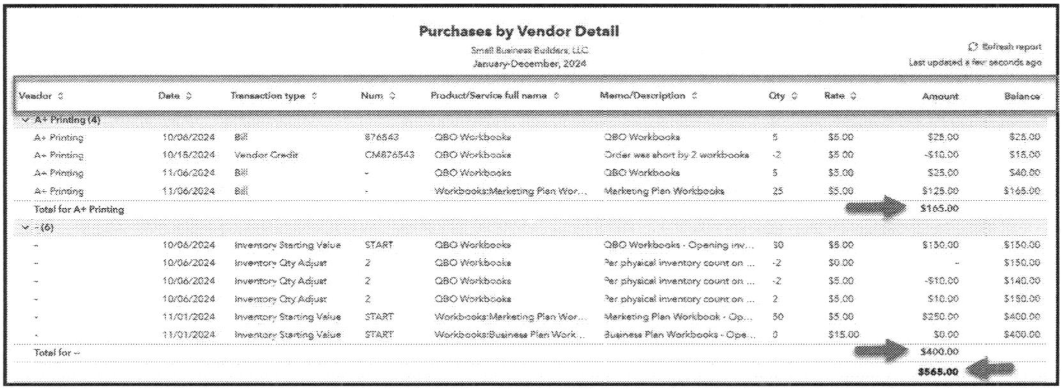

Purchases by Vendor Detail

Small Business Builders, LLC

January-December, 2024

Refresh report

Last updated a few seconds ago

Vendor	Date	Transaction type	Num	Product/Service full name	Memo/Description	Qty	Rate	Amount	Balance
A+ Printing (4)									
A+ Printing	10/06/2024	Bill	876543	QBO Workbooks	QBO Workbooks	5	$5.00	$25.00	$25.00
A+ Printing	10/15/2024	Vendor Credit	CM876543	QBO Workbooks	Order was short by 2 workbooks	-2	$5.00	-$10.00	$15.00
A+ Printing	11/06/2024	Bill	-	QBO Workbooks	QBO Workbooks	5	$5.00	$25.00	$40.00
A+ Printing	11/06/2024	Bill	-	Workbooks:Marketing Plan Wor…	Marketing Plan Workbooks	25	$5.00	$125.00	$165.00
Total for A+ Printing								$165.00	
- (6)									
-	10/06/2024	Inventory Starting Value	START	QBO Workbooks	QBO Workbooks - Opening inv…	30	$5.00	$150.00	$150.00
-	10/06/2024	Inventory Qty Adjust	2	QBO Workbooks	Per physical inventory count on …	-2	$0.00	-	$150.00
-	10/06/2024	Inventory Qty Adjust	2	QBO Workbooks	Per physical inventory count on …	-2	$5.00	-$10.00	$140.00
-	10/06/2024	Inventory Qty Adjust	2	QBO Workbooks	Per physical inventory count on …	2	$5.00	$10.00	$150.00
-	11/01/2024	Inventory Starting Value	START	Workbooks:Marketing Plan Wor…	Marketing Plan Workbook - Op…	50	$5.00	$250.00	$400.00
-	11/01/2024	Inventory Starting Value	START	Workbooks:Business Plan Work…	Business Plan Workbooks - Ope…	0	$15.00	$0.00	$400.00
Total for -								$400.00	
								$565.00	

Figure 18.20: Generating a Purchases by Vendor Detail report

The **Purchases by Vendor Detail** report is grouped by vendor and includes the following information:

- Vendor
- Date of purchase
- Transaction type: bill, vendor credit, or inventory adjustment

- Transaction number
- Product/service purchased
- Memo/description
- Quantity purchased
- Cost per unit
- Total purchase amount

Physical Inventory Worksheet summary

In *Chapter 16, Closing the Books in QuickBooks Online,* we discussed the importance of taking an annual physical inventory count. We also covered how to record inventory adjustments. The **Physical Inventory Worksheet** summary provides you with the quantity on hand, the reorder point, and the quantity on order for all your products. You can also export this worksheet to Excel to facilitate the physical inventory count.

Figure 18.21 shows a screenshot of a **Physical Inventory Worksheet** summary:

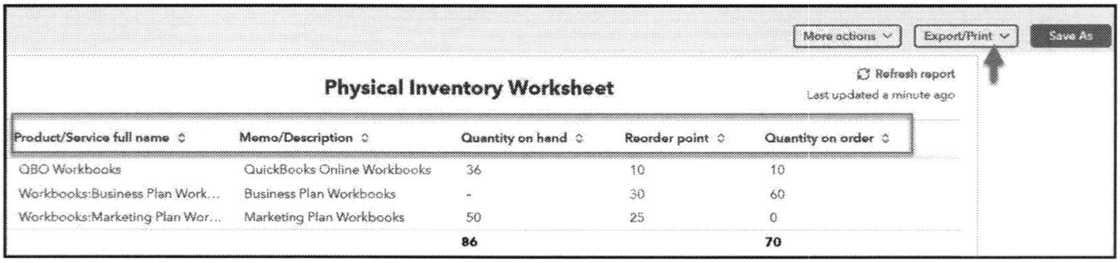

Figure 18.21: Generating a Physical Inventory Worksheet summary

The **Physical Inventory Worksheet** summary includes the following information:

- Product/service name
- Memo/description of the product
- Quantity on hand
- Reorder point
- Quantity on order, if any

You can export this report to Excel and use it for your physical inventory counts. Simply click on the **Export/Print** button shown earlier in *Figure 18.21* and follow the on-screen instructions to download the report, which should resemble the following figure:

	A	B	C	D	E
1	Physical Inventory Worksheet				
2					
3	Product/Service full name	Memo/Description	Quantity on hand	Reorder point	Quantity on order
4	QBO Workbooks	QuickBooks Online Workbooks	36	10	10
5	Workbooks:Business Plan Workbooks	Business Plan Workbooks		30	60
6	Workbooks:Marketing Plan Workbook	Marketing Plan Workbooks	50	25	0
7			**86**		**70**
8					
9					
10					

Figure 18.22: Downloading the Physical Inventory Worksheet summary to Excel

After exporting the report to Excel, create a column next to the **Quantity on hand** column, label it `Inventory Count`, and hide the **Quantity on hand**, **Reorder point**, and **Quantity on order** columns. Print the worksheet with only the **Inventory Count** column showing and have the counters write in their counts. Plug the counts into the spreadsheet and create a column to calculate the difference. The variance calculated will be the inventory adjustments required to get your books to match what is on the shelf. As mentioned previously, please refer to *Chapter 16, Closing the Books in QuickBooks Online*, for instructions on how to record inventory adjustments.

> It's important to take a physical inventory at least once a year, if not more often. This is important as a control for inventory management and ensures that, at least at the end of the year (and the beginning of the next), your books match the products that you have in stock.

Summary

In this chapter, we covered all aspects of managing inventory in QBO. First, we showed you how to ensure that the inventory is turned on, and then we went through the process of adding products to QBO. After you have added products to QBO, you are ready to record product sales to your customers, so we showed you how to do that using an invoice. When you are running low on products and need to order, you will create a purchase order and email it to your vendor supplier. Once the products are received, you will record the inventory receipt on the bill form and pay your vendor supplier before the bill is due. Finally, we covered six reports that will help you stay on top of managing your inventory.

This is the last chapter in *Mastering QuickBooks 2026*. It has been a pleasure to be your guide as you learn how to confidently manage your business finances. Congratulations on taking an important step in helping your business to be successful! Don't forget to download your free bonus items using this link: https://github.com/PacktPublishing/Mastering-QuickBooks-2026-Seventh-Edition.

Next steps

1. Be sure to head over to my YouTube channel for step-by-step product demos in QBO. Use this link to access the channel:

   https://packt.link/du2BR

2. If you have a bookkeeper or accountant who manages your books, schedule time to meet with that person each month. However, make sure that you have already reviewed your financial reports and made a list of your questions prior to this meeting. In other words, schedule your "money date" before you meet with your bookkeeper or accountant, if applicable.
3. Create an Excel spreadsheet with a list of the products that you sell. It should include the following information: purchase price, sales price, description, quantity on hand, and reorder quantity.
4. Using the list you created in step 3, add your products to QBO.

19

Appendix 1 – Intuit QuickBooks Online Certified User Exam Objectives

The **Intuit QuickBooks Certified User certification** is a credential that is recognized in the industry as a way for bookkeepers and accountants to demonstrate their proficiency in the Intuit QuickBooks accounting software. Once you have achieved this certification, you will receive access to a digital badge that you can put on your resume, social media profiles, and website. This certification will automatically set you apart from other candidates looking to obtain employment as a bookkeeper or accountant.

In this chapter, we have included a list of the objectives that are covered on the exam. In addition, we have provided the corresponding chapter in which you can find the information on each topic in our book, *Mastering QuickBooks® 2026, Seventh Edition*.

Objective		**Chapter**
1	**Intuit QuickBooks Online Administration**	
1.1	**Set up Intuit QuickBooks Online**	
1.1.1	Recognize features and benefits of Intuit QuickBooks Online Plus	2
1.1.2	Describe licensing requirements for setting up an entity in Intuit QuickBooks Online	2
1.1.3	Describe the process of migrating a company to Intuit QuickBooks Online	**N/A**

Objective		Chapter
1.1.4	Describe the access of each default user role	4
1.2	**Manage Intuit QuickBooks Online**	
1.2.1	Identify the company information that you can and can't edit	3
1.2.2	Recognize the benefits of the Close the Books feature	16
1.2.3	Compare and contrast the cash and accrual accounting methods	1
1.2.4	Identify the purpose of project tracking, class tracking, and locations	3
1.2.5	Describe how to activate project tracking, class tracking, and locations	3
1.2.6	Identify the tasks performed by automation	2
1.3	**Manage lists**	
1.3.1	Identify the lists that you can import	4 and 5
1.3.2	Identify the content of various lists	4 and 5
1.3.3	Identify the appropriate lists for different purposes	4 and 5
1.3.4	Identify when and how to add, edit, delete, and merge list items	4 and 5
1.3.5	Manage the Chart of Accounts	4
1.4	**Manage recurring transactions**	
1.4.1	Describe reasons for making transactions recurring	9
1.4.2	Define types of recurrence	9
1.4.3	Describe how to implement recurring transactions	9
1.5	**Manage journal entries**	
1.5.1	Identify the information required for journal entries	16
1.5.2	Describe how to implement journal entries	16
1.6	**Connect Intuit QuickBooks Online to apps**	
1.6.1	Identify the purpose of apps	4
1.6.2	Identify where to get apps	4
1.6.3	Identify the risks and benefits of extending functionality through apps	4

Objective		Chapter
2	**Sales and Money In**	
2.1	**Set up customers**	
2.1.1	Identify the importance of the Display Name field	5
2.1.2	Differentiate between billing and shipping addresses	5

Objective		Chapter
2.1.3	Define and describe the use of customer payment terms	5
2.1.4	Identify taxable and non-taxable customers	5
2.1.5	Define and describe the correct use of sub-customers	5
2.2	**Set up products and services**	
2.2.1	Describe and differentiate between products and services	5
2.2.2	Identify the information required to set up products or services	5
2.2.3	Describe reasons for setting up products or services	5
2.2.4	Contrast inventory products and non-inventory products	5
2.3	**Manage sales settings**	
2.3.1	Customize sales forms	4
2.3.2	Customize email message forms	4
2.3.3	Describe the purpose of activating customer discounts	3
2.3.4	Describe the Intuit QuickBooks Payments feature and how it differs from traditional payments	3 and 7
2.4	**Record basic money-in transactions**	
2.4.1	Describe the money-in transaction workflow	7
2.4.2	Record and manage invoices and sales receipts	7
2.4.3	Receive, record, and manage payments, undeposited funds, and deposits	7
2.4.4	Record credit memos and refund receipts	7

Objective		Chapter
3	**Vendors and Money Out**	
3.1	**Manage vendor records**	
3.1.1	Describe how to identify existing customers as vendors	5
3.1.2	Describe when and how to merge vendor accounts	5
3.1.3	Describe how to add or change vendor payment terms	5
3.1.4	Describe how and why to identify vendors as 1099 contractors	5,12
3.2	**Manage expense settings**	
3.2.1	Describe how and why to activate expense tracking by customer	3
3.2.2	Describe when and how to make expenses and items billable	3
3.2.3	Describe how to identify unbilled billable expenses	3

Objective		Chapter
3.3	**Record and manage basic money-out transactions**	
3.3.1	Describe the money-out transaction workflow	9
3.3.2	Identify types of money-out transactions	9
3.3.3	Compare and describe the appropriate use of checks and bill payments	9
3.3.4	Describe the effects of recording bills, checks, and credit card transactions	9
3.3.5	Differentiate between expense transactions and bank feed transactions	9
3.3.6	Describe how to record check, credit card, and debit card expense transactions	9
3.3.7	Describe the use and effects of vendor credits and refunds	9
3.3.8	Describe why and how to void, delete, and edit money-out transactions and the impact thereof	9

Objective		Chapter
4	**Bank Accounts, Transaction Rules, and Receipts**	
4.1	**Implement financial account connections**	
4.1.1	Identify the types of financial accounts Intuit QuickBooks Online can connect to	4
4.1.2	Describe the benefits of connecting Intuit QuickBooks Online to accounts	4
4.2	**Manage bank feeds**	
4.2.1	Process bank feed transactions	11
4.2.2	Define and describe the use of bank rules	11
4.3	**Manage receipts**	
4.3.1	Identify methods of uploading receipts	9
4.3.2	Describe how to record transactions from uploaded receipts	9

Objective		Chapter
5	**Basic Reports and Views**	
5.1	**Describe the content and purpose of reports**	
5.1.1	Describe the content and purpose of financial reports	14
5.1.2	Describe the content and purpose of money-in reports	8

Objective		Chapter
5.1.3	Describe the content and purpose of money-out reports	10
5.2	**Customize and deliver standard reports**	
5.2.1	Customize standard reports	14
5.2.2	Identify report delivery formats	14
5.3	**Access other reports and views**	
5.3.1	Describe the content of the audit log	15
5.3.2	Describe the content and functionality of the dashboards	2

For more information on how to take the exam, visit the Certiport website:

`https://certiport.pearsonvue.com/Certifications/Intuit/Certifications/Certify/QuickBooks-Certified-User`

20

Appendix 2 – Shortcuts and Test Drive

In this chapter, we will introduce you to two tools that can help you get the most out of QBO. The first tool is keyboard shortcuts. Similar to many other software programs, you can use keyboard shortcuts to help you quickly navigate within QBO. This is also ideal if you are not a fan of using the mouse. The second tool that we will introduce you to is the QBO Test Drive. The Test Drive allows you to access QBO without setting up an account of your own. You can use the QBO Test Drive to enter practice transactions and to see what QBO looks like before you make a purchase. After using the Test Drive, if you decide to purchase QBO, we've included a link you can use to get a discount on your purchase.

To sum up, in this chapter, we will cover the following topics:

- QBO keyboard shortcuts
- QBO Test Drive

QBO keyboard shortcuts

Keyboard shortcuts help speed up navigation, which will save you time when you're using QBO. For example, instead of using the mouse to click multiple times before you get to the chart of accounts or a new invoice template, you can use the keyboard shortcut to display these areas of QBO a lot faster.

The following screenshot shows a list of the QBO keyboard shortcuts. To access them directly in your QBO file, press the `Ctrl` + `Alt` + `?` keys simultaneously (keys may differ on a Mac).

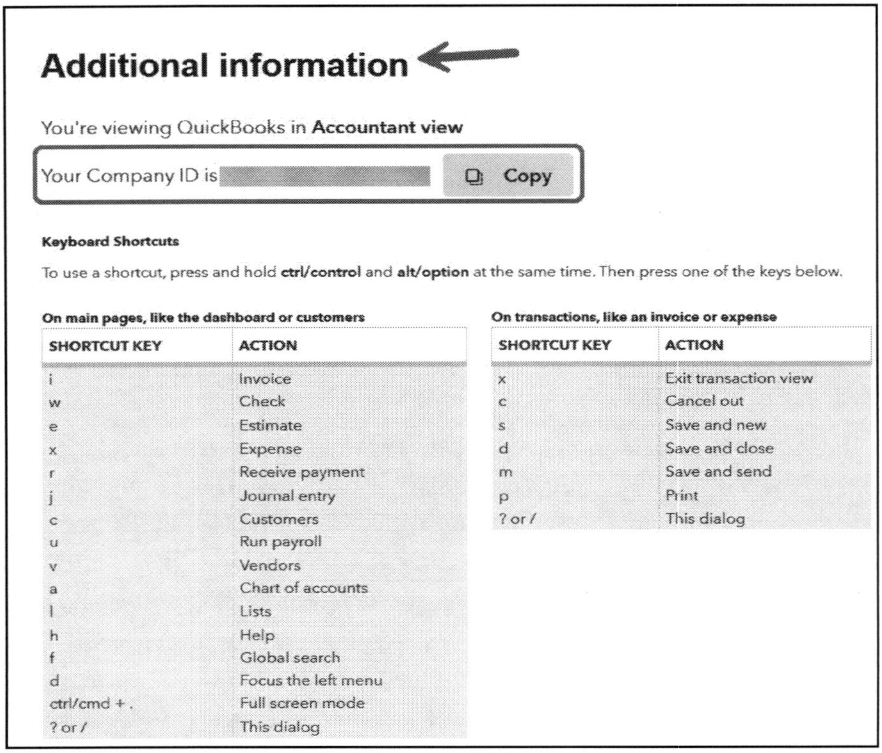

SHORTCUT KEY	ACTION
i	Invoice
w	Check
e	Estimate
x	Expense
r	Receive payment
j	Journal entry
c	Customers
u	Run payroll
v	Vendors
a	Chart of accounts
l	Lists
h	Help
f	Global search
d	Focus the left menu
ctrl/cmd + .	Full screen mode
? or /	This dialog

SHORTCUT KEY	ACTION
x	Exit transaction view
c	Cancel out
s	Save and new
d	Save and close
m	Save and send
p	Print
? or /	This dialog

Figure 20.1: Keyboard shortcuts

You can also access keyboard shortcuts from the gear icon. Within the gear menu, select **Additional info**, which is located below the **Settings** column.

At the very top of the screen, you will notice a reference to **Your Company ID**. This Company ID is your 16-digit QBO license number (not shown in *Figure 20.1* for security purposes). If you contact the Intuit Support team, this is one of the ways they will be able to identify you. Be sure to copy and save this information in a secure location. It will come in handy if, for some reason, you are not able to log into your QBO file.

QBO Test Drive

Before signing up for a QBO subscription, you can check out the QBO Test Drive, which we introduced in *Chapter 2, Getting Started with QuickBooks Online*. The Test Drive account contains sample data for a fictitious company.

Here, you can enter test transactions before you put them in your actual QBO file. For example, you can enter a credit memo or a journal entry to see how it affects the books before entering the transaction in your QBO file. Just click on the following link (depending on your region) and follow the onscreen instructions:

- **United States QuickBooks Online Plus:** `https://qbo.intuit.com/redir/testdrive`
- **United States QuickBooks Online Advanced**: `https://qbo.intuit.com/redir/testdrive_us_advanced`

The US edition of QBO was used to create this book. If you are using a version that is outside the United States, results may differ.

Discount on a QBO account

As a QuickBooks ProAdvisor, I can save you 30% off of the regular-priced QBO plans. You can get in touch with me for more details here: `https://www.crystalynnshelton.com/`.

21

Unlock Your Exclusive Benefits

Your copy of this book includes the following exclusive benefits:

- Next-gen Packt Reader
- DRM-free PDF/ePub downloads

Follow the guide below to unlock them. The process takes only a few minutes and needs to be completed once.

Unlock this Book's Free Benefits in 3 Easy Steps

Step 1

Keep your purchase invoice ready for *Step 3*. If you have a physical copy, scan it using your phone and save it as a PDF, JPG, or PNG.

For more help on finding your invoice, visit `https://www.packtpub.com/unlock-benefits/help`.

> **Note**: If you bought this book directly from Packt, no invoice is required. After *Step 2*, you can access your exclusive content right away.

Step 2

Scan the QR code or go to `packtpub.com/unlock`.

On the page that opens (similar to *Figure 21.1* on desktop), search for this book by name and select the correct edition.

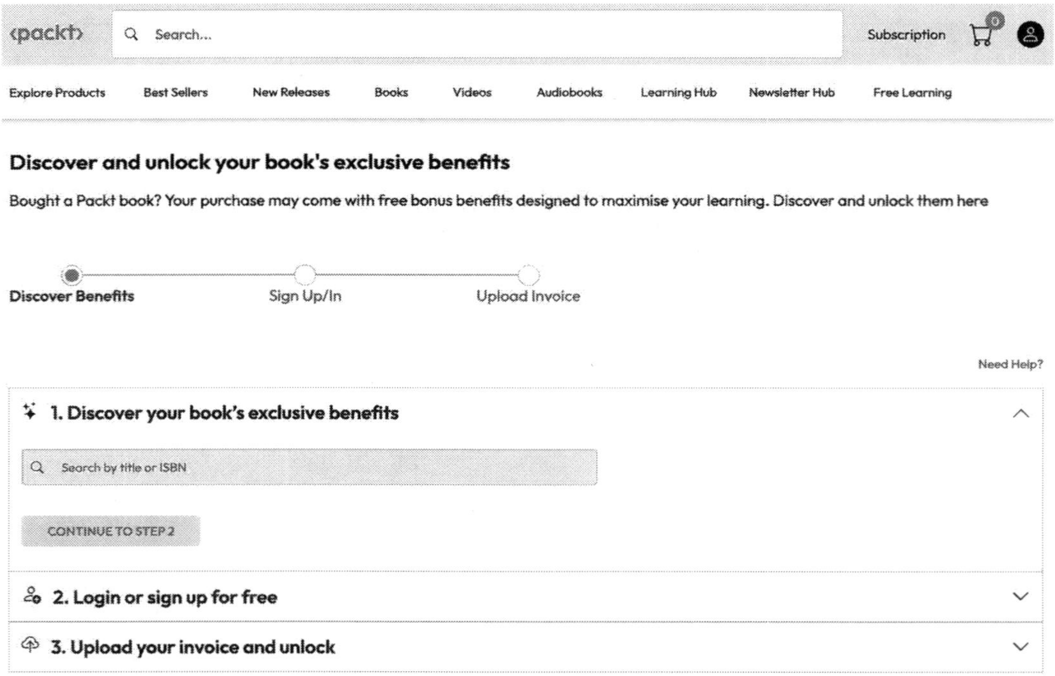

Figure 21.1: Packt unlock landing page on desktop

Step 3

After selecting your book, sign in to your Packt account or create one for free. Then upload your invoice (PDF, PNG, or JPG, up to 10 MB). Follow the on-screen instructions to finish the process.

Need help?

If you get stuck and need help, visit `https://www.packtpub.com/unlock-benefits/help` for a detailed FAQ on how to find your invoices and more. This QR code will take you to the help page.

Note: If you are still facing issues, reach out to `customercare@packt.com`.

Other Books You May Enjoy

If you enjoyed this book, you may be interested in these other books by Packt:

Mastering Microsoft Dynamics 365 Business Central

Stefano Demiliani, Duilio Tacconi

ISBN: 9781837630646

- Developing a customized solution for Dynamics 365 Business Central
- Writing performant code following extensibility patterns
- Handling reporting, files, and printing on a cloud environment
- Handling Business Central telemetries with Azure
- Writing APIs and integrations for Dynamics 365 Business Central
- Applying DevOps and CI/CD to development projects by using GitHub
- Integrating Business Central with Power Platform
- Publishing your solutions to AppSource marketplace
- Manage Copilot capabilities and create your own generative AI copilot

Workflow Automation with Microsoft Power Automate

Aaron Guilmette

ISBN: 9781836649632

- Build cloud flows using triggers, connectors, and actions
- Use Copilot and generative AI to create and edit flows
- Automate desktop tasks with Power Automate for Desktop
- Create approval processes for Teams, Slack, and email
- Connect Power Automate to Dataverse, Forms, and SQL
- Implement error handling, monitoring, and troubleshooting
- Govern and scale automations using best practices

ChatGPT and AI for Accountants

Dr. Scott Dell, Dr. Mfon Akpan

ISBN: 9781835466537

- Understand the fundamentals of AI and its impact on the accounting sector
- Grasp how AI streamlines and enhances the auditing process for high accuracy
- Uncover the potential of AI in simplifying tax processes and ensuring compliance
- Get to grips with using AI to identify discrepancies and prevent financial fraud
- Master the art of AI-powered data analytics for informed decision-making
- Gain insights into seamlessly integrating AI tools within existing accounting systems
- Stay ahead in the evolving landscape of AI-led accounting tools and practices

Packt is searching for authors like you

If you're interested in becoming an author for Packt, please visit authors.packt.com and apply today. We have worked with thousands of developers and tech professionals, just like you, to help them share their insight with the global tech community. You can make a general application, apply for a specific hot topic that we are recruiting an author for, or submit your own idea.

Share your thoughts

Now you've finished *Mastering QuickBooks 2026*, we'd love to hear your thoughts! Scan the QR code below to go straight to the Amazon review page for this book and share your feedback or leave a review on the site that you purchased it from.

https://packt.link/r/1806386895

Your review is important to us and the tech community and will help us make sure we're delivering excellent quality content.

Index

C

E

F

I

Q

R

U

V

W

Y

Made in United States
Orlando, FL
10 November 2026

90510179R00299